# The Story of God Bible Commentary Series Endorsements

"Getting a story is about more than merely enjoying it. It means hearing it, understanding it, and above all, being impacted by it. This commentary series hopes that its readers not only hear and understand the story but are impacted by it to live in as Christian a way as possible. The editors and contributors set that table very well and open up the biblical story in ways that move us to act with sensitivity and understanding. That makes hearing the story as these authors tell it well worth the time. Well done."

**Darrell L. Bock**

Dallas Theological Seminary

"The Story of God Bible Commentary series invites readers to probe how the message of the text relates to our situations today. Engagingly readable, it not only explores the biblical text but offers a range of applications and interesting illustrations."

**Craig S. Keener**

Asbury Theological Seminary

"I love The Story of God Bible Commentary series. It makes the text sing and helps us hear the story afresh."

**John Ortberg**

Senior Pastor of Menlo Park Presbyterian Church

"In this promising new series of commentaries, believing biblical scholars bring not only their expertise but their own commitment to Jesus and insights into today's culture to the Scriptures. The result is a commentary series that is anchored in the text but lives and breathes in the world of today's church with its variegated pattern of socioeconomic, ethnic, and national diversity. Pastors, Bible study leaders, and Christians of all types who are looking for a substantive and practical guide through the Scriptures will find these volumes helpful."

**Frank Thielman**

Beeson Divinity School

"I'm a storyteller. Through writing and speaking I talk and teach about understanding the Story of God throughout Scripture and about letting God reveal more of his story as I live it out. Thus I am thrilled to have a commentary series based on the story of God—a commentary that helps me to Listen to the Story, that Explains the Story, and then encourages me to probe how to Live the Story. A perfect tool for helping every follower of Jesus to walk in the story that God is writing for them."

**Judy Douglass**

Director of Women's Resources, Cru

"The Bible is the story of God and his dealings with humanity from creation to new creation. The Bible is made up more of stories than of any other literary genre. Even the psalms, proverbs, prophecies, letters, and the Apocalypse make complete sense only when set in the context of the grand narrative of the entire Bible. This commentary series breaks new ground by taking all these observations seriously. It asks commentators to listen to the text, to explain the text, and to live the text. Some of the material in these sections overlaps with introduction, detailed textual analysis and application, respectively, but only some. The most riveting and valuable part of the commentaries are the stories that can appear in any of these sections, from any part of the globe and any part of church history, illustrating the text in any of these areas. Ideal for preaching and teaching."

**Craig L. Blomberg**

Denver Seminary

"Pastors and lay people will welcome this new series, which seeks to make the message of the Scriptures clear and to guide readers in appropriating biblical texts for life today."

**Daniel I. Block**

Wheaton College and Graduate School

"An extremely valuable and long overdue series that includes comment on the cultural context of the text, careful exegesis, and guidance on reading the whole Bible as a unity that testifies to Christ as our Savior and Lord."

**Graeme Goldsworthy**

author of *According to Plan*

# JOSHUA

# Editorial Board
of
# The Story of God Bible Commentary

Old Testament general editor
**Tremper Longman III**

Old Testament associate editors
**George Athas**
**Mark J. Boda**
**Myrto Theocharous**

New Testament general editor
**Scot McKnight**

New Testament associate editors
**Lynn H. Cohick**
**Michael F. Bird**
**Joel L. Willitts**

**Zondervan editors**

Senior acquisitions editor
**Katya Covrett**

Senior production editor, Old Testament
**Nancy L. Erickson**

Senior production editor, New Testament
**Christopher A. Beetham**

# The Story of God Bible Commentary

## JOSHUA

Lissa M. Wray Beal

Tremper Longman III & Scot McKnight
*General Editors*

ZONDERVAN ACADEMIC

*Joshua*
Copyright © 2019 by Lissa M. Wray Beal

ISBN 978-0-310-49083-8 (hardcover)

ISBN 978-0-310-49084-5 (ebook)

Requests for information should be addressed to:
Zondervan, *3900 Sparks Dr. SE, Grand Rapids, Michigan 49546*

Unless otherwise indicated, Scripture quotations are taken from The Holy Bible, New International Version®, NIV®. Copyright © 1973, 1978, 1984, 2011 by Biblica, Inc.® Used by permission of Zondervan. All rights reserved worldwide. www.Zondervan.com. The "NIV" and "New International Version" are trademarks registered in the United States Patent and Trademark Office by Biblica, Inc.®

Any internet addresses (websites, blogs, etc.) and telephone numbers in this book are offered as a resource. They are not intended in any way to be or imply an endorsement by Zondervan, nor does Zondervan vouch for the content of these sites and numbers for the life of this book.

No part of this publication may be reproduced, stored in a retrieval system, or transmitted in any form or by any means—electronic, mechanical, photocopy, recording, or any other—except for brief quotations in printed reviews, without the prior permission of the publisher.

*Cover design: Ron Huizinga*
*Cover image: iStockphoto.com*
*Interior composition: Kait Lamphere*

*Printed in the United States of America*

19 20 21 22 23 24 25 26 27 28 29 /LSC/ 15 14 13 12 11 10 9 8 7 6 5 4 3 2 1

For our Godchildren
Sheena, Jamie, Molly, and Lillian
(and their siblings: Ian, Tess, Fiona, and Markus)
May you in your generation have the bold faith of Caleb, Aksah,
or those persistent five (Mahlah, Noah, Hoglah, Milcah, and Tirzah—
let their names be remembered)
But more than that,
may you at the end
cross the Jordan
in the company of Joshua

## Old Testament series

1 ▪ Genesis—*Tremper Longman III*
2 ▪ Exodus—*Christopher J. H. Wright*
3 ▪ Leviticus—*Jerry E. Shepherd*
4 ▪ Numbers—*Jay A. Sklar*
5 ▪ Deuteronomy—*Myrto Theocharous*
6 ▪ Joshua—*Lissa M. Wray Beal*
7 ▪ Judges—*Athena E. Gorospe*
8 ▪ Ruth/Esther—*Marion Taylor*
9 ▪ 1–2 Samuel—*Paul S. Evans*
10 ▪ 1–2 Kings—*David T. Lamb*
11 ▪ 1–2 Chronicles—*Carol M. Kaminski*
12 ▪ Ezra/Nehemiah—*Douglas J. Green*
13 ▪ Job—*Martin A. Shields*
14 ▪ Psalms—*Elizabeth R. Hayes*
15 ▪ Proverbs—*Ryan P. O'Dowd*
16 ▪ Ecclesiastes/Song of Songs—*George Athas*
17 ▪ Isaiah—*Mark J. Boda*
18 ▪ Jeremiah/Lamentations—*Andrew G. Shead*
19 ▪ Ezekiel—*D. Nathan Phinney*
20 ▪ Daniel—*Wendy L. Widder*
21 ▪ Minor Prophets I—*Beth M. Stovell*
22 ▪ Minor Prophets II—*Beth M. Stovell*

## New Testament series

1 ▪ Matthew—*Rodney Reeves*
2 ▪ Mark—*Timothy G. Gombis*
3 ▪ Luke—*Kindalee Pfremmer DeLong*
4 ▪ John—*Nicholas Perrin*
5 ▪ Acts—*Dean Pinter*
6 ▪ Romans—*Michael F. Bird*
7 ▪ 1 Corinthians—*Justin K. Hardin*
8 ▪ 2 Corinthians—*Judith A. Diehl*
9 ▪ Galatians—*Nijay K. Gupta*
10 ▪ Ephesians—*Mark D. Roberts*
11 ▪ Philippians—*Lynn H. Cohick*
12 ▪ Colossians/Philemon—*Todd Wilson*
13 ▪ 1, 2 Thessalonians—*John Byron*
14 ▪ 1, 2 Timothy, Titus—*Marius Nel*
15 ▪ Hebrews—*Radu Gheorghita*
16 ▪ James—*Mariam J. Kamell*
17 ▪ 1 Peter—*Dennis R. Edwards*
18 ▪ 2 Peter, Jude—*C. Rosalee Velloso Ewell*
19 ▪ 1, 2, & 3 John—*Constantine R. Campbell*
20 ▪ Revelation—*Jonathan A. Moo*
21 ▪ Sermon on the Mount—*Scot McKnight*

# Contents

# Acknowledgments

When Joshua went into the land, he had the support of many people and encouragement came from some surprising quarters. I imagine that made the task easier, especially when the going got tough. That pretty much describes my experience of the family, friends, and mentors who have walked with me through this project. They made it immensely easier, often enjoyable, and eased the times when the text seemed daunting. I am grateful for their support throughout.

My thanks go to Dr. Mark Boda, who made the initial request that I write this volume. His question was timely, for it came on the heels of a determination to engage this troubling book more deeply. Thanks to Mark for the invitation, and for his generous mentorship exercised toward me and many other scholars. Dr. Tremper Longman was a wonderful general editor. He gathered a team for The Story of God Bible Commentary project, and though the task of writing is an isolated one, he brought us together as a community through meetings, updates, and encouragements. I am also grateful to Dr. Longman for providing access to the pre-publication manuscript of his new volume, *Confronting Old Testament Controversies*; thanks, Tremper, for letting me think with you on the difficult subject of violence in Joshua! Thanks also go to Dr. Myrto Theocharous who served as associate editor for my volume. Her comments on the finished manuscript, together with those of Tremper Longman, were wise, encouraging, and very valuable. I appreciate the time they took in their own busy schedules to work on this project. Finally, I wish to extend my thanks to Katya Covrett and Dr. Nancy L. Erickson at Zondervan. As Executive Acquisitions Editor, Katya's interest in the Story of God Bible Commentary series and her interactions with authors were encouraging. As Executive Production Editor, Nancy's insight and keen editor's eye were invaluable. Thank you both for your ministry at Zondervan.

Writing this volume was a scholarly venture for the academy but also for the church. During the years of the project I made my own ecclesial journey, settling in a new denomination. That journey was graced by the mentorship of two very different, but incredibly gifted priests. The Reverend Linda Parsons and the Reverend Canon Donna Joy shared their wisdom, their time, their vision, and their experience. They are godly leaders. I can only say how encouraged I was by their ministry to me during that time, and even more, how blessed I am now to count them as friends.

I shared the material in this volume with my Joshua classes taught at Providence Theological Seminary. Students ask the best questions: insightful, honest, funny, and often difficult, helping me and their colleagues consider the text. For their engagement in class, and for their interest and contribution to this project, I give them my thanks. I still can't answer all the questions they posed, and I hope they continue to ponder Joshua. Like all of Scripture, its riches are deep and life-giving, and worthy of study. My dean, Dr. Stan Hamm, and the leadership of Providence Theological Seminary and University College granted precious sabbatical time to devote to this research, and my colleagues continue to grace my ministry with their examples of faithfulness, and their friendship.

This volume is dedicated to our godchildren and their siblings. They live in far-flung places: New Zealand, Toronto, Hamilton, and Vancouver. This book is what your Aunty has been up to these past years. During that same time, she has prayed for you (and will continue to do so). May God in his grace draw you to himself!

Finally, how can I adequately thank my husband, Steven Beal? Once again, he has walked with me through another multi-year project. He continues to be the best of God's grace-gifts.

Joshua speaks of events within the life of Israel, but the church has also read it typologically as pointing to the latter Joshua who leads his people into God's Sabbath-rest. My prayer is that this volume honors him, and that God's people are challenged, encouraged, and edified as they live in the Sabbath-rest of God, awaiting its eschatological fulfillment.

# The Story of God Bible Commentary Series

Why another commentary series?

In the first place, no single commentary can exhaust the meaning of a biblical book. The Bible is unfathomably rich and no single commentator can explore every aspect of its message.

In addition, good commentary not only explores what the text meant in the past but also its continuing significance. In other words, the Word of God may not change, but culture does. Think of what we have seen in the last twenty years: we now communicate predominantly through the internet and email; we read our news on iPads and computers. We carry smartphones in our pockets through which we can call our friends, check the weather forecast, make dinner reservations, and get an answer to virtually any question we might have.

Today we have more readable and accurate Bible versions in English than any generation in the past. Bible distribution in the present generation has been very successful; more people own more Bibles than previous generations. However, studies have shown that while people have better access to the Bible than ever before, people aren't reading the Bibles they own, and they struggle to understand what they do read.

The Story of God Bible Commentary hopes to help people, particularly clergy but also laypeople, read the Bible with understanding not only of its ancient meaning but also of its continuing significance for us today in the twenty-first century. After all, readers of the Bible change too. These cultural shifts, our own personal developments, and the progress in intellectual questions, as well as growth in biblical studies and theology and discoveries of new texts and new paradigms for understanding the contexts of the Bible—each of these elements work on an interpreter so that the person who reads the Bible today asks different questions from different angles.

Culture shifts, but the Word of God remains. That is why we as editors of The Story of God Bible Commentary, a commentary based on the New International Version 2011 (NIV 2011), are excited to participate in this new series of commentaries on the Bible. This series is designed to speak to this generation with the same Word of God. We are asking the authors to explain what the Bible says to the sorts of readers who pick up commentaries so they can understand not only what Scripture says but what it means for today.

The Bible does not change, but relating it to our culture changes constantly and in differing ways in different contexts.

As editors of the Old Testament series, we recognize that Christians have a hard time knowing exactly how to relate to the Scriptures that were written before the coming of Christ. The world of the Old Testament is a strange one to those of us who live in the West in the twenty-first century. We read about strange customs, warfare in the name of God, sacrifices, laws of ritual purity, and more and wonder whether it is worth our while or even spiritually healthy to spend time reading this portion of Scripture that is chronologically, culturally, and—seemingly—theologically distant from us.

But it is precisely here that The Story of God Commentary Series Old Testament makes its most important contribution. The New Testament does not replace the Old Testament; the New Testament fulfills the Old Testament. We hear God's voice today in the Old Testament. In its pages he reveals himself to us and also his will for how we should live in a way that is pleasing to him.

Jesus himself often reminds us that the Old Testament maintains its importance to the lives of his disciples. Luke 24 describes Jesus' actions and teaching in the period between his resurrection and ascension. Strikingly, the focus of his teaching is on how his followers should read the Old Testament (here called "Moses and all the Prophets," "Scriptures," and "the law of Moses, the Prophets and Psalms"). To the two disciples on the road to Emmaus, he says:

> "How foolish you are, and how slow to believe all that the prophets have spoken! Did not the Messiah have to suffer these things and then enter his glory?" And beginning with Moses and all the Prophets, he explained to them what was said in all the Scriptures concerning himself. (Luke 24:25–27)

Then to a larger group of disciples he announces:

> "This is what I told you while I was still with you: Everything must be fulfilled that is written about me in the law of Moses, the Prophets and the Psalms." Then he opened their minds so they could understand the Scriptures. (Luke 24:44–45)

The Story of God Commentary Series takes Jesus' words on this matter seriously. Indeed, it is the first series that has as one of its deliberate goals the identification of the trajectories (historical, typological, and theological) that land in Christ in the New Testament. Every commentary in the series will, in the first place, exposit the text in the context of its original reception. We will interpret it as we believe the original author intended his contemporary audience to read it. But then we will also read the text in the light of the death and resurrection of Jesus. No other commentary series does this important work consistently in every volume.

To achieve our purpose of expositing the Old Testament in its original setting and also from a New Testament perspective, each passage is examined from three angles.

**Listen to the Story.** We begin by listening to the text in order to hear the voice of God. We first read the passage under study. We then go on to consider the background to the passage by looking at any earlier Scripture passage that informs our understanding of the text. At this point too we will cite and discuss possible ancient Near Eastern literary connections. After all, the Bible was not written in a cultural vacuum, and an understanding of its broader ancient Near Eastern context will often enrich our reading.

**Explain the Story.** The authors are asked to explain each passage in light of the Bible's grand story. It is here that we will exposit the text in its original Old Testament context. This is not an academic series, so the footnotes will be limited to the kinds of books and articles to which typical Bible readers and preachers will have access. Authors are given the freedom to explain the text as they read it, though you will not be surprised to find occasional listings of other options for reading the text. The emphasis will be on providing an accessible explanation of the passage, particularly on those aspects of the text that are difficult for a modern reader to understand, with an emphasis on theological interpretation.

**Live the Story.** Reading the Bible is not just about discovering what it meant back then; the intent of The Story of God Bible Commentary is to probe how this text might be lived out today as that story continues to march on in the life of the church.

Here, in the spirit of Christ's words in Luke 24, we will suggest ways in which the Old Testament text anticipates the gospel. After all, as Augustine famously put it, "the New Testament is in the Old Testament concealed, the Old Testament is in the New Testament revealed." We believe that this section will be particularly important for our readers who are clergy who want to present Christ even when they are preaching from the Old Testament.

The Old Testament also provides teaching concerning how we should live today. However, the authors of this series are sensitive to the tremendous impact that Christ's coming has on how Christians appropriate the Old Testament into their lives today.

It is the hope and prayer of the editors and all the contributors that our work will encourage clergy to preach from the Old Testament and laypeople to study this wonderful, yet often strange, portion of God's Word to us today.

Tremper Longman III, general editor Old Testament
George Athas, Mark Boda, and Myrto Theocharous, editors

# Abbreviations

| | |
|---|---|
| *ABD* | *Anchor Bible Dictionary* |
| ACCS | Ancient Christian Commentary on Scripture |
| *ANEP* | *The Ancient Near East in Pictures Relating to the Old Testament.* 2nd ed. Edited by James Pritchard. Princeton: Princeton University Press, 1969 |
| *ANET* | *Ancient Near Eastern Texts Relating to the Old Testament.* Edited by James Pritchard. 3rd ed. Princeton: Princeton University Press, 1969 |
| AOTC | Apollos Old Testament Commentary |
| *BAR* | *Biblical Archaeology Review* |
| BCBC | Believers Church Bible Commentary |
| *Bib* | *Biblica* |
| BST | The Bible Speaks Today |
| *CBQ* | *Catholic Biblical Quarterly* |
| *CCEL* | *Christian Classics Ethereal Library* |
| *COS* | *The Context of Scripture*. Edited by William W. Hallo. 3 vols. Leiden: Brill, 1997–2002 |
| *CT* | *Christianity Today* |
| *EA* | El-Amarna tablets |
| *ExAud* | *Ex Auditu* |
| *Hom* | Origen, *Homilies on Joshua*. Translated by Barbara J. Bruce. Fathers of the Church 105. Washington: The Catholic University of America Press, 2002 |
| *JBL* | *Journal of Biblical Literature* |
| *JETS* | *Journal of the Evangelical Theological Society* |
| JSOTSup | Journal for the Study of the Old Testament Supplement Series |
| LHBOTS | The Library of Hebrew Bible/Old Testament Studies |
| NASB | New American Standard Bible |
| NET | New English Translation Bible |
| NICOT | New International Commentary on the Old Testament |
| NIV | New International Version |
| NLT | New Living Translation |
| NRSB | New Revised Standard Bible |
| OTL | Old Testament Library |

| | |
|---|---|
| *RA* | *Revue d'assyriologie et d'archéologie orientale* |
| TOTC | Tyndale Old Testament Commentaries |
| *TynBul* | *Tyndale Bulletin* |
| *VT* | *Vetus Testamentum* |
| VTSup | Supplements to Vetus Testamentum |
| WBC | Word Biblical Commentary |
| *ZAW* | *Zeitschrift für die alttestamentliche Wissenschaft* |
| ZIBBC | Zondervan Illustrated Bible Backgrounds Commentary |

# Introduction to Joshua

For many people, what is known of the book of Joshua could be summarized by one verse of the African-American spiritual:

*Joshua fought the battle of Jericho, Jericho, Jericho*
*Joshua fought the battle of Jericho,*
*And the walls came a-tumbling down.*

If pressed, Rahab also might be mentioned as a contributing character. There is some truth in this portrayal. Joshua is a main character, and the battle of Jericho one of the book's pivotal events, but it is a sad reduction of the book's twenty-four chapters and nuanced theology to two people and events that are often cast in heroic, summer-blockbuster tones.

For others, the book of Joshua is the source of all kinds of evils and best avoided. Its warfare and calls for total destruction, and its removal of the Canaanite inhabitants and the gifting of their land to Israel, are cited as the basis for past and present colonial oppression and religious violence. There is some truth in this portrayal also. The book has been so used in the past and present. But this portrait tends to reduce the book to certain texts and does not attend to the protestations that such readings significantly misread the book's message. Much scholarly work is currently being done to answer these very misreadings; many of these are referenced in this commentary.

Given these two common portraits of the book of Joshua, it is no wonder the church generally neglects it, or significant portions of it. In a world in which violent warfare is live-streamed to us, we are perplexed or embarrassed by the book's violent warfare. Additionally, Joshua and the walls are too often fraught with questions raised by archaeology and history—and when we get to those endless lists of Joshua 13–21, we are stumped. What does one do with them?

This commentary works with the conviction that this book is, indeed, an important one. Its primary story is quickly sketched: Israel enters the land with the assurance that God has given it to his people. As Israel carefully follows God's law and walks in covenant relationship, God promises to be with Israel, fighting on its behalf. This is the focus of the first half of the book (chs. 1–12). In the second half of the book (chs. 13–21), Joshua distributes the land under God's direction. The final chapters (chs. 22–24) call the community in the land to prioritize and guard its worship of the Lord.

The importance of Joshua is reflected in its status as a "hinge" book in Genesis–Kings. It stands as the fulfillment of promises made to Abraham, for in Joshua Israel receives the long-promised land. Joshua starts again the narrative action of Numbers, which was put on hold for Moses' last sermon in Deuteronomy; this significantly shapes Joshua's message. Joshua also stands at the start of Joshua–Kings, setting down a paradigm for life in the land that governs the story that concludes with Israel's exile in 2 Kings 25.

This commentary seeks to show the importance of the book while acknowledging that Joshua has real interpretive challenges: its warfare and the command for total destruction, the conflicting accounts that Israel has taken the land but also has not, the problem of when Jericho had walls (and whether they fell down), the messy question of who really is an Israelite, the endless lists and what to do with them. All of these make Joshua a challenge to read and preach. And, within the context of the church, holding this book to be the Word of God and thus a trustworthy account of God and his people heightens the import of each of those difficulties.

The interpretive challenges of Joshua are worth engaging, for the book has much to say to the church. Joshua stands within the story of God, the Scriptures that stretch from Genesis to Revelation. This commentary seeks to listen to Joshua's particular contribution to that larger story. And, especially *because* Joshua presents so many difficult challenges to the reader, this commentary consciously positions itself within a churchly reading tradition. With a challenging text, it is immensely helpful to listen to the wisdom of past interpreters and to ponder a text within the church's recitation of, and reflection on, the story of God.

A churchly reading tradition is not a position that avoids the challenges of Joshua—one need only read Origen's third century AD *Homilies on Joshua* to hear how aware this church father was of the challenge presented by the book's warfare. Nor is a churchly reading one that neglects past or present scholarship; this commentary engages scholars from the church and the academy for the wisdom they bring to the task. Rather, a churchly reading tradition consciously affirms the church's great story found in the Scriptures of the Old and New Testaments, summarized in the catholic creeds of the church, and reflected in statements such as "Jesus is Lord" or "Christ has died; Christ has risen; Christ will come again." It is a reading tradition that engages Joshua to ask how it prepares for Christ and informs the church. This is the perspective from which this commentary begins, and it is within this context that the challenges of Joshua are engaged.

Not only does Joshua stand within the story of Scripture, but it is contextualized in the "story" of the ancient Near Eastern world. The ways and styles of writing (genres) of that ancient world illuminate the book of Joshua in very many ways. These are explored throughout this commentary.

## Composition, Transmission, and Canonicity

### Authorship, Audience, and Date

The Babylonian Talmud Baba Batra 15a credits Joshua with the book that bears his name, excepting the final verses that record his death (24:29–30). These are credited to Eleazar. The account of Eleazar's death (v. 33) is then credited to his son, Phinehas.

The book of Joshua, as the other books in the Former Prophets (Joshua–Kings), makes no claim of authorship. While Joshua is credited with writing a copy of the law on stones (8:32) and the words of the covenant renewal (24:26), the book as a whole remains anonymous. The book's own internal evidence makes it unlikely that Joshua was the author, for a couple of reasons. First, several notations throughout the book explain phenomena and speak of them having influence "to this day" (4:9; 5:9; 6:25; 7:26; 8:28–29; 9:27; 10:27; 13:13; 15:63; 16:10). The notations seek to enshrine a memory in people for whom the events appear to be long past and in danger of being forgotten. This suggests a compositional date later than Joshua's era. Second, in at least one instance the book relies on an earlier source for events in Joshua's day (10:13), once again placing the author's work later than the source document.

The scholarly discussion of the authorship of this book is extensive and often tied to the larger question of the authorship of the whole of the Former Prophets, as well as the authorship of Deuteronomy, for all of these books share similarities of language and outlook. Outlining this larger discussion is not the purpose of this commentary. While affirming the idea that Joshua has a lengthy and complex history of composition that could stretch from Joshua to the exile or beyond, the book comes to us now in its canonical form. That form does not consider the question of authorship, one that must be addressed in order for the book to communicate its message. Whatever one concludes about the authorship of Joshua, this commentary works with its canonical form as presented in the NIV 2011 version (see Textual Witness below).

As noted earlier in this introduction, Joshua is a "hinge" book in Genesis–Kings. This commentary will explore how Joshua takes up the language, laws, and ideas presented in the canonical books that precede it. Additionally, Joshua is part of the continuous history of Israel's life in the land (Joshua–Kings), so this commentary will also explore the shared theological and linguistic landscape of those books. The narrative's terminus in the exile suggests that era as a likely context in which the final form of Joshua–Kings took shape. This does not, however, preclude the possibility of a developing composition before its final form.

The exilic terminus of Joshua–Kings also suggests an initial exilic or postexilic audience for the final form of Joshua. While this initial audience remains conjectural, one can ask how such an audience might hear the book of Joshua. If Joshua brought the people in to the promised land, what does that mean to those who have recently been taken out of that land? What does it mean as Israel returns to the land?

Many of the book's own emphases suggest concerns pertinent to an exilic audience. God's promise of land is apparent in the book; would this encourage an exilic audience to trust God's ability to return them to the promised land? The question of Israelite identity is also apparent in the book through the tension surrounding the status of the Transjordanians and of the status of professing foreigners (Rahab) and disobedient Israelites (Achan). If ethnicity and location are not the defining factor of Israelite identity, what is? These are questions that would concern an exilic audience outside the promised land, as they would a postexilic audience returning to the land as a mixed multitude. The book's own emphasis on the law of Moses suggests that Israelite identity lies in covenant obedience. Would this instruct exiles and postexilic returnees in renewed faithfulness to that law as central to their identity as God's people?

There are, of course, accounts in Joshua that describe realities present in Israel long before the exile. One example is the Gibeonites (ch. 9), who appear elsewhere in Israel's story (2 Sam 21:1–9; 1 Chr 12:4). It may be that audiences prior to the exile engaged the account now found in Joshua 9. Whatever earlier audiences there might have been, the exilic terminus of the larger story still raises the question of what the Gibeonite narrative might communicate to that exilic audience.

Positing an exilic audience as the possible first audience for the canonical form of Joshua does not limit interpretive meanings to ones intended for that audience. The book addresses multiple audiences beyond an exilic one. Each successive generation comes to the book with its questions and concerns, historical place, and theological understandings. Pondering how an exilic audience heard the text is only a starting point for pondering how this text addresses successive audiences. Affirming this book as the Word of God is to affirm that Joshua has spoken and continues to speak. Considering how these various audiences have heard Joshua becomes a part of faithful listening, bringing richness to our own understanding of how the text continues to speak today.

## Textual Witnesses

This commentary works with the NIV 2011 English translation of Joshua, which is based on the Masoretic Text of the Leningrad Codex. This Hebrew text dates from the early eleventh century AD and is the basis for the standard critical edition of the Hebrew text, the *Biblia Hebraica Stuttgartensia*. Footnotes in the NIV indicate where the translation team has made choices that differ from this standard Hebrew text. On the whole, the MT (Masoretic Text of the Leningrad Codex) is a well-preserved text with little need for proposed emendations in order to make sense of it as it stands.

A comparison of the ancient Greek translation (the Septuagint, or LXX) with the Hebrew text reveals some variations in detail and order. These are perhaps evidence that a different Hebrew text underlies the Greek translation. Examples of differences in detail can be found in Josh 20:4–5 where the process for claiming refuge is not included in the LXX. Elsewhere, some details in the land allocation chapters differ, or the order of the text varies. For instance, the covenant renewal (8:30–35) in the LXX is found after 9:1–2, and the book's ending differs in order and detail. The NIV replicates the Hebrew text with Joshua's death and burial followed by a statement of Israel's faithfulness. The LXX moves this statement before Joshua's death. It also adds additional details of Joshua's burial and extends the conclusion to note Israel's apostasy and deliverance into the hand of Eglon of Moab. The details added in the conclusion anticipate events in the book of Judges.

None of these differences significantly alter the message of the book of Joshua, although they demonstrate the tradition's varied development in these textual witnesses. The tradition as presented in the NIV is a coherent and logically ordered narrative, and it is this canonical form with which this commentary engages.

## Canonicity and Title

In the Hebrew and Greek traditions as in the English Bible the book is named after its main character. Joshua's name means "Yahweh (that is, the Lord) saves," and it is a witness to the role of the Lord in the life of Israel and its entry to the land.

In the Hebrew Bible, the book is part of the second section of Scripture known as the Former Prophets (Joshua, Judges, Samuel, and Kings). The Former Prophets were an accepted part of the Hebrew canon by 200 BC, appearing in Hebrew and Greek versions of the Hebrew Scriptures. The Former

Prophets, together with the Torah (Genesis–Deuteronomy) and possibly some of the Latter Prophets, were likely included in an exilic canon for Babylonian Jews prior to 400 BC.[1]

The inclusion of Joshua as a prophetic book can be accounted for differently. While there are no designated or recognized prophets in Joshua, Joshua himself does speak prophetically, even using the standard prophetic messenger formula, "This is what the LORD . . . says" (24:2). He issues a curse over Jericho (6:26) that, in the course of events, comes to pass (1 Kgs 16:34). The book of Kings comments that the event occurred "in accordance with the word of the LORD spoken by Joshua son of Nun," a clear citation of Joshua's prophetic role. More importantly, the book shows the fulfillment of God's will and his promises made to the patriarchs. There is no sense that the book merely records random events that happened to bring Israel into the land. It presents events from God's perspective, showing that it is his involvement that brought to completion what was promised his covenant people.

In the formation of the Christian two-testament canon, the books of the Former Prophets were included in the section of Historical Books. This placement does not reject the prophetic character of Joshua but reflects the church's particular viewpoint. That is, that the prophetic books including Joshua reveal God's unfolding work within history. From the church's perspective, that history finds its telos in Jesus Christ. For this reason, the church affirms that "when the set time had fully come, God sent his Son" (Gal 4:4). It is the astounding incarnation of God in history that moves the church to this historically-oriented assessment of the Hebrew canon. There is also a sense that the Historical Books present historical rather than fictional events. The historiographical nature of Joshua is taken up below in the discussion of genre.

## Literary Analysis

### Genre

What kind of book is Joshua? We understand that reading a newspaper report is different than reading poetry or a fairy tale. Each genre has its own cues and rules for reading and missing those cues can lead to false readings. For instance, reading Hansel and Gretel as a news report might cause you to forbid your children going outside to play lest they be kidnapped by the woman with the gingerbread house, and the emotive style of a love poem would make

1. A succinct exploration of the canonization of the Former Prophets can be found in Lee M. McDonald, *The Formation of the Christian Biblical Canon* (Peabody: Hendrickson, 1995), 32–34.

for an unhelpful account of a parliamentary debate! Within the biblical context, the question of genre is also important, and genres as diverse as poetry, law, and narrative each have different characteristics and reading cues. So, answering the question of genre is helpful for rightly hearing a communication, and this is no less the case when reading Joshua.

There are a number of different types of genres found within the book itself. These include boundary and town lists (chs. 13–21), curses (6:26), aetiological explanations (4:9; 5:9; 6:25; 7:26; 8:28–29; 9:27; 10:27; 13:13; 15:63; 16:10), historical retrospectives (24:2–13), and covenant renewal ceremonies (24:1–27). None of these provide a genre-category for the book as a whole, and each is subsumed into and serves the genre of the whole book.

The genre of Joshua is complex and extends over the categories of narrative, historiography (that is, history writing), and theology. In addition, Joshua carries the hallmarks of ancient Near Eastern conquest accounts. Each of these is commented on in the following discussion, as together they inform the genre of Joshua and shape interpretive practice.

### *A. Joshua as Narrative*

The book is a narrative of Israel's entry into the land. Even the long lists of boundaries and towns are incorporated into a narrative structure in which the main human character, Joshua, responds to God's commands by leading Israel into the land and dividing it for their possession. The study of Hebrew narrative reveals common defining characteristics.[2] In addition to the expected narrative element of plot, Hebrew narrative utilizes a narrator who (in the world of the story) is omniscient. This is not to credit to the narrator omniscience such as is given to God; rather, it acknowledges that the narrator knows all there is to know about the world of the story so that when we read a story we are in the hands of the narrator. "[Like a movie director] the external narrator . . . decides what is to be filmed, for how long, where, and how. He or she is the final authority, and we the viewers depend on it and on the work of the film crew."[3]

With this view of the narrator's omniscience we can see that it is the narrator who reveals information at crucial moments to create suspense or surprise, or withholds information as a means of engaging the reader by raising questions or creating ambiguity about events and characters. Hebrew narrative also utilizes complex methods of characterization. Characterization

2. See Robert Alter, *The Art of Biblical Narrative* (New York: Basic Books, 1981) for a classic study. See also Yairah Amit, *Reading Biblical Narratives: Literary Criticism and the Hebrew Bible* (Minneapolis: Augsburg Fortress, 2001).

3. Amit, *Reading Biblical Narrative*, 94.

in Hebrew narrative rarely is achieved through direct narrative description of appearance, motives, or inner thoughts. Rather, the reader is invited to draw conclusions through the character's words, actions, and interactions. In addition to techniques of plot and characterization, Hebrew narrative works effectively with varying points of view, key words, and repetitions. All of these techniques help the attentive reader discern the main points a narrative seeks to communicate. Many of these characteristic marks of Hebrew narrative are noted in this commentary.

### *B. Joshua as Theological Historiography*

Joshua has all the artistic hallmarks of Hebrew narrative. It utilizes them in recounting events from Israel's past, that is, historiography. Immediately, this label presents challenges for modern readers. The first is that ancient historiography does not adhere to the same standards as does much modern historiography. For instance, modern presentations of history writing are concerned with chronological exactitude, while ancient historiography is not attached to norms of chronological order or exactitude. So, events might be related in linear time but could also trace one event along a trajectory and then backtrack in time to follow another event (a technique commonly used in 1–2 Kings). Events might also be related by moving back and forth in time without signaling the presence of disordered chronology. If we read with the expectation of chronological exactitude, our reading may miss the complex nature of the presentation.

Another standard that differentiates ancient from modern historiography is that modern historiography is generally committed to a materialist worldview. That is, facts are presented and events explained without resort to the supernatural. Ancient historiography, by contrast, assumes both the existence of the gods and their direct participation in human affairs. Everywhere in Joshua, God's presence and agency is assumed. In Joshua 1 God speaks to Joshua; in Joshua 6 it is God's power that brings down the walls; in Joshua 10 God directs the heavenly elements to fight Israel's enemies; in Joshua 14–19 God directs the lot by which land is distributed. Similar understandings are apparent throughout the ancient world, as evidenced by artifacts such as the Mesha Stele, in which Moab credits victory in battle to its god, Chemosh.[4]

A second challenge when reading ancient historiography arises from the fact that Joshua is a *narrative* historiography. This again differentiates it from modern historiography, which is generally not told in story form. All history writing takes the biases of its writers, but modern history writing attempts a

4. Bill T. Arnold and Bryan E. Beyer, *Readings from the Ancient Near East* (Grand Rapids: Baker, 2002), 160–62.

self-conscious objectivity. Such a stance is impossible, but moderns do consider aiming for it a mark of good historiography. By contrast, the narrative form of ancient historiography consciously eschews such objectivity. By the nature of narrative, the ancient historiographer exercises selectivity and artistry in presenting people and events. In short, the narrative presentation is not "just the facts," but is a conscious shaping of the presentation to forward the writer's interpretation of events. Thus, ancient historiography is intentionally persuasive literature that draws the reader in and seeks to convince them that the historiographer's viewpoint is a true presentation of reality. More telling, the historiographer seeks to persuade the reader that the god (or gods/goddesses) of whom they write are ones to which the reader should give allegiance.

This is the world of narrative historiography, and it describes the genre of Joshua. This genre results in a logical corollary and raises one further challenge. Joshua assumes that the God of Israel is both present to and active for Israel. This makes Israelite historiography (as any other ancient historiography) necessarily *theological* in nature. It is not attempting scientific assessment of the world. Rather, it acknowledges God as powerful and unique. It explains Israel's experience through that lens and by doing so presents the God of Israel as deserving of both praise and covenant loyalty. This characteristic, and not chronological exactitude or the simple presentation of historical events, is its guiding principle.

This, then, raises the final challenge of the genre of theological history writing such as we find in Joshua. It is a challenge that is particularly acute for modern (and perhaps especially for many evangelical) readers. With the emphasis on historical accuracy and verifiability within modern historiography, many today would cite this as a necessary hallmark of trustworthiness for Joshua's account. This, however, unfairly places modern notions of historiography back upon the ancient historiography of Joshua. Furthermore, the license for narrative artistry inherent in narrative historiography and its theological rather than antiquarian focus raises the question of how Joshua relates to real events in history. What is the relationship between a narrative, theological historiography, and the reality of the events it presents? Put another way, must a degree of correlation to known historical events be demonstrable to affirm this account as true historiography?

This is a fraught question today and responses to it are placed on a spectrum between a maximalist approach (Joshua is a wholly trustworthy representation of factual, real events) and a minimalist approach (Joshua is a theologically-inspired story that contains few or no events of a factual nature). The argument involves questions of the historical intentionality of the book and the archaeological and epigraphic record. It is often connected to deep commitments to the Bible as God's Word and what that entails.[5]

Some of these issues, such as the archaeological record, are addressed later in this introduction. Here, it is proposed that the idea of *theological* history does not pit theology and history against one another but requires a nuanced understanding of how such history is presented. Joshua, as ancient historiography, is by nature theological in character. It assumes and speaks of God. This does not prevent it from also speaking of real events in history. However, the account's narrative genre, its theological focus, and the parameters of ancient historiography move it away from a *primary* concern of presenting just the facts, just as they happened.

This commentary engages the events described as grounded in historical reality but also affirms that these events are recorded with theological aims in mind and artistically narrated with the persuasive intent common to narrative accounts. This does not, therefore, bind the author to a primary concern of presenting "just the facts." This can be readily illustrated with a few examples from Joshua. First, the account of the Jordan crossing (chs. 3–4) is notoriously convoluted in its chronology. Little is said of the mechanics of the parted waters, and the crossing is communicated to show the Jordan as another Red Sea. The real event of the Jordan crossing is presented not as bare fact but as carefully shaped theology, revealing God's power accomplishing the miraculous crossing as a second Red Sea crossing.

Second, the capture of Jericho is presented in chapter 6 as if no battle took place. Instead, Israel shouts, the trumpets are blown, and God's power defeats the city. Yet Joshua himself asserts that Jericho did indeed battle against Israel (24:11). The account of Jericho in chapter 6 is crafted to show that God went before Israel and by his presence the city was taken. For this reason, scenes of battle are not included. The theological focus of Joshua 6 is especially apparent when compared to Joshua 8 and the battle of Ai. That encounter reads much more like a military treatise, although God remains active in the battle. Both Jericho and Ai relate battles and both reveal God's power, but they do so in very different, selective, and nuanced ways.

Third, a final example is found in Joshua 10, in which the Israelites pursue the five-king coalition. As the narrative unfolds, the coalition is "defeated . . . completely at Gibeon" (v. 10), but later, they are again "defeated . . . completely"

5. A helpful primer on this issue remains V. Philips Long, *The Art of Biblical History* (Grand Rapids: Zondervan, 1994). See also Iain Provan, V. Phillips Long, and Tremper Longman, *A Biblical History of Israel* (Louisville: Westminster John Knox, 2003), and V. Philips Long, David W. Baker, and Gordon J. Wenham, eds., *Windows into Old Testament History: Evidence, Argument, and the Crisis of "Biblical Israel"* (Grand Rapids: Eerdmans, 2002).

(v. 20). How can an enemy be defeated completely twice? And, in both instances, how is it that survivors remain from such complete destruction? The account is not ignoring the facts: there was warfare; there were survivors. But the idea of complete defeat is emphasized as a means of showing God's power, for God had assured Joshua that "I have given them into your hand. Not one of them will be able to withstand you" (v. 8). The story is shaped to demonstrate that theological truth.

It may not always be easy to tease out the bare event from what is told with selectivity and artistry, but this commentary assumes that the two realities of theology and historiography work together to show the powerful presence of Israel's God demonstrated in the real events of Israel's past.

### *C. Joshua as Ancient Near Eastern Conquest Account*

A final genre category aids understanding of the characteristics of the theological historiography found in Joshua. This is the category of ancient Near Eastern conquest accounts. Engagement with this genre shows how well Joshua fits within the genre's parameters.[6]

Extant conquest accounts are available from contemporaneous Egyptian, Hittite, Mesopotamian, Ugaritic, and Moabite battles. These accounts show remarkable similarities to what is presented in Joshua, including depictions of the god fighting on behalf of his people and often utilizing cosmic phenomena, including hailstones, the sun, moon, and stars. In addition, the people are urged to trust in their god and not military might and to not be afraid. The enemy is generally depicted as an "Other" who is to be destroyed for the good of the god's people. Conquest is generally described in hyperbolic terms: "all" the enemy is destroyed; destruction is "complete"; "no survivors" remain. Destruction is often inclusive of all living things (the concept of *herem*; see further below at Ancient Near Eastern Background: The Problem of Warfare).

The use of hyperbolic language is not meant to deceive. It was a recognized rhetorical strategy intended to elevate the victor's god. The god's power was demonstrated by the account and was both a call for his adherents to honor and serve him as well as a justification for the demotion of the defeated god and his people.

These characteristics are apparent throughout Joshua and are particularly apparent within chapters 6–12. They are noted in this commentary as they appear, and their hyperbole is a key characteristic of Joshua's historiography. Recognizing these characteristics helps explain some of the tensions and

---

6. See K. Lawson Younger, "Ancient Conquest Accounts: A Study in Ancient Near Eastern and Biblical History Writing," JSOTSup 98 (Sheffield: Sheffield Academic Press, 1990).

contradictions within the book. Further, the characteristics of ancient Near Eastern conquest accounts make an important contribution to the book's message of the unique power of Israel's God. Shown to be a powerful God who won the land for Israel, the book's call to exclusive service of this God should be heard and obeyed.

In summary, the genre of Joshua works within several categories. As an ancient Near Eastern conquest narrative, it utilizes many of the same tropes found in conquest accounts produced by its neighbours. Using these tropes, it employs the artistry of Hebrew narrative to tell Israel's story of entry into the land. It does so as a self-consciously theological historiography so that its primary aim is to show that God was active within those events. All of this is done within the context of the overarching narrative of Genesis–Kings so that what is said in Joshua is only one moment in that larger narrative and within which it must be heard.

## Structure

At the macro level, Joshua has two distinct sections. The first (chs. 1–12) is primarily narrative and relates the taking of the land. These chapters contain familiar stories such as Rahab and the spies, the parting of the Jordan, and the taking of Jericho. The second (chs. 13–24) is primarily lists of boundaries and towns and relates the tribal allocations that Israel is to possess. The repetitive nature of these lists and the unfamiliarity of the places named often leaves the latter half of the book unengaged by many readers. Chapters 22–24 conclude the book's second part, turning from tribal allocations to matters of worship and covenant renewal. For this reason, they are sometimes considered an epilogue to the whole book.

A more detailed structure breaks the book into four sections.[7] Each section expands upon ideas found in God's commission to Joshua (1:2–9) and improves upon the previous macro structure by accounting for the difference in form between chapters 13–21 and chapters 22–24. This structure traces Israel crossing the Jordan (1:1–5:12), taking the land (5:13–12:24), distributing the land (13:1–21:45), and committing to covenantal worship within the land (22:1–24:33). The following expansion on this four-fold structure outlines the structure with which this commentary works:

7. The four-fold outline of the book proposed here is found in a published dissertation by H. J. Koorevaar, "De Opbouw van het Boek Jozua" (PhD diss., Leuven: University of Brussels, 1990) and is outlined in Provan, et al., *Biblical History*, 151–52. See the outline also in Herbert H. Klement, "Modern Literary-Critical Methods and the Historicity of the OT," in *Israel's Past in Present Research: Essays on Ancient Israelite Historiography*, ed. V. Philips Long (Winona Lake: Eisenbrauns, 1999), 456.

**Crossing the Jordan (1:1–5:12)**

| | |
|---|---|
| 1:1–18 | Promises made: Commissioning Joshua and the people |
| 2:1–24 | Spying out the land |
| 3:1–5:1 | Crossing the Jordan |
| 5:2–12 | Covenant Issues: Circumcision and Passover |

**Taking the Land (5:13–12:24)**

| | |
|---|---|
| 5:13–8:29 | The Jericho Cycle: Success and Sin, Failure and Repentance, Success Renewed |
|     5:13–6:27 | Taking Jericho |
|     7:1–26 | Achan's sin at Jericho; failure at Ai |
|     8:1–29 | Success at Ai |
| 8:30–35 | Covenant Issues: Renewal of covenant |
| 9:1–27 | Gibeon crafts a covenant |
| 10:1–43 | Defending Gibeon: the southern coalition of kings |
| 11:1–15 | Defending against the northern coalition of kings |
| *11:16–23* | *Summary: entire land taken* |
| 12:1–24 | List of kings defeated |

**Distributing the Land (13:1–21:45)**[8]

| | |
|---|---|
| 13:1–33 | Eastern allocations remembered: Reuben, Gad, and Manasseh |
| 14:1–15:63 | Western allocation: Judah |
| 16:1–17:18 | Western allocation: Ephraim and Manasseh |
| 18:1–19:48 | Western allocation: Remaining tribes |
|     18:1–2 | Tent of Meeting set up at Shiloh |
|     18:3–10 | Joshua urges allocation of remaining land |
|     18:11–28 | Allocation for Benjamin |
|     19:1–9 | Allocation for Simeon |
|     19:10–16 | Allocation for Zebulun |
|     19:17–23 | Allocation for Issachar |
|     19:24–31 | Allocation for Asher |
|     19:32–39 | Allocation for Naphtali |
|     19:40–48 | Allocation for Dan |
| 19:49–50 | Allocation for Joshua |
| *19:51* | *Summary: tribal allocations completed* |
| 20:1–21:42 | Additional allocation: Cities within the tribes |
|     20:1–9 | Designation of Cities of Refuge |
|     21:1–42 | Designation of Levitical Cities |
| *21:43–45* | *Summary: God's promises fulfilled* |

8. Presented in greater detail in Chapter 13, the Introduction to chs. 13–21.

**Covenant and Worship in the Land (22:1–24:33)**

| | |
|---|---|
| 22:1–34 | Conflict with Transjordanian tribes |
| 23:1–16 | Joshua's parting words: warning and encouragement |
| 24:1–28 | Covenant Issues: Renewal at Shechem |
| 24:29–33 | Joshua and Eleazar die; Israel's future is open |

It is helpful at this point to note three aspects of this structure that point toward the book's themes. First, the taking of Jericho stands as a unit with the initial failure at Ai and the success of the second attempt (5:13–8:29). The fall of Jericho takes up extensive narrative space for it is the first action in the land and highlights God's power on Israel's behalf. When correlated with the account of Ai, the unit demonstrates a crucial maxim for Israel's life in the land: covenant obedience meets with success, while covenant disobedience results in failure. It is a maxim throughout Joshua as well as all of Joshua–Kings. This covenantal focus of the Jericho cycle is further signified by the attention to issues of covenant that surround this unit (5:1–12; 8:30–35).

Second, the centrality of Israel's covenant relationship with the Lord is communicated by the book's first and last chapters (Josh 1, 22–24). Together, they set a context for the whole book as they highlight covenantal law and worship, the identity of the covenant people, and the binding nature of the covenant. As Joshua prepares to lead Israel into the land (ch. 1) and as its leaders die (ch. 24), it is the covenant that endures. Bound to the God of the covenant, Israel's future life in the land depends on its commitment to that covenant.

Third, several summaries appear at crucial points in the structure. The first concludes the first half of the book, in which the land is taken. The summary (11:16–23) and the accompanying list of royal powers overthrown (ch. 12) gives strong testimony that the land is taken. The second summary (19:51) briefly concludes the tribal allocations, separating them from the Cities of Refuge and the Levitical cities (chs. 20–21). A final summary (21:43–45) concludes the third section and exceeds the testimony of the first conclusion (11:16–23). It states that all God's promises are fulfilled, no enemy stands against Israel, and Israel has rest. The sense that these summaries speak of total and rapid conquest stands in contrast to the book's testimony that not all the land is taken and that enemies still remain. The tension between these two testimonies is a source of much confusion for many readers who affirm a coherent and trustworthy biblical text. These tensions will be explored in the commentary, presenting them as theologically motivated and more apparent than real.

# Historical Background

## Historical Setting of the Contents of the Book

In Genesis–Kings, Joshua follows the era of Moses in which Israel experienced the exodus and the forty years of wilderness wandering. The book begins immediately after Moses' death and concludes with Joshua's death. This sets the events of Joshua within one generation of the parting of the Red Sea, and the Israelites Joshua leads across the Jordan witnessed God's provision, grace, and discipline in the wilderness. Joshua's time is followed by the era of the judges depicted in the book of Judges.

Placing the events of Joshua in the extrabiblical historical record is not an easy task, although it would at first appear to be so. While the book of Joshua gives no date for Israel's entry to the land, 1 Kings 6:1 counts four hundred eighty years from the exodus to Solomon's fourth year and the commencement of the temple project. The consensus places Solomon's fourth year at 967 BC and thus the exodus is calculated to the mid-fifteenth century. By this reckoning, entry to the land occurred in the late fifteenth century and no later than the early fourteenth century. Yet even among those for whom Joshua represents real history, this date is not uncontested, and a thirteenth century entry to the land is often preferred. A thirteenth century entry understands the four hundred eighty years (1 Kgs 6:1) as figural, calculated as forty (representing a number of fullness for one generation) times twelve generations (representing the twelve tribes). The number thus symbolizes the passage of the fullness of time, which culminates in the temple project. Alternately, this approach tallies the four hundred eighty years as a schematic aggregate of the time spans noted within Numbers–Kings. By this reckoning, the schematic four hundred eighty years equal three hundred years of real time, setting the land entry in the thirteenth century.[9]

The material evidence provided by the epigraphic and archaeological record is no less opaque when attempting to locate the time of the land entry. Much of the evidence supports a thirteenth century land entry. The epigraphic Merneptah Stele (c. 1208 BC) records Egyptian action in Canaan. The stele names Israel as a people group and not as a nation; this identification accords well with a recent, thirteenth century entry, before Israel's national formation. Conceivably, it could describe Israel which, having entered in the fifteenth century, remains yet unformed as a nation (perhaps descriptive of the time of the judges).

9. Both options are adopted as viable explanations by Kenneth Kitchen, who diligently upholds the historicity of the biblical exodus and land entry. See *On the Reliability of the Old Testament* (Grand Rapids: Eerdmans, 2003), 159–60, 307–10.

The archaeological evidence centers on issues such as the dating of Jericho and its walls, the presence and dating of destruction layers in the cities of Hazor and Jericho, and surface surveys that note burgeoning thirteenth century settlements in the highlands. Each of these lines of evidence can be applied for or against different theories of the time and means of Israelite entry to the land. None incontrovertibly prove the narrative account as presented in the biblical text, but they do provide a reasonable backdrop with which the biblical text, to varying degrees, accords.

Utilizing the witness of biblical text, epigraphy, and archaeology, various models have developed to explain the emergence of Israel in Canaan. These include full-out conquest of the land, gradual peaceful infiltration, internal peasant revolt, and various combinations of these models. Some, such as the conquest model, are based on inattentive readings of the biblical text that assume it presents wholesale and complete conquest of the land (this issue is dealt with in several places in this commentary; see particularly Explain the Story at 11:23 and 21:43–45). Other entry models are discounted for applying modern sociological and political models onto an ancient society. While none of the models fully accounts for the evidences of text, epigraphy, and archaeology, each model sheds light on some aspect of the historical reality. Israel's emergence in the land did include warfare and conquest; indigenous peoples did join with Israel; cities and royal power were targeted by Israel; and Israel's possession of the land was indeed gradually realized over many years.

Placing Israel's entry in the land within the historical record is a challenging task. It is also a task that is particularly modernist in its orientation, seeking material verification of the biblical account (or pointedly seeking to dismiss the historicity of the biblical account). These are important questions but answering them is not a requirement for discerning the message of the book. In general, Joshua fits well against the backdrop of the ancient Near Eastern world, but there are many particulars that resist an easy fit (such as the date at which the walls of Jericho existed and when and how those walls were destroyed). There are helpful studies and commentaries that fully engage these challenges.[10]

This commentary engages the text from a different perspective. It works with the premise that real events underlie the account in Joshua. It also reckons

10. See Kitchen, *On the Reliability* and Provan, et al., *Biblical History*. Helpful commentaries that engage the historical and archaeological challenges include Richard Hess, *Joshua* TOTC 6 (Downers Grove: InterVarsity Press, 1996); Richard Hess, "Joshua" in ZIBBC, ed. John H. Walton (Grand Rapids: Zondervan, 2009); Pekka M. A. Pitkänen, *Joshua*, AOTC 6 (Nottingham/Downers Grove: Apollos/InterVarsity Press, 2010); Trent C. Butler, *Joshua 1–12*, WBC 7A (Grand Rapids: Zondervan Academic, 2014); and Trent C. Butler, *Joshua 13–24*, WBC 7B (Grand Rapids: Zondervan Academic, 2014).

with the theological intent of ancient conquest accounts. This allows for an artful telling that may not unfold in strictly chronological order and that utilizes techniques such as hyperbole and narrative characterization to shape events for theological purposes. This commentary focuses on what it discerns is the primary goal of Joshua: a theological account of Israel's past that reveals Israel's God and his purposes and calls Israel and all subsequent audiences to faith in that God.

## Ancient Near Eastern Background: The Problem of Warfare

The book of Joshua reflects an ancient Near Eastern background not only in its genre of conquest account but in many of its customs and names. These are explored in this commentary in the Listen to the Story sections where examples from ancient Near Eastern texts illustrate the ancient context of Joshua.

It is helpful at this point to examine in detail one issue that makes Joshua a problematic book: warfare. The warfare in Joshua, the call for total destruction of the inhabitants (the *herem* command), and the dispossession of the inhabitants makes this a reprehensible book for many. It is in these aspects of Joshua that the cultural distance between the ancient and modern world is especially felt. The challenge is particularly acute for those for whom Joshua is Scripture. Questions of how to understand Joshua as the Word of God, account for the warfare texts, and read such texts today is engaged by scholars in a variety of ways.[11]

The present discussion addresses the warfare in Joshua within its ancient Near Eastern context. Later in this Introduction, the theological integration of Joshua into the message of the Old and New Testaments will be explored, together with consideration of the warfare in current contexts (see Theological Message). In the commentary proper, particular passages that include warfare are dealt with, building on the foundation of this present, more general discussion. This present discussion accounts for how this commentator reflects on the warfare passages. While it may not satisfy all readers, it offers one way

11. Stanley N. Gundry, ed., *Show Them No Mercy: Four Views on God and Canaanite Genocide* (Grand Rapids: Zondervan, 2003). This volume presents four different approaches by scholars within the evangelical tradition. Additional engagements with these texts can be seen in Paul Copan and Matthew Flannagan, *Did God Really Command Genocide?: Coming to Terms with the Justice of God* (Grand Rapids: Baker, 2014); Eric A. Seibert, *The Violence of Scripture: Overcoming the Old Testament's Troubling Legacy* (Minneapolis: Fortress, 2012); Gregory A. Boyd, *Crucifixion of the Warrior God: Interpreting the Old Testament's Violent Portraits of God in Light of the Cross*, 2 vols. (Minneapolis: Fortress, 2017); Tremper Longman, *Confronting Old Testament Controversies: Pressing Questions about Evolution, Sexuality, History, and Violence* (Grand Rapids: Baker Books, 2019); and John H. Walton and J. Harvey Walton, *The Lost World of the Israelite Conquest: Covenant, Retribution, and the Fate of the Canaanites* (Downers Grove: InterVarsity Press, 2017).

of attending to the challenge of warfare so as to move to other aspects of the book that are also paramount.

The pattern of warfare in Joshua is intimately connected to its religious life, as is the case for warfare throughout the ancient Near East. War was undertaken by peoples on the understanding that their god fought on their behalf and in this respect, ancient Near Eastern warfare was considered holy or religious war. This orientation is apparent in three aspects of Israel's battles: its preparation for war, its conduct of war, and its rituals and requirements following war.[12] Attention to the religious nature of Israel's warfare is attested to in Israel's laws (especially Deut 7, 20) and historical narratives (Exodus–Joshua).

In preparation for warfare, Israel's engagement was to be by God's direction, for he was the leader of Israel's army. God could fight as a warrior on Israel's behalf (Exod 14:14; 15:3; 23:22–23, 27–30), but he could also command Israel to not fight (1 Kgs 12:22–24). Engagement with the inhabitants of Canaan came under God's decree (Deut 7:1–2) and God's oversight, and direction in battle is clearly seen before the engagement at Jericho (5:13–6:5), Ai (8:1–2), and the northern coalition (11:6). Israel might also prepare for war through oracular discernment (Judg 20:18–28; 1 Kgs 20:13–14). Because ancient warfare involved the gods and was conceived as a holy activity, it required consecration and purity of the participants (Deut 23:9–14; Josh 3:5; 2 Sam 11:8–13) and observance of covenantal requirements such as circumcision (Josh 5:2–9) and sacrifice (1 Sam 13:7–12; 2 Kgs 3:26–27).

In divinely sanctioned battle, God fought on Israel's behalf. Therefore, Israel's trust was not to be in horses or chariots but in God's name (Ps 20:7). Repeatedly, Israel won battles against great odds (Josh 11:4; Judg 7:1–8, 12; 1 Kgs 20:26–28) and through weakness (Judg 6:14–16). Israel would march into battle singing praise (2 Chr 20:20–23) and carrying the ark, the symbol of God's presence in their midst (Num 10:3–56; Josh 6:3–5; 2 Sam 11:11). The battle involved not only earthly combatants but heavenly armies (Josh 5:13–15; 2 Kgs 6:17), and nature itself fought on behalf of God's people (Josh 10:11–14; Judg 5:20–21).

After the battle, Israel praised God, acknowledging victory belonged to him (Exod 15:1–18; Judg 5:1–31). Further acknowledgement of God's victory was evident in the disposition of the plunder. Plunder could be divided among the Israelites (Deut 20:14; Josh 8:27; Judg 5:30; 1 Sam 27:9), but it could also be dedicated to God for holy use. This was known as the *herem*, the total dedication to God of plunder, people, or livestock (Deut 20:17;

12. See this outlined in Tremper Longman and Daniel G. Reid, *God is a Warrior* (Grand Rapids: Zondervan, 1995), 31–47.

Josh 6:24). When plunder was involved, it was dedicated to the LORD's use. When people within the cities of the promised land were taken, they were killed (Lev 27:29; Josh 6:21) out of concern that they might lead Israel into idolatry (Deut 20:18).

The *herem* command was included in legislation that anticipated warfare as part of Israel's experience ("when you go to war . . ." [Deut 20:1]) and is often translated as "total destruction" (Deut 7:2; 20:17). The practice was not legislated as part of Israelite warfare outside of the promised land (Deut 20:10–15) nor did it legislate complete annihilation of all people in the promised land. Inhabitants did survive Israelite battle (Josh 10:36–39 compared with 15:13–15; 1 Kgs 9:21), and, rather than total destruction of all inhabitants, the aim may have been to destroy or cripple any sense of national identity. As a "pragmatic . . . [and] standard procedure of ancient warfare,"[13] it not only "strip[ped] away anything the conquered people could rally around in order to stage rebellion,"[14] but in the biblical context the removal of the inhabitant's national identity hindered Israel identifying itself with the inhabitants.

Within the promised land, the law of *herem* was applied only against cities (Deut 20:16–18). This bears out in Joshua, where the practice is mentioned almost exclusively in connection with cities (2:10 [referring to Num 21:2–3, 25]; 6:17, 18, 21; 8:26; 10:1, 28–40; 11:11, 12, 20–21). Only in the summaries of Josh 10:40 and 11:20 might the context (which does also reference cities) extend the action beyond cities. Outside of Joshua the concept also refers almost exclusively to cities taken in battle (Num 21:2–3; Deut 2:34; 3:6; 13:15[16];[15] 20:16–17; Judg 1:17; 21:10–11), although 1 Samuel 15:2–5 shows a more extensive application of the *herem*. It appears that the command of "total destruction" was leveled against those in cities in the promised land which were taken by Israel.

Three additional lines of argumentation support the idea that the *herem* command was not a general call to wipe out all the inhabitants in the land. First, it is true that the command to "destroy them totally" in Deuteronomy 7:2 does not limit the action to cities. However, in light of Deuteronomy 20:17 and the application of the *herem* throughout Joshua to cities, it is warranted to apply such a limitation to Deuteronomy 7:2. Further, immediately following the command in Deuteronomy 7:2, Israel is prohibited from ongoing interactions with the Canaanites (v. 3). This is very odd if verse 2 intended

13. John H. Walton and J. Harvey Walton, *The Lost World of the Israelite Conquest: Covennat, Retribution, and the Fate of the Canaanites* (Downers Grove, IL: InterVarsity Press, 2017), 191.

14. Ibid., *The Lost World of the Israelite Conquest*, 191.

15. At times, the versification in the Hebrew text differs from the English Bible and is placed in brackets following the English versification.

the utter destruction of all inhabitants. A likely scenario is that the command in Deuteronomy 7:2 focused on cities (as occurred in Joshua), leaving alive those inhabitants who fled to the surrounding countryside and villages. It is ongoing interaction with the remaining population that verse 3 prohibits.

Second, entry to the land did not envision total destruction of all the population. This is apparent from the many texts that speak of God "driving out" the inhabitants (Exod 23:27–31; 33:2; 34:11; Lev 18:24–28; 20:22–23; Num 33:51–56; Deut 4:37–38; 6:18–19; 7:1, 20–23). Rahab speaks of the peoples' fear (Josh 2:9–11), and texts such as Exodus 23:20–33 anticipate this response. The Exodus passage reveals that God sent "great fear" (cf. Josh 2:9) and a "hornet" (cf. Deut 7:20; Josh 24:12) that threw people into "confusion" (cf. Exod 14:24; Josh 10:10) so that they would "turn their backs and run" (cf. 2 Sam 22:41; Ps 18:40[41]). All of this was part of God driving the peoples out of the cities and the land. Yet this action was also incomplete for God vowed he would not drive them out all at once, lest the "land . . . become desolate and the wild animals too numerous" (Exod 23:29–30; Deut 7:22). Instead, Israel would dwell among the Canaanites. This is a scenario that many texts in Joshua affirm (13:1–6, 13; 15:63; 16:10; 17:12–13). As Israel increased, it would take the land over time.

Finally, the hyperbolic nature of ancient Near Eastern conquest accounts aligns with the above evidence that the *herem* command was not genocidal in its scope. Several ancient Near Eastern accounts of destruction are discussed in Listen to the Story in Joshua 6. One of those, the ninth century BC Moabite Stele, is particularly illustrative of the point.

> Israel has utterly perished forever. . . . I fought against [Nebo] from the break of dawn until noon; and I took it; and I killed everyone in it, seven thousand men and women, both natives and aliens, and female slaves; because I had dedicated [the word uses the same root as in *herem*] it to Ashtar-Chemosh [the Moabite god].[16]

The stele describes a battle in which Israel is said to have "utterly perished forever" and in which "everyone" was killed because they had been "dedicated" (using the same word that underlies *herem*). The account's intentional hyperbole is clear, for Israel did not utterly perish. It remained after this battle concluded.

It is inaccurate, then, to charge the text with describing genocide, for neither the text's claims nor the ancient Near Eastern context supports such a conclusion. Warfare in Joshua, even with the *herem* command, does not

16. *ANET*, 320–21.

empty the land completely or destroy all the inhabitants. God went ahead of Israel to drive out the inhabitants, and Israelite action was directed against the cities. Not all the inhabitants were killed, and even in the face of "utter destruction" of cities, survivors remained. Israel's possession of the land was accomplished over several years while Israel dwelt in the midst of the remaining Canaanite inhabitants.

## Theological Message: Reading Joshua with the Old and New Testaments

### Warfare and *Herem*: A Canonical Perspective

We have sought to clarify what ancient Near Eastern warfare entailed and how the battles in Joshua align with that background. Yet this alone does not fully address the challenge the text presents. How should the text be read in light of the New Testament? Does it paint a portrait of God at odds with Jesus' command to "love your enemies," do good, turn the other cheek, and be merciful (Matt 5:43–44; Luke 6:27–36)? Does the text in any way provide a paradigm for action today? The Story of God series affirms that the "New Testament does not replace the Old Testament; the New Testament fulfills the Old Testament. We hear God's voice today in the Old Testament. In its pages, he reveals himself to us and also his will for how we should live in a way that is pleasing to him" (see Preface). This calls us to address this challenge.

First, this challenge can be addressed through consideration of the text's command for *herem*. Despite the limited character of *herem* as described above, it still portrays God as commanding the death of at least some of the inhabitants. Calvin, in the early modern period, chided those who questioned God's actions in the *herem* command. Commenting on Joshua 6:20, he argues "as [God], in whose hands are life and death, had justly doomed those nations to destruction, this puts an end to all discussion."[17]

Calvin's approach has some merit, reminding us that a just God applies judgment as he sees fit. But given the challenge presented by the text, Calvin's injunction to silence is neither fair nor wise—and even he does not abide by it but proceeds to provide an explanation.

Perhaps a way forward begins by acknowledging the challenge the command presents. It can be hard to accord with other texts that speak of God's love and mercy. In this, the command does remind us that God's ways are not ours. It seems that much of the difficulty is tied to one's starting point: if it is assumed that humans are good and deserving, then the command, as well

17. John Calvin, *Commentary on Joshua*, CCEL (https://www.ccel.org/ccel/calvin/calcom07), 79.

as God's decision to remove the inhabitants from the land, seems arbitrary and unfair. But if one's starting point is that all humans are sinful and under judgment, then judgment against the Canaanites is within God's just acts. Notably, even Israel can fall under the *herem* by God's command (see commentary on Josh 7; Deut 13:12–18); there is no special treatment for Israel or against the Canaanites. Further, if all humans are sinful and under judgment, then all humanity is deserving of destruction. It is God's mercy that limits the extent and use of the *herem*.

The *herem* command is present elsewhere in the Old Testament. Israel is no stranger to warfare after it settles in the land, both in the era of the judges and the kings. Yet the warfare practice of *herem* is almost virtually limited to Joshua. It does appear in 1 Samuel 15, and prophetic texts speak of the total destruction of armies and nations (Isa 34:2–5; Jer 50:21; 51:3) as well as Israel (Isa 43:28; Jer 25:9), but the practice is concentrated on the era of Israel's entry to the land.

While these considerations of *herem* help to place the practice within its Old Testament context, they do not fully address the challenge of reading these texts within the context of a two-testament canon. For that, a second consideration is needed and calls for reflection on the reality of warfare in Joshua and in the Old and New Testaments. Christians before now have been troubled by it. Origen, in a series of homilies on Joshua from the third century AD, applied allegorical and spiritual interpretation under the conviction that "unless those physical wars bore the figure of spiritual wars, I do not think the books of Jewish history would ever have been handed down by the apostles to the disciples of Christ, who came to teach peace, so that they could be read in the churches."[18]

Whatever is said about warfare in Joshua must be set within the whole canonical narrative. The events in Joshua are part of God's plans and purposes to restore humanity to relationship with its creator; there is much more at stake than carving out a safe land for one group of people. While working within physical, human contexts, God's plan deals with spiritual realities: sin, death, redemption, and the restoration of humanity to God.

In the pursuit of these spiritual realities, God works in different eras and in different ways. Restoration takes shape in promises made to Abraham that include land gifted to a nation, Israel (Gen 12:1–3, 7; 15:18–21; 17:8; Exod 3:8, 17; 6:8; 33:1; Deut 1:6–8; 4:1). In the land Israel was to live as a light and a kingdom of priests in the midst of the nations, drawing them to the Lord (Exod 19:5–6). At the time of Joshua, God forwards his plan through

18. Origen, *Hom* 15.1.

a nation and land and within an ancient context that includes warfare. This is, however, only one step in the fulfillment of God's plan that eventuates in the work of Christ and finds its eschatological conclusion in the earthly kingdom of God. It is this plan that provides the necessary context for the warfare in Joshua.

Throughout the Old and New Testaments, God is presented as a warrior. In the Old Testament, that role is expressed in flesh-and-blood realities. To redeem his nation Israel, God acts as a warrior on its behalf. He battles Pharaoh to rescue Israel and covenant with it at Sinai (Exod 14:14; 15:1–5). God brings Israel into the land and secures a place by battling against the inhabitants. In times of Israel's apostasy, God battles against it, using foreign nations as his agents in battle against apostate Israel. When God ejects Israel from the land, he uses Babylon as his weapon to send Israel into the judgment of exile (Jer 21:3–10). In all these contexts, God the warrior acts through flesh-and-blood battle to further his plan.

In the New Testament, however, God's plan moves into a different phase and context. Battle is engaged directly with spiritual realities and is not worked out in the context of nations and land. Instead, God comes in the flesh to continue the battle through the work of Christ. Using vivid battle imagery, Christ battles principalities and powers, winning victory through the cross. He disarms the "powers and authorities [and] made a public spectacle of them, triumphing over them by the cross" (Col 2:15).

While Christ moves away from the realm of flesh-and-blood battle to spiritual battle, this is not to say that the New Testament knows nothing of physical violence. It is a false dichotomy to consider the Old Testament as violent and the New Testament as non-violent. The New Testament does at times specifically avoid violence (such as when Jesus commands his disciples to *not* defend him or prevents violent engagement on his behalf; in doing so, he acknowledges that the hour of darkness has come, that he has angelic forces at his command, and that events are unfolding in fulfillment of Scripture [Matt 26:51–54; Luke 22:50–53; John 18:10–11]). Despite these instances when Christ avoids violence, violence remains an intrinsic part of the New Testament message. For instance, John the Baptist speaks of God's coming wrath (Matt 3:7–10), and Jesus also speaks of violent ends for the body (Matt 10:28; Luke 12:5). These New Testament expressions of violence are not, however, within military contexts nor directed to or conducted by nations. Rather, they are outcomes of the larger battle now effected in the person and work of Christ.

In the New Testament Christ battles against principalities and powers and wins victory over sin and death. This decisively moves warfare into spiritual contexts as is borne out by the New Testament's use of militaristic imagery. Paul describes himself battling as a soldier (2 Tim 4:7). His weapons wage war not "as the world does" but by "divine power to demolish strongholds" (2 Cor 10:3–5). He urges Timothy to "fight the battle well" (1 Tim 1:18), like a soldier strengthened by God's grace and enabled to please his commander (2 Tim 2:1–4). The battle is fought against false teaching and against Satan and his human agents and is won by confession of faith and by Christ (1 Tim 1:15–20; 6:12–16).

These texts call Christians to spiritual warfare against unrighteousness. Yet, while the power of sin, death, and the devil were defeated at Calvary, they remain a reality in the world until their final defeat at the end of time. Until then, Christians take up spiritual armor and battle against "the rulers, . . . authorities, . . . powers of this dark world and against the spiritual forces of evil in the heavenly realms" (Eph 6:10–18). This spiritual battle finds its culmination in John's revelation. There a great, final battle is depicted (Rev 19:11–20:6). Whether a vision of an actual future battle or a powerful image of Satan's future overthrow, it reveals Christ gaining final victory through battle. With Satan defeated the book turns to the eschatological consummation of Revelation 21. Here are realized the ideals of the promised land: peaceful rest, righteous living, and God's rule in the midst of humanity.

Warfare is present throughout the biblical text. It is part of God's plan that deals with sin, death, redemption, and restoration. In the Old Testament, God works through a nation and a land. In this context God as a warrior engages in warfare on the physical plane. Joshua and the *herem* warfare in it is contextualized within that. But the Old Testament is part of the larger story that comes to completion in the New Testament. In it Christ moves the battle from the physical realm to the spiritual realm when he wins victory over principalities and powers. The church takes up that battle. Being neither a nation or possessed of land, the church fights not on the physical plane but the spiritual.[19]

Within this larger story, the battles of Joshua—though real—also serve as types and shadows of the greater battle fought by God the divine warrior. There is a sensus plenior—a fuller reading—that in light of the larger canon sees in the Canaanites a figure for the enemy of this greater battle.

For God's people in ancient Israel warfare was part of taking the land. This moment in redemption history has passed. Now, the church engages in

19. This discussion does not grapple with the reality that the church lives out this mandate in the context of a world of nations in which war still occurs, or in which violence is mounted against the vulnerable and oppressed. The possibility of "just war" and whether the church or its individuals should engage in warfare or violence within such contexts is a crucial question, but one that takes this discussion much further afield than is possible in this introduction.

spiritual warfare. The battle having moved from the physical to the spiritual context, there can be no justification for battles such as mounted in Joshua. God does not command them; God does not need them. With Christ his work proceeds otherwise. Past or present readings of Joshua that use the book to justify warfare by any nation or people against another fail to read the text within its canonical and redemptive contexts.

In all the depiction of warfare throughout the biblical text, the ultimate expression of the divine warrior's battle is that of the servant-king freely giving himself to death on a cross. This recognizes that Christ's self-giving in battle is the culmination of and the final expression of God's redemptive plan. As summarized by Stephen N. Williams,

> In our day, it is the servant-king that gives guidance on how to relate to friend and antagonist alike. This is to contextualize and not to scorn the Old Testament. It is to allow God to give Joshua the instructions fitting for him when there was a land to be possessed and allow God to give us the instructions fitting for us when Christ is possessed.[20]

**Whose Land?**

The gifting to Israel of land inhabited by the Canaanites is extremely difficult to understand in a culture such as ours. Upholding the rights of sovereignty and self-governance, land is understood as an entity under the control of its citizens. When a nation encroaches on another nation's land, it is an encroachment on that nation's sovereignty, self-governance, and ownership.

This is not the understanding of land that undergirds the book of Joshua. In it is presented the clear understanding that the land belongs to God and therefore is his to give as he wills. This is in keeping with what is presented throughout the Old Testament. It opens with God as creator of the heavens and earth, under whose directions the nations are scattered to their appointed lands (Gen 11:8; 10:1–32).

God is the owner of the "earth . . . , and everything in it" (Ps 24:1). This is the tenet that undergirds Joshua's emphasis on the land as given by God to Israel. God's gift to Israel is one that was promised to Abraham and the patriarchs (Gen 12:1–3, 7; 15:18–21; 17:8; 26:2–3; 28:13–15; 35:12; 46:3–4) and reiterated to Moses (Exod 3:8, 17; 6:8; Deut 1:6–8) and Joshua (Josh 1:2, 3, 6, 11, 15). Israel holds the land only as a steward and not as an owner. Charged with demonstrating the uniqueness of the LORD, Israel must live in the land according to God's ways.

---

20. Stephen N. Williams in J. Gordon McConville and Stephen N. Williams, *Joshua* (Grand Rapids: Eerdmans, 2010), 124.

The gift of land to Israel is not solely for the benefit of Israel. The land provides a place of safety and rest within which it might function as a priestly nation (Exod 19:5–6). It is for this reason that Israel is not to serve idols and is enjoined to rid the land of them (Exod 20:3–4; Deut 4:15–16; 7:3–6, 25–26; 13:1–18; 16:21–22; 20:18), serving the Lord alone. It is Israel's life in the land that is to witness to its covenant Lord. From this witness, the promise of blessing to all nations would find fulfillment.

The gift of land to Israel affirms this understanding of God as owner of the land, distributing it for his purposes. Yet within Joshua there is a counter voice that tempers the idea that land is Israel's by some intrinsic right or that it is held by Israel without regard to others within it. This counter voice reflects the larger canon's attention to the welfare of the nations and the culmination of that welfare in their participation in worship of Israel's God. It is found in Rahab, an inhabitant incorporated into Israel and who shares in the rest the land offers (6:25). Elsewhere it is found in the foreigners included as part of Israel and who participate in the covenant with God for life in the land (8:33, 35).

There is also a future hope for all the lands owned by God. The hope anticipates all peoples in all nations worshiping the Lord. God's ownership of the whole world will be recognized and all will experience blessing from the God of the covenant. This will take place both in Jerusalem (Isa 2:2–4; 66:18–22) and in all lands (Isa 19:19–22; 42:4; 49:6; Zeph 2:11; Mal 1:11).

## God's People: Insiders and Outsiders

Throughout Joshua, the question of the criteria for identification as God's people is a repeated theme. Clearly, inclusion as a part of Israel is not by ethnic criteria alone. Rahab is a Canaanite, yet she praises the God of Israel and is incorporated into Israel (chs. 2, 6). Caleb's family is non-Israelite, but he stands as a supreme example of Israelite faithfulness and wholehearted devotion to the Lord (ch. 14). The Gibeonites also are ethnic outsiders, yet they enter into covenant with Israel and throughout their generations serve in the holy places of the Lord's presence (ch. 9). Further, Israel and God honor the covenant commitment made to these Gibeonite outsiders, rescuing them from the southern coalition of kings (ch. 10). Conversely, the Israelite Achan acts against the Lord and his people when he sins at Jericho (ch. 6–7).

If inclusion in Israel is not determined by ethnic criteria, neither is it determined by habitation within the promised land. This is apparent in Joshua from the treatment of the Transjordanian tribes. These tribes choose land east of the Jordan, outside of the promised land. This distinguishes them from the western tribes, and their status within Israel is contested throughout the book.

The western tribal challenge over the Transjordanian's altar (ch. 22) is the culmination of that contestation. In it the western tribes reveal their assumption that the Jordan acts as a dividing line between outsiders and true Israelites. It is a viewpoint countermanded by repeated inclusion of the Transjordanians with "all Israel"—in their commitment to assist their western brothers (1:12–18), in their inclusion in the Jordan-crossing (4:12–13), and in their inclusion in land distribution alongside all Israel (ch. 13).

The categories of insider and outsider are not, then, ethnically or geographically determined. Instead, the defining criterion is response to the God of Israel. Rahab, Caleb, and even the Gibeonites recognize the God of Israel and are incorporated into the covenant people of God. The Transjordanians likewise demonstrate faithfulness under the covenant and so their identity as insiders is upheld. Achan, despite his ethnic and geographic pedigree, acts unfaithfully under the covenant, disregarding the LORD. He acts as an outsider and is therefore purged from the people of God.

Defining insiders as those who walk in covenant faithfulness by adhering to the LORD has significant implications for the book of Joshua. First, it is a reminder that Israel is not God's elect, covenant people because of some intrinsic right or deservedness. Moses reminded the people of this as they prepared to enter the land (Deut 7:7–8; 9:4–6). Israel is chosen by God's electing grace and as part of his covenant with Abraham. There is a mystery to this election, based solely on God's choice and without regard to ideas of Israel's deservedness. But election comes with responsibility, and as God's chosen people, Israel must live in the land according to his law. Having willingly entered the covenant, they must eschew idolatry, demonstrating devotion to the LORD. By these they respond to God's saving and electing grace.

Election and covenant are the basis of the gift of land to Israel. Where Israel turns from the LORD in covenant disobedience, unfaithfulness reaps God's discipline and wrath. This is true whether unfaithfulness is found in individuals, tribal groups, or leaders. The necessity of covenant faithfulness is clearly demonstrated in chapters 6–7. There, Israel through obedience takes Jericho, but through disobedience loses Ai. Only by returning to covenant obedience does Israel show its commitment to be God's covenant people, thereby ensuring God's continuing presence and power in Israel's midst.

A second significant implication arises from defining covenant obedience as the primary identifier of God's people. This implication touches on the disposition of the Canaanites and the possession of the land. In Genesis 15:16 Abraham is told that his people will return to the promised land "in the fourth generation . . . for the sin of the Amorites has not yet reached its full measure." This associates the gifting of land to Israel with the moral state of the Canaanites (here, generically labelled "Amorites"). This is something later affirmed by Moses when he says that God will drive out the inhabitants "on account of the wickedness of these nations" (Deut 9:5).

Here, the previous comments about Israel's election are crucial to note: Israel does not receive the land because it is morally superior to the Canaanites. Moses is careful to point this out, reminding Israel the gift comes "not because of your righteousness or your integrity" (Deut 9:5). Israel is as morally bankrupt as the Canaanites, and the gift of land is only because of God's election.

While the book never specifically names Canaanite sin as the reason Israel receives the land, this understanding lies fully behind the text. What the book does acknowledge is that the state of the Canaanites is not fixed, nor is the state of the Israelites fixed. Through covenant disobedience, Israel can remove itself from God's presence, protection, and care. Likewise, the book of Joshua keeps open the possibility that Canaanites can participate in the election of Israel, coming with them into God's presence, protection, and care. The account of Rahab, placed so early in the book, makes this clear. It is possible that the Canaanites, like Rahab, could have aligned with Israel, and this commentary explores that possibility where it is presented.

The permeability of any barrier between insider and outsider is a consistent theme in Joshua. That entry into the covenant is possible regardless of ethnic or geographic identity anticipates the gospel message and the new covenant. In Christ, God's people are those "purchased for God . . . from every tribe and language and people and nation" (Rev 5:9), and Christ commissions the gospel be shared so that disciples be made "of all nations" (Matt 28:19).

The inclusion of all peoples within Christ's kingdom is signalled by the arrival of the foreign magi who do homage to the child (Matt 2:1–2). Mary and Zechariah recall the promise to Abraham—a promise that included blessing for the nations (Luke 1:55, 73). Zechariah also anticipates that those "living in darkness" will know peace—a reference to Isaiah's prophecy for those living in "Galilee of the nations" (Luke 1:70–79; Isa 9:1–2). Jesus' ministry reaches to gentiles (Matt 8:5–10, 28–34; 15:21–28; Luke 17:12–19), and it is a visitation of Greeks that prompts his prediction of his death (John 12:20–23) and the assertion that it would "draw all people to myself" (John 12:32).

In the book of Ephesians Paul speaks of the inclusion of all peoples in the church—a great mystery that has now been revealed. He says:

> This mystery is that through the gospel the Gentiles are heirs together with Israel, members together of one body, and sharers together in the promise of Christ Jesus. (Eph 3:6)

This mystery was apparent in the Old Testament, embedded in Israel's calling to be a priest-nation, and bound up in the promise to Abraham of blessing for all nations. The inclusion of so-called outsiders in Joshua reflects the same message: incorporation into God's people relies not on ethnic or geographic realities but depends on God's initiative and human response to the God of the covenant. In this, Joshua anticipates what is fully revealed in the New Testament.

### Living by the Law

Joshua begins by citing obedience to the Book of the Law (1:7–9). Obedience is crucial to Israel's successful life in the land. The reference to the Book of the Law is to Moses' words in the book of Deuteronomy (Deut 28:61; 29:21; 30:10; 31:26). It also has in mind the larger narrative of Genesis–Deuteronomy and the story of God's redemption of his people (see Listen to the Story, Chapter 1). Within this story, Israel's commitment to the law is always a response to God's prior act of redemption.

At Sinai the command to follow the covenant law is preceded by a statement of God's redemption: "you yourselves have seen . . . how I carried you on eagles' wing and brought you to myself" (Exod 19:4; cf. Deut 29:2). In response to that, Israel is called to covenant obedience to the law: "you have seen. . . . Now . . . obey me fully and keep my covenant" (Exod 19:5; cf. Deut 29:2–9). Even the Ten Commandments reflect this pattern of God's saving action (Exod 20:2; Deut 5:6) followed by covenant law (Exod 20:3–17; Deut 5:7–21). The pattern of God's redemptive acts calling forth covenant obedience to the law prevents the law's construal as legalistic. Rather, it is a joyful response: an affirmation of life given by God and now lived fully as befits a redeemed people. In following it, Israel chooses life (Deut 30:15–20).

Throughout Joshua Israel is called to life lived by the law. This is evident in how the land is to be taken (chs. 1–12), how it is to be divided (chs. 13–21), and how worship is to be conducted (chs. 22–24). When Israel abides by the law, God's presence remains with them and Israel receives all the blessings promised under the covenant (Deut 28:1–14). Conversely, Israelite disobedience shuts Israel off from those same realities (Deut 28:15–68).

It is the formulation of the law in the book of Deuteronomy that most influences the book of Joshua, as well as Judges, Samuel, and Kings. Within these books, the status of Israel's covenant life is always gauged by its obedience to the law. As Joshua–Kings proceed, it is apparent that Israel fails under the law much more than it succeeds. Yet repeatedly, God remains faithful, rescuing Israel in battle, sending prophets to warn them and woo them back to covenant life, and even allowing a king (despite the inherent danger kingship poses to Israel [1 Sam 8:1–18]). God's faithfulness is evident in that exile (the most extreme punishment for covenant disobedience) is forestalled for centuries. It is not until the eighth century that the Northern Kingdom of Israel is sent to exile (2 Kgs 17:1–6) and not until the sixth century that the Southern Kingdom of Judah is sent to exile (2 Kgs 25:1–21).

Joshua begins this long history with the urging to follow the Book of the Law. It is a hopeful beginning, but one that even the book of Joshua suggests will not be maintained—and indeed the history unfolds to show Israelite unfaithfulness in spite of God's faithfulness. Even when Israel is removed from the land gifted in Joshua, God's faithfulness does not end, for to the exiles God speaks of renewal of covenant—a new covenant (Jer 31:31–34).

Under that new covenant the law will be imprinted on Israel's mind and heart. This will enable true mutuality in the covenant relationship. God will be their God and Israel his people. Sin and wickedness, which so compromised the old covenant, will be forgiven and remembered no more. This is an incredible hope to have in mind throughout Joshua. The book begins Israel's life in the land with an emphasis on promises fulfilled and hope for the future. Yet we know the ongoing story moves in a very different direction.

In the face of covenant failure, the new covenant anticipates a new redemptive act of God. The New Testament reveals that the new covenant is inaugurated through the redemptive blood of Christ (Luke 22:20; 1 Cor 11:25; 2 Cor 3:6; Heb 8:8–12; 10:15–17). Under the new covenant both Jew and gentile are redeemed and set free from sin. Both now live in the covenant life of Christ. As with the old covenant, the new covenant calls its members to a life of obedience yielded now to a new law: the law of the Spirit.

### Joshua: God's Leader

Joshua begins his ministry alongside Moses and stands with him at significant events in Israel's exodus and wilderness experience (Exod 17:8–15; 32:17–18; 33:7–11; Num 13–14). He is commissioned by Moses as his successor (Deut 31:1–13) and this is affirmed by God (Josh 1:1–9). Throughout the book, Joshua takes up Moses' ministry and, in the end, his faithful service is recognized in the title ascribed to him: the "servant of the Lord" (24:29).

Joshua is often remembered for his deeds in battle, and these are an important aspect of his role in the book. As a warrior, he leads the people into the "rest" the land affords. This rest was promised and provided by God (1:13, 15; 11:23; 21:43–45; 23:1). In addition to his role as warrior, there are many other characterizations of Joshua that are profitably noted. He serves a prophetic role, using the standard prophetic formula, "This is what the Lord says" (24:2), and issuing prophecies (6:26; 1 Kgs 16:34). Like a king, he is not to "turn from [the law] to the right or to the left" (1:7; Deut 17:20). Like the righteous man of Psalm 1 he is to "meditate on [the law] day and night" (v. 8; Ps 1:2).

In characterizing Joshua, it is his stance vis-à-vis his devotion to God and God's law that is of primary importance. Joshua is charged to follow the law (1:7–8), and he is exalted in the peoples' eyes for his obedience to God (3:7; see Explain the Story, Chapter 3). Throughout this commentary, Joshua is shown to be commanded by God and then obediently exercising such commands. In the end, he reveals his wholehearted commitment to God by affirming his allegiance through covenant (24:15).

In the Epistle to the Hebrews, the author speaks of a Sabbath-rest for the people of God. He notes that Joshua ultimately failed to provide such a rest due to the peoples' disobedience (Heb 4:8–9). This failure, then, is taken typologically as indicative of a future rest still to come and now provided through the work of Christ. It is this rest into which Christians are brought, a rest won by Christ's battle and victory over sin and death.

In light of the typological association of Joshua to Jesus, further reflection opens on the various roles in which Joshua is cast. Each provides typological connections to Jesus. Thus, as one who fulfills the ministry of Moses, Joshua anticipates Jesus, the one who provides the greater fulfillment of Moses' ministry. As final covenant mediator and lawgiver, Christ is the new Joshua, completing Moses' ministry. Joshua is exalted for his obedience to God and, in a similar way, Christ's obedience even unto death marks him as worthy of all exaltation (Phil 2:8–9). The charge to Joshua to meditate day and night upon the law, not turning from it to the right or the left, finds its fullest expression in Christ. Paradoxically, in the mystery of Christ as the eternal Word, he is himself the word of God and law of God upon which Joshua was to meditate. Finally, as Joshua's meditation evokes the law for kings in Deuteronomy 17 and the words of Psalm 1, Jesus demonstrates the perfect devotion of a king before the law and the perfect righteousness adjured in Psalm 1.

None of these typological associations detracts from the reality of the person and ministry of Joshua. Rather, they open the reading of the book of Joshua to deeper reflection and consideration of God's imprint of his life and purposes upon those through whom he worked in the Old Testament.

# Resources for Teaching and Preaching

There are many good resources for the study of the book of Joshua. These include very academic treatments as well as more popular writings. Many of these are found in the footnotes. Some that may be especially helpful include:


Butler, Trent C. *Joshua 1–12*. Word 7A. Grand Rapids: Zondervan, 2014.

Butler, Trent C. *Joshua 13–24*. Word 7B. Grand Rapids: Zondervan, 2014.

Copan, Paul and Matthew Flannagan. *Did God Really Command Genocide? Coming to Terms with the Justice of God*. Grand Rapids: Baker Books, 2014.

Creach, Jerome F. D. *Joshua*. Interpretation. Atlanta: John Knox, 2003.

Firth, David G. *The Message of Joshua: Promise and People*. BST. Downers Grove, IL: IVP Academic, 2015.

Franke, John R. ed, *Joshua, Judges, Ruth, 1–2 Samuel*. ACCS 4. Downers Grove, IL: InterVarsity Press, 2005.

Hawk, L. Daniel. *Every Promise Fulfilled: Contesting Plots in Joshua*. Eugene, OR: Wipf & Stock, 1991.

________. *Joshua*. Berit Olam. Collegeville, MN: Liturgical Press, 2000.

Hess, Richard, *Joshua*. TOTC 6. Downers Grove, IL: InterVarsity Press, 1996.

________, "Joshua." Pages 2–93 in ZIBBC. Edited by John H. Walton. Grand Rapids: Zondervan, 2009.

Longman, Tremper, *Confronting Old Testament Controversies: Pressing Questions about Evolution, Sexuality, History, and Violence*. Grand Rapids: Baker Books, 2019.

Matties, Gordon H. *Joshua*. BCBC. Kitchener, ON: Herald Press, 2012.

McConville, J. Gordon. *Joshua: Crossing Divides*. Phoenix 6. Sheffield: Sheffield Phoenix, 2013.

Pitkänen, Pekka M. A. *Joshua*. AOTC 6. Leicester/Downers Grove, IL: Apollos/InterVarsity Press, 2010.

Walton, John H., and J. Harvey Walton, *The Lost World of the Israelite Conquest: Covenant, Retribution, and the Fate of the Canaanites*. Downers Grove: InterVarsity Press, 2017.

Woudstra, Marten H. *The Book of Joshua*, NICOT. Grand Rapids: Eerdmans, 1981.

CHAPTER 1

# Joshua 1:1-18

## LISTEN to the Story

[1]After the death of Moses the servant of the LORD, the LORD said to
Joshua son of Nun, Moses' aide: [2]"Moses my servant is dead. Now then,
you and all these people, get ready to cross the Jordan River into the land
I am about to give to them—to the Israelites. [3]I will give you every place
where you set your foot, as I promised Moses. [4]Your territory will extend
from the desert to Lebanon, and from the great river, the Euphrates—all
the Hittite country—to the Mediterranean Sea in the west. [5]No one will
be able to stand against you all the days of your life. As I was with Moses,
so I will be with you; I will never leave you nor forsake you. [6]Be strong
and courageous, because you will lead these people to inherit the land I
swore to their ancestors to give them.

[7]"Be strong and very courageous. Be careful to obey all the law my
servant Moses gave you; do not turn from it to the right or to the left,
that you may be successful wherever you go. [8]Keep this Book of the Law
always on your lips; meditate on it day and night, so that you may be
careful to do everything written in it. Then you will be prosperous and
successful. [9]Have I not commanded you? Be strong and courageous. Do
not be afraid; do not be discouraged, for the LORD your God will be with
you wherever you go."

[10]So Joshua ordered the officers of the people: [11]"Go through the camp
and tell the people, 'Get your provisions ready. Three days from now you
will cross the Jordan here to go in and take possession of the land the LORD
your God is giving you for your own.'"

[12]But to the Reubenites, the Gadites and the half-tribe of Manasseh,
Joshua said, [13]"Remember the command that Moses the servant of the
LORD gave you after he said, 'The LORD your God will give you rest by
giving you this land.' [14]Your wives, your children and your livestock may
stay in the land that Moses gave you east of the Jordan, but all your fighting men, ready for battle, must cross over ahead of your fellow Israelites.

You are to help them [15]until the LORD gives them rest, as he has done for you, and until they too have taken possession of the land the LORD your God is giving them. After that, you may go back and occupy your own land, which Moses the servant of the LORD gave you east of the Jordan toward the sunrise."

[16]Then they answered Joshua, "Whatever you have commanded us we will do, and wherever you send us we will go. [17]Just as we fully obeyed Moses, so we will obey you. Only may the LORD your God be with you as he was with Moses. [18]Whoever rebels against your word and does not obey it, whatever you may command them, will be put to death. Only be strong and courageous!"

*Listening to the Text in the Story*: Genesis-Deuteronomy; see especially Genesis 12:1–3, 7; 15:4–21; Numbers 32; Deuteronomy 31:1–13, 23–26; 32:44–47; Annals of Thutmose III

The book of Joshua continues the story of Genesis to Deuteronomy, bringing Israel into the land promised Abraham in Genesis 12. Joshua's emphasis on the LORD's gift of the land, the conduct of warfare and the treatment of Canaan's inhabitants, and the importance of obedience to the law of Moses all arise out of this long narrative. Joshua is closely tied to the book of Deuteronomy, taking up several of its key words, phrases, and themes. Several connections to the larger narrative are especially prominent in Joshua 1. These are noted here.

### Joshua and Moses

Joshua begins by noting the death of Moses, the "servant of the LORD" (v. 1). Moses died in Deuteronomy 34, where his role as the "servant of the LORD" is noted (Deut 34:5). These references to Moses immediately connect the book of Joshua to the people and events of Deuteronomy. Although Moses is dead, his presence as "servant of the LORD" continues throughout the chapter (vv. 1, 13, 15; in vv. 2 and 7 he is "my servant") and the book (8:31, 33; 11:12; 12:6 [2x], 13:8; 14:7; 18:7; 22:2, 4, 5). Joshua continues the ministry of Moses, and his initial speech to the Transjordanian tribes (vv. 12–15) reveals his understanding of the binding nature of Moses' ministry. At the end of the book, after Joshua's long and obedient ministry, he himself earns the appellation "servant of the LORD" (Josh 24:29; see also Judg 2:8). The title is high recognition, placing him in the company of Moses and other servants of God such as Abraham (Gen 26:24) and David (1 Kgs 8:66). Joshua as "servant of the LORD" is recognized for his faithful service, by which the ministry of Moses, the servant of the LORD, is accomplished and the people brought into their inheritance.

The connection of the ministries of Moses and Joshua as well as the reliance of Joshua on Deuteronomy is also apparent through comparison of Deuteronomy 31:1–13 and Joshua 1:1–9. Deuteronomy 31 records Moses' commissioning of Joshua; in Joshua 1, Joshua is commissioned, but now by the LORD himself. Several themes are shared between thc passages: crossing the Jordan, inheriting the land given by the LORD as sworn to the ancestors, and obedience to the LORD's instruction or law. In both, commands are to be obeyed: Moses' in Deuteronomy 31:5, 10 and Joshua's in Joshua 1:16, 18. Beyond the thematic similarities, key words and phrases are shared: "crossing" the Jordan (Deut 31:2, 3, 13; Josh 1:2), the Lord's assurance that he is "with" his people and Joshua (Deut 31:6, 8 [cf. v. 23]; Josh 1:5, 9, 17), and he will never "leave or forsake" them (Deut 31:6, 8; Josh 1:5). Moses encourages Joshua to not be "afraid or terrified" (Deut 31:6). The LORD's encouragement is to not be "afraid" or "discouraged" (the Hebrew verb is translated "terrified" in Deut 31:6).

The resonance between the two passages is intentional. The commission issued by Moses is echoed by the LORD in Joshua 1. In this way, the transition of leadership occurs by the highest authority. The reader and the Israelites are to understand the LORD's hand is upon Joshua.

### The Book of the Law

Joshua is commanded to obey the law (in Hebrew, *torah*) of Moses, and this law is central in the book of Joshua. This provides another connection to the Pentateuch.

In its narrowest sense, this law points to the law code given to Moses by which Israel's conduct was regulated (such as in Exod 20:22–23:33; Lev; Deut 12–26). But to limit the understanding of law only to the law codes is to miss the law's full sense. "The law" is really the long narrative of God's gracious redemption and covenant with Israel recorded in Genesis–Deuteronomy.

Israel's conduct and its laws are only rightly viewed within this narrative. In this narrative, God graciously acts and Israel is invited to a response of covenant life. It is covenant life that is expressed through the narrative and in the ancient Near Eastern categories of the laws the narrative contains. *Torah* will be translated "law" in this commentary, following common convention. Such usage, however, understands Israel's law cannot be construed outside of this narrative of redemption and covenant. Israel's law is not an abstract ideal but relational imperative and loving response.

The importance of the law within Joshua is apparent: Joshua and Israel are to obey it in order to find success. Most often, the law referenced in Joshua is the law of Moses recorded in the (or "this") "Book of the Law" (v. 8). This is a self-conscious reference to the words of Moses in the book of Deuteronomy. There, Moses' oral instruction is written down in a book (Deut 30:10; 31:9, 24) that is to be read and obeyed (Deut 30:10; 32:46). It is this book which is called the "Book of the Law (Deut 28:61; 29:21[20] 30:10; 31:26).[1] The LORD's law given in the book of Deuteronomy is the standard of measure applied to Joshua and Israel as they enter the land.

## The Promise of Land: Back to the Garden

Joshua 1 emphasizes the land given by the LORD (vv. 2, 3, 6, 11, 15). The land is given to fulfill ancient promises made to Abraham (Gen 12:1–3, 7; 15:18–21; 17:8) and reiterated to Isaac (Gen 26:2–3) and Jacob (Gen 28:13–15; 35:12; 46:3–4). The promise of land is likewise reiterated to Moses (Exod 3:8, 17; 6:8; 33:1; Deut 1:6–8; 4:1).

The promises given Abraham were God's response to the sin begun in the garden and escalated through Genesis 3–11. Through these promises, God worked to restore his people to Eden—the garden-place of God's presence and provision. That place of God's presence came, in time, to be depicted in the tabernacle (and later, the temple). In these places of worship, fashioned to look like the garden (with gold and precious jewels [Gen 2:12, Exod 25:3, 7], guarding cherubim [Gen 3:24, Exod 25:18], and garden symbols [Exod 25:33–36, 1 Kgs 6:18, 32, 35; 7:18–20, 23–24, 36]), God met with his people, as he had met with Adam and Eve. These places of worship are associated with the concept of "rest," made possible by the communion with God that occurs in them. In the garden, this rest is marked by God's own Sabbath rest; the Sabbath command is enjoined upon Israel after the tabernacle is commanded (Exod 31:12–18) and built (Exod 35:1–3). Even the historic moment of temple building is marked by rest (2 Sam 7:1; 1 Kgs 5:4–5).

The land into which Israel enters is a place of "rest" (1:15; 21:44; 22:4; 23:1). The fulfillment of the promise of land is not simply entry into a geographical place; it is also entry into a typological ideal of rest, provision, and the presence of God. The book begins with the emphasis on the LORD's promise to give the land; it ends with acknowledgment that these promises are fulfilled (Josh 23:14; 24:8–13). The book of Joshua contains the hope that the blessing of "rest" experienced in the garden will be reinvigorated in the promised land.

1. Elsewhere, Joshua refers to the "Book of the Law of Moses" (Josh 8:31; 23:6).

## The Transjordanian Lands

Reuben, Gad, and the half-tribe of Manasseh settle east of the Jordan, outside the promised land (Josh 1:4). This request was granted by Moses (Num 32), though he characterized it as a sin on par with Israel's refusal to enter the land. Although Moses says the request angers the LORD, he grants it. The proviso is that the eastern tribes assist Israel to possess the promised land.

The Transjordanian request is negative, and the status of the eastern tribes and their land, being outside the promised land, remains problematic throughout Joshua. The questionable Transjordanian status is heightened given the henotheistic culture in which Israel exists. Within that ancient Near Eastern culture, a people belong to a god only within the territorial boundaries claimed by that god. Within this cultural context, the relationship of the Transjordanians to Israel, which dwells in land determined by the national God, is in question. The question of the Transjordanian status appears throughout Joshua and comes to a head in Joshua 22.

## The Style of Conquest Accounts

The structure of Joshua 1–11 shows similarities to the Egyptian conquest accounts in the Annals of Thutmose III. The Annals combine lengthy, detailed reports and short, repetitive accounts, such as this excerpt from Thutmose's Sixth Asiatic Campaign:

> Regnal year 30. Now his majesty was in the foreign land of Retenu on this 6th victorious campaign of his majesty. Arriving at the city of Kadesh, destroying it, cutting down its trees and plucking its barley. Proceeding from Shesryt, arriving at the City of Djamer, arriving at the city of Irtjet. Doing likewise against it.[2]

Such short accounts may be those referred to elsewhere in the annals as "recorded daily . . . on a leather scroll"[3] and may have been later included in the annals as-is, or as an expanded narrative.

Joshua likewise has lengthy descriptive accounts (Joshua 1–8) and short, stylized, repetitive summaries (e.g., Josh 10:28–11:14). Beyond the broad structural similarities, Joshua 1 resembles the Annals by beginning with victory credited to divine aid and commission. Thus, Thutmose begins his campaign "in order to expand the borders of Egypt according to what his [brave] and victorious father [Amun-Re] ordained that he conquer."[4] The parallels might

2. *COS* 2.2A:13.
3. Ibid., 2.2A:12 (lines 93–94).
4. Ibid., 2.2A:9.

be explained by Israelite reliance on Egyptian scribal traditions for recording military actions.[5]

Entry into the land begins with Joshua commissioned by the LORD to lead Israel. As noted above, this confirms the commission bestowed by Moses (Deut 31:1–8) by authoritatively using the LORD's voice. Thus confirmed, Joshua commands Israel, preparing them to enter the land. The land west of the Jordan had been gifted to all Israel, so the choice of the Transjordanian lands by Reuben, Gad, and Manasseh is here addressed. An ongoing concern of the book will be the status of these tribes: are they still part of Israel?

### The Preparation of Joshua (1:1–9)

These verses provide a short summation of the four major sections of the book:

| | |
|---|---|
| First | God commands Joshua to cross the Jordan (v. 2); this Israel does in chapters 1:1–5:12. |
| Second | Israel is to take the land given by God (vv. 2–3); this is the content of chapters 5:13–12:24. |
| Third | The distribution of land is assumed in verse 4; this is accomplished in chapters 13:1–21:45. |
| Fourth | Joshua is urged to covenant obedience according to the law given by Moses (vv. 7–9); this is the focus of the book's epilogue which details:<br>the peoples' ongoing service to God, signified in the narrative of the second altar (ch. 22),<br>Joshua's farewell address (ch. 23) and<br>the renewal of covenant (ch. 24).[6] |

Joshua 1 begins by recalling Moses, the "servant of the LORD." Moses plays a major role in Exodus to Deuteronomy as Israel's deliverer, leader, mediator, lawgiver, and judge. In Deuteronomy Moses rehearses the peoples' history, delivers laws to constitute their life in the land, and gives direction for taking possession of the land. Yet Moses does not enter the land but dies east of the

5. See the pertinent sections of the Annals, together with brief commentary by James K. Hoffmeier in *COS* 2.2A:7–13. See also Hoffmeier's treatment of the phenomenon in "The Book of Joshua as a Land Grant," in *Faith, Tradition and History*, ed. A. R. Millard (Winona Lake: Eisenbrauns, 1994), 165–79.

6. As set out in Koorevaar, *De Opbouw van het Boek Jozua*; see also Provan, *Biblical History*, 151–52.

Jordan according to the LORD's command (Num 20:9–12; 27:12–14; Deut 1:37; 31:2). Joshua becomes the new leader as one in whom is the "spirit of wisdom" (Deut 34:9).

Joshua is introduced as "son of Nun," a family name (patronym) known from prior accounts (Exod 33:11; Num 11:28; 13:8, 16; 26:65; Deut 1:38; 31:23; 32:44: 34:9). As a "son of Nun" he is of the tribe of Ephraim (1 Chr 7:20–27). In Numbers 13–14 he is named "Hoshea" (Num 13:8; see also Deut 32:44), which is a variant of "Joshua," meaning "The LORD saves." He is one of the twelve spies and Moses renames him Joshua in that account (Num 13:16). Of the spies, only Joshua and Caleb give a good report and trust the LORD for the land (Num 13:30; 14:6–9). They are two of the wilderness generation who, because of their faith, survive to enter the land (Num 14:38; 26:65; 32:12–13).

Joshua is "Moses' aide" (*mesharet*), a designation that appears in previous texts. As Moses' aide, Joshua accompanies Moses up Sinai (Exod 24:13; 33:11; see also Num 11:28; Deut 1:38; Josh 1:1) and waits upon Moses when he encounters the LORD in the tent of meeting (Exod 33:7–11). His zeal for the LORD is apparent, for he lingers after Moses leaves the tent (Exod 33:11). Joshua later demonstrates similar zeal when, jealous on Moses' behalf, he urges Moses to stop those who are prophesying (Num 11:26–30).

It is perhaps not accidental (given the warfare recorded in the book of Joshua) that his first appearance in the biblical text is as a military leader, victorious over Amalek (Exod 17:8–16). That victory is commemorated in a scroll, and Joshua is particularly advised to hear and remember. Perhaps this memory serves as a source of encouragement as he leads the people into the land. When Moses and Joshua descend from Sinai, it is Joshua who alerts Moses to the noise of the unruly Israelites; as a military leader, he initially concludes there is war in the camp (Exod 32:17).

Although both Caleb and Joshua enter the land, it is Joshua whom the LORD elects to lead the people, for he has the "spirit of leadership" (Num 27:12–23). Moses lays hands on Joshua, and in the sight of the people some of his authority is granted Joshua. The people are now to obey him. At the end of Deuteronomy, the succession is confirmed by Moses in terms that are echoed by the LORD in Joshua 1 (Deut 31:1–8; Josh 1:2–9). Joshua is to lead the people across the Jordan and secure possession of the land (Deut 1:38; 3:28), enabled by the LORD's presence and promise (Deut 31:23). In anticipation of securing the land, Joshua and Eleazar the priest are appointed to apportion the land among the tribes, including those lands granted the tribes east of the Jordan (Num 32:28–30; 34:17). This apportioning occurs in Joshua 13–21.

Although the first chapter of Joshua transfers leadership from Moses to

Joshua, Joshua's ministry does not negate or supersede that of Moses, who remains the "servant of the LORD" or "my servant." Joshua's leadership continues Moses' leadership, Joshua is promised God's presence as the LORD was "with Moses" (vv. 5, 17), and the peoples' commitment to obey Moses is extended to Joshua (vv. 17–18). Although Joshua continues Moses' ministry, Moses' death marks the passing of an era. It remains to be seen what new leadership will look like and how Joshua's gifts and experiences will be utilized.

The LORD commands Joshua to cross over the Jordan. This is according to the word of Moses, even though Moses himself does not cross over (Deut 3:27; 31:2; 34:4). Instead, with the LORD going ahead (Deut 31:3) Joshua will lead the people across (Deut 3:28; 31:3). The land is gifted to the Israelites in fulfillment of the ancient promises made to the patriarchs and reiterated to Moses (see Listen to the Story). Israel will engage in battle, but that alone is not sufficient to secure the land. The land is gifted; Israel receives it by God's mercy and covenant faithfulness.

The theme of the land as a gift "given" is highlighted in this chapter. The word "give" (from the Hebrew root *ntn*) occurs eight times (vv. 2, 3, 6, 11, 13, 14, 15 [2x]), and the emphasis falls on what God gives. In most instances, the land is given by the LORD and is clearly west of the Jordan (vv. 2, 3, 6, 11, 15 [the first occurrence]). Only once does the LORD give land east of the Jordan but even then, the giving is mediated by Moses (v. 13); twice those same eastern lands are given by Moses (vv. 14, 15 [the second occurrence]).

Collating these occurrences with those throughout the book reveals a similar pattern. Several characters give land,[7] such as Caleb (15:19) and the people (19:49, 50; 20:2, 8 [in the Transjordan]; 21:3, 8, 9, 11, 12, 13, 21). Joshua gives the land as Israel's inheritance (11:23; 12:7) and gives specific portions or bequests (14:12, 13; 15:13; 17:14; 22:7). Once, Joshua gives the Transjordanian land, in fulfillment of the LORD's command to Moses (17:4; cf. 11:15, 23; 14:2).

Besides these instances, overwhelmingly, it is the LORD who gives in the book. Most often, it is the promised land God gives (1:2, 3, 6, 11, 15; 2:9, 14, 24; 5:6; 18:3; 21:43 [2x]; 23:13, 15, 16; 24:13). As noted above, he once gives the Transjordanian land although it is a gift mediated by Moses (v. 13). God also gives cities (6:2, 16 [Jericho]; 8:1, 7, 18 [Ai]; 10:32 [Lachish]), kings (8:1; 10:8, 30; 11:6, 8), and people (10:12, 19; 21:44; 24:8, 11). The picture is very different, however, when comparing to what Moses gives. Only once is Moses commanded to give the promised land (9:24). Elsewhere, it is the Transjordanian land Moses gives (1:14, 15; 12:6; 13:8 [2x], 15, 24, 29; 14:3; 18:7; 22:4, 7). The implication is clear: God's intent is to give the promised

7. Different words are used in NIV to translate *ntn*, "give," including "delivered" (6:2; 8:1, 18), "hand over" (11:6), "assigned" (13:8), "designate" (20:2, 8) and "allot" (21:8, 9).

land—the land west of the Jordan—and he does so. The giving of the land east of the Jordan is God's concessionary will (Num 32:22), and it is enacted through Moses.

As God indicated to Moses, the giving of the land fulfills the ancient prophecies made to the patriarchs (Deut 34:4). Reiterating the words of Moses (Deut 11:24–25), Israel will take "every place where you set your foot" (Josh 1:3) so that "no one will be able to stand against you" (v. 5). The area of Canaan is that given in Deuteronomy 11:24 and agrees with the boundaries sketched for the province of Canaan in Egyptian sources of the second millennium.[8] The inclusion of the Hittite country in Josh 1:4 reflects a Late Bronze Age (1550–1200 BC) reality for, at that time, the Hittite Kingdom, centered in Anatolia, contested Egypt for control of northern Canaan.[9] A more detailed outline of the boundaries is found in Numbers 34:3–12. From the south end of the Dead Sea, the boundary arced south through the Wilderness of Zin, then curved northwest to the Brook of Egypt. The Mediterranean provided the western boundary north to Mount Hor. There, the boundary turned east toward the Euphrates River, where it turned south again toward the land east of Galilee. There, it turned to join the Jordan River, which served as the eastern boundary.

Three times in this chapter Joshua is commanded by God to be "strong and courageous" (vv. 6, 7, 9). A fourth time the command is issued by the Transjordanian tribes (v. 18). The first command calls Joshua to strength and courage to lead the people to inherit the land promised the ancestors. The same command was earlier given by Moses and the LORD at Joshua's commissioning (Deut 31:6–8, 23). The repetition here affirms God is passing the leadership to Joshua. He assures Joshua that he is with him as with Moses and will "never leave or forsake" him. Joshua witnessed God's presence with Moses through the exodus and wilderness wanderings; now Joshua is assured of that same presence. That God will be with him to accomplish the promise made to the ancestors is to be the basis of Joshua's strength and courage, not any military prowess or might (Deut 20:1–4).

In light of God's promises, Joshua is to respond (v. 7). The imperative "be

---

8. Several of the Amarna Letters attest to this understanding of the land of Canaan. See the discussion in Benjamin Mazar, *The Early Biblical Period: Historical Essays* (Jerusalem: Israel Exploration Society, 1986), 191–94; Yohanan Aharoni, *The Land of the Bible: A Historical Geography*, rev. (Philadelphia: Westminster, 1979), 67–77; Richard Hess, "Occurrences of Canaan in Late Bronze Age Archives in the West Semitic World," in *Israel Oriental Studies 18: Past Links: Studies in the Languages and Cultures of the Ancient Near East*, ed. Sh. Izre'el, I. Singer, and R. Zadok (Winona Lake, IN: Eisenbrauns, 1998), 365–72.

9. In the Merneptah Stele dated 1209/8 BC, reference is made to "Hatti," (the Hittites) with respect to northern Canaan. *COS* 2.6:40–41.

strong and very courageous" is in Hebrew preceded by the word *raq*, "only," indicating that what follows is the desired response to God's presence and promise in verses 2–6.[10] The imperative response is further heightened by the inclusion of "very," which appears only in this iteration of the command to be strong and courageous. Joshua's strength and courage is in this instance directed toward one goal. He must obey "all the law of Moses" and "everything written in it." Verse 8 clarifies the law of Moses is the Book of the Law, that is, the statutes and instructions as recorded in the book of Deuteronomy (see Listen to the Story).

Through obedience to this law Joshua will be "successful" and "prosperous" (vv. 7–8). Not only does this include land entry ("wherever you go"; v. 7), but it suggests prosperous success in all areas of leadership and life in the land. So important is this law that Joshua is to be "careful to obey" (in Hebrew, "to keep to do"; a similar construction appears in v. 8). He is not to turn from it "to right or left" but should "meditate on it day and night." It is wholehearted commitment to study the law that leads to right action that eventuates in success.

In the desired attitude toward the law, Joshua is characterized in the same way as are kings and righteous individuals. In Deuteronomy 17:14–20 one finds requirements placed on kings. Once enthroned, a king is to read the law "all the days of his life" so that he will "follow carefully" (using Hebrew *lišmōr*) all the words of the law and not "turn (from Hebrew *swr*) from the law to the right or to the left" (Deut 17:19–20). Joshua is commanded to similar wholehearted attention, meditating on the law "day and night" (v. 8). He does so for the same purpose: to "be careful" (also using Hebrew *lishmor*) to obey the law. Joshua is, like the kings, not to "turn (also from Hebrew *swr*) from it."

Not turning aside from the law to the right or left is a quality laid particularly upon kings, though it is valued throughout Deuteronomy (5:32; 17:11, 20; 28:14). Yet only one king is credited with completely fulfilling this command. David comes close, for he "does not turn aside" (1 Kgs 15:5 [NIV translates as "he had not failed"]). But it is never said of David that he never turns aside to either right or left. The only king who completely fulfills the kingly charge is righteous Josiah (2 Kgs 22:2). Joshua is commanded to act according to the highest possible kingly standards.

God's command also characterizes Joshua under the guise of the righteous and wise person. Psalm 1 is a wisdom psalm that opens the Psalter, inviting the wise attitudes by which the Psalter is rightly heard.[11] It characterizes the

10. While this Hebrew word is not translated in the NIV, *raq* is translated "only" in some English versions, including the NASB and NRSV.

11. See such an approach in J. Clinton McCann, *A Theological Introduction to the Book of Psalms: Psalms as Torah* (Nashville: Abingdon, 1993).

righteous person in tones strikingly similar to Joshua. The righteous person delights in the "law (*torah*) of the LORD . . . meditating on his law day and night." By so doing, "whatever they do prospers." In light of the larger story of God, Joshua's leadership is to be that of the righteous and wise individual found in Psalm 1.

For a final time, God commands Joshua to strength and courage, adding that he should neither be afraid or discouraged (v. 9). But Joshua's success is not dependent solely on his boldness. Rather, he is reminded once again that God is "with him" (v. 9; cf., v. 5). Earlier, Joshua was commanded to obey the law so that he might have success "wherever you go" (v. 7); now, God is with Joshua "wherever you go" (v. 9). Certainly, Joshua's obedience and boldness are requisites for success, for it is in them that God's powerful presence works. Without God's powerful presence, Israelite strength or boldness alone will not take the land. Through Israelite obedience, God's promise of land is realized because God's presence with Israel enables their victory.

### The Preparation of the People (1:10–11)

Once Joshua is commissioned and prepared, he prepares the people. Moses had commanded the people (Deut 1:3, 18; 3:18, 21; 4:2, 40; 6:2, 6; 7:11, et passim; Josh 1:7, 13; 4:10; 8:31, 34, et passim) and now Joshua does so (v. 10; "ordered" in this verse uses the same Hebrew root earlier translated as "gave" [v. 7] and "commanded" [v. 9]). He passes on to the people God's command to "cross" the Jordan (v. 2). Officers are to "go through" the camp and command the people that they will soon "cross" the Jordan (v. 11; "cross" and "go through" share the same Hebrew root [*ʿbr*]). The command does not change. God commands Israel to "cross" the Jordan and this is exactly the command Joshua and the officers obediently communicate to Israel.

The officers appear here and later in the narrative at crucial moments of covenant renewal and transition (Josh 8:33; 23:2; 24:1; cf., Deut 29:9). It is a word that elsewhere describes supervisors of work (Exod 5:14), legal administrators (Deut 16:18), and military leaders (Deut 20:5). The officers are certainly using administrative skill as they prepare Israel to cross the Jordan. However, their role as military leaders is also in view—a fact that the military preparation noted in verse 14 confirms. The officers prepare Israel to cross the Jordan to "take possession" of the land; this will require military action (Deut 11:23–25). As the book unfolds, "taking possession" will be seen as more than military action, involving settlement and habitation.

The crossing is to take place in three days' time. A similar three-day period of preparation is indicated in Joshua 3:2, and another as the spies hide (Josh 2:16, 22). How the various three-day periods correspond to one another has challenged commentators. They may refer to the same three-day period, with the spies dispatched on the same day Joshua issues this command to the officers. The phrase may alternately refer to an undetermined short period of a few days, with no intent that the notices correspond to one another.

Joshua communicates what he has been told: they are entering a land that is gifted to them (vv. 11; cf. vv. 13, 15). Any military action undertaken is at God's command; any military action that is successful depends on their obedience; any military action that procures land is because it has already been promised and given. There is a tension here that maintains throughout the book: God gives out of grace but also calls his people to actively participate in the execution of what he has planned and promised.

Receiving the land that is given to them, Israel is to "take possession" (from the Hebrew root *yrsh*). The root appears five times in the chapter (as a verb it appears twice in v. 11 and v. 15; as a noun it appears once in v. 15)[12] and is a thematic root in the book. It means much more than military action or conquest. The verbal form of the root appears twenty-nine times and most frequently (fifteen of twenty-nine occurrences) in chapters 13–21. There, the land given by God is distributed among the tribes and they "take possession" through settlement and habitation. Land division and habitation is intrinsically part of land possession.

### The Commitment of the Transjordanian Tribes (1:12–18)

Preparation for entry raises the question of the role and status of the Transjordanian tribes. In receipt of the eastern lands, will they remain true to the commitment made to Moses (Num 32)? Do they still understand themselves as part of Israel and thus bound by commitments made before Israel's God? This section reveals the Transjordanian tribes remain committed to the promises they have made, understanding themselves fully as part of covenantal Israel.

The status of the eastern tribes as fully a part of Israel is made apparent in the chapter's one instance in which the Lord is noted as giving them land. It is given that they might have "rest" (v. 13). This is no different than the "rest" promised the tribes who settle west of the Jordan in the promised land (v. 15). This theme of the land as "rest" is an important one. It opens the book and reappears at its conclusion once the land is possessed (21:44; 22:4). "Rest" is the culminating legacy of Joshua's ministry (23:1). The concept of the land as rest was part of God's promise to Israel (Exod 33:14; Deut 3:20; 12:10; 25:19). The rest provided by the land was the same rest of the Sabbath day

---

12. The repetition of the root in vv. 11 and 15 is not apparent in NIV. The Hebrew in verse 11 reads "take possession of the land . . . to possess it," while v. 15 reads "until they have taken possession. . . . After that you may go back to the land of your possession and possess it."

(Exod 20:11; Deut 5:14). That the Transjordanian tribes experience "rest" as did their brothers in the promised land is a sure sign of their ongoing status within Israel, despite their location.

Joshua urges the Transjordanians to "remember" their pledge to help Israel take the land (citing Deut 3:18–20 almost verbatim). Although the land is given by God, Joshua makes clear that Israel's participation includes warfare. The fighting men are to cross over in battle formation. The response of the Transjordanian tribes affirms their full commitment to Joshua's leadership and their sense of full inclusion in Israel. Whatever and wherever Joshua commands, they pledge obedience such as they gave to Moses. They will follow through and support their brothers, and those who "rebel" will face death. The anticipation of such rebellion is not an especially hopeful word, however. Moses uses the word "rebel" repeatedly to characterize Israel (Deut 9:7, 24; 31:27; cf. Ps 106:7), especially its response to God's commandments (Deut 1:26, 43; 9:23). The ongoing narrative shows that entry to the land does not free Israel of this rebellious attitude.

Two final responses indicate the Transjordanian tribes' hopes for Joshua's leadership and suggest the further conditions under which they will obey. Each is preceded by the word *raq*, the same word that precedes the command "be strong and courageous" in verse 7. In each, the tribes echo the words of the LORD, serving as a final reminder of the type of leadership to which Joshua is called. First, the tribes again equate Joshua's leadership with Moses, petitioning the LORD only (*raq*) be with Joshua "as he was with Moses." This is the requirement for successful leadership and is the very promise the LORD has made to Joshua (vv. 5, 9). Second, the tribes echo the LORD, urging Joshua to only (*raq*) "be strong and courageous." The chapter thus ends on a high note: the Transjordanians are fully included in Israel and fully committed to Joshua.

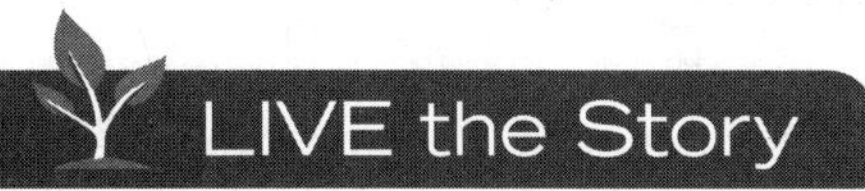


### Finding Strength and Courage: Hidden in Joshua

Be strong! Be courageous! How often sermons on Joshua 1 urge listeners to this kind of response. But the inherent danger of such exhortation is very real because often we are more like weak Israel without strength or courage. The exhortation to strength and courage can suggest that we simply need to try harder and screw courage to the sticking point. This is a "pull yourself up by the bootstraps" message, moralism that binds up the hearers in anything but the freeing good news of the gospel.

It is true that Joshua and Israel needed to do things—to respond and act—if they were to be faithful, strong, and courageous. But the requisite strength does not simply come because they drum it up out of their own depths. Rather, it comes from God: his promises, his presence, his instruction, his enabling. God is the key and source of the courage and strength to which Joshua is called.

In the New Testament, Hebrews 3–4 suggests a way of reading this command of courage and strength. In those chapters, the author works typologically with Joshua, who was to bring Israel into rest in the land. Israel ultimately fails to enter into this rest because of their disobedience. Because of that failure, the promise of rest still awaits God's people (Heb 4:8). It is now Jesus who brings God's people into the Sabbath rest of life in Christ. In this typology, Jesus is the new Joshua.

A Joshua-Jesus typology has long been recognized and developed out of this New Testament reading. In patristic writings, further license for such reading was underpinned by the fact that in the Greek Old Testament (LXX), the names "Joshua" and "Jesus" are the same Greek word, giving a translation of the underlying Hebrew name meaning "God saves." This led to much typological interpretation of Jesus as Joshua.[13]

Such typological reading provides a faithful way to address the inherent difficulty noted above in exhortations to strength and courage. In all of Scripture, there is only one who has fully heeded God's command to Joshua. Only Jesus has shown utter obedience to the Father; only he has fully kept the "Book of the Law," not turning aside from it to the left or right but meditating on it day and night. It is his obedience that enables him to bring God's people into Sabbath rest as the book of Hebrews argues. Only Jesus is found to be fully courageous and strong. In this he is the true Joshua, always strong and courageous in his obedience and faithfulness and thus fully able to bring God's people into new lands and provide rest.

That becomes good news for God's people who would walk with courage and strength today. We are now identified with Christ, baptized into him, and have been given his own Spirit. Our lives and efforts are now taken up into his, and it is his faithfulness, strength, and courage from which we live. When we are called to undertake those things that are new, difficult, or challenging, we do not simply need to drum up strength and courage from our own meager resources. We have been brought into rest in Christ and any work we now do is in his power and by his Spirit.

---

13. Origen, *Hom* 1. Origen begins with this observation, and his twenty-six homilies on Joshua develop a typological reading for edification and encouragement of believers. See also Richard Ounsworth, *Joshua Typology in the New Testament*, WUNT 328 (Tübingen: Mohr Siebeck, 2012), for a critical defense of this typological reading and exploration of it in the Book of Hebrews.

The action might be ours, but the strength is not. It comes from the one able to fully command it and us: Jesus as Joshua, the one who leads his people, and resources them beyond their ability to the fulfillment of great things. It is precisely in our weakness that he is strong and courageous, able to bring us into promised "new lands."

## Stepping into God's Story

New beginnings can be scary. Choosing to step into an as-yet unknown future calls for courage and boldness. As Israel prepares to enter the land, the people have the memory of the wilderness spies' report and its tragic result. Israel knows that there is much that can daunt as it enters the land. It is no wonder that this chapter, on the brink of new beginnings, speaks so much of courage and boldness.

The chapter's sense of a new era is certainly apparent: Moses has passed from the scene and a new leader is appointed. In another sense, the new era is not so new after all, for the story of Israel that unfolds in this book is only a continuation of a long, old story. It is a story grounded in promise (Gen 12:1–3) and whose execution is overseen by God himself. Within Israel, those who understood that story and chose to have faith in it (such as Joshua and Caleb) are those who enter the land and continue the story.

Not only is the story one that long ago began in promise and was executed in faithfulness through the years, but it is a story of God that has a far-distant outcome. That outcome is blessing to all the people on earth (Gen 12:3). The land is given to Israel so that it might be a nation set apart as holy and ministering as a priest to the whole earth. In this, Israel would draw people to the God of blessing.

The story's assured past and certain future is a strong antidote to the fear that might waylay Israel. As Israel crosses the Jordan, it is a new step in the story written and executed by God. God goes with Israel, and it is his presence with them that assures the progress of the story toward its outcome.

The church of which I am a member has, for the last several months, been working through a visioning process. Beginning with Scripture, the process has challenged the congregation to consider its past, assess its present, and listen for God's direction for its future. A collegial process centered in prayer, Scripture, and conversation, it has been instrumental in setting long- and short-term ministry goals. But the process has not been always easy or smooth. We have read and looked honestly at the reality of post-Christendom in which the church now ministers. We noted shrinking resources, increasingly complex social questions, biblical illiteracy (both within and without the church), and societal disregard for the church. Like many churches, we have faced a choice: continue to proclaim the gospel as if we still lived in Christendom and through forms that that social reality supported or dare to re-envision what a community of Christ-followers—the church—looks like in post-Christendom. It has often felt like standing at the river, waiting to go in to an unknown land. I suspect that many churches are feeling this place of dis-ease.

In my ministry within an evangelical seminary, I speak with students who have risked much to answer a call to ministry. Many students are now entering seminary later in life, leaving secure jobs and paychecks to do so. Many have come from other countries in Africa, South America, or Asia to brave Canadian ways and winters as they study. All have come in the dis-ease of the unknown and unknowable future. They, too, stand at a Jordan crossing, uncertain of but committed to an unknown future.

One encouragement that speaks to these and many other situations of the unknown is the same encouragement that Joshua 1 presents to us: our acts of faith might feel new to us. They might be terrifying and costly. They might lead us places we never imagined. But they are not really new, for they are only steps in a long, ongoing story of God and his people. What really counts in that story *is* certain: God. His power. The story's outcome. And a certainty that God is already *in* that future, awaiting the arrival of his people who pluck up the courage to step forward in faith and by Christ's power.

Countless people of faith took that step before Joshua and Israel at the Jordan: Sarah and Abraham, Shiphrah and Puah (those midwives-of-courage), Moses. Countless took that step after Joshua: Manoah and his wife (unnamed but not forgotten), the company of the prophets, John the Baptist, Barnabas. The history of the church is crowded with others: Irenaeus, Hilda of Whitby, Bonhoeffer. Each of these has stepped forward—with great or little faith—but with a sense that it is God's story in which they walk, an ongoing story assured and accompanied by God himself.

### The Land as God's Gift

The story of God's gift of land to Israel is encouraging. It reveals God's commitment to this particular nation that God rescued from slavery. Landless and oppressed Israel receives land as a place of freedom from slavery and oppression. Within this land, covenanted Israel is free to live as God's people, serving as a "kingdom of priests and a holy nation" (Exod 19:6).

Yet this encouragement can be overshadowed by the difficult questions raised by God's gift of inhabited land to Israel and the violent warfare and dispossession that gift entails. Discomfort with the violence of the book has long troubled interpreters, so that Origen claimed in the third century that

> unless those physical wars bore the figure of spiritual wars, I do not think the books of Jewish history would ever have been handed down by the apostles to the disciples of Christ, who came to teach peace, so that they could be read in the churches.[14]

The question of the book's violence and the command to annihilate the land's inhabitants is a larger question considered in the Introduction. But connected to this question is how the command to take the land has fueled past and modern colonial enterprise. Joshua has been used as justification for colonial acquisition in North and South America, South Africa, and present-day Palestinian territory, to name a few.[15]

The use of Joshua for these ends is reprehensible: a gross misinterpretation and misapplication of these texts. It completely misunderstands the particularity of the text to ancient Israel. Ancient Israel was, as a nation, covenanted to a particular God and promised a national land within which that covenant was to be lived out. At that particular time in salvation history, the covenanted nation was called to receive and inhabit the land granted them under covenant by the national deity. This involved warfare. However, once the land was taken, the commands for warfare in Deuteronomy and Joshua do not set a pattern for all time. Not even later Israel followed this command as a matter of course.

Under the new covenant, Christ comes as covenanted lord of all peoples, rather than covenanted to one nation. More, the church expresses that lordship as it is gathered from all nations and is not itself defined by geographical boundaries. To appropriate the commands to violence and warfare in these contexts is to misconstrue their role at one point in time for national, covenanted Israel. The commands are not a directive for all time by which self-appointed "God's people" argue *carte blanche* for the dispossession of others' land.[16] For such misuse of the text in the shaping of worldviews and strategies, repentance is necessary to open dialogue and repair relationships.

Even within Joshua, dispossession is not the only narrative thread; inclusion is also part of the book's message. Thus, Rahab (ch. 2) provides a model by which an individual family finds life with Israel and is not dispossessed according to the norms of Deuteronomy (Deut 7:1–2, 20–24). Further, the

---

14. Origen, *Hom* 15.1.

15. For use of the book of Joshua in colonial enterprises, see Jean Comaroff and John Comaroff, *Of Revelation and Revolution: Christianity, Colonialism and Consciousness in South Africa*, vol. 1 (Chicago and London: University of Chicago Press, 1991); Michael Prior, *The Bible and Colonialism: A Moral Critique* (Sheffield: Sheffield Academic Press, 1997).

16. See a fuller discussion in Paul Copan, *Is God a Moral Monster?: Making Sense of the Old Testament God* (Grand Rapids: Baker Books, 2011), 186–97.

inclusion of the Gibeonites (ch. 9) is honored within Israel, even though achieved through deceit.

This model of inclusion is a reminder that God's gift of land to ancient Israel was toward his larger purpose of inclusion of all peoples within his blessing. In the ongoing biblical narrative, Israel does live with others within its borders, and its laws provide justice for these people (Exod 23:9; Lev 19:33–34; Deut 1:16; 10:19; 16:11; 24:20–21). The prophetic hope is one of inclusion. All people come to Zion to worship God (Isa 2:1–5; 19:23–25; see also Ps 87:3–6) and, in a surprising reversal of the land division in Joshua 13–21, the foreigner is included in the eschatological distribution of land (Ezek 47:21–23). In the New Testament, this inclusion as equals is apparent in texts such as Ephesians 3:1–11 and Acts 15:16–17 and finds eschatological resonance in Revelation 21:22–26. By all these, the gift of land to Israel is shown not to be paradigmatic for repeated land conquests but a particular moment in God's larger plan of inclusion and salvation.

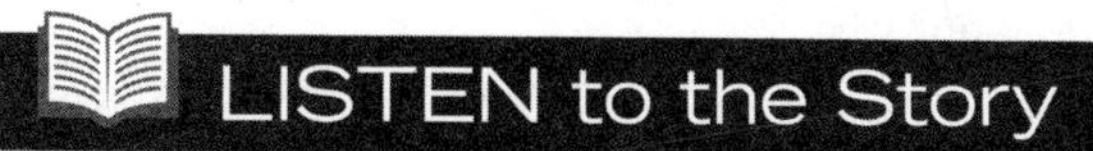

## LISTEN to the Story

1Then Joshua son of Nun secretly sent two spies from Shittim. “Go,
look over the land,” he said, “especially Jericho.” So they went and entered
the house of a prostitute named Rahab and stayed there.
2The king of Jericho was told, “Look, some of the Israelites have come
here tonight to spy out the land.” 3So the king of Jericho sent this message
to Rahab: “Bring out the men who came to you and entered your house,
because they have come to spy out the whole land.”
4But the woman had taken the two men and hidden them. She said,
“Yes, the men came to me, but I did not know where they had come from.
5At dusk, when it was time to close the city gate, they left. I don’t know
which way they went. Go after them quickly. You may catch up with
them.” 6(But she had taken them up to the roof and hidden them under
the stalks of flax she had laid out on the roof.) 7So the men set out in
pursuit of the spies on the road that leads to the fords of the Jordan, and
as soon as the pursuers had gone out, the gate was shut.
8Before the spies lay down for the night, she went up on the roof 9and
said to them, “I know that the LORD has given you this land and that a
great fear of you has fallen on us, so that all who live in this country are
melting in fear because of you. 10We have heard how the LORD dried up
the water of the Red Sea for you when you came out of Egypt, and what
you did to Sihon and Og, the two kings of the Amorites east of the Jordan,
whom you completely destroyed. 11When we heard of it, our hearts melted
in fear and everyone’s courage failed because of you, for the LORD your
God is God in heaven above and on the earth below.
12“Now then, please swear to me by the LORD that you will show
kindness to my family, because I have shown kindness to you. Give me
a sure sign 13that you will spare the lives of my father and mother, my
brothers and sisters, and all who belong to them—and that you will save
us from death.”

14“Our lives for your lives!” the men assured her. “If you don’t tell what we are doing, we will treat you kindly and faithfully when the LORD gives us the land.”

15So she let them down by a rope through the window, for the house she lived in was part of the city wall. 16She said to them, “Go to the hills so the pursuers will not find you. Hide yourselves there three days until they return, and then go on your way.”

17Now the men had said to her, “This oath you made us swear will not be binding on us 18unless, when we enter the land, you have tied this scarlet cord in the window through which you let us down, and unless you have brought your father and mother, your brothers and all your family into your house. 19If any of them go outside your house into the street, their blood will be on their own heads; we will not be responsible. As for those who are in the house with you, their blood will be on our head if a hand is laid on them. 20But if you tell what we are doing, we will be released from the oath you made us swear.”

21“Agreed,” she replied. “Let it be as you say.”

So she sent them away, and they departed. And she tied the scarlet cord in the window.

22When they left, they went into the hills and stayed there three days, until the pursuers had searched all along the road and returned without finding them. 23Then the two men started back. They went down out of the hills, forded the river and came to Joshua son of Nun and told him everything that had happened to them. 24They said to Joshua, “The LORD has surely given the whole land into our hands; all the people are melting in fear because of us.”

*Listening to the Text in the Story*: Numbers 13–14, 25; Deuteronomy 1:22–28; Joshua 7:2–5; Judges 4:17–24; Law Code of Hammurabi; Laws of Eshnunna; Bulletin Text on the Battle of Qadesh; Amarna Letters

## Telling Tales: Bad News/Good News Spies

Joshua 2 is a happy reversal of Israel’s history of “spying out the land” and consciously evokes the events of Numbers 13–14. There, Moses sends twelve spies from Kadesh. Joshua is one of the group. They are to explore Canaan, noting the terrain and vegetation, the disposition and fortification of the towns, and the number and strength of the population. The survey affirms that the land is good and its crops plentiful. The spies, however, daunted by the peoples' strength and the cities' fortifications, give a bad report that the land cannot be taken by Israel: the people are stronger and larger, and the land (though flowing with "milk and honey" [Num 14:8]) devours those who live in it. The people rebel, and Joshua and Caleb alone urge obedience to the LORD's command to take the land (Num 13:30; 14:6–9). Only Moses' intercession saves the people from immediate destruction, but they are consigned to desert wanderings until the rebellious generation dies. The LORD commands that only Joshua and Caleb will enter the land (Num 14:30).

Of course, the spies now sent by Joshua bring back a good report. It is interesting that very little "spying" actually takes place! There is no report from these spies as to the terrain, disposition of the cities, the people, or their preparedness for war. None of that really matters to this account. Rather, the focus is on the actual report that is returned by the spies: "The LORD has surely given the whole land into our hands" (Josh 2:24). Whereas the previous bad report issued in rebellion, in light of the assurances from God in Joshua 1, the present good report anticipates obedience. Israel's previous history regarding land entry will be reversed.

Moses' recap of the wilderness spy mission in Deuteronomy 1:22–28 strengthens the evocation in Joshua 2 of the episode with the spies. Moses recalls Israel was sent to spy (from the root *hpr*) out the land, and the word is exactly that used in Joshua 2:2–3. Later, the same word will appear again in Joshua 7:2 as the men spy out Ai; in each of the spying missions, the outcome is dependent on Israel's obedience to the LORD's commands. Moses' recollection of the events in Numbers 13–14 further informs the reversals in Joshua 2. He recalls the peoples' hearts were "made to melt in fear" (from the root *mss*; Deut 1:28) by the spies' report. Now, the new spies hear that it is the inhabitant's hearts that "melted in fear" (from *mss*; Josh 2:11; v. 9 records the same response using a different word). The crowning irony of the reversal is that the spies in Joshua 2 receive their good report from a Canaanite. Rahab's understanding matches that of Joshua and Caleb: God has given the land to Israel and by his power Israel will take it.

### Hospitality

Several texts in the Old Testament are concerned with hospitality given to strangers and against which Rahab's hospitality is fruitfully read. The hospitality offered the angels (Gen 19) and that offered the Levite and his concubine (Judg 19) are such stories. However, in them hospitality is offered by Israelites and (in the latter instance) to Israelites. Nor are their outcomes salutary for both host and guests as in Joshua 2. A more comparable story is that of Jael's hospitality to Sisera (Judg 4:17–24). This narrative is also one in which a non-Israelite woman unexpectedly offers hospitality and protection to outsiders amidst war. In both narratives, the protection is offered in the woman's home and is accompanied by trickery: Rahab tricks the king's men while Jael tricks Sisera. In both narratives there are hints of sexuality, as the spies and Sisera enter a woman's domain and lie down (see Explain the Story below).

There are differences in the narratives as well, for the spies live while Sisera dies. Yet each outcome furthers the LORD's purposes. These purposes are achieved at the hands of women. Women were generally noncombatants in ancient warfare but here, in the midst of war, they are instruments of the LORD's hidden sovereignty.[1] A further striking difference is that Rahab states her motivation to action. She is guided by an understanding of God's power and his role as lord of heaven and earth.

The noteworthy nature of Rahab's actions is heightened when considered alongside Numbers 25. There, at Shittim, Israelite men engaged sexually with Moabite women, and Israel began to worship the Baal of Peor. Rahab is another foreign woman, but she does not seduce the spies or subvert their worship. Instead, she rescues them and praises their God.

### Rahab: Prostitute or Innkeeper?

Rahab is introduced as an *'ishah zonah*, commonly translated as "prostitute." There is, however, a tradition that Rahab was not a prostitute but an innkeeper or tavern keeper (see Josephus *Antiquities* 5.1.2). The tradition may arise from a desire to redeem a key character in Israel's history, but there is an ancient Near Eastern context within which Rahab as innkeeper/tavern keeper would fit. D. J. Wiseman assigns the Old Babylonian role of tavern keeper (*sabitu*) to men and women, noting that due to changing social and economic forces, the tavern disappeared in the twelfth century BC. Wiseman finds in the *sabitu* a model for Rahab.[2] Providing further ancient Near Eastern context for such a reading, Hammurabi's code requires on pain of death that "women wine sellers" report to the king any outlaws in their establishment.[3] Also, within the Eshnunna law code, women who sold beer were limited in allowable items of additional commerce and were required to sell beer at current prices.[4] Taverns undoubtedly provided accommodation for travelers

1. As discussed in Elie Assis, "The Choice to Serve God and Assist His People: Rahab and Yael," *Bib* 85 (2004): 82–90.

2. D. J. Wiseman, "Rahab of Jericho," *TynBul* 14 (1964): 8–11.

3. §109 in *ANET*, 170.

4. §§15, 41 in Ibid., 162–63.

and messengers and, although they could also serve as brothels, they were not necessarily viewed as disreputable. Rather, as social centers they were places of community news.[5] Had Rahab run a tavern or inn, she could also have worked as a prostitute in that context. Certainty is impossible. However, whatever Rahab's occupation, it does not exclude her ability to respond as she does in the narrative.

## Military Spies

The use of spies in times of war appears common in the ancient Near East, providing a context for the spies' mission to Jericho. In a series of eighteenth century BC letters detailing military conflicts in Mari, the use of spies is detailed. In letter ARM 26.420 a commander, Ishme-Dagan, sends spies preparatory to an attack against the enemy encampment of Suhum. The letter conveys this news, seeking direction from an overlord.[6] Another record comes from the thirteenth century BC Battle of Qadesh. Pharaoh Ramesses II captures and interrogates two Hittite spies who provide vital information on the Hittite location, muster, and weaponry. Pharaoh calls up reinforcements and ultimately gains the victory.[7]

## Kings

The Amarna Letters is a collection of fourteenth century BC correspondence, the majority of which are from Pharaonic vassals, petty-rulers of city states in the Levant, petitioning Pharaoh their overlord. These rulers were charged with administration and defense, and were referred to variously as "mayors," "rulers," "kings," and "princes."[8] In one such letter, the ruler of Tyre (described with the same word used of the king of Jericho) refers to himself as Pharaoh's "commissioner," charged with "guarding Tyre."[9] In another letter, the same word describes Pewuru, a "counselor" of Pharaoh.[10] The "king" of Jericho is likely such a figure, exercising power over the city-state or garrison of Jericho.

5. See Samuel A. Meier, *The Messenger in the Ancient Semitic World*, Harvard Semitic Monographs 45 (Atlanta: Scholars Press, 1988), 93–96.

6. The text of Mari letter ARM 26.420 appears in a series of letters arising out of the conflict and is translated by Wolfgang Heimpel in *Letters to the King of Mari: A New Translation with Historical Introduction, Notes, and Commentary*, Mesopotamian Civilizations 12 (Winona Lake: Eisenbrauns, 2003), 359. The larger context of this letter is discussed in this volume on pages 135–41.

7. *COS* 2.5B:38–40. See also K. A. Kitchen, *On the Reliability*, 167.

8. William L. Moran, *The Amarna Letters* (Baltimore: The Johns Hopkins University Press, 1992), xxvii.

9. *EA* 149 in Ibid., 236.

10. *EA* 131 in Ibid., 212.

## EXPLAIN the Story

Much time is spent on the taking of Jericho, indicating its importance within the book (chs. 2, 6–7). The city has strategic importance, for its location on the eastern frontier guards access to the highlands. Yet the narrative in chapter 2 provides no significant military details concerning the city, or strategy for its capture; these are not provided until chapter 6. The book could, in fact, move cohesively from chapter 1 to chapter 3. The inclusion of chapter 2 suggests the narrative has significant value for the story. It is a value that is symbolic, for Jericho is the first city taken and serves to demonstrate that God is indeed with Joshua and giving Israel the land. These are theological concerns: the affirmation of the Lord's power to take the land and the possibility of including the Canaanites in Israel.

### The Mission (2:1)

The Lord commanded Joshua to "get ready to cross the Jordan River" (Josh 1:2), promising the land is given to Israel (Josh 1:3, 6, 11, 15). Joshua instead sends a covert mission to spy out the land. Is this evidence of lack of faith on the part of Joshua? Considering the previous spy mission was disastrous (Num 13–14) and Joshua has no word from the Lord to implement another such mission (as did Moses in Num 13:1), does Joshua err in sending the spies? It seems not. The narrative gives no hint of disapproval for Joshua's actions. Instead, by this action, Joshua mirrors the earlier dispatching of spies by his predecessor, Moses. Moreover, Joshua was first introduced as a successful military commander (Exod 17:10–13), and he now acts accordingly. Certainly the Lord has given the land, but Israel must move forward and act.

Joshua dispatches the spies secretly, hoping to protect their mission from exposure to the inhabitants. He may also hope to keep the mission secret from Israel for they know what happened when Moses earlier sent spies. Joshua may hope to avoid speculation and worry on their part and keep the promises of chapter 1 uppermost in their minds. The spies' report, if favorable, will bolster Israelite faith.

The spies are sent to "look over the land" (v. 1). The intent is not a wholesale canvassing of Canaan, which is signified by "especially Jericho" (v. 1). It is the city that is the spies' objective, and its strategic and symbolic value brings it to the forefront of the narrative, with three full chapters devoted to its capture and the outcome (chs. 2, 6–7). The site of Jericho lies ten miles (approximately fifteen km) northwest of the Dead Sea, identified as Tell es-Sultan at present-day er-Riha. Archaeologically, existing remains and their interpretation engender a complex debate as to the nature of the city and what walls (if any) existed at the time of Israel's entry to the land, regardless of whether one affirms a fifteenth century or thirteenth century BC entry (See Introduction).

In addition to the conflicted archaeological record, the problem is compounded by popular conceptions of Jericho that overextend the claims of the biblical text and whatever archaeological record is accessible. The walls did fall down, but the reality of the city is very different than the usual popular conception. The story is told to children with massive, medieval-style walls surrounding a vast city, and that image is held by many adults as well.[11] Yet the biblical text requires no such picture.

Jericho is presented as a city (*'ir*) thirteen times in Joshua 6 (vv. 3 [2x], 4, 5, 7, 11, 14, 15 [2x], 16, 17, 20, 26; the term does not occur in Josh 2).[12] The Hebrew term can refer to a large urban center, but it can also refer to small villages (Josh 3:16; Ruth 3:15; 1 Sam 20:6), towns (Judg 10:4; 1 Chr 2:22–23), and citadels or fortresses (2 Sam 5:7, 9; 12:26; 1 Chr 11:5, 7). Jericho is certainly small enough that an army marches seven times around it in one day with time and energy left for battle (Josh 6:15, 20). It is also small enough that the spies are quickly discovered and reported to city officials. Additionally, in contrast to Gibeon (which is called a "great ["important" in NIV] city"; Josh 10:2) and Hazor (which stood at the "head of all these kingdoms"; Josh 11:10), Jericho is not referred to in these grand terms. Nor need the walls of the era be understood as massive in height or breadth. Within the narrative's Late Bronze Age setting, typical casemate walls could be as modest as one or two stories, with homes constructed into the space between the interior and exterior walls. Even more common in this era are settlements ringed by houses of one to two stories. These structures were set edge-to-edge and their outer walls formed a barrier against invaders. Casemate walls or ringed houses could be set upon the base of previous walls or defensive systems. This would give some added height, but even these would not be the towering walls of popular conception. In sum, the city was likely modest in size, possibly a fortress outpost guarding roads leading up to the highlands

11. One need only view the popular Veggie Tales video *Josh and the Big Wall* (Phil Vischer et al, [Lombard Ill.: Big Idea Productions Inc., 2007]) to see such a depiction. Of this misconception Kenneth Kitchen, an author known for maximalist views of Israelite historiography, writes "There has always been too much imagination about Jericho by moderns (never mind previous generations), and the basic factors have ironically been largely neglected. The town was always small, an appendage to its spring and oasis, and its value (for eastern newcomers) largely symbolic as an eastern gateway into Canaan" (*On the Reliability*, 188).

12. In Joshua 6:3, "city" appears only once in the NIV; it appears twice in Hebrew which reads "march around the city once with all the armed men circling the city once."

and larger centers such as Jerusalem. By such roads eastern-invading peoples would seek entry.[13]

Arriving in Jericho, the spies enter the house of Rahab, an *'ishah zonah*, a term likely identifying her as a prostitute (Lev 21:7; Judg 11:1; 16:1; 1 Kgs 3:16; Prov 6:26). Rahab may have also been a tavern or innkeeper and perhaps not a prostitute at all (see Listen to the Story). If an innkeeper, her establishment would draw locals and be a logical place to gather news and information. As the story unfolds, expectations surrounding her profession play a crucial role in gaining the spies' safety.

The spies are dispatched from Shittim and, given Israel's history with foreign women there (Num 25), it is an ominous note. With the introduction of Rahab the prostitute, the possibility of another dangerous liaison is hinted. The danger is heightened by the use of suggestive and ambiguous language. First, the spies "entered" the house of the prostitute. The word "enter" (from the Hebrew root *bw'*) can be used of sexual liaisons (Gen 16:2; 30:3; 38:8; Deut 22:13; 2 Sam 16:21). Second, they "stayed there" (v. 1) and "lay down" (v. 8). In both cases, the Hebrew verb used (imperfect form of *shkb*) can also be used of sexual intercourse. The language is intended to be suggestive; the danger inherent in Rahab, a foreign woman and a prostitute, is clearly intended. But the language ultimately undercuts the suggestion of sexual liaison. Sexual intercourse would be signaled by the spies entering "her" and not "her house"—the latter phrase precludes a sexual connotation (Judg 9:5; 2 Sam 12:20; 2 Kgs 19:1). Similarly, they lie down "there" (v. 1), and not "with her" (which would connote sexual intercourse). The point is that the dangerous foreign prostitute acts against common Israelite perceptions of such a liminal woman (Num 25:1; Prov 2:16; 5:3–11; 7:5; 22:14). She further undercuts the negative stereotype by allying with Israel, giving an affirmation of faith worthy of a true Israelite. She, the only character named in this chapter besides Joshua, is the chapter's heroine, faithful to the LORD.

### The Mission Threatened (2:2–7)

Immediately on the heels of the spies' entry to Rahab's house, the king of Jericho (cf. 12:9) is alerted to their presence. A king (*melek*) may be a sovereign over an extensive kingdom (e.g., Pharaoh, and later David and Solomon), but such a kingdom is not mentioned here. The "king" is more likely a ruler of

13. Richard Hess, "The Jericho and Ai of the Book of Joshua," in *Critical Issues in Early Israelite History*, ed. R. Hess (Winona Lake: Eisenbrauns, 2008), 33–38. See also Kitchen, *On the Reliability*, 187–88; Anthony J. Frendo, "Was Rahab Really a Harlot," *BAR* 39 (2013): 63–5. For a different reading of the evidence, see Bryant G. Wood, "Did the Israelites Conquer Jericho? A New Look at the Archaeological Evidence," *BAR* 16 (1990): 44–58. See also T. A. Holland, "Jericho," *ABD* 3:723–40.

a city-state of Jericho, a governor or administrator exercising rule on behalf of another, or a commissioner holding responsibility for a region's military security.[14] It is such "kings" that petition Pharaoh in the Amarna Letters (see Listen to the Story above). Significantly, the king is never named (vv. 2, 3; 6:2) and his anonymity here contributes to his lowered narrative status: he is not the main character; Rahab is. He may introduce the narrative conflict by demanding Rahab "bring out the men" (v. 3), but she does not comply. It is Rahab who directs the chapter's remaining action, not the king.

The Israelite spies are there "to spy out" the land (v. 3), as were the spies sent by Moses (Deut 1:22; see Listen to the Story above). The word connects the two missions, adding a note of danger: will this mission fail as did the earlier one? Once alerted to their presence, the king sends to Rahab, as Joshua had sent the spies (v. 1) to Rahab. The king calls for the spies who "came to you" and "entered your house" (v. 3), creating ambiguity around the nature of their presence in Rahab's house. Does the king understand them to be customers of the prostitute, or simply lodgers in her house? He notes the mission "to spy out" the land is against the "whole land" (v. 3), an indication of the significance of Jericho for the security of a larger region.

The NIV prefaces Rahab's response with an aside that she "had taken the two men and hidden them" (v. 4). By this reading, the spies are safely hidden before the king's men arrive. The grammar, however, need not require this sequencing, and Rahab may have hidden the spies while the king's men await her response. This more dramatic sequence increases the threat of discovery, as it pictures Rahab hiding the spies while the king's men wait at the door. In either case, should Jericho's laws be similar to those of Hammurabi (see Listen to the Story above), her actions make her liable to execution. Perhaps she has personal, social, or class reasons to work against those in charge. No reasons are given however, and one can only speculate.

Rahab plays her cards shrewdly. First, she asserts that the men "came to me" (v. 4). The phrase plays on the sexual ambiguity in the king's inquiry and plays along with any expectations of her as a prostitute. Keeping in mind the caveats against a sexual liaison discussed in verse 1 above, Rahab is providing herself an alibi: she tells the king's men what they expect to hear, and they are ready to believe her. Second, she asserts a double innocence: "I do not know" from where they came or where they are going (v. 4). (Meanwhile, the king's

14. Hess, "Jericho and Ai," 40–41. Kitchen, *On the Reliability*, 165 uses the term "petty king." Lawson G. Stone comments that the term "king" could likewise apply to a "typical Canaanite city 'mayor,' warlord, or outlaw quite at home in the hinterlands of Canaan" ("Early Israel and Its Appearance in Canaan" in *Ancient Israel's History: An Introduction to Issues and Sources*, ed. Bill T. Arnold and Richard S. Hess [Grand Rapids: Baker Academic, 2014], 144).

men might assume that only sexual "knowing" took place!). What Rahab here twice avers she does *not* know will be offset by what she avers she *does* know in verse 9: the Lord has given the land. Finally, she commands (the verb is an imperative) the king's men to "go after" (from the Hebrew root, *rdp*, "pursue") the spies quickly. She stresses the need for haste, twice noting the time of their departure: "at dusk" and "when it was time to close the gate" (v. 5). This is very close to the time the king's men arrive at her doorstep for, when they leave in pursuit, the gates are shut behind them. She creates the sense that the spies are only steps ahead of the men, making them certain of success if only they act swiftly.

Once again, the narrative interjects an aside showing the spies hidden on the roof just steps from the king's men. Commonly used as living or working space (here, drying flax as part of the process of producing fiber for linen cloth), roofs were accessible by wooden steps or ladders.[15] Hidden under the flax, the spies might readily overhear the conversation below. The aside heightens tension, as it is yet unclear whether the king's men believe Rahab and will follow her command. They may yet enter and pursue the spies to the rooftop. The tension resolves when the men obey Rahab. Urged to "go after" (from *rdp*, "pursue"; v. 5) they go "in pursuit" and are now called "the pursuers" (v. 7; the Hebrew root *rdp* is used for each word). Thinking they are moments behind the spies, the men high-tail it after them, tracking the spies' anticipated route to the Jordan. The gates close behind them. Shrewd Rahab has controlled these men from the moment they showed up at her door.

### Melting Hearts and a Sure Sign (2:8–21)

Once she gets rid of the king's men, she engages the spies before they "lay down" (v. 8)—but not for sex (for the reasons argued above). She is a prostitute, yes, but she has more important business to attend to. An emphatic pronoun emphasizes and contrasts the characters, reading, "Now *they*, before they lay down . . . but *she*, she went up" (v. 8; author's translation). Rahab remains the active character while the spies are passive, trusting to her actions on their behalf. Their passivity is also a reminder that victory comes through the Lord (the very thing Rahab tells them), rather than their own efforts. The conversation proceeds in two sections. The first (vv. 9–14) outlines the basic agreement between the parties. The second (vv. 17–21) negotiates crucial further details. Between the two sections (vv. 15–16) is a preview of the spies' escape.

Ironically, the foreign prostitute begins the conversation with a statement of faith one might expect from the Israelites. Except for Joshua's speech (ch. 24),

15. Philip J. King and Lawrence E. Stager, *Life in Biblical Israel* (Louisville: Westminster John Knox, 2001), 34–5, 150.

it is the longest and strongest statement of faith in the book. She rehearses Israel's history, its effect on her fellow Canaanites, and her own conclusions. She earlier stated she did *not* know who the Israelites were or from where they came. Now, she states what she *does* know, and this belies her earlier declaration of innocence. Her words can be helpfully diagrammed; each item she affirms she knows begins with the Hebrew particle *ki* ("that," "for") and is mirrored in repeated affirmations that lead to her faith claim. Many of the words Rahab uses arise from Israel's own tradition, particularly the exodus tradition in which the LORD fights as a warrior against Pharaoh (Exod 15:3). The use of such words suggests she understands current events are themselves part of the LORD's war.[16]

> 9 I know
> A THAT (*ki*) the LORD has given you this land
> B AND THAT (*ki*) a great fear of you has fallen on us,
> C SO THAT (*ki*) all who live in this country are melting in fear because of you.
> D 10 FOR (*ki*) we have heard
> E how the LORD dried up the water of the Red Sea for you when you came out of Egypt
> E' and what you did to Sihon and Og, the two kings of the Amorites east of the Jordan, whom you completely destroyed.
> D' 11 When we heard of it,
> C' our hearts melted in fear
> B' and everyone's courage failed because of you,
> A' FOR (*ki*) the LORD your God is God in heaven above and on the earth below. (emphasis added to author's translation)

Rahab testifies that the land is given to Israel by God, as confirmed to Joshua in chapter 1. She then reports on the inhabitants' emotional state, in words that evoke the exodus events. She notes the Canaanites' "great fear" (v. 9). This is the same word used for the Canaanites' fear prophesied in Exodus 15:16. It is also the same fear God sends before the Israelites as they enter the land so as to terrorize their enemies (Exod 23:27; translated in NIV as "terror"). Rahab also notes the Canaanites' hearts are "melting in fear" (v. 9; from *mwg*; a different root [*mss*] describes a similar phenomenon in v. 11). Again, this word in verse 9 is that of the prophesied response in Exodus 15:15.

The Canaanites' reaction is to the news that God "dried up" the Red Sea in his victory over Pharaoh and thus Israel "came out of Egypt" (v. 10). Although

16. See the ensuing commentary and Dennis J. McCarthy, "Some Holy War Vocabulary in Joshua 2," *CBQ* 33 (1971): 228–30.

"dried up" does not appear in the Exodus account and is infrequently used elsewhere with respect to water (Ps 74:15; Isa 44:27; Jer 51:36; Zech 10:11), it appears twice more in Joshua to describe the Jordan crossing, which is specifically likened to the Red Sea crossing (Josh 4:23; 5:1). The Jordan crossing evokes the Red Sea crossing through this word use, through Joshua's leadership that mirrors Moses', and through the demonstration of the LORD's power at the sea and the river.

The Canaanites also respond to Israel's victories over Sihon and Og (Num 21:21–35; Deut 2:24–3:11). East of the Jordan, these peoples are given the generic label "Amorites" (see similarly in Gen 15:16; Josh 9:10; 24:8, 12). Rahab notes they were "completely destroyed" (v. 10). This is in accordance with the command given Israel that it is to destroy the inhabitants (Deut 7:2; 20:17). There is no use in the Numbers account of this word, although the summary states that Sihon and Og are left with "no survivors" (Num 21:34–5). Moses' recounting of the events recalls that no survivors were left to Sihon or Og (Deut 2:34; 3:3). He then adds that they were "completely destroyed" (Deut 2:34; 3:6). The word figures prominently in the account of Jericho's fall, appearing several times in both nominal and verbal forms, and the inhabitants of Jericho are completely destroyed (Josh 6:21). It is ironic, then, that the word first appears in Joshua in the mouth of one of Jericho's inhabitants. Apart from Rahab's commitment to Israel and the LORD, she and her family would be subject to destruction.

Having stated the source of the Canaanites' panic, she repeats each element: on hearing, hearts "melted in fear" (v. 11; now the root used is *mss*). Once again, the irony is great. When the spies brought back a bad report, Israel was debilitated by this same fear (Deut 1:28); now at Jericho, Israel's response will be different. When Israel crosses the Jordan (encouraged in some part by Rahab's words), it is the Canaanites who experience this fear (Josh 5:1). But Israel's victory does not make it immune to fear. When Israel disobeys God and is routed at Ai, the peoples' hearts once again melt in fear (Josh 7:5).

Rahab earlier spoke of the "great fear" on Canaan (v. 9). Now she returns to that idea and attests to the inhabitant's lack of courage. This is "because of you" (v. 11)—although Rahab is quick to connect the Israelites to the God who leads them. Having recited what was heard and the panic it evokes, Rahab concludes that the God behind all of this is "God in heaven above and on the earth below" (v. 11). The phrase is striking for its shrewd insight and its orthodoxy (Deut 4:39; 1 Kgs 8:23, cf. v. 60).

Convinced of the coming events and acknowledging Israel's God, she makes what is a logical request (signaled by the phrase, "Now then", v. 12). She speaks to them with authority and as an equal, boldly demanding a covenant with the spies.[17] She asks that they pledge reciprocal "kindness" (*hesed*), a term of covenant fidelity attributed to God himself (Exod 20:6; Deut 5:10). She further seeks a sure sign (*'ot 'emet*) of their covenanted faithfulness, asking them to spare the lives of her extended family (parents, siblings, and "all who belong to them"). To ensure there is no mistaking her request she asks additionally that they be saved from death. Her boldness is marked by the imperative command that they "swear" to her by the LORD she has just acknowledged. She acts on behalf of her family, a role usually exercised by the father.[18] She has spoken of a father (v. 13), and her action here perhaps reflects her role as the family's economic head or as a response to the opportunity of the moment.

The spies' oath is the first word they utter in the chapter. But even here, they only respond to Rahab's words; the active role remains hers. The oath is the sign Rahab requests and the spies pledge it with their lives. Their words employ the same covenantal terms she used. They will deal "kindly" (*hesed*) and "faithfully" (*'emet*) should she remain silent (v. 14; silent regarding their presence? regarding Israelite plans to invade?). In response, Rahab once more takes charge, facilitating their escape from her home on the city walls (see the discussion of wall construction at Josh 2:1). She gives her final commands; they are to "go"and "[h]ide" in the hills west of the city to avoid the search party (v. 16).

At this point (vv. 17–21), the narrative takes up the obvious gaps in the plan: how will Rahab's family be spared? How will the oath be accomplished? The NIV, translating the Hebrew "and they said" (v. 17) as a pluperfect ("they had said") sets the conversation *before* the spies depart via the window. Without this, the conversation takes place as the spies shinny down the rope. While such a conversation might add to the chapter's comedic effect, it would do little to preserve the secrecy the spies desire! The sense of the NIV is correct; this second conversation takes place in real time before the spies exit via the window in verse 15. The narrative is structured so that the basic outlines of the covenant are set (vv. 12–14) and a forward glance shows the positive outcome for the spies (vv. 15–16). There is a hurried feel to this forward glance—a sense that the spies need to escape quickly. Only after this forward glance does the narrative turn from the main outlines of the covenant to communicate the details of its execution (vv. 17–21).

---

17. K. M. Campbell, "Rahab's Covenant: A Short Note on Joshua ii 9–21," *VT* 22 (1972): 243–44, notes the constituent parts of a covenant present in the interchange between Rahab and the spies: a preamble noting the God in whose name the covenant is made (v. 11), the prologue (vv. 9–11), the stipulations imposed by the parties (vv. 12–13 by Rahab; vv. 18–20 by the spies), sanctions for breaking the covenant terms (vv. 18–20), the oath (vv. 14, 17), and the covenantal sign (vv. 18–21; the scarlet cord).

18. King and Stager, *Life in Biblical Israel*, 38.

In these details the spies are not seeking to renege on their agreement or insinuate that it was made under duress.[19] They seek to share responsibility for the successful completion of what they have sworn. Rahab negotiated with them as an equal, and the covenant arose out of her initiative. They honor that by making her a full participant in the oath's accomplishment. This is apparent from the repeated reference to their freedom from sole responsibility:

| | |
|---|---|
| v. 17–18 | "We are free (*neqim*) from this your oath which you made us swear . . . unless . . . you" (NIV: "This oath you made us swear will not be binding . . . unless . . . you") |
| v. 19 | "If any go outside . . . their blood will be on their own heads; we are free (*neqim*)" (NIV: "we will not be responsible") |
| v. 20 | "If you tell . . . we will be free (*neqim*) from the oath you made us swear" (NIV: "we will be released") |

The spies confirm they have sworn an oath to her and they consider it binding if certain actions are taken by Rahab (v. 17). She asked for kindness; they agreed (v. 14). She sought a sign; they gave their oath (v. 15). She asked that the lives of her extended family be spared; they tell her to gather them into the house. She asked that her family be saved from death; they tell her this can only occur if they remain in the safety of the house. They thus stress the mutual responsibility for the oath's success, and this mutuality is clear in the dual conclusion: "their blood will be on their own heads," and "their blood will be on our head" (v. 19).

In addition to the sign inherent in the oath, they mutualize the oath's responsibility by appointing the scarlet cord as a sign—now, not a sign from *them* to *her*, but a sign from *her* to *them*. They call for a "scarlet cord" (literally, "cord of thread of scarlet" [*tiqwat hut hashani*] in v. 18; "thread of scarlet" [*tiqwat hashani*] in v. 21) to be set in the window. They designate the cord as "this" scarlet cord, as if it was something already present in the narrative.

It is unlikely they are pointing to the "rope" (*hebel*; v. 15) in their hands and by which they escape; the words are different.[20] Others speculate the scarlet cord is some sort of identifying signage for the prostitute's house which she now places in this particular window overlooking the wall.[21] Thus the familiarity of the sign to the townspeople might not attract attention in this (apparently) new location.

---

19. This is the reading of L. Daniel Hawk, *Joshua*, Berit Olam (Collegeville: Liturgical Press, 2000), 47.

20. Contra Marten H. Woudstra, *The Book of Joshua*, NICOT (Grand Rapids: Eerdmans, 1981), 75, n. 31 who thinks the rope was part of the spies' kit, prepared for "various eventualities."

21. So Phyllis A. Bird, "The Harlot as Heroine: Narrative Art and Social Presupposition in Three Old Testament Texts," *Semeia* 46 (1989): 130.

With all details in place, the spies refer again to their pressing need: secrecy (v. 20; cf. v. 14). This cannot refer to secrecy surrounding their mission for that is already well known (vv. 2–3). The need for secrecy surrounds the days of hiding in the hills. At Rahab's command they will move further away from their camp. This leaves them vulnerable should Rahab choose to expose them. Their concern seems unwarranted however. There is no benefit to Rahab should she expose them: who would then communicate the negotiated plan to Israel's army? Rahab has every incentive to keep the spies hidden and alive lest hope of life for herself and her family be lost.

One might wonder what prompts Rahab to attach herself to Israel. Are her words those of a pragmatic woman who shrewdly surfs events to a place of safety for herself and her family? Is she a survivor at any cost? Or are her words true recognition of Israel and her God? Is her story included because it shows that even Canaanites can recognize and respond to God—a counterpoint to the command to annihilate the Canaanites that resurfaces in Joshua 6? The writer of the Epistle to the Hebrews understands that faith motivated Rahab and thus she was "not killed with those who were disobedient" (Heb 11:31). Perhaps there was some measure of self-preservation in Rahab's actions; faith can grow through less than altruistic means. But since the interlude with Rahab is not necessary to the downfall of Jericho, it seems best to consider her story to be included for this theological end: even the Canaanite can ally with Israel and its God. This woman and her family prove that possibility. The inclusion of Rahab in Scripture points to God's purposes of salvation extended to all peoples. It is indeed possible to become part of his people, regardless of who one is.

### Mission Accomplished (2:22–24)

The spies are obedient to Rahab's commands. They hide in the hills three days (that is, the rest of the first day, and two days thereafter), returning safely to Joshua in Shittim as the three days set in Joshua 1:10 draw to a close. They report to Joshua "everything that had happened" (v. 23). This may well include realities of warfare: numbers, fortifications, preparations within Jericho. But nothing of this is recorded. Only the words gained from Rahab, the woman who read the news, her own people, and the God of Israel rightly. "The LORD has surely given the whole land into our hands; all the people are melting in fear because of us" (v. 24). To her words they have added their own "surely." Perhaps this reflects their experience in Jericho. If God could so orchestrate their meeting with the faithful prostitute, then surely he is indeed working for Israel.

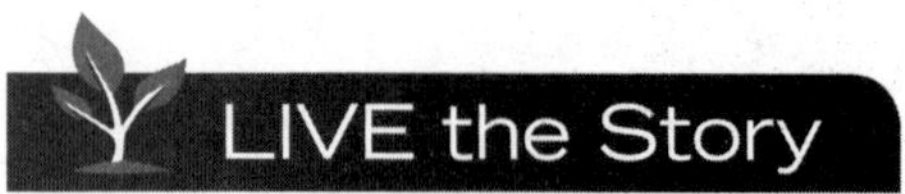


**Rahab as a Forerunner in the People of God**

Rahab is the heroine of this chapter: the foreign woman who affirms the God of Israel and assists the Israelites in taking the land. By so doing, she upends stereotypes of foreign women found in Israel's own history (particularly Num 25). Even more, and in light of God's instructions regarding the Canaanites, she affirms a deeper reality in God's economy: God's plan and purpose to bring blessing to all peoples of the earth.

Rahab is incorporated into the people of Israel following the destruction of Jericho (6:25) as the genealogy of Jesus later attests (Matt 1:5). But even in the book of Joshua, she is not the only foreigner within Israel. Caleb's family appears to have been incorporated earlier into Israel (see Listen to the Story for Josh 14–15, in Chapter 15), the Gibeonites are covenanted to Israel (see ch. 9), and foreigners are present as participants in the covenant renewal (8:33).

The inclusion of foreigners into the people of God is noted throughout the Old Testament. It is present in the everlasting covenant made with Noah, by which God commits himself to "all living creatures of every kind on the earth" (Gen 9:16). Later, in the covenant made with Abraham, God envisions that "all peoples on earth will be blessed through you" (Gen 12:3). This same covenant, with its universal vision for all peoples, is reaffirmed with Abraham, Isaac, and Jacob (Gen 15, 17; Gen 26:3–4; 28:13–14; 35:11–12). It is the Abrahamic covenant that undergirds all successive covenants. Each successive covenant extends in new ways God's commitment to Abraham on behalf of God's purposes for the fulfillment of this universal blessing. Thus, in the Mosaic covenant God affirms that for the whole earth (which belongs to God), Israel will be appointed a kingdom of priests (Exod 19:5–6), and through the Davidic covenant "all nations will be blessed through [the Davidic king]" (Ps 72:17b).

Within the Mosaic Covenant, care for foreigners is enshrined in the Ten Commandments (Exod 20:10) and reiterated in their Deuteronomic formulation (Deut 5:14). The Deuteronomic law articulates the Mosaic covenant in preparation for Israel's life in the land. In the Deuteronomic code, the foreigner within Israel is extended care, justice, and inclusion in worship (Deut 10:18–19; 16:11; 23:7–8; 24:14–21; 26:11–13; 27:19; 31:12). God's care for the foreigner is similarly apparent under the Davidic covenant as Solomon's Temple dedication prayer affirms God's ear will incline toward the foreigner who calls upon God, with the result that "all peoples of the earth may know your name and fear you" (1 Kgs 8:41–43).

The writing prophets also voice God's commitment to bless all people on earth. Their eschatological vision shows the nations turning to God and streaming to him (Isa 2:2–4; Zech 2:11; 8:20–22). In the eschatological glory that shines upon Zion, Isaiah envisions the fulfillment of Israel's priestly calling as nations and kings flock to Zion's light, participating in God's blessings (Isa 60:1–5). Likewise, God's "servant" acts for the inclusion of the gentiles into God's purposes (Isa 42:6; 49:6).

The covenants provide a structure for the narrative account of Israel's life. Within that account, the work and witness of gentiles is apparent. At times, gentiles are depicted in free association with Israelites, supporting and encouraging their plans—one thinks of Ephron the Hittite, who sold a cave and its adjacent field to Abraham for the burial of Sarah (Gen 23:10–16). Long before Israel's entry to the land, this one parcel stood as a witness to God's promise of future land possession. At other times, gentiles supported Israelite plans and voiced praise, acknowledging Israel's God—one thinks of Hiram of Tyre providing materials and labor for the temple (1 Kgs 5:1–12[15–26]), while giving "Praise, to the Lord . . . for he has given David a wise son to rule over this great nation" (1 Kgs 5:7[21]). The Queen of Sheba, likewise, seeing the greatness of Solomon's rule, acknowledged Israel's God, saying, "Praise be to the Lord your God, who has delighted in you and placed you on the throne of Israel" (1 Kgs 10:9). In a similar way, the great pride of Nebuchadnezzar is humbled, and he "praised the Most High; [he] honored and glorified him who lives forever" (Dan 4:34).

These words of praise do not suggest incorporation into the people of Israel, as occurred with Rahab. In other accounts, gentiles are shown not only praising God, but committing themselves to worship the God of Israel. Naaman the Aramean takes his praise beyond the acknowledgement of God given by Hiram and the Queen. Like Rahab, he acknowledges God's power and uniqueness, stating "there is no God in all the world except in Israel" (2 Kgs 5:15). Even though dwelling in the land of Israel's enemy, he commits himself to worship only the Lord, though he petitions the prophet that he might perform external rites of worship to Rimmon in his service to his overlord (2 Kgs 5:17–18). While Naaman is not incorporated into the people of Israel, the prophet apparently accepts his commitment to the Lord and grants the exception for his unique situation. Naaman stands as an example of the nations blessed alongside Abraham's people.

Rahab's story of incorporation into God's people is strongly paralleled by the incorporation of Ruth into Israel. Both are foreign women. Both are connected to Israel's negative association with Moabite women (Num 25): Rahab by narrative association with Shittim, and Ruth by identification as a Moabite (an identification made fourteen times in Ruth 1–4). Like Rahab, Ruth was of a people with whom Israel was barred association (Deut 23:3–6). Yet both women join themselves by oath to Israel's God and people (Ruth 1:16–17) and were received into the people of Israel on that basis. Their inclusion with three other women (Tamar, Bathsheba, and Mary) in Jesus' Matthean genealogy (Matt 1) attests to their full inclusion in Israel and the honor and importance attributed to their stories. They truly were women who instantiated God's purpose that through Abraham, all nations would be blessed.

The appearance in Jesus' genealogy of gentile women is fitting, for in the Christian tradition it is in Jesus that all the covenants find their fulfillment. Through Jesus, the blessing to the nations promised Abraham is enabled and released. As Paul says,

> The promises were spoken to Abraham and to his seed [citing Gen 12:7]. Scripture does not say "and to seeds," meaning many people, but "and to your seed," meaning one person, who is Christ. (Gal 3:16)

The Gospel writers demonstrate the fulfillment of blessing to all nations through Jesus, the long-promised seed of Abraham. Repeatedly, gentiles are featured in the Gospels. Not only does Matthew begin with a genealogy that includes Rahab and Ruth, but foreign "Magi from the east" seek out the new child to worship him (Matt 2:1–12). Matthew concludes his gospel with Jesus commissioning his disciples to go into "all nations" to share the good news (Matt 28:18–20). Luke also highlights the blessing for all nations early in his gospel as Simeon takes Jesus in his arms and praises God for the "light for revelation to the Gentiles" (Luke 2:32). All the Gospels include Jesus' encounters with gentiles. These include Samaritans brought to faith (John 4), the daughter of a Greek woman of Syrophoenicia delivered (Mark 7:24–30; it is of note, given the context of Joshua, that this same woman is a Canaanite in the Matthean account [Matt 15:21–28]), and Greeks brought to Jesus—an event that marks the "hour has come for the Son of Man to be glorified" (John 12:20–23). Amidst the struggle of the disciples to understand Jesus' identity in Mark, it is the Roman centurion who professes the good news: "Surely this man was the Son of God!" (Mark 15:39).

The inclusion of gentiles in the fledgling church (Acts 6:1–5) and the definitive breaking of the ethnic boundary in Acts 10, reveal the blessing promised to Abraham was part of the early church's DNA. It is this inclusion of the gentiles into the body of Christ, the church, that Paul describes as a mystery long hidden yet now revealed (Eph 3:6; cf. 2:11–22). The full revelation of that mystery is unmistakable in the final throne-room praise offered the lamb of God in Revelation 5:9–10:

> You are worthy to take the scroll and to open its seals, because you were slain, and with your blood you purchased for God persons from every tribe and language and people and nation. You have made them to be a kingdom and priests to serve our God, and they will reign on the earth.

The fullness of this praise is anticipated in Rahab's own words of praise, affirming that "the LORD your God is God in heaven above and on the earth below" (Josh 2:11). Rahab stands as a testimony to the inclusion of gentiles into God's promises; a type of those of every tribe and language and people and nation who are taken up into the people of God.

In Origen's homilies on Joshua, he reflects on the typological nature of Rahab, seeing in her a type—not of individual gentiles who will worship God—but of the church. Working with the etymology of her name ("Rahab" contains the Hebrew root meaning "breadth"), he exposits:

> Let us see, finally, who that prostitute is. She is called Rahab, but Rahab means "breadth." What is breadth, therefore, if not this Church of Christ, which is gathered together from sinners as if from prostitution? She says, "That place is too narrow for me. Make me a place where I may dwell. Yet who has nurtured these for me [citing Isa 49:20–21]?" And again, it is said to her, "Lengthen your stakes and enlarge your tents [citing Isa 54:2]." Therefore, that one is "breadth," the one who received the spies of Jesus.[22]

One might not affirm Origen's etymological approach, but he does recognize something of God's purposes in the character of Rahab. This woman—Canaanite though she is—is not barred from God's people. Rather, at the moment Israel moves to possess its land in which it is to live as God's kingdom of priests for the sake of the nations, her witness speaks to the end purpose of God's promises to Israel: that all the nations might be blessed. Rahab is a foretaste of that fulfillment brought about through Christ, a type of all those brought in by God's grace to Christ's body, the church. In it, all are welcome and freed to worship the lamb who has bought them—without regard to their status as Jew or gentile—with his own blood.

### The "Other" and God's People

I teach at a seminary on the Canadian prairie. Winters are cold. And long. For students who come from warm climates and plan to start in the year's second semester, the January start date is always a shock. For some, they arrive at the Winnipeg airport and step out into -40 weather (Celsius, that is!) without

22. Origen, *Hom* 3.4.

winter coats, toques, or mitts. Some have never seen snow, much less experienced the cold prairie winds.

It is a constant marvel to me that a small seminary attracts students from many cultures and nations. In recent memory, we have had students from Brazil, Paraguay, South Korea, Sudan, Nigeria, South Africa, Spain, Myanmar, England, Ireland, First Nations, and the United States. Our varied cultures make for interesting classroom discussions. We discover that sometimes, we do not easily understand one another's contexts. Culture gaps feel impossible to bridge. Those different contexts and cultures and our different national histories color our interpretation of Scripture and how we think it best applied. Our ways of studying can be very different, and as a professor I sometimes must help students learn the expectations of Canadian academia. Even our prayer modes can be very different. It makes for vibrant and stimulating learning. Integration of these different cultures can prove a challenge in class and in seminary life, and the Canadian ideal of multiculturalism is a reminder that perhaps these different cultures are best not monochromatically integrated but valued and shared. Even that ideal goes only so far to help us negotiate the gaps.

As disparate as our cultures may be, the commonality we share is life in Christ. All can speak of a gracious salvation experienced in their own lives. Under persecution, in ease, through family, friends, or the serendipitous happenings of life, Christ has found out each one and brought them into his kingdom. Some of the stories are heartwarming, some heartbreaking. Some speak of loss and hardship for the sake of the kingdom of God. Some speak of home-finding and mending. But all speak of a God who sought them out—from every tribe, tongue, people, and nation—and united them in his Son. None was outside the reach of God's gracious will.

Rahab is one such story, in a book in which the Canaanites are characterized as the Other. She is a reminder to us today: the church is the place where each of us is the Other: Outsiders opposed to God's goodness who have been invited in. The invitation has not come on the basis of our ethnicity, gender, social status—or any other marker we might claim—but solely on the basis of God's grace and Christ's work. However challenging are our interactions due to our many differences, it is this common identity that should shape our love for one another. We together are the mystery now made known, as Paul writes in Ephesians. We are called to radical unity as the one body. And it is our love for one another—born out of the love we each have received from the one in whom we are united—that should mark us as the one people of God. By this love we should be known.

CHAPTER 3

# Joshua 3:1–5:1

## LISTEN to the Story

[1]Early in the morning Joshua and all the Israelites set out from Shittim
and went to the Jordan, where they camped before crossing over. [2]After
three days the officers went throughout the camp, [3]giving orders to the
people: "When you see the ark of the covenant of the LORD your God, and
the Levitical priests carrying it, you are to move out from your positions
and follow it. [4]Then you will know which way to go, since you have never
been this way before. But keep a distance of about two thousand cubits
between you and the ark; do not go near it."

[5]Joshua told the people, "Consecrate yourselves, for tomorrow the
LORD will do amazing things among you."

[6]Joshua said to the priests, "Take up the ark of the covenant and pass
on ahead of the people." So they took it up and went ahead of them.

[7]And the LORD said to Joshua, "Today I will begin to exalt you in the
eyes of all Israel, so they may know that I am with you as I was with Moses.
[8]Tell the priests who carry the ark of the covenant: 'When you reach the
edge of the Jordan's waters, go and stand in the river.'"

[9]Joshua said to the Israelites, "Come here and listen to the words of
the LORD your God. [10]This is how you will know that the living God is
among you and that he will certainly drive out before you the Canaanites,
Hittites, Hivites, Perizzites, Girgashites, Amorites and Jebusites. [11]See, the
ark of the covenant of the Lord of all the earth will go into the Jordan
ahead of you. [12]Now then, choose twelve men from the tribes of Israel,
one from each tribe. [13]And as soon as the priests who carry the ark of the
LORD—the Lord of all the earth—set foot in the Jordan, its waters flowing
downstream will be cut off and stand up in a heap."

[14]So when the people broke camp to cross the Jordan, the priests
carrying the ark of the covenant went ahead of them. [15]Now the Jordan is
at flood stage all during harvest. Yet as soon as the priests who carried the
ark reached the Jordan and their feet touched the water's edge, [16]the water

from upstream stopped flowing. It piled up in a heap a great distance away, at a town called Adam in the vicinity of Zarethan, while the water flowing down to the Sea of the Arabah (that is, the Dead Sea) was completely cut off. So the people crossed over opposite Jericho. [17]The priests who carried the ark of the covenant of the LORD stopped in the middle of the Jordan and stood on dry ground, while all Israel passed by until the whole nation had completed the crossing on dry ground.

[4:1]When the whole nation had finished crossing the Jordan, the LORD said to Joshua, [2]"Choose twelve men from among the people, one from each tribe, [3]and tell them to take up twelve stones from the middle of the Jordan, from right where the priests are standing, and carry them over with you and put them down at the place where you stay tonight."

[4]So Joshua called together the twelve men he had appointed from the Israelites, one from each tribe, [5]and said to them, "Go over before the ark of the LORD your God into the middle of the Jordan. Each of you is to take up a stone on his shoulder, according to the number of the tribes of the Israelites, [6]to serve as a sign among you. In the future, when your children ask you, 'What do these stones mean?' [7]tell them that the flow of the Jordan was cut off before the ark of the covenant of the LORD. When it crossed the Jordan, the waters of the Jordan were cut off. These stones are to be a memorial to the people of Israel forever."

[8]So the Israelites did as Joshua commanded them. They took twelve stones from the middle of the Jordan, according to the number of the tribes of the Israelites, as the LORD had told Joshua; and they carried them over with them to their camp, where they put them down. [9]Joshua set up the twelve stones that had been in the middle of the Jordan at the spot where the priests who carried the ark of the covenant had stood. And they are there to this day.

[10]Now the priests who carried the ark remained standing in the middle of the Jordan until everything the LORD had commanded Joshua was done by the people, just as Moses had directed Joshua. The people hurried over, [11]and as soon as all of them had crossed, the ark of the LORD and the priests came to the other side while the people watched. [12]The men of Reuben, Gad and the half-tribe of Manasseh crossed over, ready for battle, in front of the Israelites, as Moses had directed them. [13]About forty thousand armed for battle crossed over before the LORD to the plains of Jericho for war.

[14]That day the LORD exalted Joshua in the sight of all Israel; and they

stood in awe of him all the days of his life, just as they had stood in awe of Moses.

[15]Then the LORD said to Joshua, [16]"Command the priests carrying the ark of the covenant law to come up out of the Jordan."

[17]So Joshua commanded the priests, "Come up out of the Jordan."

[18]And the priests came up out of the river carrying the ark of the covenant of the LORD. No sooner had they set their feet on the dry ground than the waters of the Jordan returned to their place and ran at flood stage as before.

[19]On the tenth day of the first month the people went up from the Jordan and camped at Gilgal on the eastern border of Jericho. [20]And Joshua set up at Gilgal the twelve stones they had taken out of the Jordan. [21]He said to the Israelites, "In the future when your descendants ask their parents, 'What do these stones mean?' [22]tell them, 'Israel crossed the Jordan on dry ground.' [23]For the LORD your God dried up the Jordan before you until you had crossed over. The LORD your God did to the Jordan what he had done to the Red Sea when he dried it up before us until we had crossed over. [24]He did this so that all the peoples of the earth might know that the hand of the LORD is powerful and so that you might always fear the LORD your God."

[5:1]Now when all the Amorite kings west of the Jordan and all the Canaanite kings along the coast heard how the LORD had dried up the Jordan before the Israelites until they had crossed over, their hearts melted in fear and they no longer had the courage to face the Israelites.

*Listening to the Text in the Story*: Exodus 12–17; 2 Kings 2; Psalms 66, 74, 114; Baal Epic

Crossing the Jordan River is a crucial transition: from wilderness wandering to promised land of rest. So crucial is this crossing in Israel's history that the account covers two chapters. Before the great event, three days of preparation are required. The importance of the Jordan crossing is apparent within the larger Old Testament canon by its connection to other biblical texts and events.

## The Red Sea Revisited

The recounting of the Jordan crossing likens it to the Red Sea crossing. This occurs through specific reference (4:23) and also through a web of words and allusions that recall the Red Sea. There is the obvious parallel of the parted waters and the passage through them, which in both instances is a "wonder" (Josh 3:5 [translated in NIV as "amazing thing"]; Exod 3:20; Pss 78:4 with v. 13; 106:22 ["miracles"]). The miracle of the people passing through on "dry ground" is emphasized in both accounts (Josh 3:17; 4:18; Exod 14:21, and with a different Hebrew word in Josh 4:22; Exod 14:16, 22, 29; 15:19; Neh 9:11; Ps 66:6). In both accounts the waters are piled up in a "heap" (Josh 3:13, 16; NIV "wall" in Exod 15:8 and Ps 78:13). The Psalter places the two events in parallel relationship. Thus, in Psalm 66:6 the events at the sea and the water (better translated as "river") are parallel, while in Psalm 114:1–3 God's power over the Red Sea and Jordan river is highlighted.

The ordering of the two events is comparable. In Exodus, the people celebrate the Passover, pass through the waters, and then enter the wilderness. Joshua reverses the sequence, moving the people from wilderness through the water to Passover (Josh 5:10–12). Entry into both the wilderness and promised land are closely followed by warfare and victory by God's power (Exod 17:8–16; Josh 6). Manna, given in the wilderness (Exod 16:15), ceases when Israel crosses into the promised land (Josh 5:12).

The pairing of the Red Sea and Jordan crossings reverberates in 2 Kings 2. The story is that of Elijah and Elisha—two prophets who mirror Moses and Joshua. Like Moses, Elijah mediates the covenant, meets God at Sinai, and comes to a mysterious end in the land of the Transjordan. Joshua's name ("the Lord saves") is mirrored by Elisha's ("God saves"). Both served their predecessor (Exod 24:13; 33:11; Num 11:28; 1 Kgs 19:21) and completed their predecessor's ministry. Given these and many other resonances, it is not surprising that when Elijah strikes the Jordan, the river parts and a crossing is made on "dry ground" (2 Kgs 2:8; Exod 14:21; Josh 3:17). Elisha's crossing similarly evokes the divided waters of the Red Sea (2 Kgs 2:13–14). Like a new Joshua, Elisha symbolically enters the land—not to do battle against the inhabitants but against the Canaanite god, Baal.

### Cosmic Waters and the Power of God

God's power to divide the waters of the Jordan finds its primary biblical resonance with the Red Sea events, but there is another, less apparent, biblical resonance. In the previous section, several psalms were noted that speak of God's power in taming the waters, with explicit reference to the Red Sea and Jordan river in Psalm 78 and 114. Other psalms speak of his power exercised over the waters at creation (Ps 95:5) or in the supra-historic or mythic realm (Ps 74:13–15). Notably, the same word used to describe the "heap" of water in Josh 3:13, 16 is that used in Psalms 33:7 in which God at creation piles the waters in a "heap."[1] The power exercised in many of these psalms reveals God's cosmic, eternal power over all creation—a cosmic power that is later revealed in the realm of history at the parting of the Red Sea and Jordan river.

In the creation account of Genesis 1, the waters are ordered, revealing land and thus providing a place for the sustenance of life. In the creation account in Genesis 2, this life is experienced by humans in a garden. It is a place of safety and provision at God's hand and in his presence.

The parting of the Jordan waters echoes the creation account. The waters part because God rules them in power. That power ensures God will make good on the promise that Israel will indeed possess the land. And, as at creation, the "tamed" waters of the Jordan bring Israel into a land that (like the original creation) is to be a place of rest, provision, and fellowship with God.

## Deities Victorious over Water

Several of the biblical passages noted above show God's power to tame the water. This power demonstrates God's rule and dominion. It is helpful to note that this idea is not unique to the pages of Scripture. In the ancient world, gods gained and demonstrated power by conquering the waters. Often, these waters were themselves gods who fell to the superior power of the conqueror. Thus, in the *Enuma Elish*, a creation account in Babylonian mythology, the supreme god Marduk kills the sea goddess Tiamat.[2] In Canaanite mythology, the powerful god Baal likewise gains ascendency by conquering the god of sea and river. This is related in the Baal myth from ancient Ugarit, in which parallel lines describe this god as Prince Sea and Judge River:[3]

> And the club danced in Baal's hands,
> like a vulture from his fingers.
> It struck Prince Sea on the skull,
> Judge River between the eyes.
> Sea stumbled;
> he fell to the ground;
> his joints shook;
> his frame collapsed.
> Baal captured and drank Sea;
> he finished off Judge River.
> Astarte shouted Baal's name:
> Hail, Baal the Conqueror!

---

1. In NIV the word is translated as "jar," with the marginal note using "heap."
2. Arnold and Beyer, *Readings from the Ancient Near East*, 31–50 (see p. 40 for Tiamat's death by Marduk's hand).
3. Ibid., 51–52.

Hail, Rider on the Clouds!
For Prince Sea is our captive,
Judge River is our captive.

Baal's victory over the waters marks his superiority in the pantheon and results in kingship and dominion. Within this ancient context, the power of the Lord displayed at the Jordan (as at the Red Sea) is a clear declaration of God's supreme power and kingship. As Israel enters a land in which Baal is worshiped, the Lord's power over the Jordan indicates he has—and demonstrates in history—the power credited to Baal. More, as Lord over "all the earth" (Josh 3:13), the Lord owns the territory claimed by Baal and his worshipers. These allusions thus serve as a powerful apologetic against Israelite syncretism to Canaanite Baalism.

## EXPLAIN the Story

These chapters take up the command issued by Joshua in 1:10: "cross the Jordan to go in and take possession of the land." Several preliminary observations help us enter the text.

The Jordan crossing is a significant boundary and transition. It ends the wilderness period with a second miraculous water crossing. In crossing the Jordan, Israel moves from wilderness to landedness, from wandering to rest, and from manna to the fruits of the land. Crossing this boundary is the first step toward fulfillment of God's promise to give Israel the land. The significance of the event is indicated by the frequent use of the Hebrew root meaning "to cross over" (*'br*). Although it is translated in different ways, the root occurs twenty-four times in these 2 chapters (3:1, 2, 4, 6, 11, 14, 16, 17 [2x]; 4:1, 3, 5, 7, 8, 10, 11 [2x], 12, 13, 22, 23 [2x]; 5:1 [2x]).[4] We are to take note: Israel is crossing over!

The "Israel" that crosses over is carefully delineated to emphasize unity: it is the "whole nation" (3:17; 4:1), "all" Israel, and "all" the people (3:1, 7, 17; 4:11, 14). Further emphasis on unity is apparent in that twelve men are chosen, "one from each tribe" (3:12; 4:2, 4), and twelve stones represent each of the tribes (4:3, 5, 8, 9, 20). The specific mention of Reuben, Gad, and

---

4. The root here most frequently signifies people crossing the Jordan (3:1, 11, 14,16, 17 [2x]; 4:1, 5, 7, 10, 22 [2x], 12, 13, 22, 23 [2x]; 5:1). It also signifies the other side (west) of the Jordan (5:1), walking movement across or through groups of people (3:2, 4, 6), or carrying stones over the Jordan (4:3, 8). The last three uses are not strictly about the people crossing the Jordan. On a narrative level however, repeated reference to other acts of passing over/crossing, and the aural experience of the crucial root serves to emphasize the main action of crossing the Jordan.

the half-tribe of Manasseh (v. 12) is a noteworthy mark of unity given their choice of the Transjordanian lands. Although the two and a half tribes will return across the Jordan, the land was given to all Israel, and at this watershed moment all Israel symbolically enters it.

The action of crossing is communicated through a series of commands: the LORD commands Joshua (3:8; 4:2, 3, 15), and Joshua commands the people and priests (3:5, 6, 9, 12; 4:3, 5, 17). Once, a command is issued by the officers (3:3), who pass along the command issued by Joshua in 1:10. Almost without exception, every command is explicitly or implicitly obeyed. The command and obedience sequence as they cross into the land recalls God's words to Joshua regarding obedience as necessary for success in the land (1:7). Additionally, Joshua's obedience to God and the peoples' obedience to Joshua affirm Joshua as the new leader who hears and communicates God's instructions.

Joshua might command the people, but the priests and the ark lead the crossing. The centrality of priests and ark is apparent from the number of times they are named: the priests are identified fourteen times (fifteen times in the Hebrew). Most frequently, they are identified in relation to the ark (i.e., they "carry the ark", or are commanded to carry the ark; see 3:2, 6, 8, 12, 14, 15, 17; 4:9, 10, 15, 18). The centrality of priests and ark reveals the account records an event that is one of ritual and worship. The ark is the locus of God's presence and power amidst the Israelites and requires of them due reverence.

Finally, the events are not recorded in linear fashion. For instance, there are five notices of the people crossing over (3:16, 17; 4:1, 10–11, 13). One wonders whether the priests stood near the edge of the river (3:8, 15) or in the middle (3:17; 4:3, 10) and whether they left the riverbed once or twice (4:11, 18). The twelve men are mentioned (3:12) but not utilized until later in the narrative, and there is confusion as to how many memorials are erected and where they are situated. These observations can be largely answered by recognizing that the events are viewed from several vantage points, and the action backtracks to accommodate them. Important themes are mentioned repetitively, and prolepsis prepares the reader for later exposition. Yet for all these difficulties, the events can be discerned and sketched as follows:

A. The people set out from Shittim and encamp at the Jordan;
B. After three days, further preparatory orders are issued;
C. Joshua commands the priests to set out and the march begins;
D. Bearers of the memorial stones are selected;
E. The priests' feet touch the Jordan and the waters are stopped;
F. The priests stand in the middle of the Jordan until the people pass over;
G. The twelve men take up the stones from the Jordan;
H. Joshua commands the priests to come up out of the Jordan;

I. The priests reach the west side and the waters flow again;
J. The people camp at Gilgal and set up the memorial.

**Preparing to Cross the Jordan (3:1–5)**

After the developments of chapter 2 and hard on the heels of the spies' report (2:24), Joshua hastens to execute the LORD's command (1:2). Leaving the encampment at Shittim (Num 22:1; 33:49)—a place of past covenant failure (Num 25)—Israel marches to the Jordan and its last Transjordanian encampment. Three days pass before the officers give their final orders for the march. These days might be a backward reference to the three days of preparation commanded in 1:11 and undertaken at Shittim. More likely they signal a further three-day preparation at the Jordan encampment. While the chronology is difficult to ascertain, the reference evokes the three days in 1:11 and connects the two chapters.

The officers (see discussion at 1:10) give orders for the march. The order of the tribes during marches had long been known, providing for the ark's safety in their midst (Num 10:14–28). Now, a new order is given: the ark will precede the tribes, carried by the Levitical priests (specifically the Kohathite clan, Num 3:27–31; 4:1–15; 10:21). The priests are here introduced in passing; as the narrative progresses, they become central characters in their role as bearers of the ark. In the initial commands, it is the ark that is in focus, mentioned five times in two verses: "When you see the *ark of the covenant of the* LORD *your God* and the Levitical priests carrying *it* . . . follow *it* . . . keep a distance between you and the *ark*, do not go near *it*" (3:3–4, emphasis added).

The ark's importance during the march hinges on three factors. First, the "ark of the covenant" contains the tablets of the law (Exod 25:21; Deut 10:1–5) together with the Deuteronomic law (Deut 31:26). Obedience to this law is the sign of Israel's covenant relationship with God and a reminder of God's promises (including land) and Israel's obligations. Second, the ark has military significance, going before Israel into battle in the same way ancient kings led their people into battle (Num 10:35; 14:44; 1 Sam 4–6; 2 Sam 11:11). Israel enters the land as a military force, commanded by God. Third (and most significantly), the ark represents the presence of the LORD (Lev 16:2; Num 7:89; 1 Sam 4:21–22). It is God's presence that makes the ark holy, and it is God's presence that goes before Israel into the land (Deut 9:3) to give it victory.

The ark's holiness requires it be set apart from the people by two thousand cubits (5/8 mile; 1 km.). This is similar to the limits that were put around Sinai in preparation for God's presence upon it (Exod 19:12–13, 23). In the NIV translation, the officers set this limitation *after* advising the people to follow the ark that will lead them into the unknown land. But in Hebrew, the limitation *begins* the verse, a reminder of the importance of revering God's holy ark. It is as they observe the ark's holiness and follow it that Israel knows the way to go.

Joshua gives further command that the people consecrate themselves in preparation for the "amazing things" the LORD will do (v. 5). These are yet unknown but require the people be consecrated to holiness as their LORD is holy (Lev 11:44). Consecration might include the washing and sexual abstention prescribed at Sinai (Exod 19:10–15), although here Joshua calls for only a one-day period of consecration rather than the three days at Sinai. The consecration also has in mind that Israel enters the land as a battle unit (a reality Joshua notes in v. 10); once they cross the Jordan they engage in battle at Jericho. Israel's conduct in the LORD's wars required the warriors' consecration (see, for instance, the laws for the war camp in Deut 23:9–14). It is this concern for holiness that likely stands behind Uriah's refusal to sleep with his wife—an act that would bring ritual uncleanness upon him and prevent his immediate participation in battle (2 Sam 11:11; cf., Lev 15:16–18).

### The Miraculous Crossing (3:6–17)

Having prepared the people, Joshua prepares the priests. The people must already have completed their consecration, for the priests immediately obey Joshua and the procession begins (v. 6). This provides further confirmation of Joshua's leadership.

The priests are to "take up" the ark and "pass on ahead" (literally, "cross over") before the people (v. 6). The priests are defined in this narrative by their role as bearers of the ark, and the goal of the narrative is for Israel to "cross over" the Jordan. The priests bear the ark and pass ahead of the people, but it is the ark that shows the way to go (v. 4). The narrative does not yet reveal the priests' destination; like the Israelites, we as readers see the procession set in motion without a clear understanding of what will take place. Like the Israelites, we know that the barrier of the Jordan stands between Israel and the promise.

After the chapter's several opening speeches, the LORD finally addresses Joshua (v. 7). As in chapter 1, the LORD first gives a promise, then issues a command. The promise will be fulfilled "today" and is of Joshua's exaltation. Such elevation comes only by God's hand (1 Chr 29:12) and elsewhere is experienced by Abraham (Gen 12:2) and Solomon (1 Chr 29:25). Yet no indication is given of *how* that exaltation occurs. We (like Israel) must wait for the unfolding events to reveal that. It is clear, however, that the exaltation has a purpose: to grant Israel knowledge. Israel has been promised knowledge of "which way to go" (v. 4); the exaltation will give knowledge of God's presence with Joshua. This knowledge will further confirm to Israel that Joshua has assumed Moses' mantle of leadership.

After the promise of Joshua's exaltation, a further command is given the priests. Not only are the priests to pass on ahead of the people (v. 6), they are to "stand in the river" (v. 8). Again, the coming miracle is not yet revealed and therefore no reason is provided for the bizarre act of wading into the waters. Joshua then commands the people to "come and listen" to the LORD's words (v. 9). In this, he is (like Moses before him) the LORD's prophet.

Joshua does not yet spell out the miracle to take place, referring to it only as "This is how" (v. 10). The delay increases narrative tension, leaving the best (or the most terrifying?) to last. Whereas the LORD earlier told Joshua that by the events the people will "know that I am with you" (v. 7), now Joshua's words assure the people that they "will know that the living God is among you" (v. 10). This is a certain comfort given the next words: a list of the seven nations Israel will face in the land. The list is familiar (Deut 7:1; Josh 24:11; see less complete lists at Exod 3:8, 17; 13:5; 33:2; Deut 20:17; Josh 9:1; 11:3; 12:8) and might be daunting (certainly the nations daunted the spies in Numbers 13–14). Joshua wisely reminds them that God's presence with Israel will drive them out.

God's power to do so is heightened by the descriptors Joshua applies to God. God is, first, the "living God" (v. 10), a phrase found only elsewhere in Hosea 1:10[2:1] and Psalms 42:2[42:3] and 84:2[84:3] (similar phrases are found in Deut 5:26; 1 Sam 17:26, 36; 2 Kgs 19:4, 16; Isa 37:4, 17; Jer 10:10; 23:36). The nature of Israel's God as "living" is in contrast to the gods of the nations who are viewed as empty idols, unresponsive vanities of wood and stone (Lev 19:4; Deut 32:21; Isa 44:9–20; Jer 2:5; 10:8–16). That God is a living God is particularly pertinent in the land of Canaan where Baal is worshiped. The mythology of Baal relates how, in a yearly cycle, the deity was killed but then broke free from his rival, death. The return of rain and fruitful crops (and thus another season of life) was taken as proof of Baal's return to life. In this context, the God of Israel—the true living God of power and life—is with Israel to overcome the foreign nations and their gods. In a second descriptor, God is the "Lord of all the earth" (vv. 11, 13), a phrase that echoes that of Rahab (2:11) and acknowledges God's dominion over all the earth. As such, he can claim the land of Canaan for Israel.

Finally, in a further narrative delay before revealing the miracle, Joshua anticipates the role to be played by the twelve men. In the same way the priests were introduced in passing (v. 3) to become central characters as the narrative progresses, so the twelve men are introduced in passing and their more central role revealed later. With priests and people prepared, Joshua finally delivers the punch line: the priests carrying the ark are to "stand" in the waters of the Jordan (v. 8). The moment their feet touch the waters, the waters will respond. They will be dramatically cut off and "stand" in a heap, as did the Red Sea (Exod 15:8; Ps 78:13).

All is prepared for the people to "move out" (v. 3), and they now "break camp" (v. 14; the two expressions come from the same Hebrew root, *nsʿ*) with the priests carrying the ark to lead the way. Priests and people are now in motion, and the crossing is narrated in verses 14–17. Four times within those verses we are told that Israel "crosses over" or "passes by" (*qal* variations of the same Hebrew root, *ʿbr*), which is the purpose of the miraculous parted waters. The action slows in these verses and water—miraculously stopped by the ark's passage—is described in several ways. Joshua has prophesied that the water would be "cut off," "stand up," and form a "heap" (v. 13), and each of these words features in the account.

As the people and priests set out, a digression again delays the action and increases the wonder of the miracle. The usual harvest flood stage of the Jordan swells it with winter rain beyond its normal ninety to one-hundred-foot width and three to ten-foot depth. Some estimates taken from a nineteenth century AD flood observation suggest the harvest flood could make the river as much as a half-mile wide.[5] Despite this obstacle, Joshua's word proves true: "as soon as" the priests' feet touch the waters, the miracle occurs (v. 15).

The miraculous stoppage is viewed in two directions. Upstream from the priests, the waters "stopped flowing" (v. 16). The word used is that of Joshua's prophecy (v. 13; "stand up"). The waters stand up in a "heap," again echoing Joshua's words and recalling the Red Sea crossing. The text pinpoints the location of the stoppage, and Adam can be identified with modern Tell ed-Damiyeh, about fifteen miles north of the Jordan at Jericho. Adam is a site at which the Jordan's high banks have periodically collapsed due to earthquakes and mudslides that have stopped the water's flow for as long as seventy-two hours.[6] Such explanations (while providing an account of the mechanics of the miracle) fail to explain the precision of its timing and duration. On this, the text makes clear its claim: it is the presence of the ark of the covenant of the Lord of all the earth that causes the waters to stop flowing. The text calls its audience to mark the wonder of the crossing.

If the waters upstream are stopped, the waters downstream are "cut off" (v. 16) as Joshua had said (v. 13). The miracle is emphasized by noting the waters are "completely" cut off. A twenty-mile stretch of riverbed is thus exposed and the people "cross over opposite Jericho" (v. 16). The courage of Jericho melted away when they heard of the long-ago Red Sea crossing

5. Hess, "Joshua" in ZIBBC, 25; see also Colin J. Humphreys, *The Miracles of Exodus: A Scientist's Discovery of the Extraordinary Natural Causes of the Biblical Stories* (London/New York: Continuum, 2003), 25–26.

6. Stoppages are noted as early as 1267 AD, and as recently as 1906 and 1927. The 1927 stoppage lasted seventy-two hours. See Kenneth Kitchen, *On the Reliability*, 19–21.

(2:10–11); one can only imagine their state of mind on hearing the report of the current event.

The miracle is viewed once again (v. 17), focusing on the priests and people. In this view, the priests have moved to the middle of the Jordan where they stand on "dry ground" as Israel likewise passes by on "dry ground." Once again, the language recalls the dry ground of the Red Sea crossing (Exod 14:21) and anticipates Elijah's own Jordan crossing (2 Kgs 2:8). In fulfillment of God's promise, Israel crosses as "all Israel" and the "whole nation." It is a defining moment for the people, Israel. In covenant with God they will always be his "people"; now in the crossing, they are for the first time in the passage identified as a "nation." As a nation, they enter the land to claim a territory deeded by God. The priests remain in place until the nation "had completed" the crossing, just as the waters were "completely" cut off.

### Twelve Stones for a Sign (4:1–9)

Before the priests exit the waters, the narrative pauses to provide for a memorial of the event (4:1–9). The importance of this memorial is signaled by a repetition (4:19–24) that is communicated from a different perspective. In the same way, the crossing's importance was signaled by retellings from various perspectives. The segue to recount the memorial remains connected to preceding events by referring to the "whole nation" crossing over (3:17; 4:1) and recalling the twelve men selected in 3:12. Once again, the unity of the nation is evident: the "whole" nation crosses over; the men are representative of "each tribe."

The priests earlier took up the ark and crossed over the Jordan (3:6). Now the men's actions mirror and commemorate that event as they take up stones and cross over. The stones are selected from the very spot where the priests and ark stood as the nation crossed. The Hebrew pointedly references the spot three times: the men are to take up stones "from this *place*, from the middle of the Jordan, where the priests are standing" (v. 3, author's translation).

The twelve men, previously selected, have apparently waited with Joshua on the east side while the nation crossed over. Now Joshua commissions them to each gather a stone. Again, the nation's unity is apparent: the men are "one from each tribe" (4:2, 4), and the stones are "according to the number of the tribes of the Israelites" (4:5, 8). No tribe—whether settled in the Cisjordan or Transjordan—is neglected in the memorial. The Israelites obey Joshua, fulfilling the LORD's word (v. 8). The stones are removed to that night's camp and subsequently erected at Gilgal (v. 20).

The stones are to be a "sign" (v. 6) and "memorial" (v. 7) to present and future generations. A "sign" is a token that commemorates and evokes rich memories of past events, much as a treasured souvenir draws our minds back to a past holiday. Some signs might be ritual acts, such as eating unleavened bread to commemorate the exodus and prompt the retelling of its story (Exod 13:3–10). Other signs, such as Aaron's rod that buds, serve as reminders of God's power and a warning to the community (Num 17:10[17:25]); the curses of Deuteronomy 28:46 are similar signs to remind and warn against covenant disobedience.

"Memorials," like signs, prompt remembrance of past events. Very often, memorials are situated within the realm of the cult. Memorials include the day of Passover (Exod 12:14; 13:9), the stones set in the shoulder of the High Priest's ephod and breastplate (Exod 28:12, 29; 39:7), the bronze censers of Korah, Dathan, and Abiram hammered out to cover the altar as a reminder of the prerogatives of the Aaronic priests (Num 16:40[17:5]), and even scrolls or items of plunder from the LORD's wars (Exod 17:14; Num 31:54). The cultic character of the memorial stones acknowledges the LORD's presence as intrinsic to land entry. Israel's passage is therefore one of holiness and worship.

The standing stones will prompt the future question, "What does this mean?" It is a question also found in Exodus 12:26 and 13:14 in response to Passover rituals and in Deuteronomy 6:20 in response to God's instructions. In each instance, the question prompts the telling of Israel's story: deliverance out of Egypt by God's power. In the same way, the sign and memorial of the stones prompts a brief story (v. 7):

> The flow of the Jordan was cut off
>     before the ark of the covenant of the LORD.
>     When it crossed the Jordan
> The waters of the Jordan were cut off.

The shape of the story remembers the essentials of the miracle: the outer brackets tell of the water cut off, and the inner core reveals the means by which the miracle was effected: the ark of God by which his powerful presence goes before the people. This story is to be remembered and recounted "among you . . . your children . . . and the people of Israel forever" (v. 6–7).

The memorial passage is concluded with a review of several key items concerning the selection, transport, and disposition of the stones (vv. 8–9). As in verse 3, the stones are taken up and brought over, mirroring the priest's own action with the ark. The point is that the Israelites are obedient to Joshua. The review highlights two levels of obedience: the people obey Joshua, acknowledging his leadership, while Joshua commands the people "as the LORD had told Joshua" (v. 8).

In some translations (NASB, NRSV, NLT), the twelve stones set up in verse 9 are understood to be a *second* memorial where the priests stood in the Jordan. A literal reading of the Hebrew leads in this direction. However, it would be odd to suddenly and briefly introduce a second memorial in the midst of the narrative's flow. No further elaboration of a second memorial is provided, and the narrative has an established pattern of revisiting previous elements. The NIV translation follows this pattern, understanding verse 9 to speak of the twelve stones removed from the river. The reference highlights the stones' special nature, for they came from the place where the priests "who carried the ark of the covenant" stood (v. 9).

Finally, attesting to the endurance of the memorial, the writer notes the stones are there "to this day." Since then, the stones have disappeared, but the memorial remains in the narrative before us.

### The Miraculous Crossing: The View from the West Side (4:10–18)

The crossing is rehearsed once again, continuing several themes and introducing new ones. The priests are still those who "carry the ark" (vv. 10, 16, 18) and the ark is still primarily referenced as the "ark of the LORD" or the "ark of the covenant of the LORD" (vv. 11, 18). But the ark is also called the "ark of the covenant law" (v. 16), a phrase found in Joshua only here but common in Exodus. In Exodus, the ark containing the tablets of the covenant law (Exod 25:16, 21) is the "ark of the covenant law" (Exod 25:22; 26:33–34; 30:6, 26; 39:35; 40:3, 5, 21; see also Num 4:5; 7:89).

The emphasis on "crossing" remains as the people "hurried over" (v. 10), "had crossed" (v. 11), "came to the other side" (v. 11), and "crossed over" (v. 12, 13). They cross as a unified whole ("all of them" [v. 11], "all Israel" [v. 14]), but this is in tension with the explicit mention of the Transjordanian tribes. All may cross over, but not all have chosen to remain in the promised land. This tension runs through the whole of the book of Joshua. The mention of the tribes and the unusual "ark of the covenant law" are attributable to the prominence of Moses in this crossing account (vv. 10, 12, 14). Moses' history is intimately tied to the covenant document placed in the ark, and he is the crafter of the Transjordanian agreement (Num 32).

Joshua is shown to continue Moses' ministry. The people follow Joshua's direction as they had Moses' (v. 10). Joshua had affirmed the Transjordanian agreement (1:12–15) and these tribes cross over "as Moses had directed them" (v. 12). The awe in which Joshua is held is the same as that given Moses (v. 14).

Joshua is also shown to be the new leader who does "everything the LORD had commanded" (v. 10). It is in this context of obedient ministry that Joshua is exalted by the LORD (v. 14). He is not exalted for performing the miracle—that is all God, as the sustained emphasis on the ark's power makes clear. Joshua is exalted for his obedience. God is with Joshua as he was with Moses

(Josh 1:5) and Joshua exhibits the obedience God required for entry to the land (Josh 1:7). For these reasons he is exalted.

For the first time in the crossing account, battle is specifically mentioned. The Transjordanian tribes cross "ready for battle" (v. 12; Josh 1:14; Num 32:17). The forty thousand "armed for battle" may further describe these tribes or refer to those of all Israel prepared for battle. The forty thousand may be an accurate number as per census numbers in Numbers 26. Such round numbers can also be used to simply suggest a very large group (as in Judg 5:8; 2 Sam 10:18; 1 Kgs 4:26[5:6]). The Hebrew word here translated "thousand" can also be translated "unit," thus, "forty units (of undisclosed numbers)" cross the Jordan "for war." The war is cultic: the warriors cross "before the Lord" (v. 13).

Finally, the narrative perspective shifts conclusively to the Jordan's west side. The crossing is completed (4:11 reads "as soon as all of them had crossed," utilizing the same Hebrew word translated "completed" in 3:17). From the west bank, the people watch as the ark exits the riverbed. A series of commands, from the Lord to Joshua (vv. 15–16) and then from Joshua to the priests (v. 17), facilitate this final movement. These commands follow on Joshua's exaltation and further demonstrate his obedient leadership. As the priests' feet touch the banks, a second miracle occurs and the waters again flow. The miracle's power lies not in the priests themselves, but in the fact they carry the "ark of the covenant" (vv. 16, 18), the locus of God's presence amidst his people. The magnitude of the miracle is revisited for the priests arrive on "dry ground" (v. 18), which is no different than the ground of the exposed riverbed (Josh 3:17; cf. Exod 14:21). More, the reference to the "flood stage as before" is a reminder of the magnitude of the miraculous stoppage.

### Twelve Stones: The Memorial at Gilgal (4:19–24)

The miraculous crossing occurs on the tenth day of the first month: the day of the Passover preparation (Exod 12:3). The notation anticipates the Passover that will be held in the land (5:10). Israel camps at Gilgal, its base of operation (5:9–10; 9:6; 10:6–9, 15, 43; 14:6), until the tent is moved to Shiloh (18:1).

In close proximity to Israel's first battle target (Jericho), Gilgal is the place of the memorial stones. The first account of the memorial (4:1–9) noted their value for present and future generations; this account focuses solely on their value for future generations. The descendants' question is that of the first account (vv. 6, 21). The first answer spoke of the ark and the arrested waters. This second, lengthier answer speaks of the dry ground and God's action of drying the waters. Here, the answer given in vv. 22–23 is set out showing the clear emphasis on the dry ground:

> 'Israel crossed the Jordan **on dry ground**.'
> For the LORD your God **dried up** the Jordan . . .
> until *you* had crossed over.
> The LORD your God did to the Jordan what he had done to the Red Sea when he **dried it up** before *us* until *we* had crossed over (vv. 22–23; emphasis added).

The verses make an explicit reference to the Red Sea. They also refer implicitly to the Red Sea through the use of "dry ground" which also appears in the Red Sea account (Exod 14:16, 22, 29; 15:19). In comparing the two events, Joshua distinguishes between the Red Sea generation ("us," "we") and the present generation ("you"). Each has now experienced God's power over the waters; each has experienced an "exodus."

The stones invoke remembrance for Israel, and as the story is remembered Israel is to respond with reverent fear as it did at the Red Sea (Exod 14:31). The recounting of the Jordan miracle will go beyond Israel, and the nations too will know God's mighty power. How the nations might respond is not indicated here but comes in the very next verse.

### Melting Hearts (5:1)

The Amorite and Canaanite kings west of the Jordan hear of God's power that dried up the river (4:23). They know of the Israelite crossing, but their response is not the reverent fear to which Israel is called (4:24). Their response echoes that of the Jericho inhabitants. With them, they "melt in fear" (2:11; 7:5) and have no courage (2:11). Such fear and dread was anticipated at the Red Sea (Exod 15:15–16; Deut 2:25; 11:25). Sadly, the kings west of the Jordan do not respond as did Rahab.

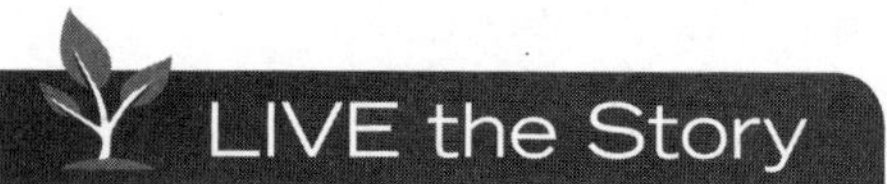


### Crossing into Rest: The Baptism Imagery

The Jordan crossing is a decisive transition moment in Israel's history. Paired with the Red Sea crossing, these two transitions bookend the wilderness time. That the wilderness wanderings are concluded and the Jordan crossed is indicative of God's ongoing commitment to the promises made to his covenant people despite their sinfulness. As Israel crosses the Jordan, they move from landlessness to landedness and the rest, safety, and provision the land represents. The land offers these physical realities, but it also offers rest, safety, and provision on a symbolic level (see Listen to the Story, Chapter 1). That is, the land holds out the promise of the same "rest" experienced in the garden and figured in the tabernacle (and later, the temple). This rest is the experience of the presence of God, fellowship with him, and the goodness of life lived under his covenant. The land serves as a symbolic cipher of these spiritual realities so that, in the Jordan crossing, Israel crosses over into "rest."

The Jordan continues as a symbol of transition in the Bible. In the Old Testament, it is most notable (outside of Joshua) in the Elijah-Elisha account (see Listen to the Story, The Red Sea Revisited above). In 2 Kings 2, Elijah transitions east across the Jordan to his mysterious end, and Elisha transitions back imbued with Elijah's power to engage in battle against the forces of Baal in the land. In a lesser way, Naaman experiences his own transition "through" the Jordan (2 Kgs 5) when God's cleansing power is mediated by its waters. The enemy from Aram becomes a worshiper of the Lord, acknowledging "there is no God in all the world except in Israel" (v. 15). In the New Testament, the Jordan is associated with Jesus' transition into his public ministry. In each Gospel (Matt 3:13–17; Mark 1:9–13; Luke 3:3, 21–22; John 1:28–34), Jesus is baptized in the Jordan with an accompanying testimony of his Sonship. In the synoptic tradition, the Father attests to the Son, being "well pleased" in him; in John, the Baptizer provides the testimony.

The Jordan crossing's symbolic transition into "rest" is a key component in a Christian interpretation of Joshua 3–4. In Hebrews 3–4, Israel's unbelief is held up as an example Christians should not imitate. The author reminds the listener that Israel's unbelief barred its entrance into the land and the rest it provided. Even though rest was a possibility for Israel, the wilderness generation "did not share the faith of those who obeyed" (4:2). They were unlike those Israelites (such as Caleb and Joshua) who did enter the land. Yet, even those who entered the land failed, ultimately, to enter its promised rest because of ongoing unbelief. The epistle attests to this by saying:

> For if Joshua had given them rest, God would not have spoken later about another day. There remains, then, a Sabbath-rest for the people of God. (Heb 4:8–9)

This Sabbath rest, the epistle argues, is made available to believers only by faith, in and through the work of Christ, not by any work of the believer. The Christian enters life in Christ by God's work and participates in the rest that God provides, for "anyone who enters God's rest also rests from their works, just as God did from his" (Heb 4:10).[7]

Within the Christian tradition, it is baptism that is the sign of transition

7. See Ounsworth, *Joshua Typology*, 78–95.

into the new life Christ provides. Working with the connection in Hebrews of the Jordan crossing and rest and given Christ's own transition by baptism in the Jordan, it is not surprising that the Jordan crossing typologically prefigures Christian baptism into the rest of life in God. This figural connection is heightened through a typological reading of Joshua as Jesus. This typology rests in part on the fact that only these two figures have (in the Greek) the same name (see Live the Story, Chapter 1). The figural connection of the Jordan crossing and baptism is clear in Origen's homily on Joshua 3–4:

> Lest you marvel when these deeds concerning the former people are applied to you, O Christian, the divine word promises much greater and loftier things for you who, through the sacrament of baptism, have parted the waters of the Jordan.[8]

Further development of Origen's image of baptism as Jordan-crossing is seen in his treatment of the parting of the Red Sea. As noted above, the two crossings are linked by shared words, themes, and structure (although reversed). At times, Origen likens the Red Sea crossing to baptism. More often, Origen likens the Red Sea to a believer's entry into a time of Christian instruction known as the Catechumenate. For this initiatory period Origen utilizes the image of 1 Corinthians 10 in which Israel is baptized into Moses "in the cloud and in the sea" (v. 2) and given spiritual food and drink. Origen sees in the new catechumens those who have been baptized into Moses to receive the spiritual food and drink of Christian teaching. Of these catechumens Origen says,

> [you have] undertaken to submit to the precepts of the Church, you have parted the Red Sea and, placed in the stations of the desert, you daily devote yourself to hearing the Law of God and looking upon the face of Moses, through which the glory of the Lord is revealed.[9]

It is at the completion of this initiation (during which the believer has learned of the faith and tested the desire to join the church), that the believer is admitted to the sacraments (baptism and the Lord's Supper). In likening baptism to the Jordan crossing, Origen simply extends his figural reading of 1 Corinthians 10: if passage through the Red Sea figures entry to Christian initiation, then, by extension, passage through the Jordan figures baptism.

For sinful Israel, entry to the land was an act of God's grace, revealing God's commitment to fulfill the promise given Abraham. The promised land was a place of rest and safety in which Israel would live the fullness of

---

8. Origen, *Hom* 4.1. A similar figure is explored in *Hom* 4.2, 5.3.
9. Ibid., 4.1. See also *Hom* 1.7 for a similar figure.

covenant life. The crossing was a wondrous event; a miracle wrought by God's power and presence. It was a decisive turning from the sinful wilderness time to the covenant life envisioned in the land. In a similar way, baptism is a passage from the old life of sin and death to the fullness of new life in Christ. Like the Jordan crossing, it is a wondrous passage, unveiling the surprising grace of God.

The connection of the Jordan crossing and Christian baptism is powerfully made in the Great Vigil of Easter. This is a liturgical service held on the Saturday between Good Friday and Easter Sunday (Holy Saturday, as it is known). Held after sundown, it is considered the first service of Easter, and it incorporates four elements drawn from the ancient practices of the church. Each element highlights Christ's transition from death to life and our transition through baptism to new life in him.

First, a new paschal candle is lit, signifying Christ's resurrected life in the tomb's darkness. This light is processed into the darkened church, and congregants light tapers from the paschal candle, symbolizing their life is found in Christ's life. Second, the history of salvation is surveyed through readings from the Old and New Testaments. The Old Testament readings trace God's creation, the outworking of God's promises to Abraham, and God's salvation of Israel through the Red Sea. One of the New Testament readings in this survey is Romans 6:3–11, which recounts our baptism as a death-to-life reality accomplished through our identification with Christ. Of note is that alongside the Romans passage, Psalm 114 is offered. This psalm praises God, recalling the turning back of the Red Sea and the Jordan. It is an effective typological pairing of the baptismal passage in Romans with the parted waters of the Jordan. Finally, the history of salvation culminates with a gospel account of the resurrection, focusing the fulfillment of God's promise of rest in the one who conquered sin and death.

Third, after these readings, those who have prepared are baptized, and the congregation renews its baptismal vows. Again, the liturgy remembers significant scriptural transitions effected through water, including Christ's own baptism in the Jordan. Fourth and finally, the Easter Eucharist is shared, and those gathered at the Lord's Table are reminded that only by Christ's death and resurrection is their own transition into life made possible.

The whole liturgy is mindful of the mysterious miracle of Easter: Christ's transition from death to life that enables our transition through water into life. For those familiar with Joshua 3–4 and the role it plays in the church's understanding of baptism, the liturgy is pregnant with meaning, arising out of God's promises to Israel on behalf of the world and demonstrating the church's figural participation in those narratives.

### Treading the Verge of Jordan: Eschatological Hope

Joshua 3–4, as noted in the commentary above, is filled with indications of Joshua's and Israel's obedience to God's commands. There is the hope that this new generation enters the land to fully appropriate the promised rest (1:15). The book's own affirmation is that this hope is achieved (see commentary at 21:43–45, in Chapter 19). Of course, the book also notes that while God's promise of rest is accomplished, the land is not fully possessed, even in Joshua's old age (13:1; 23:1–5), and disobedience on the part of the people remains a real threat to land possession. There is a tension in the book: the promises are both fulfilled and awaiting fulfillment; now and not yet. This opens the Jordan crossing typological reading in a new, eschatological direction. In this eschatological reading, the Jordan crossing is the believer's crossing from life through the "Jordan" of physical death into the fullness of heaven, the place of rest and full communion with God.

One sees this eschatological reading in Bunyan's allegorical classic, *Pilgrim's Progress*. As the character named Christian comes to the end of his pilgrimage (his life), he is confronted by a river that he must cross to reach his goal, the city on a mighty hill, heavenly Jerusalem. Christian begins passage of the river. Midstream, he is frightened but remembrance of Christ's presence encourages him and

> the enemy was after that as still as a stone, until they were gone over. Christian, therefore, presently found ground to stand upon, and so it followed that the rest of the river was but shallow. Thus they got over. . . . Thus they went along towards the gate. Now you must note, that the city stood upon a mighty hill; but the pilgrims went up that hill with ease, because they had these two men [angels] to lead them up by the arms: they had likewise left their mortal garments behind them in the river; for though they went in with them, they came out without them. They therefore went up here with much agility and speed, though the foundation upon which the city was framed was higher than the clouds; they therefore went up through the region of the air, sweetly talking as they went, being comforted because they safely got over the river, and had such glorious companions to attend them. The talk that they had with the shining ones was about the glory of the place; who told them that the beauty and glory of it was inexpressible. There, said they, is "Mount Sion, the heavenly Jerusalem, the innumerable company of angels, and the spirits of just men made perfect."[10]

10. John Bunyan, *Pilgrim's Progress*, *CCEL*, 112–13, https://www.ccel.org/ccel/bunyan/pilgrim.html.

The identification of this eschatological river as the Jordan is made explicit in the great hymn, *Guide Me, O Thou Great Jehovah*, written by the eighteenth century hymnist William Williams.[11] The first verses speak of the wilderness wanderings and God's provision of manna and water. It petitions God as "fire and cloudy pillar [to] lead me all my journey through." But it is the third verse that clearly reveals the wanderer is a Christian and the wilderness the pilgrimage of life. In this context, the petition for guidance "all my journey through" is that God would lead the believer up to the Jordan-crossing of death and over to possess Canaan, the promised land of heaven:

*When I tread the verge of Jordan,*
*Bid my anxious fears subside;*
*Death of death and hell's destruction,*
*Land me safe on Canaan's side:*
*Songs of praises, songs of praises,*
*I will ever give to thee,*
*I will ever give to thee.*

## Joshua: Exalted through Obedience

> "Today I will begin to exalt you in the eyes of all Israel, so they may know that I am with you as I was with Moses" (3:7). That day the LORD exalted Joshua in the sight of all Israel; and they stood in awe of him all the days of his life, just as they had stood in awe of Moses. (4:14)

The commentary above argued that the exaltation of Joshua was in no way due to his effecting of the miracle of the Jordan. That act was wholly God's doing. Rather, Joshua's exaltation was due to his obedience to God's commands, ensuring Israel crossed the Jordan so as to honor God's holy presence that led the way in the ark. Several elements in the narrative emphasize the obedience of Joshua: he fulfills God's commands, and he passes along God's commands to the people which they then fulfill. The ark of the "covenant of the LORD" (4:18), the symbol of God's presence and power, and in which God's law is housed, is highlighted throughout the narrative, and Joshua carefully ensures the memorial of the event is built as God instructed.

Earlier, the typological association of Joshua to Jesus was explored (see Listen to the Story, Chapter 1). In that vein, the exaltation of Joshua leads to reflection upon the exaltation of Jesus. As with Joshua, Jesus' exaltation is connected to his obedience, an attitude apparent in the Gospel accounts.

At the baptism of Jesus, the Son is approved by the Father. Immediately,

11. Written by William Williams, translated by Peter Williams. Public Domain.

Jesus is led by the Spirit into the wilderness where Satan tempts him. For each test, Jesus grounds his obedience in God's word, and he uses Deuteronomy to refute Satan (Matt 4:4–10 and Luke 4:4–12 cite Deut 8:3; 6:13, 16). Deuteronomy—the law of Moses—is the very text Joshua was urged to obey (1:7–8; see Explain the Story and Listen to the Story, Chapter 1).

Throughout his ministry, Jesus claims he has come to do the Father's will (John 4:34; 6:38), and at his transfiguration the Father once again voices his approval of the Son (Matt 17:1–8; Mark 9:2–8; Luke 9:28–36). In the garden, while praying the cup of suffering would pass from him, this same obedience enables Jesus to pray "not my will, but yours be done" (Matt 26:39; Luke 22:42). It is this obedience, by which Jesus humbles himself and commits to humiliation and death, that the Christ hymn acknowledges (Phil 2:6–11). The hymn lauds the great reversal of God's economy: Christ in obedience humbled himself to death on a cross and *therefore* "God exalted him to the highest place" (v. 9).

Christ's ministry culminates in his death. His baptism inaugurates that ministry, and his transfiguration marks the final journey to the cross. These two events, at which the Father voices full approval of the Son, anticipate this final exaltation through the cross.

Origen, preaching on the Jordan-crossing, meditates upon this typological connection to Christ. He also draws out the connection of exaltation to obedience, citing Christ's obedience in baptism and through death as worthy of exaltation:

> Indeed, Jesus is not exalted before the mystery of baptism. But his exaltation, even his exaltation in the sight of the people, assumes a beginning from then on. If "all who are baptized [into Christ Jesus] are baptized into his death," and the death of Jesus is made complete by the exaltation of the cross, deservedly then, Jesus is first exalted for each of the faithful when that person arrives at the mystery of baptism. Because thus it is written that "God exalted him, and gave him a name that is above every name, that at the name of Jesus every knee should bend, in heaven and on earth, and below the earth."[12]

As Israel was called to the obedience of Joshua, their leader, so Christians are called to the obedience of Christ. Following Christ calls us to the obedience of baptism, the sign and symbol of our death in him. It is our death to self and to the world. Only through this death is the new birth in Christ made possible. This is exaltation, indeed!

---

12. Origen, *Hom* 4.2.

## Catechesis: The Power of Living Memory

"What do these stones mean?" (4:6, 21)

On April 9, 2017, Canada solemnly observed the one-hundredth anniversary of the Battle of Vimy Ridge, fought in World War I France. The ceremony was held at the memorial site in France, and an attendance of twenty-five thousand people was expected, though no one now living fought at Vimy Ridge. At the memorial site is a monument of terrible beauty, familiar by sight to most Canadians. The monument, along with the mention of "Vimy Ridge," evokes a sense of Canadian identity: the battle and its memorial monument are part of the Canadian story. Whether one affirms the necessity of war or not and whether one agrees with the mythology attached to the monument, it is a truly Canadian icon. The memorial monument has power; it engages us in our own story.[13]

This is the nature of all good memorials. They are part of an ongoing story. They raise questions of meaning, drawing the observer into a narrative and connecting them to their own past. Ultimately, a powerful memorial enables people to existentially experience the past event so as to live out its demands and implications in the present. This is the power of the stones drawn out of the river. A memorial for future Israelites, they are *aides memoire* that draw people into the story and its present day implications. Reflecting on God's wonders (including the Jordan crossing), the psalmist calls for a present day response when he calls listeners to "put their trust in God and . . . not forget his deeds but . . . keep his commandments" (Ps 78:7).

For the Christian, this memorial power is particularly evident in the ordinance or sacrament of the Lord's Supper. It is not simply a remembrance of what occurred in the past, however sacred that memorial is. Rather, in the Lord's Supper we activate the past in the present: the Lord is present with the gathered community around the table; within a sacramental context, the elements themselves mysteriously communicate God's grace. In our actions around the table we "proclaim the Lord's death until he comes" (1 Cor 11:26), thus existentially entering the narrative. It is at the Lord's Table that we again are called to live out of the narrative we proclaim. In faith, in obedience, in love, our actions will show we have both heard and entered the memorial's story.

13. The power of the Vimy Ridge monument, and the contested role it plays in Canadian identity and mythology, is well explored by Robert Everett-Green in the *Globe and Mail* newspaper's April 5, 2017 article, "Vimy Ridge: Birthplace of a nation—or of a Canadian myth?" (http://www.theglobeandmail.com/news/national/battle-of-vimy-ridge-first-world-war/article34515113/).

# CHAPTER 4

# Joshua 5:2–12

## LISTEN to the Story

[2]At that time the LORD said to Joshua, "Make flint knives and circumcise the Israelites again." [3]So Joshua made flint knives and circumcised the Israelites at Gibeath Haaraloth.

[4]Now this is why he did so: All those who came out of Egypt—all the men of military age—died in the wilderness on the way after leaving Egypt. [5]All the people that came out had been circumcised, but all the people born in the wilderness during the journey from Egypt had not. [6]The Israelites had moved about in the wilderness forty years until all the men who were of military age when they left Egypt had died, since they had not obeyed the LORD. For the LORD had sworn to them that they would not see the land he had solemnly promised their ancestors to give us, a land flowing with milk and honey. [7]So he raised up their sons in their place, and these were the ones Joshua circumcised. They were still uncircumcised because they had not been circumcised on the way. [8]And after the whole nation had been circumcised, they remained where they were in camp until they were healed.

[9]Then the LORD said to Joshua, "Today I have rolled away the reproach of Egypt from you." So the place has been called Gilgal to this day.

[10]On the evening of the fourteenth day of the month, while camped at Gilgal on the plains of Jericho, the Israelites celebrated the Passover. [11]The day after the Passover, that very day, they ate some of the produce of the land: unleavened bread and roasted grain. [12]The manna stopped the day after they ate this food from the land; there was no longer any manna for the Israelites, but that year they ate the produce of Canaan.

*Listening to the Text in the Story*: Genesis 17:1–14; Exodus 12:1–30, 43–51; 16:1–18, 31–35; Saqqara Bas-Relief; Story of Sinuhe

This short passage reinstates two rituals necessary to complete the transition from wilderness to landedness. The reinstated rituals identify Israel's covenant nature. The manna ceases once the rituals are completed, confirming the transition's end.

### Circumcision: The Sign of the Covenant

The sign of circumcision seals God's covenant with Abram and is required of every male in Israel, including slaves or other non-relatives attached to Israelite households (Gen 17:9–14). The rite is performed in the family setting by the father on the child's eighth day (Gen 21:4). Circumcision is the crucial covenantal sign, and Israelites who forego it have broken the covenant and are cut off. However, the external sign is useless without a concomitant internal covenant commitment (Lev 26:41; Deut 10:16; Jer 4:4). Circumcision is necessary to participate in the Passover feast (Exod 12:48), and this is reflected in the order of the Joshua passage.

Circumcision in Genesis 17 is accompanied by Abram's name change, signaling the covenant's transformative nature. For post-wilderness Israel, the circumcision rite marks a transformation, transitioning from the generation of wilderness disobedience to the generation of landed obedience. Additionally, the sign of circumcision was given Abram immediately following the promise of land (Gen 17:7–11). Now, once again, the promise of land and circumcision are presented together as Israel's renewal of the covenant sign prepares them to receive the covenant promise of land.

### The Passover Renewed

Passover commemorates God "passing over" the land of Egypt. Held in conjunction with a seven-day feast of Unleavened Bread, the two commemorate the exodus (Exod 12:1–30; see also Lev 23:4–8; Num 28:16–25; Deut 16:1–8). Israel departs Egypt on the day after the Passover (Exod 12:31; Num 33:3). Instituted by God as a perpetual annual festival (Exod 12:14, 24, 42), the feast is celebrated in a family setting (Exod 12:3–11, 46), although Deuteronomy places the sacrifice in a cultic setting (Deut 16:2, 5–7). The Passover and exodus are intrinsic to Israel's identity and mark the calendar's first month (Abib). Preparations begin on the tenth day, and no males may participate unless circumcised (Exod 12:48). Passover is observed the evening of the fourteenth day, with Unleavened Bread continuing another seven days.

Israel is particularly enjoined to observe Passover in the promised land (Exod 12:25; 13:5). A child's question, "What does this mean?" prompts an accounting of God's deliverance (Exod 12:24–27). Similarly, the question of Joshua 4:6–7, 21–22 connects miraculous events to the story of God's fulfillment of covenant promises.

Passover was observed at least once in the wilderness (Num 9:1–14). While Israel did "everything just as the LORD commanded Moses" (v. 5), some in the community were unable to participate due to uncleanness. This contrasts to the account in Joshua 5 that emphasizes "all" the new generation (v. 5) and the "whole" nation (v. 8) celebrated. No exclusion is noted in Joshua's Passover celebration.

### Manna for the Wilderness

Manna is the food given to the grumbling wilderness generation (Exod 16:3–4). The gift of manna tested Israel's obedience (v. 4) but was also God's gracious provision for forty years. Its cessation when Israel entered the land (Exod 16:35) ends Israel's transition into the land as the new generation.

### Circumcision, Festivals, and Provision in the Ancient World

Circumcision was widely practiced in West Semitic cultures (Israel, Ammon, Moab, Edom). It was also practiced in Egypt, and a third millennium bas-relief found in a tomb in Saqqara, Egypt depicts Egyptian priests using obsidian knives to circumcise young boys.[1] The antiquity of the practice may account for Israel using flint knives at a time when metal was widely available.

In Emar (a northern Syrian city whose texts date from the fourteenth-twelfth centuries BC), the *zukru* festival begins, like Passover, on the fourteenth day of the first month. Passover is followed by the seven-day feast of Unleavened Bread; *zukru* also continued for a further seven-day festival. Beyond the similarity in date and length, the *zukru* festival does not commemorate a god's great saving acts. Instead, offerings are made to the god Dagan and the pantheon of Emar.[2]

Canaan is described as "flowing with milk and honey" (v. 6). Food is important to this passage and is variously described (vv. 11–12). An account of Sinuhe, an exiled Egyptian official in the second millennium, describes the bounty of land situated in northern Palestine and Syria. Honey, barley, and milk are all mentioned; each is noted in Joshua:

> Figs were in it, and grapes. It had more wine than water. *Plentiful was its honey*, abundant its olives. Every (kind of) fruit was on its trees. *Barley* was there, and emmer. There was no limit to any (kind of) cattle. . . . . Many [meals] . . . were made for me, *and milk in every (kind of) cooking*.[3]

1. *ANEP*, 206.
2. *COS* 1.123:431–34
3. *ANET*, 19–20. Emphasis added.

## EXPLAIN the Story

These verses sketch Israel's final transition into the promised land. The narrative completes the wilderness/crossing/Passover sequence of Joshua 3–5, noted in Chapter 3 above, and is a reversal of the Passover/crossing/wilderness sequence of the previous generation. The new generation also reverses the experience and fate of the earlier, disobedient generation who died outside the land. Instead, the new obedient generation enters the land and lives.

The passage's transitional character partakes of the past while anticipating the future. The past is wilderness disobedience but also covenant promises, the sign of circumcision, and deliverance ritualized in Passover. The new generation identifies with its covenantal past by reinstituting circumcision and Passover. It is an obedient generation that anticipates land possession. That these events occur on the "plains of Jericho" (v. 10) foreshadows the next step to land possession: Jericho.

The taking of Jericho, and the related account of Ai (chs. 7–8), is set off by two interludes. Joshua 5:2–12 is the first. In it, Israel addresses covenantal lacunae. The second is Joshua 8:30–35, in which Israel renews the covenant after its first failure in the land.

### A Cut Above: The New Generation Is Not the Old Generation (5:2–9)

"At that time" (v. 2), that is, during Israel's encampment at Gilgal, the LORD commands Joshua to reinstate circumcision. Joshua's response uses the same words as the command, thus illustrating his obedience. Oddly, although the text declares the new generation had not been circumcised (vv. 5, 8), God directs Israel be circumcised "again" (v. 2). Perhaps in the wilderness an Egyptian form of circumcision (which did not fully remove the prepuce) was practiced. On this understanding, Joshua performs a second circumcision according to the Israelite practice.[4] However, because the text explicitly states circumcision was not the wilderness practice (vv. 5, 8), it is more fitting to consider that after a period of neglect, Israel is to "again" practice circumcision.

"Flint knives" (vv. 2–3) are used. It is a word combination unique to these two verses, highlighting the action's special nature. Flint was earlier used to circumcise Moses' son (Exod 4:25), and obsidian flints are depicted in the Saqqara Bas-Relief (see Listen to the Story). Metal was widely available during Joshua's time, but stone implements continued in use. The use of stone for circumcision may relate to the ancient origin of the practice or to practical

4. Jack M. Sasson, "Circumcision in the Ancient Near East," *JBL* 85 (1966): 474.

reasons of ease of availability and concerns for hygiene.[5] The circumcision is performed at Gibeath Haaraloth or the "Hill of Foreskins." The hill may be an existing cult site; certainly the name conjures images of very many males being circumcised. Its location is unknown although narrative context suggests proximity to Gilgal.

Verses 4–8 set out the reasons Joshua performed the circumcision. They can be stated simply: the generation of Egypt had all been circumcised; the generation born in the wilderness had not. But the text expands this explanation, comparing and contrasting the two generations in several ways and giving theological reflection.

The discussion moves from the old generation (vv. 4–5a) to the new (v. 5b), back to the old (v. 6) and again to the new (vv. 7–8), a movement the following commentary presents graphically:

Verses 4–5a: **The old generation** is described in several ways (vv. 4–5). To emphasize their unity, they are twice called "all the people" (NIV has "all those," v. 4). They are three times described as those who "came out (the Hebrew root is *yts*) from Egypt" (NIV has "leaving Egypt," v. 4). They are also the "men of military age." All these descriptors are given to those to whom two things happened: they "had been circumcised," and they "died in the wilderness."

In v. 5b **the new generation** is contrasted ("but") to the old. Initially, many of the descriptors are the same. The new generation is likewise a unified whole—"All the people." They also "journey from Egypt" (the Hebrew root is *yts*, as in the old generation "coming out"). The difference between the two generations is made clear as the new generation was "born in the wilderness" and "had not been circumcised."

5. A. R. Millard, "Back to the Iron Bed: Og's or Procrustes'?," in *Congress Volume Paris 1992*, VTSup 59, ed. J. A. Emerton (Leiden/New York/Köln: E. J. Brill, 1995), 196.

Both generations wander for forty years (v. 6). Then the narrative reviews the two generations and includes some theological reflection on their two fates:

> Verse 6: The forty years are on account of the **old generation**, described now as "all the men" (the Hebrew word is *goy*), those of "military age" who "left Egypt" (*yts*). Again, these died, but now a theological reason is provided: their disobedience.

Several instances of disobedience are recorded in the wilderness, but the crowning instance (and the one that prompts the judgment of non-entry) is the peoples' rebellion after the spies' report (Num 13–14). For their refusal to take the promised land, Israel faces judgment and death in the wilderness (Num 14:30–35; Deut 1:34–40). The audacity of Israel's refusal is that God had promised the land on oath to their ancestors (Gen 12:7; 15:18; 17:8; 26:3; 28:13; Exod 32:13). It is theirs and, as a nation equipped for battle (note the many references to the military character of the old generation), they can take it by the LORD's command. He has prepared for them an abundant land to meet their needs, for it "flows with milk and honey" (Exod 3:8, 17; 13:5; 33:3; Num 13:27; 14:8; Deut 6:3; 11:9; 31:20; Jer 11:5; Ezek 20:6).

> Verse. 7–8: For the disobedience of the old generation the land is given to **the new generation** (Num 14:31). This generation is now described as "sons raised in their place," as "still uncircumcised" in the wilderness and "not circumcised on the way." Once again, the defining element that sets them apart from the old generation is their obedience to covenant law, for they are the "ones Joshua circumcised." Following circumcision, they are the "whole nation" (v. 8, echoing the word *goy* used of the old generation), thus replacing the old. And, if the fate of the disobedient old generation was death in the wilderness, by implication the obedient new generation will experience life in the promised land.

The defining issue in the comparison is that of obedience. One generation disobeys and dies; the next obeys and lives to receive the promise given the ancestors.

The circumcision requires a healing period during which Israel rests in the camp. This period extends at least through the Passover observance and probably through the seven-day feast of Unleavened Bread that follows. In response to their full obedience and covenantal identification, God removes the reproach of Egypt. This reproach is likely the stigma of Israel's Egyptian slavery or their covenantal disobedience in the wilderness. Now, Israelite obedience and the mark of the covenant "rolls away" that stigma. In a word play, Gilgal sounds similar to the Hebrew root for "roll away" (*gll*).

### Passover Food, New Food (5:10–12)

Newly circumcised, they are now able to participate in the Passover (Exod 12:48). The fourteenth day of the first month (Abib) is the date God set for the Passover (Exod 12:6). The date here is a reminder that Israel now acts according to covenant stipulations. The notation also forges a connection to the date of the Jordan crossing, which occurred on the tenth of the first month (Josh 4:19). This date is set as the first day of Passover preparations (Exod 12:3). The connection draws the Jordan crossing into the preparatory phase of this Passover, tying it together with the circumcision at Gilgal as an intrinsic part of this Passover. It is a Passover celebrated by the reconstituted nation (*goy*), the people of God. Despite Israelite disobedience in the wilderness, the miraculous Jordan crossing, the circumcision, and the Passover all reveal a new attitude of obedience. This is a hopeful Passover. Celebrated on the plains of Jericho, it looks ahead with anticipation to continued obedience and therefore successful possession of the land, as Joshua 1:7 promised.

Passover is celebrated, but no mention is made of the Passover lamb. In the reference to unleavened bread (v. 11) there may be an oblique reference to the feast of Unleavened Bread that follows Passover. But neither the lamb nor Unleavened Bread is highlighted. The omission is intentional. Instead, emphasis is placed purposefully on eating the food of Canaan ("they ate" occurs three times in vv. 11–12). They ate "the produce of the land," "this food from the land," and "the produce of Canaan." The repetition signals the land's abundance; after all, it is a land flowing with milk and honey—a reality noted in the context of the Passover command (Exod 13:5), the wilderness sin (Num 13:27; 14:8), and in Moses' words preparing the people for land entry (Deut 6:3; 11:9; 26:9; 27:3; 31:20). That reality is mentioned for the first time in Joshua in this passage (v. 6).

The emphasis on eating goes beyond merely demonstrating the land's abundance. The unleavened bread and roasted grain represent staple foods of the region and are contrasted to manna, the food that sustained Israel in the wilderness. This contrast shows in the structure of the verse:

> They ate some of the produce of the land: unleavened bread and roasted grain.
> The manna stopped the day after they ate this food from the land;
> there was no longer any manna for the Israelites
> but that year they ate the produce of Canaan. (5:11–12)

The wilderness is over; the wilderness generation is dead. Israel's change of diet dates from the Passover, the last moment of transition into the land. "That very day" the wilderness food ceases, and they enjoy the food of the land long promised.

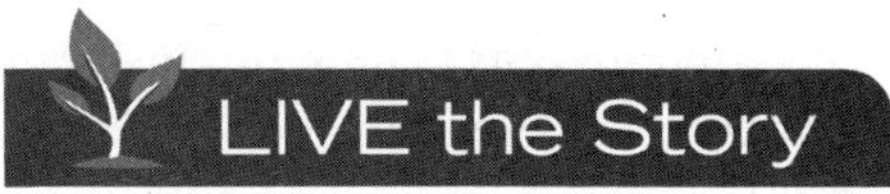


### Circumcision: External Sign and Internal Reality

Circumcision, Passover feast, and partaking of the food of the land complete the transition from wilderness to promised land. Throughout the transition, the narrative emphasizes the necessity of obedience. Only through obedience does Israel successfully transition from wilderness to land.

Transition into the land follows the sequence wilderness-crossing-Passover and reverses the earlier Passover-crossing-wilderness sequence. For Passover to be observed in obedience, the covenant lacuna of circumcision must be overcome. Joshua circumcises the Israelites in the flesh, but circumcision is not only an external rite. Passages such as Leviticus 26:41 and Deuteronomy 10:16 reveal that the external rite is emblematic of a more essential reality of the heart and mind. Only through circumcision of heart is the Deuteronomic ideal of loving the LORD with heart and soul possible; it is this internal circumcision—performed by God—that enables obedience to the law (Deut 30:6–10). The internal reality alongside the external mark identifies Israel as God's people and, while external circumcision continues as a mark of Israel's covenant status, Israel's disobedience in the land reveals hearts that have not submitted to internal circumcision.

The prophets refer to Israel's lack of internal circumcision. Jeremiah includes Israel along with the nations as "uncircumcised in heart" and warns that the state of Israel's heart will lead to punishment (Jer 9:25–26 [9:24–25]). In a plea for repentance, Jeremiah urges Israel to circumcise themselves to the LORD—a circumcision performed in the heart (Jer 4:4). Jeremiah's later words of a new covenant take up the state of Israel's heart. In an apparent reference to essential internal circumcision, God promises that he will himself write his laws on Israel's heart. This new covenant addresses the breach between Israel and God and envisions all Israel knowing God and walking in obedience to his covenant (Jer 31:33–34).

Both Isaiah (52:1) and Ezekiel (44:7–9) envision a restored Israel in which only those circumcised in heart and flesh and who walk in cleanness will enter the temple. Ezekiel echoes the language of Jeremiah and expands on this understanding of circumcised hearts: God will give a new heart and spirit to Israel, removing their heart of stone so they walk in God's law (Ezek 11:19–20; 36:26–28).

Thus, as Israel transitions into the land, and with narrative attention given to the centrality of obedience, the command to circumcise the Israelites affirms *both* external circumcision *and* the circumcision of the heart, which enables obedience. The obedience of the new generation suggests that for this moment at least, internal and external circumcision is an achieved reality.

The New Testament takes up the fundamental necessity of internal circumcision, and, as in the Old Testament, links it to obedience and righteous living. Paul compares internal circumcision to the carrying out of the law's precepts. Those who are externally circumcised but do not carry out the law are not internally circumcised; those who are not externally circumcised but do carry out the law's precepts are considered to be internally circumcised (Rom 2:25–29). These are the ones who are "inward Jews" for they have "circumcision of the heart, by the Spirit, not by the written code" (v. 29). As in Jeremiah and Ezekiel, the circumcision of the heart is performed by God through the Spirit. Elsewhere, God's act of internal circumcision is through Christ, by which the "whole self ruled by the flesh was put off when you were circumcised by Christ, having been buried with him in baptism" (Col 2:11–12).

In these passages, Paul equates internal circumcision with freedom from the "self ruled by the flesh" (Col 2:11) and with keeping "the law's requirements" (Rom 2:26), a reality that is now realized for those baptized into Christ. Origen likewise takes up the ethical focus of circumcision of the heart, arguing that through baptism (typologically related to the Jordan crossing; see Live the Story, Chapter 3), circumcision cuts off "every defect of wrath, pride, jealousy, lust, greed, partiality, and other such things"[6] Without such circumcision, one is "not able to put aside the reproach of Egypt, that is, the allurement of fleshly vices."[7] This internal circumcision occurs "through 'the baptism of regeneration'" by which believers are freed from enslavement to

6. Origen, *Hom* 1:7.
7. Ibid., 5:5.

base desires and pleasures.[8] For circumcised believers, Origen understands that the food of the land is an eschatological promise of full, future communion with Christ.[9] Manna is no longer needed as, in the future, all spiritual needs are met in the place of rest, security, and full provision of the believer's union with Christ.

While the circumcision cited in Joshua 5 is an external one, it cannot be separated from the necessity of internal change that results in obedience. This linkage is apparent elsewhere in the Old Testament canon and it is taken up and developed in the New Testament. Christians are baptised into Christ and are therefore called to obedient discipleship. This can only arise from hearts circumcised by the life-giving Spirit.

---

8. Ibid., 5:6.
9. Ibid., 6:1.

CHAPTER 5

# Joshua 5:13–6:27

## LISTEN to the Story

13Now when Joshua was near Jericho, he looked up and saw a man
standing in front of him with a drawn sword in his hand. Joshua went up
to him and asked, "Are you for us or for our enemies?"
14"Neither," he replied, "but as commander of the army of the LORD I
have now come." Then Joshua fell facedown to the ground in reverence,
and asked him, "What message does my Lord have for his servant?"
15The commander of the LORD's army replied, "Take off your sandals,
for the place where you are standing is holy." And Joshua did so.
6:1Now the gates of Jericho were securely barred because of the Israelites.
No one went out and no one came in.
2Then the LORD said to Joshua, "See, I have delivered Jericho into your
hands, along with its king and its fighting men. 3March around the city
once with all the armed men. Do this for six days. 4Have seven priests carry
trumpets of rams' horns in front of the ark. On the seventh day, march
around the city seven times, with the priests blowing the trumpets. 5When
you hear them sound a long blast on the trumpets, have the whole army
give a loud shout; then the wall of the city will collapse and the army will
go up, everyone straight in."
6So Joshua son of Nun called the priests and said to them, "Take up the
ark of the covenant of the LORD and have seven priests carry trumpets in
front of it." 7And he ordered the army, "Advance! March around the city,
with an armed guard going ahead of the ark of the LORD."
8When Joshua had spoken to the people, the seven priests carrying the
seven trumpets before the LORD went forward, blowing their trumpets,
and the ark of the LORD's covenant followed them. 9The armed guard
marched ahead of the priests who blew the trumpets, and the rear guard
followed the ark. All this time the trumpets were sounding. 10But Joshua
had commanded the army, "Do not give a war cry, do not raise your voices,
do not say a word until the day I tell you to shout. Then shout!" 11So he

had the ark of the LORD carried around the city, circling it once. Then the army returned to camp and spent the night there.

[12]Joshua got up early the next morning and the priests took up the ark of the LORD. [13]The seven priests carrying the seven trumpets went forward, marching before the ark of the LORD and blowing the trumpets. The armed men went ahead of them and the rear guard followed the ark of the LORD, while the trumpets kept sounding. [14]So on the second day they marched around the city once and returned to the camp. They did this for six days.

[15]On the seventh day, they got up at daybreak and marched around the city seven times in the same manner, except that on that day they circled the city seven times. [16]The seventh time around, when the priests sounded the trumpet blast, Joshua commanded the army, "Shout! For the LORD has given you the city! [17]The city and all that is in it are to be devoted to the LORD. Only Rahab the prostitute and all who are with her in her house shall be spared, because she hid the spies we sent. [18]But keep away from the devoted things, so that you will not bring about your own destruction by taking any of them. Otherwise you will make the camp of Israel liable to destruction and bring trouble on it. [19]All the silver and gold and the articles of bronze and iron are sacred to the LORD and must go into his treasury."

[20]When the trumpets sounded, the army shouted, and at the sound of the trumpet, when the men gave a loud shout, the wall collapsed; so everyone charged straight in, and they took the city. [21]They devoted the city to the LORD and destroyed with the sword every living thing in it—men and women, young and old, cattle, sheep and donkeys.

[22]Joshua said to the two men who had spied out the land, "Go into the prostitute's house and bring her out and all who belong to her, in accordance with your oath to her." [23]So the young men who had done the spying went in and brought out Rahab, her father and mother, her brothers and sisters and all who belonged to her. They brought out her entire family and put them in a place outside the camp of Israel.

[24]Then they burned the whole city and everything in it, but they put the silver and gold and the articles of bronze and iron into the treasury of the LORD's house. [25]But Joshua spared Rahab the prostitute, with her family and all who belonged to her, because she hid the men Joshua had sent as spies to Jericho—and she lives among the Israelites to this day.

[26]At that time Joshua pronounced this solemn oath: "Cursed before the LORD is the one who undertakes to rebuild this city, Jericho:

"At the cost of his firstborn son
he will lay its foundations;
at the cost of his youngest
he will set up its gates."

[27]So the LORD was with Joshua, and his fame spread throughout the land.

*Listening to the Text in the Story*: Exodus 3:1–10; Judges 6:11–14, 22; Genesis 32:22–32; Numbers 22:23; 1 Chronicles 21:16; Deuteronomy 7:1–6; 20:10–18; Annals of Ashurbanipal; Kirta Epic; Ugaritic Entry Rituals; Victory Stela of King Piye; Mesha Inscription; Geba Barkal Stela of Thutmose III; Annals of Ashurnasirpal II; Annals of Tiglath-Pileser I

**Mysterious Meetings**

Joshua's encounter with the LORD's commander is comparable to encounters with the "angel of the LORD" experienced by Moses (Exod 3:1–10) and Gideon (Judg 6:11–14). Similarities exist between the three accounts, suggesting adherence to a stylized genre known as a "commissioning report." Such reports typically include a human-divine encounter, a human response of worship or fear, a specific task appointed, and divine assurance provided. Each account provides interesting variation on the pattern, and exploration of how the pattern varies in Joshua helps bring understanding of the narrative's purposes.

Moses and Gideon encounter the "angel of the LORD," while Joshua encounters "the commander of the LORD's army." Specifically identifying who this commander is can be challenging (see Explain the Story below) but despite the different possibilities, the commander is one from the divine realm. Moses and Joshua each are confronted by something surprising (surprise is signaled by a small Hebrew word, left untranslated in the NIV) and approach with interest and an initial question. Both are told to remove their sandals for they stand on holy ground, and they respond in reverence and fear. While Moses and Joshua approach with a question, Gideon is himself confronted by the angel who initiates the conversation with a greeting. Like Moses and Joshua, Gideon responds with worship and fear.

To this point, the accounts clearly work with the same elements, as follows:

| | Exodus | Judges | Joshua |
|---|---|---|---|
| **Divine-human encounter** | 3:2 | 6:12 | 5:14 |
| **Response of reverent fear** | 3:6 | 6:22–24 | 5:14–15 |

The final two elements of the commissioning report in the Moses and Gideon accounts are readily apparent:

| | Exodus | Judges |
|---|---|---|
| **Commission to specific task** | 3:10 | 6:14 |
| **Divine assurance** | 3:6–9 | 6:16 |

In the Joshua account, the placement of the chapter break (after 5:15) makes these final elements harder to notice. More, because chapter 6 begins with background information about Jericho (6:1), it could be concluded the verse begins a new account. But considering chapter 6 a continuation of the narrative (the chapter divisions are not part of the original text, after all), the missing elements are apparent as follows:

| | Exodus | Judges | Joshua |
|---|---|---|---|
| **Commission to specific task** | 3:10 | 6:14 | 6:3–5 |
| **Divine assurance** | 3:6–9 | 6:16 | 6:2 |

While the anticipated elements of the stylized genre are apparent in Joshua, there are differences to the similar accounts in Exodus and Judges. These differences, and their effect within the narrative, are explored below (see Explain the Story).

### A Sword in the Hand

Joshua sees a man with a "drawn sword in his hand." The phrase appears elsewhere twice. In Numbers 22:23 the "angel of the LORD" bars Balaam's way with a "drawn sword in his hand." In 1 Chronicles 21:16 the angel holds a "drawn sword in his hand" as plague devastates Jerusalem. Both instances are ominous and indicative of God's judgment. In Joshua, the sword is held by a different figure, but should the same sense of judgment and threat be construed? Or, in keeping with many ancient Near Eastern texts (see Drawn Swords and Victory below), should the drawn sword signal assurance of victory? If judgment, against whom: Joshua and Israel, or the Canaanites and Jericho? This is not specifically stated. In Joshua 6 the sword is active against Jericho. But Israel is called to obedience (Deut 4:1–2; 5:32–6:25; 8:1, 6; 11:22–25) and is not exempt from God's judgment. This is proven true in the aftermath of Jericho (chs. 7–8).

### Devoted to the LORD

Rahab earlier referred to the complete destruction (from the root *hrm*) of peoples in the Transjordan (Josh 2:10; cf. Deut 2:34; 3:6). Joshua 6 now explicitly commands this action against Jericho. Additionally, the city is burned and left as a perpetual ruin. The Introduction to this commentary explores more fully the question of the *herem*—those things devoted to God; comments here speak more specifically to the issue in Joshua 6. Deuteronomy, which most fully informs Joshua's practice of *herem*, calls for the total annihilation of the peoples of the land who dwell in the cities, along with the destruction of their cult sites, lest Israel bow to Canaanite idols (Deut 7:1–6; 20:16–18). Deuteronomy 7:2–3, by forbidding intermarriage and treaties with the peoples of the land, tacitly acknowledges their ongoing existence, thus supporting the hyperbolic nature of the *herem* law; the law itself acknowledges the peoples' continuance. More, the law stands alongside other texts that show the inhabitants would be driven from the land, indicating they were not all killed (Exod 23:27–31; 33:2; Lev 18:24–28; 20:22–23; Num 33:51–56; Deut 4:37–38; 6:18–19; 7:1, 20–23; see Introduction). One could also argue that the intent of the *herem* law was the destruction of any sense of national identity, thus preventing regrouping and rebellion by the subdued people.[1] Certainly this would have been a pratical effect of killing significant numbers of people in a city or area.

The exercise of the *herem* laws at Jericho is unusual in its inclusion of animals and booty. Being set outside the realm of ordinary use, living things are killed and consecrated items are put into the LORD's house without possibility of redemption (Lev 27:28–29). The application of *herem* laws to animals and booty is not part of the Deuteronomic law for cities within the promised land (see further in commentary below). The unique, extended application of the law at Jericho may be explained by considering that this city (as the first city taken in the land) stands as a first fruits offering (Lev 23:9–14), acknowledging God's gift of land.

1. This is the argument of Walton and Walton, *The Lost World of the Israelite Conquest*; see Part 5, Proposition 15 and 16 (pp. 169–94).

Set against this total offering, the exception of Rahab is extraordinary. A Canaanite is spared because of her kindness extended to Israel and requested in return (Josh 2:12). Her acknowledgement of Israel's God is such that she no longer exists as a threat to Israel's holiness. More, her confession challenges the view that only those of the nation of Israel can be faithful to the covenant. In the next chapter, one of Abraham's descendants will act against the covenant; Rahab acts in accord with the covenant and is spared.

## Drawn Swords and Victory

Swords proffered by gods in assurance of victory are common in the ancient world. Temple drawings in Medinet Habu show the twelfth century BC Pharaoh Ramesses III receiving a sword from the god Amon-Re. The text reads, "Take to thee the sword, my son, my beloved, that thou mayst smite the heads of rebellious countries."[2] Likewise, the god Ptah offers the thirteenth century BC Pharaoh Merneptah a sword with the accompanying words, "Take now [this sword] and banish from yourself your troubled heart!"[3] While the sword in Joshua 5 is not offered to Joshua (but only held by the enigmatic commander of the Lord), the account fits well within this ancient context. An account that aligns more closely with the biblical presentation is found in the Annals of Ashurbanipal, a seventh century Assyrian king. Before battle with Elam, a vision is granted the king's seer in which "the goddess Ishtar who dwells in Arbela came in. Right and left quivers were hanging from her. She held the bow in her hand and a sharp sword was drawn to do battle." Ishtar assures Ashurbanipal of victory won wholly by the goddess: "you shall stay here. . . . while I go and do that work in order that you attain your heart's desire."[4] The parallel to the Joshua account is striking, although unlike Ashurbanipal's account, the battle against Jericho is God's idea, not Joshua's, and Joshua is called to action, although not action one might expect in battle.

## "Seven" in Military and Cultic Contexts

The number seven is characteristic of the Jericho account and is found elsewhere in biblical military accounts (1 Sam 11:3; 13:8; 1 Kgs 20:29; 2 Kgs 3:9). Ancient Near Eastern military and cultic texts also feature the number seven.

In the Kirta epic, a mid-second millennium text from the kingdom

2. Described and quoted in W. F. Edgerton and J. A. Wilson, *Historical Records of Ramses III* (Chicago: University of Chicago Press, 136), 4 (http://oi.uchicago.edu/sites/oi.uchicago.edu/files/uploads/shared/docs/saoc12.pdf).

3. A. Leo Oppenheim, *The Interpretation of Dreams in the Ancient Near East* (Chicago: University of Chicago, 1956), 251, 192.

4. *ANET*, 451.

of Ugarit north of Canaan, the king is commissioned by the god El to divinely-planned military action. The seven-day march and siege effects the enemy's submission by aligning military effort with sacred time and the will of the commissioning god:

March a day, and then a second
A third day, and a fourth;
A fifth day, and a sixth.
Then, at sunrise, on the seventh,
When you arrive at Udum the great
Arrive at Udum majestic
Attack its outlying town, assault the surrounding villages!
Then halt, a day and a second
A third day, and a fourth
A fifth day, and a sixth . . .
Then, at sunrise, on the seventh,
King Pabuli will sleep no more . . .
Then he'll send two messengers,
To Kirta in the night-camp . . .
Take, O Kirta, offerings—offerings of peace![5]

A similar emphasis is found in cultic entry rituals that bring the deity to the king's palace by a grand procession and sacrifices. One such ritual found in Ugaritic literature reads, "The king will go take the gods. Everyone will follow the gods on foot; the king himself will go on foot, seven times for all of them."[6] The parallel to the procession of the ark around Jericho is apparent, setting Israel's action in the cultic as well as military sphere.

### Warfare Practices and Total Destruction

The warfare practices represented in Joshua 6 are part and parcel of their ancient Near Eastern context. For instance, Jericho is barred and "no one went out and no one came in" (6:1), terms similarly used in siege accounts such as the eighth century Egyptian victory stele of King Piye. He imposes sieges, "not letting goers go, not letting entrants enter."[7] Once a city is taken, the consecration of booty to the god is known from thirteenth century BC Egyptian texts. For instance, Sethos I dedicates booty to Amun:

5. Excerpts from lines 2–27 of Column III of the Kirta Epic. Recorded in *Ugaritic Narrative Poetry*, ed. Simon B. Parker (Atlanta: Scholars Press, 1997), 15–17.

6. Lines 23–26 in RS1.005 found in Dennis Pardee, *Ritual and Cult at Ugarit*. Writings from the Ancient World 10 (Leiden/Boston/Köln: Brill, 2002), 69–72.

7. *COS* 2.7:43–44.

> [booty including] every sort of precious vessel from their lands, silver, gold, lapis-lazuli, turquoise, red jasper, and every (kind of) precious stone . . . by the valor that you [Amun] granted me.[8]

Once consecrated, these items are not for common use. A cautionary text citing the danger of such misuse (as in Josh 6:18) is found in a fourteenth–twelfth century BC Hittite text:

> Whatever silver, gold, clothing, and bronze implements of the gods you hold, (you are) their guards (only). (You have) no (right) to the silver, gold, clothing (or) bronze implements of the gods. What is in the house of the gods (is) not (for you). It is for the gods. Be very careful. There is to be no silver or gold for the temple official.[9]

The practice of destruction of life was also common. Several texts speak of the utter destruction of populations, although the hyperbolic nature of the claims is evident in that the populations continued.[10] The ninth century BC Moabite Mesha Inscription presents a very close parallel to the biblical text, even utilizing the terminology of *herem*:

> Israel has utterly perished forever. . . . I fought against [Nebo] from the break of dawn until noon; and I took it; and I killed everyone in it, seven thousand men and women, both natives and aliens, and female slaves; because I had dedicated [the word uses the same root as in *herem*] it to Ashtar-Chemosh [the Moabite god].

The fifteenth century Gebal Barkal Stele of Thutmose III reads:

> The great army of Mitanni, it is overthrown in the twinkling of an eye. It has perished completely, as though they had never existed.

And the ninth century Assyrian Annals of Ashurnasirpal II relate:

> I approached the city of Kinabu, the fortified city of Hylaya. I besieged with the mass of my troops (and) my fierce battle array; I conquered the city. I slew with the sword 800 of their combat troops; I burned 3,000 captives from them. I did not leave one of them alive as a hostage . . . I razed, destroyed, (and) burned the city.

The Ashurnasirpal text also highlights the practice of razing a conquered city (as in Josh 6:24). The practice appears repeatedly in the twelfth century

8. Ibid., 2.4A:25, 2.4C:27; 2.4E:29; 2.4F:31.

9. Ibid., 1.83:218.

10. The examples below are taken from Younger, "Ancient Conquest Accounts," 227–28, 236. The Mesha Inscription can be found also in *ANET*, 320–21.

BC Assyrian Annals of Tiglath-Pileser who "burned, razed, and destroyed" many cities. He also curses conquered Hunusu:

> [I] conquered that city. I took their gods; and I carried off their booty, possession and property. I burned the city. Three great walls which were constructed with baked bricks and the entire city I razed and destroyed. I turned it into a ruin hill and a heap. . . . I inscribed . . . a warning not to occupy that city and not to rebuild its wall.[11]

### Commissioned and Assured (5:13–6:5)

With the Jordan crossed and Israel prepared through circumcision and Passover, the taking of Jericho is next. Before that, Joshua is confronted by the Lord's commander and a reminder that in God's battle Joshua and the army must participate as holy people.

"Near" Jericho (5:13; the Hebrew can be translated as "in" Jericho, but this makes no sense in the narrative's flow) Joshua is surprised by the appearance of a soldier. Joshua makes the logical inquiry: for whom does he fight? The unequivocal "neither" introduces an element to this battle beyond the we/they, Israel/enemy categories in which Joshua's question is framed. That new element is the supernatural realm the commander represents.

The word "commander" (5:14) can be translated several ways including "leader," "official," or "prince." Here, the military context is apparent and "commander" or "general" might be expected (Gen 21:22; Judg 4:7; 2 Sam 2:8; 10:16; 1 Kgs 2:32; 16:16; 2 Kgs 5:1). He commands an "army (*tsaba'*) of the Lord" (5:14). Such an "army" could designate a human army in service of God (Num 31:21; Deut 20:9; 2 Sam 3:23), or the Lord's heavenly army (Dan 8:11; and see the narrative depiction of this army in 2 Kgs 6:17). Elsewhere, the same term, "army" can be used in the sense of "host" (as in the heavenly host of stars; Deut 4:19; 17:3; 2 Kgs 17:16), or the host of angels attending in the Lord's heavenly court (1 Kgs 22:19; Pss 103:21; 148:2).

Encamped at Jericho and purposed to take the land, Joshua's human army stands at the ready. The context suggests that this is the army to which the commander refers. Joshua's army is indeed heavenly, for it is the Lord's. The commander "has come," seemingly to ensure Joshua is attuned to these greater, unseen realities of the battlefield.

---

11. Younger, "Ancient Conquests Accounts," 79–89, includes twenty notices of cities "burned, razed, and destroyed." Episode 19 (p. 81) includes the cursing of Hunusu.

Joshua falls in reverence. Such reverence can be offered to God Himself (Pss 5:7[8]; 99:5, 9) and to humans of superior rank or power (Gen 33:7; 1 Sam 2:26; 2 Sam 14:33; 2 Kgs. 4:37). The "commander of the LORD's army" appears in a context similar to those in which the "angel of the LORD" appears (see Listen to the Story). Often, the distinction between the angel and the LORD is not clearly drawn (Gen 16:7–14; 18:1–2; 22:11–16; Exod 3:2–4; Judg 2:1; 6:11–14, 20–22; 13:3–21), and the same could be said of the commander and the LORD. The commander is certainly supernatural, and Joshua's reverence and his request for a message communicate he feels his inferiority. Addressing the commander as "my lord" reinforces that inferiority while falling short of ascribing deity.

If the narrative concluded at 5:15, no commission or divine assurance would be given Joshua as expected in a commissioning account (see Listen to the Story above). But the narrative continues on, and in this continuance is both commission and divine assurance. What is apparent by this point is a message that Joshua must hear: this battle will be won by God and his army, not Joshua and his. Joshua cannot hope to see victory if he does not see—and respond appropriately—to God's holiness. The drawn sword, representing a threat where it elsewhere appears (Num 22:23; 1 Chr 21:16) cuts both ways: it can be raised against Jericho, but it can likewise be raised against Joshua and Israel should they dishonor God's holiness and the battle God commands. Joshua removes his sandals, acknowledging the heavenly being stands in God's presence and ushers Joshua into the holy sphere. Joshua's immediate obedience bodes well for the battle's outcome.

From the holy encounter near Jericho, the narrative digresses and describes Jericho: barred tightly. "No one went out and no one came in" (6:1) because the Israelites are encamped before the city. The barred gates confirm the inhabitants' melted hearts and failed courage (2:9–11; 5:1). The placement of the digression emphasizes the difficulty of taking Jericho. Can any feasible commission or divine assurance be given in the face of this obstacle?

Part of the assurance is what has already transpired: the commander's words and the holy presence of God (5:14–15). But the LORD gives a specific word of assurance: barred gates are ironically ineffective, for the LORD "has delivered [literally "given"] the city"—it is a *fait accompli*. God will give the land as promised (1:3, 6, 11, 15; see also Josh 24:8, 12). Passage in and out of the city is only temporarily barred. The LORD's victory changes this (the "in/out" language of verse 1 is taken up later to prove the point; vv. 22–23). A further assurance is that Jericho will be given "into [Joshua's] hand" (v. 2; see Josh 2:24) together with its king. The king is never named and thus shorn of import and power. Further dismissing the king, his fate is not recounted in this chapter. One must wait until Josh 8:2, 29 and 10:1 for a glimpse of it. The fighting men are likewise delivered to Joshua, although some armed resistance is mounted (Josh 24:11). That such resistance is not recorded in this chapter heightens the narrative effect of the LORD's victory: it is achieved by God's power, and without apparent resistance.

Finally, Joshua is commissioned (vv. 3–5). Interestingly, it is not a command (such as "take the city"). God has already indicated the objective—which he will accomplish. Rather, the commission assumes the objective and turns to battle tactics. God summarizes the strategy, and further details are provided as the narrative unfolds. Military and cultic language appears in God's commands and throughout the chapter. Both army and priests participate, for the presence of the ark sets warfare in the realm of the holy. The plan is simple, supernatural, and startling. While later battles are fought with more conventional strategies (chs. 8, 10), Jericho is different. Uniquely placed as the first battle in the land, it showcases God's power and commitment to give Israel the land. Israel's battle task is obedience.

The "armed men" (v. 3, later simply the "army" [vv. 5, 7, 10, 16, 20]; also "the people" [v. 8]) are to march, circling the city as common in military practice (2 Kgs 6:14–15; 8:21; Ps 118:10). Including the ark reframes the action as cultic; represented in the ark, God's presence and power encircle the city. The action is completed daily for six days, and seven times on the seventh day, completing a holy week of divinely-ordained time.

The narrative gives no sense of a chronological gap between the Passover (5:10) and the siege. The consecutive presentation sets the siege as continuous with the Passover. The seven-day march corresponds to the seven days of the Feast of Unleavened Bread, setting both river crossing and Jericho into a cultic context (4:19; 5:10). The seventh day falls on the festival's final consecrated assembly (Lev 23:8), further hallowing the event. The centrality of the number seven is echoed in several other "seven's": seven priests (vv. 4, 6, 13), seven trumpets (vv. 4, 6, 8, 13), a seventh day (vv. 4, 15) and seven circuits on the seventh day (vv. 15 [2x], 16).

Seven priests are commanded to precede the ark, continuously sounding trumpets on the seventh day. Only later is it clarified that the trumpets sound continuously during each march (vv. 8–9). During the Jordan crossing, the priests were "those who carry the ark" (3:8, 12, 15,17; 4:9, 10, 18). At Jericho, they are more frequently those who "carry the trumpets" (vv. 4, 6, 8, 12) and sound them (vv. 4, 8, 9, 13, 16, 20). The ark is of course carried (vv. 6, 11, 12), but most often no bearers are mentioned (vv. 4, 7, 5, 9, 13 [2x]). The narrative focus makes it seem as if the powerful ark needs no human assistance to make the circuit.

The trumpets of ram's horn and the shouting reveal the march is both military and religious. Ram's horns are the same instrument that sounded God's presence at Sinai (Exod 19:16–19). These trumpets were used in military action (Judg 3:27; 6:34; 1 Sam 13:3; 2 Sam 2:28) but also during religious festivals and fasts (Lev 25:9; Num 10:10; Ps 81:3[4]) and when the LORD's ark was in procession (2 Sam 6:15; 1 Chr 15:28; Ps 47:5[6]; cf. 98:6). The priests are instructed to "blow" the trumpets (vv. 4, 8, 9 ["blew" and "sounding"], 13 ["blowing" and "sounding"], 16 and 20 ["sounded"]), and this word too is found in military (Judg 3:27; 6:34; 7:18–20; 2 Sam 18:16) and religious (Num 10:3; 2 Kgs 11:14) settings. Likewise, nominal and verbal forms of "shout" (vv. 5 ["give a loud shout" is more literally translated, "shout a loud shout"], 10 ["war cry", "shout"], 16, 20) are used in military (Judg 7:21; 1 Sam 17:20, 52; 2 Chr 13:15; Isa 42:13) and religious (Pss 27:6; 47:5[6]; 89:15[16]) settings.

God states the outcome of Israel's obedient march (v. 5). The walls will fall down. The army will enter.

## Joshua Commands Priests and Army (6:6–7)

Joshua immediately relays the needed information to the priests and army, demonstrating his obedience to God; subsequent verses show Joshua's commands are likewise obeyed by each group.

Joshua is identified by his patronym, as when he earlier received God's commands (1:1) and sent the spies to reconnoiter (2:1). Now, God's new command is given, and Joshua initiates the next phase of the military operation. God commanded they "march around the city" (vv. 3, 4), and Joshua issues the same order with the same words (v. 7). Priests will "carry the ark of the covenant" as they did in chapters 3–4. A select group of seven priests will "carry seven trumpets." They are prominent actors in the march, signaling God's presence and prompting the final shout that overcomes the city walls (v. 20).

The army likewise is commanded with a select group appointed to precede the ark. The "armed guard" is a troop perhaps selected from all Israel (Num 31:5; Josh 4:13; 1 Chr 12:23[24]), or from the Transjordanian tribes who had earlier been commanded to arm themselves and cross over the Jordan before the LORD (Num 32:21–32; Deut 3:18). If the latter group is intended, it again speaks of their ongoing inclusion in Israel. Together with the rear guard (v. 9) the armed guard ensures safe, consecrated space around the ark. The command to "advance" (v. 7), the armed guard "going ahead" (v. 7), together with "went forward" (v. 8) share the same Hebrew root as in the word "cross" (*ʿbr*).[12] A key

12. In verse 7 the army is to "advance" (cross over terrain), while the guards "go ahead" and the priests (v. 8) "went forward" (that is, cross over in front of the army).

word in the crossing account, its use here holds the crossing and the Jericho march together as two parts of Israel's entry to the land.

**Around for Six Days (6:8–14)**

The commands given, the action begins. The priests carrying the trumpets go forward (*'br*) and the ark follows—no mention is made in this initial circuit of those who carry it. The armed guard preceding the priests is now joined by the rear guard. One circuit is made and then an unremarkable return and a quiet night in the camp. The second day proceeds in the same fashion. Joshua's early start shows his commitment to obediently fulfill God's command. The priests carrying the ark follow the lead of the priests carrying trumpets. The armed men and rear guard are stationed as before. A second circuit is made. They return for a quiet night in the camp. The laconic "they did this for six days" (v. 14) hints at the march's simplicity—but also its astonishing power.

Three things stand out from the account of the daily circuits. First, there is an emphasis on the trumpets "blowing" and "sounding." The emphasis is more apparent in Hebrew, for the same Hebrew root (*tq'*; in different formulations) underlies the different translations in the NIV (in vv. 8, 9 [2x],13 [2x]). At Sinai, the trumpet blast produced fear and trembling as it heralded God's holy presence (Exod 19:16; 20:18–19). One can imagine Jericho—already melting in fear (5:1)—experiencing increasing terror with each circuit of the ark. Second, in contrast to the trumpets' sounding is the army's utter silence. Joshua commands this silence (v. 10) in between verses recording the trumpets' noise (vv. 8–9, 12–14). The counterpoint makes for marked contrast. Joshua three times gives a negative command (v. 10):

> Do not give a war cry,
> do not raise your voices,
> do not say a word.

This is followed up with a positive qualifier: the people shall raise their voices only at Joshua's command.

The final emphasis in the daily circuits is the procession's movement, signaled by various forms of the Hebrew root *hlk* (meaning "to walk", "go"). These are not all translated in the NIV but are shown here to capture the emphasis in verses 8–14:

> **Day 1** (vv. 8–9):
> The seven priests carrying the seven trumpets . . . went forward blowing trumpets
> the ark *followed* (*hlk*) them

the armed guard *marched* (*hlk*) ahead of the priests who blew the trumpets
the rear guard *followed* (*hlk*) the ark
the [priests carrying the] trumpets were *walking* (*hlk*) and sounding.

**Day 2–6** (v. 13):

The seven priests carrying the seven trumpets went *forward* (*hlk*)
*marching* (*hlk*) before the ark . . . and blowing the trumpets
the armed men *went ahead* (*hlk*)
the rear guard *followed* (*hlk*)
[the priests were] *marching* (*hlk*) while the trumpets kept sounding.

The account of each day's procession is imbued with movement and initiated by the priests with the trumpets proclaiming the LORD's presence. Whereas the river crossing focused on the priests who carried the ark, here the focus is on the priests leading the procession before the ark—those who carry the ark recede into the background. All other players follow the lead of the priests, and it is the priests who are last mentioned in each day's procession.

### Seventh Day and Seven Circuits (6:15–26)

The climactic seventh day arrives. The order of the march and the outcome of the seventh day is known; we anticipate Joshua's command to release the victory cry (v. 10). But the taking of the city does not proceed in quick narrative succession. New commands interrupt the narrative flow and heighten tension. The narrative pace is further slowed by repeated sidebars regarding Rahab's fate. These alternate with the main action of destroying the city. The sidebars bring a vital contribution to the chapter's message.

The seventh day's unique character is marked by Israel arising not just "early" (v. 12) but (by an additional modifier) "at daybreak" (v. 15). The desire to demonstrate obedience continues high and is highlighted. As they were commanded they "march around" (v. 4) and "circle" the city (v. 15; the words are the same Hebrew word) seven times—a detail noted three times in two verses (vv. 15–16). The priests sound the trumpets a final time with the "long blast" commanded in verse 5. It is the same "long blast" given at Sinai to signal the Israelites might approach the consecrated mountain; its reappearance at this moment indicates in yet another way that Jericho is set aside as consecrated to God. Approach to it must be signaled by God.

Following the trumpet blast, Joshua gives the command and affirms the victory is God's (v. 16). The shout goes up but the walls do not come down . . . yet. A narrative delay postpones the inevitable until verse 20. In verses 17–19, Joshua issues further commands for the destruction of the city.

Joshua's commands implement the Deuteronomic law of the *herem* (Deut 7:1–6; 20:10–18; see also the Introduction). The city and "all that is in it" is to be set apart as *herem*, that is, "devoted to the LORD." In these verses, the noun, *herem* is used three times (v. 17 "devoted to the LORD"; v. 18 "devoted things" and "liable to destruction"), and a verbal form once (v. 18 "bring about your own destruction"). The word refers to devoted items, a state of being devoted, or the action of devoting. Those things that are set apart as *herem* are consecrated to God and removed from the ordinary realm. According to the ancient context, consecration of people means death. Property can be set apart as holy and stored or used in holy places (as was practiced in the ancient Near East; see above under Listen to the Story). None of the consecrated items could be redeemed from such use (Lev 27:28–29).

The application of the law at Jericho is unique, for people, animals, and materials are devoted to the LORD. This exceeds the Deuteronomic law that requires only the people be killed (note that Deut 20:16–17 qualifies "anything that breathes" with the following verse in which people—not animals—are intended). The usual practice is that animals and goods are taken as plunder, as is practiced elsewhere (Josh 8:1–2; 11:12–14; Num 31:8–12). As the first city taken in the land, Jericho is offered up as a "first fruits" offering; everything is set apart for the LORD. It marks the land as belonging to God alone and as a holy land for a holy people. Israel's holiness arises only out of its covenant relationship with God and that relationship is evidenced by Israel's obedience to its covenant partner.

Joshua commands the city's destruction but then commands two exceptions, each signaled by the same word, *raq* ("only" in v. 17; "but" in v. 18). The first is positive: he spares Rahab and her household. His stated reason for doing so is not what we might expect (Rahab's affirmation of Israel's God). This may be in the background—certainly it is a central element of Rahab's account (2:9–11). Joshua instead cites her action: she "hid the spies we sent" (v. 17). Rahab "hid" the spies from the king's men and urged the spies to "hide" for three days (2:6, 16). The two words are different in Hebrew, and Joshua uses the second word. Because of Rahab's actions, the spies pledged "our lives for your life" to Rahab (2:14), and it is this Joshua honors.

The second exception is negative. Israel is warned not to take anything devoted to God. To do so lays claim to what is God's alone. Such high-handed disobedience would result in Israel herself becoming an item of *herem*, devoted to God for destruction, and the recipient of "trouble" (v. 18). The notion of Israel "troubled" by this violation anticipates Achan's sin in chapter 7. Achan (together with Saul and Ahab) are the only people of whom it is said they brought "trouble" on Israel (Josh 7:25; 1 Sam 14:29; 1 Kgs 18:17).

The devoted items from Jericho are to be consecrated (that is, made holy), as Israel was holy to God (Josh 3:5; cf. 5:15). The booty is committed to the treasury that housed dedicated items and monies. It was located in the sacred precincts of the tabernacle (and later, the temple). Sadly, some of the holy items are taken (ch. 7) and Israel's own holiness is compromised. Through this, Israel becomes *herem*.

The *herem* command is interspersed with the command to spare Rahab:

v. 17 the city and all in it to be devoted to the LORD
    v. 17 Rahab and all in her household shall be spared
v. 18 caution against taking items devoted to the LORD

Later, the enactment of the *herem* is likewise interspersed with the sparing of Rahab:

v. 21 the city is devoted; living things are destroyed
    vv. 22–23 Rahab and all her household spared
v. 24 the city is razed; consecrated items put in the treasury
    v. 25 motivation for sparing Rahab; her ongoing story
v. 26 the city is cursed

It is clear that the terrible destruction of Jericho is held in tension with the redemption of Rahab from it. The interspersion also acknowledges the tragedy by suggesting a different possible outcome for the city. Rahab recognized Israel's God as "God in heaven above and on the earth below" (Josh 2:11) and thus welcomed the spies. She showed a Canaanite could acknowledge Israel's covenant God. Had Jericho's inhabitants done so, they likewise may have been spared. All is not determined by ethnicity as is proven in the next chapter where an Israelite acts against the covenant . . . and brings upon him and all Israel the *herem* law.

After the narrative pause of verses 17–19, action is restarted by reiterating elements of verse 16 (the trumpets, the shouting). With the shout, the walls fall. These are not the oft-pictured substantial walls of great height and breadth. During this era, the walls were perhaps casemate walls or houses built in a continuous ring with their backs forming a barrier to invaders (see Explain the Story, Chapter 2). The miracle is not that walls of immense height fell, but that they fell on cue, at God's command, and by his power.

The walls collapse upon themselves and the army goes "straight in"—as God had said (v. 5). After seven days of marching and substantial narrative build-up, the city falls with little fanfare and even less narrative space. But this is, perhaps, the point: God having given the city (v. 2) and issued his commands, and Israel having obediently followed those commands, what else could have happened?

Israel takes the city and fulfills the Deuteronomic command of destruction. Using hyperbolic, formulaic terms common in ancient Near Eastern conquest accounts (see the Introduction), "every living thing" is destroyed. The qualifying "men and women, young and old, cattle, sheep and donkeys" is a formulaic way of heightening the hyperbole of "every" (similarly, hockey fans might say, "We totally annihilated that team! All of them—forwards, defense, goalie—were begging for mercy!"). The hyperbolic nature of this qualifier appears to be supported not only by the genre markers found in such ancient Near Eastern conquest accounts, but by the biblical evidence. The specific formulation of the qualifier (which in Joshua 6 reads "men and women, young and old, cattle, sheep and donkeys") utilizes a particular prepositional phrase (*min . . . weʿad*) that in similar contexts occurs only eight times in the Old Testament (Josh 6:21; 8:25; 1 Sam 15:3, 22:19; 2 Sam 6:19; 1 Chr 16:3; 2 Chr 15:13; Esth 3:13).[13] In every instance except 1 Samuel 22:19, the qualifying phrase follows after the descriptor *kol* ("all," "every") and appears to be a stereotypical way to describe "all, everyone" without intending specific and accurate comments on the gender and age of those involved.

Despite the hyperbole, there is no reason to doubt widespread slaughter in Jericho. But for Rahab and her family the destruction is countermanded. She had asked the spies to swear they would deal kindly with her in return for her kindness, and they had sworn, "our lives for your life." Joshua now activates that oath (v. 22). The word "oath" derives from the same root as the number "seven." In a narrative that has stressed that number (twelve occurrences in the NIV), it is striking to see it now in such a different context.

The rescue of Rahab takes up again the "in/out" language of verse 1. Jericho's barred gates prevented anyone going in or out. God's victory changes that: Israel has indeed gone in, and because of an oath sworn in response to Rahab's kindness, some Canaanites have come out. This, too, is a victory of God.

Rahab and her house are put (in Hebrew, "made to rest") "outside the camp" for as covenantal outsiders they are not admitted within its holy boundaries. This is not the final word, for she comes to live "among" the Israelites (v. 25). She is "made to rest" outside the camp but comes to experience a fuller rest by incorporation into the covenant people. Even more, she is an ancestor of Christ (Matt 1:5), who gives true rest (Heb 4:1–11).

The full devotion of the city is accomplished, for it is offered up by fire.

---

13. The phrase "men and women" appears in all occurrences except in Esther (which lists young and old, women and children). Often, other items are added to the phrase, such as young/old, small/great, child/infant, and various livestock designations. All occurrences have the specific prepositional formulation "*min . . . weʿad*."

This action is noted in other ancient Near Eastern accounts, as is Joshua's curse against the city. The curse sets Jericho's destruction in perpetuity (see Listen to the Story) and is uttered as a solemn "oath." This is the chapter's last use of the Hebrew root noted in verse 22 but now Joshua's oath promises death, not life, as was previously the case with Rahab. The city's fate is that of idolatrous Israelite cities burned as "whole burnt offerings to the LORD" (Deut 13:16). Joshua prophetically proclaims the city must remain a ruin forever, never to be rebuilt. The oath's fulfillment is noted in 1 Kings 16:34. Hiel, who undertakes to rebuild Jericho, does so with the loss of his firstborn and youngest sons, possibly as idolatrous sacrifices made in the hope of strengthening the foundations.

### The Report (6:27)

The events at Jericho show the LORD is with Joshua, as he had promised (1:5, 9; 3:7). A report of the events circulates, as had the report of the Red Sea crossing (2:10). Joshua's fame spreads, but it is a reflection of God's fame (2:10; 9:9). The inhabitants must have increased in fear—but not so much that it prevents them attacking at a later date (9:1–2).

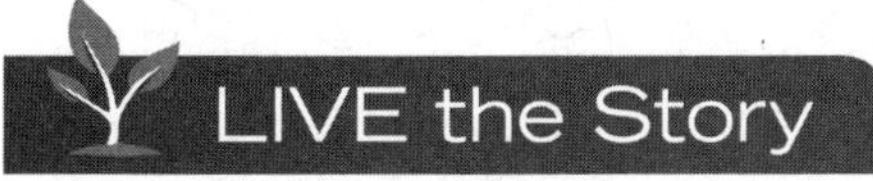


### *Herem*: Not the Last Word

The destruction of Jericho is the first and most extreme application of the *herem* command in Joshua. Reading the *herem* text within the context of ancient Near Eastern conquest accounts aids in understanding what is (and is not) intended by the words of these texts and the purposes for which these texts were written (see the Introduction for an extended discussion). But such understanding does not preclude the reality these texts communicate: people died, and cities were burned by the command of God.

The challenge of Jericho is not unique to our modern context (as if moderns are somehow more sensitized to the destruction of war). Origen, writing in the third century AD showed full awareness of the difficulty, seeing it as necessarily requiring spiritual reading:

> Unless those physical wars bore the figure of spiritual wars, I do not think the books of Jewish history would ever have been handed down by the apostles to the disciples of Christ, who came to teach peace, so that they could be read in the churches.[14]

---

14. Origen, *Hom* 15.1.

A similar discomfort is apparent in Eric Seibert's recent comments on Joshua 6–11:

> By any standard of measure, the narrative describing the conquest of Canaan in Joshua 6–11 is one of the most morally troubling texts in the entire Old Testament. Historically, it has also been one of the most toxic. This text has had an extremely harmful afterlife and has been used to provide religious rationale for some of the most heinous acts of violence in human history. People have repeatedly utilized the conquest narrative to justify colonialism and its attendant evils of warfare, killing, theft, and dispossession.[15]

Interpretative attention to this problematic aspect of Joshua is important, as the extended discussion in the Introduction indicates. But much more can be said of Joshua 6 (as the first of the warfare texts in the book); to focus primarily upon the *herem* in fact moves in a direction that the biblical text itself does not take. Not only is the *herem* a reality limited in time primarily to this era of Israel's life, but in books canonically following Joshua, it is downplayed, and focus is directed in other ways.[16] This is suggestive of the biblical writers' own discomfort with this aspect of Israel's past life and their ability to come to terms with it. The canon, in its references and allusions to Joshua, plots a trajectory away from the *herem* of Joshua 6 toward an attitude of inclusion of the foreigner. This in turn provides a context in which Jesus' call to "love your enemies and pray for those who persecute you, that you may be children of your Father in heaven" (Matt 5:44–5) is easily located.

A brief survey of such texts follows and affirms that the *herem* command is not the final word. In doing so, the survey reveals the trajectory toward the New Testament and also opens space to reflect upon other theological aspects of Joshua 6.[17]

First, while Joshua is the main human character in the book, the canon rarely names him in the ongoing story (Judg 1:1; 2:6–8, 21, 23; 1 Kgs 16:34;

---

15. Seibert, *The Violence of Scripture*, 95. Seibert's argues these texts should be read as pointers toward non-violent reading strategies. His approach engages in troubling ways with the issue of biblical authority, an outcome that he acknowledges and seeks to mitigate. Similar acknowledgement of the negative legacy of these texts and varying ways to responsibly read them (all of which affirm the texts give no license to present-day violence) are found in the four essays and responses in Gundry, *Show Them No Mercy*.

16. A significant exception is the application of *herem* in 1 Sam 15 when *herem* is enacted against the Amalekites and their king on account of an historic offense against Israel (vv. 2–3). For that offense, God decrees that he will blot out the name of Amalek (Exod 17:8–16). It is this decree that lies behind Samuel killing Amalek's king, the symbol of Amalek's power.

17. Much of the material in this section is indebted to Robert L. Hubbard, Jr., "Only a Distant Memory: Old Testament Allusions to Joshua's Days," *ExAud* 16 (2000): 131–48.

1 Chr 7:27; Neh 8:17). Moses and Aaron remain key characters, even at times receiving credit for Israel's entry to the land (1 Sam 12:8). Second, several historical retrospectives are provided in the narrative following Israel's entry to the land. Some of these speak of land entry in a way that glosses over Joshua and the conquest. For instance, Judges 6:8–10 rightly credits land entry to the LORD driving out the inhabitants. This is true. But it is odd that no mention is made of Joshua, Israel's battles, or the destruction of the enemy mentioned alongside God's action. A similar omission is apparent in the history recounted in 1 Samuel 12. There, Israel moves directly from escape from Egypt to settlement in the land, with no mention of land entry, battle, or destruction. Again, Joshua is not mentioned. Instead, settlement is credited to Moses and Aaron.

A similar absence of Joshua and/or battle and destruction of the inhabitants is found in historical retrospectives in the prophets. Thus, Amos 2:9–10, while acknowledging the destruction of the Amorite, credits the action solely to God. The action of Joshua and the Israelites is not mentioned in possessing the land. In Jeremiah 2:6–7 the LORD brings Israel out of Egypt, leads them through the wilderness, and brings them into a fertile land. Again, the leadership of Joshua and the action of Israel is not mentioned. Finally, the historical retrospective in Micah 6:4–5 begins by naming leaders and a contest: God bringing Israel up out of Egypt under the leadership of Moses, Aaron, and Miriam, and the contest with Balak and Balaam. Then, the retrospective moves to land entry. But this event is not related with an eye to leaders and a contest. Had it done so, Joshua and Eleazar would be mentioned as leaders and Jericho or the leaders of the southern and northern coalitions (Josh 10–11) taking the role of the contest. Instead, the account glosses over both leaders and contest. The events of Jericho are subsumed in the phrase "your journey from Shittim to Gilgal." The omission is striking.

Each of the apparent omissions could be accounted for logically. It may be the accounts seek to highlight the greater leadership of Moses. Perhaps they pursue particular rhetorical intents within which the omission makes sense. Certainly, the omissions direct the focus to God as the one responsible for successful land-entry. Despite these possible reasons for the omission, they remain notably absent. Their absence could even signal later Israel's own discomfort with the *herem* or be an acknowledgement that the time for *herem* has passed.

Third, it appears the ongoing canonical narrative confirms the hyperbolic nature of the Deuteronomic law of *herem*. Instead of calling for their destruction, there is marked acceptance of the nations under the ban as a "given" within Israelite society. In 2 Samuel 21:1, David upholds the rightness of the Gibeonite covenant by which these Canaanites were granted a place in Israelite society. Texts such as 2 Samuel 24:7 and 1 Kings 9:20–21 (cf. 2 Chr 8:7–8) speak without embarrassment or justification of the presence of Canaanites within Israel. The inclusion of the Canaanites is brought to an astounding consummation in Ezekiel 47:21–23. In a passage of land distribution that is modeled on Joshua 13–19, the prophet envisions a future of full inclusion and parity for foreigners within Israel. Along with the tribes of Israel, foreigners receive an "inheritance" (*nahalah*; the word is that used of the "inheritance" granted Israel in Joshua [see Chapter 13, Introduction to chs. 13–19]):

> You are to distribute this land among yourselves according to the tribes of Israel. You are to allot it as an inheritance for yourselves and for the foreigners residing among you and who have children. You are to consider them as native-born Israelites; along with you they are to be allotted an inheritance among the tribes of Israel. In whatever tribe a foreigner resides, there you are to give them their inheritance, declares the Sovereign LORD.

Clues such as these reveal that in the Old Testament, the *herem* exercised at Jericho was not a command for all time. Instead, the canonical narrative moves in a direction that affirms the great promise to Abraham that "all peoples on earth will be blessed through you." This does not remove the challenge Joshua 6 presents, nor are warfare and destruction absent from the New Testament; these are taken up in the Introduction's discussion. It is, however, the call for inclusion that is more descriptive of the whole Old Testament's attitude. The inclusion granted foreigners within Israel (and even within Josh 6 in the person of Rahab) overturns a legalistic and unchanging reading of the *herem* command and anticipates the attitude of Jesus' call to love the enemy.

Texts that downplay the *herem* at Jericho open other avenues of engagement with influential aspects of Joshua 6. One reality that Joshua 6 engages, which Joshua 7 then affirms in reverse, is the correlation of obedience to success. As explored in Explain the Story above, Joshua 6 is crafted to highlight obedience: of Joshua to God; of Israel to Joshua and thus to God. The call to obedience regarding things devoted to the LORD is taken up in Joshua 7 and shows the reverse side of the equation: disobedience correlates to failure. Within the literature of Deuteronomy and Joshua–Kings, this same correlate applies and is known as "retribution theology." Repeatedly, Israel's response of obedience or disobedience to the law directly correlates to the success or failure of their life in the land. It is abundantly clear that disobedience can (and does) lead ultimately to Israel's expulsion from the land (Deut 28:58–68; Josh 24:20; 1 Kgs 8:46–49; 2 Kgs 17:1–20; Jer 11:1–8).

Reading Joshua 6–7 should not lead people to think that, if they only obey God, life will always go well. One thinks of Job's comforters, kicking the poor guy when he is down. They insist his sickness must be a sign of God's retribution—and conclude Job must therefore be sinful or disobedient (Job 4:7–9; 8:2–6; 11:13–20). New Testament believers can also fall into this fallacy, especially as Jesus calls his disciples to obedience (John 14:15, 21–23). I recall a conversation with two elderly ladies at church years ago. One lady had recently lost her husband to cancer. The second lady (who subscribed to a common misunderstanding of this kind of retribution theology) flatly stated that the widow's husband must not have had enough faith and that his disobedience resulted in God punishing him with untimely death. It was a moment of great pain for the new widow.

Under the covenant, retribution theology does have a place. But this way of speaking of God's actions in the world needs a balance. Wisdom literature adds a new perspective to that of retribution theology: that the blameless (such as Job [1:8]) may indeed suffer. For people under God's covenant, retribution theology describes covenantal consequences. But even Israel in its disobedience receives mercy and blessing by the patient hand of God, and even the obedient can suffer. In Joshua, the emphasis falls on retribution theology, but within Israel's own history, and as wisdom literature reveals, it is not the only way that God operates within his world.

### Jericho as "The World, the Flesh, and the Devil"

Not only has the Christian interpretive tradition taken the Jordan crossing as a type for baptism and Rahab as a type for the church (see Live the Text, Chapters 2, 3), but Jericho also has been interpreted typologically or symbolically as the world, the flesh, and the devil overcome by Christ and the believer.

Origen's preaching on Joshua includes the figure of Jericho as the world, out of which the church (Rahab) is saved. The trumpets blown against the city are a figure of the gospel preached by its priests or ministers. It is the word of God, sounded out in the ministry of preaching, that proclaims judgment against the world.[18] In a further reflection on this typological reading of Jericho, Origen reads the battle as a call to holy living in which each believer battles against his or her sins.[19] Origen also extends this figure eschatologically, so that Jericho (the world) falls at the end of the age—an end signaled by the trumpet blast of 1 Corinthians 15:52.[20] Out of this world, Rahab (the church) is saved at the end of time.

---

18. Origen, *Hom* 6.4, 7.1.

19. Ibid., 7.4, 7.6. Similarly, Origen's homilies often figure the inhabitants of the land as figures of sin against which the believer battles (see *Hom* 1.6, and *Hom* 13–14 on Joshua 10–11).

20. Ibid., 6.4, 7.1.

Origen is not alone in such figural readings. The fifth century Maximus of Turin also likened the trumpet to the word preached. Maximus likened the walls that fall to "evil thoughts [that] have been destroyed" so that the preaching of the priests "penetrates to the bare parts of the soul, for the soul is found bare before the Word of God when its every evil deed is destroyed."[21] Maximus sums up the figure:

> In this regard, before the soul knows God and accepts the truth of the faith, it veils itself, so to speak, under superstitious works and surrounds itself with something like a wall of perversity, such that it might seem to be able to remain impregnable within the fortifications of its own evil-doing. But when the sacred sound thunders, its rashness is overthrown, its thinking is destroyed, and all the defenses of its superstitions break asunder in such a way that, remaining unprotected, as it is written, the Word of God might penetrate even to the division of its spirit and its inmost parts . . . . so also now the priestly preaching subjugates, captures and takes vengeance on a sinful people.[22]

Maximus also follows Origen's eschatological reading. In his reading, the seven days of marching figures the fullness of time after which the world will perish, with the one who does the will of the LORD enduring forever (citing 1 John 2:17).[23] This eschatological reading also appears in the nineteenth century writer, Charlotte Maria Tucker. Despite the growing predominance of historical and historical-critical readings of the time, Tucker continues with common figural readings. She construes Rahab as the church, anxiously watching for the fullness of time:

> There is much that reminds us of Christ's church, in the position of the pale, anxious woman of Jericho, watching from her casement the Israelites encircling the city doomed to destruction, she herself secure in a promise, saved by faith. . . . A thousand years with the Lord is but as a day, and for nearly six such periods has the silent, solemn march of events, brought nearer the grand consummation before us. . . . She [Rahab/Church] is listening with trembling expectation for the sound of the *shout, and the voice of the archangel, and the trump of God* [citing 1 Thess 4:16]. . . . She has nothing to fear in that day: the blood of Christ is her salvation—the angel of destruction will see the token of living faith [Tucker here making

21. Maximus of Turin, cited in John R. Franke, ed., *Joshua, Judges, Ruth, 1–2 Samuel*, ACCS 4 (Downers Grove, IL: Inter Varsity Press, 2005), 34.

22. Maximus in Franke, *Joshua*, 35.

23. Ibid., 36.

> a common figural association of the scarlet cord and the blood of Christ], and touch not the redeemed of the Lord.[24]

In a recent class on Joshua, readings representing this approach were shared with students preparing for a variety of church and parachurch ministry. Students expressed varying degrees of resonance with such figural reading of the Canaanites and the inhabitants of Jericho. There was recognition that the helpfulness of such figural reading was not an attempt to sidestep historical questions but opened up yet another way to engage the text for Christian reading. Comparison was made to a similar appropriation of the many enemies presented in the Psalter. These enemies might be flesh-and-blood enemies but could also be enemies such as sickness, rejection, and even the discord of psychological pain. The broad range of presentation of the enemy in the Psalter becomes a means of entry into the Psalter's words and experience: one was readily able to read one's own challenges into the enemy presented in the psalms.

Granted that the psalms and Joshua are two very different genres, the engagement with the enemies of the psalmists provides a way to consider the enemies in Joshua. Such a reading could be considered an extension of the figural reading in which Joshua stands as a type for Jesus. As Joshua led Israel against its flesh-and-blood enemies, so Jesus leads the church and its individual members against the spiritual forces in heavenly places arrayed against it. Such a figural reading, by which the church considers the Canaanites as types of the soul's enemies, need not be wholly abandoned.

### Rahab: An Enduring Memory

What is the hallmark of faith? Why is Rahab remembered within the Christian tradition? For one reason, she is placed within the family tree of Jesus (Matt 1:5–6). Matthew presents her as the wife of Salmon, the father of Boaz who married Ruth. Rahab is thus the ancestress of David and Jesus:

> Salmon the father of Boaz, whose mother was Rahab, Boaz the father of Obed, whose mother was Ruth, Obed the father of Jesse, and Jesse the father of King David.

The lineage of David through Boaz is traced in the book of Ruth (Ruth 4:21). The inclusion of Rahab (as well as Ruth) in this family line places her in the context of a very human story: the outsider brought in (Ruth no

---

24. Charlotte Maria Tucker, in Marion Ann Taylor and Christiana de Groot, eds., *Women of War, Women of Woe: Joshua and Judges through the Eyes of Nineteenth-Century Female Biblical Interpreters* (Grand Rapids: Eerdmans, 2016), 40 (emphasis original).

less than Rahab). In some way, this is a description of all who come to faith in Jesus Christ. Both Jew and gentile are alike "under the power of sin" (as Rom 1–3 inexorably argues) and all are outsiders, standing in need of God's merciful inclusion. Naming Rahab in Jesus' family line is a hopeful reminder that in God's economy, none need be excluded from faith, but all can be brought into the very human story of Jesus, the hidden king born to a young virgin girl in a backwater Roman province. His story is one that encompasses all humanity, inviting all into God's family as brothers and sisters.

Rahab is remembered in the Christian tradition for a second reason. Perhaps surprisingly, it is not on account of her great confession of faith in Joshua 2:9–11. Rather, it is because of what her confession resulted in: action. This is the reason Joshua instructs she be saved out of Jericho: "because she hid the spies we sent" (6:17), and for her action she is remembered in the New Testament. Within the faith chapter of Hebrews 11, Rahab stands alongside all those who acted, and thus confessed their faith. She was preserved "because she welcomed the spies." This is characterized as obedience for "she was not killed with those who were disobedient" (Heb 11:31). In similar fashion, James argues that "faith without works is dead" (Jas 2:26) and points to Rahab as an example of lively faith because of "what she did when she gave lodging to the spies and sent them off in a different direction" (Jas 2:25). True faith—faith that pleases God (Heb 11:6)—is faith that acts.

Rahab's confession of praise for Israel's God is noteworthy. But it is the action arising out of her conviction that is honored in the church's memory.

### Heavenly Beings, Heavenly Perspectives

Dr. Gordon Franklin was the New Testament professor at Northwest Bible College in Edmonton, Alberta. Although I attended there thirty years ago, I still remember several of his ideas and ways of capturing truth. Some of his one liners were priceless, pithy, and still ring true today. He once commented that churches can forget that they are on the front lines of a battle and in doing so, forget what really matters and perhaps lose sight of the battle itself. He would say, "Only those far behind the front lines complain of warm beer." I often recall that saying when churchgoers grumble about things that are, in the grand scheme of God's action, inconsequential. Perhaps they grumble because they've left the battle and are far away from Christian action. Or perhaps they've forgotten they stand on the front lines where beer (warm or otherwise) is not the issue. Those who see themselves on the front lines know the real issue is the spiritual battle in which Christians are engaged. This is their focus (Eph 6:10–17).

Joshua's query to the heavenly commander, and the response he receives, are reminders of that heavenly battle. Joshua initially fails to recognize the heavenly nature of this commander, reducing him to earthly concerns of "whose side are you on?"

It is not uncommon in the Christian tradition to understand the commander as the preincarnate Christ. Calvin makes this identification in his commentary on Joshua 5:13–15, "it was thus a special pledge of the divine favor that the Captain and Head of the Church, to whom Moses had been accustomed, was now present to assist."[25] Whether this identification is correct, or whether the commander is heavenly but only of an angelic order (see Explain the Story above), the point is clear. There are things more important for Joshua to know than whether the commander was Israelite or Canaanite.

The commander's response directs Joshua to the more important reality of the unseen realm. It is Joshua's recognition of this new, heavenly perspective that precipitates his openness to listen. It likewise precipitates his response to the holy. Israel's battle fought in the human sphere dealt with heavenly realities: God was near and the ground holy. Recognizing this, Joshua removed his shoes, heard God's direction, and acted accordingly.

This discussion can be added to the earlier consideration of a Christian reading of the Canaanites as spiritual enemies. As the church and its members attend to the heavenly realities of frontline warfare, it sees beyond the human manifestation of such battle. The church is invited to see the heavenly realities behind the human realm so that it not be blind to God's presence. The church is called to fight not against flesh-and-blood enemies but against spiritual forces in heavenly places. In such battles (as in all of life), the church acknowledges it walks in the power and presence of God and fights with the weapons he has provided: dependent prayer and humble action.

---

25. Calvin, *Joshua*, CCEL (https://www.ccel.org/ccel/calvin/calcom07.pdf). Calvin makes the argument that this commander is the same as the presence of God that went before Israel after the Golden Calf incident, and which Paul names as the Christ (1 Cor 10:4).

CHAPTER 6

# Joshua 7:1–26

## LISTEN to the Story

1But the Israelites were unfaithful in regard to the devoted things;
Achan son of Karmi, the son of Zimri, the son of Zerah, of the tribe of
Judah, took some of them. So the LORD's anger burned against Israel.
2Now Joshua sent men from Jericho to Ai, which is near Beth Aven to
the east of Bethel, and told them, "Go up and spy out the region." So the
men went up and spied out Ai.
3When they returned to Joshua, they said, "Not all the army will have
to go up against Ai. Send two or three thousand men to take it and do not
weary the whole army, for only a few people live there." 4So about three
thousand went up; but they were routed by the men of Ai, 5who killed
about thirty-six of them. They chased the Israelites from the city gate as
far as the stone quarries and struck them down on the slopes. At this the
hearts of the people melted in fear and became like water.
6Then Joshua tore his clothes and fell facedown to the ground before
the ark of the LORD, remaining there till evening. The elders of Israel
did the same, and sprinkled dust on their heads. 7And Joshua said, "Alas,
Sovereign LORD, why did you ever bring this people across the Jordan to
deliver us into the hands of the Amorites to destroy us? If only we had
been content to stay on the other side of the Jordan! 8Pardon your servant,
Lord. What can I say, now that Israel has been routed by its enemies? 9The
Canaanites and the other people of the country will hear about this and
they will surround us and wipe out our name from the earth. What then
will you do for your own great name?"
10The LORD said to Joshua, "Stand up! What are you doing down on
your face? 11Israel has sinned; they have violated my covenant, which I
commanded them to keep. They have taken some of the devoted things;
they have stolen, they have lied, they have put them with their own possessions. 12That is why the Israelites cannot stand against their enemies;
they turn their backs and run because they have been made liable to

destruction. I will not be with you anymore unless you destroy whatever among you is devoted to destruction.

13“Go, consecrate the people. Tell them, ‘Consecrate yourselves in preparation for tomorrow; for this is what the LORD, the God of Israel, says: There are devoted things among you, Israel. You cannot stand against your enemies until you remove them.

14“ ‘In the morning, present yourselves tribe by tribe. The tribe the LORD chooses shall come forward clan by clan; the clan the LORD chooses shall come forward family by family; and the family the LORD chooses shall come forward man by man. 15Whoever is caught with the devoted things shall be destroyed by fire, along with all that belongs to him. He has violated the covenant of the LORD and has done an outrageous thing in Israel!’ ”

16Early the next morning Joshua had Israel come forward by tribes, and Judah was chosen. 17The clans of Judah came forward, and the Zerahites were chosen. He had the clan of the Zerahites come forward by families, and Zimri was chosen. 18Joshua had his family come forward man by man, and Achan son of Karmi, the son of Zimri, the son of Zerah, of the tribe of Judah, was chosen.

19Then Joshua said to Achan, “My son, give glory to the LORD, the God of Israel, and honor him. Tell me what you have done; do not hide it from me.”

20Achan replied, “It is true! I have sinned against the LORD, the God of Israel. This is what I have done: 21When I saw in the plunder a beautiful robe from Babylonia, two hundred shekels of silver and a bar of gold weighing fifty shekels, I coveted them and took them. They are hidden in the ground inside my tent, with the silver underneath.”

22So Joshua sent messengers, and they ran to the tent, and there it was, hidden in his tent, with the silver underneath. 23They took the things from the tent, brought them to Joshua and all the Israelites and spread them out before the LORD.

24Then Joshua, together with all Israel, took Achan son of Zerah, the silver, the robe, the gold bar, his sons and daughters, his cattle, donkeys and sheep, his tent and all that he had, to the Valley of Achor. 25Joshua said, “Why have you brought this trouble on us? The LORD will bring trouble on you today.”

Then all Israel stoned him, and after they had stoned the rest, they burned them. 26Over Achan they heaped up a large pile of rocks, which remains to this day. Then the LORD turned from his fierce anger. Therefore that place has been called the Valley of Achor ever since.

*Listening to the Text in the Story*: Deuteronomy 1:19–3:11; 13:12–18; 20:10–18; Baal Epic; Die of Yaḥali; Law Code of Hammurabi; Old Babylonian Heptascopic Texts

## Narrative History Repeats Itself

Through Achan's sin, Israel is counted unfaithful. Joshua 7–8 has striking similarities to another episode of Israel's unfaithfulness in the wilderness (Deut 1:19–3:11).[1] The similarities invite comparison of the new generation and the wilderness generation and raise the ominous possibility that the new generation also could suffer the fate of their ancestors. The victory at Jericho does not excuse Israel from covenant faithfulness.

Both accounts present a similar schema of failure followed by repentance, restoration, and victory. Although the particular order of events is not identical, both open with the leader (Moses, Joshua) dispatching spies (Deut 1:22–24; Josh 7:2); in both the spies are to "go up and spy out" the land (Deut 1:24; "explored" is the same Hebrew word as Josh 7:2 "spy out"). Each account gives the spies' good report (Deut 1:25; Josh 7:3) and in both Israel advances against the enemy. It is an advance that Deuteronomy explicitly (1:43) and Joshua implicitly (7:3) characterize as arrogant. In both, Israel is pursued and routed and mourns before the LORD (Deut 1:44–45; Josh 7:4–6). Tellingly in both, Israel's heart "melts in fear" before its enemies (Deut 1:28; Josh 7:5). In response to Israel's unfaithfulness, God's anger is roused (Deut 1:34, 37; Josh 7:1), and he is no longer with them in battle (Deut 1:42; Josh 7:12). Although the guilty in each account confess their sin (Deut 1:41; Josh 7:20–21), this does not prevent their complete annihilation (Deut 1:35–39; 2:14–15; Josh 7:15, 24–26). Only then is God's anger turned away and victory assured. Israel advances against the enemy (Deut 2:16, 24–25; Josh 8:1–2), is victorious, and implements *herem* (Deut 2:31–3:11; Josh 8:18–25) with only the cattle and plunder excepted at God's command (Deut 2:35; 3:7; Josh 8:2, 27).

## Booty: The Practice at Jericho

As explored earlier in this commentary (see Ancient Near Eastern Background: The Problem of Warfare in the Introduction and Explain the Story,

1. This is fully explored by Christopher T. Begg, "The Function of Josh 7,1–8,29 in the Deuteronomistic History," *Bib* 67 (1986): 320–34.

Josh 6:15–26), the requirement at Jericho that no booty be taken appears to be an extreme application of the booty and *herem* laws. Achan's expectation of booty was not out of the ordinary, as evidenced by the granting of booty in Israel's next successful battle at Ai (ch. 8). Achan's crime is one of disobedience to the specific application of the law in Israel's initial battle against Jericho. As a first-fruits of all Israel's conquests in the land, the battle against Jericho is unique.

**Extreme Measures against a Sinful Town**

At first glance Deuteronomy 13:12–18[13–19] does not seem comparable to Joshua 7. Deuteronomy 13:1–11 gives guidelines for prophets and family members who entice Israel to idol worship. The penalty is severe: death. Then, Deuteronomy 13:12–18 provides guidelines for dealing with a whole town that turns to idolatry.

Joshua 7 does not address idolatry, but the procedure it follows is similar to that outlined in Deuteronomy 13:12–18. First, inquiry is carefully made to determine the town's guilt. Once guilt is established, the town is to be completely destroyed (in Deut 13:15 the verbal form of *herem* is used). The people and livestock are put to the sword and the town's plunder burned as a whole burnt offering to God; nothing is reserved. Only then is the LORD's anger turned away, and mercy and compassion extended to God's people. Finally, the town is to remain "a ruin forever" and "none of the condemned things are to be found in your hands" (13:17).

Achan's story describes the fate of one who has the condemned things "found in his hand." Possession of the consecrated items contravenes God's command and holiness. The presence of the consecrated items in the camp defiles the people and makes them *herem*. To rectify the covenant breach, Israel makes inquiry to expose the truth (as in Deuteronomy). The offender is not pardoned; like the town, he is completely destroyed, wholly offered up to God by stoning and (as in Deut 13) by burning. Only then does God "turn from his fierce anger" (Josh 7:26), the proof of which is the taking of Ai. Ai is rendered a "ruin forever," a phrase that occurs only in Deuteronomy 13:16 and Joshua 8:28, further aligning the two accounts. The rocks piled over Achan and the perpetual ruin of the idolatrous town are a reminder to Israel of the offender's sin.

The similarities suggest that Achan's sin is as heinous as that of idolatry. Like idolatry, the hidden plunder infects Israel's holy state and threatens its covenant relationship. Action against idolaters "purges the evil from among you" (Deut 13:5) so that "no one among you will do such an evil thing again" (Deut 13:11) and so that God's "fierce anger" will be turned away from Israel

(Deut 13:17). Achan's execution similarly purges evil from Israel's midst. It serves to warn Israel of the correlation between covenant obedience and success in the land. Only as Israel walks in covenant obedience can it anticipate God's power exercised on Israel's behalf.

### Signs of Mourning

Joshua's torn clothing and prostration and the elders' dust-strewn heads are clear signs of mourning. Such signs are elsewhere evident in the biblical text (see below, at 7:6–15) and are found in extrabiblical texts as well. In the Ugaritic Baal epic, even the gods mourn in these ways. When El learns of Baal's death "the Gracious One, the kindly god, descends from the throne, sits on the footstool, (descends) from the footstool, sits on the earth. He pours dirt of mourning on his head, dust of humiliation on his cranium."[2]

### Casting of Lots

Achan's sin is revealed through a process of selection which, while not stated, is likely accomplished by the casting of lots. In the reign of the Assyrian king, Shalmaneser III (ninth century BC), an inscription reveals the annual practice of selecting the king's high officer of state by casting lots. The year is then named after the selected official. In this role, the officer would cast lots for legal and commercial purposes. The inscription of Yaḥali records his plea for the lots he casts in his year:

> The Die (Pūru) of Yaḥali: Aššur, the great lord! Adad, the great lord! (This is) the die of Yaḥali, the Chief Steward of Shalmaneser, king of Assyria . . . In his [Yaḥali's] eponymy (assigned to him by) his die, may the harvest of Assyria prosper and thrive. Before Aššur and Adad, may he throw his die.[3]

Of course, the lot cast by Joshua is commanded by God. The selection of Achan is superintended—it is not a chance throw of the dice.

### Stealing from the Gods

The misappropriation of items consecrated to the gods was a serious offense in the ancient Near East. The Old Babylonian (eighteenth century BC) law code of Hammurabi reveals this. The king charges that "if a seignior stole the property of church or state, that seignior shall be put to death; also the one who received the stolen goods from his hand shall be put to death."[4] The extension of guilt beyond the thief to the one who receives the goods sheds

2. *COS* 1.86:267.
3. Ibid., 2.113I:271.
4. *ANET*, 166.

light on the extension of guilt to Achan's family. Had they known of the hidden goods—or assisted in secreting, rather than disclosing them—they would be equally implicated in the crime.

Further evidence for the serious nature of theft from the gods is apparent in Old Babylonian heptascopic texts (liver-omen texts). Several of these texts speak of sacrilege against devoted items that are similar to the items of *herem*. This sacrilege could be met with fines of silver and gold but could also merit execution—even by burning. One text attests that "a high priestess who continually steals from the consecrated items is to be seized and burned," while in another text a similar crime committed by a high-priestess, priest, or priest's wife is punishable by execution, though the means of execution is left unspecified.[5]

## EXPLAIN the Story

Joshua 7 stands between two great Israelite victories. Though different in tactics—Jericho's victory stresses the presence of God's ark; Ai's victory is won through shrewd human battle—both victories reveal God's power to give Israel the land. The chapter looks back to Jericho for it is Achan's theft of consecrated and thus prohibited items (Josh 6:18) that is the reason for the first defeat at Ai and the nation's status as *herem*. Joshua 7 also looks further back to chapter 2 as it raises the questions, "Who is a true Israelite?" and "How is covenant keeping expressed?" Rahab, the outsider by birth and profession, speaks and acts faithfully as if an ideal Israelite. Achan, the insider, acts unfaithfully, as if he is the stereotypical Canaanite. By their choices, they secure the fate of both their families. The chapter also looks ahead to the destruction of Ai—a battle only won because Israel reverses the effects of Achan's sin. The victories at Jericho and Ai are tainted, therefore, with the remembrance of this first sin after Israel's entry to the land.

The chapter clearly demonstrates the necessity of obedience to success in taking the land. Jericho is taken because Israel is obedient to God's strategy, and God's power is freely exercised in the midst of his holy people. When Achan steals items consecrated to God, he mars the nation's purity. A holy God dwells in the midst of a holy people (Lev 11:44; 19:2; 20:26; Deut 7:6; 14:2; 23:9–14; 26:19; 28:9; Isa 12:6; Jer 2:3; Ezek 20:41) and cannot remain with defiled Israel or go with his people to battle Ai. Israel must remove impurity for God to exercise once again his power on their behalf. It is a hard-won lesson.

5. M. Anbar, "Le châtiment due crime de sacrilège d'après la Bible et un texte hépatoscopique paléo–babylonien," *RA* 68 (1974): 172–73.

Setting the account early in the book emphasizes the centrality of the lesson for all that Israel seeks to accomplish in the land.

### Defeat at Ai (7:1–5)

The chapter begins by informing readers of the behind-the-scenes theft. This is only slowly revealed to the characters, and the delay creates narrative tension. The "spoiler" verse (v. 1) picks up on Joshua's warning not to "take" the "devoted things" (*herem*; Josh 6:18). These key words appear throughout the chapter. The "devoted things" are the chapter's problem and appear eight times (vv. 1 [2x; "some of them" is *herem* in Hebrew]; 11, 12 [2x]; 13 [2x; Hebrew reads "until you remove the *herem*"]; 15). "Take" appears five times (vv. 1, 11, 21, 23, 24). The word "take" initiates the problem, sketches the interactions between Achan and Israel, and finally resolves the problem:

Achan **takes** the items<br>
    Israel is implicated in **taking** them<br>
Achan confesses he **took** them<br>
    The messengers **take** the items from the tent<br>
    Israel **takes** Achan to stone him.

As the chapter concludes, it confirms the truth of Joshua's warning regarding "trouble" (6:18). Achan has brought "trouble" on Israel and is in turn visited with "trouble" (7:25). The troubling events are memorialized in the name "Valley of Achor," for "Achor" sounds like the Hebrew word for trouble.

Achan steals the sacred items (Josh 6:19), but it is all Israel that is charged with unfaithfulness (v. 1). This corporate accountability reveals the unique power of the *herem* items. Their presence within the camp infects the whole camp. But there are also cues in the narrative that reveal Achan's arrogant sinfulness in appropriating the banned items is an arrogance—a self-centered overconfidence—that characterizes more than this one man. The recommendation of the scouts, and even the words and actions of Joshua, suggest they have forgotten their utter dependence upon God and the necessity of obedience to success.

Achan is introduced with a full patronymic (v. 1). Identified with four generations, it is the longest identification in all of Joshua and sets the offender firmly within widening social contexts of family, clan, and tribe. These widening circles may also suggest what has been stated: that culpability is shared by all Israel for it is "the Israelites" who have acted unfaithfully. Later, when all Israel seeks the identity of the individual perpetrator, the lots begin with the larger group and work down to the individual. There can be no doubt that Achan is part of all Israel.

The culpability of all Israel becomes clear in verse 11 where Israel is indicted, and its sin is detailed with verbs having a plural subject. The misappropriation of items dedicated to God and their presence in the midst of Israel brings impurity upon the whole people. Corporate sin is met with corporate punishment as the whole nation becomes *herem* and so falls before its enemies (v. 12). Corporate sin must be rectified by corporate action.

Israel has "acted unfaithfully" (v. 1), a term describing serious transgressions. These may be in the realm of human interactions including infidelity, enticement to idolatry, and unjust judgments (Num 5:12, 27; 31:16; Lev 6:2[5:21]; Prov 16:10). Most frequently, it describes covenant violations against God such as improper worship (2 Chr 26:16) and idolatry (1 Chr 5:25; 2 Chr 28:23; Ezek 20:27–28). In Joshua, the term is elsewhere found only in 22:16, 31, describing the altar built by the Transjordanian tribes. Initially understood as a false altar, it is therefore a covenant offense and unfaithful.

The "anger of the LORD burns" against Israel for the egregious offense. Only after Israel removes the offender does God's anger abate (v. 26). To understand the depth of the offense, it is helpful to note the severity of other crimes that elicit God's anger. It elsewhere burns against Israel for complaints and rebellion (Num 11:10; 25:3; 32:10–13) and especially the worship of other gods (Deut 29:27[26]; Judg 2:14, 20; 3:8; 10:7; 2 Kgs 13:3; 2 Chr 25:15). In a narrative that shows similarities to Joshua 7 (see Listen to the Story above), God's anger burns against the town fallen into idolatry (Deut 13:17[18]).

When the spies are dispatched, Israel is unaware of its position before God; the reader, however, knows. The mission begins in the shadow of God's anger, which does not bode well for its outcome. Joshua commands the spies "go up and spy out the region." The command evokes the recent mission to Jericho (2:1) and could be construed in a positive light. But the command differs from that given at Jericho, which was "go up and look over the land." The difference aligns the current command more closely to the ill-fated spy mission of the wilderness where the spies "went up . . . and explored" (Deut 1:24; the NIV word "explored" is the same as "spy out" in Josh 7:2). For the reader privy to verse 1, the reference continues the ominous tone of the chapter's opening. The spies are sent to Ai. The name of this town translates as "The Ruin," perhaps so called because of its disposition in Joshua 8:28. In light of Joshua 7:1, the name adds to the chapter's foreboding tone.

Ai is traditionally identified with Et-tell. Like Jericho, its archaeological record is problematic. It was likely a military outpost guarding the larger center of Bethel just a mile to the northwest. Ai stood three miles north of Beth-aven.[6]

6. For further discussion of the archaeological and textual record for Ai, see Hess, "Jericho and Ai of the Book of Joshua," 33–46 in *Critical Issues in Early Israelite History*.

These towns may be mentioned simply to place Ai geographically and to prepare for the further mention of Bethel in Joshua 8. But both towns have a troubled history: Bethel ("House of God") begins as the place of Jacob's vision (Gen 28:10–17) but becomes better known as a place of apostasy (1 Kgs 12:25–33). Beth-aven ("House of Wickedness") is likewise remembered as a place of apostasy (Hos 4:15; 5:8; 10:5). Once again, an ominous note is sounded by these names.

The spies' confident report initially sounds positive: the city is sparsely populated (as one might expect of a military outpost) and easily taken with two to three thousand men (or two to three "units" as the word might also be translated; if so, an unknown number of soldiers is dispatched). The point is that the whole army is not needed. This would be the first act not conducted by "all Israel" since Joshua 1. This might signal the spies' confidence or indicate their misunderstanding of the importance of Israel's unity in the land (and which the book has carefully emphasized). Even more telling is what is missing from the spies' report: there is no recognition here that "God has given the city" (as at 2:24; 6:16); there is no acknowledgement of God's presence or power. It is quite possible that Achan's wrong views regarding his right to Jericho's plunder stem from an arrogance more broadly shared among the people. The spies' recommendation suggests they have forgotten the source of the Jericho victory and wrongly estimate their own ability to win. By the fact that Joshua does not speak of God nor petition God's instructions, he may share in Israel's forgetfulness and arrogance.

Under God's anger, and wrongheaded about the ease of victory, Israel is soundly routed. Without even breaching the city gate, they run from the Ai contingent, chased ignominiously to "the stone quarries," an undisclosed location perhaps identified as the steep slopes of Wadi el-Makkuk on the road back toward Jericho. There, they are struck. In total, thirty-six of three thousand are lost. Despite the limited casualties, the rout leaves the Israelites as fearful as the Canaanites (Josh 5:1)—but only more so, for the Israelites' hearts melt and are "like water." So much for Israel's triumphant entry into the land.

### Devoted to Destruction (7:6–15)

Joshua responds immediately, tearing his clothes and falling before the ark. He is joined by the elders who sprinkle dust on their heads. These actions are typical signs of mourning (Gen 37:34; 44:13; 1 Sam 4:12; 2 Sam 1:2; Job 1:20; 2:12; Lam 2:10; Ezek 27:30). After a lengthy time, Joshua's mourning turns to intercession.

Initially, Joshua appears once again to be fulfilling the ministry of Moses. A similar scene of mourning and intercession occurred in the wilderness after Israel's rebellion and refusal to enter the land. There, Moses and Aaron fell down before the people, and Joshua and Caleb tore their clothes (Num 14:5–6). These signs of mourning were followed by Moses' intercession on behalf of the people (Num 14:10–19). By this intercession, he won forgiveness for them, although the LORD forbade the wilderness generation entry to the promised land (Num 14:20–23).

Even Joshua's opening words ("Alas, Sovereign LORD") are an appropriate opening to intercession. However, as Joshua's intercession continues, he sounds suspiciously like the wilderness generation complaining against Moses and Aaron. Each complaint begins with an accusatory "why," blames God for defeat, and states preference for lands other than the promised land:

> The wilderness generation: "If only we had died in Egypt! Or in this wilderness! **Why** is the LORD bringing us to this land only to let us fall by the sword? Our wives and children will be taken as plunder. Wouldn't it be better for us to go back to Egypt?" (Num 14:2–3; similar accusations although without the "why" appear in Exod 14:11; 16:3; Deut 1:27)
>
> Joshua: "Alas, Sovereign LORD, **why** did you ever bring this people across the Jordan to deliver us into the hands of the Amorites to destroy us? If only we had been content to stay on the other side of the Jordan!" (Josh 7:7)

Joshua's similarity to the complaining wilderness generation places him in a critical light. In the face of God's repeated promises to be with Israel and to give them the land, and God's repeated reminders of the necessity of obedience to these ends, it might be more appropriate for Joshua to fall down with the question, "How have we sinned?" or "In what way has disobedience brought about this failure?" Instead, after addressing God he begins with wilderness-style accusation. He first asks "why?" and then accuses God of delivering Israel to destruction by the hand of the "Amorites" (here used as a general term signifying the people in the land; see Josh 24:8, 12). In an ironic twist, he uses the key words "across" and "the other side," both of which come from the Hebrew root *'br*. This is the same word that features so prominently in Joshua 3–4 as Israel "crosses" (*'br*) into the land to possess it. Joshua now reverses that victorious crossing, regretting it occurred, and pining after the lands of the Transjordan—even though those lands are not the promised land but only a concessionary gift (Num 32)!

Joshua's intercessory focus is also very different than Moses'. Moses bases his request for forgiveness first on concern for God's reputation and fame (Num 14:13–16) and then on the basis of God's character (Num 14:17–19). Israel's destruction is raised only because it would be interpreted by the nations as evidence of God's powerlessness (vv. 15–17). But Joshua focuses on Israel and its survival: Israel's destruction (v. 7), Israel's ease (v. 7), Israel's rout (v. 8), and Israel's name (v. 9). Almost as an afterthought, he wonders about God's name (v. 9). The afterthought seems a manipulative maneuver in comparison to Moses' focused concern for God's name.

God's response suggests he is none too impressed with Joshua's words and actions, although there is no word of rebuke (vv. 10–11). He peremptorily rejects his mourning: "Stand up! What are you doing down on your face?" Joshua had asked "why" (v. 7), and God overturns that with his "what"—the words are the same in Hebrew. Instead of assurance or forgiveness, God reveals the depth of the problem. Israel has sinned. That sin is clarified in v. 11 with a series of five phrases each beginning with the same Hebrew word, *wegam* ("and also" or "that is"), which the NIV leaves untranslated. All of the verbs have a plural subject, indicting Israel and not only Achan:

Israel has sinned . . .
. . . *and also* violated my covenant
. . . *and also* they have taken
. . . *and also* they have stolen
. . . *and also* they have lied
. . . *and also* they have put them with their own possessions.

To "violate the covenant" is literally "to cross over the covenant." The word used is from the same root (*'br*) as in verse 7 and in chapters 3–4 and adds further irony to Israel's sin. After crossing over the Jordan into the land, they quickly "cross over" the covenant under which they are to live in the land. The severity of the offense is apparent, for "crossing over" or violating the covenant also describes worshiping other gods (Deut 17:2–3; Josh 23:16; Judg 2:19–20; Hos 8:1) for which sin the land is lost (Josh 23:16; Judg 2:19–20; 2 Kgs 18:12). God had commanded Israel to keep the covenant (v. 10). The disobedient theft has transgressed the camp's holiness, and all Israel now stands in violation of covenant relationship.

Israel also has "taken" the devoted items (v. 11), which is the word of Joshua's warning (6:18) and Achan's action (Josh 7:1). Now applied to Israel, it highlights the corporate nature of the offense. The covenant nature of the violation is also apparent for Israel has "stolen" (a word found in the Ten Commandments [Exod 20:15; Deut 5:19] and in a list that echoes the Ten Commandments [Lev 19:11]) and "lied" (Lev 19:11).

By misappropriating items consecrated to God and totally off limits to Israel, Israel forfeits its holiness before God and is now itself devoted to destruction. The rout before Ai is but the first fruits of that new status, for

God will "not be with them anymore" (v. 12). God's presence in the midst of a holy people has been the source of Israel's victory, as shown at Jericho. Now, Israel is promised that they will not "stand before their enemies," and further retreat and rout can be anticipated.

Only one route is offered to restore God's presence—and attendant victory in the land (v. 12–13). They must "destroy whatever" in their midst is devoted to destruction and "remove" it (v. 13). Both verbs are strong actions; similar "destroying" is enacted against hostile nations (Deut 2:12; 7:24; 33:27; Josh 11:14, 20), apostate dynasties (1 Kgs 15:29; 16:12; 2 Kgs 10:17), and Baal and other idols (Num 33:52; 2 Kgs 10:28). It is an action that Israel herself may experience (Deut 6:15; 7:4; 9:8; 28:48; Josh 23:15). "Removal" is often of idols (Gen 35:2; Josh 24:14, 23; Judg 10:16; 1 Sam 7:3–4), those involved in idolatry (1 Kgs 15:12–13) or unauthorized places of worship (2 Kgs 18:4; 23:19). But Israel, too, could experience removal from God's presence on account of its sins (2 Kgs 17:18, 23; 23:27; Jer 32:31). The LORD is prescribing drastic action for Israel.

In preparation for the next day, Joshua is to consecrate the people, and the people are to consecrate themselves (v. 13). The double mention of this act suggests it is a crucial prerequisite to the lot casting. Israel had been consecrated before crossing the Jordan (3:5), but the presence of the devoted items has made the people unholy. After consecration, Israel is to submit to a process of selection superintended by God. Moving from larger to increasingly smaller social units within Israel, tribes, clans, and families draw near to God who then "chooses."

A similar system of "choice" is employed elsewhere, at times involving the Urim and Thummim (1 Sam 10:20–21; 14:41–42). Joshua elsewhere utilizes lot casting (Josh 14:2; 15:1; chs. 18–19, 21), and it could be the mechanism of selection here.

Once the individual perpetrator is selected, corporate Israel must take the final step to destroy and remove the one devoted to destruction. Destruction by fire is imposed infrequently in Israel (Lev 20:14; 21:9; see also in Philistia, Judg 15:6). It is imposed on the idolatrous town (Deut 13:15–17), an account with affinities to Joshua 7 (see Listen to the Story above). The town in Deuteronomy 13 is wholly destroyed, reflecting the serious nature of the crime. The prescription for total destruction of the town acknowledges that unchecked, the town's idolatry could spread in Israel.

Achan's theft carries a similar weight of seriousness for it has already spread to infect Israel. The theft is a violation of Jericho's status as the first fruits of Israel's occupation of the promised land, and a contravention of the LORD's direct command regarding items consecrated to holy use. All of these reasons make the crime a "violation of the covenant" (vv. 11, 15), contravening the covenant of Sinai by which Israel was made God's special possession. As a final judgment of the theft, the LORD calls it an "outrageous thing" (v. 15), a phrase used of heinous sexual crimes (Gen 34:7; Judg 19:23–24; 20:6; 2 Sam 13:12), sexual immorality (Deut 22:21; Jer 29:23), and lies (Jer 29:23). The outrageous nature of Achan's crime is heightened for it is something outrageous "in Israel," God's holy people (v. 15; see also a similar judgment of "outrageous things" in Gen 34:7 and in 2 Sam 13:12 where such things are "not done in Israel").

The penalty is to be exacted against Achan and "all that he had," which includes not only his sons and daughters (no reason is given for his wife's omission; perhaps she is not living), but also his flocks, tent, and all his possession (v. 24). Various reasons can be given for the inclusion of his children along with his possessions and livestock. Possibly his children were complicit in the crime; after all, the items are hidden in the ground in the midst of the family tent, and it is difficult to think they were not aware of the theft. They may even have assisted in the concealment. But "complicity" would not account for the inclusion in the penalty of the livestock and inanimate possessions. The family may be complicit, but something more appears to be at work.

Joshua's warning (6:18) reckons with the contaminating nature of the devoted items: possession of the devoted items brings *herem* upon the possessor. The Jericho items are consecrated and thus part of the realm of the holy and subject to the ritual laws of that realm. Within the realm of the holy, an Israelite who comes in contact with unclean or impure items is rendered unclean (Lev 11:39–40; 14:33–36; 15:4–12). This is at issue in Deuteronomy 7:25–26 concerning images of foreign gods. They are to be burned in the fire, lest their silver and gold make them coveted and they are taken. If taken, their possessor will be set apart for destruction. It appears that a similar dynamic of contamination is at work in both cases. Achan, his family, and "all that he has" have been in close, if not direct, contact with the consecrated items. That improper and close proximity brings contamination. For this reason, the penalty is exacted against Achan and "all that belongs to him."

The narrative of Achan is comparable (unfavorably) to that of Rahab. The outsider Rahab acted with covenant kindness (*hesed*), acknowledging the powerful God of the covenant (2:9–13). By this, she won her own life and that of "all who belong to her" (6:17, 22). Achan, the covenant insider, acts against the covenant. By this, he forfeits his life and that of "all who belong to him."

### Troubling the Troubler (7:16–26)

Joshua begins the process of selection "early" on the next day as a sign of his commitment to God's command. Israel is fully cooperative, coming forward for selection. Achan's introduction in verse 1 placed him in ever-widening social circles, which concluded with his tribal affiliation. Now, he is selected through a narrowing process. Beginning with tribes, then clans, then families, the perpetrator is identified. The lengthy process keeps Israel in suspense. The reader (who already knows the outcome) experiences the anxiety of the slow process through the slow and specific narrative delineation. God promised he would "choose" through the lot (v. 14 [3x]). Now, that same verb is used in a passive sense as tribe, clan, family, and individual "are chosen." By this, God's superintendence of the lot is apparent.

Joshua addresses Achan as "my son," as an elder or superior would address one of younger or inferior station (Gen 22:7, 8; 43:29; 1 Sam 26:17). A note of sadness tinges the address, for Joshua knows the threat Achan has brought upon Israel and that Achan must die. Joshua urges Achan to glorify and honor God by telling the truth without "hiding" it. Achan's reply provides another contrast to Rahab. She spoke of God's miracles, his power to give the land, and his position as "God in heaven above and on the earth below" (2:9–11). Achan offers no words of praise or acknowledgement of God's power and appears less a true Israelite than Rahab.

Achan does acknowledge the truth that he "has sinned" and uses the same word as God's indictment (v. 11). But his description of what he has taken is of note. He does not refer to the stolen items as "devoted" (as in vv. 1, 11, 13, 15), but as "plunder." In the normal course of warfare, plunder was Israel's right (Num 31:27; Deut 2:35; 3:7; 20:14; 1 Sam 30:20), and the appropriation of plunder was the usual practice even in Joshua (8:2; 11:14; 22:8). By referring to the devoted items as plunder, Achan reveals he thinks of them as his right. He not only has disregarded the direct command of God but has not fully grasped the unique holiness of the Jericho battle. Instead, he asserts a claim.

Achan's claim is asserted over items of value: a robe whose value is its foreign origin in Babylon (the Hebrew word is "Shinar"; see Gen 10:10; 11:2; 14:1, 9; Dan 1:2), six to seven pounds of silver, and approximately one pound of gold. Achan "covets" these valuables. It is a covenant offense, for "covet" is the word used in the tenth commandment (Exod 20:17; Deut 5:21). This is also the word used to warn Israel not to "covet" the silver and gold of idols lest they take it and become ensnared, bring it into their house, and become "set apart to destruction." Instead, the idols are to be burned (Deut 7:25–26). Achan's theft of silver and gold evokes this offense but with a tragic difference. By his covetousness he brings silver and gold into his home, becomes devoted, and is himself burned.

Achan "took" the items, and for the third time in this chapter the key word of Joshua's warning (6:18) is used. Achan may have asserted a claim to plunder, but he knows he has done wrong for he has "hidden" the items. The word he uses for hiding the items is not that of Joshua's invitation to disclosure (v. 19). It is the word used to describe Rahab "hiding" the spies under the flax (2:6); once again, Achan and Rahab are contrasted. The Canaanite prostitute acted in covenant faithfulness, but the Israelite acted in covenant unfaithfulness—and attempted to hide the evidence.

Achan provides details of the hiding place (v. 21), and messengers are quickly dispatched and quickly return, having found the items as described. Even though Achan has already indicated the hiding place "in the tent," the location is three more times indicated in just two verses (vv. 22–23). This is perhaps a subtle implication of Achan's whole family in preparation for their appearance in the next scene (vv. 24–26). The items are spread "before the LORD," returning them to the sphere to which they were earlier consecrated (6:19, 24).

Once the devoted items are returned to their rightful place, Joshua and "all Israel" act corporately to deal with "whoever is caught with the devoted things" (v. 15). As discussed above, this includes his children as possible accomplices and as those contaminated by close association to the holy things. His livestock, tent, and all his possessions are included in the ritual execution. Joshua had earlier asked God, "Why?" and, before the execution proceeds, he directs the same question to Achan, perhaps in bewilderment, sadness, anger—or all three.

The execution takes place outside the camp in the Valley of Achor. The name, through a word play, memorializes the connection between the perpetrator, trouble, and the place of execution (vv. 25–26). "Achor" sounds similar to "Achan" as well as the "trouble" (*'akar*) he brought on Israel. Now, through Israel, God will visit trouble (*'akar*) upon Achan. He joins the company of only two others of whom it is said they "troubled" Israel: Saul (1 Sam 14:29) and Ahab (1 Kgs 18:17). A member of this triumvirate of infamy, Achan is remembered in Joshua's time as one whose actions threatened the whole community of Israel (Josh 22:20). It will be left for the later canon to comment whether his name might be redeemed.

The terrible consequence for infringing on God's holiness and bringing Israel to the brink of destruction is laid upon Achan and "all that he had." God had commanded destruction by fire (v. 15), a penalty that is known in the ancient Near East for theft of consecrated items (see Listen to the Story above). It is found infrequently in the biblical text (Lev 20:14; 21:9; Judg 15:6; Deut 13:15–17), suggesting its reservation for crimes holding particular consequence for Israel's covenant life.

Before burning Achan, Israel stones him to death. Whether this was assumed in the prescribed penalty (v. 15) or whether Israel wishes to kill Achan before committing him to flames is uncertain. This form of capital punishment (here, *wayyirgemu*) is a penalty reserved for crimes such as blasphemy (Lev 24:23), offering one's children to Molech (Lev 20:2), and Sabbath breaking (Num 15:35)—all crimes which threatened the fabric of covenant life. In addition to stoning Achan, the NIV notes that Israel "stones (here a different word, *wayyisqelu*) the rest." Though the word is different than that applied to Achan, this too is a form of capital punishment reserved for serious covenant breaches such as enticing other gods (Deut 13:10), worshiping other gods (Deut 17:5), and blasphemy (1 Kgs 21:13). After Israel stones the guilty, they are then committed to the flames (v. 25).

Israel's corporate action removes what compromised their holiness before God. His fierce anger is turned away, a phrase that describes similar situations in which egregious sins are atoned for (Num 25:4; Deut 13:17; 2 Chr 29:10; 30:8). Standing under God's anger, Israel learned that "you cannot stand against your enemies" (v. 13). The next chapter shows that when God's anger is turned away, judgment is also reversed; obedient Israel will win a decisive victory over Ai at God's command.

The rock pile raised over Achan is described in the same way as those raised over the king of Ai (8:29) and Absalom (2 Sam 18:17). In those instances, the stones served as burial mounds. Stone piles could also serve as a witness or memorial (Gen 31:46–48), and this connotation could also be applied to the rocks raised over Achan (as also to the rocks over the king of Ai; 8:29). The notation that they remain "to this day" suggests a memorializing function. Earlier, Israel had placed a stone memorial commemorating the Jordan crossing (4:4–7, 20–24). It served as a reminder and teaching aid, a memorial to God's power and a call to Israel to "fear the LORD your God" (4:24). The tragedy of Achan's memorial is that it commemorates one who neglected to hold God in reverence. Instead, violating God's holiness, Achan would be remembered as a dark mark on Israel's identity. The memorial nature of the rocks over Achan is joined by the commemorative name, "The Valley of Achor."

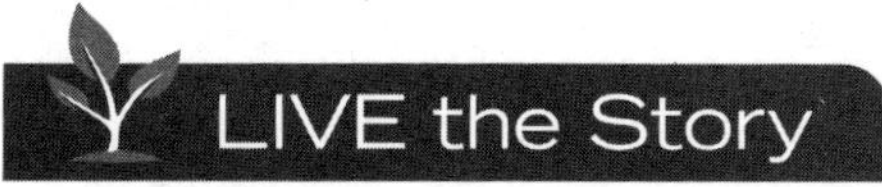


### The Cost of Sin; the Good of the Body

The terrible cost of Achan's sin and its effect on the larger community present a complex problem in this passage. The above commentary has sought to engage the biblical and cultural context to explore Israel's shared culpability and the reasons for Achan's penalty. While not wholly easing the text's difficulty, the contextual approach seeks to faithfully open the text's logic and meaning to modern audiences. But what of ongoing interaction with these challenging ideas of the cost and scope of sin? How might the church continue to reflect on this text and the ideas it presents? Does it in any way call the church to similar action?

There are many places in the biblical text that speak to the serious cost of sin and its expansive effects in the world. Relational alienation, violence, hardship and toil: these are just some of the effects revealed in Genesis 3. Sin and its effects shape the whole Old Testament narrative.[7] Because of sin's horrific nature by which the whole world came under its sway (Rom 1–3; 1 John 5:19), Christ died on the cross. This is, ultimately, the cost of sin and its remedy. Only by this death was it possible that "whoever believes in him shall not perish but have eternal life" (John 3:16).

Beyond the broad sweep of creation-fall-redemption, sin and its effects are clearly seen on an individual scale. Sins occur within families (Rebecca and Jacob deceive Isaac; Gen 27), kings sin against their subjects (David against Bathsheba; 2 Sam 11), and servants sin against their masters (Gehazi against Elijah; 2 Kgs 5).

The psalms of lament provide some especially pertinent interactions with the reality of sin's effects. Many of these psalms are those of an individual lamenting an experience of judgment for personal sin (Pss 25:18; 32:3–10; 38:1–8; 51:1–4). Other laments reveal that righteous individuals suffer as part of the community and on account of that community's sins (Pss 12:1–8; 58:1–5, 10–11). This aspect of corporate culpability and the corporate experience of discipline for sin is especially apparent in the prophetic corpus. Jeremiah was God's righteous prophet, but as part of the covenant community he suffered alongside the people on account of communal sin. His message was rejected by the people, and with them he lived through the horrors of siege and conquest. Ezekiel, deported with the exiles, likewise suffered with the people for corporate covenant sins.

In a marvelous act of substitution for the guilt of corporate sin, Isaiah's righteous sufferer takes on the community's guilt and punishment (Isa 53:4–12). In the New Testament, this passage is applied to Jesus: he is viewed as the ultimate substitution, taking upon himself the culpability of not just the Old Testament covenant community but of the whole world (Matt 8:17 [citing Isa 53:4]; Luke 22:37 [citing Isa 53:12]; John 12:38 [citing Isa 53:1]; Acts 8:32–33 [citing Isa 53:7–8]; Rom 15:21 [citing Isa 52:15]; 1 Pet 2:22–25

7. A valuable resource that traces the reality and effects of sin throughout the Old Testament and God's provision for its remedy is Mark J. Boda, *A Severe Mercy: Sin and Its Remedy in the Old Testament*, Siphrut 1 (Winona Lake: Eisenbrauns, 2009).

[citing Isa 53:4–9]).[8] Unlike Achan, who suffered for his own sin and whose death released the community from culpability, Jesus suffered for no sin of his own and paid the price to release all communal *and* individual sin.

The above passages sketch out (1) that disobedience and sin receive discipline and punishment; and (2) that one individual's sin can affect the whole community and that righteous individuals within that community can suffer as part of the community. In this way, the realities inherent in the Achan narrative find broader resonance throughout the biblical text.

The New Testament interacts further with this narrative in instructive ways. Achan's account is set at the beginning of Israel's entry to the land and provides, as the entry begins, a crucial message: that obedience leads to success in the land while disobedience leads to failure. Additionally, Achan's sin and its effect is a reminder that Israel does not act on its own accord but as God's people for God's ultimate purposes for the world. Because God is a holy God, Israel must act in holy ways. It is Israel's holiness that enables God's ongoing presence and power in its midst.

These aspects of Joshua 7 find resonance in Acts 5. There, a new covenant community begins its life as God's people. Constituted a community by the indwelling Holy Spirit, God's presence and power are in its midst. The community is thus a holy people and is to act in holiness. The sin of Ananias and Sapphira contravenes that holiness. Free to sell property and give what they wish to God, they apparently let people think they had consecrated all the proceeds. Their arrogant conspiracy to withhold funds and lie about it is met with swift and fearful retribution. Both die by God's hand when the word of judgment is pronounced against them. The result within the community is that "great fear seized the whole church and all who heard about these events" (v. 11). As in Joshua 7, the fate of Ananias and Sapphira served a purpose early in the church's life. They are a stark reminder of the holy nature of the church and the necessity of faithful living. Dealing falsely with consecrated items marred the community and was met with judgment.

In 1 Corinthias 11:17–34, those whose actions do not rightly regard the church as Christ's body face similar judgment. In that passage, the love feast prior to the Lord's Table had become a place to flaunt wealth. Some brought and ate much while others went hungry. By such inequity and mistreatment of the body, Paul charged they came to the Lord's Table in an "unworthy manner" by sinning against the "body and blood of the Lord" (v. 27). Such sinful disregard for the body of Christ was met with judgment as "many among you are weak and sick, and a number of you have fallen asleep [died]" (v. 30).

8. Several of these New Testament citations rely on the Greek version (Septuagint; LXX) of the Old Testament.

The sin of some had corporate effect by "despise[ing] the church of God by humiliating those who have nothing" (v. 22). For this sin, the arrogant face the strong judgment of the Lord (vv. 32, 34). The judgment is evidence of the seriousness of individual sin. It touches the community in profound ways. The judgment also reveals the lengths to which God goes to chastise and discipline actions that adversely affect the body.

Two final texts reveal how individual sin adversely affects the body of Christ: 1 Corinthians 5:1–8 and Galatians 5:1–12. Each text enjoins strong discipline upon the sinner for the sake of the church's welfare. Each text also likens the presence of sin in the church to a leavening agent. Left unchecked, it will leaven the whole lump of dough. This is very close to the concept of *herem* in Joshua 7. Common to these two texts are realities the church shares with Israel. That is, the church (like Israel) is a covenant community in which God's presence dwells. The church (like Israel) has been contaminated by sin through individual action. The church (like Israel) must expunge the source of that sin. The difference in these texts is how the church is to deal with the perpetrators.

In 1 Corinthians 5:1–8 the leaven is the man involved in gross sexual immorality. The group's tolerance of him is proof of the leavening effect of sin. As in Achan's story, the church is to get rid of the old yeast: the immoral man (v. 7). This is accomplished not by stoning (as for Achan), but by putting the individual out of the group, effectively casting him outside the realm of God's Spirit and presence and into the realm of Satan. The discipline was remedial for the individual, seeking the "destruction of the flesh"—the fleshly attitudes, desires, and actions opposed to God's Spirit, so that his "spirit may be saved on the day of the Lord" (v. 5). The discipline was also remedial for the church. As they rid themselves of old yeast, they were returned to their true identity: a holy people for God's dwelling ("Get rid of the old yeast, so that you may be a new unleavened batch—as you really are"; v. 7).

In Galatians 5:1–12 the leavening agent is false teachers who taught believers they must be circumcised to be justified. Paul again warns the church they are in danger of the leavening power of this false teaching. Its effect is that the church has "been alienated from Christ; you have fallen away from grace" (v. 4). Paul (in contrast to the prescription given to the Corinthian church), is vague regarding the discipline. He says only that the false teacher will have to "pay the penalty" (v. 10). So dangerous is the leavening effect of the teaching, however, that Paul graphically describes the penalty he thinks appropriate: that those who teach the necessity of circumcision for justification would "go the whole way and emasculate themselves!" (v. 12).

In Achan's story and in these texts, the importance of preserving the corporate body as the place of God's presence and power is uppermost. An individual whose sin threatens the integrity of that body must be summarily—and strongly—dealt with. In various ways they are to be cut off from the body so it can regain health, becoming in practice what it really is: God's holy people.

Sin is serious business, leavening the holy people of God. Attending to Achan's narrative as it speaks to sin's power and the community's identity should bring the church to ponder its own understandings and practices of what it tolerates without comment, to its harm.

### The LORD Is a Warrior

Israel's defeat at Ai demonstrates the flip side of the maxim "obedience leads to success in the land" demonstrated in Joshua 6. It also demonstrates the flip side of the truth that "God fights for Israel."

The portrayal of God as a warrior is common in the Old Testament. A paradigmatic portrait of God as warrior is his deliverance of Israel from Egypt. Once delivered, Israel celebrates the "LORD is a warrior; the LORD is his name" (Exod 15:1–3). The whole concept of "holy war" (see Introduction) utilizes the metaphor of God as warrior. God brings Israel into the land "by war" (Deut 4:34) and directs warfare (Deut 7:1–2; Josh 5:13–15). By his presence through the ark, God precedes Israel into battle (Num 10:35; Joshua 3–4). Repeatedly, God fights for Israel, often utilizing supernatural weapons against the enemy (Josh 10:10–14; 23:9–10). God's action on Israel's behalf is noted at Jericho (6:2, 16, 27) and at Ai (8:1, 7).

God as the divine warrior is most often conceived as fighting on behalf of Israel against its enemies. Joshua 7 shows the other side of this reality and is a reminder that God's action for Israel should not be presumed. God has, under the covenant, committed to fight on Israel's behalf (Lev 26:7–8; Deut 28:7). But covenant blessings are not Israel's prerogative; they require Israel's commitment and covenant obedience. When that commitment fails, the covenant blessings are withdrawn. In warfare, the divine warrior sets his face against Israel and they will be defeated (Lev 26:17; Deut 28:25).

This aspect of God as divine warrior is at work in Joshua 7 as Israel enters the land. It is the same aspect that appears again as Israel nears its exile from the land. The exile was the ultimate covenantal discipline for Israel's failure under the covenant. In Jeremiah 21, under Babylonian siege, King Zedekiah hopes God will again "perform wonders for us as in times past so that he [Nebuchadnezzar] will withdraw from us" (Jer 21:2). Zedekiah's words recall the great exodus event when God as divine warrior worked "wonders" (Exod 3:20; Ps 106:22, "miracles") and delivered Israel from its great enemy.

Jeremiah's response likewise references the exodus imagery, telling the king that God's "outstretched arm and mighty hand," extended on Israel's behalf at the Red Sea (Exod 6:6; Deut 4:34; Ps 136:12), will now be extended against Israel:

> I myself will fight against you with an outstretched hand and a mighty arm in furious anger and in great wrath. . . . I will give Zedekiah king of Judah, his officials and the people in this city . . . into the hands of Nebuchadnezzar king of Babylon and to their enemies who want to kill them. He will put them to the sword; he will show them no mercy or pity or compassion. (Jer 21:5–7)

The paradigm of God as a warrior involves much more than his actions for or against Israel; such a limited paradigm would offer little good news for a sinful world. Thankfully, there is more to the paradigm than this. The paradigm is one that extends throughout the Old and New Testaments, and can be identified in five phases:[9] (1) God fights on behalf of Israel against its enemies (as evidenced at the Red Sea and Jericho); (2) God fights against disobedient Israel (as evidenced at Ai, and in Jeremiah); (3) hope arises in Israel for a future divine deliverer (most apparent in the prophetic corpus); (4) Jesus fights the principalities and powers; and (5) God's ultimate victory at the final battle.

Israel's failure at Ai is instructive of the theology of Joshua regarding the role of obedience for success in the land. But it also informs the canonical expression of the divine warrior paradigm. Israel's disobedience under the covenant and the cause of its failure at Ai was an expression of human sinfulness. However committed Israel might be, it remained a sinful people whose hearts went astray from God and his covenant. Israel's experience was not unique, for such waywardness and sin is the experience of all humankind; the failure at Ai is not a unique phenomenon.

It is the fourth phase of the divine warrior paradigm that answers this problem. In the victory of Jesus on the cross, all principalities and powers raised up against God are defeated (Col 2:15; cf. Eph 1:21; Phil 2:10). Through this defeat, Christ opens the way for his disciples to live in the fullness of the new covenant, freed from sin and enabled by the Spirit to live a life pleasing to God.

The covenantal failure at Ai and God's action against Israel is not God's final word. The divine warrior has defeated the ultimate enemy of sin and now forever fights on behalf of his own people, winning both their freedom and their obedience.

---

9. An accessible exposition of this paradigm is found in Longman and Reid, *God is a Warrior*.

**Merciful History: Redeeming Sin**

Achan's sin, and the threat of destruction for all Israel, is intentionally related as Israel begins to possess the land. Together with Joshua 6 and 8, it powerfully communicates the retributive theology that underlies the book: obedience = success; disobedience = failure.

Achan's sin and its effect also became a powerful memory within Israel, appearing twice more. The first time is as the eastern tribes return home after the land is taken (Josh 22). They build an altar at the Jordan and, when this becomes known, Israel voices its fear that the altar contravenes the covenant. This would again open Israel to the consequences of disobedience and the divine warrior once again acting against them. To voice this fear, they recall the episode of Achan:

> "[D]o not rebel against the Lord or against us by building an altar for yourselves, other than the altar of the Lord our God. When Achan son of Zerah was unfaithful in regard to the devoted things, did not wrath come on the whole community of Israel? He was not the only one who died for his sin." (22:19–20)

This episode, as the book draws to a close, shows Israel has learned well the lesson of Achan. They are fearful that his error will be repeated and thus challenge the Transjordanian altar. Achan serves as a touchstone of the terrible consequences of covenant disobedience.

The second time Achan appears is in the prophet Hosea, who wrote in the eighth century BC, many years after Israel settled in the land. The record of the intervening centuries which are contained in Joshua–Kings shows Israel's ongoing covenant failures. In Hosea 1 the prophet enacts Israel's covenant history by marrying a woman who turns to adultery. In the same way, God "married" Israel at Sinai, but she turns to other lovers—the foreign nations and their gods. In naming Hosea's children, God communicates the terrible consequences due Israel under the covenant. The covenant demonstrated God's love toward them and made them his people. Now, they will be "Lo–ruhamah" ("Not loved") and "Lo–Ammi" ("Not my people"). It is a very bleak ending for the people rescued out of Egypt, sustained by God in the wilderness, and gifted with the land.

Hosea 2, however, shows that God's judgment under the covenant was not the last word. After a time of punishment, Israel would experience again God's love for his people (Hos 2:23). Hosea utilizes the marriage metaphor again; now a marriage renewed and love quickened. God will allure his bride and speak tenderly to her as he did in the wilderness. His bride will respond with love and delight (Hos 2:14–20). The images are incredibly hopeful as, out of punishment and darkness, a new lease on the covenant is discovered. Even the heavens and earth rejoice at the wonder of it (2:21–23.)

In the midst of this incredible restoration and love, this verse appears:

> "I am now going to allure her; I will lead her into the wilderness and speak tenderly to her. There I will give her back her vineyards, and will make the Valley of Achor a door of hope." (Hos 2:14–15)

The terrible Valley of Achor, a place marked by Israel's disobedience, by failure and death, is now redeemed as a symbol of hope and restoration. Achan's "trouble" (Josh 7:25) did continue in Israel, for Israel continued to sin against the covenant as Achan had. This "trouble" eventually led to Israel's exile, but God's mercy looks beyond disobedience to renewal, turning symbols of trouble and death into symbols of peace and life.

CHAPTER 7

# Joshua 8:1–29

## LISTEN to the Story

[1]Then the LORD said to Joshua, "Do not be afraid; do not be discouraged. Take the whole army with you, and go up and attack Ai. For I have
delivered into your hands the king of Ai, his people, his city and his land.
[2]You shall do to Ai and its king as you did to Jericho and its king, except
that you may carry off their plunder and livestock for yourselves. Set an
ambush behind the city."

[3]So Joshua and the whole army moved out to attack Ai. He chose thirty
thousand of his best fighting men and sent them out at night [4]with these
orders: "Listen carefully. You are to set an ambush behind the city. Don't
go very far from it. All of you be on the alert. [5]I and all those with me will
advance on the city, and when the men come out against us, as they did
before, we will flee from them. [6]They will pursue us until we have lured
them away from the city, for they will say, 'They are running away from
us as they did before.' So when we flee from them, [7]you are to rise up
from ambush and take the city. The LORD your God will give it into your
hand. [8]When you have taken the city, set it on fire. Do what the LORD has
commanded. See to it; you have my orders."

[9]Then Joshua sent them off, and they went to the place of ambush and
lay in wait between Bethel and Ai, to the west of Ai—but Joshua spent
that night with the people.

[10]Early the next morning Joshua mustered his army, and he and the
leaders of Israel marched before them to Ai. [11]The entire force that was
with him marched up and approached the city and arrived in front of it.
They set up camp north of Ai, with the valley between them and the city.
[12]Joshua had taken about five thousand men and set them in ambush
between Bethel and Ai, to the west of the city. [13]So the soldiers took up
their positions—with the main camp to the north of the city and the
ambush to the west of it. That night Joshua went into the valley.

[14]When the king of Ai saw this, he and all the men of the city hurried

out early in the morning to meet Israel in battle at a certain place overlooking the Arabah. But he did not know that an ambush had been set against him behind the city. [15]Joshua and all Israel let themselves be driven back before them, and they fled toward the wilderness. [16]All the men of Ai were called to pursue them, and they pursued Joshua and were lured away from the city. [17]Not a man remained in Ai or Bethel who did not go after Israel. They left the city open and went in pursuit of Israel.

[18]Then the LORD said to Joshua, "Hold out toward Ai the javelin that is in your hand, for into your hand I will deliver the city." So Joshua held out toward the city the javelin that was in his hand. [19]As soon as he did this, the men in the ambush rose quickly from their position and rushed forward. They entered the city and captured it and quickly set it on fire.

[20]The men of Ai looked back and saw the smoke of the city rising up into the sky, but they had no chance to escape in any direction; the Israelites who had been fleeing toward the wilderness had turned back against their pursuers. [21]For when Joshua and all Israel saw that the ambush had taken the city and that smoke was going up from it, they turned around and attacked the men of Ai. [22]Those in the ambush also came out of the city against them, so that they were caught in the middle, with Israelites on both sides. Israel cut them down, leaving them neither survivors nor fugitives. [23]But they took the king of Ai alive and brought him to Joshua.

[24]When Israel had finished killing all the men of Ai in the fields and in the wilderness where they had chased them, and when every one of them had been put to the sword, all the Israelites returned to Ai and killed those who were in it. [25]Twelve thousand men and women fell that day—all the people of Ai. [26]For Joshua did not draw back the hand that held out his javelin until he had destroyed all who lived in Ai. [27]But Israel did carry off for themselves the livestock and plunder of this city, as the LORD had instructed Joshua.

[28]So Joshua burned Ai and made it a permanent heap of ruins, a desolate place to this day. [29]He impaled the body of the king of Ai on a pole and left it there until evening. At sunset, Joshua ordered them to take the body from the pole and throw it down at the entrance of the city gate. And they raised a large pile of rocks over it, which remains to this day.

*Listening to the Text in the Story*: Exodus 14:15–28; 17:8–15; Judges 20:36–48; Annals of Thutmose III; Battle of Qadesh; Deeds of Šuppiluliuma; Nubian War Stele; Sennacherib's First Campaign against Merodach Baladan

## Hands of Power: Moses and Joshua

The battle of Ai highlights human battle tactics, but the victory is still achieved by God (8:1, 18). A similar blend of divine power and human execution is evident in Joshua's first battle (Exod 17:8–16). In that battle, human effort is apparent for Joshua "overcame the Amalekite army with the sword" (v. 13), and God's presence and power is apparent in Moses' upheld hand grasping the symbolic staff of God (Exod 17: 9). At Ai, Joshua likewise holds up the javelin until the battle is won (8:26).

A similar sign of God's power is also present at the Red Sea. There, Moses takes God's staff in his hand and holds it aloft (Exod 14:15–28). At this sign of power, the seas are parted, Israel is rescued, and Egypt defeated. Once Israel is safely through the waters, Moses again holds up his hand so that the waters return. At Ai, Joshua's action echoes that of Moses and reveals yet again that his ministry is continuous with Moses' ministry.

## Benjaminite Gibeah as Ai

The battle of Ai is a chilling paradigm for the later battle against Benjamin (Judg 20). In response to the horrific death of the Levite's concubine in Benjaminite Gibeah, Israel engages Benjamin at Gibeah and (as at Ai) is unexpectedly defeated (Judg 20:19–25). Israel then comes before God with weeping, fasting, and sacrifice in a display of penitence that surpasses Joshua's ambiguous supplication (Judg 20:26; see Josh 7:6–9). Reparation in both accounts is followed by an assurance of victory (Judg 20:28). After penitence, Israel again engages Benjamin, having first set an ambush (Judg 20:29). Benjamin is lured out of the city by Israel's feigned retreat (Judg 20:32; the same word is used in Josh 8:6, 16). In the midst of the battle the ambush enters and burns the city (Judg 20:36–38). The rising smoke alerts Israel, which launches the counterattack; terrified by the smoke, Benjamin flees (Judg 20:39–42) but is soundly defeated in battle (Judg 20:33–36, 42–46). A virtual *herem* takes place as Israel puts Benjaminite towns to the sword, "including the animals and everything else they found" (Judg 20:48). In a final resonance with the Ai paradigm, Israel burns "all the [Benjaminite] towns they came across" (v. 48).

Once these similarities are known, they affect the reading of Joshua 8. In addition to the victorious battle at Ai, the reader anticipates the foreboding future battle in which Benjamin is reconfigured as Canaanite Ai. At Ai, obedient Israel is victorious because restored covenant relationship is met by God's presence and power on Israel's behalf. But covenant obedience does not endure. By the time of the judges, Israel will be caught in repeated cycles of sin, degenerating until "everyone did as they saw fit" (Judg 21:25). The battle against Benjamin responds to such non-covenantal actions. Thus, reading canonically, the similarities to Judges 20 are a reminder that the battle of Ai is only a temporary victory; soon, covenant disobedience will return and Israel—in the tribe of Benjamin—will face Ai's fate.

## Ambush and Impalement: Common Battle Tactics

The ambush set by Joshua is not unique in the ancient Near East. Several accounts of surprise attack and ambush are available to us. In one report from the Annals of Thutmose III (fifteenth century BC), the pharaoh attacks Megiddo. He considers moving troops along a narrow road to arrive by a surprise route before the city:

> What is it like, traveling on this road which becomes narrow, since it is reported, the enemies are there, standing [outside], [and they are] becoming more numerous? Will not the horses have to go in single file and [the army] and people likewise? Will our lead troops be fighting (there) while those at the rear are standing around here in Aruns, not able to fight?[1]

After assessing other routes, Thutmose considers the element of surprise is worth the danger and time necessary in the surprise route. Once his troops have all traversed the narrow road, he mounts a successful attack against Megiddo.

Another pharaoh, Ramesses II, records a thirteenth century BC battle against Qadesh in which a Hittite ambush is set against Egyptian reinforcements marching to join Ramesses:

> Now, the despicable Fallen (chief) of Hatti, along with the many lands that were with him, stood hidden and ready, on the North-East of the (town) of Qadesh. . . . See, they had been made to stand hidden behind the town of Qadesh. Then they emerged on the South side of Qadesh, and attacked the division of Pre at its middle, as they were marching, unaware, and not prepared for fighting. Then His Majesty's troops and chariotry collapsed before them.[2]

Luckily for the Egyptian troops, Ramesses captures Hittite scouts, learns of the ambush, and rides to the rescue.[3]

Another account of a Hittite ambush is preserved in the fourteenth century BC Deeds of Šuppiluliuma. His son gives this account:

---

1. *COS* 2.2A:9.
2. Ibid., 2.5A:34.
3. Ibid., 2.5A:34; 2.5B:39

> [My father] laid an ambush [for them] and [attacked] the Ka[ška men]. [He also attacked] the auxiliaries who had come, (so that) the Kaška troops and the au[xiliary] troops [suffered many casualties].[4]

The impalement of dead bodies on stakes is also attested in ancient Near Eastern accounts. Impalement was not simply a means of execution. Its goal was utter humiliation of the enemy by imposing the dreaded fate of non-burial. Thus, Sennacherib's account of his campaign against Merodach-Baladan concludes by saying that "the enemy warriors . . . who had not submitted to my yoke, I cut down with the sword and hung on stakes."[5] Another account from the Nubian War Stele notes that enemy Libyans are "cast to the ground by hundred-thousands and ten-thousands, the remainder being impaled ('put to the stake')."[6] Joshua's vicious act is in keeping with his times.

## EXPLAIN the Story

The defeat at Ai ("The Ruin") occurred because of Achan's disobedience. In this chapter, God's "fierce anger" has turned away (7:26), and he promises to deliver Ai into Israel's hands. To emphasize the correlation between obedience and success, this chapter highlights in several ways Israel's obedience to God's commands. First, the action is commenced by God's command (vv. 1–2) and new instructions are likewise initiated by God (v. 18). Second, Joshua's actions and his own commands to the army (vv. 3–8) follow God's instructions, often presented in the same words:

1. God commands the "whole army" (v. 1); Joshua and the "whole army" move to attack Ai (v. 3);
2. They are to "go up and attack" (v. 1); the army "moved out to attack" (v. 3; the words are the same in Hebrew)
3. God promises "I have delivered" (v. 1); Joshua affirms God "will give" the city (v. 7; the words are the same in Hebrew);
4. God commands they "Do to Ai and its king as you did to Jericho and its king" (v. 2); Joshua charges that Ai be set on fire, which was the fate of Jericho (v. 8, 28). Additionally, Ai's inhabitants are destroyed (the important root *ḥrm*, so prominent in the Jericho account, is used) and the king executed (vv. 26–28);

4. Ibid., 1.74:186.
5. Ibid., 2.119A:302.
6. K. A. Kitchen, ed., *Merneptah & the Late Nineteenth Dynasty*, vol. IV of *Ramesside Inscriptions: Translated & Annotated* (Oxford, UK/Malden MA, U.S.A.: Blackwell Publishing, 2003), 1 (line 34:10).

5. God excludes (*raq*) the plunder from destruction (v. 2); for reasons of narrative tension, Joshua does not immediately communicate this key command. Only in v. 27 is the exception noted ("But" [*raq*] Israel did plunder);
6. God commands the ambush (v. 2); Joshua sets it up in verses 3–7a, 13.

**Instructions for Battle (8:1–9)**

God's first words are reassuring: Joshua is to be neither afraid nor discouraged. The encouragement is that of Deuteronomy 1:21, where it accompanied the command to take the land according to God's promises. The use of the same words is a strong reminder that the promise of land is still in force. The encouragement is also similar to that given Joshua when commissioned by Moses (Deut 31:6) and God (Josh 1:9). These echoes remind Joshua that he is still the appointed leader and, by recalling the words of Joshua 1, that a new beginning is underway after the covenant breach of chapter 7.

Emphasizing that taking the land was a task for all Israel, God commands Joshua to employ the "whole army" (v. 1). This is a marked contrast to the abortive first attempt in which Joshua dispatched a small contingent (7:4). After commanding the attack, God promises victory over Ai. The Hebrew promise can be rendered, "See! I have delivered into your hands" (v. 1). This precise formulation is found only in two other places. In Deuteronomy 2:24, after the wilderness generation dies, God commands the new generation to their first action. He promises Sihon to Israel using the same words. In Joshua 6:2 God uses the same formulation to promise Jericho and its king to Israel. The action against Ai thus begins in confident company, bolstering Israel's courage after the earlier failed attack. The delineation of success to include "his people . . . and his land" goes beyond the king and city promised at Jericho. This would further bolster Israel's courage.

The "king" of Ai (as at Jericho; see comments on Josh 2) is not necessarily a powerful sole ruler but may be a petty ruler or an administrator whose power is granted by a larger city (possibly Bethel). Such a connection to Bethel would explain Bethel battling alongside Ai (v. 17). The extent of Ai's "people and land" is unknown and the phrase may simply intend to assure Israel of total victory.

Ai and its king are to be dealt with as Jericho and its king. The fate of Jericho is stated in chapter 6, but the king's fate is not. That must be extrapolated from 8:29: death and impalement (if not also burial) at the city gates (see also 10:1, 28, 30). The great difference in the disposal of Ai is that now Israel is allowed its plunder and livestock; the exception is granted with the strong word *raq* ("except"). The exception is a reminder that Ai is different than

Jericho, which was wholly devoted to the LORD (6:17–19, 21). The violation of Jericho's ban was disastrous. Now the LORD makes clear the usual terms of warfare apply here. These allowed the taking of plunder (Deut 20:16–18; see also Deut 2:35; 3:7). Thus, at Ai, Israel is granted latitude in comparison to Jericho. Nevertheless, obedience to the different command remains crucial to Israel's success.

Finally, almost as an afterthought, God commands an ambush be set "behind" the city—that is, to the west of the city between Ai and Bethel (vv. 9, 12). The details of the ambush and the general attack strategy are left to Joshua and are slowly revealed as the narrative progresses. No mention of the upheld javelin is made here. Only in the need of the moment does God reveal this aspect of the plan.

Given God's promise and instructions, Joshua acts immediately. He and the "whole army moved out to attack" (v. 3) as God had instructed. Joshua's commands first turn to the last item of God's instruction: the ambush. Joshua details its deployment (v. 4) and then relates the strategy of the main force (vv. 5–6) before describing the ambush strategy (vv. 7–8). The directions for the ambush begin and end Joshua's words, suggesting the importance of the ambush to the mission's success.

Joshua's instructions in verses 3–8 are enveloped by attention to obedience, signified by the Hebrew word for "command" in verses 4 (here translated "with these orders") and 8 ("Do what the LORD has commanded . . . you have my orders [in Hebrew, "I have commanded you"]"). As God's leader, Joshua communicates God's commands. Israel's success (a lesson learned at Jericho and the first attempt at Ai) is dependent on following God's commands through his leader Joshua. Joshua's instructions are also enveloped by the call to "See!" in verse 4 (NIV has "Listen carefully") and verse 8 ("See to it"). Israel "sees" the whole plan; later, the king of Ai will "see" the Israelite main force (v. 14) but not the ambush. Short-sightedness will broker destruction.

The ambush force of thirty thousand (v. 3) is exceptionally large and it is difficult to think how so many could be positioned secretly. It is better understood as thirty "units" as the word *'eleph* (here translated as "thousand") can also denote a military unit of undisclosed size, perhaps ranging from five to fourteen men.[7] While this reading significantly reduces the numbers, it does nothing to align with the five thousand men (or five units) designated for the ambush in verse 12. Perhaps the difficulty in one or other of the

7. The word may be so used in places such as Num 1:16 (and in the census lists that follow); Num 10:4; Judg 6:15; 1 Chr 12:20. This conclusion is based on a careful assessment of the census lists of Num 1 and 26 within their historical context. See particularly pp. 60–63 in G. E. Mendenhall, "The Census Lists of Numbers 1 and 26," *JBL* 77 (1958): 52–66.

numbers lies with a scribal error. The ambush is deployed at night to ensure its secrecy and positioned west of Ai, close enough to mount a swift attack. They are to be "on the alert," perhaps for some prearranged signal or for the army's exit from Ai. We are left to speculate that some sign is agreed upon that unleashes the ambush. The javelin is not revealed until the heat of the battle but even then, its role as a signal is difficult to determine (see discussion at v. 18 below).

The plan turns to the action of the main force. Their success relies on Ai coming out "as they did before" and thinking Israel flees "as they did before" (vv. 5–6). In the earlier failed attempt, Israel "fled" (Josh 7:4; from the root *nws*; NIV translates as "were routed") before Ai and Ai "pursued" (Josh 7:5; from the root *rdp*; NIV translates as "chased") them. Joshua's instructions and the event itself repeatedly use these same words so that the narrative itself recreates the "as before-ness" of the first attempt:

Joshua's plan (vv. 5–6) in the words of the first attempt.
—"We will flee (*nws*) from them" (8:5)
—Ai will say, "They are running (*nws*) as before" (8:6)
—"So when we flee (*nws*) from them . . . (8:6)
The event (vv. 15–17) in the words of the first attempt.
—Israel "fled (*nws*) toward the wilderness" (v. 15)
—"All the men of Ai were called to pursue (*rdp*) them" (v.16)
—"They pursued (*rdp*) Joshua" (v. 16)
—"They left the city open and went in pursuit (*rdp*) of Israel" (v.17)

The success of the plan is that Israel will "lure" Ai from the city (v. 6). The plan succeeds; Israel follows Joshua's commands, recreates the first attack, and Ai is indeed "lured" from the city (v. 16).

The ambush is then instructed to "take" (from the root *yrsh*) the emptied city (vv. 7–8). The word has theological import in this chapter, reaffirming Israel in its covenant status and the concomitant gift of land. The word has the same root as used in 1:11, 15 when Israel was to "take possession" of the land, and the root last appeared in 3:10 when Israel was to "drive out" the nations. After five chapters, it appears again as a reminder of the ongoing covenantal promise of land. Israel will "take" the land through its obedience and God's presence and promise. The ambush is also to "set [the town] on fire" (v. 8) and they do so in verse 19. Later, different words are used to describe a second action, as Joshua "burned Ai" (v. 28).

After the instructions are given, the narrative backtracks to the action of verse 3, noting again that Joshua sent off the ambush. Having done so, Joshua remains that night with the people (v. 9).

## Deployment for Battle (8:10–13)

The ambush force deployed, Joshua sets out "early in the morning." This phrase has been used three times in the book thus far (3:1; 6:12; 7:16), and each time it demonstrates Joshua's quick obedience; the phrase characterizes him similarly here. He and the "leaders of Israel" lead the army. Joshua last appeared with the leaders in 7:6 as they sought the reason for the failure at Ai. It is fitting that as that failure is reversed, the leaders again appear with Joshua. Joshua and the leaders march with the army and camp before Ai with a valley (*gay'*) between them and Ai. This valley gives the camp some protection (vv. 10–11). Once again, the ambush is noted (v. 12).

Several difficulties are apparent in connection with the deployment of the ambush and the army's march to Ai. First, there is a chronological difficulty: was the ambush deployed at night (vv. 3–4)? Or, are those in the ambush part of the army's march to Ai, to be deployed after its arrival before the city (v. 11)? NASB, NET, NLT, and NRSV take the latter option, a translational decision that awkwardly deploys the ambush twice (in vv. 3–4, and v. 12). Second, Joshua appears to deploy the ambush, and then spend the night in two different ways (and possibly places): "with the people" (v. 9) and by going "into the valley" (v. 13). Third, the numbers cited for the ambush are discrepant (see discussion at v. 3). It is no wonder that very different pictures are sketched in commentaries, and the narrative can be judged "rough and confused."[8]

Granted, the narrative presents challenges, but it is not so "rough and confused" that a clear picture cannot be gained, albeit not one that fully resolves all difficulties. Two common approaches show a responsible way forward. In the first, verses 3–9 preview the plan: the whole force will go up to Ai, from there the ambush will be deployed at night, but Joshua will remain with the people. These events then take place in "real time" in verses 10–12 as the whole army moves to Ai during the day, the ambush is dispatched at night, and Joshua remains with the people (army). Later that night Joshua moves into the valley. One of the very real difficulties of this reading, however, is that one imagines that the army encamped at Ai would be under very close surveillance by Ai. This would make it difficult for an ambush to be deployed undetected.

A second common approach is that taken by the NIV translators. In it, verses 3–9 unfold events in real time. The ambush is instructed and deployed under cover of darkness, far from Ai's watchful walls. The remaining force ("the entire force that was with him") sets out the next morning and camps before Ai (v. 11). At the moment the main army makes camp, the reader is reminded of the larger plan through a recapitulation. Joshua "had taken . . .

8. This is the judgment of Richard D. Nelson, *Joshua*, OTL (Louisville: Westminster John Knox, 1997), 110.

and set" (v. 12) the ambush, and it lies hidden west of the city—out of sight of both Bethel and Ai. Verse 13 then summarizes the whole scenario of troop deployment: the main camp north of the city and the ambush west of it. This reading follows a more natural narrative flow. It is not, however, without its difficulties. Significantly, it requires the ambush be hidden for all of a day and a night, placing it at risk of discovery.

After moving to Ai Joshua goes that night into the "valley" (v. 13; *'emeq*). This is a different geographical feature than the valley in verse 11. An *'emeq* is a broad, flat valley suitable for battle, being large enough for troop muster (Judg 7:8, 12) and the movement of iron chariots (Judg 1:19, 34; Isa 22:7). Joshua may be making a reconnaissance trip to survey the battlefield. More likely, under cover of darkness, Joshua moves his troops into the valley, positioned for battle.

### Victory Achieved (8:14–23)

In these verses, the narrative replicates the hurry and confusion of battle. Narrative action moves quickly and is presented with continuously shifting perspectives. One sees the battle first from one side and then from the other; by verse 22, the perspectives are confused and unclear:

v. 14 the king of Ai sees; he and his men hurry out
v. 15 Joshua and all Israel feign retreat
v. 16–17 all the men of Ai pursue
v. 18 Joshua holds up the javelin
v. 19 the ambush attacks
v. 20 the men of Ai see the smoke and panic
v. 21 Joshua and all Israel see the ambush is successful
v. 22 the melee of battle blurs the action (see discussion at v. 22 below)

While shifting perspectives recreate the confusion of battle, the language reveals the battle unfolding exactly as Joshua planned. The similarity of language between Joshua's plan and its execution is generally apparent in the NIV, and the following reference to the use of particular Hebrew words clarifies this further:

| | | |
|---|---|---|
| v. 5 | Plan | Joshua plans they "will come out after us" (using the Hebrew roots *yts'* and *qr'*; literally, "come out and meet us") |
| v. 14 | Action | Ai hurries out to "meet Israel in battle" (using the same Hebrew roots); |

| | | |
|---|---|---|
| v. 5 | Plan | Joshua plans that Israel "will flee" (using the Hebrew root *nws*) |
| v. 15 | Action | Israel is driven back and "fled" (using the same Hebrew root); |

| | | |
|---|---|---|
| v. 6 | Plan | Joshua plans that Ai "will pursue us" (using the Hebrew roots *yts'* and *'hr*; literally, "go out after") |
| v. 16 | Action | Ai is called to "pursue them" and "pursued Joshua" (using the Hebrew roots *rdp* and *'hr* in both cases; literally, "pursue after") |
| v. 17 | Action | There was none who did not "go after" Israel; Ai "went in pursuit" of Israel (using first the Hebrew roots *yts'* and *'hr*; and then *rdp* and *'hr*); |

| | | |
|---|---|---|
| v. 6 | Plan | Joshua plans that they will "lure them away from the city" (using the Hebrew root *ntq*) |
| v. 16 | Action | Ai is "lured away from the city" (using the same Hebrew root). |

It may be that the battle is a tumultuous melee, but God empowers Israel's battle strategy: it is utterly successful, working according to plan.

Joshua had repositioned his troops during the night, ready for battle. Seeing this in the morning, the king of Ai quickly deploys his troops, but because he does not "see" (v. 14) all the plans that Joshua had earlier commanded his troops to "see" (vv. 4, 8), his hurried action (v. 14) will be defeated by the hurried action of the ambush troops (v. 19). The two forces meet "at a certain place overlooking the Arabah." This is possibly the *'emeq* of verse 13 and is a place from which ready retreat could be made toward the camp at Gilgal, perhaps even along the route of Israel's earlier retreat (7:5).

The feigned retreat is so successful that verses 16–17 pile clause on clause to show how completely Ai thinks the battle is "as before" (vv. 5–6) and is taken in by the ruse:

v. 16 "All the men . . . were called to pursue them"
v. 16 "they pursued Joshua and were lured away from the city"
v. 17 "Not a man remained in Ai or Bethel"
v. 17 there was none "who did not go up after Israel"
v. 17 "they left the city open"
v. 17 "and went in pursuit of Israel"

At this point, Bethel suddenly appears to fight alongside its near neighbor, Ai. Bethel's support is likely as Bethel could expect an attack, should Ai fall. While this makes Bethel's appearance understandable, no previous hint prepares for Bethel's arrival. The point of Bethel's sudden appearance is to show how completely Israel's ruse works. It draws out all possible defenses for "not a man remained in Ai or Bethel who did not go out after Israel" (v. 17). The suggestive hyperbole (given there remain people in Ai in v. 24) forces the point: Israel's attack is a real threat and must be stopped. Should Bethel and Ai fail, Israel will win the city.

With so many in pursuit and Israel on the run, one might wonder if feigned retreat is about to become full out rout. The battle is at the turning point. At this crucial juncture, the LORD once again shows up, but in an unexpected fashion. He commands Joshua to hold out the javelin, a curved scimitar-like weapon (it is the type of weapon wielded by Goliath in 1 Sam 17:6, 45), toward Ai. In obedience, Joshua does so, and this serves as a signal to the ambush.

It is difficult to understand how a weapon lifted up in battle east of Ai could be seen by those in hiding west of the city, and suggestions such as a string of pre-arranged scouts at strategic locations transmitting the signal to those in ambush might be considered. But while the javelin does somehow precipitate the ambush, its greater power is its symbolic meaning. The javelin in Joshua's upraised hand echoes the ministry of Moses holding up the staff of God in Exodus 14 and 17. In those instances, God's power won the battle for his people. Additionally, according to the iconography of the ancient Near East, an upraised hand symbolizes power. It is not surprising, then, that the two references to Joshua's upraised hand in verses 17–18 form an envelope surrounding confirmation of victory:

> "Hold out toward Ai the javelin that is in your hand
>     for into your hand I will deliver the city."
> So Joshua held out toward the city the javelin that was in his hand.

The javelin held up in Joshua's hand signals the doom of the city (indeed, it is not lowered until the city is destroyed in v. 26). God had promised to deliver Ai (v. 1), a promise Joshua reiterated (v. 7). Now, with the sign of God's power in Joshua's upraised hand, the promise is reaffirmed. Ai will fall by God's power exercised through his people.

The king of Ai had moved quickly (v. 14) but did so without seeing the full plan and therefore without success. The ambush now moves quickly and, having seen the whole plan (vv. 4, 8), success is guaranteed. At the signal of doom, they enact Joshua's command. They "rose quickly . . . rushed forward . . . entered the city . . . and captured it." Their success is clear; they "set [the city] on fire" just as Joshua had ordered (vv. 8, 19).

The battle suddenly turns against Ai. Looking back, they see the smoke and finally "see" the full plan. A small Hebrew word left untranslated communicates their surprise: "The men of Ai looked back and *behold* (!!) saw the smoke . . ." (v. 20). Their shocked surprise turns to panic as they are caught in a pincer movement. Israel, once routed (*hpk*) by Ai (7:8), now "turned back" (*hpk*) and routs Ai (v. 20). The confusion on the battlefield is somewhat replicated in the Hebrew (v. 22), for the subject and object of the phrases, "came out of the city against them" and "cut them down" is not explicitly stated. The context clarifies this, as does the NIV, by specifying that it is "those in the ambush" and "Israel" who act against fighters from Ai. Ai is cut down in the confusion with no survivors or fugitives (v. 22; the phrase also occurs in Jer 42:17; 44:14; Lam 2:22; "no survivors" is found in Deut 2:34; 3:3; Josh 10:20–40; 11:8; 2 Kgs 10:11; "no fugitives" is found in 2 Kgs 9:15; Ezek 6:8; Amos 9:1). The king is seized (that is, "taken") to Joshua; the verb used echoes Joshua's initial command to take the city (v. 8).

**After the Battle (8:24–29)**

The chapter draws to a close by returning to the opening command to "do to Ai and its king as you did to Jericho and its king." Verse 24 expands on the "no survivors nor fugitives" of verse 22, describing the pursuit and death of the army on the battlefield and in the wilderness. Then, "all the Israelites" kill the inhabitants of Ai. The description is hyperbolic, emphasizing the totality of the work (vv. 24–25): "everyone had been put to the sword," "killed those who were in [Ai]," "twelve thousand men and women," "all the people of Ai," "Joshua did not draw back his hand . . . until he had destroyed all who lived in Ai."

The twelve thousand killed is questionable as an accurate tally. The city had been described as having few people in it (7:3), and twelve thousand is perhaps an inflated number intended to highlight the scope of Israel's victory. It might designate not thousands killed but military units (as noted above at v. 3). Such a designation would be expected if Ai was a military outpost to Bethel. The twelve thousand is said to include "men and women." But once again, this appears to be the hyperbole of ancient Near Eastern accounts; a way of emphasizing Israel's great victory without providing specific reference to the actual gender of those killed (see commentary at 6:21 for further discussion).

Whatever the accounting, the inhabitants, as at Jericho, are "destroyed." The term is that used in the Jericho accounts and is yet another hyperbolic marker of such ancient Near Eastern conquest accounts (see Introduction and

Listen to the Story in Josh 6). Finally (v. 26), the javelin is held up in Joshua's hand until the action against Ai is completed, symbolizing God's power in the battle.

The narrative now comes to the crucial point of failure at Jericho: the plunder (v. 27). God had commanded Israel might take plunder at Ai according to the normal procedure of warfare (see discussion at v. 2). For all Joshua's careful communication of battle plans, the narrative has given no indication Joshua communicated anything about the disposition of plunder. The silence creates narrative tension: had Joshua communicated the command? Would the people obey it now, or would they fail as at Jericho? This verse relieves the tension: "But (*raq*) Israel did carry off for themselves . . . the plunder." Utilizing *raq* employs the same word as the Lord's "except" in verse 2, making apparent Israel's obedience. Israel has indeed acted "as the Lord had instructed Joshua" (v. 27). They have learned at Jericho that, even regarding plunder, there is a correlation of obedience to success.

Like Jericho, Ai is burned. It is also made a "permanent heap of ruins," a phrase applied only to Ai and to the apostate city in Deuteronomy 13:16[17]. Its fate matches it name, for Ai means "The Ruin." Ai remains desolate "to this day" and is for Israel a permanent memorial to the hard lesson of Ai: disobedience is costly. Only obedience takes the land.

The first word in God's command to Joshua was that God would deliver Ai's king into Joshua's hands (v. 1). His fate was to be that of Jericho's king (although that king's fate was not recorded in Joshua 6). Ai's king is killed and his body impaled (see also Josh 10:26–27). The brutal display is intended as a post-death shaming of the body. At sunset, the body is taken down and disposed. The action is similar to the law dealing with criminals who have been executed and their bodies exposed. In that law, the body is not to be left hanging overnight but is to be buried, lest the land be desecrated (Deut 21:22–23). Although that law does not here apply (as it concerns criminals, not captured kings), it reflects the concern behind Joshua's action. Though a body may be shamed in punishment, whether it is that of a criminal (as in Deut 21:22–23) or a defeated enemy, it should not be left to decay and defile the land.

As a testimony at the gate of his ruined city, a burial cairn is placed over the king's body. They "raised a large pile of rocks over it, which remains to this day." The phrase is identical to that which describes the large pile raised over Achan (7:26). Thus, the ending of this chapter mirrors the ending of the tragic Achan narrative. In each, two signs commemorate the events: the place is named (the Valley of Achor; The Ruin), and a large pile of rocks becomes a witness "to this day."

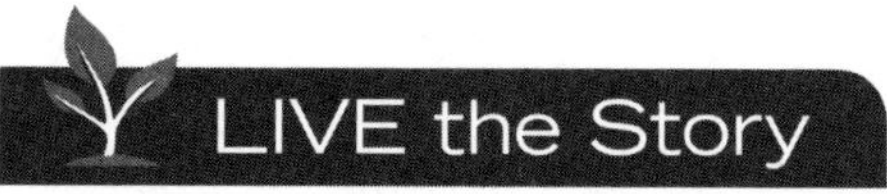


### God's Anger, and God's Commitment

Joshua 7 and 8 together make a point crucial to Israel's successful entry to the land: obedience leads to success, while disobedience leads to failure. In Joshua 7, Israel's failure is specifically tied to Achan's sin, which rouses God's anger that "burns against Israel" (7:1). Under God's anger, Israel is defeated in its first attempt against Ai.

The defeat at Ai is not Israel's first experience of God's holy anger. Even though Joshua leads the new generation into the land, the failure at Ai could easily fit into the experiences of the wilderness generation. Many times in those years God's anger burned against his people for their covenant failures. Despite the provision of manna, the Israelites complained—a complaint that Moses characterizes as evidence Israel has "rejected the Lord, who is among you" (Num 11:20). The rejection is met by God's anger (Num 11:10). When Aaron and Miriam challenge Moses' role as God's representative, God's anger burns against them (Num 12:9). The great sin at Baal Peor (Num 25:3) and the Transjordanian rejection of the promised land (Num 32:10) are each met by God's burning anger. In time, God's anger is turned away through the intercession of Moses, through acts of penitence, or by purging the offense from the people. In each instance, God remains committed to Israel because of the covenant.

Israel's experience of God's covenant is illuminated by events at Mount Sinai. Even while Moses was receiving God's law by which the people would be distinguished as his covenant partner, the people sin with the golden calf. God proposes to let his anger burn against Israel (Exod 32:10), but Moses' intercession averts this outcome. It is during this defining episode that God reveals the complexity of his character. He is a God

> compassionate and gracious . . . , slow to anger, abounding in love and faithfulness, maintaining love to thousands, and forgiving wickedness, rebellion and sin. Yet he does not leave the guilty unpunished. (Exod 34:6–7)

God's character is, from this description, weighted toward gracious acts. More is said of his compassion, grace, love, and faithfulness than of his anger. Anger is present but "slow," suggesting God's longsuffering character. Likewise, God notes the reality of wickedness, rebellion, and sin that calls for punishment. But this is accompanied by his commitment to forgiveness.

The initial failure at Ai arises out of God's slow anger directed against his covenant people. Entry to the land came with Moses' urging to

> "[f]ear the LORD your God, serve him only. . . . Be sure to keep the commands of the LORD your God and the stipulations and decrees he has given you. Do what is right and good in the LORD's sight, so that it may go well with you and you may go in and take over the good land the LORD promised on oath to your ancestors." (Deut 6:13, 17–18)

At Ai, Israel has turned from this urging and experiences the consequences.

Joshua 8 tells the other side of God's covenant character. Israel's second, successful attempt at Ai arises not only because they are obedient to God's commands. It is also because the purging of Achan's sin has turned God's anger in a manner similar to that described in Deuteronomy 13:17–18. Israel atones for its sin, and forgiveness is extended. God's presence and power again accompany the Israelites, and they are successful.

Israel's psalmists knew well God's mercy extended after sin. God's anger "lasts only a moment, but his favor lasts a lifetime" (Ps 30:5). Iniquity is met with forgiveness, and favor comes upon the land as God's fierce anger turns away (Ps 85:1–2). There is even the testimony that God's compassion and grace "does not treat us as our sins deserve" (Ps 103:10). As at Ai, Israel's repentance is met with God's presence and forgiveness. There is once again the experience of covenantal blessing.

God's anger against sin is also a New Testament reality. Any characterization of God in the Old Testament as solely a God of wrath, and God in the New Testament as solely a God of mercy, is a poor reading of both Testaments.

In the Old Testament as well as the New, God shows both anger and mercy. In the New Testament, God's anger is expressed as a present reality (John 3:36; Rom 1:18; Eph 5:6; 1 Thess 2:16). More frequently, God's anger is anticipated as a future reality (Matt 3:7; Luke 3:7; 21:23; Rom 2:5–8; Col 3:6; 1 Thess 1:10; Rev 6:16–17; 14:10, 19; 15:1, 7; 16:1, 19; 19:15). The New Testament also shows God's mercy. Under the first covenant, Israel experienced God's mercy following intercession, penitence, and purification—and sometimes, even in the absence of these actions! Under the new covenant God now provides a way that his anger might be forever turned aside and his full presence experienced. This occurs through the sacrifice of Jesus the Christ. By it, the believer is justified and removed from God's wrath both in the present and in the future (Rom 5:9; 1 Thess 1:10; 5:9). Rather than alienation, there is the presence and power of God, and the experience of the "rest" promised Joshua, but fully achieved through Christ (Heb 4:8–11).

## Remembering to Remember

Israel's victory at Ai can never be recounted without a tone of regret. It can never be simply a thrilling story of clever battle won against a duped enemy; a second try that redeems earlier defeat. This is no Saturday matinee movie of derring-do in battle. It is too terrible for that.

It is terrible because it involves death: of thirty-six Israelites (7:5) and many more Canaanites. Even though it is difficult to determine exactly the number intended in 8:25 (see Explain the Story above) and even though influenced by hyperbole, it is clear that many people died. Even the long purposes of God for the redemption of the world that called for Israel's habitation within a secured land; even the sinful culture of the Canaanites against which God brings judgment (see Gen 15:16; see the discussion of both in the Introduction) do not change the fact presented in this account: people died in the land entry. These are people who—however fallen—are made in the *imago Dei*, the image of God. Surely, we must mourn such loss and consider that God also mourns over the destruction of that which he created.

The terrible cost of Ai for Israel is clear in the memorial embedded in each of Joshua 7 and 8. Achan's death in the Valley of Achor is memorialized by a "large pile of rocks, which remains to this day" (7:26); the King of Ai's death at the gate of Ai is also memorialized by a "large pile of rocks . . . which remains to this day" (8:29). The phrasing is identical. Together with the fact each event is associated with a fateful name (Valley of Achor, Ai ["The Ruin"]), the two memorials mark this one story with somber warning.

The warning is that Achan's sin threatened all Israel. Penitential action was costly. The warning is that victory over Ai and its king came only after initial defeat: covenant sinfulness resulted in failure. The warning "to this day" is that Israel must remain faithful under the covenant if they are to be God's people in God's land for God's purposes.

Israel can never assume itself to be inherently righteous—Israel is, in fact, no more righteous than the Canaanites (Deut 9:4–6). Israel receives the land because of God's grace and his promises to Abraham. It is only the covenant that sets Israel apart as God's people. It must remember God's grace and respond with thankfulness expressed through covenant obedience. Otherwise, it will be as sinful as the Canaanites and fall under God's judgment.

As explored in Listen to the Story above, the structure of Joshua 8 anticipates the account in Judges 20 in which Benjamin appears to have forgotten the warning memorialized at Achor and Ai. In Judges 20, Benjamin sins. It is only one episode in Judges depicting the downward spiral of sin in which Israel repeatedly forgets the covenant. Throughout Judges–2 Kings this is Israel's story: forgetfulness and sin. Ultimately, forgetfulness and covenant failure on their part leads to the discipline of exile.

The church must also be a people of remembrance, for remembrance can inform present faithfulness. We remember the cross, of course, at the Lord's Table. We proclaim the terrible cost that God himself paid in battling sin and we anticipate the final battle in which death itself will be defeated (1 Cor 15:24–28; Rev 20:14).

But the church must also be a student of its own family history, seeking greater faithfulness and not repeating the sins of the past. In the Canadian context, many churches were participants in the Residential School system—a government and church-sponsored system begun in the 1870s that was not fully abandoned until 1996.[9] First Nations children were systematically removed from their homes and placed in residential schools, robbed of family, home, and culture, and suffering many forms of abuse. The system was designed to "kill the Indian in the child."[10]

Given the fact that misapplication of the text of Joshua undergirded much colonial expansion and contributed to attitudes that fostered such schools, the call to remember "to this day" found in Joshua 7–8 provides a chilling call to these churches. There must be acknowledgement that Joshua has been horribly misused, particularly in the justification of colonial expansion that could equate First Nations people with the Canaanites. Any system that arose out of such thinking must be vigorously opposed.

In 2014, while Canadians awaited the results of The Truth and Reconciliation Commission's report on Residential Schools, a ceremony took place near the Museum of Human Rights in Winnipeg, Canada. The ceremony was on the grounds of The Forks, at the confluence of the Red and Assiniboine Rivers, a location at which First Nations gathered for centuries and which is now parkland. The ceremony installed a stone monument honoring survivors of Residential Schools. Conceived by a group of concerned individuals and churches, the monument was donated by a member of a local Anglican Church (one of the denominations that participated in running Residential Schools).

---

9. The system included not only the Residential Schools but through the decades 1960–1980, the "Sixties Scoop." This was another iteration of government policy against First Nations. It involved government workers taking children (without consent, and often without warning) from their homes and placing them in (most often) non-aboriginal foster homes. The effects of both Residential Schools and the Scoop are long-term and devastating. See Andrew Russell, "What was the '60s Scoop'? Aboriginal children taken from homes a dark chapter in Canada's history," *Global News* report posted August 23, 2016 at https://globalnews.ca/news/2898190/what-was-the-60s-scoop-aboriginal-children-taken-from-homes-a-dark-chapter-in-canadas-history/.

10. This reference is found on pages 130, 369, 375, and 376 in *Honouring the Truth: Reconciling the Future. Summary of the Final Report of the Truth and Reconciliation Commission of Canada.* Available online at http://nctr.ca/assets/reports/Final%20Reports/Executive_Summary_English_Web.pdf.

Among the attendees were First Nations peoples, Christians, and church leaders. As the hole for the monument was dug, Elder Sylvia James (a First Nation elder who collaborated on the monument project) commented:

> We were witness to reconciliation taking place. . . . It was an awesome feeling watching this unfold. . . . When I looked into the hole I was reminded of the hurt, shameful damaged awful dreams being laid to rest and new beginnings for new life coming up. . . . We are sending the nightmares away and beginning the healing journey in remembering those who didn't get a chance to witness this.[11]

This monument in its memorial, penitential, and reconciling power is a vivid modern-day example of the "large pile of rocks" of Joshua 7–8.

In 2015, the Truth and Reconciliation Commission of Canada released its report on residential schools, which included many calls for ongoing action toward reconciliation.[12] One response to the report came from the Anglican Church in Canada. It set aside June 21 each year as National Aboriginal Day of Prayer, a day to remember the church's role in the Residential School system, repent of attitudes that contribute to such actions, and pray together with our Aboriginal brothers and sisters in the faith.

Appointed for that day is the following prayer:

> *Creator God,*
> *from you every family in heaven and on earth takes its name.*
> *You have rooted and grounded us in your covenant love,*
> *and empowered us by your Spirit*
> *to speak the truth in love,*
> *and to walk in your way towards justice and wholeness.*
> *Mercifully grant that your people,*
> *journeying together in partnership,*
> *may be strengthened and guided*
> *to help one another*
> *to grow into the full stature of Christ,*
> *who is our light and our life.*
> *Amen.*[13]

---

11. Elder Sylvia James in Meagan Fiddler, "Residential school students honoured with monument in Winnipeg," *CBC News* report and video posted May 26, 2014 at http://www.cbc.ca/news/canada/manitoba/residential-school-students-honoured-with-monument-in-winnipeg-1.2654447.

12. The Truth and Reconciliation Report can be accessed at http://nctr.ca/reports.php. The response to that report by the Anglican Church of Canada can be found here at http://www.anglican.ca/news/response-of-the-churches-to-the-truth-and-reconciliation-commission-of-canada/30010922/.

13. Found at http://www.anglican.ca/faith/worship/resources/nadppropers/.

The above prayer and the National Aboriginal Day of Prayer are very small steps toward truth and reconciliation in Canada. But as these words are prayed, they too can serve as a memorial; a "large pile of rocks, which remain to this day," marking a profound past wrong that must never be repeated and pointing forward to new faithfulness, acknowledging our covenant Lord created and cares for all peoples.

## LISTEN to the Story

[30]Then Joshua built on Mount Ebal an altar to the LORD, the God of
Israel, [31]as Moses the servant of the LORD had commanded the Israelites.
He built it according to what is written in the Book of the Law of Moses—an altar of uncut stones, on which no iron tool had been used. On it they offered to the LORD burnt offerings and sacrificed fellowship
offerings. [32]There, in the presence of the Israelites, Joshua wrote on stones
a copy of the law of Moses. [33]All the Israelites, with their elders, officials
and judges, were standing on both sides of the ark of the covenant of the LORD, facing the Levitical priests who carried it. Both the foreigners living among them and the native-born were there. Half of the people stood in front of Mount Gerizim and half of them in front of Mount Ebal, as Moses the servant of the LORD had formerly commanded when he gave instructions to bless the people of Israel.

[34]Afterward, Joshua read all the words of the law—the blessings and the
curses—just as it is written in the Book of the Law. [35]There was not a word
of all that Moses had commanded that Joshua did not read to the whole assembly of Israel, including the women and children, and the foreigners who lived among them.

*Listening to the Text in the Story*: Genesis 12:7; Exodus 24:3–11; Deuteronomy 11:26–32; 27:1–26; Joshua 24

**A Covenant People**

At Shechem between Ebal and Gerizim Israel renews its covenant with God. Israel's covenantal nature traces back to the covenant promises of land, descendants, and blessing made to Abraham (Gen 12:1–7; cf. Gen 15, 17) and reaffirmed to all the patriarchs (22:15–18; 26:3–4, 23–25; 28:13–15; 35:11–12; 48:3–4). Abraham responds to God's promise of land by building an altar at Shechem (Gen 12:7). Now, Israel renews its covenant in this historic location.

The Sinai covenant develops and extends the Abrahamic covenant, forming Israel as God's chosen people. Its ratification ceremony (Exod 24:3–11) is similar to that of Joshua 8. An altar is built by Moses, burnt and fellowship offerings are made (vv. 4–5), and God's word is communicated verbally (v. 3), written down (v. 4) and read to the people (v. 7). The twelve stones Moses sets up to commemorate the tribes parallel the stones on which Joshua inscribes the law. While Joshua 8 does not specifically speak of covenant, the parallels indicate a covenantal context.

Joshua 8:30–35 enacts a ceremony commanded in Deuteronomy 11:26–32. More complete details are given in Deuteronomy 27:1–26. The two passages provide an envelope around the core of Deuteronomy that contains the covenant laws, obedience to which is necessary for possessing the land (Deut 11:22–25, 31–32; 27:1; cf. Josh 1:7–8). When Israel under Joshua enacts this ceremony, it does so having personally experienced the necessity of obedience to taking the land. The events of Joshua 6–8 have proven it.

The ceremony in Joshua 8 includes inscribing the law upon stones, building an altar of uncut stones that have not been shaped by iron tools, offering burnt and fellowship offerings, and pronouncing blessings and curses on Gerizim and Ebal. Despite some minor variations (noted below), Joshua's ceremony is that prescribed in Deuteronomy 11 and 27.

The placement of the covenant renewal at this narrative juncture is a reminder that Israel receives the land as a covenant gift and for the covenant purposes outlined to Abraham. God's presence with his people and thus their ability to take the land was jeopardized by Achan's sin. Only by purging that sin was Israel able to take Ai. Now, fully restored to covenant relationship, Israel stands poised to take the remaining land. The elements of the ceremony emphasize the ongoing place of the law of Moses to direct the people as they take and live in the land.

## EXPLAIN the Story

Although the city is not mentioned here, Ebal and Gerizim lie respectively just north and south of Shechem. Israel travels 20 miles north of Ai and even further from its base camp at Gilgal, to which they return and remain for several chapters (9:6; 10:6, 15, 43; 14:6). The likelihood and feasibility of a lengthy journey into territory yet unclaimed raises questions regarding this pericope's placement. It is connected to the preceding narrative by a Hebrew word that allows but does not require strict chronological placement. In light of the extended covenant ceremony in chapter 24, it might better be placed there. Such a location would mitigate the difficulty of the return journey early in Israel's entry into the land. That the difficulties of this pericope's placement have been long recognized is indicated by the fact it appears after 9:2 in the LXX and before 5:2 in the Dead Sea Scrolls. However, the repeated reference to enacting this first ceremony "when they have crossed over (the Jordan)" (Deut 27:2, 3, 4, 12) fits the present location of this pericope. Certainly, there is no compelling reason Israel could not have made the journey at this point, despite its difficulties.

There are also compelling theological reasons for the covenant renewal after Jericho and Ai. The journey to Shechem shows Israel's commitment to perform the prescribed ceremony and, after Achan and Ai, reflects the restored covenant relationship. The penetration into the central highlands may also be a symbolic journey asserting claim to the land. In this case, the altar built at Shechem (as Abraham's earlier altar) underlines the claim.

The pericope, together with 5:2–12, brackets the Jericho-Ai account. The brackets relate cultic events that define Israel's identity as a covenant people (circumcision and Passover; covenant renewal before the ark). Narratively, this is a fitting way to set off this primary Jericho-Ai account in which the lessons of obedience and land possession are so strikingly experienced. Together, Jericho and Ai show that on the question of taking the promised land, obedience = success while disobedience = failure. (Additionally, the account's placement immediately before Israel's covenant with Gibeon contributes to that chapter's questions of obedience and covenant status). All else in Joshua works within this paradigm, and Israel experiences the full blessings of its covenant identity when it is obedient to the law.

One expects such a journey would encounter resistance or that battle would be joined at Shechem. The absence of battle reports may reflect the text's selective nature or that the inhabitants' fear has (for now) forestalled attack (2:9–11; 5:1). The book records no report of battle against Shechem, and its king does not appear in any listing of defeated kings (12:9–24). Israel has a long history at Shechem (e.g., Gen 12:6–7; 33:18–20; 34; 35:1–5), and the Shechemites may have willingly accepted the Israelite presence and readily assimilated. The dual mention of assimilated "foreigners" (vv. 33, 35) may acknowledge that possibility.

Three significant emphases are found in this short passage. First, the emphasis on "all Israel" continues. The "Israelites" are named (vv. 31, 32), and it is "all the Israelites" who are present at the ceremony (v. 33). A cross section of the group includes leaders: elders, officials, judges, and Levitical priests (v. 33), as well as the powerless and vulnerable (v. 35). The inclusiveness of Israel continues beyond Rahab to other "foreigners who lived among them" (vv. 33, 35). The whole nation is represented in the two halves that stand before the priests (v. 33). All of these comprise the "people" (*'am*) of Israel; the term is that applied to the LORD's covenant people. Finally, it is the "whole assembly" that gathers to hear the law.

The second emphasis, communicated in various ways, is Joshua's fulfillment of the ministry of Moses. Moses has not been mentioned in the narrative since the Jordan crossing (3:7; 4:10, 12, 14); as the "servant of the LORD" Moses has not appeared since 1:1, 13, 15. After the failure and recovery of Jericho-Ai, his narrative reappearance is a reassuring reminder that Israel is restored to the covenant life instituted under him. All that takes place in this pericope answers the "command of Moses" (vv. 31, 33, 35), and it is the "law of Moses" (v. 32) or the "Book of the Law of Moses" (vv. 31, 34) by which each constituent part of the narrative is directed: the altar's construction (vv. 30–31), the laws copied on the stone (v. 32), the blessing pronounced upon the people (vv. 33–34), and the reading of the book (vv. 34–35). Yet for all the prominence of Moses and his law, it is Joshua who builds the altar, conducts the ceremony, and writes and reads out the law. Joshua is named four times in the NIV (although only twice in the Hebrew text; vv. 30, 35) and is revealed as the one who fulfills the law of Moses and—by writing and reading the law—wholly occupies the ministry of his predecessor.

The final emphasis is on the law as a written text (vv. 31, 34) to be copied (v. 32) and read (vv. 34–35). This emphasis on writing is found in Deuteronomy where, in addition to the command to write the law on these stones (27:3, 8), the law is written on the stone tablets (4:13; 5:22; 9:10; 10:2, 4), on doorposts (6:9; 11:20), in a copy for the king (17:18), in a song (31:19, 22) and most frequently, in a book (28:58, 61; 29:19–20, 27; 30:10; 31:9, 24). The emphasis on writing in Joshua 8:30–35 reveals the influence of Deuteronomic thought that values the place of writing to communicate and witness to the law's power within Israel.

Joshua writes "a copy of the law of Moses" on the stones (v. 32) and in this, he is presented in the guise of Israelite kings who were commanded to write out a "copy of this law" (Deut 17:18). Joshua had earlier been commanded to obey the law of Moses (see 1:8 and commentary there); now he reads it to the people, instructing them for life in the land. Like a good king, he knows the written text has the power to shape life.

### An Altar from the Book (8:30–31)

The altar is described in the words of Deuteronomy 27:5–6. It is also like the altar at Sinai (Exod 20:25). Burnt and fellowship offerings are offered as commanded (Deut 27:6–7; see also Exod 20:24). These two types of offering were paired at times of great public significance such as covenant ratification (Exod 24:5), ceremonials concerning the ark and temple (2 Sam 6:17–18; 1 Kgs 8:64; 9:25), and other events of national importance (Judg 21:4; 1 Sam 10:8; 2 Sam 24:25).

Burnt offerings are whole burnt offerings that atone for sin (Lev 1:4), while fellowship offerings are for celebration and feasting (Lev 3:1–17; 7:11–21; Deut 27:7). Both are particularly apt at this time in Israel's life. The offerings and the reading of the law would remind Israel of its sin—most tragically encountered in Achan's theft. The renewal ceremony and its sacrifices hold together the reality of sin and provision for its remedy. Perhaps it is for this reason that the altar stands on Ebal, the mountain of curses: the altar is a reminder of sin's curse and the need for atonement. But it is an equal reminder of sin's reversal by God's grace through sacrifice. Given the renewed covenant and the atonement for sin, Israel has much to celebrate.

### Law and Blessing on the Mountains (8:32–35)

In Deuteronomy, the command to write the law precedes the command to build the altar (27:1–8). In Joshua, the execution is reversed: first the altar is built and then the law is written and read. There are two reasons for this reversal. First, the sacrifices are the final step in restoring Israel to right relationship with God and thus look backward to the events of chapters 6–8. Second, the reading of the law prepares for the ongoing narrative, for it is by obedience to the law that the people will continue in covenant and possess the land.

From Deuteronomy 27:2 it can be assumed the stones are plastered. Unlike the uncut altar stones, these stones would be smoothed to provide a writing surface. Similar plastered surfaces for writing are known from the ninth century Deir ʿAlla and Kuntillet ʿAjrud inscriptions.[1] The stones are not the forbidden cultic stones that Israel was to destroy in the land and not build for herself (Exod 23:24; 34:13; Lev 26:1; Deut 7:5; 12:3; 16:22; 1 Kgs 14:23; 2 Kgs 17:10). Nor are the stones like the steles Israel would set up to commemorate vows and covenants (Gen 28:18, 22; 31:13, 45; 35:14; Exod 24:4). Rather, these stones set up by Joshua are unique, being inscribed with the words of the law. Whether the inscription contained the legal core of Deuteronomy (chs. 12–26) or a fuller version of the book, comparison with the Law Code of Hammurabi suggests that one or two stones would provide sufficient space. Joshua may have commanded the actual writing be done by skilled scribes, but he is credited with the action. In this, he is Moses' successor, bringing God's law to the people.

---

1. These inscriptions can be found in *COS* 2.27:141, 173. The Deir ʿAlla plaster inscription talks about Balaam, son of Beor (possibly the same seer as in Numbers 22–24); the Kuntillet ʿAjrud plaster inscription notes (with a companion depiction) Yahweh and "his Asherah" or consort, applying to Israel's God characteristic ancient Near Eastern ideas of gods having consorts.

The tribes and the leaders are arrayed before the two mountains. On Gerizim, the mountain of blessing, stand the tribes of Leah's first four children (Reuben is excluded, presumably for his sin [Gen 35:22; 49:3–4]; thus Simeon, Levi, Judah and Issachar) and Rachel's children (Joseph and Benjamin). On Ebal, the mountain of cursing, stand the tribes of the excluded Reuben, Leah's last child (Zebulun), and the children of the handmaids Zilpah and Bilhah (Gad, Asher, Dan, Naphtali; Deut 27:12–13; see Gen 29:31–30:24). Although the mountain of cursing is named and the curses are read (v. 34), only Moses' instruction for blessing (and not cursing) is recalled (v. 33). This significantly reframes the instructions given for this renewal. The instructions spoke of both blessing and cursing but proclaimed only curses (Deut 27:12–26). While the focus on cursing in Deuteronomy realistically anticipates the peoples' failure, here in the midst of covenant renewal, the emphasis falls on blessing. In this way, the correlation between Israel's recent obedience and blessing is heightened.

Present at the ceremony but not mentioned in Deuteronomy are the "foreigners living among Israel." From the time of the exodus, Israel had foreign people living in their midst and participating in Israel's festivals (Exod 12:19, 48–49; 20:10; Lev 16:29; 18:26; 19:33–34). Several of the laws Joshua read to the people consider the foreigner's wellbeing (Deut 5:14; 14:29; 16:11; 24:17; 26:12); even the curses pronounced in Deuteronomy 27 contain one that upholds the rights of the foreigner (v. 19). People such as Rahab and her family could find a welcome and place within Israel. The double-mention of foreigners in the face of Israel's actions against the land's inhabitants is a needed reminder of this reality.

Similarly, unmentioned in Deuteronomy 11 and 27 is the ark of the covenant. Joshua places it between the two groups of people who face it. Levitical priests "carry the ark of the covenant of the LORD" (v. 33), which is the description repeatedly used in the Jordan crossing (chs. 3–4). There the ark symbolized God's powerful presence enabling Israel's miraculous entry to take the land. The covenant renewal ensures God's presence is fully restored within Israel, and the ark symbolizes that. Additionally, the priests "who carried the ark of the covenant of the LORD" are those who were entrusted with the Book of the Law of Moses (Deut 31:9, 24–26). By this association Israel is reminded of the book and the pressing need for obedience to it if the covenant relationship is to continue with all its blessings. With these symbols before them, Israel again is set to take the land.

Finally, Joshua undertakes to read all the words of the deuteronomic law to the assembled community, taking up a Levitical responsibility. In Deuteronomy 27 the Levites are only commanded to recite the curses, to which the people give their affirmation. Joshua appears to appropriate to himself Deuteronomy

31:9–13 in which the Levitical priests are to read the law to the assembled people every seven years during the Feast of Tabernacles. The purpose given in Deuteronomy 31:12–13 for the reading can be applied to Joshua's action: the people are to listen, learn to fear the LORD their God, and carefully follow all the words of the law. They are to do this "as long as you live in the land you are crossing the Jordan to possess." The covenant relationship has been restored by sacrifice, by witnessing the written law, and by affirming its blessings and curses. This reading is one final way that Joshua seeks to plant the covenant law within the peoples' hearts as they continue to take the land.

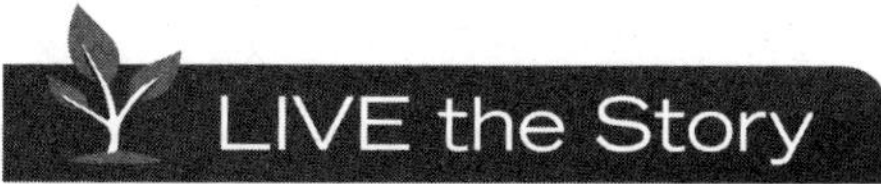


### The Covenant Identity of God's People

This short passage, together with 5:1–12, brackets the covenant failure of Achan's sin at Jericho and the concomitant military failure at Ai. The brackets contrast Israelite failure with those things that mark Israel as an obedient covenant people: circumcision and Passover (5:1–12), sacrifice and the law of Moses (8:30–35). Each of these is an identifier given by God; obedience to them marks God's people as his covenant partner.

The community is released from its failure at Jericho and its initial military attempt at Ai only after, in obedience to God, it takes steps to right Achan's wrong. This return to covenant obedience removes judgment from the community and enables their second, victorious attempt at Ai. The sequence of events at Jericho and Ai demonstrate the crucial link of covenant obedience to success in the land. This link was stated in Joshua 1 where the role of the law of Moses in Israelite obedience and land possession was clearly made (1:7–9).

The placement of the covenant renewal at this point in the narrative confirms that Israel's relationship to God is fully "reset." After failure, there is a new beginning, and the gathered community is renewed in its covenant identity. This affirmation of identity is facilitated through God's word to Moses, for the law is read and sacrifice offered according to its precepts. Together, word and sacrifice serve as aural and visual reminders of to whom Israel belongs and what that identity requires of them.

This reaffirmation of identity after failure, marked by word and sacrifice, has a message for the Christian church—both as a corporate entity and in its constituent individuals. Corporately and individually, sin and failure remain part of Christian experience. The church and its members are called to repentance and restitution, but as in Joshua, it is God's covenant that enables ongoing relationship—now a new covenant facilitated through Christ's blood.

This new covenant calls its people to continually reaffirm its power and claims. This is especially so after the experience of personal or corporate sin. In these instances, as in the covenant renewal ceremony in Joshua 8, the church gathers around God's word and God's sacrifice as the markers of its covenant identity. In the church, it is the Lord's Table that most clearly holds up word and sacrifice; as the community gathers around the table, hearing the words of institution, and proclaiming through word and act the death of Christ, it reaffirms its identity. With a renewed sense of identity in Christ, the church is also renewed in Christ's call to live as his people.

Many years ago during my seminary education in a Baptist seminary, our worship class watched a video featuring Robert E. Webber.[2] I remember his lecture positively, but the only thing I clearly recall is his assertion that Christians—especially those conscious of their sin and unworthiness—should "run to the table." It was the Lord's Table that, through word and action, proclaimed the power of Christ's death for the forgiveness of sin. As the community participates in the rite of the Lord's Table, it is reminded of the new covenant in which it stands and is reaffirmed in its covenant identity. Reaffirmed, the people of God again are sent out, conscious of their freedom, and released to joyfully live out the goodness of covenant life.

### The Powerful Word

As noted above, there is in this passage an emphasis on the word *written* (vv. 31, 32, 34). The law of Moses, prominent in Joshua 1 (see Listen to the Story, Chapter 1), is revisited at this moment of covenant renewal. The written law of Moses directs how the ceremony is to be conducted; it is an *aide memoire* directing the ceremony of renewal. Joshua also reinscribes the law on stones in the presence of the people; it provides ongoing instruction for covenant people. The written word again appears as Joshua gives his farewell speech (23:6) and in the covenant ceremony as the book closes (24:26). In both instances, it is the written word that provides direction for the life in the land.

The written word—represented in this chapter by the law of Moses—plays a significant role as Israel enters the land, marking that crucial moment. When Israel is expelled from the land to exile, that crucial moment is similarly marked by the written word in the book of Jeremiah.

Jeremiah names Israel's covenant failure as the reason for expulsion, while

2. Robert E. Webber (1933–2007) was an American theologian who wrote extensively about worship, drawing on ancient church practice and liturgy. He founded the Robert E. Webber Institute for Worship Studies, and his several volumes include *Common Roots: The Original Call to an Ancient-Future Faith* (Grand Rapids: Zondervan, 1978); *Evangelicals on the Canterbury Trail: Why Evangelicals are Attracted to the Liturgical Church* (Waco: Word Books, 1985); *Ancient-Future Worship: Proclaiming and Enacting God's Narrative* (Grand Rapids: Baker, 2008).

also speaking of future hope and return. It does so self-consciously, confessing that in the written words of Jeremiah are presented the word of God (1:1–2; 51:64). Jeremiah contains words written in letters to encourage exiles (29:1) and on scrolls as prophetic promise (45:1). Written deeds of land attest to future hope (32:10–12, 44), and the great book of consolation (chs. 30–33) begins with the directive to "Write in a book all the words I have spoken to you" (30:2). The inscribed hope for Israel in this book of consolation is matched by inscribed words against the nations (25:13) and even Babylon, God's instrument (51:60).

The enduring power of God's word, attested through a written text, is the subject of Jeremiah 36. King Jehoiakim's attempts to destroy the prophet's written message are futile: the king is judged (36:29–31); the word endures. The enduring power of this written word is apparent: the book of Jeremiah remains, a written text that reveals the word of God in the words of Jeremiah.

Andrew Shead explores in Jeremiah the emphasis on the word *written*. It is a theme he also discerns in Deuteronomy and Joshua.[3] His work draws conclusions about the value and power of written words, arguing that (1) written words remain as a permanent witness in the absence of the speaker. They attest to the truth of what is spoken, enabling remembrance and internalization of the written message; (2) in the process of reading, one is able to hear the word of the LORD, turning to the LORD from the heart.

Joshua and Jeremiah stand at significant moments of land entry and expulsion. Each is influenced by the book of Deuteronomy, the law of Moses. In this regard, Shead's conclusions regarding the value of the written word in Jeremiah are apt for the covenant renewal ceremony in Joshua as well. In Joshua's covenant renewal, the written law of Moses is obeyed, reinscribed on stones, and read to all the people. The written word attests to truth, prompts remembrance and internalization of the message, and enables Israel to turn to the LORD from the heart.

The same dynamic is at play in the written *book* of Joshua. It now stands far removed from its original authors and audience and functions within the canon of the Old and New Testaments. But the power of Joshua as a written word remains. It attests to truth, prompts remembrance and internalization of the message, and enables listeners to the turn to the LORD from the heart. Joshua may present interpretive challenges around issues of warfare and the disposition of the Canaanites and land, but perhaps the greatest challenge it presents to us lies not in these but in our willingness to be addressed by the powerful and enduring written word of God inscribed in the book of Joshua.

3. Andrew Shead, *A Mouth Full of Fire* (Downer's Grove: InterVarsity Press, 2012); see particularly ch. 6, "Word and Permanence," pp. 233–36.

## LISTEN to the Story

[1]Now when all the kings west of the Jordan heard about these things—
the kings in the hill country, in the western foothills, and along the entire
coast of the Mediterranean Sea as far as Lebanon (the kings of the Hittites,
Amorites, Canaanites, Perizzites, Hivites and Jebusites)—[2]they came
together to wage war against Joshua and Israel.

[3]However, when the people of Gibeon heard what Joshua had done to
Jericho and Ai, [4]they resorted to a ruse: They went as a delegation whose
donkeys were loaded with worn-out sacks and old wineskins, cracked and
mended. [5]They put worn and patched sandals on their feet and wore old
clothes. All the bread of their food supply was dry and moldy. [6]Then they
went to Joshua in the camp at Gilgal and said to him and the Israelites,
"We have come from a distant country; make a treaty with us."

[7]The Israelites said to the Hivites, "But perhaps you live near us, so
how can we make a treaty with you?"

[8]"We are your servants," they said to Joshua.

But Joshua asked, "Who are you and where do you come from?"

[9]They answered: "Your servants have come from a very distant
country because of the fame of the LORD your God. For we have heard
reports of him: all that he did in Egypt, [10]and all that he did to the
two kings of the Amorites east of the Jordan—Sihon king of Heshbon,
and Og king of Bashan, who reigned in Ashtaroth. [11]And our elders
and all those living in our country said to us, 'Take provisions for your
journey; go and meet them and say to them, "We are your servants;
make a treaty with us."' [12]This bread of ours was warm when we packed
it at home on the day we left to come to you. But now see how dry
and moldy it is. [13]And these wineskins that we filled were new, but see
how cracked they are. And our clothes and sandals are worn out by the
very long journey."

[14]The Israelites sampled their provisions but did not inquire of the

Lord. [15]Then Joshua made a treaty of peace with them to let them live,
and the leaders of the assembly ratified it by oath.
[16]Three days after they made the treaty with the Gibeonites, the Israelites
heard that they were neighbors, living near them. [17]So the Israelites set out
and on the third day came to their cities: Gibeon, Kephirah, Beeroth and
Kiriath Jearim. [18]But the Israelites did not attack them, because the leaders
of the assembly had sworn an oath to them by the Lord, the God of Israel.
The whole assembly grumbled against the leaders, [19]but all the leaders
answered, “We have given them our oath by the Lord, the God of Israel,
and we cannot touch them now. [20]This is what we will do to them: We
will let them live, so that God’s wrath will not fall on us for breaking the
oath we swore to them.” [21]They continued, “Let them live, but let them
be woodcutters and water carriers in the service of the whole assembly.”
So the leaders’ promise to them was kept.
[22]Then Joshua summoned the Gibeonites and said, “Why did you
deceive us by saying, ‘We live a long way from you,’ while actually you
live near us? [23]You are now under a curse: You will never be released from
service as woodcutters and water carriers for the house of my God.”
[24]They answered Joshua, “Your servants were clearly told how the Lord
your God had commanded his servant Moses to give you the whole land
and to wipe out all its inhabitants from before you. So we feared for our
lives because of you, and that is why we did this. [25]We are now in your
hands. Do to us whatever seems good and right to you.”
[26]So Joshua saved them from the Israelites, and they did not kill them.
[27]That day he made the Gibeonites woodcutters and water carriers for the
assembly, to provide for the needs of the altar of the Lord at the place the
Lord would choose. And that is what they are to this day.

*Listening to the Text in the Story*: Deuteronomy 20:10–18; 29:1–15; Joshua 2:8–14; Bulletin Text on the Battle of Qadesh; Ten Year Annals of Great King Muršili II of Hatti

## A Page from the Playbook of Deuteronomy

The Gibeonites act and speak as if they had a copy of the Book of the Law available to them. This is unlikely, but their actions and words, and the passage as a whole, are shaped to reflect Deuteronomy 20:10–18 and 29:1–15. The references to the Book of the Law throughout the chapter reveal that Israel is in danger once again of disobeying the law of Moses.

Deuteronomy 20:10–15 prescribes action against "distant" cities (20:15) as the Gibeonites repeatedly characterize themselves (vv. 6, 9, 22). Israel could offer "peace" to distant cities, as Joshua offers Gibeon (v. 15). Once peace is negotiated, the distant peoples are to "work" for Israel (Deut 20:11; a verbal form from the root *'bd*). The related nominal form is found in the "service" to which Joshua commits the Gibeonites (v. 23) and their self-reference as "servants" (vv. 8, 9, 11, 24).

Deuteronomy 20:16–18 prescribes action against cities in the land. Six nations are listed and include the Hivites (the people group to which the Gibeonites belong; v. 7). Variant lists are found elsewhere (e.g., Exod 3:8, 17; 13:5; 33:2; Deut 7:1; Josh 11:3; 24:11), but only in Deuteronomy 20:17 and Joshua 9:1 and 12:8 are these six nations listed in this particular order. No treaty should be made with near nations (Exod 23:32; Deut 7:3); they are to be "utterly destroyed" as the Gibeonites acknowledge (although using different wording; v. 24).

Deuteronomy 29:1–15[28:69–29:14] is the covenant renewal before Israel's entry into the land. Israel commits to "[c]arefully follow the terms of this covenant, so that you may prosper in everything you do" (v. 9), and it is such covenant obedience that is at stake in the negotiation with the Gibeonites. As part of covenant renewal, Moses relates Israel's history (29:2–8), a history that Israel was unable to understand, see, or hear (29:4). It is this same lack of perception that leads to the Gibeonite treaty. The Gibeonites present themselves in clothes and shoes that are "worn" and "old" (from the Hebrew *blh*; v. 5); the verbal form of this same root describes Israel's clothes and shoes that did not "wear out" in the wilderness (29:5). The charade may intend to arouse Israel's sympathy for others who have likewise traveled far. Gibeon's wine and bread also echo the account of Israel's history (Deut 29:6). Most telling, only in Deuteronomy 29:11 and Joshua 9:21 are woodcutters and water carriers listed together. In Deuteronomy, these foreigners serve Israel and are included in the covenant, and similar future participants are named (v. 15). The covenant forged in Joshua 9 thus raises the question: are the Gibeonites these anticipated future foreigners? If so, does the Gibeonite covenant draw them into Israel's covenant with God?

### Not Quite Rahab

Both Rahab and the Gibeonites have "heard" of God's mighty acts (2:10; 9:3). Both cite the exodus and the victories over Sihon and Og. Both seek a covenant with Israel to ensure life (2:12–13; 9:6, 11). But the two cases are not the same. The Gibeonites have only "heard" of the LORD's acts while Rahab gives personal testimony: she begins her testimony with "I know" (2:9). This places her in the company of other foreigners who align themselves with Israel and its God and whose testimony likewise begins "I know" (see Jethro [Exod 18:11], Naaman [2 Kgs 5:15], the widow of Zarepath [1 Kgs 17:24], and the Shunammite woman [2 Kgs 4:9]).[1]

The Gibeonites and Rahab also respond differently to their knowledge of God. The Gibeonites devise a ruse while Rahab acts with kindness—the word is that used for covenant faithfulness (see Explain the Story at 2:12 in Chapter 2). And, while both attest to God's mighty acts, only Rahab invokes the Lord in the oath she seeks (v. 12). Both Rahab and the Gibeonites are "inhabitants of the land" who are in some way incorporated into Israel. Rahab appears to be personally invested in Israel and its God and becomes one who dwells "in the midst" of Israel. Gibeon becomes a treaty ally to Israel, but are they (like Rahab) "outsiders" who become "insiders"? This is explored below.

**Staying Alive: Making Treaties**

The complexity of the Gibeonite ruse finds no clear ancient Near Eastern parallels, but there are examples of treaty delegations that demonstrate shrewdness and deception to gain a treaty. The fourteenth century BC Annals of Muršili record the king's response to the plea of the lord of Šeha:

> [W]hen [Manupa-Tar ḫunta] heard about me: "The Hittite king is coming," [he became] afraid and so [he did not] then [come] against me. He sent [to] me his mother and old men and old women. They came and [fell down] at my feet. Because the women fell down at my feet, I had mercy on the women and so I did [not] enter the Šeḫa-River Land. They handed over to me the Hittite transplantees who were in Šeḫa-River Land. . . . Manapa-Tar ḫunta and the Šeḫa-River Land I made into my subjects.[2]

The delegation includes the aged, and the king's mother who rely on wisdom and royal position to forward the negotiations. But sending the elderly and the women may also intend to deceive the Hittites as to Šeha's strength, or (as is the case) arouse mercy. Whether by wisdom or cunning deception, the delegation achieves its end. Šeha becomes subject by treaty, the terms of which include the return of Hittite fugitives.

There may be a similar cunning, and a desire to evoke mercy in Jacob's actions as he prepares to meet his brother whom he had cheated. Hearing that Esau approached with four hundred men (Gen 32:6), Jacob sent ahead gifts to "pacify" him (Gen 32:20) and "find favor" (Gen 32:5; cf. 33:8). Jacob also

---

1. As noted in Sarah Lebhar Hall, *Conquering Character: The Characterization of Joshua in Joshua 1–11*, LHBOTS 512 (New York/London: T & T Clark, 2010), 40.

2. *COS* 2.16:86.

sent ahead his wives and children who might deceive his brother as to the force of armed men traveling with Jacob. While the brothers craft no formal treaty, Jacob's actions are illuminated by the account of the delegation from Šeha.

Clearer evidence of deception in treaty negotiations is apparent in the thirteenth century BC Qadesh Bulletin Text recording Pharaoh's march north toward Qadesh. Enroute, two Shasu present themselves as negotiators:

> They say, "It is our brothers, who are tribal chiefs with the Fallen One of Hatti, who have sent us to His Majesty, saying: 'We shall become servants of Pharaoh, LPH [an acronym for "Life, Prosperity, Health"], and we shall separate ourselves from the Ruler of Hatti.'"

The Bulletin Text continues, exposing the delegates' deception:

> Now, these (two) Shasu said these things, and lied to His Majesty. (For) it was the Fallen One of Hatti who had sent them, to find out ("see") where His Majesty was, so as to prevent His Majesty's army from being prepared to fight with the Fallen One of Hatti.[3]

## EXPLAIN the Story

Joshua 9–12 is a unit in which Israel successfully completes a southern and a northern campaign. Each of chapters 9–11 begins with the opening phrase, "when X heard" a report of Israelite activity. This continuity joins the chapters together. Chapter 12 concludes the unit with a summary of Israelite victories against kings both east and west of the Jordan. Chapters 9–12 draw the second section of Joshua to a close. In it, Israel is depicted as "taking" the land (see Chapter 1). With Joshua 13, the third section (and second half) of Joshua opens and the narrative focus turns to land allotment.

Joshua 8 ends with covenant renewal that commits Israel to follow the law of Moses. In juxtaposition, chapter 9 clearly shows Israel's ongoing failure to live fully its covenant life. As well, Joshua 8:33, 35 notes the foreigners living among Israel. The Gibeonites become one of these foreigners, incorporated by treaty and the reframing of Israel's oath. Joshua 9 is a story of compromise and its outcome ambiguous concerning the status of Gibeon. How are the actions of Israel and Gibeon to be judged in this narrative? Joshua 9 testifies to Israel's failure, but it also testifies to Israelite commitment to honor oaths made; it testifies to Gibeonite deception, but it also honors Gibeonite shrewdness in effecting the ruse.

3. Ibid., 2.5B:39.

## A Response of Aggression (9:1–2)

The chapter begins with the same language as 5:1: "When all the kings . . . heard." The two notations form a bracket around the events of Jericho which include cultic preparation (5:2–12), success at Jericho (5:13–6:27), failure at Ai (7:1–5), reparation (7:6–26), success at Ai (8:1–29), and cultic conclusion (8:30–35). These kings of ch. 9 are "west" of the Jordan. The word literally means "across" (the same word is translated as "east" in v. 10, reflecting the perspective of the Gibeonites). It is the thematic word of chapters 3–4 as Israel "crossed" the Jordan; its reappearance here is a reminder that Israel "crossed" the Jordan to gain the lands of these western kings.

Although similar, chapters 5 and 9 do not begin identically. The kings are here more extensively enumerated as to their geographic territory and ethnic makeup, signifying the report of Israel has spread even further. Their response has also changed: from fear in chapter 5 to gathering "together" for war against Israel. The unity of the group is never realized, for in chapters 10–11 the extensive geographic coalition fractures into smaller, more localized campaigns. Unity is instead realized in the Gibeonites' concerted effort against Israel.

In chapter 5, it is the report of the Jordan crossing that elicits fear. The content of the report in 9:1 is not specified ("these things") nor why it elicits resistance rather than fear. Following immediately after the covenant renewal, it could be that the kings have heard of this event and rightly construe the altar as a symbolic claim over the land of Canaan. More likely, they respond to the events of Jericho and Ai (10:1) and are determined to arrest Israel's progress into the land. Given Israel's initial defeat at Ai, the kings now realize that Israel is not invulnerable. Joshua has commented on this very possibility (7:8–9).

The kingly coalition is introduced in verse 1, but its action is postponed until chapter 10. In the interim, the Gibeonites reveal a different response to the Israelite presence.

## A Treaty by Deception (9:3–15)

The Gibeonites are like the kings in one respect: they "hear" a report. But in many respects the report they hear and the response they give is very different than that of the kings. First, the report's content is clearly noted: the victory against Jericho and Ai. Thus, the Gibeonite response is to Israel's stunning victory. Second, the report is heard by the people of Gibeon and they, with their elders, respond (v. 11). No Gibeonite king appears in Joshua, and perhaps this accounts for the description of them as only "like" a royal city" (10:2). Third, the Gibeonites respond with a ruse rather than aggression. The contrast to the kings' action is sharpened by the inclusion of an emphatic Hebrew particle: the kings gather for war, but Gibeon—even they—resort to a ruse.

The word "ruse" (*'ormah*) can be either negative (with the sense of trickery or deception [Exod 21:14]) or positive (with the sense of cleverness or prudence [Prov 1:4; 8:5, 12]). The related adjective is similarly ambiguous (Gen 3:1; Job 5:12 compared to Prov 12:16, 23; 13:16). The less ambiguous term "deceit" (*mirmah*; Gen 27:35; 2 Kgs 9:23; Pss 5:6[7]; 10:7; 24:4) is not used in chapter 9, and this leaves Gibeon's actions open to construal. Are they negatively deceitful or prudently ensuring life through clever trickery?

The ruse is mounted by Gibeon, a city 8 miles northwest of Jerusalem and identified as modern el-Jib. It is an important city with at least three associated cities (v. 17). Larger than Ai, its men are good fighters (10:2). Given its advantages, mounting resistance against Israel would be a logical option. That they resort to a ruse shows how greatly they fear (v. 24).

During the treaty negotiations and the reframing of the oath (vv. 16–27) different Israelite parties take the lead in the negotiations: Joshua (vv. 6, 8–13, 22–27), the Israelites (vv. 6, 7, 14, 16–18), the leaders of the assembly (vv. 15, 19), and the whole assembly (v. 18). Rather than evidence of the blending of sources behind the current narrative (as is sometimes argued), these different voices represent the logical participation of Israelite parties during negotiations. Thus, Joshua and the Israelites execute the negotiations (vv. 6–14). As leader, Joshua contracts the treaty (v. 15) that is then publicly ratified by the leaders of the assembly on behalf of the whole assembly (v. 15). When the ruse is discovered, the Israelites set off for Gibeon, presumably to attack it (vv. 16–17). This attack is forestalled by the leaders. They receive the assembly's grumbling (v. 18) and propose a compromise solution that benefits the whole assembly (vv. 19–21). Joshua once again acts on behalf of Israel, ratifying the compromise with the Gibeonites. By his prerogative as leader, he shapes the compromise somewhat differently and also places a curse upon Gibeon (vv. 22–27).

In presenting their case, the Gibeonites speak and act in ways that align them with Israel. Having no king, the delegation indicates their decisions are made by the people and elders (v. 11), a situation not dissimilar to Israel. Likewise, the Gibeonites know something of Israel's covenant and its promises (v. 24), and their ruse plays out as if they know details of the law (such as Deut 20, 29; see Listen to the Story above). With their worn clothes, sandals, battered luggage, and dry and moldy bread, they are a picture of people who have traveled a long journey. Their condition is, in fact, that of Israel's own desert experience had it not been for God's provision. Perhaps the Gibeonites hope to stir up a sense of fellow-feeling in the Israelites.

They present themselves to Joshua and the Israelites at Gilgal, Israel's first camp in the land (4:19) and from which Israel launches its campaigns until it decamps to Shiloh (18:1). Seeming to work with knowledge of Deuteronomy 20:10–18, the Gibeonite petition has two foci: (1) that they are from a distant country (vv. 6, 9, 13); and (2) that they wish to become vassals under treaty to Israel (vv. 6, 11). Throughout a series of exchanges, Gibeon does not stray from these two foci.

They present their request for a treaty to Joshua and the "Israelites" (vv. 6, 7; the Hebrew reads "man of Israel"). The term is frequently used in places where the collective "Israel" is clearly meant and not just one man (Judg 7:23; 8:22; 9:55; 20:20; 1 Sam 17:25; 2 Sam 15:13; 19:42–42[43–44]; 23:9; 1 Chr 10:1). This is the sense in Joshua 9.

The Gibeonites present their petition, carrying their "long-distance" props. In the Hebrew text, it is the fact of their distant homeland that is first noted: "From a distance country we are; make a treaty with us." This sounds awkward in English but reveals their shrewdness. They first address the Deuteronomic tenet so crucial to treaty-formation: distance. The Israelites are perhaps suspicious, and their question presses on this tenet (v. 7). That the narrative here notes the Gibeonites are Hivites—not only one of the near peoples who have gathered against Israel (v. 1) but a group with whom Israel is particularly forbidden to ally and should destroy (Deut 20:17)—signals the covenant danger presented to Israel. Will they discern the ruse or be taken in by Gibeonite scheming?

The Gibeonites dodge the question, turning from the Israelites to address Joshua. They tell Joshua "We are your servants." This is not mere polite address. In vassal treaties, the inferior party is the "servant" of the superior party. The Gibeonites are pushing their request for a treaty. Joshua pushes back. Although his question is less pointed than the Israelites', he still asks the crucial questions of "who" and "where" (v. 8). The Gibeonites respond vaguely, for a truthful response would reveal they are near neighbors and therefore not treaty candidates.

Their response continues to focus on their two crucial issues (vv. 9–13): (1) they are a distant people; and (2) they want a covenant. On the first issue, they repeat that they are from a distant country—but now a *very* distant country (v. 9)—from which they have made a *very* long journey (v. 13). Once again, they offer their props as proof. On the second issue, they repeatedly insist on their servant status (vv. 8, 9, 11) and again request a treaty (v. 11). They even manage to reveal that their delegation represents the elders and "all those living in our country." The effect is to suggest that should a treaty be made, it will be with a unified people. No Gibeonite will contest it.

Finally, the Gibeonites provide a motivation for their request. They have heard of the Lord's fame in Egypt and east of the Jordan. Shrewdly, they give no hint of the local events at Jericho and Ai, for travelers from a far country may not yet have heard such recent news. The motivation they provide has nothing of personal commitment to Israel's God but only a statement of the LORD's power against the inhabitants. This same reality is later stated in more visceral and negative terms: they fear for their lives (v. 24). For now, to an unsuspecting ear (which undiscerning Israel appears to have in spades at the moment), Gibeon's praise of the LORD makes them sound Israelite. By word and action, Gibeon has amply shown its wish to be ratified as Israel's vassal.

Israel appears convinced. The stale provisions are sampled, possibly as a final confirmation of the story (v. 14). Their reliance on their physical senses is immediately contrasted to what should have taken place: inquiry of the LORD.

True to its history, Israel does not hear, see, or understand (Deut 29:4). Even Joshua is taken in. He makes a treaty, committing Israel to leave Gibeon in peace and life. On behalf of the assembly, the leaders ratify the oath and invoke God (v. 18). By this oath, Israel skewers itself on the horns of a dilemma: the sworn oath cannot be broken; the commitment to Gibeon's life directly contravenes the Deuteronomic law in Deuteronomy 20:16–17.

### Reframing the Oath (9:16–27)

Now it is Israel's turn to "hear" (v. 16; cf. vv. 1, 3, 9), and the news is not good. The very thing the Israelites asked of Gibeon, "Perhaps you live near us; how can we make a treaty?" is what Israel learns: they live near them; they have made a treaty. The news breaks just three days after the treaty is made, and Israel reacts quickly, traveling in one day the 20 miles to Gibeon. The news is, in fact, worse than anticipated. They discover that Gibeon has three satellite cities that now stand under Israelite protection. An attack against Gibeon is only forestalled by the oath sworn before the LORD, the God of Israel. Knowing they have broken the law of Moses, Israel is unwilling to add further error to the bill.

All the elders and people of Gibeon united to preserve their lives (vv. 3, 11). Now, the "whole assembly" of Israel unites to grumble against all the leaders (vv. 18–21). It is an ironic echo of the wilderness. There, unfaithful Israel repeatedly "grumbled" against the leadership of Moses and Aaron (Exod 15:24; 16:2, 7–11; 17:3; Num 14:2, 27, 29, 36; 16:11, 41[17:6]; 17:5[20]); now, it is the leadership that has acted unfaithfully. The reason for Israel's present grumbling is not specified. Perhaps (as in the wilderness when they grumbled over not getting the food and water they wanted) at issue is the booty they are denied by not attacking Gibeon. Perhaps (as in the wilderness when they felt Moses and Aaron were lording it over them) they are unhappy that the leaders insist on abiding by the oath. Perhaps they are just angry they've been duped. Whatever the cause, they respond forcefully against their leadership.

The leaders' response is interesting in what it lacks. There is no open confession that the law of Moses has been broken; surely this should be uppermost at this narrative point given the recent covenant renewal (8:30–35). Neither do the leaders inquire of the LORD to seek his solution, nor is any sign of repentance or regret given as after the failure at Ai (7:6–7). Instead, the leaders propose a solution that is a choice among difficult choices. They let the offense against the LORD's covenant stand. They do not add another wrong by reneging on the covenant with Gibeon; instead, they reframe it.

The leaders had not considered the LORD when the original covenant was made with Gibeon. Now that omission is rectified as the leaders acknowledge the oath is sworn by Israel's covenant God, the "LORD, the God of Israel" (vv. 18–19; cf. Exod 3:14–15; 6:1–8; 20:2). It is with this same "LORD, the God of Israel" that Israel itself has just renewed covenant (8:30). This God is a covenant-making God, who keeps the oaths he has made. Not least of these oaths is his promise of land to Israel (Gen 26:3; Exod 33:1; Num 14:23; Deut 1:35; 10:11; 34:4; Josh 1:6; 21:43–4). Oaths made in the name of this God must be honored, and the leaders seek to avoid the LORD's wrath for oath breaking (v. 20). This "wrath" (*qetseph*) was most recently experienced over Achan's sin (*qetseph* is used in recollecting this event in 22:18–20).

The leaders propose Israel keep the oath. Their proposal also seeks to appease the assembly and punish the Gibeonites. It invokes the law by which distant nations are to "serve" Israel (Deut 20:11). The leaders, however, reframe the idea of Gibeonite service (vv. 8, 9, 11) toward literalism. No longer "servants" (that is, covenant inferiors), they are to "serve" as woodcutters and water carriers. In the biblical text (Gen 24:11; Judg 16:21; Lam 5:13), as in the ancient Near East, such tasks are performed by women. Should men perform such tasks, they could be characterized as women—a shameful characterization in the ancient world (Jer 48:41; 49:22; 50:37; 51:30; Nah 3:13).[4] The leaders seek shame for the Gibeonites and benefit for the Israelites.

Once the proposal is accepted, Joshua summons the Gibeonite vassals and chides them. He asks why they "deceived" Israel. The word is less ambiguous than the "ruse" of verse 4 and elsewhere negatively describes Laban's deception of Jacob involving Leah (Gen 29:25), Michal's deception enabling David's escape (1 Sam 19:17), and Saul's disguise to manipulate the medium of Endor

4. Note that the NIV uses "weakling" to translate the Hebrew word "women" in Jer 50:37; 51:30 and Nah 3:13. In all the verses the context is one of warfare, which amplifies the shame factor: not only are men characterized as women, but the men thus characterized are "big, strong warriors." The comparison portrays a negative stereotype of men and women that (sadly) can still be found today.

(1 Sam 28:12). In each of these cases, the victim (Jacob, Saul, the medium) is not wholly innocent. A similar judgment may be applied to Israel in the case of the Gibeonite ruse, and perhaps this accounts for the somewhat defensive tone in Joshua's question: he knows Israel was deceived through its own neglect.[5]

The Gibeonite's bid for life is granted but secured by a curse (v. 23). This is the usual penalty for breaking a treaty (Deut 27:15–26). The Gibeonites sought to make (in Hebrew, "cut" [*krt*]) a treaty (vv. 6, 11) and become Israel's "servants" or inferiors in the vassal relationship. The curse reverses what they sought. Gibeon lives but will never be "released" (*krt*) from "service."

The Gibeonite response reveals their willingness to continue the vassal relationship, even with the additional curse. They continue the treaty terminology, calling themselves "servants" (v. 24). Their plea that Joshua "do to us whatever seems good and right to you" (v. 25) is likewise treaty terminology. The eighth century BC Sefire Stele records a treaty in which the Assyrian conqueror Tiglath-Pileser III makes a treaty with the King of Arpad. Under that treaty, Arpad must deliver any traitors to their Assyrian overlord who will do to them "whatever is good in my sight."[6] The Gibeonites' willingness to remain in treaty relationship stems from what they now relate as their real motivation (v. 24). They cite what they have been told of the LORD's command through "his servant Moses" regarding the gift of land and the disposition of its inhabitants. It was fear that prompted the Gibeonite ruse; now, it prompts their ongoing submission to Joshua's ruling.

As Israel's leader, Joshua is ultimately credited with saving the Gibeonites (v. 26). It is a "salvation" of their lives, and in it one might discern future possibilities of grace. Although cursed to perpetual servitude (a servitude that is still in place under David's rule [2 Sam 21:1–6]), Joshua changes the terms of their labor. The leaders had promised only that the Gibeonites would serve the assembly (v. 21). Joshua locates that service in the "house of my God" (v. 23), directing that Gibeon will serve "for the assembly" at "the altar of the LORD at the place the LORD would choose" (v. 26). The "altar of the LORD" is that place at which God calls his people to worship him and where he presences himself with them. This can be in the tent of meeting (Lev 17:6), the tabernacle (Josh 22:19, 29), and on Mount Ebal (Deut 27:6). Once the temple is built, it is designated as the place of God's choosing, and the ark resides there (Deut 12:5, 14; 1 Kgs 8:12–22). Until that time, Gibeon's service will be wherever the ark resides: (Shiloh [18:1], Kiriath Jearim [1 Sam 7:1–2]; the City of David [2 Sam 6:16–17], and finally the Jerusalem temple [1 Kgs 8:6]).

---

5. The defensive nature of Joshua's question and the culpability of the deception's victims in these cases is noted in Hall, *Conquering Character*, 155.

6. *COS* 2.82:216.

Possibly, the Gibeonites served also at the great high place at Gibeon, their hometown (1 Kgs 3:4).

There is a paradox in Joshua's application of the compromise. Gibeon remains a cursed people, yet they serve at the very heart of Israel's covenant life in the place of God's choosing. Perhaps the curse is Joshua's attempt to keep the Gibeonites separated from the Israelites. This would mitigate the possibility they would lead Israel astray with their gods. However, their exposure to Israelite worship and priestly ministries may have provided an avenue toward active participation in Israel's covenant life. Perhaps, over time, they move from their present acknowledgement of only the power of Israel's God, to active participation in Israel's covenant life and worship.

The perpetual nature of the curse is reminiscent of the curse against Jericho (6:26). At Jericho, one woman and her family were saved from destruction because of Israel's oath, and the city was perpetually cursed. Now, the Gibeonites live because of Israel's oath, but Gibeonite deception garners their perpetual curse. How differently the narrative would have unfolded had Gibeon affirmed the LORD as had Rahab and, rather than deception, displayed Rahab's *hesed*.

The Gibeonites remain a marked people. To Israel, they remain a reminder of Israel's covenant failure. As those who are covenanted to Israel and serve in holy places, they are a reminder that even the foreigner—woodcutters and water carriers—can be part of the covenant life of Israel.

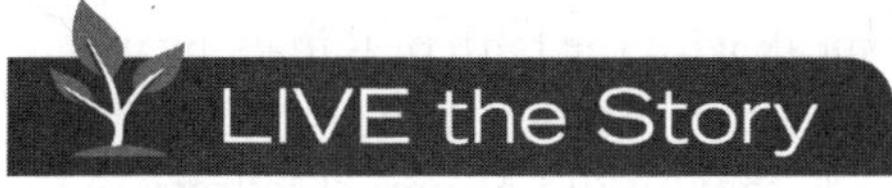


### Messing Up: The Human Way of Things

Martin Scorsese's 2016 movie, *Silence*, is based on the 1966 novel by the same name written by Shusaku Endo. In the movie, Kichijiro is an ambiguous character, despicable in some ways, but also filled with sadness and regret. In seventeenth century Japan, this alcoholic fisherman, an apostate and guilt-ridden Christian, serves as a guide to Jesuit priests seeking their mentor. At a time when Japan actively persecutes Christians, Kichijiro repeatedly betrays the priests into hostile hands. Each time, he repents—apparently, genuinely so. Whether he does not fully comprehend the depth of God's love and forgiveness or whether he is simply driven by his survival instinct is not entirely clear. He is a Judas-figure who settles for the pragmatic, unable to enjoy the peace and security available in God. His story is a graphic portrayal of humans "messing up" in their choices. The outcome for him, as for others, is tragic.

The commentary on the Gibeonites explores the ambiguity in this narrative, both around the Gibeonite ruse (should it be judged as deceitful manipulation? applauded as clever shrewdness? recognized as the *modus operandi* of a fellow underdog?) and the Israelite covenant (does it deal fairly with the Gibeonites? what status does it really afford them within Israel?). One's determination on these ambiguities does not change their underlying cause: human action that does not understand what God offers or disregards what God requires. This is the human way: whether intentionally or not, humans are adept at leaving God out of the equation and so messing up.

Israel messes up in this passage by not inquiring of God—a lesson one would hope they had learned by now. There are accounts in Israel's history of inquiry directed to God (Gen 25:21–22; 2 Sam 7; 2 Kgs 19), but there are many more of Israel not inquiring of God. From Adam and Eve's choice in the garden, to Abraham and Sarah using Hagar in an attempt to fulfill God's promise; from Israel demanding a king "like the nations" (1 Sam 8:5), to King Jeroboam disregarding God's promise of a dynasty (1 Kgs 11:30–31, 37–38) and seeking to establish his own kingdom (1 Kgs 12:25–33), Israel's story is filled with those making choices without consulting God. Too often, those choices result in widespread harm (for Israel and the world) and heartache through generations. In Joshua 9, Israel's failure to consult with God results in a covenant with Gibeon they must honor, but by which they again fall foul of their covenant with God. One can imagine that for the Gibeonites the failure is attended by heartache and regret.

Gibeon messes up in this passage by acting from fear. Able to speak only of God's fame and power, they do not speak with the faith of Rahab, by which they could have been incorporated into Israel. Rather than the potential of inclusion as worshipers, their ruse gains them a life of perpetual servitude. Contrasted to the foreigners renewing the covenant in the preceding chapter (8:33, 35) and paired with Rahab's own act of faith, the Gibeonite action is a picture of something much less than what *could have been.*

"Messing up" is a New Testament reality, too. It comes with the same heartache and damage as it did in the Old Testament. Paul's summary of the state of all humanity puts the problem clearly:

> There is no one righteous, not even one; there is no one who understands; there is no one who seeks God. All have turned away, they have together become worthless; there is no one who does good, not even one. . . . There is no fear of God before their eyes. (Rom 3:10–12, 18)

Not just Israel and Gibeon, but all humanity falls short and lives with much less than what could have been. Only God's grace can intervene in the "could have been" places of life.

## Who Can Be Included?

Commenting on Matthew's parable of the Workers in the Vineyard, Robert Farrar Capon imaginatively and cheekily retells the story of the generous landowner. The landowner surprisingly pays the workers who worked only an hour exactly the same as those who had "borne the burden of the work and the heat of the day" (Matt 20:12). Responding to those workers who object to his grace toward the latecomers, Capon places these words in the landowner's mouth:

> You're telling me I can't do what I want with my own money? I'm supposed to be a stinker because you got your nose out of joint?. . . . I decided to put the last first and the first last to show you there are no insiders or outsiders here: when I'm happy, everybody's happy, no matter what they did or didn't do.[7]

Capon's exploration of the categories of insider/outsider in this parable touches on a persistent interpretive question raised by the Gibeonite covenant: who can be brought in to Israel? What criteria are necessary for inclusion?

Already, Joshua has raised the question of insiders and outsiders. Joshua 2 dealt with Rahab, a Canaanite who sounds like an Israelite insider. She is brought in to God's people. Joshua 6–7 dealt with Achan, an Israelite insider who acts like a Canaanite outsider. He brings grief to himself, his family, and Israel. How should the Gibeonite ruse be read alongside these two accounts? In making a covenant with Israel, are they now insiders? Or, do they remain outsiders because (1) they are Canaanite; (2) they acted with deception; and (3) what they say of God has not included the words of faith exhibited by Rahab?

The first reason they might be considered outsiders is their Canaanite ethnicity. In answer to this, there are other foreigners living within Israel as part of the covenant people (as noted in 8:33, 35). This weighs against Gibeonite exclusion on ethnic grounds alone. Indeed, once the covenant is made, Israel stands by its covenant partner, even going to battle to defend it (Josh 10). The Gibeonites remain part of Israel during its history (see 2 Sam 21:1; 1 Kgs 9:20–21; 2 Chr 8:7–8), and a future of greater inclusion is anticipated by Ezekiel (Ezek 47:21–23; see also Live the Story, Josh 2). The ethnic identity of the Gibeonites does not preclude them from being covenanted to Israel and receiving benefit from that covenant. They appear to become insiders.

The second reason they might be considered outsiders is their deception. Yet there are cues in the narrative that suggest this is not really an issue for

7. Robert Farrar Capon, *The Parables of Judgment* (Grand Rapids: Eerdmans, 1989), 54.

Israel (or for God, who in the next chapter fights to uphold Israel's covenant commitment to Gibeon). The narrative uses an ambiguous term for their actions, rather than a morally negative word (see above, at 9:3–15). Even if the morally negative word (*mirmah*) had been used, that word elsewhere describes the acts of Israelites who are used by God for his purposes: Jacob's deceit (Gen 27:35) does not preclude him from God's blessing (Gen 28:10–15), and he becomes the progenitor of the twelve tribes of Israel; Jehu's treachery (2 Kgs 9:23) does not prevent God's approval (although the approval is, ultimately, lost; 2 Kgs 10:30–31). It seems that the issue of deceit does not exclude one from covenant relationship with God and his people.

The narrative even suggests a grudging approval for Gibeonite ingenuity. This is not surprising, as Israel has at times survived on its wits. Even its founding father, Jacob the trickster, schemed to best Laban (Gen 30:25–43). Contributing to this sense of grudging approval is the depiction of the Gibeonites: worn clothing, moldy provisions. These evoke Israel's own wilderness wanderings in a sympathetic way, suggesting solidarity with the Gibeonites. Neither ethnicity nor, apparently, deception prevents Gibeonite participation by covenant in Israel.

This leaves the third reason that the covenant between Gibeon and Israel might be excluded: the Gibeonites do not appear to have the same faith as evidenced by Rahab. While they enter covenant without voicing Rahab's faith, Israel and God remain committed to them as covenant partners (as ch. 10 proves!). On this level, Gibeon appears to be an insider. Now, of course, the covenant made with Gibeon was not one intended to make them Israelite or automatically invest them as worshipers of God. It was not a covenant of salvation but a covenant of loyalty. By it, Gibeon submitted herself to Israel, and Israel committed to an overlord's responsibilities.

As the covenant with Gibeon was lived out, one wonders what effect the victories of Joshua 10 might have in moving the Gibeonites to greater faith. Similarly, one wonders whether the proximity to the cult added Gibeonite service (that is, worship) to their service (that is, labor). This is speculative, of course, but others in the Old Testament, the New Testament, and the church have come to faith as they have seen God's power, or as they have participated (even as observers) in services of worship.

The covenantal inclusion of Gibeon, however achieved, does raise the question of the right to inclusion; of deservedness. It is on this point of deservedness that the Gibeonite narrative touches the New Testament, in two ways. The first is evident in Origen's homily on Joshua 9. Origen reads the Gibeonites as a type of those in the church who are "in," but without the whole-hearted dedication and purity Origen approves:

> There are in the Church certain ones who believe in God, have faith in God, and acquiesce in all the divine precepts. Furthermore, they are conscientious toward the servants of God and desire to serve them, for they also are fully ready and prepared for the furnishing of the Church or for the ministry. But, in fact, they are completely disgusting in their actions and particular habit of life, wrapped up with vices and not wholly 'putting away the old self with its actions' [citing Col 3:9]. Indeed they are enveloped in ancient vices and offensive faults, just as those persons were covered over with old garments and shoes. Apart from the fact that they believe in God and seem to be conscientious toward the servants of God or the worship of the Church, they make no attempt to correct or alter their habits. For those, therefore, our Lord Jesus certainly permits salvation, but their salvation itself, in a certain measure, does not escape a note of infamy.[8]

Origen's disapproval is evident in a subsequent comment:

> I myself was unwilling to pursue salvation by means of the arrangement of the Gibeonites and to be numbered among 'hewers of wood' or 'carriers of water'; but I wish to seize the inheritance in the midst of the Israelites and to receive a portion of the land of promise.[9]

The value of Origen's reading is its call to deeper discipleship. Its danger is in deciding who within the body measures up; who is an "Israelite," and who is a "Gibeonite." There seems little room in Origen's reflection for the weaker sister or brother, and all too much room for the measures of legalism: a human rule by which other Christians are strictly measured and either approved, or discounted.

The Gibeonite narrative and the question of inclusion and deservedness touches the New Testament in a second way. It, too, thinks of the Gibeonites within a Christian context and brings us back to Capon's treatment of the Workers in the Vineyard. The parable asks, "are you envious because I am generous?" (Matt 20:15), and Capon explores the kind of extravagantly generous bookkeeping in which God engages. Capon notes that the parable challenges those who think they are more deserving of God's grace than others. Rather, all come into God's kingdom as undeserving, holding nothing in their account which merits their inclusion as an "insider." Capon writes of God's bookkeeping that

8. Origen, *Hom* 10.1.
9. Ibid.

> in that book [ie. God's ledger], nothing stands against you. There are no debit entries that can keep you out of the clutches of the Love that will not let you go. There is no minimum balance below which the grace that finagles all accounts will cancel your credit. And there is, of course, no need for you to show large amounts of black ink, because the only Auditor before whom you must finally stand is the Lamb.[10]

In the context of Joshua 9, we are all Gibeonites: deceitful perhaps, looking only for gain perhaps—or with any other number of disqualifying traits. But those disqualifying traits only prevent entry into covenant with God and receipt of all its blessings, *if the covenant is based on merit, rather than grace.* Reading the Gibeonite covenant in counterpoint with this New Testament parable reveals the bookkeeping of God's economy. Outsiders become insiders not on the basis of merit (or ethnicity, or honor). The covenant holds grace for all—even for the Israelites, even for the Gibeonites, and (as Capon points out) even for those who come to the vineyard one hour before the day is done.

---

10. Capon, *Parables of Judgment*, 55.

# CHAPTER 10

# Joshua 10:1–43

## LISTEN to the Story

[1]Now Adoni-Zedek king of Jerusalem heard that Joshua had taken Ai
and totally destroyed it, doing to Ai and its king as he had done to Jericho
and its king, and that the people of Gibeon had made a treaty of peace
with Israel and had become their allies. [2]He and his people were very
much alarmed at this, because Gibeon was an important city, like one of
the royal cities; it was larger than Ai, and all its men were good fighters.
[3]So Adoni-Zedek king of Jerusalem appealed to Hoham king of Hebron,
Piram king of Jarmuth, Japhia king of Lachish and Debir king of Eglon.
[4]"Come up and help me attack Gibeon," he said, "because it has made
peace with Joshua and the Israelites."

[5]Then the five kings of the Amorites—the kings of Jerusalem, Hebron,
Jarmuth, Lachish and Eglon—joined forces. They moved up with all their
troops and took up positions against Gibeon and attacked it.

[6]The Gibeonites then sent word to Joshua in the camp at Gilgal: "Do
not abandon your servants. Come up to us quickly and save us! Help us,
because all the Amorite kings from the hill country have joined forces
against us."

[7]So Joshua marched up from Gilgal with his entire army, including
all the best fighting men. [8]The LORD said to Joshua, "Do not be afraid of
them; I have given them into your hand. Not one of them will be able to
withstand you."

[9]After an all-night march from Gilgal, Joshua took them by surprise.
[10]The LORD threw them into confusion before Israel, so Joshua and the
Israelites defeated them completely at Gibeon. Israel pursued them along
the road going up to Beth Horon and cut them down all the way to
Azekah and Makkedah. [11]As they fled before Israel on the road down from
Beth Horon to Azekah, the LORD hurled large hailstones down on them,
and more of them died from the hail than were killed by the swords of
the Israelites.

[12]On the day the LORD gave the Amorites over to Israel, Joshua said to
the LORD in the presence of Israel:

"Sun, stand still over Gibeon,
  and you, moon, over the Valley of Aijalon."
[13]So the sun stood still,
  and the moon stopped,
  till the nation avenged itself on its enemies,

as it is written in the Book of Jashar.

The sun stopped in the middle of the sky and delayed going down about
a full day. [14]There has never been a day like it before or since, a day when
the LORD listened to a human being. Surely the LORD was fighting for Israel!

[15]Then Joshua returned with all Israel to the camp at Gilgal.

[16]Now the five kings had fled and hidden in the cave at Makkedah.
[17]When Joshua was told that the five kings had been found hiding in the
cave at Makkedah, [18]he said, "Roll large rocks up to the mouth of the
cave, and post some men there to guard it. [19]But don't stop; pursue your
enemies! Attack them from the rear and don't let them reach their cities,
for the LORD your God has given them into your hand."

[20]So Joshua and the Israelites defeated them completely, but a few
survivors managed to reach their fortified cities. [21]The whole army then
returned safely to Joshua in the camp at Makkedah, and no one uttered a
word against the Israelites.

[22]Joshua said, "Open the mouth of the cave and bring those five kings
out to me." [23]So they brought the five kings out of the cave—the kings
of Jerusalem, Hebron, Jarmuth, Lachish and Eglon. [24]When they had
brought these kings to Joshua, he summoned all the men of Israel and said
to the army commanders who had come with him, "Come here and put
your feet on the necks of these kings." So they came forward and placed
their feet on their necks.

[25]Joshua said to them, "Do not be afraid; do not be discouraged. Be
strong and courageous. This is what the LORD will do to all the enemies you
are going to fight." [26]Then Joshua put the kings to death and exposed their
bodies on five poles, and they were left hanging on the poles until evening.

[27]At sunset Joshua gave the order and they took them down from the
poles and threw them into the cave where they had been hiding. At the
mouth of the cave they placed large rocks, which are there to this day.

[28]That day Joshua took Makkedah. He put the city and its king to the

sword and totally destroyed everyone in it. He left no survivors. And he
did to the king of Makkedah as he had done to the king of Jericho.
29Then Joshua and all Israel with him moved on from Makkedah to
Libnah and attacked it. 30The LORD also gave that city and its king into
Israel's hand. The city and everyone in it Joshua put to the sword. He left no
survivors there. And he did to its king as he had done to the king of Jericho.
31Then Joshua and all Israel with him moved on from Libnah to
Lachish; he took up positions against it and attacked it. 32The LORD gave
Lachish into Israel's hands, and Joshua took it on the second day. The city
and everyone in it he put to the sword, just as he had done to Libnah.
33Meanwhile, Horam king of Gezer had come up to help Lachish, but
Joshua defeated him and his army—until no survivors were left.
34Then Joshua and all Israel with him moved on from Lachish to
Eglon; they took up positions against it and attacked it. 35They captured
it that same day and put it to the sword and totally destroyed everyone in
it, just as they had done to Lachish.
36Then Joshua and all Israel with him went up from Eglon to Hebron
and attacked it. 37They took the city and put it to the sword, together with
its king, its villages and everyone in it. They left no survivors. Just as at
Eglon, they totally destroyed it and everyone in it.
38Then Joshua and all Israel with him turned around and attacked Debir.
39They took the city, its king and its villages, and put them to the sword.
Everyone in it they totally destroyed. They left no survivors. They did to
Debir and its king as they had done to Libnah and its king and to Hebron.
40So Joshua subdued the whole region, including the hill country, the
Negev, the western foothills and the mountain slopes, together with all
their kings. He left no survivors. He totally destroyed all who breathed,
just as the LORD, the God of Israel, had commanded. 41Joshua subdued
them from Kadesh Barnea to Gaza and from the whole region of Goshen
to Gibeon. 42All these kings and their lands Joshua conquered in one
campaign, because the LORD, the God of Israel, fought for Israel.
43Then Joshua returned with all Israel to the camp at Gilgal.

*Listening to the Text in the Story*: Exodus 14; Numbers 21:21–35 and Deuteronomy 2:24–3:11; Ten Year Annals of Great King Muršili II of Hatti; Gebel Barkal Stela and the Annals of Thutmose III; Sargon's Letter to the God; Karnak Inscription; Qadesh Inscription; Azatiwata's Royal Inscription; Aramaic Text in Demotic Script

**The Divine Warrior Fights for the Outsider's Cause**

God's power is exercised on behalf of Israel at the Jordan crossing and the Jericho battle. In Joshua 10 for the first time it is explicitly stated that the Lord "fights for" Israel (vv. 14, 42). This was anticipated in Deuteronomy (1:30; 3:22; 20:4) and recalled in Joshua's final words (23:3, 10). Only rarely is it elsewhere stated specifically that God "fights" (from *lhm*). Most often, the divine warrior fights for Israel against nations and peoples (2 Chr 20:29; 32:8; Neh 4:20; Isa 30:32; Zech 14:3); occasionally, the warrior fights against Israel (Isa 63:10; Jer 21:5).

Prior to Joshua, the Lord explicitly "fights for" Israel only at the Red Sea (Exod 14:14, 25), a text instructively read alongside Joshua 10. Both at the Sea and at Gibeon, God utilizes nature to fight on Israel's behalf. By so doing, God brings "confusion" (from *hmm*; v. 10; Exod 14:24) to the enemy and they "flee" (from *nws*; v. 11, 16; Exod 14:27) without escape. In both cases, the Lord hardens the hearts of the foreign leaders to achieve God's purposes (11:20 [in a summary of Israel's southern and northern campaigns]; Exod 14:4).

Despite the similarities, there are differences between the accounts. In Exodus, God fights for Israel because their previous overlord acts in deceit and aggression against them. God fights so that Israel might escape Egypt. In Joshua, God fights for Israel against the southern coalition so that Israel might enter. In both cases, the aggressor is not Israel: it is Pharaoh and the southern coalition that raise the battle. Significantly, Israel fights to honor its covenant with deceitful Gibeon. Though the Gibeonite covenant was ill-advised (see Chapter 9 above) and contradicts God's commands in Deuteronomy, God acts in power to preserve Gibeon—outsiders who have become insiders through covenant.

**Sihon and Og: West Side Story**

Joshua 10 introduces the coalition kings by name and region (v. 3, 5, 23) and calls them the "kings of the Amorites" (v. 5–6). The phrase "king(s) of the Amorites" occurs only twenty-five times in the Old Testament. In most cases it refers to Sihon, "king of the Amorites" (Num 21:21, 26, 29, 34; 32:33; Deut 1:4; 2:24; 3:2; 4:46; Josh 12:2; 13:10, 21; Judg 11:19; 1 Kgs 4:19; Pss 135:11; 136:19) or Sihon and Og, the "kings of the Amorites" (Deut 3:8; 4:47; 31:4; Josh 2:10; 9:10; 24:12). In Joshua 5:1 it refers to the frightened western kings—perhaps the same Amorite kings mentioned in Joshua 10:5–6. Only in Joshua 5:1; 10:5, 6 are kings other than Sihon and Og named as Amorite kings. The evocation in Joshua 10 of Sihon and Og, kings defeated by Israel (Num 21:21–35; Deut 2:24–3:11), is ominous. Even before God promises to give the coalition into Israel's hand (v. 8), the evocation anticipates the coalition's defeat.

The defeat is also anticipated by several other connections between the accounts of the eastern and western battles.[1] For instance, Israel's leader is not to fear and is assured that God has delivered the enemy into Israel's hand (Num 21:34; Deut 3:2; Josh 10:8). Israel battles the enemy and leaves no survivors (Num 21:35; Deut 2:34; 3:3; Josh 10:28, 30, 33, 37, 39–40). *Herem* is applied (Deut 2:34; 3:6; Josh 10:28, 35, 37, 39–40), and action in battle is commanded in accordance with past precedent (Deut 3:2; Josh 10:28, 30, 32, 35, 39).

The connections between these battles against the "kings of the Amorites" anticipate the same outcome—Israel's victory—on both sides of the Jordan. The connections also tie the east/west battles together as part of the one action of taking the land, even though the Transjordanian lands were not part of the original grant to Israel. God fights for Israel east and west of the Jordan. This creates ambiguity regarding the delineation of the land and Israelite identity: *does* the promised land now include the Transjordanian lands? *Are* the eastern tribes part of Israel, or does Israel dwell only west of the Jordan? This is the same ambiguity noted in Joshua 1, which persists through the distribution of the land (chs. 13–19) and the eastern tribes' departure back across the Jordan (ch. 22).

Finally, the connections to the eastern battle are a reminder that Joshua continues the ministry of Moses: both lead Israel toward promise; both miraculously cross waters; both accomplish similar victories over Amorite kings.

## Ancient Near Eastern Warfare Accounts

The account of the battle against the southern coalition (as well as the northern coalition in ch. 11) is wholly contextualized within the ancient world. The miraculous intervention of God, the significance of the events occurring on one day, the hyperbolic language, the pursuit, capture, and method of execution of the kings, the summary of the battle, and the terse and stereotypical language found particularly in verses 28–39 all find counterparts in the ancient literature. Often these counterparts shed light on what is communicated by the Bible's textual code. Because so many examples could be considered, the following are simply a few of the most pertinent.[2]

1. For a fuller discussion of connections summarized here, see Hall, *Conquering Character*, 182–83. Hawk, *Joshua*, 159–67, explores the structural connections between the campaigns recounted in Deut 2–3 against Sihon and Og, and those of Joshua 8, 10–11.

2. An invaluable scholarly work that shows the accounts to be wholly contextualized within the ancient Near Eastern world is Younger, "Ancient Conquest Accounts." Access to similar materials at a more popular level (often citing Younger) can be found in Kitchen, *On the Reliability*, and commentaries such as those by Hess, *Joshua*, and "Joshua" in ZIBBC, and Pitkänen, *Joshua*.

***Heavenly Intervention***

Ancient gods are often depicted as participating in warfare on behalf of their people. This occurs through miraculous interventions in the realm of nature, such as the hail or the arrested sun in Joshua 10. Credited to the gods, these phenomena are interpreted as reflections of their glory. Thus, King Muršili II of Hatti writes in the Ten Year Annals:

> When I had gone and when I had arrived in Lawa-ša, the victorious Stormgod, my lord, showed his divine power. He shot a lightning bolt. . . . The lightning bolt went and struck Arzawa. It struck Apāša, the city of Uḫḫaziti. When Uḫḫaziti became ill, he did not subsequently come against me for battle. . . . the Sungoddess of Arinna, my lady, the victorious Stormgod, my lord, Mezzulla and all the gods ran before me.[3]

Similarly, Thutmose III notes a miracle of Amun-Re, by which the Egyptian army gains victory:

> Pay attention . . . then you will know the miracle of Amun-Re in the presence of the Two Lands. . . . sentries were in the very act of being posted at night in order to do their regular watch. There were two astronomers (present). A star approached, coming to the south of them. The like had not happened before. It shot straight toward them (the enemy), not one of them could stand . . . falling headlong. . . . Not one of them retaliated; no one looked back. Their chariotry is gone, they (the horses?) having bolted . . . in order that all foreigners might see the awe of my majesty.[4]

Sargon's Letter to the God is an Assyrian account of Assur's divine intervention with hailstones. The account includes events that are particularly similar to those of the biblical record: the miracle precipitates the enemy's flight over many miles and up and down mountains. During the pursuit many enemy troops are slaughtered. The enemy kings hide in mountain recesses, but ultimately the enemy is annihilated and the land subdued. Of the miracle Sargon writes:

> I pursued them at the point of the javelin. The rest of the people, who had fled to save their lives, whom [the enemy king] had abandoned that the glorious might of Assur, my lord, might be magnified, Adad, the violent, the son of Anu, the valiant, uttered his loud cry against them; and with the flood cloud and hailstones (lit. "the stone of heaven"), he totally annihilated the remainder.[5]

3. *COS* 2.16:85.
4. Ibid., 2.2B:17.
5. Cited in Younger, "Ancient Conquest Accounts," 210.

These excerpts show the biblical account participates wholly in the tropes and expressions common to ancient Near Eastern battle accounts.

### *Structure and Language*

The Annals of Thutmose III provide good comparison to the accounts of Joshua 1–11. In the Annals, a detailed and lengthy account is provided of a key battle. This is followed by short, stereotypically-phrased accounts of several actions (see Listen to the Story, Chapter 1). These brief summaries are so distinct from what precedes that it has been supposed they represent "day book" entries—brief daily scribal records.[6] For instance, the Sixth Asiatic Campaign reads:

> Regnal year 30. Now his majesty was in the foreign land of Retenu on this 6th victorious campaign of his majesty. Arriving at the city of Kadesh, destroying it, cutting down its trees and plucking its barley. Proceeding from Shesryt, arriving at the City of Djamer, arriving at the city of Irjet. Doing likewise against it.[7]

Joshua 10–11 provides an abbreviated battle account when compared to Joshua 6–9, but it is the succinct summaries in 10:28–39 with repetitive, stereotypical language that are so similar to the so-called "day book" entries.

Finally, the summary at 10:40–43 (and also at 11:16–20, 23) aligns with the protocols expected in ancient conquest accounts. Such summaries use hyperbolic language that glorifies the victor and, especially, the victor's god. Such hyperbole must be read with an understanding of the genre's ideological intentions rather than as a literal account of "what actually happened."

### *A Single Day*

The idea of several great events occurring in a "single day" is part of the hyperbole of ancient Near Eastern conquest accounts (see vv. 12–14, 28, 35). Tiglath-Pileser boasts of plundering from the "edge of the land of Suhu to Carchemish of Hatti-land" in a single day—a distance of approximately two hundred miles. Puzur-in-Šušinak, a governor of Susa, claims the conquest of seventy towns in a single day, and the Egyptian Seti I claims the taking of three cities "in the space of a single day."[8] The purpose of the hyperbole is to heighten the victor's grandeur and prove they have their god's support.

---

6. The distinctive style and the "Day-book" idea are explored by James K. Hoffmeier, "The Structure of Joshua 1–11 and the Annals of Thutmose III," in *Faith, Tradition, and History: Old Testament Historiography in Its Near Eastern Context*, ed. A. R. Millard (Winona Lake: Eisenbrauns, 1994), 165–79.

7. *COS* 2.2A:7–13 provide the sustained battle accounts as well as the terse, stereotypical summaries. The *Sixth Asiatic Campaign* is found at lines 1–103a.

8. All cited in Younger, "Ancient Conquest Accounts," 215–16.

### *Triumph "Over" Enemies*

Joshua calls his commanders to put their feet on the necks of the apprehended kings (v. 24; see also Ps 110:1). This symbol of dominance is alluded to in such works as the Karnak Inscription of Sethos I, where it is proclaimed that "your enemies are beneath you," and in the Qadesh Inscription of Ramesses II, where in victory the enemies are "under your feet."[9] Similar sentiment is found in the Hittite Royal Inscription in which Azatiwata proclaims "I, Azatiwata, put them under my feet."[10] These declarations are shorthand for the longer idea of putting one's feet on the neck of the enemy, an idea fully expressed in the Aramaic Text in Demotic Script. Of note in this inscription is the god's encouragement and commitment to save his servant, as is found in Joshua 10:

> Mar [the god] speaks up and says to me: "Be strong, my servant, fear not. I will save . . . I shall destroy [your] [enemy in] your days and during your years [your] advers[ary] will be smitten. [Your foes] I shall destroy in front of you; your foot on their necks [you will place]."[11]

## EXPLAIN the Story

Joshua 9–12 is a unit, concluding the first half of Joshua (see Explain the Story, in Chapter 9). In Joshua 10, Adoni-Zedek heads the southern coalition against Israel. The military action of chapter 10 parallels that of the northern coalition in chapter 11. These chapters take up the narrative begun at 9:1 and interrupted by the Gibeonite ruse. Joshua 10 and 11 are clear companion narratives, as is evident by their shared stylized structure:[12]

**Introduction:**

Ch. 10 Amorite coalition organized by Adoni-Zedek, King of Jerusalem

Ch. 11 Canaanite coalition organized by Jabin, King of Hazor

**Oracle of Assurance to Joshua:**

Ch. 10: "Do not be afraid . . . I will hand them over" (v. 8; author's translation)

Ch. 11 "Do not be afraid . . . I will hand . . . them . . . over" (v. 6)

9. *COS* 2.4A:24; 2.5A:37.

10. Ibid., 2.21:125.

11. Ibid., 1.99:313.

12. Noted in K. Lawson Younger, "The Rhetorical Structuring of the Joshua Conquest Narratives," in *Critical Issues in Early Israelite History*, ed. Richard S. Hess, Gerald A. Klingbeil, and Paul J. Ray Jr. (Winona Lake: Eisenbrauns, 2008), 3–32.

**Victory gained in one decisive, open-field battle:**
Ch. 10 At Gibeon
Ch. 11 At the waters of Merom
**Pursuit to tribal boundaries:**
Ch. 10 Southernmost boundaries
Ch. 11 Northernmost boundaries
**Capture of leading cities:**
Ch. 10 Multiple cities (vv. 28–39)
Ch. 11 Hazor and royal cities (vv. 10–12)
**Campaign summary: 10:40–43; 11:23**

Despite the shared structure, each chapter works toward different goals. Chapter 10 is a longer, more detailed account of battle and demonstrates intertwined themes: victory comes because God fights for Israel, and because Israel is obedient to God's commands. Chapter 11 gives a briefer account of battle and focuses on Moses' commands, revisiting a theme that began in Joshua 1 and informs chapters 1–12.

The intertwined themes of Joshua 10 have appeared in the preceding chapters, and several other elements tie the chapter to those which precede it. Mention of Gibeon, Jericho, Ai, and Gilgal recall key events, as does the language of "total destruction" (*herem*; see 2:10; 6:17–19, 21; 10:1, 28, 35, 37, 39, 40). God's assurance that Joshua not fear (v. 8) becomes Joshua's assurance to the people (v. 25). These assurances echo the opening chapter (1:6, 7, 9, 18; cf. 8:1) and are a reminder that despite all that has transpired, God remains committed to Israel and will act on its behalf.

As in Joshua 3–4, the narrative does not proceed in linear fashion but retraces its steps at several points. Thus, while verses 1–15 give a summative overview of the whole battle, verses 11–14 are a retrospective of one phase of the action. The overview concludes with the army's return to camp at Gilgal (v. 15) before backtracking with two further retrospectives. These recount particular aspects of the battle. The first (vv. 16–27) disposes of the kings of the alliance; the second (vv. 28–39) takes major cities in the southern region. This is followed by a stereotypically-phrased conclusion and a resumptive statement of the army's return to Gilgal. This chapter can be sketched as follows:

Amorite alliance attacks Gibeon (vv. 1–5)
Gibeonite plea for assistance (v. 6)
Israelite victory: movement from Gilgal to Azekah to Makkedah (vv. 7–10)
  Retracing Israelite steps: the pursuit to Azekah (vv. 11–14)
Battle's end: return to Gilgal (v. 15)
  Retracing Israelite steps: kings at Makkedah (vv. 16–27)

Retracing Israelite steps: from Makkedah to Debir (vv. 28–39)
Concluding summary (v. 40–42)
Battle's end: return to Gilgal (v. 43)

### Help Pleas (10:1–6)

For the first time west of the Jordan, Israel battles a coalition of kings. Israel has battled western kings before at Jericho and Ai, but those kings fought alone. Can Israel win against a coalition? The seriousness of the threat is marked by the careful naming of the kings and the cities they rule (vv. 3, 5, 23)—a contrast to the unnamed kings of Jericho and Ai (2:2; 8:2, 29). Despite the coalition's strength, the narrative subtly anticipates Israelite victory simply by designating the coalition "the five kings of the Amorites" (v. 5, 6). Elsewhere applied almost exclusively to the defeated Sihon and Og (see Listen to the Story above), this linguistic "alliance" suggests a similar fate awaits the coalition.

Adoni-Zedek assembles and leads the coalition, comprised of five kings of significant cities. Adoni-Zedek's name (which means "my lord is righteous") is similar to that of Melchizedek ("my king is righteous") who earlier ruled from Jerusalem (Gen 14:18–20). Yet while Melchizedek honored Abram, Adoni-Zedek resists God's people. He recognizes that Gibeon's alliance threatens Jerusalem's northern approaches. The cities of the coalition, west and south of Jerusalem, have a vested interest in assisting Jerusalem.

As in 9:1, resistance is precipitated by what is "heard" (v. 1), with the content of the report now specified. Ai was "taken" (from *lkd*), *herem* applied, and the king executed (the fate of Jericho and its king is also revealed). The hope is to prevent Israel "taking" the coalitions' cities and kings. The coalition will be unable to win, and they will indeed be "taken" (*lkd* is used repeatedly in vv. 28–39).

Great alarm (v. 2; in Hebrew, "they greatly feared") is raised at the report of Gibeon's "treaty of peace" (v. 1; 9:15), which allies them to Israel. It is Gibeon's "peace" with the enemy that is the gist of Adoni-Zedek's appeal (v. 4). Although not a royal city (no king is ever cited), Gibeon is important, large, and a military force. This force no longer stands between Israel and the coalition cities. Adoni-Zedek acts prudently: an attack that reclaims Gibeon will provide a buffer zone. It will also punish Gibeon and warn other Canaanite cities against forging a treaty with Israel.

Adoni-Zedek's "appeal" (from *shlh*) is "Come up" (from *'lh*) and "help" (from *'zr*). The strong coalition responds promptly (five kings are noted once again, but with the ominous reference to the "Amorite kings"). "All their troops . . . move up" (from *'lh*) and "attack" (from *nkh*). Gibeon manages to get a message out to its treaty partner and, as the lesser partner ("your servant"), claims its right of military aid in words that mirror Adoni-Zedek's plea. Gibeon "sent word" (*shlh*) saying "Come up" (*'lh*) and "help" (*'zr*). Gibeon adds a note of urgency (come "quickly") and (as in ch. 9) a touch of creativity through the hyperbolic "all" the kings (rather than five!). Gibeon appeals to Joshua to live up to his name (v. 6): he is to "save" them ("Joshua" and "save" both come from the root *ysh'*).

**Israelite Victory (10:7–15)**

Gibeon's plea echoed Adoni-Zedek's appeal. Now, Joshua's response echoes the kings' response. He too "marched up" (from *'lh*) with "his entire army" and all his best fighters. But Joshua brings what the five kings do not have: the LORD's three-fold assurance (v. 8). First, Joshua is commanded not to fear. The words are those given before Ai (8:1) and similar to those of 1:9. Second, Gibeon's plea was that Joshua not "abandon" them, which literally reads "withdraw (*rph*) your hand." Now God promises that he will give the Amorite kings and their troops into "your hand." The same assurance was made before Jericho (6:2) and Ai (8:1). In another suggestive allusion, by this deliverance into Joshua's hand, God upholds his promise to not "fail" (*rph*) Joshua (1:5). Finally, Joshua is assured the enemy will not "withstand" him, as was promised in 1:5. These assurances are given as Israel marches out to uphold its covenant with Gibeon. Even though contracted against Moses' law, God honors the covenant. He commits to fight as Israel battles on behalf of Canaanite Gibeon.

By traveling the twenty miles from Gilgal at night (a tactic also attested in the Mesha Inscription), Joshua's morning arrival has the element of surprise. Its tactical advantage is increased as God "threw the enemy into confusion" (from *hmm*). God had earlier promised Israel success through this strategy (Exod 23:27; Deut 7:23) and, of the fifteen times this action occurs in the Old Testament, in most cases God is the actor in a warfare context. A primary example occurs at the Red Sea when God throws the Egyptians into confusion and they conclude "The LORD is fighting for Israel against Egypt!" In other contexts, the LORD confuses the enemy with thunder (1 Sam 7:10) and lightning (2 Sam 22:15).

The confusion occurs "at Gibeon" (v. 10) and is perhaps only a response to the surprise attack. Surely, however, the confusion is due to more than the element of surprise. The sun stopping still over Gibeon is the LORD's work (vv. 12–14), as are the hailstones (v. 11). Surely the narrative intends that these, too, were instrumental in throwing the enemy into confusion. If so, the confusion that enables the complete victory "at Gibeon" (v. 10) extends to include events narrated during the subsequent pursuit. Whatever the cause and extent of the confusion, Israel's success is due to the divine warrior (v. 11) who fights for Israel (v. 14). As in ancient Near Eastern conquest accounts, God gains victory and praise through the supernatural weapons he wields against the enemy.

The LORD fights for Israel, but Israel is wholly involved in the battle. The confusion "at Gibeon" enables Israel to "defeat them completely" (v. 10). The greatness of Israel's victory is marked in verse 10 by three occurrences of the Hebrew root *nkh* (with the idea of "to strike"): Israel "defeated them completely" (in Hebrew, "struck them" with "a great strike") and "cut them down" ("struck them") from Azekah to Makkedah. That the enemy (although "defeated completely" and "cut down") survives to flee toward its cities demonstrates the hyperbolic nature of the text. The hyperbole makes the rhetorical point that with God fighting for Israel, Joshua successfully "strikes" the enemy that sought to "strike" (NIV "attack," v. 4) Gibeon.

Israel pursues the enemy through the pass at Beth Horon. This pass leads to the Elah Valley and south toward the coalition cities. The pursuit passes Jarmuth and reaches Azekah (approximately 15 miles south of Beth Horon) before continuing south to Makkedah, which is situated on a major route. From there, the Amorites could flee to their cities of Lachish, Eglon, and Hebron.

Reaching Makkedah, the narrative pauses for a retrospective look at the pursuit and the "large hailstones" God wielded against the kings' armies. The identical phrase occurs in verse 18 when Joshua commands the placement of "large rocks" to trap the kings. The identical wording is part of the intertwined theme (see Explain the Story above for the structure and themes of chs. 10–11): God fights for Israel, and Israel fights, too. God and man use the same weapons, each appropriate to their spheres of heaven and earth.

The account next turns to the miraculous stoppage of the sun and moon. This takes place "on that day," an expression meaning "around the time" of the preceding events. Chronological progression is not required by the phrase and here provides a retrospective of earlier events. Given the relative positions of the sun (east over Gibeon) and moon (west over Aijalon), Joshua's command is given in the morning, perhaps when the battle at Gibeon is underway, or early in the pursuit toward Beth Horon. However, a request made early in the day seems odd, for the full day is yet before Joshua. Why would he make such a request when the day is young and the battle hardly begun? This difficulty is addressed further below.

"On that day" the LORD gives the Amorites to Israel (v. 12). If "that day" is the same day as that of verse 28 and the day in view in verse 13, then the defeat at Gibeon, the pursuit, and the defeat of Makkedah all occur within one calendar day. It may even be that all the cities in verses 28–39 are intended as included in the one day. The improbability of this is clear: not only would these events take more than even a lengthened day, verse 32 specifically indicates that Lachish alone took two days to subdue. Perhaps "that day" in verse 12 has in view only the initial battle with the kings during which their power is broken, or includes the initial phases of the pursuit. A better solution suggests itself from the genre cues of ancient Near Eastern conquest accounts. In them (see Listen to the Story above), a hyperbolic "single day" encompasses events and military marches that in reality took much longer. Through this literary device, the power of the LORD who fights for Israel is made apparent.

Joshua acts in a mediating role in verses 12–13 as he speaks to the LORD words that are also intended for Israel's hearing. The words addressed to God are not given, but Joshua's apostrophe to the sun and moon are included in them. Like Moses before him, who spoke to the rock in the presence of the people (Num 20:8), Joshua's words are a sign to the people that creation is obedient to God—even through his appointed servant.

The sun and moon are both commanded to "stand still" (v. 12), which is further described in a poetic couplet as "stopped" so that the sun "delayed going down about a full day" (v. 13). What actually happened? The traditional view is that the sun and moon actually stop, enabling time for Israel to "avenge itself on its enemies." In reality, it would be the earth that stopped; the words are a description of what is observed visually, much as we might say the "sun rose" or the moon "stood on the horizon." If the earth actually stopped, there are very real challenges that accompany the phenomenon, indicated by the correlation between the earth's rotation and gravity. Whether or not one believes God performs miracles (which this author does), the traditional view is challenged not only by the phenomenological problems, but the need to account for the timing of the request: why there would be any need to make this unusual request so early in the battle (as noted above)?[13]

Other ways of understanding this text have been proposed. Several involve natural phenomena such as eclipses or dust storms obscuring the sun and moon. None of these really provide a good explanation, for the text says nothing about such occurrences. Other solutions note the hyperbolic nature of ancient conquest accounts and their depiction of the gods utilizing nature as a weapon. Hyperbole has been explored elsewhere in this chapter, and it is likely at work in this text as well.

---

13. For a helpful discussion of the questions surrounding miracles, science, and what God could or might do, see Stephen N. Williams, "God of Miracle and Mystery" in McConville and Williams, *Joshua*, 154–70.

A helpful line of research explores Mesopotamian omen texts. These describe the sun and moon "standing" and "stopping" in the sky, using the same words as in the biblical account. In these texts, the appearance of the sun and moon together on particular days serves as an omen. The nature of the omen for good or ill is dependent on the day of the month on which the confluence occurs. This suggests the text is working polemically with known ideas, revealing what would be a bad omen for the Amorites and showing that it is God who controls such phenomena. One problem with the solution these omen texts provide is that none of them refer to lengthened days. Thus, while they go a long way to contextualize the biblical text, they are not completely parallel.[14]

None of the possible explanations fully satisfies all questions, leaving the event somewhat allusive and mysterious. The poetic form of this event adds to the event's mystery, for poetry is by nature allusive and figurative. In the end, the text itself is not overly concerned to detail or explain what happens or how—these are not questions on which the text focuses. Rather, it focuses on the theological conclusions to be drawn from the event.

Whatever happened with the sun and moon may remain a mystery forever, but the two-fold theological point is clear. First, the day is proclaimed as unique. Its uniqueness is not due to the miracle, but due to the fact the "LORD listened to a human being" (v. 14). This is not (of course!) the only time the LORD has ever attended to humans! The Old Testament is filled with instances of God listening to his people, from Israel's cry from Egypt (Exod 2:24) to Hagar's distress (Gen 16:11). God is a God who hears prayer (1 Kgs 8:27–53). In this instance, however, a particular Hebrew phrase is used ("the LORD listened to the voice of X"). This phrase is found only two other times in the Old Testament. Once, the "LORD listened to Israel's plea" (Num 21:3) and victory in war resulted. Only one other time, however, has the "LORD listened to the voice of X" (when "X" is an individual): Elijah (1 Kgs 17:22).[15] Elijah petitioned the LORD for a miracle, and the LORD listened and responded so that life was restored. In the context of Elijah's narrative (1 Kgs 17–18), the miracle is for the purpose of proving God's power before the showdown at Mount Carmel. The comparison to Joshua is especially interesting. In both cases, the LORD's power is proven. And in both cases, the individuals are

14. The omen texts are discussed by John H. Walton, "Joshua 10:12–15 and Mesopotamian Celestial Omen Texts," in *Faith, Tradition, and History: Old Testament Historiography in Its Near Eastern Context*, ed. A. R. Millard (Winona Lake: Eisenbrauns, 1994), 181–90.

15. Note that the NIV translates 1 Kings 17:22 as "the LORD heard Elijah's cry." In addition to the three verses in which "the LORD listened to the voice of X" (Num 21:3; Josh 10:14; 1 Kgs 17:22), two additional verses note that "*God* listened to the voice of X" (Gen 30:6; Judg 13:9—both in the context of the miraculous).

intentionally presented as fulfilling the ministry of the Lord's servant, Moses. In Joshua, the unique day proves God's power while also proving the ministry of Joshua-*qua*-Moses.

The second theological point is boldly made: "Surely the Lord was fighting for Israel!" (v. 14; cf. v. 42). Israel does not stand alone in fulfilling its covenant obligations toward Gibeon. God fights on Israel's behalf as Moses had promised (Deut 1:30; 3:22; 20:4) and as occurred at the Red Sea (Exod 14:14, 25). Israel does fight, but it is the presence of God with Israel—evident in the enemies' confusion and the elements acting very un-elementally—that enables Israel's victory.

The main outlines of the battle summarized, Israel's return to Gilgal is noted. Joshua went up with "his entire army" (v. 7) and returns "with all Israel" (vv. 15, 43), suggesting the magnitude of their success—not one of their number is lost.

From this conclusion, all that follows is retrospective (vv. 16–39) and summative conclusion (vv. 40–43). The retrospective shows Israel fighting alongside the divine warrior in a battle already won.

### Exposing the Five Kings (10:16–27)

Israel had pursued the enemy troops from Azekah to Makkedah (v. 10). This retrospective returns to Makkedah to continue the pursuit (vv. 10, 16–19). As with the first retrospective (vv. 11–15), this one begins with the enemy's flight (v. 16). The focus turns from the defeat and pursuit of the enemy army to the five kings who began the action. They are mentioned seven times in these few verses (vv. 16, 17, 22, 23, 24 [2x], 26), with an additional mention naming their cities (v. 23). The chapter focuses on kingly power, showing it to be utterly ineffective against the Lord and his troops. The kings began by planning Israel's demise (vv. 3–5); now those plans are dashed, and the kings are "hiding" in a cave at Makkedah (vv. 16, 17, 27).

The intertwined theme of God fighting/Israel fighting continues in this section. While the previous retrospective highlighted God's acts in battle—the hail, the sun and moon—this retrospective examines Israel's acts in battle. Yet the Lord remains very much "fighting for Israel" (v. 14), for he gives the enemy into Israel's hand (v. 19) and achieves victory against future enemies (v. 25).

This divine/human interaction is also apparent as Joshua delivers words to Israel that he himself received from God:

> God encourages Joshua (v. 8):
> 
> Do not be afraid
> 
> I have given them into your hand

Not one . . . will be able to withstand (from *'md*) you;

and then Joshua gives that same encouragement to Israel (vv. 19, 25):

Do not be afraid (v. 25)

God has given them into your hand (v. 19)

Don't stop (from *'md*, in Hebrew, "don't stand"); pursue your enemies (v. 19)

Joshua's words to Israel (vv. 19, 25) are those he received as this action began (v. 8). To them he adds additional words of encouragement (v. 25), which he had himself received from God. God had encouraged Joshua to "not be discouraged" (1:9; 8:1) and to "be strong and courageous" (1:6, 7, 9; 8:1). Now Joshua includes those same encouragements in his words to Israel. In doing so, he once more takes on the role of Moses, speaking God's words to his people.

Earlier, Israel had pursued the Amorite army while the LORD hurled hailstones (in Hebrew, "large rocks") from heaven. Now, Joshua commands Israel to hole up the kings with "large rocks" blocking the cave. Focused on pursuit, only one verse is given to the command (v. 18), and the action does not pause to note its accomplishment. Hot on the enemies' heels, Israel attacks from the rear to prevent them reaching their walled cities. The LORD gives the fleeing armies into the hand of Israel who "defeated them completely" (v. 20). This is the same phrase as used in verse 10 and (as in v. 10) is hyperbolic for, although Israel "defeats them completely," survivors escape (vv. 10, 20). A few reach their cities, but the fate of these survivors is left until verses 28–39.

The pursuit ends, and the "whole army" returns safely to Joshua at Makkedah (v. 21). The "whole army" not only continues an emphasis on "all Israel" entering the land and fighting together (1:12–15), but it also contrasts the defeated and dispersed Amorite troops. In like manner Israel's safe return contrasts the fugitive survivors and the kings who, though "hidden," are anything but safe. Confirming the magnitude of the Israelite victory is the comment that "no one uttered a word against the Israelites" (v. 21). The comment is similar to that uttered in Exodus 11:7 when, after God's great Passover victory, a distinction was made between Israel and Egypt and no utterance was made against Israel. In the present context, the great victory over the Amorite troops stops the mouths of the inhabitants. This is another expression of the fearful awe in which the land holds Israel (2:9–11; 5:1; 9:24).

Joshua deals with the kings according to the conventions of the ancient world (see Listen to the Story, Chapters 7 and 10). The whole army witnesses as their leaders symbolically place their feet on the necks of the defeated kings. The repeated reference to "the five kings," "these kings," and the naming of their towns emphasizes that royal power cannot stand against the Lord and his army (vv. 22–24). Joshua encourages the troops for future battle (v. 25), using the symbolic moment of humiliation of the foe to affirm that this (and all future) victory is accomplished by the Lord's hand. If any of the peoples choose to fight Israel, the Lord will defeat them.

The kings are executed and impaled, exposed until evening as an act of humiliation. Joshua does not leave the bodies indefinitely (as would be the usual ancient Near Eastern practice of humiliation) but removes them at evening. This honors the human body, a concern evident in the law (Deut 21:22–23; see discussion of the similar action at 8:29). The final resting place for the five kings is, ironically, the cave in which they sought refuge. The rocks placed there are a reminder of the events and a testimony that Israel and God fought together against the inhabitants' supposed kingly power.

## Taking the Cities (10:28–39)

After executing the five kings at Makkedah, verses 28–39 note cities taken before Israel returns to Gilgal (vv. 15, 43). The action begins at Makkedah where the kings were executed, and the narrative continuity is particularly apparent in the Hebrew word order that reads, "Now Makkedah Joshua took that day."

Makkedah is geographically in the midst of the cities named in the list. From it, Israel moves northwest to Libnah then turns south to Lachish, east to Eglon, northeast to Hebron, and finally south to Debir. Three of the cities are those of the five kings. Excluded are Jerusalem (no mention of taking Jerusalem is made until Judg 1:8) and Jarmuth (passed during the pursuit). Cities other than those of the five kings are taken (Makkedah, Libnah, Debir). That this may be a selective account is clear from 12:15 where the king of Adullam is enumerated. Adullam is a southern city and most likely taken as part of this action.

The account offers no narrative exposition, and the rapid pace heightens the sense of Israel's invincibility; no city can stand because God fights for Israel. This is furthered by the account's highly stylized, iterative nature. One by one and in the same manner, city after city falls. The repetitive format offers a clearly discernible pattern, even though not all elements are always present for each city and may appear in different order. This pattern is familiar as it is found in similar conquest accounts from the ancient Near East, including Egyptian, Hittite, and Assyrian records. The patterning shared by these accounts and present in the biblical text includes the following elements:[16]

16. The patterning is based on the Hebrew wording. Where English translation obscures this, the different English words are shown. A discussion of the patterning of such accounts can be found in Younger, "Rhetorical Structuring," 17–24. See also Hess, *Joshua*, 223.

| **Building Blocks Utilized** | **Makkedah** | **Libnah** | **Lachish** | **Gezer** | **Eglon** | **Hebron** | **Debir** |
|---|---|---|---|---|---|---|---|
| Joshua and all Israel moved on from city A to city B | | X | X | | X | X | X |
| took up positions against it | | | X | | X | | |
| attacked it | | X | X | | X | X | X |
| the LORD gave [city/king] into their hand | | X | X | | | | |
| took it/captured it | X | | X | | X | X | X |
| put the city/king to the sword | X | X | X | | X | X | X |
| *a king comes up to help* | | | | *X* | | | |
| *Joshua defeated him* | | | | *X* | | | |
| totally destroyed everyone | X | | | | X | X | X |
| left no survivors | X | X | | *X* | | X | X |
| as they did to [city/king] | X | X | X | | X | X | X |

The account includes cities belonging to the five kings and new cities ruled by unnamed kings. These could be sketched as follows:

Makkedah and its king (non-coalition city)<br>
Libnah and its king (non-coalition city)<br>
    Lachish (coalition city; king not here mentioned; killed in v. 26)<br>
        King of Gezer<br>
    Eglon (coalition city; king not here mentioned; killed in v. 26)<br>
Hebron and its king (coalition city; king also killed in v. 26)<br>
Debir and its king (coalition city)

Kings are a clear focus in the list. Their futile actions and their fate demonstrate the theme of ineffective kingly power. The list has an outer frame of four kings specifically noted as killed in the action of vv. 28–39. Hebron's king was already mentioned as killed (v. 26). The repetition is perhaps for narrative symmetry or may indicate that an additional ruler or a ruler from a satellite city is in view. Within this frame, two kings (Lachish and Eglon) are killed in Israel's earlier action. At its center the list has a unique entry, noting a king who has not yet appeared in the narrative: the King of Gezer. He travels south to aid Lachish but is defeated. Although Gezer is not mentioned as taken, the king is killed. His troops suffer what is not included in the Lachish and Eglon accounts: "no survivors were left" (see above table).

The kings of Makkedah and Libnah are executed and compared to the king of Jericho, the first king taken in the land. This provides a retrospective assessment of the king of Jericho's power—it was as ineffective as that of the present kings. The final city, Debir, compares the fate of its king to that of Libnah (and, by extension, Jericho). From the list's beginning to its end, royal power is maligned as ineffective against Israel and its God. By contrast, the passage focuses on Israel's more egalitarian structure of "Joshua and all Israel" (vv. 29, 31, 34, 36, 38). Under its divine king, Israel has success against all opposing kings.

The list also shares the hyperbole common to ancient conquest accounts. Thus, the accounts speak of total destruction (see the discussion of hyperbole and *herem* in Listen to the Story, Chapter 5; see also Introduction). Cities are attacked and although none are burned (as were Jericho and Ai), no survivors are left; all are put to the sword. Without recognizing the rhetorical use of hyperbole common to such accounts, the claim of total destruction would be puzzling at best. For instance, Hebron and Debir are "totally destroyed" with "no survivors," but just one chapter later the cities are still inhabited. Joshua engages them again and executes *herem* a second time (11:21)! This second "total destruction" similarly reflects the hyperbole of such texts—for later still, Caleb continues the task of battling the inhabitants of these same cities (14:6–15; 15:13–15). This is not an example of the biblical text contradicting itself. Rather, as in other ancient conquest accounts, hyperbole is a standard rhetorical strategy. In this instance, it makes a dual theological point: (1) as Joshua fulfills the command of total destruction (Deut 20:16–17) the crucial relationship of obedience to success is made clear (1:7–8); and (2) Israel's success shows that God fights on its behalf.

### "Because God Fought for Israel" (10:40–43)

As noted above (see Listen to the Story), the concluding summaries in ancient Near Eastern conquest accounts work to make a rhetorical point, often affirming the power of the victor's god. This is the case here. The very real battles Israel fought in this campaign are summarized and victory is credited to God, who fought for Israel (v. 42). This is a theological claim the chapter has already made (v. 14). Additionally, the conclusion revisits the chapter's intertwined theme of Israel's full participation in the battle. Here, successful participation is credited to obedience to God's command (v. 40).

The hyperbolic nature of the summary's claims is clear in its language. It is the language employed at several points in the chapter and whose hyperbole has already been discussed. Thus, "the whole region" (vv. 40, 41), "all their lands" (v. 42), and "all these kings" (vv. 40, 42) are "subdued" (v. 40, 41; translated as "defeated" in vv. 10, 20, 33). They are also characterized as "conquered" (v. 42; the same word is translated "taken" in vv. 1, 28, 32, 37, 39 and "captured" in v. 35). All this has been accomplished in "one campaign" in which "no survivors" were left (v. 40; cf. vv. 28, 30, 33, 37, 39) but all were "totally destroyed" (v. 40; cf. vv. 1, 28, 35, 37, 39). It is through these claims that the theological point of God's power and Israel's obedience is made. While the summary's claims are grand, no claim is made of full occupation of the land—that is yet to come, and Israel pointedly remains camped at Gilgal (vv. 15, 43; 14:6).

The conclusion continues its focus on kingly power (vv. 40, 42) but moves the focus from "Joshua and all Israel" in the previous section to Joshua alone. His leadership is lauded as he is noted as the sole human actor. The territory Joshua has "subdued" is sketched in two different ways. First, the regions of the southern sweep are noted and include the central hills (Hebron, Debir), the western foothills and mountain slopes (Lachish, Libnah, Makkedah), and the Negev, or at least the city whose location controls access to this area (Eglon). The regional summary may also envision a more extensive campaign than described in the chapter's selective account. Second, the boundaries of the territory subdued by Joshua are sketched. These stretch from Kadesh Barnea in the south to Gaza in the western foothills. Kadesh Barnea is the point from which Israel made its ill-fated reconnaissance (Num 13:26). The boundary also includes Goshen (not the Egyptian territory of the same name in Gen 46:28–34; 47:1–10 but a southeastern boundary toward the Negev and the Dead Sea). The boundary returns finally to Gibeon where the chapter's action began.

This bounded territory Joshua has conquered in "one campaign," a characterization that suggests the inevitability and ease with which the land was taken. With this, the chapter concludes its summary with the crucial point: God has faithfully fought for his covenant people; by this, Israel has received the land.

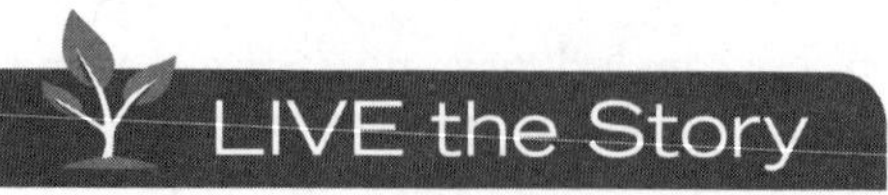


### The Power of the King

Several aspects of Joshua 10 open reflection on the idea of God's kingship. "God as King" may be an unfamiliar or uncomfortable idea for many Christians.

In a modern democracy, "rule" is something considered best shared among the people. For those in a constitutional monarchy (such as the Canadian context), royalty is part of the system of governance. But the sovereign lives far away—in London, England—and visits rarely, while the sovereign's representative (in Canada, the Governor General) is not a frequent part of daily life and government. For others, kingship conjures images of despotic, absolute rule, examples of which have wrought great suffering, even in our century. For reasons such as these, the concept of God's kingship often is an unexplored metaphor. This is unfortunate, for it is a pervasive image throughout the Bible and opens exploration of Christ's identity and work in helpful ways.

In Joshua 10 (as in Josh 11), there is an emphasis on the overthrow of royal power. The five-king coalition formed against Gibeon and Israel (v. 3) is defeated and the kings killed (v. 26). The death of four additional kings is noted (vv. 28, 30, 33, 39), and the death of Jericho's king is twice recalled (vv. 28, 30). The chapter's summary (vv. 40–43) states "All these kings . . . Joshua conquered." The chapter reveals royal power is ineffective against a sovereign God and the army he commissions.

God's ability to overturn royal power is a constant Old Testament theme. God's power is exercised over foreign kings (as in Josh 10) and Israelite kings. Over Israelite kings, God exercises his power several ways. First, the institution of kingship begins in Israel by God's permission, granted as a concession to the peoples' sinful request (1 Sam 8:1–7). Second, God selects kings such as Saul (1 Sam 9:17; 10:1) and David (1 Sam 16:11–13), designating them by prophetic anointing. Third, after the kingdom divides into northern (Israel) and southern (Judah) nations, the LORD's power over kings is exercised through appointing and deposing successive dynasties, particularly in the northern kingdom (1 Kgs 11:29–31, 37; 14:6–14; 16:1–4; 21:20–22; 2 Kgs 9:1–13).

God similarly exercises power over foreign kings. They can be appointed by God's hand (1 Kgs 19:15; Isa 45:1; Jer 25:9; Dan 5:18) as well as deposed by him (Dan 4:31 with 5:20–21, 25–28). God's power over foreign kings is often (as in Josh 10–11) exercised in the context of battle. The LORD uses foreign kings and their armies as instruments to test Israel (Judg 3:1–4) or to exercise discipline (Judg 2:11–15; 2 Kgs 19:25–26; Jer 21:4–7, 10). When foreign powers boastfully take credit for their victory or overextend their mandate with excessive violence, God's sovereign power brings his instrument down (2 Kgs 19:22–24, 27–28; Jer 51:7–9, 20–25).

The source and prerogative of God's power over kings resides in the fact that he is the greater sovereign. In the Old Testament, God's kingship is attested by his creative power, eternally enthroning him over the world and its inhabitants (Pss 24:1; 93:1). Miriam praises God's kingship at the Red Sea (Exod 15:18), celebrating his victory over Egypt's king and the waters themselves. The Psalms also celebrate God's power over the Red Sea water (Ps 77:16–20; 114:1–3), understanding that this power is the expression in history of his power over the cosmic waters (Pss 18:14–15; 24:1–2; 29:10; 74:12–17; Isa 27:1; Nah 1:4). It is in light of God's absolute kingship over Israel that its request for a human king is reckoned sinful (1 Sam 8:7).

God's kingship and his rule over the nations is the subject of Psalm 2. Even though the "nations conspire [and] the kings of the earth rise up and the rulers band together against the LORD and against his anointed" (vv. 1–2), God remains the "One enthroned in heaven" (v. 4). As this all-powerful king, God's response toward the nations' conspiracy is scorn and rebuke:

> The One enthroned in heaven laughs;
> the LORD scoffs at them.
> He rebukes them in his anger
> and terrifies them in his wrath (vv. 4–5).

Rather than conspiring against God, the nations are called to "be wise. . . . Serve the LORD with fear and celebrate his rule with trembling" (v. 10–11). The psalm could serve as commentary on the events of Joshua 10. It provides a ready description of the action of the Canaanite kings and the more appropriate response they could have rendered. It also speaks of the ease with which God's sovereign power overthrows their opposition.

The New Testament applies Psalm 2 to the work of God in Christ. In Acts 4, Psalm 2 reveals God's sovereign power demonstrated through the resurrection of Jesus. The apostles name Herod, Pontius Pilate, the gentiles, and Israel as those who "raged and plotted in vain" against the Lord and his anointed, Jesus Christ (Acts 4:25–27). The nations have apparent success in opposing the Lord's anointed, Jesus, for he is crucified by their hand, but it is God's power that triumphs. In another use of Psalm 2, Paul preaches the resurrection in Pisidian Antioch (Acts 13). In his sermon, he cites Psalm 2 as attesting to the resurrection of Christ (v. 33). The psalm's use in both Acts 4 and 13 interprets the resurrection as the evidence that God is the one enthroned in heaven (Ps 2:4). Through the powerful resurrection he "laughs . . . scoffs . . . rebukes . . . and terrifies" the earthly power of the nations (Ps 2:4–5).

For a final time in the book of Revelation, the nations rage against God and his anointed. As in Joshua 10, the nations gather for battle against God's army (19:11–21). Leading that army is the "King of King and Lord of Lords" (v. 16). This king is revealed to be the word of God—Jesus—who strikes down the nations with his sword, to rule in righteousness with a scepter of iron (v. 15; cf. 20:4), an apparent echo of Psalm 2:9. Throughout the book of

Revelation, God's rule has been praised (5:13; 7:10, 15; 19:6). Following the final battle, the Son-King hands all power over to the Father who reigns as all in all (1 Cor 15:24–28).

In a final and lasting demonstration of his sovereign power, the king who created the world will now make "everything new" (Rev 21:5) and dwell with his people in the perfected Jerusalem. His sovereignty will be glorious. As Psalm 2:11 anticipates, and in an amazing reversal of the kingly opposition in Joshua 10, the raging nations will become willing subjects, bringing their splendor to honor the Great King:

> The city does not need the sun or the moon to shine on it, for the glory of God gives it light, and the Lamb is its lamp. The nations will walk by its light, and the kings of the earth will bring their splendor into it. (Rev 21:23–24)

### Symbols of Power: All Things under His Feet

Joshua utilizes a common ancient Near Eastern image of conquest when he instructs the men of Israel to put their feet on the necks of the conquered kings (v. 24; see Listen to the Story above). A similar (but not identical) figure of humiliating conquest is found in Isaiah 51:23 where Israel's enemies call them to "fall prostrate that we may walk on you."

Another related image is found in Psalm 110. This is a messianic psalm and is utilized by Peter (along with Joel 2 and Ps 16) in his Day of Pentecost sermon (Acts 2). With it, Peter argues that Christ has ascended to heaven, thus proving that "God has made this Jesus, whom you crucified, both Lord and Messiah" (Acts 2:34–36).

The specific citation Peter makes is:

> The Lord said to my Lord:
> 'Sit at my right hand
> until I make your enemies
> a footstool for your feet' (Acts 2:34–35 citing Ps 110:1).

The phrasing is not identical to that of Joshua 10:24 but provides an evocative analogy. In both instances, a powerful enemy is overthrown and humbled by God's power. In a literal reading of Joshua 10, the enemies are human kings. The Christian interpretive tradition also works figurally with the passage. Origen sees in the Canaanite kings a figure of "opposing powers and spiritual iniquities." God defeats them through Joshua, who is a figure of the true Joshua (Jesus) who defeats all opposing spiritual powers.[17] Such a

17. Origen, *Hom* 11.2.

reading aligns with Peter's interpretation of Psalm 110, where victory is won in the spiritual realm.

The New Testament takes up the image of enemies defeated and put under Christ's feet. Jesus himself utilizes Psalm 110 in Luke 20:41–44. In an honor-shame contest with the Sadducees (who deny the resurrection), Jesus undercuts their challenge by arguing the dead indeed rise, for the LORD is the God of Abraham, Isaac, and Jacob. That is, "He is not the God of the dead, but of the living, for to him all are alive" (Luke 20:38). As further proof of his claim, Jesus cites Psalm 110:1, using it to show that the Messiah, the one who is both David's lord and son, must be the eternal, living God. It is this one whose feet are on his enemies, triumphant over them.

Psalm 110:1 also is used in similar fashion in Hebrews 1:13. In verses 5–14 several psalms (2:7; 104:4; 45:6–7; 102:25–27) are brought together with Psalm 110:1. Through this, the author argues for the superiority of Christ. The Son is God whose "throne . . . will last for ever and ever" (v. 8) and who has been made to sit at God's right hand until his enemies are made his footstool (v. 13). Once again, it is the sovereign God whose power is exercised in triumph over his enemies, bringing them under his feet.

Calvin examines Psalm 110, seeing the defeat of Christ's enemies that throughout time fight against Christ's rule. Each will fall, humiliated and overcome under the feet of the victor:

> By these words the prophet affirms that Christ would subdue all the opposition which his enemies in their tumultuous rage might employ for the subversion of his kingdom. At the same time, he intimates that the kingdom of Christ would never enjoy tranquillity until he had conquered his numerous and formidable enemies. And even should the whole world direct their machinations to the overthrow of Christ's royal throne, David here declares that it would remain unmoved and unmoveable, while all they who rise up against it shall be ruined. From this let us learn that, however numerous those enemies may be who conspire against the Son of God, and attempt the subversion of his kingdom, all will be unavailing, for they shall never prevail against God's immutable purpose, but, on the contrary, they shall, by the greatness of his power, be laid prostrate at Christ's feet. And as this prediction will not be accomplished before the last day, it must be that the kingdom of Christ will be assailed by many enemies from time to time until the end of the world.[18]

18. John Calvin, *Commentary on the Psalms*, vol. 4, CCEL (https://www.ccel.org/ccel/calvin/calcom11.html), 266–67.

Calvin acknowledges that Christ's enemies will be undone. He emphasizes that in Christ "all will be unavailing, for they shall never prevail against God's immutable purpose." Reading Psalm 110:1 in light of Joshua 10, all that opposes the Christian church will ultimately face the same fate as the Canaanite kings. But Calvin does not assert that all enemies are presently under Christ's feet. The church cannot walk in a here-and-now triumphalism for there are "many enemies from time to time until the end of the world." The endpoint for all opposition is rightly placed by Calvin in the future. In this, he looks to 1 Corinthians 15:20–28 where only at the consummation are all enemies—including the great enemy, death—finally and forever placed under the feet of the sovereign Lord:

> Then the end will come, when he hands over the kingdom to God the Father after he has destroyed all dominion, authority and power. For he must reign until he has put all his enemies under his feet. The last enemy to be destroyed is death. For he "has put everything under his feet." (1 Cor 10:24–27)

These are words of hope: hope to raise up in the face of persecution and martyrdom; hope to hold up at the graveside. Christ is the victor—risen, ascended, and at God's right hand; all enemies are forever under his feet. Thanks be to God!

### Supernatural Battle and Spiritual Warfare

The entries above have touched on figural readings of the battle in Joshua 10. This section takes up such readings again, first looking at God's supernatural power in battle, and then turning to the spiritual battle in which Christians are to engage.

Popular culture readily displays the supernatural in battle. In Steven Spielberg's 1981 movie, *Raiders of the Lost Ark*, Indiana Jones warns Marion Ravenwood not to look as the ark of the covenant is opened by the archaeologist René Belloq and his Nazi associates. Indy and Marion keep their eyes tightly shut as eerie, angelic figures fly out of the ark. Suddenly, they are revealed as horrible angels of death and, along with bolts of raw energy emanating from the ark, they fly about in a cinematic depiction of God's power unleashed against enemy forces. Melting faces and exploding heads ensue! Invisible, supernatural armies are also movie fare: one thinks of Aragorn's timely arrival at the Battle of the Pelennor Fields in Peter Jackson's 2003 version of *The Lord of the Rings: The Return of the King*. With him is the ghost army of the Dead Men of Dunharrow. The glowing horde traverses the field and city. Swift death ensues!

The Old Testament also includes the supernatural in battle, although it is not included (as in our culture) merely for entertainment value. Instead, it makes theological claims regarding the power and presence of God in Israel's midst.

Several accounts show God's supernatural utilization of creation in battle. Joshua 10 reveals God battling on Israel's behalf through the forces of nature (hailstones, sun, moon). At the Red Sea, God fights for Israel against Egypt using the wind and water to defeat a powerful enemy (Exod 14:14, 21–28; see also The Power of the King above). In a similar fashion, God brings his battle-ready Israelites through the Jordan (see Chapter 3). Elsewhere, water is part of a supernatural battle strategy (2 Kgs 3:16–20), and God uses a loud wind to frighten the enemy army (2 Sam 5:22–25; 2 Kgs 7:6–7).

The involvement of God in battle is part and parcel of the biblical record. After God battles the Egyptians, Miriam describes him as a "warrior" (Exod 15:3). At the final battle, Christ appears as a warrior, with the word coming as a sword from his mouth (Rev 19:15). Joshua has already encountered the "commander of the army of the LORD" (Josh 5:13–15), and God is known as the "LORD Almighty, the God of the armies of Israel" (1 Sam 17:45). For this reason, the ark of the covenant, the symbol of God's presence and power, goes before Israel into battle (Num 10:33–36; Josh 3–4, 6; 1 Sam 4:3–4).

God leads Israel into battle, but there are also accounts of supernatural, heavenly armies (2 Kgs 6:6–23) that are led by heavenly commanders (Josh 5:13–15). Daniel even speaks of heavenly beings battling one against the other (Dan 10:4–6, 20). Prophets also are part of the supernatural reality of God's warfare. The writing prophets recorded many prophetic words of battle against the nations (Isa 13–21; Jer 46–51; Ezek 25–32). Prophets are solicited prior to battle (1 Kgs 20, 22; 2 Kgs 3:11–19) and supernaturally predict victories (2 Kgs 13:14–19). The title, "The chariots and horsemen of Israel!" is applied to Elijah and Elisha (2 Kgs 2:12; 13:14), both of whom were part of God's battle against Baal, disobedient Israel, and foreign nations.

In the New Testament, the warrior God remains, now battling not against flesh and blood enemies, but against spiritual forces (see the fuller discussion in the Introduction, and The Power of the King above). Paradoxically, the battle over dark principalities and powers, and even death itself, is won through the warrior's self-sacrifice on the cross (Col 2:13–15; Eph 4:8, citing Ps 68 [a battle-psalm]). The resurrection and ascension of Christ marks this decisive victory, ushering in the reign of God. Yet, until the final battle, the world lives in an in-between time; a now and not yet time between victory won and victory realized. The kingdom of God *is here*, but the kingdom of God *awaits its final consummation.*

During this in-between time, the spiritual battle is engaged by Christ's followers, who, through identification with Christ, are taken up in the battle of God. For this reason, Paul urges Christians to

> Put on the full armor of God, so that you can take your stand against the devil's schemes. For our struggle is not against flesh and blood, but against the rulers, against the authorities, against the powers of this dark world and against the spiritual forces of evil in the heavenly realms. Therefore put on the full armor of God, so that when the day of evil comes, you may be able to stand your ground, and after you have done everything, to stand. (Eph 6:11–13)

It is the Christian's present spiritual warfare through which Origen reads Joshua 10 (and 11). He broadly conceives of the warfare in Joshua as a figure for spiritual warfare for

> [e]ven now my Lord Jesus Christ wars against opposing powers and casts out of their cities, that is, out of our souls, those who used to occupy them. And he destroys the kings who were ruling in our souls 'that sin may no longer reign in us,' so that, after he abolishes the king of sin from the city of our soul, our soul may become the city of God and God may reign in it.[19]

Within Origen's allegorical framework, the kings of chapters 10–11 find more specific meaning. The five kings of Joshua 10 are figures for the five senses, through which people are tempted to sin. The senses—the five kings—"Fight the Gibeonites, that is, carnal persons."[20] Later, Origen will liken the northern leader, Jabin (Josh 11:1), to the devil against whom Christians "wage war properly under the leadership of Jesus."[21] Victory involves the hamstringing of the enemies' horses (human passions such as lust, petulance, pride, fickleness), achieved "when the body is humbled by fastings and vigils and by every pain of self-denial."[22]

In the context of the Christian's spiritual warfare, Joshua 10 offers assurance. The Christian does not fight the battle in his or her own strength. Christ stands with them, fighting on their behalf, and empowering them in the midst of the battle. While individual battles may be won or lost, the outcome is assured when every "king" will be defeated. In that time, the Christian will know the true freedom of victory over sin, death, and the devil.

---

19. Origen, *Hom* 13.1.
20. Ibid., 11.4.
21. Ibid., 15.3.
22. Ibid.

CHAPTER 11

# Joshua 11:1–23

## LISTEN to the Story

[1]When Jabin king of Hazor heard of this, he sent word to Jobab king of
Madon, to the kings of Shimron and Akshaph, [2]and to the northern kings
who were in the mountains, in the Arabah south of Kinnereth, in the western
foothills and in Naphoth Dor on the west; [3]to the Canaanites in the east and
west; to the Amorites, Hittites, Perizzites and Jebusites in the hill country;
and to the Hivites below Hermon in the region of Mizpah. [4]They came out
with all their troops and a large number of horses and chariots—a huge army,
as numerous as the sand on the seashore. [5]All these kings joined forces and
made camp together at the Waters of Merom to fight against Israel.

[6]The LORD said to Joshua, "Do not be afraid of them, because by this
time tomorrow I will hand all of them, slain, over to Israel. You are to
hamstring their horses and burn their chariots."

[7]So Joshua and his whole army came against them suddenly at the
Waters of Merom and attacked them, [8]and the LORD gave them into
the hand of Israel. They defeated them and pursued them all the way to
Greater Sidon, to Misrephoth Maim, and to the Valley of Mizpah on the
east, until no survivors were left. [9]Joshua did to them as the LORD had
directed: He hamstrung their horses and burned their chariots.

[10]At that time Joshua turned back and captured Hazor and put its king
to the sword. (Hazor had been the head of all these kingdoms.) [11]Everyone
in it they put to the sword. They totally destroyed them, not sparing
anyone that breathed, and he burned Hazor itself.

[12]Joshua took all these royal cities and their kings and put them to
the sword. He totally destroyed them, as Moses the servant of the LORD
had commanded. [13]Yet Israel did not burn any of the cities built on their
mounds—except Hazor, which Joshua burned. [14]The Israelites carried
off for themselves all the plunder and livestock of these cities, but all
the people they put to the sword until they completely destroyed them,
not sparing anyone that breathed. [15]As the LORD commanded his servant

Moses, so Moses commanded Joshua, and Joshua did it; he left nothing undone of all that the LORD commanded Moses.

[16]So Joshua took this entire land: the hill country, all the Negev, the whole region of Goshen, the western foothills, the Arabah and the mountains of Israel with their foothills, [17]from Mount Halak, which rises toward Seir, to Baal Gad in the Valley of Lebanon below Mount Hermon. He captured all their kings and put them to death. [18]Joshua waged war against all these kings for a long time. [19]Except for the Hivites living in Gibeon, not one city made a treaty of peace with the Israelites, who took them all in battle. [20]For it was the LORD himself who hardened their hearts to wage war against Israel, so that he might destroy them totally, exterminating them without mercy, as the LORD had commanded Moses.

[21]At that time Joshua went and destroyed the Anakites from the hill country: from Hebron, Debir and Anab, from all the hill country of Judah, and from all the hill country of Israel. Joshua totally destroyed them and their towns. [22]No Anakites were left in Israelite territory; only in Gaza, Gath and Ashdod did any survive.

[23]So Joshua took the entire land, just as the LORD had directed Moses, and he gave it as an inheritance to Israel according to their tribal divisions. Then the land had rest from war.

*Listening to the Text in the Story*: Exodus 1–14; Numbers 13:26–33; Deuteronomy 9:1–3; Poem and Bulletin Text on the Battle of Qadesh; Zakkur Inscription; Armant Stele

## Hardened Hearts

In the crossing of the Jordan, the Red Sea crossing is evoked (see Listen to the Story, Chapter 3). In this chapter, the evocation of the exodus is renewed in the reference to God "hardening their hearts" (v. 20). In Exodus 4–14, God hardens Pharaoh's heart (Exod 4:21; 7:3; 9:12; 10:1, 20, 27; 11:10; 14:4, 8, 17) while Pharaoh hardens his own heart (Exod 8:15[11], 32[28]; 9:34; 13:15). Before this occurs however, there are hints that this hardened heart is already at work. In Exodus 1–2 Pharaoh's actions and thinking are already harsh and oppressive. At the burning bush, God says of Pharaoh that "I know that the king of Egypt will not let you go unless a mighty hand compels him" (3:19). Something strong must take place for Pharaoh to relent and let God's people go. Pharaoh's first words to Moses' command to release Israel reveal the source of his heart attitude:

> "Who is the LORD, that I should obey him and let Israel go? I do not know the LORD and I will not let Israel go." (Exod 5:2)

Pharaoh will not acknowledge God. Instead, he actively resists God's purposes. Even when God reveals himself through miraculous power, Pharaoh's heart is set in this attitude of arrogant rebellion.

The Canaanite coalition is likewise hardened by the LORD, but this hardening only strengthens ("hardens") a prior attitude. Rahab and the Gibeonites yielded to God, acknowledging his grant of land to Israel (2:9–11; 9:24). By contrast, the Canaanite kings oppose that plan by engaging Israel in battle. Though they have reports of God's fame at the Sea, the Jordan, and Jericho, they will not yield. To achieve his purposes, God confirms their attitude, and the Canaanites persist in engaging in battle. Elsewhere, Canaanite wickedness and idolatry are given as reasons for their dispossession (Gen 15:16; Deut 7:4; 9:4–5); these are not reasons specifically named in Joshua. Instead, Joshua notes their failure to acknowledge God and his purposes regarding the land. The Canaanite kings and their power will be broken, as was that of Pharaoh before them.

### Anakites Again

The reference to the Anakites in 11:21–22 singles out a specific people in the midst of broad summaries (vv. 16–19, 23). The reference might be considered a disconnected digression since Anakites are not elsewhere named in chapters 10–11. However, their presence in this summary is a reminder of their role in Israel's entry (or non-entry!) to the land.

It was because of the descendants of Anak—the Anakites—that Israel shrank in fear from entering the land. In Numbers 13 the spies' report that the inhabitants live in large fortified cities and are of "great size." Beside them, the Israelites appear like "grasshoppers in our own eyes" (Num 13:26–33). These giants are the Anakites.

As Moses prepares the people to enter the land, the Anakites are again mentioned as a fearful memory:

> "Hear Israel: You are now about to cross the Jordan to go in and dispossess nations greater and stronger than you, with large cities that have walls up to the sky. The people are strong and tall—Anakites! *You know about them and have heard it said: 'Who can stand up against the Anakites?'*" (Deut 9:1–2; emphasis added)

Moses then gives encouragement, lest the memory have power to once again hinder Israel's entry to the land:

> "But be assured today that the LORD your God is the one who goes across ahead of you like a devouring fire. He will destroy them; he will subdue them before you." (Deut 9:3)

Mentioning the Anakites in the concluding verses of Joshua 11 is especially meaningful. As the first half of the book draws to a close and the focus turns from taking the land to possessing the land, the citation of Anakite destruction marks the extent of Israelite victory—over peoples and over fear. Trusting in God's promise, they acted in obedience. Not even the dreaded, giant Anakites had power to prevent what God had promised.

### As the Sand on the Seashore

The huge army that challenges Joshua is "as numerous as the sand on the seashore" (v. 4). The terrifying aspect of an army too numerous to count is elsewhere similarly described. Ramesses II describes the armies of Hatti at Qadesh as "men and chariotry, abundant, exceedingly numerous like the sand."[1] This is the description in the poetic record of Ramesses' battle. In the summative Bulletin Text they are "furnished with their infantry and chariotry, [bearing their combat weapons]; they are more numerous than the sands of the seashore."[2]

### Fear Not

The Zakkur Inscription from northern Syria, likely dated to the eighth century BC, is a petition made by Zakkur, king of Hamath to his god Baʿlshamayn. Zakkur is besieged by a coalition of seventeen kings and receives assurance:

> Baʿlshamayn said to me, "Do not be afraid! Since I have made [you king, I will stand] beside you. I will save you from all [these kings who] have besieged you."[3]

While the inscription's assurance to not fear is similar to several given Joshua (1:9; 8:1; 10:8), it is especially pertinent to the present context because Joshua, too, is confronted by a large coalition.

### Summaries for Glory

Summaries of military activity, such as the Armant Stele of Thutmose III, are styled to glorify both the military leader and the sponsoring god. The rhetoric of these passages is similar to that found in Joshua 11:

1. *COS* 2.5A:34.
2. Ibid., 2.5B:39.
3. Ibid., 2.35:155.

> Regnal year twenty-two, second month of winter, day 10. A summary of the acts of bravery and victory of that which this good god performed comprising every act of athleticism beginning with the first generation of that which the Lord of the gods and the Lord of Armant, who exulted in his victories, did for him in order to have his bravery recounted for millions of years to come, besides the acts of athleticism which his majesty performed through time. If they were reported specifically by occurrence, they would be too many to record.[4]

## EXPLAIN the Story

As in chapter 10, Joshua responds to royal aggression. Joshua 10 and 11 have the same structure (see Explain the Story, Chapter 10) but are diverse in thematic focus. Joshua 11 is less detailed and contains none of the supernatural interventions of chapter 10. Its thematic focus links success with obedience to Moses' commands, closing the first half of the book with a crucial theme introduced in chapter 1. The chapter also continues chapter 10's focus on kings but moves from focusing on "all Israel" fighting a coalition of kings to presenting Joshua as the main actor. This facilitates the chapter's theme of obedience, for Joshua's leadership operates in obedience to Mosaic law.

### The Northern Campaign (11:1–15)

For the final time in Joshua, kings "hear" a report which, in context, is of the southern coalition's defeat. "Hearing" begins each of chapters 9, 10, and 11 and unites them as a unit. In each chapter, kings respond with aggression. This is different than their initial response of fear when Israel crossed the Jordan (5:1). The response also differs from that of Rahab (2:9–11) and the Gibeonites (9:24), who acknowledge Israel's claims and God's power.

The northern coalition is the final large-scale military action recorded in Joshua and concludes the first half of the book, which is focused on "taking" the land. Headed by Jabin, the king of Hazor, the coalition is larger than the five-king coalition of chapter 10. Jabin is joined by Jobab, the king of "Madon" ("Madon" elsewhere occurs only in 12:19 and may be a copyist's error for the "Merom" named in 11:5, 7), and unnamed kings from several geographic areas. These unnamed kings represent areas north and west of the Jezreel Valley (Shimron and Akshaph, respectively), mountainous areas north and south of the Jezreel Valley, the area south of Kinnereth (the Sea of Galilee/ Kinnereth or alternately the city of Kinnereth on the northwest side of the

4. *COS* 2.2C:18 also *ANET* 234.

Sea), the Shephelah or western hills, and the area near the coastal city of Dor, south of Mount Carmel. In addition, six Canaanite peoples are included, demonstrating the breadth of the coalition. The list is familiar (see 9:1 and 3:10 [with the addition of the Girgashites]).

The coalition represents areas from the east, through to the coast, and north to Mount Hermon. It is a vast force (described as "all their troops," "huge army," "all these kings"), innumerable as the "sand on the seashore" (vv. 4–5). Making the enemy even more formidable, it is fortified with a great number of horses and chariots—weapons of war against which Israel has not yet been tested. Despite terrifying odds and superior weaponry, significant clues anticipate Israel's victory. First, Pharaoh had earlier utilized horses and chariots, yet he was defeated by God's power (Exod 14:9, 23; 15:1, 19, 21; Deut 11:4). For this reason, Israel is not to fear such weapons (Deut 20:1). Second, God is present with and fights for Israel against the nations (10:14, 42). No coalition, however daunting, poses any real threat (3:10). In light of these realities, Joshua is not to fear (v. 6; cf. 8:1; 10:8, 25). As Israel earlier saw Egypt slain by the waters (Exod 14:30), God will likewise hand this enemy to Israel at the waters of Merom. Israel is to ensure the armies' chariots are demobilized by hamstringing the horses.

The waters of Merom is likely a site on the border of Hazor to the north and Shimron to the west.[5] Joshua attacks with the whole army and does so "suddenly" (v. 7), utilizing the tactic of surprise as at Gibeon (10:9). No further battle tactics are provided, but the victory is the Lord's. He gives the coalition into Israel's hand as promised (vv. 6, 8).

The defeated army flees and is pursued toward the territorial boundaries; the rhetorical effect is that Israel sweeps the enemy over the boundaries and from the land. The rhetoric emphasizes Israel's victory; in reality, the Canaanites continue as an ongoing presence in the land allotted for possession (see 15:63; 16:10; 17:12–13). The boundaries sketch out a broad area (vv. 8–10). Moving to Greater Sidon in the region of Tyre, eastward along the Litani River and the Misrephoth Maim to the Valley of Mizpah, Israel turns south along the valley to Hazor.

The pursuit utilizes the stereotypical phrasing found in chapter 10: Israel "defeated them," striking until "no survivors were left" (v. 8). In the pursuit, Joshua's obedience and leadership is highlighted, for he alone is credited with demobilizing the horses and chariots (v. 9). These weapons are an important piece of Canaanite resistance, an importance signaled by unusual Hebrew word order that (unlike the NIV translation) places the object before the verb:

5. For discussion of the placement of the locations in this chapter together with archaeological data, see Hess, *Joshua*.

"*their horses* he hamstrung and *their chariots* he burned" (emphasis added). The kings might trust in chariots and horses, but Joshua obediently trusts in the LORD and prevails (Ps 20:7[8]).

Joshua is credited with taking Hazor, the city which spearheaded the coalition. The account (vv. 10–11) utilizes the stereotypical phrasing of ancient Near Eastern accounts (see table and commentary in Chapter 10) and includes:

> Joshua turned back to Hazor . . .
> captured it . . .
> put the king to the sword *and* put everyone in it to the sword . . .
> totally destroyed them . . .
> left no survivors.

The formulaic phrases are rhetorically employed. They show total victory as in Joshua 10, because the LORD fought for Israel. To these phrases is added the notation that Hazor was head of "all these kingdoms" (v. 10). The importance of the city may account for the dual notice that both its king and its people are "put to the sword" (vv. 10–11). Of all the southern and northern coalition cities only Hazor is burned, further marking its importance. The burning of Hazor stands with the burning of Jericho as the first and last cities taken in Joshua 1–12. They dramatically frame the account of Israel "taking" the land.

The action concludes with a summary statement (vv. 12–15). The cities taken are "royal cities," which is a reminder of the "kings" of verses 1–3. While the summary notes several cities are taken, no battle account is given and only Hazor is named as burned. The familiar phrasing and hyperbole of such summaries continues (see Listen to the Story, Chapter 10) for the cities are "taken," "put to the sword," and "totally destroyed" not sparing "anyone that breathed."

The brevity of the conquest account directs attention to the chapter's different thematic focus. While chapter 10 focused on "all Israel," chapter 11 focuses on Joshua as the primary actor. The summary's first verse credits Joshua alone with taking the cities and kings, putting them to the sword, and totally destroying them (v. 12). This he does as "Moses the servant of the LORD commanded." Joshua's obedience to the law of Moses is taken up again in verse 15, which gives an explicit chain of command:

> The LORD commanded his servant Moses
> → so Moses commanded Joshua
> → and Joshua did it.

That the point not be lost, the verse concludes by restating the chain of command: Joshua "left nothing undone of all that the LORD commanded

Moses" (v. 15). Joshua is shown as the obedient servant of 1:7–9, fulfilling the commands of the Book of the Law of Moses and thus of the Lord himself. By this obedience his leadership finds success as he leads Israel into the land.

Although focused on Joshua, the summary does not forget Israel. Between the statements of Joshua's obedient leadership (vv. 12, 15), two verses detail Israel's part in the campaign, styled to highlight their obedience. First, Israel burns no city except for Hazor, which led the attack (v. 13). The norm of not burning cities aligns with the law of Moses (Deut 20:16–18) and is a tactic by which Israel gains furnished accommodation as envisioned in Moses' law (Deut 6:10–11; cf. Josh 24:13). Second, while at Jericho a specific command against taking plunder was issued; no such command is here given. This allows Israel to take plunder and livestock (v. 14). This, too, aligns with the law of warfare (Deut 20:16–18). Israel's earlier failure on this point (Josh 7) makes this present obedience especially noteworthy. Success has come to Israel (as to Joshua) through their obedience. Finally, Israel is obedient to the law of *herem* or total destruction (v. 14). Much has already been said regarding the hyperbolic nature of this command and its fulfillment (see Introduction and Chapters 5 and 10 above). Using the language of ancient conquest accounts, more is stated than actually occurs in order to heighten the theological point of Israel's victory by the power of its God.

### Southern and Northern Campaigns Summarized (11:16–22)

Two further summaries are given, each beginning with "So Joshua took all the/this land" (vv. 16, 23). In them the perspective widens to include both southern and northern campaigns as well as earlier actions at Jericho, Ai, and Gibeon. Each summary recalls past events and anticipates the future.

The first summary (vv. 16–22) notes the "entire land" taken by regions (v. 16). These are listed in a south-to-north direction, representing the action of chapters 10–11. The hill country, Negev, Goshen, and western foothills represent the southern campaign; the Arabah and mountains of Israel represent the northern campaign. A notable exception is the coastal plain, an area which Israel has not engaged to date. After this brief regional sketch, two significant landmarks set the boundaries of the action: Mount Halak in the south and Mount Hermon in the north. The summary credits Joshua with capturing and executing "all their kings" (v. 17), that is, those of Jericho, Ai, and the southern and northern cities. Thus far, the summary aligns with the rhetoric of the book (and particularly chs. 10–11) in which rapid, total victory is emphasized.

In verse 18 however, the rhetoric's hyperbole is revealed. A surface reading of the campaigns suggests Israel has completely and rapidly taken all the land and destroyed all the inhabitants. At times, the text has undercut this presentation (for instance, survivors remain after complete defeat [10:20]; the battle-action is only in prescribed areas and not the whole land). Now, the idea of rapid, total "conquest" is held in tension with the statement that Joshua waged war against "all these kings for a long time." The lengthy battle is emphasized in the Hebrew text by noting the time frame first: "*for a long time* Joshua waged war against all these kings" (emphasis added).

The tension between rapid conquest and long-term engagement might be explained by asserting the summary is prospective. That is, it credits Joshua with all subsequent action until the land is indeed subdued and possessed. This would need to be a very long view of the matter, for even in Joshua's old age large areas of the land are yet to be taken (13:1). Not even after Joshua's death is the land fully possessed (Judg 1:1).

Another way to explain the tension is to consider the genre characteristics of ancient Near Eastern conquest accounts. Using hyperbole, such texts show the power of the sponsoring god and elevate the victor's status. Such language has been noted in several places in Joshua 10–11. This language highlights the ideology of rapid and complete victory over portions of the land, while at times noting survivors and ongoing warfare. This is not an attempt at subterfuge but a recognized rhetorical strategy for making theological claims regarding Israel's God.

With such hyperbole in mind, verse 18 is an important piece of the picture. It is a reminder that while the text's primary emphasis is on victory, that victory has only initially subdued the land. It has not destroyed all kings and peoples, nor resulted in Israel's immediate and complete habitation of the land.

The strategy of taking the land over the long term is not new. Passages such as Exodus 23:27–31 and Deuteronomy 7:20–23 reveal that Israel will not eliminate the inhabitants quickly, lest the land be rendered inhospitable to Israel's life. Moreover, it appears that the lengthy action involves God not annihilating the people but slowly "driving them out" (Exod 23:29–30; Lev 20:23; Num 33:51–56; Deut 4:37–38; 6:18–19), a strategy that is elsewhere described as the land "vomiting out" the peoples (Lev 18:24–28, a fate Israel will itself experience in the exile [Lev. 18:28; 20:22]). It is within this context that Israel conducts warfare, engaging those who have chosen to remain and resist Israel's claim.

Alongside the account of protracted warfare (v. 18) is a stunning verse that recalls the deceptive (but binding) Gibeonite treaty: "Not one city made a treaty of peace with the Israelites," except Gibeon (v. 19). This appears to open the possibility that, despite the prohibition against treaties (Deut 7:2), other groups besides the Gibeonites could have negotiated peace with Israel. Perhaps the inhabitants could have responded other than with aggression.

The choice of Rahab, certainly, and the choice of Gibeon, possibly, was open to them. War was not a foregone conclusion.

Or was it? Israel took cities and kings in battle (vv. 18–19), and the reason for this is given in verse 20—perhaps the most difficult verse in the book of Joshua:

> For it was the Lord himself who hardened their hearts to wage war against Israel, so that he might destroy them totally, exterminating them without mercy, as the Lord had commanded Moses.

In what way might this verse be understood? Its challenge is heightened by the larger perspective of the canon. God has set in motion a merciful plan by which "all peoples on earth will be blessed" (Gen 12:3). The Old Testament anticipates the inclusion of the nations in the blessing of God (Isa 19:19–22; 42:4–6; 49:6; 56:3, 6–8; 60:1–3; Zeph 2:11; Zech 14:9; Mal 1:11), a reality that finds eschatological fulfillment through Jesus Christ (Matt 28:18–20; Rev 5:9–10). In what way might this verse be faithfully read within this context? A few considerations help toward greater understanding of a difficult verse.

First, the hardening is done "by the Lord himself." God does take initiative against intransigent people. These might be Canaanite (as here), but they can also be Israelite. For instance, Deuteronomy 2:15 uses a similar phrase to describe the "hand of the Lord himself" (author's translation) against the wilderness generation. For their rebellion and refusal to receive his promise of land, God acts against his own people. God's action, then, is not evidence of his hatred of the Canaanites compared to his love for Israel. Rather, God deals with intransigence wherever it is found.

Second, God "hardened their hearts," a phrase which is most often applied to Pharaoh. Here, it is applied to the kings who then lead their people into battle. Interestingly, the people themselves are not hardened. As discussed above (see Listen to the Story), this hardening takes up and strengthens what has through word and action already been exhibited by Pharaoh—and by the Canaanites. When God hardens the hearts of the Canaanite kings, he is strengthening them to carry out in the long term what they themselves have already resolved to do: oppose Israel in battle. Significantly, in the context of Joshua 11, the kings' hardened hearts are contrasted to the obedience of Joshua and Israel to the commands of Moses (see above at vv. 12–15). The kings are also contrasted—in juxtaposition with the immediately preceding verse—to the Gibeonites. The Gibeonites chose not to oppose God's purposes in granting Israel the land. Had the kings chosen the way of obedience and non-opposition, this hardening may never have occurred. But they did not so choose, and God hardens their resolve to act out their choice. By this means, God "brings low those whose eyes are haughty" (Ps 18:27[28]).

Third, the language of *herem* is employed with the same hyperbolic intent as elsewhere. The language that people be destroyed reflects Deuteronomy 7:2. In Deuteronomy, the immediately following verses show the hyperbole of the command, for they address issues of ongoing habitation with the peoples (vv. 3–5). The affirmation in Joshua that the *herem* is applied "without mercy" suggests not the intent to utterly annihilate the peoples but the inexorable pursuit of God against the intransigence of the Canaanite kings. God wills his purposes be fulfilled through Israel and toward the blessing of all nations (Gen 12:3). He will pursue and punish the kings' opposition without mercy. By contrast, mercy is shown to those in the land who align with Israel and affirm God's purposes. Rahab and the Gibeonites are examples of this mercy extended to Canaanites.

An addendum closes this first summary, citing the destruction of the Anakites within Israelite territory. This may be another piece of rhetoric lauding Joshua by crediting to him action that occurs later (14:6–15; 15:13–19) or initiated now for later completion by Caleb and Othniel. The placement of the notation heightens the point being made: God is fighting for Israel, and the terrifying Anakites have no power. Fear of them stirred Israelite rebellion in the wilderness and they did not enter the land (Num 13:26–33). Now, obedient Israel enters the land and the Anakites fall. This reversal of Israel's past affirms God's promise in Joshua 1: he is with Israel, and therefore none can withstand God's people.

### Looking Backwards; Looking Forward (11:23)

The second summary is just one verse. Like the first summary, this verse recalls Israel's past and anticipates its future. In it the centrality of Joshua is apparent through two primary actions: he "takes" the land (as in v. 16), and he "gives" it as an inheritance. This summarizes the first half of the book, for chapters 1–12 focus on taking the land. It also looks to the second half of the book, for in chapters 13–21 Joshua will give the land by lot to the Israelite tribes.

Joshua is credited with taking "the entire land" as the "Lord had directed Moses." The chapter's summaries have each cited Moses (vv. 12, 15, 20, 23), ending the first half of the book by recalling Moses' presence in its first chapter. Joshua was charged with obedience to the law of Moses, and by that obedience he has gained success (1:7–9). By careful attention to the law, Joshua is shown as Moses' true successor.

The taking of the "entire land" demonstrates God's promises are true and have found fulfillment (Gen 15:18–20). Israel has subdued the land but must now possess it as its "inheritance." The word appears here for the first time in Joshua. It signals a shift to the book's second half where "inheritance" will appear forty-nine more times as Israel receives its allotted lands. These lands are given it as an inheritance to be possessed.

Finally, the "land had rest (from *shqt*) from war." The verse concludes the first half of the book, which focused on the battles of "all Israel." All that remains is the listing of kings taken in battle (ch. 12). For now, Israel's wars are ended, and never again in Joshua does "all Israel" join in battle. There will be individual and tribal skirmishes as Israel settles into its possession; one such account records Caleb taking Anakite cities (14:6–15). That account also ends with the phrase, the "land had rest (from *shqt*) from war."

With the cessation of war, Israel begins the process of possessing the land and entering into the "rest" (from *nwh*) anticipated in Joshua's commission (1:13, 15). This is the rest promised the ancestors (21:44; 22:4) and that Israel achieves once the land is allotted (23:1). This rest is experienced in the land and dependent on covenant faithfulness. For this reason, Israel renews the covenant following land allotment (chs. 23–24). Too soon after it is renewed, the covenant will be broken and rest disrupted. This first half of the book, however, ends in expectation of lasting rest.

### Terrifying Horses and Chariots

Not only is the northern coalition greater in number than its southern counterpart, but it has a terrifying weapon: a "large number of horses and chariots" (v. 4). This is a formidable weapon of war in the ancient world and is a tactical threat to Israel whenever an enemy possesses it (Exod 14:7–9; Judg 4:3; 1 Sam 13:5; 1 Kgs 20:1). Israel even blames the presence of Canaanite horses and chariots for its inability to take the land (Josh 17:16–18; Judg 1:19). So threatening is the prospect of chariots and horses that they form part of the image of systemic, universal evil, with which the kings of the earth commit adultery (Rev 18:13).

The threat of horses and chariots is a real military threat but should not be feared by Israel. A paradigm of this counter-intuitive reality is the destruction of Pharaoh's chariots and horses: Pharaoh has them in great number; Israel should not fear them. Pharaoh and his six hundred-plus chariots pursued Israel, trapping them before the Red Sea (Exod 14:7–9), yet Israel gains victory over the formidable force. This is not because of Israel's greater weaponry or tactical force, but only because the Lord fought for Israel (Exod 14:14, 28).

By God's victory over Pharaoh's horses and chariots, Israel forever knows that "The LORD is my strength and my defense; he has become my salvation" because "horse and driver he has hurled into the sea" (Exod 15:1–2, 21). Not only Israel, but Egypt also will learn that "I am the LORD when I gain glory through Pharaoh, his chariots and his horsemen" (Exod 14:18; 15:19). Both Moses (Deut 11:4; 20:1) and Joshua (Josh 24:6) recall this event as proof of God's power and trustworthiness. This deliverance from a mighty enemy is the paradigmatic basis for Israel's continued obedience and trust in God. Years later, Isaiah cites the same paradigm as proof of God's ability to rescue his people. He urges Israel not to "trust in the multitude of their chariots and in the great strength of their horsemen" (Isa 31:1) but to instead trust that God can and will deliver his people once again (Isa 43:16–17).

Israel's trust in God's ability to deliver them from powerful enemies rests in God's power as a warrior, a power greater than Pharaoh, his horses, and his chariots (see Live the Story, Chapter 10). God's power over the chariots and horses of Israel's powerful enemies is demonstrated in battle—both at the Red Sea and in Israel (1 Kgs 20:1, 13). Israel also has a glimpse of this power exercised in the unseen realm. This realm is indicative of the spiritual battle that underlies enemy attack. Thus, at Dothan, surrounded by enemy forces, Elisha prays that God would open the eyes of his terrified servant. God does, and the servant sees an angelic host of fiery chariots and horses surrounding them (2 Kgs 6:17). Fear is dispelled, and the servant (as well as the reader) understands that God fights for Israel with his "tens of thousands and thousands of thousands" chariots (Ps 68:17[18]). Later, the Aramean army besieging Samaria is frightened off when the LORD causes them to "hear the sound of chariots and horses and a great army" (2 Kgs 7:6), surely a reference to the invisible army revealed in the prior chapter. Both Elisha and his predecessor Elijah are engaged in battle—against human armies arrayed against Israel as well as the threat of Baal—and it is not surprising that they are named as "[t]he chariots and horsemen of Israel" (2 Kgs 2:11–12; 13:14). They are both God's servants on the frontline against powerful enemies. By God, these enemies are ultimately defeated.

The psalmist proclaims "some trust in chariots and some in horses . . . but we trust in the name of the LORD our God" (Ps 20:7[8]), but the reality in Israel was not so clearly the case. Israel fails to take all the land because the Canaanites had iron chariots (Josh 17:16–18). David added chariots and horses to his arsenal (2 Sam 8:4), and his son used them as symbols of royal prerogative (1 Kgs 1:5). It is Solomon's amassing of horses and chariots (1 Kgs 4:26 [5:6]; 9:19) that reveals how deeply Israel failed in its trust of the LORD. Not only does Solomon build up a large force of horses and chariots, he purchases them from Egypt (1 Kgs 10:26–29). Both are against the Deuteronomic law for kings (Deut 17:16) and evidence of Solomon's divided heart: he loves the Lord (1 Kgs 3:3), but throughout his reign there is evidence of the divided loyalty that culminates the narrative (1 Kgs 11:1–6).[6] Solomon, by gathering thousands of horses and chariots, shows himself the anti-paradigm of one who trusts God. He amasses great weaponry, showing that trust in the Lord is easily replaced with trust in human strength.

In the great recitation of salvation history presented in the Easter Vigil on Holy Saturday (see Live the Story, Chapter 3), a list of ten possible Old Testament readings is provided from which selections are made to tell the story. Of these, at least three must be read, but only one is always required: Exodus 14. Paired with the canticle of Exodus 15, it tells of the great deliverance out of Egypt, including the defeat of Pharaoh, his horses, and chariots. The requirement that this text be read in the service rests on the understanding that the deliverance out of Egypt foreshadows the greater deliverance of the cross. At the cross, Christ delivers us from our own house of bondage to sin and death and from our own Pharaoh, the devil.

Paul, delivered from an undisclosed trouble, writes to the Corinthian church, encouraging their trust in God. Paul bases this trust on the fact of God's defeat of death through resurrection:

> We do not want you to be uninformed, brothers and sisters, about the troubles we experienced in the province of Asia. We were under great pressure, *far beyond our ability to endure*, so that we despaired of life itself. Indeed, we felt we had received the sentence of death. But this happened *that we might not rely on ourselves but on God, who raises the dead.* He has delivered us from such a deadly peril, and he will deliver us again. On him we have set our hope that he will continue to deliver us, as you help us by your prayers. Then many will give thanks on our behalf for the gracious favor granted us in answer to the prayers of many. (2 Cor 1:8–11, emphasis added)

Like the Israelites whom Moses and Joshua sought to encourage in the face of overwhelming enemies, Paul seeks to encourage a fledging church. Moses and Joshua cited horses and chariots overcome as proof of God's power; in this, they remember the great event of Israel's liberation: defeat of Pharaoh and his forces at the Red Sea. Paul cites an undisclosed enemy, but he makes the same move as did Moses and Joshua: trust God now in the face of "horses and chariots" because God has defeated them at our own "Red Sea deliverance" out of bondage.

---

6. See further exploration of Solomon's divided heart in Lissa M. Wray Beal, *1& 2 Kings*, AOTC 9 (Downers Grove: InterVarsity Press, 2014).

Given the typological correlation of the exodus deliverance and the cross, it is no wonder that a popular Christian chorus takes up Miriam's testimony. Using the type of the Red Sea and Pharaoh's horses and chariots, it testifies to God's great deliverance through the cross. But as Paul testified to his Corinthian friends, there are ongoing enemies, "horses and chariots" that are too powerful to be overcome by human strength. This is part of the ongoing spiritual warfare in which the church is engaged (see Live the Story, Chapter 10). The chorus directs each singer and each listener to the One who has delivered us, and encourages continued trust. God *has* overcome, and God *will* overcome:

*I will sing unto the LORD,*
*for he has triumphed gloriously,*
*the horse and rider thrown into the sea.*
*I will sing unto the LORD,*
*for he has triumphed gloriously,*
*the horse and rider thrown into the sea.*
*The LORD, my God, my strength and song,*
*Has now become my victory.*
*The LORD, my God, my strength and song,*
*Has now become my victory.*
*The LORD is God, and I will praise him,*
*our covenant God, and I will exalt him.*
*The LORD is God, and I will praise him,*
*our covenant God, and I will exalt him.*[7]

## Paradise Lost

James Hilton's 1933 novel, *Lost Horizon*, tells the story of a plane that crashes in the Himalayan Mountains.[8] The travelers are taken to the hidden valley paradise of Shangri-La. The novel explores the destruction of this hidden paradise through human desire and human failing. In 1937, Frank Capra produced a movie version and in 1973 a musical version was released, with music by Burt Bacharach. The musical was in many ways cringe-worthy and was panned.[9] Thankfully, I remember little of that version except one snippet of the title song. It speaks of the longing for safety and perfection:

7. Text and music at http://hymnary.org/text/i_will_sing_unto_the_lord_for_he_has_tri.

8. First published in 1933 by William Morrow & Company. The company was acquired by Harper Collins, through whom editions were published in 2004, 2012 under the HarperCollins Perennial label.

9. Roger Ebert gives it a scathing review and one star. See http://www.rogerebert.com/reviews/lost-horizon-1973.

*Have you ever dreamed of a place far away from it all?*
*Where the air you breathe is soft and clean,*
*and children play in fields of green,*
*and the sound of guns*
*doesn't pound in your ears.*[10]

It is a sentiment that underlies most utopian movies: the desire for paradise. It also underlies most dystopian movies: the threat of paradise lost. *Lost Horizon*, and the utopian/dystopian genre, unearth the human desire for perfection and the sad acknowledgement that it is beyond our reach.

In Joshua 11 the land is taken and experiences "rest" (v. 23; a verbal form from *shqt*). It seems paradise has arrived. In the context of chapters 10–11, "rest" includes cessation of war. But the land also holds the promise of rest that is much more than military peace. The land is to be (like the Edenic garden), a place of communion between God and people. In this communion Israel would experience covenant blessings and true rest (from *nwh*; see Listen to the Story and Live the Story, Chapter 1).

The "rest" of Joshua 11:23 is short-lived, being disrupted by covenant disobedience. Not only within Joshua but repeatedly in the book of Judges, covenant disobedience characterizes God's people. In Judges 2:10–19 the pattern of the book is laid out. It reveals the connection between covenant obedience and rest, and covenant disobedience and war. Covenant obedience is the prerequisite to the experience of rest in the land. When Israel wanders from the covenant and forsakes the LORD, God delivers them into the hands of their enemies. Warfare becomes the fruit of covenant failure and signals the loss of rest—communion with God under the covenant—which the land promised. When Israel repents God raises up a judge, Israel is delivered, and the land experiences peace. While the judge lives, Israel remains faithful and experiences true rest: cessation from war and the fullness of covenant communion.

In Judges, when God rescues his people from their enemies, it is reported that the land had "peace" (3:11, 30; 5:31; 8:28). The word is a related verbal form to that in Joshua 11:23 (from *shqt*). While the context is military engagement, *shqt* is not divorced from the larger concept of rest (from *nwh*) promised Israel (Josh 1:13, 15; 21:44; 22:4; 23:1). The book of Judges, working with the pattern of Judg 2:10–19 and using the key word *shqt*, emphasizes that while it is possible to reclaim peace, it does not last, and true rest is lost through covenant disobedience.

---

10. Full text can be accessed at http://www.lyricsfreak.com/b/burt+bacharach/lost+horizon_20544207.html.

The appearance of this word as Israel's wars end in Joshua 11:23 is a presentiment of that failing. "Rest" can be proclaimed in Joshua 11:23, but covenant disobedience continues—as does warfare. More, covenant disobedience increases, and Israel descends to grievous sins (Judg 17–21). No longer marked by covenant faithfulness, "everyone did as they saw fit" (Judg 21:25).

Joshua 11:23 sounds like paradise has arrived for Israel. Knowing the longer story, the reader knows paradise does not last. Human desire and human failing prevent any utopian horizon. The writer to the Hebrews recognizes the futility of Israel's "rest," noting that it was not achieved under Joshua. Rather, its achievement is possible only in Christ (Heb 4:8–9). This is the conclusion that Origen expounds. Working with his typological reading of the Canaanites as our sinful desires against which we battle, he preaches:

> [True rest] is fulfilled in my Lord Jesus Christ alone. Consider yourself—you have come to Jesus and through the grace of baptism have attained the remission of sins; and now in you 'the flesh' does not 'fight against the spirit and the spirit against the flesh.' Your land has ceased from wars if you still 'carry around the death of Jesus Christ in your body' so that, after all battles have ceased in you, you may be made 'peaceable' and you may be called 'a child of God.'[11]

Origen is not here preaching some kind of present human perfection, although he calls believers to live as people of Christ. He concludes his sermon by citing Micah 4:4 and the eschatological image of true paradise found there, when God's perfected people will sit "under their own vine and . . . fig tree." It will be a time when the Lord's mountain will be established, and peoples will stream to it; a time of swords beaten into plowshares and spears into pruning hooks. It will be paradise realized, not paradise anticipated. There will be no lost horizon, but only true rest, a rest once promised Israel but realized through Christ.

11. Origen, *Hom* 15.7.

CHAPTER 12

# Joshua 12:1–24

## LISTEN to the Story

1These are the kings of the land whom the Israelites had defeated and
whose territory they took over east of the Jordan, from the Arnon Gorge
to Mount Hermon, including all the eastern side of the Arabah:
2Sihon king of the Amorites, who reigned in Heshbon. He ruled from
Aroer on the rim of the Arnon Gorge—from the middle of the gorge—to
the Jabbok River, which is the border of the Ammonites. This included
half of Gilead. 3He also ruled over the eastern Arabah from the Sea of
Galilee to the Sea of the Arabah (that is, the Dead Sea), to Beth Jeshimoth,
and then southward below the slopes of Pisgah.
4And the territory of Og king of Bashan, one of the last of the
Rephaites, who reigned in Ashtaroth and Edrei. 5He ruled over Mount
Hermon, Salekah, all of Bashan to the border of the people of Geshur
and Maakah, and half of Gilead to the border of Sihon king of Heshbon.
6Moses, the servant of the LORD, and the Israelites conquered them.
And Moses the servant of the LORD gave their land to the Reubenites, the
Gadites and the half-tribe of Manasseh to be their possession.
7Here is a list of the kings of the land that Joshua and the Israelites
conquered on the west side of the Jordan, from Baal Gad in the Valley of
Lebanon to Mount Halak, which rises toward Seir. Joshua gave their lands
as an inheritance to the tribes of Israel according to their tribal divisions.
8The lands included the hill country, the western foothills, the Arabah,
the mountain slopes, the wilderness and the Negev. These were the lands
of the Hittites, Amorites, Canaanites, Perizzites, Hivites and Jebusites.
These were the kings:

| | |
|---|---|
| 9the king of Jericho | one |
| the king of Ai (near Bethel) | one |
| 10the king of Jerusalem | one |
| the king of Hebron | one |
| 11the king of Jarmuth | one |

| | |
|---|---|
| the king of Lachish | one |
| [12]the king of Eglon | one |
| the king of Gezer | one |
| [13]the king of Debir | one |
| the king of Geder | one |
| [14]the king of Hormah | one |
| the king of Arad | one |
| [15]the king of Libnah | one |
| the king of Adullam | one |
| [16]the king of Makkedah | one |
| the king of Bethel | one |
| [17]the king of Tappuah | one |
| the king of Hepher | one |
| [18]the king of Aphek | one |
| the king of Lasharon | one |
| [19]the king of Madon | one |
| the king of Hazor | one |
| [20]the king of Shimron Meron | one |
| the king of Akshaph | one |
| [21]the king of Taanach | one |
| the king of Megiddo | one |
| [22]the king of Kedesh | one |
| the king of Jokneam in Carmel | one |
| [23]the king of Dor (in Naphoth Dor) | one |
| the king of Goyim in Gilgal | one |
| [24]the king of Tirzah | one |
| thirty-one kings in all. | |

*Listening to the Text in the Story*: Numbers 21:21–35; 32:1–42; Deuteronomy 2:24–3:11, 12–20; Joshua 1:12–18; Sennacherib's Annals; Qadesh Inscription; Siege of Jerusalem Inscription; Armant Stele

**Transjordanian Lands: Part of One Campaign**

Included in the list of kings defeated are Sihon and Og, whose lands are east of the Jordan. Israel committed to pass peacefully through Sihon's territory, but the king challenged Israel and was defeated. Og likewise challenged Israel and was defeated. The account (Num 21:21–35) utilizes much of the same language found in the conquest accounts in Joshua. Israel put Sihon "to the sword" (v. 24) and "struck down" Og and his whole army, leaving "no survivors" (v. 35). Similar hyperbole describes the extent of the conquest: "all" Sihon's cities and "all" their surrounding settlements are taken (v. 25). Finally, the LORD's promises about the kings are the same as those given in Joshua: he will "deliver [Og] into your hands" (v. 34; see Josh 6:2; 8:1; 10:8, 19) and Moses is to "do to him what he did to Sihon" (v. 34; see Josh 8:2; 10:28, 30, 35, 37, 39). That similar language is used of campaigns east and west of the Jordan binds the conquest of Transjordanian and promised land into one extended campaign.

The eastern lands were reluctantly granted Reuben, Gad, and the half-tribe of Manasseh by Moses. The condition of possession was to assist Israel to take the land west of the Jordan. Numbers and Deuteronomy present the tribes' request in an unfavorable light, but Joshua reframes the negative account (see The Transjordanian Lands in Listen to the Story, Chapter 1). In the book an ambiguity exists regarding the status of the Transjordanian land and tribes for they are outside of the promised land yet considered part of "all Israel." For this reason, the eastern campaign is included in chapter 12's summary.

### Conquest Lists

Conquest summaries and lists of conquered territories, cities, and rulers are part of ancient Near Eastern literature, appearing at the end of conquest accounts as in Joshua. One campaign might be represented by multiple extant accounts. When compared, these lists are clearly selective and partial in nature.[1] Thus, as in Joshua 12, cities might be listed without an accompanying account detailing the city's fall. At times, a tally is provided of the cities taken, which may not match the number of cities listed. Besides providing summaries of battle (see the Armant Stele; Listen to the Story, Chapter 11), the lists provide a way of praising military leaders and their god. Joshua 12 thus concludes the first half of the book by confirming what the chapters have argued: Joshua (and Moses) is a powerful leader, and the LORD is "God in heaven above and on the earth below" (2:11).

A similar laudatory purpose is apparent in the Qadesh Inscription which lists lands taken by Ramesses and credits the conquest to the god Re:

> Beginning of the Triumph of the King of Southern and Northern Egypt, Usimare Setepenre, Son of Re, (beloved of the Gods), Ramesses II Meriamun, given life forever, which he achieved: against the Hatti-land,

1. A comparison of the Annals of Sennacherib's seventh campaign to the campaign account in the Walters Art Museum inscription is provided in Younger, "Ancient Conquest Accounts," 230–3, and demonstrates this aspect of summative lists.

> Naharina, and against the land of Arzawa; against Pidassa, (and) against the Dardanaya (land); against the land of Masa, against the land of Qarqisha, and Lukka; against Carchemish, Qode, (and the) land of Qadesh; against the land of Ugarit, (and) Mushnatu.[2]

The Siege of Jerusalem Inscription provides a similar list, noting cities taken and crediting success to Sennacherib's god Ashur:

> In my third campaign, I marched against Hatti. . . . Ashur my lord overwhelmed his strong cities, Great Sidon, Lower Sidon, Bit-zitti, Sariptu, Mahaliba, Ushu, Akzib, Akko, walled cities (provided) with food and water for his garrisons, and they bowed in submission at my feet. . . . In the course of my campaign, I surrounded and conquered Beth-Dagon, Joppa, Bene-berak, Azor, cities belonging to Ṣidqa, who did not submit quickly, and I carried off their spoil.[3]

## EXPLAIN the Story

Joshua 12 ends the first half of the book, which is structured in four acts: Jordan crossing (1:1–5:12), taking the land (5:13–12:24), land distribution (chs. 13–21), and ongoing worship (chs. 22–24; see Explain the Story, Chapter 1). The chapter's genre is recognizable from similar ancient Near Eastern lists. The genre is employed to demonstrate the strong leadership exercised by Moses and Joshua and confirm God's power attested throughout Joshua 1–11. The chapter's shape and content build on theological themes introduced in chapter 1 and explored in the book's first half.

The ambiguous status of the Transjordanian tribes and their territory, encountered earlier in Joshua (see, for instance, 1:12–18), is maintained in the list. Many features suggest the Transjordanian tribes are part of "all Israel." They are included in the list of Israelite victories, and several features suggest their equality with the Cisjordanian tribes:

- east and west tribes both "conquer" their respective territories ("conquer" [vv. 6, 7] and "defeated" [v. 1] translate the same Hebrew root, *nkh*);
- both groups are described as "Israelites" (vv. 1, 6, 7);
- the "possession" (v. 6) and "inheritance" (v. 7) allotted on either side of the Jordan is the same word in Hebrew; no distinction is made;
- both groups are led by the Lord's accredited leader. The continuity of Joshua's leadership with that of Moses "the servant of the Lord"

2. *COS* 2.5A:33.
3. Ibid, 2.119B:302–03.

is apparent as Joshua fulfills Moses' ministry, becoming the new "servant of the LORD" (24:29)

The conformity of presentation is a reminder that the Transjordanian tribes are part of "all Israel." However, other elements in the chapter (such as its structure) reflect the ambiguity that surrounds the Transjordanian tribes and lands showing that, while part of "all Israel," they are yet distinct from the Cisjordanian tribes. The fact that the Transjordanian conquests are included in the list cuts both ways: they are part of the conquests conducted by Israel, but they are pointedly separated from the account of the Cisjordanian tribes.

The accounts of eastern and western conquests are separate but share a similar structure. For the eastern tribes, the pattern is straightforward:

**A** "These are the kings of the land" . . . east
- **B** Summary of the territory, citing landmarks (v. 1)
  - **C** List of the kings (vv. 2–5)
    - Sihon, identified by
      - capital
      - territory ruled
    - Og, identified by
      - capital
      - territory ruled
    - **D** Moses and the Israelites conquered/Moses gave as a possession (v. 6)
      - **E** to the Reubenites, the Gadites and the half-tribe of Manasseh (v. 6)

The western conquest follows, reusing the same elements, but varying and providing complexity to the pattern. Greater attention is thus granted the tribal possession in the promised land proper:

**A** "Here is a list of the kings of the land" . . . west (v. 1 and v. 7 have the same Hebrew phrase)
- - **D** Joshua and the Israelites conquered (v. 7)
- **B** Summary of the territory, citing landmarks (v. 7)
  - - **D** Joshua gave as an inheritance (v. 7)
      - **E** according to their tribal divisions
- **B** Summary of the territory, by regions and peoples (v. 8)
  - **C** List of the kings (vv. 9–24)

Not only is the western account more extensive, but the dual summary description of the territory ("B") is interspersed with two references to Joshua. Whereas for the eastern tribes one notation marks Moses "conquering" and "giving" (v. 6), for the western tribes there are two notations that mark Joshua "conquering" and "giving" ("D"; v. 7). In this way, greater attention is given Joshua's leadership. Notably, the "giving" of the Transjordanian lands falls within God's concessionary will and is credited neither to God nor Joshua (here and throughout the book; see Explain the Story, Chapter 1). By contrast, the promised land is given in the book exclusively by God and Joshua (here, and also 11:23). The lists' structure thus gives marked attention to the promised land and to Joshua's leadership.

The chapter affirms the ideology of Israel's success in several ways. The land noted as taken is extensive, reflecting the actions of Israel throughout chapters 6–11. No claim of "total conquest" is made, however, for the coastal plain and Philistine lands are not included. In addition, six of the seven peoples in the land are noted (v. 8; cf. 3:10 and commentary, Chapter 3). Added to this group is Og, a "Rephaite" (v. 4). The Rephaites are first noted in God's promise to Abraham (Gen 15:19–20). By taking the lands promised Israel that are occupied by these peoples, the chapter affirms God's promises are fulfilled.

Finally, the ideology of Israel's success is seen in the extensive list of kings conquered. It traces Israel's successful campaigns in which God fought for Israel. The victories at Jericho and Ai are first recorded, and verses 10–16 cover the southern campaign. Included are kings and cities known from that campaign together with other cities that were not mentioned in chapter 10's campaign. These include Adullam, whose location between Lachish and Jerusalem makes it likely taken in the southern campaign. Geder is also otherwise unknown but is included in the list with cities of the southern campaign. The inclusion of the Negev cities of Hormah and Arad is unusual but not unaccountable. Taken during the wilderness journey (Num 14:44–45; 21:1–3; 33:40; Deut 1:44), their inclusion here refers to those events or suggests a further engagement during the southern campaign. The list moves on to the central hills (Bethel, Tappuah) and then to many northern kings spread over a wide area but likely all taken in the northern campaign (vv. 19–24). That not all of these were named in chapter 11 aligns with the summative and selective nature of such lists. Finally, Tirzah in the central hills moves the action back toward Israel's camp at Gilgal.

The list of thirty-one kings provides a broad overview of Israel's successes in the land. There is an inevitability communicated through the intonation of their names and cities and the repetitive "one." The first half of the book closes on this rhetorical note of completion: God's leaders have obediently led God's people into the land. King after king has been unable to withstand Israel as, by God's presence and power, the promises were fulfilled.

## LIVE the Story

As the first half of Joshua closes, this chapter graphically affirms what God promised as the book began: God will give the land. No one will stand against Joshua and Israel. Israel's commitment to obey the Book of the Law will ensure success, for God is with them. The repetitive intonation of kings taken east and west of the Jordan shows God has fulfilled his promise. No king was able to withstand Israel's king, the LORD, who empowered his appointed leaders and obedient people.

The context of this chapter is crucial to its message. Read without reference to what precedes it, Joshua 12 looks like an encomium to Israel's power, for no explicit reference links Israel's victories to God's power. Read without reference to what follows, Joshua 12 could easily end the book, without attention to the ongoing work of fully possessing the land. As a "hinge" chapter and in the context of the whole book, Joshua 12 is both celebration and warning. It stands between great victories gained by God's power and ongoing success in the land requiring Israel's ongoing obedience to God. Should Israel discount either God's power or the necessity of obedience, all that was gained in Joshua 1–12 will be jeopardized as the book proceeds.

In a similar way, Christians live in the full victory of what God has accomplished in Christ. God in Christ has "disarmed the powers and authorities . . . triumphing over them by the cross" (Col 2:15). By the cross, resurrection, and ascension, the kingdom of God has intruded into the here and now. These are realities to be repeatedly enumerated and celebrated.

But God's kingdom is not yet fully realized "on earth as in heaven"—as The Lord's Prayer reminds us. The kingdom is now present, and not-yet fully realized in our midst. Christians are called to pray and work, living out God's rule in our lives, our churches, and our communities. By the faithful, Spirit-empowered obedience of God's people, the rule of God is extended.

In the same way that Joshua 12 looks back and affirms God's promises fulfilled and looks ahead in anticipation of Israel's possession of the land, the church affirms the kingdom of God is present in Christ while anticipated in its fullness. The church must inhabit this context of the now and not yet: relying on God's full promises; moving ahead to possess the land. Should the church forget that it is by God's power that the kingdom has come near, it will only move ahead in its own power: human strength arrayed against forces too powerful to combat. Should the church attend only to the promise fulfilled without living to further God's kingdom, it will stagnate: introspective praise without mission. Both perspectives are necessary for the church: the powerful affirmation of God's victory won; the faithful obedience to ongoing discipleship.

# CHAPTER 13

# Introduction to Joshua 13:1–21:45

Joshua 13 begins the third section of the book of Joshua. In the first section, Israel crossed the Jordan (1:1–5:12). In the second, Israel "took" the land given by God (5:13–12:24). Joshua 11:16–23 summarizes that action, with chapter 12 providing a selective list of kings taken. In the book's third section (chs. 13–21) the land is distributed among the tribes before the concluding fourth section turns to matters of ongoing worship and covenant loyalty (chs. 22–24).

Chapters 13–21 have a coherent theme, structure, and style that set them off from sections one, two, and four. Noting these characteristics in an introduction places the chapters in the "big picture" of the book's narrative arc and theology. This is crucial to the task of reading The Story of God Bible Commentary of Joshua, lest it be overwhelmed by the section's seemingly endless lists of place names and boundaries. To this end, this introduction explores the themes, style, and structure of the chapters as a whole before the commentary turns to the discrete chapter units.

The section can also be helpfully engaged in light of the biblical and ancient Near Eastern story. Several texts are explored to contextualize the whole section; those that are pertinent to only a particular chapter in the unit are explored in the appropriate commentary chapter.

## Theme: Dividing an Inheritance for Possession

As noted above, these chapters divide the land among the tribes. The theme of land division is characterized by four words used repeatedly throughout chapters 13–21. The first is that Israel is to "possess" (from the root *yrsh*) the land. The verb appears elsewhere in Joshua (1:11, 15; 3:10; 8:7; 12:1; 23:5, 9, 13; 24:4, 8) but is clustered in chs. 13–21 (13:1, 6, 12, 13; 14:12; 15:14, 63; 16:10; 17:12, 13(2x), 18; 18:3; 19:47; 21:43). It can refer to Israel possessing the land, or of God giving the land to Israel to possess (often with the idea of driving out the inhabitants). The word can also refer to Israel's failure to possess the land. Land possession is not simply military conquest but includes Israel inhabiting the land. These chapters delineate the boundaries of the land that Israel claims and will in time inhabit.

This land is given to Israel as an "inheritance" (*nahalah*). God is the ultimate owner of the land but gifted it to Abraham and his descendants (Gen 12:7; 13:15, 17; 15:7, 18; 17:8) and confirmed the promise with an oath (Gen 24:7). "Inheritance" is used fifty times in Joshua but almost exclusively (forty-five times) in chapters 13–21.[1] "Inheritance" initially appears in 11:23 as the first half of the book closes. In its summary that Joshua "took the entire land" and "gave it as an inheritance to Israel," the verse looks back to Israel's military exploits and forward to land division. The emphasis in chapters 13–21 is on the successful division of this inheritance among the tribes. A tension becomes apparent, however, for there are several notations that Israel is unable to fully possess its inheritance.

The inheritance of land is distributed by lot (*goral*), a word used in Joshua only in these chapters. Each of the Cisjordanian tribes receives its land by lot (14:2; 15:1; 16:1; 17:1, 14, 17; 18:6, 8, 10, 11; 19:1, 10, 17, 24, 32, 40, 51). Even the Levites who are dispersed in cities throughout the land and have no fixed territory for their own receive their apportioned cities by lot (21:4, 5, 6, 8, 10, 20, 40). The Transjordanian lands, however, are not allocated by lot but by the tribes' request and Moses' command. The different means of allocation marks the eastern lands differently than those of the promised land.

Finally, the chapters employ the lot to "divide" the land so that each tribe (barring the Levites) receives a "portion." Both "divide" and "portion" arise from the same Hebrew root (*hlq*). Within Joshua, the root is most frequently found in chapters 13–21 (thirteen times, both as a verb [13:7; 14:5; 18:2, 5, 10; 19:51], and as a noun [14:4; 15:13; 18:5, 6, 7, 9; 19:9]; the root also appears in 22:8, 25, 27 without reference to land apportionment).

Land division takes into account the different needs of the different tribes but is not done by random selection or by skillful management. Rather, land division is conducted according to God's will and under the auspices of Eleazar the priest, together with Joshua and the tribal leaders (14:1; 17:4; 19:51; 21:1). Eleazar may have cast the Urim and Thummim to discern God's will for the distribution (Exod 28:30; cf. Num 27:21; 1 Sam 14:41; 28:6). Regardless of the means of discernment, land allotment was a holy matter as it fulfilled God's command to Moses (see Num 26:52–56 and Listen to the Story below). Thus, land division—no less than the Jordan crossing (the first section of the book) and the taking of the land (the second section of the book)—is a matter of obedience. Much time is given in this section to land division, a reminder that all of Israel's life in the land—entry, taking, possession, habitation—can only be successful if conducted in obedience to the word of God (1:7–8).

1. It occurs five times outside Josh 13–21, in 11:23; 23:4; 24:28, 30, 32.

## Structure: Tribes, Families, and Worship

The shape of the chapters is carefully crafted and can be sketched as follows. This careful structure reveals several theological themes:

A New Beginning: God's commission and promise (13:1–7)
  A Review of Land Taken: the eastern tribes (13:8–14)
    Inheritance of Reuben (13:15–23)
    Inheritance of Gad (13:24–28)
    Inheritance of Manasseh (13:29–31)
  Closing summary of eastern land (13:32–33)

    Introduction: distribution of western land (14:1–5)
        *Inheritance for faithful Caleb (14:6–15)*
      Inheritance for Judah: boundaries (15:1–12)
          *Inheritance for Aksah (15:13–19)*
      Inheritance for Judah: towns (15:20–63)

      Inheritance for Joseph introduced (16:1–4)
      Inheritance for Ephraim (16:5–10)
      Inheritance for Manasseh introduced (17:1–2)
          *Inheritance for Zelophehad's daughters (17:3–6)*
      Inheritance for Manasseh (17:7–13)
        *Inheritance for Joseph contested (17:14–18)*
        **Shiloh: Worship and Land (18:1–10)**
      Inheritance for Benjamin (18:11–28)
      Inheritance for Simeon (19:1–9)
      Inheritance for Zebulun (19:10–16)
      Inheritance for Issachar (19:17–23)
      Inheritance for Asher (19:24–31)
      Inheritance for Naphtali (19:32–39)
      Inheritance for Dan (19:40–48)
        *Inheritance for faithful Joshua (19:49–50)*
    Conclusion: distribution of western land (19:51)

      Tribal Contributions from Inheritance (20:1–21:42)
        For Cities of Refuge (20:1–9)
        For Levitical cities (21:1–42)
Land Possession and Rest: God's promises fulfilled (21:43–45)

This bird's-eye view highlights several foci and patterns that illuminate narrative themes. While the themes are explored further in the commentary on individual chapters, some initial observation provides a helpful guide to reading chapters 13–21.

As with chapters 1–12, chapters 13–21 have a discernible beginning and ending. The second half of the book opens by commissioning Joshua (13:1–7) in ways that recall God's commission in 1:1–9. In both, God sketches out the land to be taken as an inheritance and includes God's promise to act on Israel's behalf. The first half of the book concludes with a broad summary (11:16–23) in which the "entire land" is taken (v. 16, 23) and there is "rest from war" (v. 23). Affirming this rhetorical claim is the summative list of kings taken in battle (ch. 12). A similar ending that appropriates the same rhetoric concludes the land distribution, claiming "all the land" is given. Israel has "rest on every side," and no enemies are able to "withstand" Israel so that "not one of all the Lord's good promises to Israel failed; everyone was fulfilled" (21:43–45).

The ending found at 21:43–45 must be held alongside the obvious concluding remark at 19:51. There, the assignment of tribal territories is completed as Israel "finished dividing the land." This ending makes a distinct division between the allotment of tribal territories (chs. 13–19) and the cities allotted for refuge and for the Levites (chs. 20–21). The narrative wisely separates out the two types of allotment showing, first, that Israel is graciously allotted land by God (chs. 13–19) and second, that Israel responds by gifting cities for the needs of the Levities and the whole community (chs. 20–21). This is a response of gratitude. It is also a response of obedience, for God had commanded these cities be set aside (Num 35:1–15). Together, the two parts of chapters 13–21 show the total distribution among, and for the benefit of, all Israel.

Once Joshua is commissioned, the unit reviews the lands allotted east of the Jordan (13:8–33). This serves as a reminder that even the Transjordanian tribes are part of "all Israel." The concern for such unity is pervasive in Joshua. It is present as the book opens (1:12–18) and is the subject of chapter 22 just before Israel affirms its covenantal commitments to God (chs. 23–24).

Only after this needful reminder does the unit move to allocate the western lands. While both eastern and western lands are "all Israel," the western lands are the true promised land. Thus, this large section has its own introduction and conclusion (14:1–5; 19:51b). The tribes are listed in a generally south-to-north direction, echoing the movement of Israel into the land (chs. 2–11). Judah is listed first followed by its northern neighbor, Joseph (comprised of Ephraim and the half-tribe of Manasseh). Several reasons, in addition to replicating Israel's progress into the land, may account for the ordering of Judah and Joseph first in the allotments. The primacy may be due to the fact they are the largest western tribes, with more extensive boundaries and town lists.

The primacy may also reflect the earlier elevation of these two tribes (see Gen 48:15–20; 49:8–12). In addition, these are the tribes of Caleb (Judah) and Joshua (Joseph). This Introduction will note several ways the book of Numbers informs land distribution; this placement of the Judah and Joseph allotments suggests reflection on the fateful events of the wilderness in which Caleb and Joshua played a crucial role (Num 13–14).

The remaining tribes are likewise listed in a south-to-north pattern, beginning with the southern tribes (Benjamin, Simeon) followed by the northern tribes (Zebulun, Issachar, Asher, Naphtali). Dan is placed last, naming cities in its original southern location but also noting the loss of its tribal allotment and movement north to Leshem. The movement of this tribe to a northern city accounts for its placement with other northern tribal allotments. That this movement occurs due to Dan's failure to possess its southern allotment effectively ends the tribal allotments on a note of failure.

The allotments given Judah and Joseph (14:1–17:18) are granted from Gilgal (14:6); those for the seven remaining tribes (18:11–19:48) are granted from Shiloh (19:51). Between these two groups lies the narrative of the relocation of the tent of meeting to Shiloh (18:1–10). The narrative disrupts the lists of tribal allotments, providing a narrative center that focuses on Israel's worship. Israel possesses the land as the gift of its covenant God, and worship in the place of God's choosing and by the means of God's choosing is crucial to ongoing possession of that gift.

The themes of faithfulness and land possession are addressed throughout chapters 13–21 by the inclusion of several narrative passages. The tribal allotments are bracketed by parallel narratives of allotments granted Caleb in Judah and Joshua in Joseph (14:6–15; 19:49–50). Caleb and Joshua represent the largest western tribes, but the inclusion of these parallel accounts has deeper significance. They bracket the tribal allotments with examples of faithfulness and hope. Caleb and Joshua were the spies who urged Israel to trust in God's promise of the land (Num 14:6–9). That promise has now come to pass. For their trust and service, they receive private allotments—a witness in the midst of Israel.

Juxtaposed between these narratives is another concerning Joseph (17:14–18). Caleb boldly claimed and took his allotment, but Joseph (though "numerous and very powerful" [17:17]) is unable to do so. Like Israel in the wilderness, Joseph complains that the inhabitants are too powerful to be overcome. Joshua's response to them voices the same faith as his response to the rebellious tribes in the wilderness. The question these vignettes raises is which vision of Israel's life in the land will be established—the faithfulness of Caleb and Joshua or the fearfulness of Joseph? Despite the strong affirmation throughout these chapters that Israel possesses the land, there are hints that the latter vision has a hold within Israel. That the tribal lists end with Dan's failure confirms this reality.

Adding to the theme of these vignettes are two additional ones, that of Aksah of Judah (15:13–19) and the Josephite daughters of Zelophehad: Mahlah, Noah, Hoglah, Milkah, and Tirzah (17:3–6). Both are narratives in which women (who were—by their gender—marginalized from the process of land allotment within a patrilineal system) receive an inheritance. In each case it is granted because of their persistent faith that boldly claims land. It is this characteristic that is valorized above their gender as another example of the faith necessary to possess the land.

The vignettes of Caleb, Aksah, the five daughters, and the Josephites have been shown to share several common structural elements:[2]

- A confrontation between two parties;
- A case is made upon which the request for land is based;
  - In some of the vignettes a flashback to Moses is offered (not found in the Aksah [15:18–19] or Joseph–tribe [17:14–18] vignettes;
- The land grant is made;
  - In some of the vignettes the Lord's command is referenced (not found in the Caleb [14:6–15], Aksah [15:18–19] or Joseph-tribe [17:14–18] vignettes; and
- Summary of results (not found in the Aksah [15:18–19] vignette).

Whether the shared elements in these vignettes point to an identifiable genre such as a "land grant narrative" and whatever the source of these narratives, the shared patterning suggests that each is included to address similar concerns. The exploration of why these narratives are included and what they add to the overall narrative and theological purposes of the book of Joshua will be taken up in the commentary proper.

At points throughout the allocation of land, it is noted that the Levites do not receive an allotment. This occurs when the eastern lands are allotted (13:14, 33; 14:3), when the western lands are allotted (14:4), and when the last seven allotments are granted (18:7). These notations acknowledge that the Levitical tribe is excluded from the tribal allocations and anticipates chapter 21. There, the Levites are distributed throughout the tribes for the benefit of all Israel. The Levitical ministry is intended to guide Israel's worship so that their tenure in the land is lasting and fruitful. In addition to the several

2. Noted in Nelson, *Joshua*, 177.

notations regarding the Levites, a series of negative notations state Israel's failure to fully possess their tribal lands (13:13; 15:63; 16:10; 17:12–13; 19:47). These negative notations are further explored in the commentary below.

Within this larger structure, each tribal allotment is narrated with the same constituent parts. While there is some variation, the pattern is easily discernible. Each tribal allotment contains a heading (15:1; 16:1–4; 16:5; 17:1; 18:11; 19:1, 10, 17, 24, 32, 40), a sketch of tribal boundaries (15:2–12; 16:5b–8; 17:7–10; 18:12–20; 19:10b–14, 22, 26–29, 33–34), a list of the towns within the allotment (and most often including a tally of the number of towns; 15:21–62; 16:9; 17:11; 18:21–28; 19:2–8, 15, 18–22, 25–26, 28, 30, 35–38, 41–46), and a concluding statement (15:12b, 63; 16:10; 17:12–13; 18:28b; 19:8b–9, 16, 23, 31, 39, 47–48).

The variations to the pattern are at times readily explained. For instance, Judah heads the lists and, as a large and prominent tribe, uniquely has its towns presented in several sub-lists that group and tally the towns according to region (15:21–62); Simeon's allotment lacks a boundary delineation, but the concluding statement notes Simeon's absorption in Judah and thus accounts for the discrepancy; Dan's allotment likewise includes no boundaries, but the conclusion notes the tribe's removal from its allotment, providing a reason for the pattern variation. Elsewhere, the variations are not accounted for so readily. For instance, Asher and Issachar both list towns and boundaries but without clear delineation between the two categories. The variations are not unusual when compared with the many similar lists produced by Israel's neighbors (see Listen to the Story below).[3]

*Listening to the Text in the Story*: Genesis 12:1–3, 7; 15:18–21; 17:8; Numbers 26:52–56; 33:50–54; Alalakh Land Grants *AT*1 and *AT*456; Hittite Treaty between Tudḫaliya IV with Kurunta of Tarḫuntašša

## Land for the New Generation

Israel now receives as an inheritance the land promised to Abraham (Gen. 12:1–3, 7; 15:18–21; 17:8; see also Chapter 1, Listen to the Story). The inheritance is divided according to God's command to Moses (Num 26:52–56; 33:53–54), given in Moab before the Jordan crossing (Num 26:63). God's command is in view throughout Joshua 13–21, reflected in the vocabulary shared between the command in Numbers and its execution in Joshua:

3. Further description of the structure of the tribal lists can be found in Kitchen, *On the Reliability*, 179–80.

- the land is allotted to Israel (from *hlq*; Num 26:53, 55, 56 ["distributed" in NIV]);
- the land is Israel's inheritance (*nahalah*; Num 26:53, 54, 56; the verbal form occurs in v. 55; cf. 33:54; 34:13);
- the land is divided by lot (*goral*; Num 26:55, 56; 33:54; 34:13);
- the land is allotted proportionally according to ancestral tribes (Num 33:54).

The proportional needs of each tribe are determined in Numbers 26 by way of census (vv. 4–51; cf. 33:50–54; 34:13–15). This is the second census conducted in the wilderness and is in preparation for entry to the land. It is conducted after the wilderness generation died, leaving only Moses, Caleb, and Joshua (Num 1:1–2; 26:3–4, 64). The census is also conducted after Israel sinned at Baal Peor (Num 25) and is evidence that, despite ongoing sin, God's promise regarding the land remains. In the census, the Levitical clans are enumerated separately from the other tribes (26:57–62) and the reason for this is given: "because they received no inheritance among them" (v. 62).

The correlations with Joshua 13–21 are apparent. Joshua likewise allots (*hlq*) the land to Israel as an inheritance (*nahalah*), using the lot (*goral*). The Levitical tribes are not included in the allotments to Israel but are treated separately and last, receiving not a tribal allotment but cities as an inheritance. Even the placement of the second census after the sin of Peor has affinities with Joshua 13–21 where, despite Israel's failures (at Jericho, Ai, and with the Gibeonites), God's promises are realized and the land gifted.

## Lists! Lists! Lists!

Lists of boundaries and towns are found in documents from many different ancient Near Eastern contexts including military, religious, treaty, land grant, and administrative. Often, as in the biblical text, these lists have introductions and conclusions and may be further divided by subheadings.[4] Comparisons made between Joshua 13–21 and ancient Near Eastern treaty, land grant, and administrative lists show particular resonance, setting the biblical text within its ancient context.

4. Further discussion of the variety of lists discussed here can be access in Kitchen, *On the Reliability*, 181–82; see also Richard Hess, "A Typology of West Semitic Place Name Lists with Special Reference to Joshua 13–21," *BAR* 59 (1996): 160–70, and "Asking Historical Questions of Joshua 13–19: Recent Discussion Concerning the Date of the Boundary Lists," in *Faith, Tradition, and History: Old Testament Historiography in Its Near Eastern Context*, ed. A. R. Millard et al. (Winona Lake: Eisenbrauns, 1994), 191–205.

Several treaties from places such as Mari, Babylon, Ugarit, and Hatti include boundary and town lists. As in the biblical text, such lists have an introduction and conclusion, narrative notices interspersed with the lists, and duplicate descriptions of the same boundary. At times, the number of towns listed and the tally provided do not agree. The treaty lists help to define the covenanted relationship between parties. One such thirteenth century Hittite treaty between Tudḫaliya IV and Kurunta of Tarḫuntašša begins with a historical introduction and then, in approximately fifty lines, defines the treaty borders. A later portion of the treaty (approximately twenty-two lines) lists cities granted under the treaty. As in the biblical text, the borders may be defined by towns, geographic areas, and landmarks. The treaty reads in part:

> In the direction of Mt. Huwatnuwantam the *ḫallapuwanza* is its/his border, but the *ḫallapuwanza* belongs to the Ḫulaya River Land. In the direction of Kuwarsawants up behind, the *ḫuwaši* stone of the Dog is the boundary. In the direction of Ušša (to the N?), Azrata is its/his boundary, but the city Zarata (belongs) to the Ḫulaya River Land. In the direction of Wanzataruwa the town Harazzuwa is his boundary, but Harazzuwa (itself) belongs to the Land of Ušša. In my father's first written treaty the town Šuttasna was his boundary in the direction of Mt. Kuwakuwaliya. But later my father himself made the town Šantimma the boundary. Šantimma (itself) however, belongs to the Land of the Ḫulaya River. In the direction of the town Wanzatarwa and Kunzinasa his boundary is Mt. Arlanta and the town Alana. Alana belongs to the Land of the Ḫulaya River, but the water which is on Mt. Arlanta belongs jointly to the Land of the Ḫulaya River and Ḫatti.[5]

Land grants, in which land is gifted by a suzerain to a vassal for military aid provided, reveal points of contact with Joshua 13–21. Land grants vary greatly in style, and it is difficult to speak of one form used in all such grants. However, Richard Hess convincingly argues that two such grants from Middle Bronze Age Alalakh, *AT*1 and (even more so) the lengthy *AT*456, present one model of such a grant that can be compared favorably with Joshua 13–21.[6] In these land grants, past events are narrated as the context for the present land grant, the gifted land is delineated and cities named, and oaths are witnessed before the gods to seal the agreement. In a similar way, Joshua 1–12 provides a narrative context for the lands granted by God to Israel. The land grant delineates boundaries and cities (chs. 13–21), and Joshua concludes with a

5. *COS* 2.18:100–106, lines 29–42.

6. Ibid., 2.127:329 for *AT*1; Ibid., 2.137:369–70 for *AT*456. Helpful discussion of *AT*456 is found in Hess, "Joshua" in ZIBBC, 9–13, 58–59.

covenant sworn by Israel. In Joshua, the covenantal context of the land grant is found not only in chapters 23–24, but also in 8:30–35.

The largest sampling of available ancient lists is administrative texts. Here, the similarity of form to Joshua is most striking. Introductions and conclusion, subdivisions within longer lists, and the tallying of similar items within a list are usual markers of administrative lists. These same features are found in Joshua 13–21.

While none of the ancient list forms fully explain all the features of the lists in Joshua 13–21 (for instance, explanatory glosses such as those at 19:9, 47 are anomalous), the comparables firmly contextualize the form of Joshua 13–21 within the ancient world.

# CHAPTER 14

# Joshua 13:1–33

## LISTEN to the Story

1When Joshua had grown old, the Lord said to him, "You are now very old, and there are still very large areas of land to be taken over.

2"This is the land that remains: all the regions of the Philistines and Geshurites, 3from the Shihor River on the east of Egypt to the territory of Ekron on the north, all of it counted as Canaanite though held by the five Philistine rulers in Gaza, Ashdod, Ashkelon, Gath and Ekron; the territory of the Avvites 4on the south; all the land of the Canaanites, from Arah of the Sidonians as far as Aphek and the border of the Amorites; 5the area of Byblos; and all Lebanon to the east, from Baal Gad below Mount Hermon to Lebo Hamath.

6"As for all the inhabitants of the mountain regions from Lebanon to Misrephoth Maim, that is, all the Sidonians, I myself will drive them out before the Israelites. Be sure to allocate this land to Israel for an inheritance, as I have instructed you, 7and divide it as an inheritance among the nine tribes and half of the tribe of Manasseh."

8The other half of Manasseh, the Reubenites and the Gadites had received the inheritance that Moses had given them east of the Jordan, as he, the servant of the Lord, had assigned it to them.

9It extended from Aroer on the rim of the Arnon Gorge, and from the town in the middle of the gorge, and included the whole plateau of Medeba as far as Dibon, 10and all the towns of Sihon king of the Amorites, who ruled in Heshbon, out to the border of the Ammonites. 11It also included Gilead, the territory of the people of Geshur and Maakah, all of Mount Hermon and all Bashan as far as Salekah—12that is, the whole kingdom of Og in Bashan, who had reigned in Ashtaroth and Edrei. (He was the last of the Rephaites.) Moses had defeated them and taken over their land. 13But the Israelites did not drive out the people of Geshur and Maakah, so they continue to live among the Israelites to this day.

14But to the tribe of Levi he gave no inheritance, since the food offerings presented to the Lord, the God of Israel, are their inheritance, as he promised them.

15 This is what Moses had given to the tribe of Reuben, according to
its clans:
16 The territory from Aroer on the rim of the Arnon Gorge, and from
the town in the middle of the gorge, and the whole plateau past Medeba
17 to Heshbon and all its towns on the plateau, including Dibon, Bamoth
Baal, Beth Baal Meon, 18 Jahaz, Kedemoth, Mephaath, 19 Kiriathaim, Sib-
mah, Zereth Shahar on the hill in the valley, 20 Beth Peor, the slopes of Pisgah, and Beth Jeshimoth—21 all the towns on the plateau and the entire
realm of Sihon king of the Amorites, who ruled at Heshbon. Moses had
defeated him and the Midianite chiefs, Evi, Rekem, Zur, Hur and Reba—
princes allied with Sihon—who lived in that country. 22 In addition to those
slain in battle, the Israelites had put to the sword Balaam son of Beor, who
practiced divination. 23 The boundary of the Reubenites was the bank of
the Jordan. These towns and their villages were the inheritance of the Reubenites, according to their clans.
24 This is what Moses had given to the tribe of Gad, according to its clans:
25 The territory of Jazer, all the towns of Gilead and half the Ammonite
country as far as Aroer, near Rabbah; 26 and from Heshbon to Ramath Mizpah and Betonim, and from Mahanaim to the territory of Debir; 27 and in
the valley, Beth Haram, Beth Nimrah, Sukkoth and Zaphon with the rest
of the realm of Sihon king of Heshbon (the east side of the Jordan, the territory up to the end of the Sea of Galilee). 28 These towns and their villages
were the inheritance of the Gadites, according to their clans.
29 This is what Moses had given to the half-tribe of Manasseh, that is,
to half the family of the descendants of Manasseh, according to its clans:
30 The territory extending from Mahanaim and including all of Bashan,
the entire realm of Og king of Bashan—all the settlements of Jair in Bashan,
sixty towns, 31 half of Gilead, and Ashtaroth and Edrei (the royal cities of
Og in Bashan). This was for the descendants of Makir son of Manasseh—
for half of the sons of Makir, according to their clans.
32 This is the inheritance Moses had given when he was in the plains of
Moab across the Jordan east of Jericho. 33 But to the tribe of Levi, Moses
had given no inheritance; the LORD, the God of Israel, is their inheritance,
as he promised them.

*Listening to the Text in the Story*: Numbers 21:21–35 (cf. Deut 2:24–3:11); 22:1–24:25 (cf. Deut 23:4–5); 31:1–12; 32:33–42 (cf. Deut 3:12–20); Chapter 13, Introduction to Joshua 13–21

### Sihon and Og; The Transjordanian Tribes . . . Again

The importance of the Transjordanian tribes and the land they took from Sihon and Og has been explored above (see Listen to the Story, Chapter 1, 12). Although east of the Jordan (and thus outside the promised land), these lands are included first in a section that allocates land to the nine and a half tribes (v. 7). This is a reminder that not only was the Transjordan taken first, but that Reuben, Gad, and the half-tribe of Manasseh remain part of Israel. Their land was granted as a concession but, like the western land, is an "inheritance" (13:14 [2x], 23, 28).

### Balaam

A strange passing reference is made to the prophet Balaam (v. 22). This foreign prophet was hired by Balak to curse Israel, but Balaam committed himself to say only what God commanded. In the end, Balaam pronounced several oracles of blessing upon Israel (Num 22–24). Mentioning Balaam in Joshua 13 is not necessary to describe the eastern allocation (and does not appear at all in the same territorial summation in ch. 12). The reference to Balaam is an important contribution, however, for two reasons.

First, the narrative of Balaam includes three lengthy oracles that are introduced and concluded by narrative elements, firmly embedding them within their narrative context (23:1–12; 23:13–26; 23:27–24:14). These are followed by four short, consecutive oracles without intervening narrative, which are more loosely tied to the narrative context (24:15–25). Of the three firmly-embedded oracles, the last one ends with a recollection of promises originally made to Abraham:

> "May those who bless you be blessed
> and those who curse you be cursed!" (Num 24:9)

The words echo those spoken by God to Abraham (Gen 12:3) when the promise of land was first made. These words not only describe what happened to Moab but are a true depiction of Israel's entry to the land: those who sought to oppose Israel (Sihon, Og, Moab, Jericho, southern and northern kings) were defeated, while Israel was blessed. This blessing was not simply the gift of land, but God's own presence in Israel's midst, crossing before them, and fighting on Israel's behalf so that they might have rest in the land.

The mention of Balaam is a reminder as Israel begins to allocate the land that the ancient promise of blessing and curse has come to pass. Surprisingly, the reference to Balaam comes in the context of the Transjordanian allotment—an allotment granted by God's concessionary will to tribes who chose not to enter the land. Despite this, the reminder reveals that God's faithfulness to the promises to Abraham remains.

Balaam's second contribution to the narrative comes through the mention of his death alongside that of five Midianite chiefs, princes allied with Sihon (vv. 21–22). Although Balaam prophesied as God directed, there is no evidence his allegiance transferred to Israel or its God. He continued to practice divination, and it may be by divination that he counseled Moab to seduce Israel at Baal Peor (Num 25; 31:16). Zur, one of the five Midianite chiefs, had a daughter involved in seducing Israel (v. 21; Num 25:15). For her role in the seduction she is killed, and Israel is also commanded to kill the Midianites (Num 25:14–17). The death of the chiefs in Joshua 13 is the fulfillment of that command; the death of Balaam in the same context suggests his death is also recompense for Baal Peor.

The death of the five chiefs and Balaam is a reminder of the anticipated end for those who oppose God. Balaam practiced divination against Israel, and the Midianite kings opposed Israel. Both are killed. As Israel now allocates and settles the land they must heed the warning: should they, like Balaam or Midian, oppose God, they will be punished, regardless of their covenant identity. The lesson of Joshua 1–12 must be adhered to: allegiance to God and obedience to the law of Moses is as necessary to possessing the land as it is to taking it.

## EXPLAIN the Story

### The Land Remaining (13:1–7)

The first half of the book opens with great anticipation: Israel is promised "every place" (1:3) in the land that God gives them. The land's boundaries are extensive, with the promise that "no one will be able to stand against you" (1:5). This is the rhetorical emphasis throughout chapters 1–12 and is dominant in the conclusion (11:16, 23), although this is held in tension with ongoing efforts to take and possess the land (see above, Chapter 11, Josh 11:16–23).

It is this ongoing effort with which the book's second half begins. Both the narrator and God attest to Joshua's old age (v. 1), yet despite the passing years "very large areas" of the land remain to be possessed. The "land that remains" (v. 2) is sketched broadly and is land that lies beyond areas taken in chapters 1–12. The land still to be taken includes much of the coastal plain. From the Shihor River (the Wadi el-Arish), it includes the area of the Philistine pentapolis north to Ekron, the area of the Geshurites to the southwest, and the Avvites to the south. The location of Arah is unknown and Aphek disputed, but the Sidonian lands lie along the Phoenician coast. The border of the Amorites marks the northern boundary of these lands and perhaps indicates a border with Amurru, a northern kingdom in the Lebanon area. Byblos lies on the coast north of modern Beirut, and the area of Lebanon is identified as stretching from Mount Hermon northeast to Lebo Hamath in northern Syria. Also included are Sidonian lands within the mountainous area of Lebanon, although the precise location of Misrephoth Maim is uncertain (see 11:8).

Once the "land that remains to be taken" is noted, chapters 13–21 turn to allocation of all the land that is gifted to Israel. This is a prospective allocation, including those lands still to be taken.

In chapter 1 Joshua's success was attached to his obedience to the law of Moses (1:7–8). Through his obedience he would "lead these people to inherit the land." Joshua 13 opens with a re-commissioning. In it, the call to obedience remains, for Joshua is to "allocate this land . . . as I have instructed you" (v. 6). The land he allocates is divided "as an inheritance" (vv. 6–8) among the western tribes. The allotments are a prospective vision whose accomplishment is hindered by setbacks to land possession experienced by several tribes. Despite these setbacks there is no sense that Joshua's ministry has failed. God continues his commitment to Joshua, noting that "I myself will drive them out" (v. 6). As it appears in the NIV, the promise to "drive them out" seems limited to only the region of the Sidonians. It could, however, be understood to apply to all the land that remains to be taken (vv. 2–6).

### Eastern Boundaries (13:8–14)

The second half of Joshua begins the allocations by recapping the Transjordanian allotments. Granted by Moses east of the Jordan (v. 8; cf. v. 32), they were Moses' concession to the sinful request of the Transjordanian tribes (Num 32). The land was granted on the proviso that Reuben, Gad, and the half-tribe of Manasseh assist the western tribes in taking the promised land. When Joshua reminded the Transjordanian tribes of their commitment, they affirmed that "just as we fully obeyed Moses, so we will obey you" (1:17). The account of the eastern allotments at the head of this section is a reminder that the Transjordanian tribes remained true to their promise (Num 32:25; Josh 1:16), demonstrating their commitment to all Israel. Once this recap is completed, however, the eastern lands receive no further attention in this third section of Joshua; the focus moves to, and remains on, the western, promised land.

The part played by Moses in the eastern allotments is noted (v. 8; cf. vv. 15, 24, 29, 32). Despite the concessionary grant, Moses remains the "servant of the Lord" (v. 8; cf. 1:13, 15; 12:6; 18:7). Only at the end of Joshua's ministry, when all the lands have been allocated, is the title "servant of the Lord" applied to Joshua (24:29).

As in the boundary list of the land that remains to be taken (vv. 2–6), the boundaries of the eastern lands are broadly sketched. Many of the names given are those noted in 12:2–5. In that list, the territories of Sihon and Og are noted separately but here, while each king is named, their territories are blended into a unified whole gifted to the two and a half tribes.

Included in the boundary list are the independent kingdoms of Geshur and Maakah. These lie west of the half-tribe of Manasseh, occupying the area of the Golan Heights. Geshur lies immediately east and north of the Sea of Galilee, and Maakah stretches north from Geshur to Mount Hermon. Geshur appears later in David's family story (2 Sam 3:3; 13:37–38), and Maakah joins a coalition against David (2 Sam 10:6–8).

In Joshua 12:5 these two kingdoms were named merely as a boundary point; in 13:11 they are included as part of the allotment given the Transjordanian tribes. In a striking note of failure, 13:13 specifies that "the Israelites did not drive out the people of Geshur and Maakah." The blame is laid on all Israel rather than the eastern tribes, as a further mark of solidarity between eastern and western tribes. This is the first of many notices of Israel's failure to fully possess the land; later, the western tribes of Judah (15:63), Ephraim (16:10) and Manasseh (17:12–13) will be similarly indicted.

Despite this notation of failure, the emphasis in verses 8–33 is upon the complete taking of the eastern lands. This is achieved by the liberal use of the Hebrew word *kol*, translated as "all," "whole," and "entire" in reference to land taken (five times in vv. 8–14 and eight times in vv. 15–33). By contrast, this same Hebrew word, used to speak of extensive conquest, is found only three times in chapters 14–19 (15:46; 16:9; 19:8). By applying this emphasis in chapter 13, the need for continued narrative focus on action east of the Jordan is rendered rhetorically unnecessary. As "all" the land is taken, no more need be said of it. Focus can instead turn to the promised land.

The sketch of the eastern boundaries concludes with a notation of the Levitical "inheritance" (*nahalah*; v. 14). The Levitical allotment differs markedly from that of the other tribes and is marked by the strong "but" (*raq*) that begins the exception (v. 14). The Levites are not gifted with land, although they do receive towns throughout Israel (Num 26:62; 35:1–5; Josh 21). Their inheritance is here a pragmatic one: the food offerings made by Israel (Lev. 2:3, 10; 6:16–18, 24–30; 7:5–36; 21:22). By these offerings, the life of the Levites is sustained (Num 18:8–32; Deut 18:1–6).

The Levitical inheritance is noted periodically throughout the tribal allocations (14:4–5; 18:7) and anticipates chapter 21 in which specific towns are gifted to them east and west of the Jordan. That the first notation of Levitical inheritance (v. 14) occurs within eastern tribal allotments is a reminder that God does not leave the Transjordanian tribes without a witness. They too are part of Israel. Levites will live among them as among the tribes within the promised land proper, for all the tribes comprise God's chosen people and must be instructed in his ways.

### Eastern Tribal Allotments (13:15–33)

After tracing the boundaries in broad terms, the detailed allotments are given for the two and a half eastern tribes. Moving from south to north, for each of Reuben, Gad, and the half tribe of Manasseh boundaries, regions, and cities are named. Each allotment includes a remembrance of Sihon, Og, or the five Midianite kings (vv. 21, 27, 30) and battles successfully undertaken in obedience to God's command and through his power (Num 25:16–17; 31:1–12; Deut 2:24–3:11). The remembrance is a reminder that Israel's continuing success requires continuing obedience. Balaam's death (v. 22) is likewise a reminder; they should walk in the blessing the foreign prophet pronounced and avoid the divinatory practices which he engaged; these are prohibited to Israel (Deut 18:14). Fullness of life in the land comes as Israel walks in the promised blessing and in obedience.

As in verses 8–14, Moses is highlighted. He defeats the eastern kings (v. 21) and allocates the eastern lands (vv. 15, 24, 29, 32, 33). Moses remains the LORD's servant (v. 8), but it is always Moses and not Joshua who is cited as granting the Transjordanian lands (see Explain the Story, Chapter 1). In this way, the faithless request to remain outside the land is associated with the wilderness generation under Moses (Num 32).

The account of the eastern tribal allotments continues the emphasis on "all," "whole," and "entire." This rhetorical strategy enables the narrative to relate the eastern allocation and then turn wholly to the western lands; nothing more need be said of the eastern lands for they have been "wholly" taken (as discussed above, vv. 8–14).

Eastern allotments head the chapters of land distribution. Through significant wording, they provide a paradigm for the western allotments. First, the Transjordanian tribes receive an "inheritance" (*nahalah*, vv. 23, 28; the same word is implied in v. 32 and supplied in NIV). In this, they are no different than the western tribes who also are allotted an inheritance (Num 26:52–56; Josh 13:7).

Second, as will occur for the Cisjordanian tribes, eastern allotments are made proportionally, "according to its clans": Reuben (vv. 15, 23), Gad (vv. 24, 28), and Manasseh (vv. 29, 31). The clan is a familial unit comprised of several families, and several clans comprise a tribe. "According to its clans" takes the size and needs of each tribe into account for equitable land distribution. In this, the Transjordanian allotments follow the command given Moses (Num 26:52–56; cf. Listen to the Story in Chapter 13).

The phrase "according to its clans" first appears in Joshua in connection with the Transjordanian tribes but continues to describe all subsequent western allocations (15:1, 12, 20; 16:5, 8; 17:2; 18:11, 20, 21, 28; 19:1, 8, 10, 16, 17, 23, 24, 31, 32, 39, 40, 48).[1] In most cases, the phrase begins and ends a descriptive list. Even the Levitical cities are allocated from tribal allotments "according to its clans" (21:4, 7, 33, 40).[2] The replication of the pattern set by the initial Transjordanian allocation is one more way the narrative confirms that, despite the choice made by the Transjordanians, they are part of Israel.

As the eastern allocation ends, Moses is credited again with granting the eastern inheritance (v. 32; cf. v. 8). This takes place before the Jordan crossing (and thus outside of the land itself), for it occurs "in the plains of Moab" and "east of Jericho," and therefore pointedly "across the Jordan." The word used here for "across" is from the familiar Hebrew root *'br*, the same root repeatedly encountered in chapters 3–4 as Israel "crossed" (*'br*) the Jordan (see Chapter 3). The use of this key word ironically juxtaposes two events: the faithless choice of the eastern lands made "across" (east of) the Jordan versus Israel's triumphant journey "across" the Jordan under Joshua's leadership.

The juxtaposition separates the Transjordanian choice from Israel's crossing of the Jordan, placing a rhetorical boundary between eastern (concessionary) and western (promised) lands. Yet knowing the Transjordanian's faithful role in crossing and taking the western land (1:12–18), the juxtaposition returns the narrative to the familiar ambiguity surrounding the eastern tribes. They are part of "all Israel," remaining faithful to their promise, but they have chosen the lesser land east ("across") the Jordan.

Finally, the chapter closes with a second reference to the Levites and their lack of landed inheritance (v. 33). Earlier (v. 14) the Levitical exclusion was explained on pragmatic grounds. Now, a different reason is given for the exclusion: their inheritance is the LORD, a reality that Moses stated (Deut 10:6–9; 18:1–2). The role of the Levitical tribes' particular consecration finds its origin in Exodus 32:25–29. There, for their zeal for God they are consecrated to him for holy service. That service is outlined in Numbers 3–4 and includes ministry within the sacred precincts as well as the care and transportation of the ark, the sacred tent, and its furnishings. It is out of their devoted service to the LORD that their sustenance comes (through the offerings, as v. 14 notes).

1. The NIV provides a few variants in the translation of the Hebrew phrase, including "by their clans" (15:12; 17:2), "of the clans" (18:20), and "for its clans" (18:28).

2. NIV does not translate the Hebrew phrase in verses 33, 40.

**What Epitaph?**

How will you be remembered? What would you like inscribed on your tombstone? For a while, this somewhat morbid question became a common icebreaker given by a member of our Bible study group. Whenever that portion of the time fell to him, knowing grins would break out, anticipating it.

Answers varied, but the tombstone epitaphs likewise showed common themes. "She was a worshiper of God," said one. "A faithful husband and father," said another. "In hope of the resurrection" was common. All were statements that spoke their hope of a life lived for God and rewarded through Christ.

How might the epitaphs read for those in this chapter? Despite their desire to remain east of the Jordan, this chapter includes the Transjordanians as part of Israel, receiving an inheritance. They are remembered here (as elsewhere in Joshua) in positive terms, while yet acknowledging their choice of the Transjordan. There is something about their election under God's covenant that keeps remembrance of them on the positive side of the equation. Their epitaph might read, "Kept by God, despite their choice," or "Faithful to their promise" (referencing Josh 1:16).

Balaam, however, fares not as well. He is not remembered here for the many blessings he spoke over Israel. Instead, his violent death and his practice of divination are recalled. As explored above, remembrance of him is negative. In the New Testament Balaam is likewise negatively remembered, for Jude uses his example to describe the actions of ungodly people (Jude 11). Balaam's tombstone might read perhaps "He practiced divination," or "He enticed Israel away from faith," or even "He turned away from the God of blessing." Despite the amazing fact that God worked through this foreign prophet, Balaam did not sustain his service over the long haul. For this, his end was ignoble. On the basis of this chapter's commentary on Balaam, we might think Shakespeare's observation well describes this prophet's life:

> The evil that men do lives after them;
> The good is oft interrèd with their bones. (*Julius Caesar*, Act 3, Scene 2)

This *might* be the final assessment of Balaam in Joshua, except for the fact that (however badly he ended) for a time his ministry was empowered by God and directed to his purposes. By God's design, Balaam's more lasting legacy in Israel's life is the repeated blessing he pronounced over Israel. It is this fact that is the last remembrance of Balaam within Joshua. In God's first-person account of Israel's history, he remembers Balaam—not for his failure, but for his fulfillment of God's purposes:

> When Balak son of Zippor, the king of Moab, prepared to fight against Israel, he sent for Balaam son of Beor to put a curse on you. But I would not listen to Balaam, so he blessed you again and again, and I delivered you out of his hand. (Josh 24:9–10)

In this light, Shakespeare's observation could be reversed: the evil is interred with Balaam; the good lives after him. Not because of his own good, but because, for however brief a moment, he submitted to God's hand, giving powerful testimony to God's power and purposes.

So, perhaps, the ice-breaker of "what would you like on your tombstone?" is not such an easy or certain game. It does provide opportunity to reflect upon how we choose to live life. How blessed we are if throughout life we serve God wholeheartedly, never wavering. How much better than a life lived like Balaam: a time of glorious service that then turns away from God.

But in that darker eventuality, might not we (like God does for Balaam), well remember the good that has been done by the power of God and for his people? Not even latter apostasy can erase that memory, although it saddens the reflection.

## God in the "Boring Bits"

It can be fun to pose this question to a group of Christians: "If you couldn't sleep at night, and decided to read your Bible, to what text would you turn?" Answers range widely: from psalms of comfort, to favorite stories, to whatever is next in a devotional reading program. But there are always a few sheepish grins, and the naming of a text that is considered a certain sleep-inducer! People name different parts of the Bible and name different reasons: the Levitical laws because they have no narrative thread; the genealogies because of the soothing repetition of the "begats," Revelation because it feels incomprehensible. Often, these texts are turned to because they are considered "boring" or without spiritual value. Not far down such a list Joshua 13–21 is included.

These chapters are often skipped over because of their repetitive nature and the names and places that are unrecognized. What do these have to do with Christian faith? What is lost if these "boring bits" are skipped over?

It is true that some texts in the Old Testament are easily recognized as part of God's grand narrative. We see the importance of Abraham and Sarah's walk of faith and recognize our own human frailty in their decisions and challenges. We understand how such texts prepare for Christ, reveal God's heart, or connect with our lives. But the lists? In these, it is not so clear. And so, they are easily skipped over.

These texts are, however, part of God's story; no less "Word of the Lord" than the central text of Genesis 12:1–3 or Isaiah 53. The key is in learning *how* these texts communicate that story and speak God's word. They are not intended to enable an exact diagram of the boundaries, as that is often prevented by significant missing detail. But in the naming of towns and the sketching of boundaries, they communicate the full completion of what God promised. In the details, the land is given and claimed as a recognition that God has, indeed, given the land. In the recording of the details, we see Israel's remembrance and gratitude for God's work. God's hand is made evident in these "boring bits."

And, tucked into these "boring bits" are shining stories of the faithfulness of God's people caught up in the mundane issues of land distribution. There are also stories of the *un*faithfulness of God's people, standing as a warning and challenge to readers, asking them to choose which life of faith *they* will emulate.

This is all good news for us. For most of us, and for most of life, we live in the ordinary. It is the mundane details that color and shape our lives: packing lunches, gassing up the car, bandaging bruised knees, buying groceries, heading out once more to the office. But it is in these mundane details (as in the mundane details of the lists) that God's presence is known, and his promises are proven true, faithful, and life-giving. And it is in these mundane details of life that we are called to faithfulness and away from unfaithfulness, as was Israel.

It is in the discipline of the "boring bits" that we see the stunning hand of God, and where we can order our lives to recognize and respond to his faithfulness with our own faithfulness. So, perhaps that 2:00 a.m. sleep-inducer *isn't* Joshua 13–21. There is too much of God's promise fulfilled in it; too much challenge to walk faithfully in *our* mundane, to let us sleep easily.

# CHAPTER 15

# Joshua 14:1–15:63

## LISTEN to the Story

[1]Now these are the areas the Israelites received as an inheritance in
the land of Canaan, which Eleazar the priest, Joshua son of Nun and the
heads of the tribal clans of Israel allotted to them. [2]Their inheritances
were assigned by lot to the nine and a half tribes, as the LORD had commanded through Moses. [3]Moses had granted the two and a half tribes
their inheritance east of the Jordan but had not granted the Levites an
inheritance among the rest, [4]for Joseph's descendants had become two
tribes—Manasseh and Ephraim. The Levites received no share of the land
but only towns to live in, with pasturelands for their flocks and herds. [5]So
the Israelites divided the land, just as the LORD had commanded Moses.

[6]Now the people of Judah approached Joshua at Gilgal, and Caleb son
of Jephunneh the Kenizzite said to him, "You know what the LORD said
to Moses the man of God at Kadesh Barnea about you and me. [7]I was
forty years old when Moses the servant of the LORD sent me from Kadesh
Barnea to explore the land. And I brought him back a report according to
my convictions, [8]but my fellow Israelites who went up with me made the
hearts of the people melt in fear. I, however, followed the LORD my God
wholeheartedly. [9]So on that day Moses swore to me, 'The land on which
your feet have walked will be your inheritance and that of your children
forever, because you have followed the LORD my God wholeheartedly.'

[10]"Now then, just as the LORD promised, he has kept me alive for
forty-five years since the time he said this to Moses, while Israel moved
about in the wilderness. So here I am today, eighty-five years old! [11]I am
still as strong today as the day Moses sent me out; I'm just as vigorous to
go out to battle now as I was then. [12]Now give me this hill country that
the LORD promised me that day. You yourself heard then that the Anakites
were there and their cities were large and fortified, but, the LORD helping
me, I will drive them out just as he said."

[13]Then Joshua blessed Caleb son of Jephunneh and gave him Hebron

as his inheritance. [14]So Hebron has belonged to Caleb son of Jephunneh the Kenizzite ever since, because he followed the LORD, the God of Israel, wholeheartedly. [15](Hebron used to be called Kiriath Arba after Arba, who was the greatest man among the Anakites.)

Then the land had rest from war.

[15:1]The allotment for the tribe of Judah, according to its clans, extended down to the territory of Edom, to the Desert of Zin in the extreme south.

[2]Their southern boundary started from the bay at the southern end of the Dead Sea, [3]crossed south of Scorpion Pass, continued on to Zin and went over to the south of Kadesh Barnea. Then it ran past Hezron up to Addar and curved around to Karka. [4]It then passed along to Azmon and joined the Wadi of Egypt, ending at the Mediterranean Sea. This is their southern boundary.

[5]The eastern boundary is the Dead Sea as far as the mouth of the Jordan.

The northern boundary started from the bay of the sea at the mouth of the Jordan, [6]went up to Beth Hoglah and continued north of Beth Arabah to the Stone of Bohan son of Reuben. [7]The boundary then went up to Debir from the Valley of Achor and turned north to Gilgal, which faces the Pass of Adummim south of the gorge. It continued along to the waters of En Shemesh and came out at En Rogel. [8]Then it ran up the Valley of Ben Hinnom along the southern slope of the Jebusite city (that is, Jerusalem). From there it climbed to the top of the hill west of the Hinnom Valley at the northern end of the Valley of Rephaim. [9]From the hilltop the boundary headed toward the spring of the waters of Nephtoah, came out at the towns of Mount Ephron and went down toward Baalah (that is, Kiriath Jearim). [10]Then it curved westward from Baalah to Mount Seir, ran along the northern slope of Mount Jearim (that is, Kesalon), continued down to Beth Shemesh and crossed to Timnah. [11]It went to the northern slope of Ekron, turned toward Shikkeron, passed along to Mount Baalah and reached Jabneel. The boundary ended at the sea.

[12]The western boundary is the coastline of the Mediterranean Sea.

These are the boundaries around the people of Judah by their clans.

[13]In accordance with the LORD's command to him, Joshua gave to Caleb son of Jephunneh a portion in Judah—Kiriath Arba, that is, Hebron. (Arba was the forefather of Anak.) [14]From Hebron Caleb drove out the three Anakites—Sheshai, Ahiman and Talmai, the sons of Anak. [15]From there he marched against the people living in Debir (formerly

called Kiriath Sepher). [16]And Caleb said, "I will give my daughter Aksah in
marriage to the man who attacks and captures Kiriath Sepher." [17]Othniel
son of Kenaz, Caleb's brother, took it; so Caleb gave his daughter Aksah
to him in marriage.

[18]One day when she came to Othniel, she urged him to ask her father
for a field. When she got off her donkey, Caleb asked her, "What can I
do for you?"

[19]She replied, "Do me a special favor. Since you have given me land
in the Negev, give me also springs of water." So Caleb gave her the upper
and lower springs.

[20]This is the inheritance of the tribe of Judah, according to its clans:

[21]The southernmost towns of the tribe of Judah in the Negev toward
the boundary of Edom were:

Kabzeel, Eder, Jagur, [22]Kinah, Dimonah, Adadah, [23]Kedesh, Hazor,
Ithnan, [24]Ziph, Telem, Bealoth, [25]Hazor Hadattah, Kerioth Hezron (that
is, Hazor), [26]Amam, Shema, Moladah, [27]Hazar Gaddah, Heshmon, Beth
Pelet, [28]Hazar Shual, Beersheba, Biziothiah, [29]Baalah, Iyim, Ezem, [30]Eltolad,
Kesil, Hormah, [31]Ziklag, Madmannah, Sansannah, [32]Lebaoth, Shilhim,
Ain and Rimmon—a total of twenty-nine towns and their villages.

[33]In the western foothills:

Eshtaol, Zorah, Ashnah, [34]Zanoah, En Gannim, Tappuah, Enam,
[35]Jarmuth, Adullam, Sokoh, Azekah, [36]Shaaraim, Adithaim and Gederah
(or Gederothaim)—fourteen towns and their villages.

[37]Zenan, Hadashah, Migdal Gad, [38]Dilean, Mizpah, Joktheel, [39]Lachish,
Bozkath, Eglon, [40]Kabbon, Lahmas, Kitlish, [41]Gederoth, Beth Dagon,
Naamah and Makkedah—sixteen towns and their villages.

[42]Libnah, Ether, Ashan, [43]Iphtah, Ashnah, Nezib, [44]Keilah, Akzib and
Mareshah—nine towns and their villages.

[45]Ekron, with its surrounding settlements and villages; [46]west of Ekron,
all that were in the vicinity of Ashdod, together with their villages; [47]Ashdod,
its surrounding settlements and villages; and Gaza, its settlements and villages, as far as the Wadi of Egypt and the coastline of the Mediterranean Sea.

[48]In the hill country:

Shamir, Jattir, Sokoh, [49]Dannah, Kiriath Sannah (that is, Debir), [50]Anab,
Eshtemoh, Anim, [51]Goshen, Holon and Giloh—eleven towns and their
villages.

[52]Arab, Dumah, Eshan, [53]Janim, Beth Tappuah, Aphekah, [54]Humtah,
Kiriath Arba (that is, Hebron) and Zior—nine towns and their villages.

[55]Maon, Carmel, Ziph, Juttah, [56]Jezreel, Jokdeam, Zanoah, [57]Kain,
Gibeah and Timnah—ten towns and their villages.
[58]Halhul, Beth Zur, Gedor, [59]Maarath, Beth Anoth and Eltekon—six
towns and their villages.
[60]Kiriath Baal (that is, Kiriath Jearim) and Rabbah—two towns and
their villages.
[61]In the wilderness:
Beth Arabah, Middin, Sekakah, [62]Nibshan, the City of Salt and En
Gedi—six towns and their villages.
[63]Judah could not dislodge the Jebusites, who were living in Jerusalem;
to this day the Jebusites live there with the people of Judah.

*Listening to the Text in the Story*: Numbers 13:1–14:38; 20:22–29; 32:28–30; 34:17–19; Deuteronomy 10:6; Chapter 13, Introduction to Joshua 13–21; Emar Ritual of Installation of the Storm God's High Priestess; Imgûa Partition Document; Phoenician Cebel Ires Daği Inscription

**Priestly Participation in Land Distribution**

This is the first of several times Eleazar appears in Joshua, always in the context of land distribution (14:1; 17:4; 19:51; 21:1). In these texts he is always named with Joshua and representative tribal leaders, and his participation reflects God's original commandment given Moses (Num 32:28; 34:17–18). The deaths of Eleazar and Joshua are recorded in the final verses of the book (24:29–33), after they have faithfully completed the task of land distribution.

As a representative of the priests and Levites, Eleazar's presence is a reminder that the mundane task of land distribution is a sacred act; there is no dichotomy between sacred and secular. The priest exercises his role alongside representatives from all the other tribes so that together, they ensure the distribution is a concerted act of "all Israel." Through Israel's representatives, land is distributed equitably for the good of all.

Eleazar is one of Aaron's sons consecrated as priest (Exod 6:23; 28:1; Lev 8:1–36; Num 3:1–4). As such, he had responsibility for the care of the tabernacle, its furnishings and articles, and exercised oversight of those who cared for the sanctuary (Num 3:32; 4:16). After Aaron's death Eleazar is vested as chief priest (Num 20:22–29; Deut 10:6). With Moses, he conducted the second wilderness census as the basis for land allocation (Num 26:3–4). He witnessed Joshua's commissioning by Moses (Num 27:12–23) and, with Joshua, received Moses' commands for the allocation of the Transjordanian and western lands

(Num 32:28–30; 34:17–18). It is Eleazar's son Phineas who is dispatched to confront the Transjordanian tribes when they build an altar (22:13, 31–2).

## Faithful Caleb

Caleb is no stranger to the biblical story. He and Joshua are the two faithful spies who urge Israel to enter the land against the peoples' fearful opposition (Num 13–14). For their faithfulness, Caleb and Joshua survive the wilderness generation and enter the promised land (Num 14:26–30). Caleb is further rewarded with an inheritance of land for following God "wholeheartedly" (Num 14:24; Deut 1:36; Josh 14:8).

The inheritance granted Caleb is striking on two counts. First, of the two faithful spies, it is only Caleb who is promised this reward, perhaps an acknowledgement of his leadership as spokesperson in urging the people to faithfulness (Num 13:30; 14:24). Joshua does receive an allotment, but this is not tied specifically to his faithfulness in Numbers 13–14.

Second, Caleb is part of the tribe of Judah. In this capacity he represents Judah as one of the spies who go into the land (Num 13:6). He also represents Judah in the group of tribal leaders who, together with Eleazar and Joshua, apportion the land (Num 34:19). But though integrated into the tribe of Judah, Caleb is not an Israelite but a Kenizzite. Although it is not conclusive, the Kenizzites may trace their lineage to Esau's grandson Kenaz (Gen 36:11, 15, 42). Elsewhere, the Kenizzites are named as foreigners in the land promised Abraham (Gen. 15:19). By this account, Caleb is a foreigner whose clan had earlier incorporated in to one of Israel's tribes. Though a non-Israelite, he receives an inheritance within Israel. Like Rahab, he is another example of the inclusion and honor granted a foreigner.

## Casting Lots

The practice of lot casting appears in other contexts in the ancient Near East. In rituals for the installation of a high priestess found in the thirteenth century Amorite city of Emar,

> [T]he sons of Emar take lots from the temple of NINURTA and grasp them before the storm god. The daughter of any son of Emar may be designated.[1]

In this case, the casting of lots is conducted in the presence of the god, a practice that parallels the biblical account (18:8) and indicates the belief that the items so adjudicated were of concern to the deity and the results under his or her power.

---

1. *COS* 1.122:427.

Lot casting was part of the legal process of distributing inheritance lands as evidenced in the nineteenth century BC Old Babylonian partition document.[2] The document shows an undivided inheritance transferred to the deceased's children, the removal of any illegal claimants occupying the land, and the equitable transfer of the land by lot to the inheritors. Although Joshua is not a legal text, it reflects similar concern for equitable distribution of an inheritance, determined by lot.

### Women Gifted Together with Lands

For his victory in battle, Othniel is awarded a grant of land. Included in the award is Caleb's daughter Aksah (15:16–17). The inclusion of women in real estate transfers is part of the seventh century BC Phoenician record known as *Cebel Ires Dağı*. In it, one individual (Mutas) grants land to another (Kulas). As the record relates the subsequent history of the plot of land, it becomes apparent that included in the original grant was Mutas's daughter. She is gifted a second time to another individual along with the fields originally granted Kulas:

> Mutas gave to Kulas the field of the Prince and the vineyards within the field of the Prince below the town as well as the vineyards below ML. . . . But when he (Kulas) exiled Masanazamis . . . then King Awariku handed over to Masanazamis all these fields (of Kulas). . . . And furthermore, Mutas had given MSD, his daughter, to Kulas; but during the term of office of Aziwasis, he (Awariku) handed her over to Masanazamis.[3]

That grants of land should bundle women as part of the gift seems abhorrent to modern western readers but was accepted in the ancient Near Eastern world.

### Introduction to the Distribution of Western Lands (14:1–5)

The western allotments begin with the tribe of Judah (chs. 14–15) followed by Joseph (chs. 16–17). Only after the tribes reassemble themselves and bring the tent of meeting to Shiloh (18:1) is the land divided among the remaining seven tribes (see Chapter 13). The placement of the Shiloh account thus separates the allotments given Judah and Joseph from those granted the seven smaller tribes. This chapter explores the allotment granted Judah, noting its

2. Called the "*Imgûa* Partition Document" by Anne M. Kitz, "Undivided Inheritance and Lot Casting in the Book of Joshua," *JBL* 119 (2000): 601–18.

3. *COS* 3.55:139.

positive treatment of themes of faithfulness and obedience. Similar themes follow in the Joseph allotment but are not as strongly presented. Where they do appear, Joseph is often cast in a more negative light.

Judah's allotment is preceded by a general introduction of the inheritance Israel receives "in the land of Canaan" (vv. 1–5). This differentiates these lands from the inheritance "east of the Jordan" (13:32). Before describing Judah's allotments, which begin in 15:1, several digressions note the individuals responsible, the methods used in the allocation of land, and the exceptions and additions to the allotments. Each digression not only creates anticipation for the land-allocation proper but gives insight into the theological concerns of the Judahite allocation narrative.

The allocation of the western lands is introduced in verses 1–5 with three key words prominent in chapters 13–21 (see above, Chapter 13). The land is referred to as an "inheritance" (*nahalah*; vv. 2, 3 [2x]) and (using the same Hebrew root) the land is "received as an inheritance" and "allotted" (v. 1). The Hebrew root thus appears five times in the first five verses (compared to only four times in the rest of chs. 14–15; 14:9, 13, 14; 15:20) and clearly defines the character of the land allocation; it is indeed Israel's inheritance received from the LORD and a fulfillment of the promise of 1:6. All that takes place by way of land allotment in these chapters demonstrates God's faithfulness to his promise given to Joshua.

Two other key words highlight the obedience inherent in the process of land allocation (see Introduction, Chapter 13). The land is "divided" (v. 5) and assigned "by lot" (v. 2). This is done "as the LORD had commanded Moses" (vv. 2, 5; see Num 26:52–56; 34:13). Joshua's actions once more set him in the role of Moses' successor, fulfilling the task assigned to Moses.

Moses is credited again with granting the eastern lands (v. 3). The western allocation is conducted by Eleazar, Joshua, and the "heads of the tribal clans of Israel," a group which includes representatives of all the western tribes except Levi (v. 1). Their appointment fulfills a command given Moses (Num 34:16–29) so that both the means of allocation used (the lot), and those responsible for its execution, demonstrate Israelite obedience.

The details of allocation for the nine and a half tribes contain a retrospective glance to the two and a half tribes whose lands lie east of the Jordan (v. 3). Hearkening back to events fully described in chapter 13 binds those events to the present account. Even as the allocation moves west of the Jordan, the eastern tribes are not forgotten. They are integral to "all Israel."

The continuing concern for all Israel necessitates a comment about the Levites (vv. 3–4). The Levites receive no "inheritance among the rest" of the tribes, and the explanation offered is that the Joseph tribe is divided into two tribes (Manasseh and Ephraim). Each of these tribes is then counted within the twelve-tribe system, and allocated a tribal allotment. By this count, Levi could be construed as displaced, or an extra tribe and thus excluded from land allocation. Such a conclusion is forestalled, however, by the notation the Levites receive "towns to live in, with pasturelands." Not only does the phrase give assurance that the Levites do indeed receive something, it serves as a placeholder. The phrase "towns to live in, with pasturelands" appears here and only elsewhere in Joshua 21 where it appears repeatedly, describing the many towns and pastures received by the Levites due to their special status within Israel. The reference in chapter 14 is a reminder they are neither displaced nor forgotten.

A final comment reaffirms that the western allocation of land fulfills God's command given through Moses (v. 5).

### Inheritance for Faithful Caleb (14:6–15)

The introduction anticipates an immediate account of land allocation, but this is delayed by a lengthy digression concerning Caleb. His story is split into two pieces (14:6–15 and 15:13–19) that are interwoven with Judah's allocation (15:1–12, 20–63). The interweaving of Caleb's story with Judah's allotment is a rhetorical presentation (to Judah, and even to all Israel!) of the faith that receives the land.

The tribe of Judah approaches Joshua at the camp in Gilgal where Israel is still encamped (v. 6). Although Eleazar and the heads of the tribal clans are part of the allocation process (v. 1), Joshua alone is highlighted in the first allotment. This reflects the special nature of this first allotment granted Caleb the Kenizzite, a man of Judah with whom Joshua has a particular history.

Most of Caleb's speech (vv. 2–11) forms the basis for the claim he makes. His claim is stated in only one verse (v. 12) and is based on past history and God's promises. Caleb claims the authority of God's promise (v. 12) by noting it came through Moses the "the man of God" and "the servant of the Lord" (vv. 6, 7, 9). This is a subtle reminder to Moses' successor that the Lord's promises came through his authoritative representative and should be honored.

Caleb claims Joshua's knowledge of the promise and so does not at first repeat it (v. 6). Instead, he rehearses their shared history (vv. 7–9). Caleb's citation of his age at the time he and Joshua were spies from Kadesh Barnea (v. 7) is not extraneous detail or an old man's fond reminiscence of the exploits of youth. Rather, as his later speech reveals (v. 10), forty-five years have passed since the promise was made. This assumes the forty years in the wilderness and leaves five years for the land entry. For all these years Caleb held fast to the promise, demonstrating the "wholehearted" character God ascribed to him at Kadesh Barnea.

Referring to the good report he gave after spying out the land, he characterizes the wilderness generation's response as "melting in fear." The characterization is similar to that of the Canaanites (2:9, 11; 5:1), leaving Israel unable to acknowledge God's presence and action in their midst. Besides fear, Israel exhibited several other responses in Numbers 13–14. They "rebel" (14:9), "grumble" (14:2, 27), held the LORD "in contempt" (14:11, 23), and "refused to believe" the LORD despite many miraculous signs (14:11). In short, they "sinned" (14:19) and "were unfaithful" (14:33). Elsewhere, God summarizes their response as not following him "wholeheartedly" (Num 32:11). This is precisely the word God used to describe Caleb (Num 14:24; 32:12; Deut 1:36). The opposite of Israelite fear, grumbling, rebellion, and unbelief, Caleb the Kenizzite is of a different spirit (Num 14:24). He is the true Israelite, wholehearted and unwavering (even through forty-five years!) in his trust in God's promises.

Finally, Caleb provides his recollection of God's promise:

> The land on which your feet have walked will be your inheritance and that of your children forever, because you have followed the LORD my God wholeheartedly. (v. 9)

Caleb's recollection takes up the spirit of the original promise, but is not recounted in the precise words of Numbers 14:24:

> Because my servant Caleb has a different spirit and follows me wholeheartedly, I will bring him into the land he went to, and his descendants will inherit it.

Caleb claims the inheritance according to the LORD's promise. Although the promise was originally directed toward Caleb's descendants ("his descendants will inherit it"), Caleb claims the promise's fulfillment in his own lifetime, a reality foreseen in Moses' account of the promise:

> [Caleb] will see [the land], and I will give him and his descendants the land he set his feet on, because he followed the LORD wholeheartedly. (Deut 1:36)

Caleb's recollection of the promise (v. 9) also echoes Moses' rendition of it through the reference to the land "he will set his feet on." This phrase evokes Joshua 1:3 and the promise given Joshua that wherever Israel sets "the sole of your (plural) foot" will be given them. Caleb's words depict him as an "all Israel" figure, believing and claiming all that God has promised.

Caleb moves from the basis of his claim to the claim itself. The shift is signaled by the "Now then" in verse 10, a phrase that is repeated later in the verse

("So here I am" in NIV) and gives a sense of immediacy and urgency to his request. The phrase also occurs in an abbreviated form in verses 11 and 12 ("now"). There is eagerness in Caleb's request, as if for forty-five years he has looked forward to accomplishing that which the wilderness generation rejected. The time of that accomplishment is "now," and Caleb is eager to begin.

Through Caleb's request, he continually moves between the past and the present:

| v. 10 | Now then, | | |
|---|---|---|---|
| | | just as the LORD promised, (past) | |
| | | | he has kept me alive . . . (present) |
| | | since the time he said this to Moses, while Israel moved about in the wilderness, (past) | |
| | | | So here I am today . . . (present) |
| v. 11 | | | I am still as strong today (present) |
| | | as the day Moses sent me out; (past) | |
| | | | I'm just as vigorous to go out to battle now (present) |
| | | as I was then. (past) | |
| v. 12 | | | Now give me this hill country (present) |
| | | that the LORD promised me that day. (past) | |
| | | You yourself heard then . . . (past) | |
| | | | but, the LORD helping me, I will drive them out (present) |
| | | just as he said. (past) | |

The rhetorical effect of this alternation is to show Caleb's anticipation of present success rests in his ongoing belief that God is as present and powerful now as he was then. More, that Caleb's own faith is as vibrant today as it was then. By God's help, Caleb has faith to accomplish now what Israel failed (through fear) to accomplish then.

Caleb cites the Anakites to illustrate his present faith, reminding Joshua of their large, fortified cities (Num 13:28). Unlike the wilderness generation, Caleb is unfazed by them. He is confident he will drive them out according to God's promise (Num 14:24; 33:52–53; Deut 1:8, 21, all verses which communicate God's promise using the same Hebrew root ["drive out"] as in Caleb's speech). Earlier, the Anakites were noted as defeated by the hand of Joshua (11:21–22), an anticipatory summary of Caleb's action that is credited to the leader under whom Caleb serves. The unity of the two accounts is apparent for both conclude with the same phrase, "The land had rest from war" (11:23; 14:15).

Caleb claims the hill country, a specific location that goes beyond the original promise of simply "land" (Num 14:24). This suggests Caleb's selection of the "hill country" is his application of the promise in light of present events and personal choice. However the specific land is selected, the main point lies in Caleb's attitude. Even after many years, Caleb remains wholehearted. Even though old, he claims God's present help as the source of his strength (*hazaq*; v. 11). It is the same strength to which Joshua was urged (1:6, 7, 18). By it, Caleb anticipates victory.

Joshua responds positively to Caleb's request by granting Hebron (later designated a City of Refuge [20:7] and a Levitical city [21:11–12]). When later it is given the Levites, they are granted the city proper, while Caleb possesses its fields and villages. Hebron is linked to an earlier Anakite leader and the town's previous name (Kiriath Arba) recalls him. The practice of changing a town's name (perhaps in this case to mark Caleb's possession of it) was a not-uncommon practice (see 15:15; Gen 28:19; Judg 19:10).

Arba the Anakite's three descendants Ahiman, Sheshai, and Talmai held the city during the spies' expedition (Num 13:22), and Caleb is credited with driving them from it in 15:14 (cf. Judg 1:20). The note that Hebron has belonged to Caleb's descendants "ever since" (in Hebrew, "to this day") confirms God's promise to Caleb.

Caleb is like Rahab and Gibeon before him, who were incorporated into Israel "to this day" (6:25; 9:27). Once more, a foreigner is granted place and prominence within Israel. For a final time, Caleb's possession is attributed to his wholeheartedness (v. 14; cf. vv. 8, 9). The emphasis on his wholehearted faith sets him up as a paradigm for all Israel to emulate as they receive their allotted inheritance.

Joshua's response to Caleb includes a blessing (v. 13) that is either the inheritance or some additional blessing. Blessings are granted by a superior to an inferior and Joshua, as Moses' successor and Israel's leader, is in authority over Caleb. But Joshua also bestows a blessing upon one with whom he shared "wholeheartedness" (Num 32:12). In this attitude, they are colleagues together in faithfulness.

### Inheritance for Judah: Boundaries (15:1–12)

After this important digression, the allotment for Judah is provided. Anticipated in 14:1 and again in 14:6, the delay heightens the importance of this first allotment. Judah's land is allotted "according to its clans" (15:1, 12), ensuring equitable distribution as God commanded (Num 26:52–56). Equitable distribution was important in the Transjordanian allotments (13:15, 23–24, 28–31) and is a pattern throughout the western allotments (see Listen to the Story, Chapter 13), placing the eastern and western allotments on the same footing.

There is a difference between the eastern and western allotments, however. Judah's "allotment" (*goral*) is provided according to the "lot" (*goral*; 14:1–2) "as the LORD had commanded" (14:2). The command for the lot appears in Numbers 26:55–56 and is repeated after the Transjordanian concession (Num 32), with specific reference to the promised land (Num 33:54; 34:13). The lot is not mentioned in Joshua 13 for the eastern lands. It makes its first appearance in the book here, with the first western allocation. The use of the lot inextricably ties the allocation of the promised land to God's will, for he controls the lot.

Judah's boundary list is the most detailed and extensive of all the western allotments (ten verses; only Benjamin's boundary list is close; 18:12–20). Judah's town list is also the most extensive of all the western town lists. Interwoven with the narratives of Calebite faith and persistence, the extensive list serves as a concrete witness to the results of such faith. Caleb, the paradigmatic individual, zealous to take all the land upon which his foot trod, led the way for the western tribes to fulfill the promise given Joshua (1:3).

The detailed allotment for Judah begins in hope. Its extensive boundaries suggest the promise's fulfillment. But it does not end on this same note, for Judah is unable to fully possess the land (15:63). As the allotments to the other tribes are detailed, the boundary and town lists become shorter, and the notations of failure persist. Each suggests that the example of Caleb is not wholly embraced by his countrymen.

Judah's boundaries begin at its southeastern border. From the southern end of the Dead Sea, the boundary is first sketched from east to west. The eastern boundary is the Dead Sea. The northern boundary also is sketched from east to west, with the Mediterranean as its western boundary. Not all geographical features of the boundary have been identified, and it is not the purpose of this commentary to explore the identification challenges; other commentaries have such a mandate.[4] The biblical description is clear enough to sketch the boundary's approximate details. Several places are named that featured in Israel's entry to the land: Kadesh Barnea, from where the spies were dispatched in Numbers 13–14 (v. 3), the Valley of Achor where Achan was stoned (v. 7), and Jerusalem from which the southern coalition against Israel originated (v. 8). Jerusalem itself does not lie within Judah's allotment as the boundary is the valley immediately south of the city. Jerusalem lies within Benjamin's territory (18:16, 28).

## A Portion for Aksah (15:13–19)

Aksah's account (and that of the daughters of Zelophehad that follows), by incorporating women into the narrative of land distribution, broadens the picture of what constitutes "all Israel." To date, foreigners have been incorporated in to Israel. Rahab, the Gibeonites, and Caleb the Kenizzite are all reminders that one need not be Israelite by birth to be part of the people of Israel. Conversely, Achan's sin reveals that those ethnically Israelite can act in ways opposed to God's vision for Israel.

Aksah demonstrates that inclusion into Israel—especially with respect to possession of the land—is a matter of faith, rather than gender. In a cultural system that vests land patrilineally, Aksah is a reminder that women could receive land. Even with a patriarchal system, women could own land and play this active role as part of all Israel. Aksah's faith is comparable to Rahab's, for both women make demands for participation in Israel. Her faith is also comparable to her father Caleb's, and both are rewarded with land. Together, father and daughter present a paradigm of persistent faith that Israel can emulate.

The account begins by reprising Caleb's inheritance, noting Joshua's obedience to the LORD's command. The "inheritance" granted Caleb in the first part of the narrative (vv. 9, 13), now becomes a "portion" (*heleq*)—the word is different than the earlier description of Caleb's inheritance, but is not unique in Joshua (14:4; 18:5, 6, 7, 9; 19:9; 22:25, 27).

Caleb's acquisition of Hebron was in 14:13–15 assumed rather than detailed. The present account provides those details. Caleb "drives out" the three Anakites, a fact that is repeated in Judges 1:20 with a full account in Judges 1:9–15. Some differences appear when comparing the account in

4. Two such commentaries that have such a mandate and do it well are Richard Hess, *Joshua*, and Pitkänen, *Joshua*.

Joshua and Judges. In Judges, Judah is credited with victory against Hebron and Debir. This can be explained by narrative foci: Judges 1 focuses on Judahite claims, whereas Joshua 15 focuses on Caleb and his clan. Naming Judah as the victor in Judges 1 does not exclude Caleb as the primary actor. He is, after all, a tribesman within Judah.

The Judges account also places the action after Joshua's death (Judg 1:1). This conflicts with a straightforward narrative reading of Joshua that places the action in Joshua's time. A further conflict appears with the summary account in 11:21–22, which credits Joshua with taking Hebron and Debir. The summative nature of 11:21–22 makes the discrepancy more felt than real. Its purpose is to praise Joshua, crediting to him all action stemming from his leadership (whether completed in his lifetime or after his death). It may be that a two-stage action occurred: before Joshua's death he bestowed the inheritance upon Caleb; after Joshua's death Caleb takes Hebron.

Debir is part of the "hill country" inheritance Caleb claimed (14:12) and is part of the larger Judahite territory (15:49). Debir is also designated a Levitical city (21:15). The city was conquered during the southern campaign (10:38–39), an initial military action that did not include Israelite possession (see Chapter 10 above). Caleb's action reengages Debir for that long-term purpose.

The promise of Aksah as a reward to the victor brings to mind Saul's promises regarding his daughters (1 Sam 17:25; 18:25). The victor is Caleb's nephew and Aksah's cousin. A marriage contracted between cousins would retain property, including any land gifted as dowry, within the family. A son of Caleb's younger brother (Judg 1:13), Othniel is a man of faith in his own right, for he serves as a judge in Israel (Judg 3:7–11).

As abhorrent as the gifting of a woman as a military prize seems to modern western cultures that value personal choice and romance as the basis for marriage, the arrangement aptly reflects ancient Near Eastern values. As noted in the ancient Near Eastern example above (see Listen to the Story), women were considered "giftable" as rewards for various services rendered to a superior. This aspect of the story certainly exposes the cultural gap between it and many modern readers.

Thus far, the account has reviewed Caleb's bold faith and introduced Othniel as a military hero. Both men successfully take the land. Their success serves as background to the point of the pericope: Aksah's request (vv. 18–19). Aksah initiates the sequence by urging her husband to ask her father for a field. While some versions of the Greek text (the Septuagint, often identified with the sigla LXX) note that Othniel urges *her* to make the request, the NIV works with the Hebrew text in which Aksah is the initiator.

The requested field is, within the ancient Near Eastern context, a dowry gift.[5] A dowry was gifted when the marriage contract was concluded or when the bride moved to her husband's home. Dowries could include household items, slaves (Gen 29:24, 29), jewels or clothing (Gen 24:48–52), and sometimes land. Dowry gifts were generally given by the bride's father, but in exceptional cases (such as the poverty of the bride's family) could be given by the groom or his family. When given, they came under the control of the bride's husband, although the wife could utilize them during her husband's life. Ultimately, dowries of land would remain the bride's. In the event she was widowed or divorced, the land could provide her with a livelihood and an inheritance for her children.

Othniel apparently makes the request for the field, although the request does not appear in the narrative. The omission serves to focus the narrative on Aksah who presents a further request to her father. She dismounts her donkey, and it would be customary for her to bow to the ground (1 Sam 25:23). Like Rahab before her (2:12), her request is a bold imperative: "Give me springs of water!" The request would ensure the dowry land has ongoing viability. Located in the dry "Land of the Negev" the property—perhaps in or around Debir—would provide little sustenance without access to water. Her demand for springs she describes as a "special favor," which is the NIV translation of the Hebrew word, "a blessing" (*berakah*). She requests her father grant her this blessing, as Joshua earlier blessed her father (14:13). Caleb acknowledges her bold faith. He grants abundant springs to water the land she and her heirs receive in Israel.

Aksah's unusual narrative demonstrates that (regardless of gender) those who are persistent in claiming what is theirs possess the land. The persistent faith of father and daughter provide a context and an explanation for the extensive lists provided of Judah's allotment. The narratives show persistent faith; the lengthy lists show the result—much land is taken. Appearing at the beginning of the western allotments, the narratives suggest that should the other tribes exercise the same faith, they too will boldly possess the promised land.

### Inheritance for Judah: Towns (15:20–63)

Judah's town list is extensive and highly structured. Subsequent lists are less so, contributing to a sense of Israel's growing inability to fully possess the land.

The list begins with the phrase "this is the inheritance of." The phrase

5. A concise discussion of dowry gifts within the ancient context is provided by Raymond Westbrook in *Property and the Family in Biblical Law*, JSOTSup 113 (Sheffield: Sheffield Academic Press, 1991), 142–64. See also Joseph Fleishman, "A Daughter's Demand and a Father's Compliance: The Legal Background to Achsah's Claim and Caleb's Agreement," *ZAW* 118 (2006): 354–73.

is found throughout chapter 13–19 and always describes the inheritance of "X" tribe (13:23, 28; 16:8; 18:20, 28; 19:8, 16, 23, 31, 39, 48). It generally concludes lists and only here heads a tribal allotment. The phrase's unique placement matches the uniqueness of this first town list.

Judah's towns are given "according to its clans." The repetitive phrase found throughout chapters 13–19 most often begins and ends a list (as it does Judah's boundaries; see 15:1, 12). Here, it only precedes the Judahite town list (see Explain the Story, Chapter 14 above). As is common in ancient Near Eastern lists, the categorized items are clustered into groups and subdivisions with headings and/or conclusions (see Listen to the Story, Chapter 13). Here, towns are collected into four geographical areas (vv. 21, 33, 48, 61), each with a heading. The towns in these geographical areas are further subdivided into ten lists, each concluding with a phrase tallying that subdivision's towns, namely, "X towns and their villages." Not every tally aligns with the number of towns listed (see v. 32), a not-uncommon feature of ancient Near Eastern lists. The list can be outlined as follows:

| | |
|---|---|
| Area 1 | Southernmost region (vv. 21–32) |
| | One subdivision of "towns and their villages" |
| Area 2 | Western foothills (vv. 33–44) |
| | Three subdivisions of "towns and their villages" |
| (no heading) | Philistine area (vv. 45–47) |
| Area 3 | Hill country (vv. 48–60) |
| | Five subdivisions of "towns and their villages" |
| Area 4 | Wilderness (vv. 61–62) |
| | One subdivision of "towns and their villages" |

A fifth area is comprised of Philistine towns and their surrounding areas (vv. 45–47). No tally of its towns is provided. In place of the stock, "X towns and their villages" variants are used: "its settlements and villages" for Ekron, Ashdod, and Gaza; "together with their villages" for Ashdod. The unit's appearance at the center of the list and its difference in form set it apart, perhaps an acknowledgement that this area, while part of Judah's territory, remains firmly outside Judahite control (10:40–42; 13:2). If so, at the heart of Judah's extensive town list is a note of failure.

Failure also closes the list, for Judah "could not dislodge (from *yrsh*) the Jebusites . . . in Jerusalem to this day." In Judges 1:8, after the death of Joshua "Judah attacked Jerusalem . . . and took (from *lkd*) it." The action described in Judges is used elsewhere in Joshua to describe a military victory against a city (6:20; 8:19; 10:1, 28, 32, 35, 37, 39, 42; 11:10, 12, 17). The victory, however, may not include ongoing possession and the dispossession ("dislodging") of the city's inhabitants. Despite the act of "taking" Jerusalem in Judges 1:8, the city apparently is not possessed until the time of David (2 Sam 5:6–9).

The inability of Judah to "dislodge the Jebusites" must also be compared to Judges 1:21. There, it is Benjamin (not Judah) that is unable to "drive out" (from *yrsh*) the Jebusites. Judges 1 is itself aware of action against Jerusalem by both Judah and Benjamin (1:8, 21) and that Jerusalem was within Benjaminite territory (v. 21). The account of two different tribes attacking Jerusalem may reflect the border-city status of Jerusalem. On the border of Judah and Benjamin, both tribes appear to have made bids for the town with varying degrees of success. At any rate, the inclusion of the notation in Joshua 15:63 certainly has rhetorical force: despite Judah's size, despite the examples of Caleb and Aksah, it yet fails to possess this key city.

The allocation of the western lands begins in high hope but throughout chapters 13–21 there are notations of failure. The allocation of land concludes, however, with a strong affirmation of success (21:43–45). Throughout Joshua, Israel's success reveals the power of God fighting on its behalf and God's faithfulness to his promise of land. And throughout, Israel's failure is embedded in its inability to be "strong and courageous" in obedience to the law and in trusting God's promises. Both truths are upheld by the book of Joshua. Further discussion of the tension will wait until the final affirmation of success in ch. 21.

### The Blessings of Inheritance

The idea of "inheritance" is key to chapters 13–21 (see Chapter 13 above). Israel's inheritance is the land, intended as a place of provision, safety, and communion with God (Deut 6:1–25; see also Listen to the Story, Chapter 1 above). The inheritance of land was promised to Abraham and anticipated in the wilderness (Num 26:53–56). Moses' instructions to Israel in Moab prepared them to live in the land given as their inheritance (Deut 4:21; 26:1). Once established in the land, the land still is referred to as an inheritance (1 Kgs 8:36 [and in the postexilic parallel text, 2 Chr 6:27]; 1 Chr 16:18). The Psalter often rejoices in the land as an inheritance (Pss 78:55: 105:11; 135:12), and God's gift of this inheritance is proof of his enduring love (Ps 136:21–22).

Provision, safety, and communion with God are available in the inheritance of land. The same benefits were experienced by the Levites through a very different inheritance. In their unique consecrated role, the Lord, as well as cultic offerings received in his service, became their inheritance. Israel does provide the Levites with land holdings (ch. 21), but these are not labeled an inheritance. Repeated references throughout chapters 13–19 ensure that the Levites are not mistakenly considered overlooked in the distribution of land (13:13, 33; 14:4; 18:7).

The idea of Israel receiving an inheritance from the LORD is common in Joshua. What Joshua does not state, but which is revealed elsewhere, is that the LORD also has an inheritance. That inheritance is Israel. God brings them out of Egypt "to be the people of his inheritance" (Deut 4:20; 9:26, 29). As such, they are an inheritance that is chosen (Ps 33:12) and blessed (Ps 28:9). When anointed, kings rule over God's inheritance (1 Sam 10:1; Ps 78:71). When Israel prays and repents, God's attention and forgiveness is assured "for they are your people and your inheritance" (1 Kgs 8:50–51).

Through mutual inheritance, God and Israel are intimately connected. The mutuality of inheritance is itself a reflection of the mutuality of the covenant, by which God and Israel belong to one another (Exod 6:6–7; 19:5–6) and which is best expressed by the phrase "you are my people, and I am your God" (Lev 26:12; Ps 50:7; Jer 7:23; 11:4).

The New Testament takes up the idea of "inheritance." Inheritance is still gifted by God, although it is no longer the concrete gift of land but a spiritual reality. As the New Testament presents the whole church serving as God's priests (1 Pet 2:9; Rev 1:6; 5:10), this idea of a spiritual inheritance more closely aligns with the Levites receiving God himself as their inheritance.

Colossians, by employing a figural reading of the exodus and land entry, argues that Christians are "qualified . . . to share in the inheritance of his holy people" (1:12). In this verse, the inheritance is figured as a land, but a spiritual one: the kingdom of light. As in Joshua, this "land" is gifted by the Father who has "rescued us from the dominion of darkness [a figural reading of Egypt] and brought us into the kingdom of the Son he loves [a figural reading of Canaan]" (Col 1:12–13). Colossians extends the figure further, calling Christians who inhabit this land to obedience in it. By the Spirit, Christians are to "live a life worthy of the Lord and please him in every way: bearing fruit in every good work" (Col 1:9–10).

The call to live worthily as inheritors is explored more fully in Romans and Galatians. In both epistles, Paul argues that Christians stand as heirs not through works of the law but through faith (Rom 4:14; Gal 3:26–29). This, too, parallels the Old Testament for Israel entered the land by faith and by faith followed the law in loving response to God. In Old and New Testaments, there is faith and responsive action. Paul explains the process by which Christians live a worthy life in their inheritance: by faith, Christians receive the gift of the Spirit, being made children of God and thus co-heirs with Christ (Rom 8:15–17). By faith, the Spirit works within so as to produce the deeds of the Spirit (Rom 8:1–17; Gal 3:29–4:7). Thus, while Christians await the fullness of their inheritance in the redemption of the body, it is the life of the Spirit, expressed in suffering, in good works, and in prayer, that reveals them as inheritors.

Elsewhere, the spiritual inheritance is named as eternal life (Matt 19:29; Mark 10:17; Luke 10:25; Tit 3:7), salvation (Heb 1:14), and a blessing (1 Pet 3:9). It is in several texts named the kingdom of God (1 Cor 6:9–10; Gal 5:21), and a kingdom which is imperishable (1 Cor 15:50).

These spiritual realities find eschatological expression in the inheritance of the new heavens and earth (Rev 21:7). This eschatological inheritance, like the inheritance in the Old Testament, is one in which the mutuality of covenant is demonstrated. Using the language of covenant, the new heavens and earth are described:

> God's dwelling place is now among the people, and he will dwell with them. They will be his people, and God himself will be with them and be their God. "He will wipe every tear from their eyes. There will be no more death" or mourning or crying or pain, for the old order of things has passed away. (Rev 21:3–4)

The intimacy expressed in covenantal language in the book of Revelation is a reminder of the inheritance of land in Joshua. The land was to be a place of provision, safety, and communion with God. Israel was to be his people, and he their God. The persistent reality of disobedience and sin prevented this realization. Only through the work of the new Joshua—Jesus—could the hope of such an inheritance find its fulfillment.

### Faithful Even to Old Age

Even though Caleb's family was originally non-Israelite, his faithfulness is a paradigm for all Israel to follow. Wholehearted, he shows the enduring faith by which the land is taken. That this faithful paradigm was remembered in Israel is apparent from the intertestamental book of Sirach, or Ecclesiasticus. When praising the "famous men" of Israel (chs. 44–50), Caleb is praised alongside such luminaries as Abraham, Moses, David, and Solomon. His faithful trust in God in Numbers 13–14 is remembered as a "loyal deed" (46:7) and the events of Joshua 14 are remembered in this way:

> The Lord gave Caleb strength,
> which remained with him to old age,

so that he went up to the hill country,
and his children obtained it for an inheritance;
so that all the sons of Israel might see
that it is good to follow the Lord (Sir 46:9–10).

Sirach remembers Caleb not just for his strength, but for his endurance into old age. His strength and endurance are an example of one who follows the Lord. Sirach cites Caleb so that successive generations would see the goodness of such action and do likewise.

Caleb's fighting strength might be more readily associated with young men, but the biblical text makes a point of emphasizing his age: forty years old then . . . forty years have passed . . . eighty-five years old now . . . as strong today . . . as then (vv. 7–11). Sirach also points to his old age. It is true that Caleb stands as a paradigm for both young and old to emulate, but the particularity of his age is especially noteworthy. It is an encouragement to witness a long life of faith lived in the trust of God.

Caleb stands with others who even into old age trusted what God had said and acted on it. He might easily have been included in Hebrews 11 with people such as Noah (who built an ark when six hundred years old; v. 7; cf. Gen 7:6), Abraham and Sarah (centenarians who considered "God faithful who had made the promise"; vv. 8–11), Jacob (at one hundred forty-seven years, blessing his descendants in light of God's promises; v. 21; cf. Gen 47:28), or Moses (at eighty, leading Israel out, accompanied by eighty-three-year old Aaron; v. 29; cf. Exod 7:7). Perhaps he could be included with those who "through faith conquered kingdoms" or "became powerful in battle" (Heb 11:33–34).

Caleb trusted God's word that Israel would indeed enter the land, the place of rest, and acted on that trust. Sadly, despite his faith, Israel's disobedience prevented the full experience of rest that the land offered (Heb 4:8). So, alongside those in Hebrews 11, Caleb ultimately "did not receive the things promised . . . but only saw them and welcomed them from a distance" (11:13).

The promise of rest in the land for which Caleb trusted God is made possible in Jesus. He is the one who brings the rest of the inheritance (see above, The Blessings of Inheritance; see also Rom 5:1–2; Eph 2:14–18; Col 1:12–13). In Luke's gospel account of the events surrounding Jesus' birth, several old people are presented. Like Caleb, they are people who held faith for many years: Zechariah and Elizabeth (1:5–7), Simeon (2:25–26), and Anna (2:37). Like Caleb, they acted on their faith, ready to receive what God had promised.

For young and old, Caleb is a paradigm of faithfulness. In a society and church that often discounts the value and contribution of its elders, Caleb must be attended to. He stands as a paradigm for our own elders in the faith and calls the young to watch and listen for examples of persistent faith, held through the years, and still engaged in action. It is these elders who become living paradigms, Calebs for the next generation.

**Recovering Aksah; Nineteenth Century Women Readers**

Aksah, like Caleb, demonstrates bold faith. Much of what has been said of Caleb's influence could be said of Aksah, although the Christian interpretive tradition has focused on Caleb as the paradigmatic exemplar. Aksah has not been neglected, however, as commentaries (such as this one!) engage her story.

A recent and fruitful interpretive project has brought to light significant past writers who have engaged Aksah. This has occurred through the collegial and concerted effort of a group of scholars determined to recover women biblical interpreters. Research of publications in nineteenth century England and North America alone yields hundreds of women publishing their work in journals and with reputable publishers of monographs. Of diverse ecclesial and educational backgrounds, these women applied to Scripture interpretive strategies common to their day, engaging Scripture through a variety of genres (e.g., commentaries, poetry, sermons, and catechetical works). Most often writing for women and children, they wrote in a context where publishing was both accessible and affordable and therefore in demand.

Reading these nineteenth century women writing on Aksah opens the door to see the work of the church in a different era. One readily sees how a different era's social values and questions shaped interpretation. This in turn helps present readers examine how their own time, with its particular interpretive methods, contexts, social values, and questions shapes their interpretation. Such recovery also provides great encouragement: the church has read and been instructed by these stories in myriad ways. More, women have found ways—whether with or without the approval of church or society—to join the great engagement with Scripture that is the work of the church. In this, these women (like Aksah) have given voice to their faith.[6]

Three brief examples of women interpreting Aksah follow, each freshly engaging the story. In the process, they address common questions in the Victorian era, such as the role of women in society (Victorian women could not own property) and how to read Aksah's story as Christian Scripture.

The first author is known by the penname "Lydia," whose writings were published in the 1830s–40s in *The Christian Lady's Magazine*. Lydia holds to Victorian views on women and property ownership but does not engage this

6. Examples are taken from Taylor and de Groot, *Women of War*.

aspect of the text. Rather, she applies a figural reading. Aksah is interpreted as a Christian, making supplication to the Father. Lydia urges Christians to approach as Aksah did:

> How shall we approach the Father of Spirits? As Achsah (*sic*) approached her earthly parent, with the confidence of a child, but with the low prostration and meek reverence of an inferior, pleading his own rich gift as the ground of a further 'blessing.' Thou has given thine only-begotten Son, wilt thou not also freely give the Comforter, the Sanctifier,—the fruitful source of blessings,—the earnest of a future and far richer inheritance.[7]

A second example comes from the Englishwoman Grace Aguilar, a devout Jewess familiar with Christian worship and tradition. In her popular book, *The Women of Israel*, she interprets Aksah as affirming the right of women to own property even after marriage. She upholds typical views of the roles for men and women and does not advocate for women's ownership of property independent of her husband. Additionally, Aguilar sought to undermine the view that Judaism degrades women, while Christianity elevates women.

Her reading calls us today to ask what social issues and values color our own interpretation of Aksah:

> We learn too from this, that woman must undoubtedly have had the power of possessing landed property in her own right, and in a degree exclusive of her husband; else Caleb would have made over the portion intended for her to Othniel on his marriage. . . .
>
> The beautiful law of our God was then in full force among every rank and condition of man; and surely we can find no trace in the history of Achsah (*sic*) to confirm the false position of our [that is, women] being degraded. Does it not rather elevate us to a perfect equality with our brother man, and prove undeniably that the Israelites were the very first nation in the world to hold forth the love and hand of woman as the pure and holy incentive to deeds of manliness and valor?[8]

A final example comes from the American, Elizabeth Cady Stanton, from her contribution on Aksah in the 1898 edition of *The Woman's Bible*. Cady Stanton was an advocate for women's rights, and her reading contrasts significantly with the two prior examples, being a clarion call for women to speak out and claim their rights. Her work is a reminder that the biblical text was inextricably bound up in pressing social issues. Reading her work might

7. Ibid., 61–62.
8. Ibid., 66.

point the way for present-day advocates to examine to what use they press the Scriptures:

> Achsah's (*sic*) example is worthy the imitation of the women of this Republic. She did not humbly accept what was given her, but bravely asked for more. We should give to our rulers, our sires and sons no rest until all our rights—social, civil and political—are fully accorded. How are men to know what we want unless we tell them? They have no idea that our wants, material and spiritual, are the same as theirs; that we love justice, liberty and equality as well as they do; that we believe in the principles of self-government, in individual rights, individual conscience and judgment, the fundamental ideas of the Protestant religion and republican government.[9]

These are just some of the many examples of how women interpreters have entered the story of Aksah. Engaging the story through the pressing issues of their own day, these interpreters remind us that we all interpret through the lens of our own time. Reading these foremothers from the nineteenth century is a reminder to consider the power of our own times to shape our interpretation of Aksah's faithful persistence.

9. Ibid., 69.

# CHAPTER 16

# Joshua 16:1–17:18

## LISTEN to the Story

[1]The allotment for Joseph began at the Jordan, east of the springs of Jericho, and went up from there through the desert into the hill country of Bethel. [2]It went on from Bethel (that is, Luz), crossed over to the territory of the Arkites in Ataroth, [3]descended westward to the territory of the Japhletites as far as the region of Lower Beth Horon and on to Gezer, ending at the Mediterranean Sea.

[4]So Manasseh and Ephraim, the descendants of Joseph, received their inheritance.

[5]This was the territory of Ephraim, according to its clans:

The boundary of their inheritance went from Ataroth Addar in the east to Upper Beth Horon [6]and continued to the Mediterranean Sea. From Mikmethath on the north it curved eastward to Taanath Shiloh, passing by it to Janoah on the east. [7]Then it went down from Janoah to Ataroth and Naarah, touched Jericho and came out at the Jordan. [8]From Tappuah the border went west to the Kanah Ravine and ended at the Mediterranean Sea. This was the inheritance of the tribe of the Ephraimites, according to its clans. [9]It also included all the towns and their villages that were set aside for the Ephraimites within the inheritance of the Manassites.

[10]They did not dislodge the Canaanites living in Gezer; to this day the Canaanites live among the people of Ephraim but are required to do forced labor.

[17:1]This was the allotment for the tribe of Manasseh as Joseph's firstborn, that is, for Makir, Manasseh's firstborn. Makir was the ancestor of the Gileadites, who had received Gilead and Bashan because the Makirites were great soldiers. [2]So this allotment was for the rest of the people of Manasseh—the clans of Abiezer, Helek, Asriel, Shechem, Hepher and Shemida. These are the other male descendants of Manasseh son of Joseph by their clans.

[3]Now Zelophehad son of Hepher, the son of Gilead, the son of Makir,

the son of Manasseh, had no sons but only daughters, whose names were Mahlah, Noah, Hoglah, Milkah and Tirzah. 4They went to Eleazar the priest, Joshua son of Nun, and the leaders and said, "The Lord commanded Moses to give us an inheritance among our relatives." So Joshua gave them an inheritance along with the brothers of their father, according to the Lord's command. 5Manasseh's share consisted of ten tracts of land besides Gilead and Bashan east of the Jordan, 6because the daughters of the tribe of Manasseh received an inheritance among the sons. The land of Gilead belonged to the rest of the descendants of Manasseh.

7The territory of Manasseh extended from Asher to Mikmethath east of Shechem. The boundary ran southward from there to include the people living at En Tappuah. 8(Manasseh had the land of Tappuah, but Tappuah itself, on the boundary of Manasseh, belonged to the Ephraimites.) 9Then the boundary continued south to the Kanah Ravine. There were towns belonging to Ephraim lying among the towns of Manasseh, but the boundary of Manasseh was the northern side of the ravine and ended at the Mediterranean Sea. 10On the south the land belonged to Ephraim, on the north to Manasseh. The territory of Manasseh reached the Mediterranean Sea and bordered Asher on the north and Issachar on the east.

11Within Issachar and Asher, Manasseh also had Beth Shan, Ibleam and the people of Dor, Endor, Taanach and Megiddo, together with their surrounding settlements (the third in the list is Naphoth).

12Yet the Manassites were not able to occupy these towns, for the Canaanites were determined to live in that region. 13However, when the Israelites grew stronger, they subjected the Canaanites to forced labor but did not drive them out completely.

14The people of Joseph said to Joshua, "Why have you given us only one allotment and one portion for an inheritance? We are a numerous people, and the Lord has blessed us abundantly."

15"If you are so numerous," Joshua answered, "and if the hill country of Ephraim is too small for you, go up into the forest and clear land for yourselves there in the land of the Perizzites and Rephaites."

16The people of Joseph replied, "The hill country is not enough for us, and all the Canaanites who live in the plain have chariots fitted with iron, both those in Beth Shan and its settlements and those in the Valley of Jezreel."

17But Joshua said to the tribes of Joseph—to Ephraim and Manasseh—"You are numerous and very powerful. You will have not only one allotment

[18]but the forested hill country as well. Clear it, and its farthest limits will be yours; though the Canaanites have chariots fitted with iron and though they are strong, you can drive them out."

*Listening to the Text in the Story*: Genesis 41:51–52; 48:8–21; Numbers 26:28–34; 27:1–11; 36:1–13; Inscription of Gudea of Lagash; Codex Lipit-Eshtar; Samaria Ostraca; Amarna Letter EA 365; Hittite Treaty between Tudḫaliya IV and Kurunta of Tarḫuntašša

## Ephraim over Manasseh

These chapters describe the allotment for Joseph, Jacob's son by the beloved Rachel. Two sons were born to Joseph in Egypt: Manasseh the first-born (the name commemorates the passing of Joseph's hardships) and Ephraim (the name commemorates Joseph's fruitfulness in Egypt; Gen 41:51–52). When Joseph brought his two sons to receive a blessing from the dying Jacob, he anticipated a preferential blessing upon Manasseh as the elder son. To facilitate that, he placed Manasseh at Jacob's right hand which, had it been placed upon Manasseh's head, would signify that preference. Against anticipation, Jacob extended his right hand to Ephraim and pronounced the greater blessing upon the younger son. In answer to Joseph's objection, Jacob affirmed that although Manasseh would be great, Ephraim would be greater (Gen 48:8–21).

Manasseh does become great as evidenced by its western tribal allotment (held in addition to its Transjordanian lands). Ephraim, however, is the greater tribe throughout Israel's history. In time, "Ephraim" becomes synonymous with the northern kingdom of Israel (Isa 7:2–8; Ezek 37:16; Hos 4:17). The greater status of Ephraim is apparent in Joshua 16–17, for Ephraim's allotment is related first.

## Daughters Who Dared

The request of Mahlah, Noah, Hoglah, Milkah, and Tirzah to inherit alongside their uncles has some precedent in the ancient Near East (see Inheritance Rights below). It also has precedent in the biblical text. In the second wilderness census (one purpose of which was to ensure equitable land allocation; Num 26:53–56), Joseph's descendants are named according to their birth order. The clans descended from Manasseh are first named, followed by those of Ephraim (Num 26:28–34). Manasseh's descendants are traced through Makir to Gilead and his six sons. After naming the six sons of Gilead, Numbers further traces the line to Hepher's son Zelophehad, noting his lack of sons and naming his five daughters. This genealogy appears in Joshua 17:1–3 with a slight discrepancy in one name (Numbers names Iezer; Joshua names Abiezer; the difference between these similar names is likely a scribal error).

Naming the daughters prepares for their request immediately following the census (Num 27:1–11). Their genealogical place within the Manassehite clan is restated and, citing their father's death, they seek an inheritance alongside their uncles. The request is unusual within a patriarchal culture in which land passes patrilineally. Although unusual, their request does uphold patriarchal cultural sensibilities, for its goal is to preserve the father's name within Israel (Num 27:4). To support their request, the women refer to their father's character: he was not part of Korah's notorious rebellion in Numbers 16 (27:3). Although Zelophehad was part of the sinful wilderness generation, they argue no particular sin exists that merits his exclusion from Israel. Through Moses, God grants the unusual request and formulates inheritance laws for such cases (27:5–11).

The daughters of Zelophehad feature once more in the last chapter of Numbers (36:1–13). There, the tribes voice concern over the ruling granted the daughters. Should the women contract marriages outside their tribe, the land would be lost to Manasseh, and gained by the husband's tribe. The Lord hears the concern and provides a solution. The women are to marry only within their tribe and thus preserve the tribal inheritance. Zelophehad's daughters agree to the amendment and marry cousins on their father's side.

The two accounts of the daughters (chs. 27, 36) are important in the book of Numbers for they bracket the final chapters. These chapters provide final details for entry to the land—land which must be equitably distributed according to chapter 26. The census and the details of the final chapters affirm God's promise of land will be accomplished. The daughters' request, which brackets these final details, emphasizes the need for equitable distribution among all Israel. In Joshua, the daughters' claim what is theirs, lest it be overlooked. Alongside Caleb and Aksah, they are those who in faith claim the land God has promised.

### Inheritance Rights

The provision for inheritance by women is not unique to the biblical text. Although unusual in the ancient Near East, it is attested. A late third-millennium inscription from the Mesopotamian city of Nuzi cites such an allowance granted by Gudea of Lagash: "In the house having no son as heir, its daughter entered into its heirship."[1] The same provision is reflected in

1. Cited by Westbrook, *Property and the Family in Biblical Law*, 162.

the early second millennium Sumerian law code of Lipit-Eshtar: "If a man dies and has no son as heir, the unmarried daughter shall be his heir."[2] The rare appearance of such allowances suggests they are not part of commonly accepted legal practice. The biblical narrative's repeated attention to inheritance vested in a father's daughters is a strong affirmation of the concern for preservation of tribal inheritance. Whether the law continued to be honored in similar cases within Israelite culture cannot be determined.

### Corvée Labor

Both Ephraim and Manasseh subject the Canaanites to "forced labor" (the *mas* in Hebrew; 16:10; 17:13; cf. Judg 1:28, 30, 33, 35). Forced (corvée) labor continued in Israel and is particularly attested in the monarchic period. It most often appears as part of Solomon's extensive building projects, utilizing both Israelite and non-Israelite workers (2 Sam 20:24; 1 Kgs 4:6; 5:13–14[4:27–28]; 9:15, 21). A similar practice of forced labor is attested in the Amarna letters, fourteenth century BC correspondence between Egypt and its Canaanite and Syrian assignees. One such letter (EA 365) brings to Pharaoh's attention the complaint of a leader in Megiddo who is employing forced labor to work fields near Shunem. The official complains that other officials are shirking their contribution to the work force:

> May the king, my lord, take cognizance of his servant and his city. In fact, only I am cultivating . . . and only I am furnishing corvée workers. . . . But consider the mayors that are near me. They do not act as I do. They do not cultivate . . . and they do not furnish corvée workers.[3]

### Mixed Tribal Allotments

At times the boundary lists in Joshua 16–17 name tribal cities contained within another tribe's boundaries (16:9; 17:8–9, 11). A similar configuration appears elsewhere in ancient Near Eastern treaty arrangements, such as the treaty between Tudḫaliya IV and Kurunta of Tarḫuntašša. In Section 9 of that treaty, Hittite-controlled cities are described within the boundaries of Tarḫuntašša:

> These are cities of the king of Ḫatti which were inside the land of Tarḫuntašša: Anta, the ruined cities of Anta, Lahhuiyašši, Waštišša, Hudduwašša, Handawa, Daganza, Šimmuwa, Šahita, the men of Kammama (as Men of the Long Weapon, Walištašša (and its) Golden Charioteers, Inurta, Wattanna, Malhuwaliyata, Kašuriya, Šawiya, Pariyašša, Annauliliya, Puhanta,

2. Ibid.
3. From lines 8–23 in *EA* 365. Cited by Moran, *The Amarna Letters*, 363.

> Gurtanašša, the pomegranate-men, Aralla, the men of Araunna, Uppašša, the augurs—(insofar as) one resides within the borders of the land, they too are given (to Kurunta).[4]

These parallels, together with those discussed in the Chapter 13 above, show this chapter reflects the customs of the ancient world and enables greater understanding of the biblical text within its context.

## EXPLAIN the Story

Joshua 16–17 records the western allotment granted the tribe of Joseph in its clans of Ephraim and half-Manasseh. It is part of the land allocated prior to the relocation of the tent of meeting to Shiloh (ch. 18). Following the allotment granted Judah (14:6–15:63), chapters 16–17 continue distribution of the inheritance "in the land of Canaan, which Eleazar the priest, Joshua son of Nun and the heads of the tribal clans of Israel allotted to them" (14:1).

Comparing the presentation of the Judahite and Josephite allotments reveals that, while much is allotted to the Joseph tribe and they are faithful in claiming it, there is a sense of a falling-away from the faithfulness presented in Judah's allotment. In both allotments, boundaries and towns are named, but as explored below, Joseph's are significantly less extensive, detailed, and structured than Judah's. No town lists appear for Joseph, and some towns named for Ephraim and Manasseh lie within other tribal boundaries. Further, while both Judah and Joseph fail to wholly take the land (for Judah: 15:63; for Ephraim: 16:10; for Manasseh: 17:12–13), Joseph's failures increase in degree. Judah was unable to dislodge inhabitants of one town (15:63). This is the case for Ephraim (16:10), but Manasseh fails to take many towns (17:12). And, while Ephraim appears to apply the corvée without incident, Manasseh can only do so "when the Israelites grew stronger" (v. 13).

In some instances, the falling-away from the paradigm of Judah's allotment can be explained logically and reflects no sense of failure. For instance, that some Josephite towns lie within other tribal allotments aligns with extant ancient treaty documents. Additionally, that some of Ephraim's towns lie within Manasseh may reflect the unique nature of one tribal allotment shared by two tribal clans. Despite these explanations, the overall sense of the portrayal is that it is incomplete and characterized by disintegration. The land is allocated; the tribes move to possess it. But Joseph's achievement is less than that achieved by Judah. Much indeed remains to be done (13:1).

4. *COS* 2.18:101.

The structure of chapters 14–17 likewise contributes to this sense of lessened achievement. As noted in Chapter 13 above, Joseph's allotment structurally mirrors Judah's, particularly with respect to the placement of interspersed narratives. These narratives reveal attitudes toward the possession of promised, allocated land:

Introduction: distribution of western land (14:1–5)
*Inheritance for faithful Caleb (14:6–15)*
Inheritance for Judah: boundaries (15:1–12)
*Inheritance for Aksah (15:13–19)*
Inheritance for Judah: towns (15:20–63)
Inheritance for Joseph introduced (16:1–4)
Inheritance for Ephraim (16:5–10)
Inheritance for Manasseh introduced (17:1–2)
*Inheritance for Zelophehad's daughters (17:3–6)*
Inheritance for Manasseh (17:7–13)
*Inheritance for Joseph contested (17:14–18)*

The narrative responses span chapters 14–17 and bind the chapters together as a unit, marking it with themes of faithfulness and persistence in possessing the land. Caleb is a paradigm of faithful persistence. As such, he can be paired with the allotment given Joshua (19:49–50)—a Josephite who is Caleb's counterpart in faithfulness. This pairing is explored in Chapter 13 above. Within the Judahite-Joseph allocations of chapters 14–17, Caleb's narrative of faithfulness is paired with that of the Josephite complaint, a narrative of unfaithfulness (17:14–18). The two narratives work together, and the Josephites thus end the pre-Shilohite distribution on a negative note.

Aksah and Zelophehad's daughters are the second narrative pairing within these chapters. Like Caleb, they show faithful persistence in claiming the land. As well, these women's stories show that the "all Israel" that can possess the land includes women, despite cultural norms. Together with Caleb, these women's stories contrast the attitude displayed in the Joseph vignette.

**Introduction: The Allotment for Joseph (16:1–4)**

An allotment is drawn for Joseph, the tribe descended from Jacob's son and represented by Ephraim and Manasseh. Half of Manasseh had already claimed land east of the Jordan, and the allotment drawn in 16:1 is the "inheritance" (*nahalah*) for the other half of Manasseh and for Ephraim (16:4). The large size of the Josephite allotment and its location in the center of Israel reflects the honor Joseph held in his father's regard. As chapter 17 closes, the one allotment granted as Joseph's inheritance will become a matter of contention

(17:14). Within this one allotment, each of Ephraim and Manasseh receive their own allocation of land with its own boundaries and cities (16:5–10; 17:1–13), fulfilling Jacob's promise that Joseph would receive a double portion of land (Gen 48:22).

The "allotment" (*goral*) is a key word in chapters 13–21 (see Chapter 13 above). It is in Joshua translated both as "lot" (14:2; 19:1) and "allotment" (15:1; 16:1). Although the NIV reads "the allotment for Joseph" (16:1), the Hebrew reads "the allotment (*goral*) came out for Joseph" (also in 19:1, 17, 24, 32). The phrase suggests allocation was by the lot (perhaps the Urim and Thummim) cast out from a container. Conducted by the priest Eleazar (14:1), the lot discerned God's will, sanctifying the process and its outcome.

The boundaries for Joseph's one allotment are incompletely sketched and provide only the southern boundary (16:1–3). It moves east to west along the borders of Benjamin and Dan, sharing some of the same border markers (18:11–14; 19:40–48). Beginning at the Jordan east of Jericho, it passes north of that Benjaminite city (18:12, 21) running toward Bethel in the hill country. In the Hebrew text, Luz (v. 2) features as the next border point; the NIV conflates the two cities following the practice of the Hebrew text elsewhere (Gen 28:19; 35:6; Josh 18:13; Judg 1:23). Turning southwest enroute to Lower Beth Horon, the boundary passes through territory held by the Arkites and Japhletites, two non-Israelite peoples inhabiting the land.

The Japhletites are otherwise unknown, but an Arkite plays an important role in Israel's later history. Hushai, David's faithful counselor, is an Arkite (2 Sam 15:32; 16:16; 17:5, 14). Although Ephraim lays claim to its territory, these inhabitants remain in the midst of Joseph's allotment. They are indicative of Joseph's failure to fully possess the land, a reality that is directly stated in verse 10. Finally, the boundary passes through Gezer (whose king Israel had earlier conquered; 12:12) and reaches the Mediterranean.

The southern boundary ends, but no further boundaries are sketched for Joseph at this time. They are anticipated, however, as the introduction ends by naming "Manasseh and Ephraim" (v. 4). Together, these two are "the descendants of Joseph," and the extensive boundaries they hold are Joseph's "inheritance." Summarized in verse 4 by their birth order, the following territory descriptions name them by the order of the blessing: Ephraim, then Manasseh.

**Inheritance for Ephraim (16:5–10)**

The allotment (*goral*) of Joseph is divided between Ephraim and Manasseh. Because the one "allotment" has already been noted (16:1), Ephraim's portion is described as a "territory" (*gebul*). The description follows the pattern of other tribal allotments, using phrases filled with significance. First, Ephraim's territory is apportioned "according to its clans" (vv. 5, 8; see Listen to the Story and commentary, Chapter 14; see also Chapter 13). Throughout the tribal allotments, the phrase opens and closes territory descriptions. It is a reminder that the wilderness census numbered the clans for the purpose of equitable land distribution (Num 26:52–56). By apportioning territory according to Israel's clans, Eleazar, Joshua, and the tribal leaders distribute the land in obedience to the commands given Moses.

Second, as for all the tribes (Manasseh is an exception; see Territory for Manasseh: Boundaries below), Ephraim's territory is summarized with the words, "this was the inheritance of the tribe of 'X'" (v. 8; see also Explain the Story at 15:20) and is further described as an "inheritance" (v. 5). All that Israel receives by way of land is received as a gift from God—as inheritance, a key word in Joshua 13–21. The receipt of inherited land requires careful attention to it and to one's actions and attitudes in it. For this reason, God's commission to Joshua spoke of land as gift and the necessity of obedience for success in it (1:1–9). The numerous references to "inheritance" in Joshua 13–21 (forty-five times; see Chapter 13) evoke this necessary correlation of gift and obedience.

These are the theological parameters within which Ephraim holds its territory. The boundary description is not detailed but gives a sense of the territory's shape and scope. The southern boundary aligns with the boundary description in verses 2–3. It moves from Ataroth Addar (likely the Ataroth of v. 2) through Upper Beth Horon to the Sea. Its northern boundary is sketched in two movements. First, from Mikmethath east of Shechem (17:7) the boundary moves east and then southeast, passing Jericho to the Jordan. Then, returning to the center point of the northern border at Tappuah, it extends west to the Mediterranean. The Sea is Ephraim's western border. Ephraim controls some towns within Manassite territory. This occurs along the borders (17:8–9), perhaps an indication of disputed boundaries or the porous boundaries shared peacefully by brother-clans.

The postlude to Ephraim's territory description returns to the negative account of failure to possess the land (16:10; cf. 13:1, 13; 15:63). Called to possess (from *yrsh*) the land, Ephraim is unable to possess (that is, "dislodge" [*yrsh*]) the Canaanites). The inhabitants remain in an uneasy truce with Ephraim and are put to forced labor, an enslavement that recalls the Gibeonites. Unlike the Gibeonites (9:24), however, there is no indication these Canaanites acknowledge the power of Israel's God. Nor is there even the (slight) hopefulness of the Gibeonite experience of working within the cult and thus proximate to God's presence. These Canaanites know only forced labor. It is not an auspicious ending for the tribal account of Joseph's favored son.

## Territory for Manasseh: An Inheritance for Zelophehad's Daughters (17:1–6)

Before listing Manasseh's boundaries, a digression takes up two important items: the unique division of Manasseh into eastern and western tribes and the request of the daughters of Zelophehad.

The account begins by naming an "allotment" (*goral*) for Manasseh. As noted above, this key word was not applied to Ephraim's territory (16:5–10). Its use does not indicate an additional allotment granted to Manasseh; Ephraim and Manasseh share the one allotment granted Joseph (16:1). Its usage here is in deference to Manasseh's status as the first-born son.

The mention of Manassehite territory brings to mind this tribe's divided nature: only one half resides west of the Jordan. Although divided as to land possession, the two half tribes share common ancestry, counting both Makir and Manasseh as ancestors (Num 26:29–33). The eastern branch of this clan dwells in Gilead (v. 1b). The pause to mention the holdings of the eastern branch of this family carefully forestalls any sense of their exclusion from "all Israel"—a concern that was also apparent in chapter 13 (cf. 14:1–5). The present allotment (v. 1a, 2–5a) traces another branch of the Manasseh-Makir line, which settles in the Cisjordan.

The narrative affirms the interrelations of the two half-tribes through the structure of the account, whose perspective shifts repeatedly:

| | |
|---|---|
| v. 1a | western half-Manasseh: introduction |
| v. 1b | eastern half-Manasseh in Gilead and Bashan |
| vv. 2–5a | western |
| v. 5b | eastern |
| v. 6a | western |
| v. 6b | eastern |

Naming the clans who inherit Manasseh's western lands and the discussion of male descendants introduces the problem of Hepher. The death of his son Zelophehad threatens that clan's ongoing possession of their portion. The story of Mahlah, Noah, Hoglah, Milkah, and Tirzah resolves this threat. Their narrative is paired with that of Aksah: both stories of women; both demonstrating the persistent faith necessary to land possession. The daughters are well-remembered in Israel. Not only are Mahlah, Noah, Hoglah, Milkah and Tirzah named in each account in which they appear in the book of Numbers (26:33; 27:1; 36:11), but most of their names (together with those of their uncles) are towns and regions named in the eighth century BC Samaria Ostraca. The Ostraca contain records of wine and oil deliveries to people and places in the area of Samaria; the presence of the women's names suggests it was in this area the clans settled, with memory of the women preserved in local names.[5]

The request of five daughters to inherit land alongside their male relatives pits the five women against the patrilineal system of inheritance. The unusual nature of their request within such a system is apparent through the repeated (and often extraneous) references to men in the account (emphasis added):

| | |
|---|---|
| v. 2 | "the clans of Abiezer, Helek, Asriel, Shechem, Hepher and Shemida" reads in Hebrew with repetition of the phrase "the sons of": "the clans of *the sons of* Abiezer, *the sons of* Helek, *the sons of* Asriel, *the sons of* Shechem, *the sons of* Hepher, and *the sons of* Shemida" |
| v. 2 | "These are the other *male* descendants of Manasseh" |
| v. 3 | "Zelophehad *son of* Hepher, *the son of* Gilead, *the son of* Makir, *the son of* Manasseh" |
| v. 3 | "had *no sons* but *only daughters*" |
| v. 4 | "give us an inheritance among our relatives" reads in Hebrew "give us an inheritance *among our brothers*" |
| v. 4 | "gave them an inheritance along with *the brothers of their father*" |
| v. 6 | "*the daughters* . . . received an inheritance *among the sons*" |

There can be no doubt the narrative is shaped to highlight the uniqueness of women included alongside males as those who possess the promised land.

Although the daughters' request had been granted before Israel entered the land, they persist in claiming the allowance. They lay their request before "Eleazar the priest, Joshua son of Nun, and the leaders" which is the full group appointed to divide the land (Num 34:16–29). They recall the original ruling made by God through Moses, and Joshua—acting as Moses' successor—obediently fulfills the law.

Their inclusion alongside those who possess land—and their inclusion in "all Israel" is signaled several ways:

1. The accommodation made in Numbers has the force of a legal ruling (Num 27:11);
2. The ruling is commanded by the Lord (twice in 17:4);
3. The ruling was committed to Moses and performed by Joshua, both appointed servants of God;
4. The women request and are given an "inheritance" (*nahalah*). They also "received an inheritance" (a verbal form of the same root). The *nahalah* is a key word used throughout the land distribution

5. A translation of the entries appears in Aharoni, *The Land of the Bible*, 315–27.

(see Chapter 13). Its repeated use within the account of the daughters' claim is particularly compelling, for elsewhere in the description of Manasseh's territory (17:1–13) it is never used for the tribe's land. It once refers to Manasseh's land in the context of Ephraim's towns and villages (16:9), but the reference is not a direct statement that Manasseh received "an inheritance";

5. The five daughters stand alongside the five remaining clans (Abiezer, Helek, Asriel, Shechem, and Shemida) as equal recipients of the ten tracts of land granted the western tribe (v. 5).

Like Caleb before them, Zelophehad's daughters claim what God promised them. When Manasseh received its territory, the five women persisted in faith, anticipating their claim would be honored. Although women, they receive an inheritance in Israel equal to that of the other clans in Manasseh. The book of Joshua repeatedly shows that God notices and honors the faith of those whom others might consider outsiders. God grants land to "all Israel." This includes Caleb the foreigner, Aksah the dowered daughter, and Mahlah, Noah, Hoglah, Milkah, and Tirzah—women of faith whose names should indeed be remembered.

### Territory for Manasseh: Boundaries (17:7–13)

Finally, the narrative outlines Manasseh's boundaries, but these are even sketchier than those provided for Ephraim. The point here is not to provide a detailed map, but to set the allotment in the context of its neighbors.

From Asher—either the tribal allotment north of Manasseh, or an unknown town along Manasseh's southern border—the boundary moves to Mikmethath east of Shechem (named in Ephraim's northern boundary; 16:6) and proceeds south to En Tappuah (possibly the Tappuah named along Ephraim's northern boundary; 16:8). Tappuah and the areas along the margins of the Kanah Ravine are an area whose borders are not clearly drawn. Towns and territory along the border are mixed with Ephraimite holdings (vv. 8–10; cf. 16:8–9). The Sea forms Manasseh's western border, Asher bounds it on the north, and Issachar and the Jordan form its eastern boundary. As with Ephraim, Manasseh's border with Asher and Issachar is mixed (v. 11). Along the Jezreel Valley (Beth Shan, Iblean, Taanach, Megiddo, and possibly Endor [whose location is uncertain]) and on the coastal plain (Dor), Manassite towns lie within bordering tribal territories.

The brief details of Manasseh's territory are fewer than those provided for Ephraim. This may be due to the nature of the material used by the compiler. But in the present context it affirms the ascendency of Ephraim over

Manasseh—the ascendant tribe is described in greater detail. The "lowering" of Manasseh is also apparent in the absence of key words and phrases that elsewhere characterize the territory lists. There is no specific reference to this territory as Manasseh's "inheritance," something that is said of Ephraim's territory (16:5). Further, Manasseh's list does not contain the concluding phrase "this is the inheritance of 'X'" as in Ephraim's list (16:8). The omission is particularly apparent in the context of chapters 13–19, as for every tribe except eastern and western Manasseh this phrase describes the tribal allocation (13:23, 28; 15:20; 16:8; 18:20, 28; 19:8, 16, 23, 31, 39, 48; see at 15:20 in Explain the Story in Chapter 15). Finally, while the phrase "according to its clans" appears in respect of Manasseh in 17:2 (the phrase appears twice in Hebrew which the NIV translates "the clans of" and "by their clans"), that reference is limited to territory granted to specific descendants within Manasseh. The territory list for Manasseh in 17:7–12 completely lacks this structural phrase. For all other tribes (including Ephraim's), the phrase begins and ends the tribal allocation.

Manasseh had received Jacob's blessing that he would be a "great people" (Gen 48:19), but the blessing of the younger Ephraim included ascendancy over his brother. The paucity of expected phrasing and detail in Manasseh's tribal list aligns with the reality of Ephraim's greater blessing.

Finally, faced with Canaanite persistence, Manasseh (like Ephraim) is unable to "occupy" (from *yrsh*) several Canaanite towns (v. 12). Manasseh must wait until Israel grows "stronger" (from *hzq*) before it can act. This is the strength (*hzq*) urged on Joshua when Israel entered the land (1:6). It is the power by which God fought for Israel (4:24), which Joshua urges Israel to exhibit (10:25), and which Caleb's years could not diminish (14:11). Israel, armed with God's promises and God's power, could take the land. Manasseh did not, and even when Israel "grew stronger," could not "drive them out completely" (the phrase uses *yrsh* twice). Rather than fully occupy the land, Manasseh can only put the inhabitants to forced labour, which was intended for far distant nations with whom Israel made peace (Deut 20:11, 15).

### Joseph's Complaint (17:14–18)

The allocation to Ephraim and Manasseh (16:5–17:13) closes as it began, with a focus on the one tribe of Joseph and the one allotment granted it (16:1; 17:14). In this vignette, the "people of Joseph" complain to Joshua that they have "only one allotment" for their inheritance (17:14). Despite the fact the allocation was completed under the LORD's direction, they question its equity. Their reasons at first appear well-founded as they acknowledge the LORD's favor upon them in making them a "numerous people" (*'am rab*) who are "blessed (from root *brk*) . . . abundantly." Are they not right to request more land?

Their request is problematic for several reasons, ending chapters 14–17 on a negative note and in contrast to the accounts of Caleb, Aksah, and Mahlah, Noah, Hoglah, Milcah and Tirzah. First, the Joseph tribes request more land because the LORD has "blessed" them abundantly. This is the same word earlier used in Caleb's account (14:12), with which this account is paired (see diagram in Explain the Story above). In response to Caleb's fearless and faithful declaration that he would take the "hill country," Joshua blesses Caleb and grants him Hebron. In comparison, the Joseph tribe recognizes God's abundant blessing but is unwilling to take its own "hill country." The contrast is marked, and the Joseph tribe fares poorly in comparison to Caleb.

Second, the Joseph tribe requests more land because they are a "numerous people" (*ʿam rab*). This accords with the census tallies in Numbers 26: Ephraim and Manasseh together number eighty-five thousand, making the Joseph tribe larger than any other tribe. Joshua admits their assertion but disallows their request for more land. He uses their own words to acknowledge they are "numerous" (*ʿam rab*) but proposes a different outcome. Rather than grant them a second allotment (thus effectively rejecting the divinely-directed lot), he urges them to take the land they have already been granted, and "go up into the forest and clear land . . . [amongst] the Perizzites and Rephaites" (v. 15).

Joshua's words chide them for their failure to fully possess their allotment. Their failure is two-fold: they have not expanded into their whole territory, and they have allowed the inhabitants to remain. (The Perizzites and Rephaites are elsewhere noted in the promised land [Perizzites in 3:10; 9:1; 11:3; 12:8; 24:11; Rephaites in 15:8; cf. 12:4; 13:12]). Unlike Caleb, who was undaunted by the Anakites in Hebron, Joseph (despite boasting in its numbers) is unwilling to take on the inhabitants.

The Josephite response is telling. They effectively dodge Joshua's command to "go up . . . and clear land for yourselves" (v. 15). Instead, they return to their initial complaint: the land is not enough. Then they add another complaint, further excusing their failure to take the land: the lower plains are held by the Canaanites and their iron chariotry. These are not chariots made completely of iron (which would be too heavy and cumbersome for effective use), but chariots fitted with iron reinforcements. The Josephites apparently feel boxed in and conclude they are unable to take the plains because of Canaanite strength.

Israel has faced and defeated chariots before, although these may not have had iron reinforcements (11:4). These past victories had nothing to do with Israel's superior weaponry, or its strength of numbers. Past victory occurred because God fought on Israel's behalf (11:6–8). This is just as Moses had promised: when Israel entered the land and encountered "horses and chariots and an army greater than yours" they were not to fear "because the LORD your God, who brought you up out of Egypt, will be with you" (Deut 20:1).

The "army greater than you" that Moses describes is an *'am rab*, the very phrase Joseph has used to describe itself. Faced with a strong enemy, Israel is to "not be fainthearted or afraid"; to "not panic or be terrified by them." Israel's security does not rest in their ability but in the LORD who "goes with you to fight for you against your enemies to give you victory" (Deut 20:3–4). This is what the *'am rab* of Joseph has forgotten, or lacks faith to believe. Again, the contrast to Caleb is marked: Caleb anxiously desired to engage battle, eager to act on the LORD's promises; Joseph sidesteps action, fearful to go up to clear land and fearful to engage the Canaanites on the plain. Their fear echoes that of the unfaithful spies who, fearful of the inhabitants, counseled Israel could not take the land because the inhabitants were "stronger (from *hzq*) than we are" (Num 13:31).

Joshua's final word to Joseph continues the challenge to engage the inhabitants and take the land. Joshua again acknowledges Joseph is an *'am rab* and adds that they are "very powerful." Given the Josephite's measure of the enemy, Joshua seeks to assure them that Joseph's power is enough. Should they exercise that power as the LORD directed Israel, they could indeed expand their territory. Joseph currently occupies only the hill country within their allotment. It is indeed not enough. Should they exert themselves according to Joshua's command, they will effectively expand that allotment, taking up the forested hill country as well. Finally, and with perhaps the episode of the unfaithful wilderness spies in mind, Joshua declares that Joseph can achieve these goals even though the Canaanites are "strong" (from *hzq*). If Joseph will move beyond the fear that earlier crippled the wilderness spies, they will be able to drive the inhabitants out and possess the land.

Contextualizing their request within the several vignettes of chapters 13–17 reveals the Josephite complaint is motivated not by issues of equity but by lack of faith. Their request compares them unfavorably to Caleb, Aksah, and the daughters of Zelophehad. The Josephites sound as fearful as the wilderness spies who were afraid to enter the land. The allocation to the great Joseph tribe ends on a note of defeat.

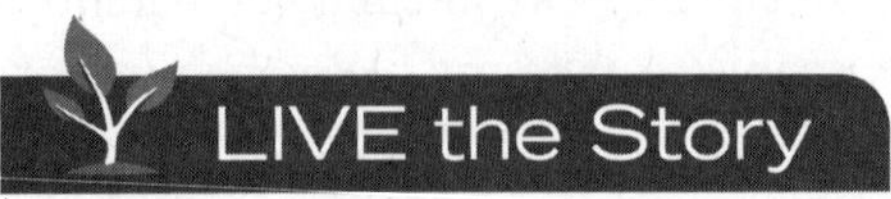


**May Their Name Be Remembered!**

Start talking about Mahlah, Noah, Hoglah, Milcah, and Tirzah, and you will likely be met by a blank stare. Who are these people (or, *are* they people)? The names of the five daughters of Zelophehad are not on the top shelf of peoples' minds. Caleb, they know. Aksah (whose story appears in Josh 15 and Judg 1) is often known, but not these daughters.

This is disconcerting, for they appear three times in the Old Testament (here, and in Numbers 27 and 36). Their story is an important one, engaging as it does issues of equitable land distribution, who is worthy to receive land (and thus counted as part of all Israel), and how God's commandments can be modified to meet new considerations. Each time these women appear, they are called the "daughters of Zelophehad," but they are also all named—all five of them (Num 27:1; 36:11; Josh 17:3).

Despite the unique place of these women—named and receiving an inheritance as part of all Israel—they are not proto-feminists. They are firmly embedded in and remain within a patriarchal system, and their request to Moses is precipitated by a thoroughly patriarchal concern: that their father's name not disappear (Num 27:4). Their appearance in Joshua (as explored above) does make their gender an important part of the story. It is as women within a patriarchal system that they make their persistent request, holding Israel to what God through Moses commanded. They make sure they are heard. And for this, they are remembered as models of the kind of faith that takes the land. They *should* be remembered.

This speaks to women of faith in all ages, called by God to many tasks. Often, these tasks are those that are deemed by society or the church as unsuitable, unseemly, or downright sinful (ask any woman whom God has called to preach, and the stories can be disheartening as to how the church too often labels or excludes them). Often, they find themselves within systems that do not want to listen to them, neither giving an ear to their testimony of God's call or opening doors so that an acknowledged calling can be given to the body of Christ. Like Mahlah, Noah, Hoglah, Milcah and Tirzah, they are outside the halls of power, trying to be heard.

Dr. Marion Taylor teaches at Wycliffe College, Toronto. She often tells the story about how the question of a student in her class changed her life as a researcher and teacher. The student asked to write a paper on an early woman interpreter of the Bible and asked for some suggestions. She recalls that, while she could think of a few modern women, few past women interpreters came to mind. This bothered her, and subsequent research revealed women had indeed interpreted the Bible throughout church history. Hundreds of published women interpreters were recovered from the nineteenth century alone. Amazed at the rich resource that was no longer heard in the church, Dr. Taylor brought their voices into her classes and to the church's attention through several publications.[6] Especially for the women in Dr. Taylor's classes,

6. See Live the Story, Chapter 15 for one example of publication by Taylor, *Women of War*.

these recovered voices were a great encouragement. Relegated to the margins by the power structures of church and society, these interpretive foremothers were a reminder to be persistent, speaking out what God had called and given. Now, through this recovery effort, these women's names will be recalled and remembered.

It is not only women that can be kept outside, asking to be heard. The challenge to be heard can be felt by many: international students in North America to train for ministry, immigrants and refugees attending our churches, our First Nations brothers and sisters, those living with mental illness. The so-called halls of power in the church have a long list of those who often are not admitted for a hearing.

The testimony of Mahlah, Noah, Hoglah, Milcah, and Tirzah is that they believed what God had said, and they acted on it. The good news of their story is that what God had gifted to them was honored. Their voice was heard, and Israel faithfully responded. We know this because Israel recorded the story of these women, not once, but three times.

The women wanted their father's name remembered. But may *their* names be remembered as an encouragement to all who struggle to have their voice heard in the midst of God's people. And may God's people have a listening ear and a responsive heart.

## The Blessing of the Lesser

Although Manasseh was the older brother and therefore due the greater blessing according to the laws of primogeniture, Jacob bestowed that blessing upon Ephraim, the younger brother. The elevation of Ephraim over Manasseh is apparent in the structure of this chapter, with Ephraim's territory presented before Manasseh's territory. Further, only Ephraim's territory is an "inheritance," as Manasseh's allocation is not labeled with that key word. Finally, Ephraim's allotment, as that of the ascendant tribe, is presented with greater detail than that of Manasseh's.

The elevation of the younger over the older is a common biblical theme. By it, God reverses expectations, opening to new possibilities. The reversals become evidence of God's mysterious electing power and purposes, as Paul's commentary in Romans 9 makes clear.

The first instance of this reversal is in Genesis 4. Of the sacrifices made by the brothers Cain and Abel, it is the younger brother Abel whom God regards, along with his sacrifice (4:4). Later in the family history Seth is born (4:25; 5:3), and it is through this youngest of the three brothers that God's promises move forward. In Abraham's family, his firstborn is Ishmael. Even when God promises another son by Sarah (17:16), Abraham pleads for honor for his firstborn, saying, "If only Ishmael might live under your blessing!" (17:18). God, however, is not bound to the system of primogeniture. While Ishmael does receive a blessing as Abraham's son (17:20), the greater blessing of covenant with God is bestowed on Isaac (17:19).

The pattern continues, and Isaac's younger son Jacob is elected over Esau. Even before they are born, God proclaims that "the older will serve the younger" (25:22–26). The ongoing narrative shows how this occurred: not because Jacob was better, kinder, or more deserving (he was in fact a liar, a cheat, and a trickster), but "in order that God's purpose in election might stand—not by works but by him who calls" (Rom 9:11–12). In a side-story that plays with the trope of primogeniture (while also hoisting the trickster Jacob on his own petard), Jacob thinks to marry the younger sister, Rachel, but Laban effects his own trickery and substitutes the older, Leah. Laban's reasoning is that "It is not our custom here to give the younger daughter in marriage before the older one" (Gen 29:26). Despite the trick, the younger Rachel still rises above her older sister in Jacob's love.

Jacob's twelve children, the progenitors of the twelve tribes, continue to subvert the expected primogeniture. Judah, who becomes the ascendant tribe and who is promised rule over his brothers (Gen 49:1–12), is Jacob's fourth child. Reuben, Simeon, and Levi are before him in birth order, but each is passed over in favor of Judah. In the same way, Manasseh is passed over in favor of Ephraim (Gen 48:13–20).

Elsewhere, the younger Moses is chosen over his elder brother Aaron to lead Israel (Exod 7:7; Miriam may also have been older, if she is the sister present in Exod 2:4), David the youngest son is anointed king over Israel by God's prophet (1 Sam 16:11–12), and it is Solomon who is anointed king and builds the temple, despite his older brother's bid for the throne (1 Kgs 1). Even the choice of the nation of Israel is made over other nations older, greater and stronger—although neither Israel's righteousness or integrity placed it ahead of other nations (Deut 9:1, 5). Rather, the choice of Israel was based on God's gracious promises given to Abraham, Isaac, and Jacob (Deut 9:5).

Each elevation of the younger moves God's plans forward. God's plans move forward not because the chosen individual was the first, the wisest, or the best. There is no deservedness by which they might boast, for God's purposes are achieved "not by works but by him who calls" and do "not, therefore, depend on human desire or effort, but on God's mercy" (Rom 9:12, 16).

In the New Testament the elevation of the younger over the older remains but is subverted in an unexpected way. In the parable of the Prodigal Son (Luke 15:11–32), the younger son demonstrates little to commend him. Greedy and profligate, he wastes his father's riches. Returning to his father, he is unexpectedly elevated. Decked out in finery he does not deserve, he is feted. This follows the pattern of the elevation of the undeserving younger brother.

It is the treatment of the older brother in this parable that is unexpected. Understandably cheesed-off, he gripes at his father's lavish grace. The churlish elder brother, by griping against his father and so misunderstanding his mercy, places himself at the same level of undeservedness as the younger brother. The father does not respond with chastisement, nor does he tell the elder brother that he's just out of luck; that all that can be lavished has been given to the younger brother. Instead, the father reminds the elder brother that all the blessings of the elevated son belong also to him: "My son, you are always with me, and everything I have is yours" (v. 31). The great grace of this parable is that two undeserving brothers receive the father's lavish grace. One is elevated beyond deserving, and one is invited to participate beyond deserving.

It seems that the New Testament utilizes these ideas of primogeniture and undeserved elevation to describe the inclusion of Jews and gentiles in the great mystery of God's purposes made known in the church. God first made himself known to the Jews, revealing himself to them through the law and the prophets (Rom 3:1–2). These are great advantages that one might expect of a "first-born son" (Exod 4:22; Jer 31:9) and are advantages of which Paul previously boasted as a Jew (Phil 3:4–5).

In the unveiling of God's great mystery and in an unexpected demonstration of God's grace and mercy, the blessings of sonship are extended. They are not extended (as in the case of the Prodigal Son) to an undeserving younger brother, but now to one wholly outside the family: to gentiles, to those "separate from Christ, excluded from citizenship in Israel and foreigners to the covenants of the promise, without hope and without God in the world" (Eph 2:12).

This is the system of primogeniture and the parable of the Prodigal Son gone wild: not the younger son, but the total outsider elevated. This elevation need not happen at the expense of the older brother, however, for both the outsider and the first-born son are brought into the same family inheritance. Both have now "in Christ Jesus . . . been brought near by the blood of Christ. . . . creating one new humanity out of the two" (Eph 2:13, 15). There is blessing enough for both the first-born and the outsider to receive by faith.

The pattern of elevation of the younger brother, present in the allotments granted Ephraim and Manasseh, is part of a larger pattern of God's unexpected grace. In the New Testament, the pattern is both subverted and redeemed, showing the great mystery by which outsider gentiles are made "heirs together with Israel, members together of one body, and sharers together in the promise in Christ Jesus" (Eph 3:6). It is an astounding sharing of the Father's family inheritance.

### Faith, Fear, and Failure

We should perhaps take some comfort in the inclusion of the Josephite grousing (17:14–18). It does stand as a negative example alongside the positive examples of Caleb, Aksah, Zelophehad's daughters, and (later) Joshua (19:49–51). The comfort lies in the fact that despite their negative example of fearful faith, they continue to be included in all Israel. God does not reject them, and this instance of fear is not the only characteristic demonstrated by the Josephites.

In fact, the Josephites continue to play an important role in Israel's history. The great northern tribe of Ephraim is Josephite. From Josephite tribes come several judges (Deborah and Abdon from Ephraim; Gideon, Jair, and Jephthah from Manasseh). In the northern kingdom of Israel (where Ephraim was the dominant tribe), kings are powerful, although uniformly disapproved for their failure to walk in covenant obedience and worship. Northern prophets are better examples of faith. Hosea likely came from Ephraimite territory, and several prophets addressed the northern kingdom. These include Elijah and Elisha, Hosea, Amos, and Micah. There is no sense that this one instance of Josephite fear disqualified them or their descendants from acting faithfully.

Every believer knows fear from time to time. We can be weak, shrink back, and grouse at many things in our situation. We can even grouse at God. There are many ways we probably have, and likely will, be like the Josephites in this passage. One need only think of Peter's denial of Christ (John 18:15–27), or the disciples hidden behind closed doors for fear (John 20:19), or John Mark deserting the work of God in Pamphylia (Acts 13:13; 15:38; although no reason is specified, Paul at least concluded Mark's reasons were unworthy) to realize that we often fall short of being great examples of faith.

Like the Josephites, these times of unfaithfulness (even if they include sin) need not exclude us from God and his people. Repentance can be undertaken if needed. Forgiveness is available, as is kindness and grace. And one instance of fear or failure does not equal a lifetime of fear and failure. Ask Peter, restored to leadership; ask the disciples, released in power to preach the gospel; ask John Mark, restored and useful to the apostle who once wrote him off (2 Tim 4:11).

CHAPTER 17

# Joshua 18:1–19:51

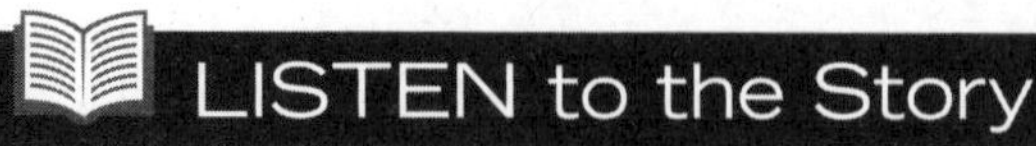

## LISTEN to the Story

1The whole assembly of the Israelites gathered at Shiloh and set up the tent of meeting there. The country was brought under their control, 2but there were still seven Israelite tribes who had not yet received their inheritance.

3So Joshua said to the Israelites: "How long will you wait before you begin to take possession of the land that the Lord, the God of your ancestors, has given you? 4Appoint three men from each tribe. I will send them out to make a survey of the land and to write a description of it, according to the inheritance of each. Then they will return to me. 5You are to divide the land into seven parts. Judah is to remain in its territory on the south and the tribes of Joseph in their territory on the north. 6After you have written descriptions of the seven parts of the land, bring them here to me and I will cast lots for you in the presence of the Lord our God. 7The Levites, however, do not get a portion among you, because the priestly service of the Lord is their inheritance. And Gad, Reuben and the half-tribe of Manasseh have already received their inheritance on the east side of the Jordan. Moses the servant of the Lord gave it to them."

8As the men started on their way to map out the land, Joshua instructed them, "Go and make a survey of the land and write a description of it. Then return to me, and I will cast lots for you here at Shiloh in the presence of the Lord." 9So the men left and went through the land. They wrote its description on a scroll, town by town, in seven parts, and returned to Joshua in the camp at Shiloh. 10Joshua then cast lots for them in Shiloh in the presence of the Lord, and there he distributed the land to the Israelites according to their tribal divisions.

11The first lot came up for the tribe of Benjamin according to its clans. Their allotted territory lay between the tribes of Judah and Joseph:

12On the north side their boundary began at the Jordan, passed the northern slope of Jericho and headed west into the hill country, coming

out at the wilderness of Beth Aven. [13]From there it crossed to the south
slope of Luz (that is, Bethel) and went down to Ataroth Addar on the hill
south of Lower Beth Horon.

[14]From the hill facing Beth Horon on the south the boundary turned
south along the western side and came out at Kiriath Baal (that is, Kiriath
Jearim), a town of the people of Judah. This was the western side.

[15]The southern side began at the outskirts of Kiriath Jearim on the
west, and the boundary came out at the spring of the waters of Nephtoah.
[16]The boundary went down to the foot of the hill facing the Valley of Ben
Hinnom, north of the Valley of Rephaim. It continued down the Hinnom
Valley along the southern slope of the Jebusite city and so to En Rogel.
[17]It then curved north, went to En Shemesh, continued to Geliloth, which
faces the Pass of Adummim, and ran down to the Stone of Bohan son of
Reuben. [18]It continued to the northern slope of Beth Arabah and on down
into the Arabah. [19]It then went to the northern slope of Beth Hoglah and
came out at the northern bay of the Dead Sea, at the mouth of the Jordan
in the south. This was the southern boundary.

[20]The Jordan formed the boundary on the eastern side.

These were the boundaries that marked out the inheritance of the clans
of Benjamin on all sides.

[21]The tribe of Benjamin, according to its clans, had the following
towns:

Jericho, Beth Hoglah, Emek Keziz, [22]Beth Arabah, Zemaraim, Bethel,
[23]Avvim, Parah, Ophrah, [24]Kephar Ammoni, Ophni and Geba—twelve
towns and their villages.

[25]Gibeon, Ramah, Beeroth, [26]Mizpah, Kephirah, Mozah, [27]Rekem,
Irpeel, Taralah, [28]Zelah, Haeleph, the Jebusite city (that is, Jerusalem),
Gibeah and Kiriath—fourteen towns and their villages. This was the
inheritance of Benjamin for its clans.

[19:1]The second lot came out for the tribe of Simeon according to its
clans. Their inheritance lay within the territory of Judah. [2]It included:

Beersheba (or Sheba), Moladah, [3]Hazar Shual, Balah, Ezem, [4]Eltolad,
Bethul, Hormah, [5]Ziklag, Beth Markaboth, Hazar Susah, [6]Beth Lebaoth
and Sharuhen—thirteen towns and their villages;

[7]Ain, Rimmon, Ether and Ashan—four towns and their villages—[8]and
all the villages around these towns as far as Baalath Beer (Ramah in the
Negev).

This was the inheritance of the tribe of the Simeonites, according to its clans. [9]The inheritance of the Simeonites was taken from the share of Judah, because Judah's portion was more than they needed. So the Simeonites received their inheritance within the territory of Judah.

[10]The third lot came up for Zebulun according to its clans:

The boundary of their inheritance went as far as Sarid. [11]Going west it ran to Maralah, touched Dabbesheth, and extended to the ravine near Jokneam. [12]It turned east from Sarid toward the sunrise to the territory of Kisloth Tabor and went on to Daberath and up to Japhia. [13]Then it continued eastward to Gath Hepher and Eth Kazin; it came out at Rimmon and turned toward Neah. [14]There the boundary went around on the north to Hannathon and ended at the Valley of Iphtah El. [15]Included were Kattath, Nahalal, Shimron, Idalah and Bethlehem. There were twelve towns and their villages.

[16]These towns and their villages were the inheritance of Zebulun, according to its clans.

[17]The fourth lot came out for Issachar according to its clans. [18]Their territory included:

Jezreel, Kesulloth, Shunem, [19]Hapharaim, Shion, Anaharath, [20]Rabbith, Kishion, Ebez, [21]Remeth, En Gannim, En Haddah and Beth Pazzez. [22]The boundary touched Tabor, Shahazumah and Beth Shemesh, and ended at the Jordan. There were sixteen towns and their villages.

[23]These towns and their villages were the inheritance of the tribe of Issachar, according to its clans.

[24]The fifth lot came out for the tribe of Asher according to its clans. [25]Their territory included:

Helkath, Hali, Beten, Akshaph, [26]Allammelek, Amad and Mishal. On the west the boundary touched Carmel and Shihor Libnath. [27]It then turned east toward Beth Dagon, touched Zebulun and the Valley of Iphtah El, and went north to Beth Emek and Neiel, passing Kabul on the left. [28]It went to Abdon, Rehob, Hammon and Kanah, as far as Greater Sidon. [29]The boundary then turned back toward Ramah and went to the fortified city of Tyre, turned toward Hosah and came out at the Mediterranean Sea in the region of Akzib, [30]Ummah, Aphek and Rehob. There were twenty-two towns and their villages.

[31]These towns and their villages were the inheritance of the tribe of Asher, according to its clans.

[32]The sixth lot came out for Naphtali according to its clans:

[33]Their boundary went from Heleph and the large tree in Zaanannim,

passing Adami Nekeb and Jabneel to Lakkum and ending at the Jordan.
34The boundary ran west through Aznoth Tabor and came out at Hukkok.
It touched Zebulun on the south, Asher on the west and the Jordan on
the east. 35The fortified towns were Ziddim, Zer, Hammath, Rakkath,
Kinnereth, 36Adamah, Ramah, Hazor, 37Kedesh, Edrei, En Hazor, 38Iron,
Migdal El, Horem, Beth Anath and Beth Shemesh. There were nineteen
towns and their villages.

39These towns and their villages were the inheritance of the tribe of
Naphtali, according to its clans.

40The seventh lot came out for the tribe of Dan according to its clans.
41The territory of their inheritance included:

Zorah, Eshtaol, Ir Shemesh, 42Shaalabbin, Aijalon, Ithlah, 43Elon,
Timnah, Ekron, 44Eltekeh, Gibbethon, Baalath, 45Jehud, Bene Berak, Gath
Rimmon, 46Me Jarkon and Rakkon, with the area facing Joppa.

47(When the territory of the Danites was lost to them, they went up
and attacked Leshem, took it, put it to the sword and occupied it. They
settled in Leshem and named it Dan after their ancestor.)

48These towns and their villages were the inheritance of the tribe of
Dan, according to its clans.

49When they had finished dividing the land into its allotted portions,
the Israelites gave Joshua son of Nun an inheritance among them, 50as the
LORD had commanded. They gave him the town he asked for—Timnath
Serah in the hill country of Ephraim. And he built up the town and
settled there.

51These are the territories that Eleazar the priest, Joshua son of Nun
and the heads of the tribal clans of Israel assigned by lot at Shiloh in the
presence of the LORD at the entrance to the tent of meeting. And so they
finished dividing the land.

*Listening to the Text in the Story*: Numbers 13–14 and Judges 18; Exodus 29:44–46; Leviticus 26:1–13; Deuteronomy 12:1–14; Chapters 13 and 15

## A Tent for Meeting

Setting up the tent of meeting is a significant event in Joshua. The tent's construction was commanded in Exodus. It was to be a place of sacrifice for successive generations (Exod 29:42). Sacrifice was a vital part of Israel's covenant, and the tent was consecrated for its role by God's presence and glory.

The sacrifices offered at the tent, conducted according to law and by the priests, were to be a safeguard against worshiping the LORD in ways influenced by the inhabitants. It was the covenant, and the holy system of approach to God instituted under the covenant, that enabled God to "dwell" (a verbal from *shkn*) among Israel and meet with them. God was, for Israel, the God "who brought them out of Egypt so that I might dwell among them" (Exod 29:46). These covenantal realities are in view in Joshua 18:1 as the whole assembly gathers to "set up" (using *shkn*, but a different verbal form) the tent.

In Deuteronomy 12:1–14, God commanded the tent be set up at a place selected from all the tribes and at which the LORD would "put his Name there for his dwelling (from *shkn*)" (Deut 12:5, 11; 14:23; 16:2, 6, 11; 26:2). Significantly, Deuteronomy commands this place be set up after Israel crosses the Jordan to the "resting place and inheritance the LORD your God is giving you" (12:9), and after the LORD grants "rest from all your enemies around you so that you will live in safety" (12:10).

The tent of meeting stands as a powerful reminder of Israel's covenant relationship with the God who has rescued them and provided a land of rest and safety. The erection of the tent of meeting in Joshua 18:1 is another way that the book of Joshua signals the fulfillment of God's covenant promises.

### A Subversive Spying Mission

The Danite allocation (19:40–48) and specifically the taking of Leshem (v. 47) is helpfully read in the context of the narration of the same event in Judges 18 (where the captured city is called Laish). The two accounts refer to the same event for in each the city is renamed Dan, and both events occur while the tent of meeting is at Shiloh.

In Judges, representative men are sent to spy out the land because Dan had not "come into an inheritance among the tribes of Israel" (18:1). The spies return a favorable report: the people live in safety, unsuspecting and secure. The people lack nothing and are prosperous, for the land is very good. The spies urge the Danites to take the land, concluding that "God has put [it] into your hands" (18:10). Dan does take the land, meeting no opposition. Following their military success, Dan sets up idols in their new city "all the time the house of God was in Shiloh" (18:31).

In addition to the obviously negative idolatry in Judges 18, other clues place the events in a negative light. First, Dan asserts the land is given by God (v. 10; NIV reads "God has put [it] into your hands"). Nowhere, however, does God actually state this. In fact, God *has* given them land: the inheritance they have failed to claim. Second, the land is superlatively peaceful: the inhabitants live in safety, unsuspecting and secure. It is also superlatively profitable in the Danites' eyes: its inhabitants lack nothing (v. 7), nothing whatever (v. 10); the land is prosperous and very good (vv. 7, 9). To their discredit, the Danites reject their own inheritance, given by God for their peace and provision. Instead, they pursue another land that looks better able to provide. What a rejection of the good land given by God!

Third, the account in Judges has telling comparisons to the disastrous wilderness spying mission (Num 13–14). The wilderness expedition was directed by God for the purpose of bringing Israel into the land; it ends badly because the scouts bring a bad report and Israel becomes fearful. The Danite expedition was directed by the Danites for the purpose of finding a land more suited to their tastes; it appears to end well (for they take the land) but ultimately ends in Danite apostasy. In both, a representative group of spies is dispatched. In both, the land is described favorably. The response of the tribes in both accounts differs, however. The Danites feel confident, for the land is peaceful and unprotected; the wilderness spies feel fearful because of the inhabitants' perceived strength and numbers. Ironically, the strength of the inhabitants really counts for nothing because the Lord was with the wilderness generation. Despite the inhabitants' strength, the Israelite attempt would have been as successful as if the land was peaceful and unprotected.

The wilderness mission began in promise and ended in judgment. The Danite mission began in the rejection of God's land and ended in the rejection of God. The account is a negative retelling of one of Israel's most negative episodes and cannot be considered positive by any reckoning.

With this background text in view, the account of Dan's allotment ends the tribal allocations on a very bad note. All is not well in Israel even though God has fulfilled his promises.

### Dividing the Land at Shiloh (18:1–10)

The gathering of the tribes to Shiloh to set up the tent of meeting is a brief but significant interruption of the tribal allocations. It divides chapters 13–19 into two major segments: allocations to Judah and Joseph (chs. 14–17) and allocations to the remaining seven tribes (chs. 18–19; see Chapter 13 above).

The tent of meeting is a reminder of Israel's covenant with the Lord. He rescued Israel from Egypt, sustained it in the desert, and brought it into the rest of the promised land. Faithful worship at the tent is necessary for Israel to maintain its covenant relationship with the Lord and its rest in the land.

This places the tent of meeting at the symbolic geographic, narrative, and theological center of land possession.

Gathered at Shiloh is "the whole assembly of the Israelites" (literally "all the assembly of the sons of Israel"), a phrase that occurs in Joshua only here and in 22:12. In chapter 22, once again the "whole assembly of the Israelites" (NIV reads simply "the whole assembly of Israel") gathers in Shiloh, although for a different, less positive purpose.

The gathering to set up the central shrine is connected to the land "brought under their control" (v. 2, from *kbsh*), a word that occurs in Joshua only here. The expression, and the gathering to the shrine, is another way of expressing Moses' directive of Deuteronomy 12:10 that Israel will receive "rest" (from *nwh*) from its enemies and should then gather at the LORD's shrine (Deut 12:11). The "rest" of Deuteronomy 12 is promised and anticipated in Joshua 1:13, 15 (the word is the same). In Joshua 11:23 and 14:15 the land had "rest" (using a different word) from war. While rest does not necessitate Israelite control and habitation of all the land, it does indicate an Israelite claim through successful warfare enabled by God's presence and power. God has been instrumental to the fulfillment of "rest," bringing the land under Israelite "control." It is this that triggers the gathering at Shiloh.

Additionally, the land "brought under their control" (from *kbsh*) evokes the Genesis command that humanity "subdue (from *kbsh*) the earth" (Gen 1:28). The phrases and verbal formulations in Genesis and Joshua are not identical, but the evocation is stunning and far-reaching. The garden is the place of God's full presence; of harmonious relationships between God and his people, and the people and the land. As Israel enters and "subdues" the land, there is no sense they are to violently exploit it (in fact, Deuteronomy calls Israel to gratefulness for the gift of the land's fullness [Deut 16:9–17; 26:1–11], and prosperity is dependent upon covenant obedience rather than exploitative husbandry [Deut 28]. As well, the land is to be respected in the midst of warfare [Deut 20:19–20]). The evocation of the Genesis command brings anticipation that the promised land will be a new garden—filled with God's presence, the perfection of all relationships, and good care and stewardship of God's gifted land (see Listen to the Story, Chapter 1).

Despite these signs that God's promises are completed, Israel's work is ongoing. Following the narrative interlude (v. 1), the concern with "inheritance" in verse 2 returns the chapter to a key word used throughout Joshua 13–21 (see Chapter 13). It is important that the remaining seven tribes receive their allotted portion of land, for they are part of all Israel.

Joshua is a primary actor throughout verses 3–10. His question, "How long will you wait before you begin to take possession (from *yrsh*) of the land?"

begins the action. It also reveals continuing tension between two ideas in chapters 13–21. On one hand the land is taken and has rest (11:23); on the other hand, much land remains to be fully taken (that is possessed through habitation; from *yrsh*; 13:1). This tension is apparent in that the land is "brought under their control" yet several tribes have not yet "received their inheritance" (vv. 1–2).

Joshua urges the remaining tribes to possess the land "the LORD, the God of your ancestors, has given you." This contrasts them with the eastern tribes who received their land from Moses (v. 7). Joshua's words also contrast the remaining tribes with Judah, which initiated the allocation of its land (14:6) without any need for prompting.

It is also Joshua who supervises the casting of lots for the remaining allocations (vv. 6, 8, 10). Although Eleazar and the heads of the tribal clans are participants (19:51; 14:1), Joshua is the primary actor, ensuring these remaining tribes receive their lands. The LORD's oversight is apparent, for the lot is "in the presence of the LORD" (vv. 6, 8, 10) and at the shrine "at Shiloh" (vv. 4 [by implication in light of v. 9], 8, 9, 10).

Further highlighting Joshua's leading role in this episode, he adds a survey as a new step in the process of land allocation. This wisely engages the tribes in the task at hand and moves them out of inaction. Joshua's instructions are repetitive: he twice instructs the land be surveyed (vv. 4–7, 8) and then his instructions are executed (vv. 9–10). The repetitions suggest the importance of obedience to the LORD's commands issued through his representative, Joshua.

The two sets of instructions issued by Joshua (vv. 4–7, 8) and their execution (vv. 9–10) show the same concern for equitable land distribution as in previous land allocations. Thus, Joshua sends out a representative group of three men from each tribe, and the survey is conducted "according to the inheritance of each [tribe]" (v. 4) and "according to their tribal divisions" (v. 10). The land is equitably divided into seven parts (vv. 5, 6, 9) and "town by town" (v. 9). All this safeguards the equity prescribed in Numbers 33:54.

A new element records the survey results in a written document (vv. 4, 8, 9). This is the third written collection referenced in Joshua, along with the Book of the Law of Moses (1:8; 8:31, 34; 23:6; 24:26) and the Book of Jashar (10:13). The previous books serve two purposes: (1) instruction for successful life in the land; and (2) as an *aide memoire* for future generations. This third "book" will act similarly, providing a record of land allocation for future generations and ensuring the ongoing possession of each allotment by its designated tribe.

Land allocation for the remaining seven tribes occurs in the context of all Israel. Joshua's initial instructions (vv. 4–7) reference land previously allocated to Judah and Joseph (v. 5) and to the Transjordanian tribes (v. 7). Similarly, the Levitical exception and its rationale are mentioned again (v. 7; see also 13:14, 33; 14:4). Earlier, the Levitical inheritance was identified as the "food offerings presented to the LORD" (13:14) and "the LORD, the God of Israel" (13:33). Now, the inheritance is specified as priestly service (in Hebrew, "the priesthood of the LORD"). The Levites will receive a gift of towns and pasturelands from the tribes (ch. 21). Until then, these references are a reminder that the Levites, too, are part of all Israel.

### Seven Allotments for Seven Tribes (18:11–19:48)

The second segment of tribal allocation continues the task begun in chapters 14–17 and utilizes several comparable structures and foci. These are here initially explored to give a sense of the whole, followed by a few comments on items of interest within the lists themselves.[1]

As in the Judahite and Josephite allotments, the land is allotted "according to its clans." The phrase begins and ends each of the seven allocations (with slight variation of translation in the NIV; [2] 18:11, 20, 21, 28; 19:1, 8, 10, 16, 17, 23, 24, 31, 32, 39, 40, 48). The tribes may be slow to begin the process, but it is conducted with a view to equitable land distribution, as God had commanded.

Structurally, the lists continue to provide boundary details, town lists, and tallies. This structure was fully apparent in the Judahite allotment, providing a lengthy and carefully structured list. The list for the Josephite allotment was, in comparison, shorter and less structured (see Chapters 15 and 16 above). In the same way, the allocation to the seven tribes begins with a lengthy and structured list of Benjaminite boundaries and a list of its towns—although both fall short of the Judahite lists in length and detail. The remaining tribal lists are much shorter and less structured, even at times combining boundaries with towns. The final allotment to Dan provides a list of towns only. An explanation is given for the omission in the Danite tribal allotment, but it is an admission of tribal failure to take the land. Thus, the second segment of tribal allocation ends in failure, as did the first segment (17:14–18).

The overall effect of the second segment is diminishment and disintegration. Benjamin begins the second segment, but not as strongly as Judah began the first; Dan ends the second segment in greater failure than Joseph did the

1. As noted in the discussion of the allotments for Judah and Joseph, the purpose of this commentary is not to focus on matters of site identification. See Hess, *Joshua,* and Pitkänen, *Joshua* for engagement with those questions.

2. See the discussion in Explain the Story, 13:15–33 in Chapter 14 for the variant translations of this phrase in the NIV.

first. If the first segment proposed two opposing visions for land possession (the bold faith of Judah, Caleb, Aksah, and the daughters of Zelophehad versus the shrinking faith of the Josephites), this segment reveals the latter vision has taken hold. The LORD may have granted rest and victory, but Israel lacks the obedience and faith to possess its allocations.

With these "large picture" elements in mind, a few highlights within the individual tribal lists are in order. Benjamin is geographically situated between Judah and Joseph. The allocation is the most detailed of all the seven tribes, although less so than Judah's lists. Benjamin's boundaries are first described (vv. 12–20a) before a concluding summary (v. 20b). The description begins with the northern boundary then moves to the western, southern, and eastern boundaries. Benjamin's relatively small territory is virtually encircled by its larger neighbors, and many of its border towns and markers are shared with Ephraim (Bethel, Ataroth Addar, Beth Horon [16:2–5]) and Judah (Kiriath Baal [Kiriath Jearim], Nephtoah, Valley of Ben Hinnom, En Rogel, En Shemesh, the Pass of Adummim, the Stone of Bohan, Beth Arabah and Beth Hoglah [15:6–9]). Like the Judahite town lists (15:21–62), the Benjaminite town lists are listed in geographical collections. Benjamin's town lists have an eastern (vv. 21–24) and western (vv. 25–28) collection. Each is tallied as in the Judahite lists.

Simeon's allotment has no boundary description, an omission explained in verse 1 and more fully in verse 9. Situated within Judah's territory, many of Simeon's cities are also noted in Judah's list (Beersheba, Hazar Shual, Ezem, Eltolad, Hormah, Ziklag, Ain, and Rimmon; see 15:28–32). By its placement within Judah, Simeon is absorbed into the larger tribe, virtually losing its tribal identity. This fulfills the curse of dispersal issued by Jacob against Simeon for its part (along with Levi) in bringing retribution against the Shechemites for the rape of Dinah (Gen 34:1–31; 49:5–7). Later (Josh 21), the dispersal of Levi (Gen 49:5–7) is dealt with through the appointment of Levitical cities. Unlike the Simeonite dispersal, the Levitical dispersal is one of honor, overriding Jacob's curse (see Listen to the Story, Chapter 19 for the explanation).

Following the standard conclusion regarding the inheritance gifted Simeon (v. 8), a verse explains why Simeon's allotment is taken from that of Judah. It is an explanation that reflects poorly upon Judah. Judah's territory is described as "more than they needed (*rab mehem*)," so a portion is granted to Simeon. This may reflect generosity or a pattern of shared tribal efforts, but it more likely reflects Judah's failure to take the land (the narrative has already noted one such failure by Judah in 15:63). Simeon's grant of land is because Judah's territory was too *rab*—big—for them. This is the word repeatedly used by the Josephites to complain about their territory: they were a numerous (*rab*) people and wanted a larger territory. Joshua told them that, being numerous, they should take more of the land already allotted to them (17:14–18). It is a suggestive possibility that Simeon receives an allotment from Judah because the tribe of Judah felt unable or unwilling to take a territory they felt was too large. This would, then, be another note of failure on Judah's part.

Zebulun is located in the western area of lower Galilee. Its boundaries are sketched, followed by an appended list of five towns (with no introductory statement). These are tallied as twelve; the discrepancy is not uncommon in such listings in the ancient Near East (see Listen to the Story, Chapter 13). Zebulun's allotment ends with the standard summary slightly modified to specify their equitable inheritance as "these towns and their villages" (v. 16). This modified summary continues in the remaining tribal lists (vv. 23, 31, 39, 48).

Issachar's list shows real deterioration in the established pattern. Its introduction and conclusion are as expected, but its boundaries are only briefly noted (v. 22) and are preceded by a listing of towns with no standard introduction. Asher's list deteriorates further still. It begins and ends in the usual way and contains a list of towns (vv. 25–26, 28, 30). These are contained within and serve as part of the boundary list (vv. 25–30). Naphtali adheres more closely to the pattern, with an introduction and conclusion (vv. 32, 39). It lists its town separately and tallies them but provides no introduction to the town list.

In summary, only Benjamin's allocation replicates the same level of detail and structure as found in Judah's list. In the first segment, Joseph's list is less detailed and structured than Judah's; in the second segment, the tribes after Benjamin reveal a more marked lessening in structure. All tribal lists from Simeon to Naphtali are either truncated or disordered. Whatever the origin and development of these lists, they can now be read as a powerful statement of disintegration and a falling-away from the task at hand: taking the land gifted and won for them through God's promise and power.

The final allotment for Dan brings this decline to a sad conclusion. It also has the expected introduction and conclusion (vv. 40, 48), but it includes only a list of towns (with no standard introduction) and no boundary list. Further, Dan's allotment is ordered after, and thus included with, the northern tribes. Its towns, however, are actually in the south (Zorah and Eshtaol are included in Judah's territory in 15:33, and Ir Shemesh, Aijalon, Timnah, Ekron, Eltekeh, Gibbethon, Baalath, and Joppa can all be placed with relative certainty in the same area).[3]

The allocation explains the discrepancy, citing Dan's migration to claim

3. Hess, *Joshua*, 302–3.

a new territory. The southern towns are those of their original allotment. The absence of boundaries acknowledges the relinquished southern allotment. While no reason is given for Dan's migration, it is striking that the taking of Leshem uses familiar warfare language: Dan "went up," "attacked," "took Leshem," and "put it to the sword" (v. 47). Instead of describing Dan taking its appointed territory, these terms describe Dan taking a territory of its own choosing. Dan moves against peaceful Leshem, battling to possess ("occupy," using the key term *yrsh*) it.

The Danite action ends the tribal allocations badly: a tribe actually rejects its gifted land and seeks out territory of its own choosing. When placed alongside the longer account in Judges 18 and that account's resonances to the wilderness generation's spying mission (see Listen to the Story above), the negative effect is further enhanced. The migration of Dan has its own spying mission—but not one commissioned by God. It is a spying mission that leads Dan to take a peaceful and unsuspecting people in a false conquest. These resonances enhance the dismal ending of the tribal allocations.

## An Inheritance for Joshua (19:49–51)

Joshua's inheritance concludes the tribal allocations of chapters 13–19. The third section of Joshua has only the Levitical and Refuge cities left to allocate (chs. 20–21). Joshua's grant begins and ends by noting the land division is "finished" (vv. 49, 51). The word occurs infrequently in Joshua and only here in relation to land.[4] The conclusion is positive in tone, a stark contrast to the final tribal allocation to Dan. Although brief, these three verses take up several threads present throughout the third section, reinforcing its theological themes.

Joshua successfully led Israel into the land God "gave" (from *ntn*) them (1:2). Now the tribes honor Joshua's leadership by "giving" (from *ntn*) land to Joshua. This is done "as the LORD commanded" (v. 50), which refers back to the LORD's promise that Caleb and Joshua would enter to settle in the land (Num 14:30). Interestingly, while there is a clear promise of land for Caleb (Num 14:24; Deut 1:36), no corresponding word appears for Joshua and might here be assumed.

Joshua is an Ephraimite and receives the town of Timnath Serah from the Josephite allotment. In the "hill country of Ephraim," it is located in the same territory about which the Josephites had earlier complained (17:15).

4. "Finished" translates a *piel* form of the Hebrew root *klh*; the root occurs three times more in Joshua, all *piel* forms. The occurrences are in 8:24 ("had finished killing"), 10:20 (not translated by NIV, but the Hebrew has the sense of "when Joshua and the Israelites had finished destroying them completely"), and 24:20 ("make an end of you").

Like Caleb, Joshua appears ready to take the land promised and given by God. These two men of faith stand at the beginning and end of the land allocation chapters (14:6–15; 19:49–51). There are several notes of failure throughout these chapters, but Joshua and Caleb (together with Aksah and the daughters of Zelophehad) demonstrate the faith by which land is taken.

Several elements in this short conclusion reveal it stands as a bracket to the opening of the western land allocation (14:1–5). First, Eleazar, Joshua, and the heads of the tribal clans assign territory to the tribes (v. 51). The same notation began the western allocations (14:1) and is a reminder that allocation west of the Jordan is conducted as God commanded (Num 34:16–29). Second, key words used throughout chapters 13–21 (see Chapter 13 above) are clustered at the commencement and conclusion of the western allocations (14:1–5; 19:49–51). In each passage, the land is an "inheritance" (from *nhl*; 14:2, 3 [2x]; 19:49, 51 [NIV translates as "territories" in 19:51]) and both passages use the same Hebrew root (*nhl*) in verbal formulations regarding the land (14:1 as "received as an inheritance," and "allotted"; 19:49 as "dividing"; 19:51 as "assigned"). While the use of the same verbal root is obscured by NIV translational choices, it is a reminder that, from beginning to end, land allocation is about land gifted to Israel as an "inheritance."

Both passages also use key words that signal equitable land distribution. Land is "divided" (from *hlq*; 14:5; 19: 51) among the tribes. This is overseen by God through the "lot" (*goral*; 14:2; 19:51) executed through Eleazar in obedience to God's command through Moses (Num 26:52–56; 34:13).

Joshua has clearly overseen land distribution according to God's command. He has obeyed the law of Moses. He receives a grant of land not only because of his faithfulness in Numbers 13–14, but because he has fulfilled Moses' ministry. He is truly a faithful Israelite.

While Joshua fulfills Moses' ministry, the real actor is the Lord who grants the land. Thus, the conclusion notes the land assigned "by lot," that is, under God's direction. This takes place "at Shiloh," significantly ending the second segment of land allocation where it began (18:1). Shiloh is the place of the tent of meeting where God meets with his people. Thus, the lot was assigned "in the presence of the Lord" and "at the entrance to the tent of meeting."

Land allocation has engaged leadership: Joshua, Eleazar, the heads of the tribal clans. It has painted Israel in its faithfulness and unfaithfulness, and its success and failure to take the land. Land allocation was conducted in anticipation of full possession and habitation, but it only occurred because of the long-ago promise made by a faithful God who, by his powerful presence, led Israel into the land. Only God can continue to empower Israel for full possession—but only as Israel continues in obedience.

**Gathered Around the Lord**

The very brief mention of the tent at Shiloh, with Israel gathered around it, is not an indication that the event holds little significance. As noted in Listen to the Story and Explain the Story above, this one verse is the book's narrative, geographic, and theological center. As such, it points to that one thing that makes Israel unique: God's presence in its midst. The tabernacle at Shiloh was the visible reminder of that presence and enabled ongoing covenant relationship through the sacrificial system. As God's people lived within that covenant, Israel served as a kingdom of priests (Exod 19:6) so that the nations would join in the worship of the Lord. Already at this point in Joshua, this is an accomplished reality in people such as Rahab and in the foreigners included in the covenant renewal ceremony (8:30–35).

When God first encamped with Israel at Sinai, the community was gathered before the Lord at the mountain. Only this presence made it unique. Moses knew this and was reluctant to begin the journey to the promised land without God's presence (Exod 33:14–16). When the tabernacle was built and dedicated, God's presence filled it (Exod 40:34–38). Solomon, too, dedicated the temple, and it filled with God's presence (1 Kgs 8:10–13). Solomon's prayer of dedication shows he realized that it was God's presence by which prayer was heard, whether offered by Israel or by foreigners (1 Kgs 8:23–53).

The centrality of the tabernacle and (later) the temple to Israel's identity as God's people is apparent. As well, God's presence in Israel's midst was not for its benefit only but for that of the nations among which she dwelt.

The gospel of John takes up the idea of temple once again but with a significant difference. It remains the place of God's presence, the center of the life of God's people, and the source of its purpose. The significant difference is that the place of God's presence is no longer a building but a person: Jesus Christ. John testifies that "The Word became flesh and made his dwelling among us" (John 1:14). The phrase takes up the Greek term used for the idea of the tabernacle and might be rendered better as "The Word became flesh and tabernacled among us." In the next chapter, John makes the connection even clearer for when Jesus says, "Destroy this temple, and I will raise it again in three days" (John 2:19), John testifies that "the temple he had spoken of was his body" (John 2:21). In the person of Christ, God has come near in a new way. Christ is the new tabernacle or temple, the place of God's dwelling. He is the center of the Christian life and community, providing its unique identity and purpose.

The First Epistle of Peter reflects on this idea, likening Christ to the cornerstone of a solid building. Peter extends the metaphor further, as believers in Christ are joined to that cornerstone to form a new tabernacle or temple in which all God's people serve as priests:

> You also, like living stones, are being built into a spiritual house to be a holy priesthood, offering spiritual sacrifices acceptable to God through Jesus Christ. (1 Pet 2:5)

It is their incorporation into Christ, the living temple, that identifies the New Testament people of God. Incorporated into this new temple, they are "a chosen people, a royal priesthood, a holy nation, God's special possession" (1 Pet 2:9). From this identity comes their purpose. It is, like Israel's purpose in the land, set among the nations. Like Israel, the church is also called to live a holy life, now by the law of God's Spirit. No longer dwelling in land designated as a possession in the midst of the nations, the church goes out into all the nations to "declare the praises of him who called you out of darkness into his wonderful light" (1 Pet 2:9).

### Joshua's Leadership

The whole book begins with Joshua, Israel's God-appointed leader. He leads Israel to possess the land (1:1–9). The allocation of the land also begins with Joshua's leadership, and focuses on land possession and distribution (13:1, 6–7). In chapter 18:3–10, Joshua addresses a delay or reluctance on the part of the seven tribes to take possession of the land. By Joshua's initiative and action, he calls these tribes to their task. The land distribution also ends with Joshua, as his leadership is recognized with a personal allocation of land (19:49–50).

Despite some setbacks, Joshua's leadership in the book is successful. In Joshua 18–19, Joshua's effective leadership is demonstrated in many ways. First, the order of the chapter reveals the source of Joshua's success. It is notable that Joshua initiates the chapter's action only after the tent is set up. Important as land possession is for Israel, this is momentarily set aside for the more important call of worship. One wonders whether, in that act of worship, God reminded Joshua of the work still to be done. Second, Joshua's effective leadership is apparent as he is not slow to engage the tribes. Once the tent is set up, he immediately chastises them for work left undone. Yet he wisely balances chastisement with encouragement, recalling for them the ancient promise of land in the appellation "the God of your ancestors" (18:2) and reminding them that the task is a *fait accompli* ("the land that the Lord . . . has given you"; v. 3). By this, he addresses their reluctance or fear to take the land. Third, Joshua's effective leadership is clear because he does not leave it to the tribes to figure out how they should proceed. Recognizing that the process has stalled (for whatever reason), he initiates action by commanding the land survey (vv. 4–6). Fourth, as an effective leader, he engages the tribes in a representative way in the land survey (v. 4).

These acts of effective leadership, together with his references to the other tribes (Judah and Joseph, v. 5; Gad, Reuben, and half-Manasseh, v. 7; the Levites, v. 7), would prompt the tribes' realization that they play a role in something bigger than just themselves, and do so as a united body. Their task is part of a task given to all Israel and as part of God's purposes through Israel. Finally, Joshua explains the task more than once, ensuring that it is fully understood (18:8). In all these ways, Joshua exercises effective leadership at a time when the tribes' vision and drive had failed.

Recognizing Joshua's leadership in the face of the tribes' stalled vision is not to hold him up as a model for all leaders in similar situations. The point of the passage is not to provide "steps to successful leadership." It may be that the steps Joshua takes might be helpful in other situations—but those situations might require other steps and a very different style of leadership. Joshua's actions should not be taken as a panacea for all leaders trying to fire up God's people when vision is lost. But for the challenge faced by the seven tribes, this is how God worked through his appointed leader, Joshua.

There are many "how to" courses and books for pastors and church leaders. Some suggest that success is measured similarly for all situations (often simply numerical growth) and can be achieved through applying set actions and leadership styles. Reflecting on Joshua's leadership in this passage, it might be more useful to simply say that in a time of need, God raised up a leader and worked through the leader he had appointed. Joshua was appointed and "trained" under the leadership of Moses, whose style and calling were different than Joshua's. That difference made Moses effective at a different moment in Israel's life. In the next generation, God worked through Joshua within his context and with his personality and gifts. Though different in style and action, he was equally effective.

In this chapter, Joshua's action brought the people back to that to which they were called. No Christian leader should feel bound to replicate Joshua's leadership style. Each is called and gifted differently, and appointed to different contexts. Each can be assured that God will work effectively in and through them, just as he did with Joshua at a crucial moment in Israel's life.

### Faith, Fear, and Failure (Reprise)

The migration of Dan ends the second segment of land allocation (chs. 18–19) on a negative note. The first segment (chs. 14–17) also ended on a negative note: the Josephite complaint (17:14–18). The earlier exploration of Josephite Faith, Fear, and Failure (see Live the Story, Chapter 16) pointed out that one such choice does not determine a destiny.

While this is true, it is also true that such choices, when repeated, can chart a negative course into the future. This appears to be the case with the Danite choice. As the Danites traveled north to take the peaceful land of Laish, they convinced an itinerant Levite to accompany them. The Levite agreed, apparently lured by the prestige the position offered (Judg 17:1–13; 18:1–6, 13–21). This same Levite brought with him an idol which Dan set up and served for many years until Israel's captivity (Judg 18:29–31).

Dan's cultic failure expanded beyond this idolatry. Later, when Israel seceded from the southern kingdom, Jeroboam set up Dan as the northern center of his infamous calf cult (1 Kgs 12:29). Dan's participation in a new idolatry suggests a pattern of thinking and action within the tribe's life. As participants for many years in the idolatry introduced by the Levite, they gave no resistance to the idolatry introduced by Jeroboam. They participated in Jeroboam's calf cult in which lay the seeds of the northern kingdom's destruction and expulsion from the land. The final peroration on the sins of the northern kingdom names not just the calf cult of Jeroboam but many sins of idolatry (2 Kgs 17:7–17). These sins are characterized as a failure to listen to God and trust him. The result was that Israel "followed worthless idols and themselves became worthless" (2 Kgs 17:15).

Dan first chose to reject the land gifted by God and sought out a land of its own choosing. This was a failure to follow God's command. To this, Dan added the sin of the Levite's idol and later, the sin of Jeroboam. In the end, Dan's descendants lived in another land: Assyria—a land Israel would never describe as good, secure, or prosperous.

Fear and lack of trust can lead to one failure of faith, but that one failure need not determine a destiny. It is the repeated, determined rejection of God's ways that led Dan (and the northern kingdom) to its destiny. The sad irony of Dan's repeated rejection is that it concludes a section that begins with the antidote to such rejection: the worship of God (Josh 18:1).

Whether God's people are those of Joshua's era or today, the central fact and driving force of life must be the worship of God. Daily attention to God: listening to his word, delighting in his love, attending to practices of devotion and consecration, remaining in fellowship with the people of God's community—these are practices that facilitate long devotion to the one God.

# CHAPTER 18

# Joshua 20:1–9

## LISTEN to the Story

[1]Then the Lord said to Joshua: [2]"Tell the Israelites to designate the
cities of refuge, as I instructed you through Moses, [3]so that anyone who
kills a person accidentally and unintentionally may flee there and find protection from the avenger of blood. [4]When they flee to one of these cities,
they are to stand in the entrance of the city gate and state their case before
the elders of that city. Then the elders are to admit the fugitive into their
city and provide a place to live among them. [5]If the avenger of blood comes
in pursuit, the elders must not surrender the fugitive, because the fugitive
killed their neighbor unintentionally and without malice aforethought.
[6]They are to stay in that city until they have stood trial before the assembly
and until the death of the high priest who is serving at that time. Then
they may go back to their own home in the town from which they fled."
[7]So they set apart Kedesh in Galilee in the hill country of Naphtali,
Shechem in the hill country of Ephraim, and Kiriath Arba (that is,
Hebron) in the hill country of Judah. [8]East of the Jordan (on the other
side from Jericho) they designated Bezer in the wilderness on the plateau
in the tribe of Reuben, Ramoth in Gilead in the tribe of Gad, and Golan
in Bashan in the tribe of Manasseh. [9]Any of the Israelites or any foreigner
residing among them who killed someone accidentally could flee to these
designated cities and not be killed by the avenger of blood prior to standing trial before the assembly.

*Listening to the Text in the Story*: Exodus 21:12–14; Numbers 35:6–34; Deuteronomy 4:41–43; 19:1–13; Law Code of Hammurabi; Hittite Laws

### A Place for Safety

The idea of enshrining in law a place of refuge for those who kill a person unintentionally is an old idea in Israel. It first appears in Israel's oldest law code, the

Covenant Code (Exod 20:22–23:33). In it, the provision is briefly described (21:12–14), directing the manslayer to flee "to a place I will designate." Some type of trial is apparently assumed, for those who do flee but are found guilty of deliberate murder are to be "taken from my altar and put to death" (21:14). The reference to the altar indicates the place of refuge is associated with a cult site, a reality that apparently stands behind Joab's act of claiming asylum by grasping the horns of the altar in 1 Kings 2:28. The law as it develops does not specifically locate the cities at cult sites, focusing rather on accessibility and equitable distribution throughout Israel (Num 35:14; Deut 19:3).

The cities are described in detail in Numbers 35:6–34, using much of the language found in Joshua. Six cities are designated, with three on either side of the Jordan. The cities are also Levitical cities and are intended to provide safety for Israelites and "foreigners residing among them" (v. 15). This provision is repeated in Joshua 20:9. The cities provide refuge for one who has killed "accidentally" so that the "avenger" may not kill them before a trial by the assembly determines the facts of the case. That a trial is prescribed shows a concern that justice is served.

Numbers 35 speaks extensively of the penalty for the murderer (vv. 16–21, 30–31) and the unintentional killer (vv. 22–29, 32). Once a trial determines the unintentional nature of the killing, the killer must remain in the city of refuge. Should they venture outside it, the avenger may kill them without guilt. Only the death of the current high priest ends the manslayer's sentence, allowing him or her to return to their property unmolested by the avenger. No ransom may be given to release the manslayer before the death of the high priest.

The high priest's death terminates the sentence, although no reason for this is given. It may be that the death of the priest (as the Lord's representative) marks the end of a period of ritual cleansing for the bloodshed. Blood is sacred, and thus shed blood "pollutes the land" and "atonement" must be made for it lest the land be "defiled." Such cleansing is necessary to enable Israel to dwell in holiness and for the holy Lord to dwell among the Israelites (vv. 33–34). Assuming the high priest's death marks the sentence's terminus for these reasons, then the law includes both a means of justice, and a reminder of the gifted and holy nature of the land due to the Lord's presence in it.

The cities of refuge appear in two locations in Deuteronomy. The first (Deut 4:41–43) names three cities in the Transjordan. These are listed immediately before the law is introduced (4:44–49) and only later are the western cities mentioned. Moses may name the eastern cities out of concern the eastern tribes not be left out, forgotten, or otherwise downgraded as not fully Israel. If this were to happen, the appointment of eastern cities might be neglected, thus eliminating ready refuge for Transjordanian tribes.

The three western cities are not mentioned until Deuteronomy 19:1–14. These cities (unlike the eastern cities) are not named. Their accessibility and equitable distribution throughout the land is underscored (v. 3) and, as in Joshua 20, the cities are for the protection of one who kills "unintentionally, without malice aforethought" (v. 4). As in Numbers 35, there is a concern for justice lest "innocent" blood be shed (vv. 6, 10, 13). Unique to Deuteronomy 19 is the provision for an additional three cities west of the Jordan. These are appointed in anticipation that God would "enlarge your territory . . . and give the whole land he promised" (v. 8). This eventuality is contingent on Israel "carefully follow[ing] all these laws I command you today" (v. 9).

### Intentionality

The penalties prescribed under the ancient law codes did take intentionality into consideration. For instance, Hammurabi's eighteenth century BC code prescribes significantly reduced penalties should one individual strike another unintentionally. In the case of a beating that results in death, the accused may also make a similar plea and receive a reduced penalty.[1] Likewise, the seventeenth–sixteenth century Hittite code prescribes penalties for those who cause injury or death. In both instances if "it is an accident," the penalty is half that of intentional injury or death.[2] Neither code provides any extant example of a provision for cities of refuge or other mechanisms to safeguard the life of those who kill when "it is an accident."

## EXPLAIN the Story

Joshua 20–21 is an addendum to the tribal allocations. The two chapters are a unit, bracketed by concluding summaries (19:49–51; 21:43–45). The first conclusion ends the allocation of land to the tribal groups (chs. 13–19), while the second ends the third section (chs. 13–21). Although chapters 20–21 are an addendum, they are important, not least because they demonstrate obedience to the commands issued by Moses (Num 35). The chapters relate the appointment by Israel of two types of cities: cities of refuge for the manslayer (ch. 20) and cities for the Levites (ch. 21).

Moses' command for the two types of cities appoints first the Levitical cities (Num 35:1–5) and second, the cities of refuge (Num 35:6–34). Joshua 20–21 reverses this order so that the Levitical cities end Joshua 13–21. In a

1. See §§195–208 in *COS* 2.131:348. §§206–07 in particular provide for unintentional injury or death.

2. See §§1–8 in Ibid., 2.19:107. Comparison of §§1, 3 and 2, 4 show the variant penalties in the case of accidental death.

book that so clearly calls Israel to obedience and right worship as necessary to land possession, the priestly teaching ministry is crucial (Deut 33:8–11). Concluding land allocation with attention to the Levites highlights their role in Israel. Additionally, it prepares for the book's final section (chs. 22–24) that focuses on worship. This is an activity in which the priestly role is paramount.

### Israel Gifts Cities of Refuge (20:1–9)

The chapter begins by emphasizing Joshua's authority to command the cities of refuge, signaled by the words, the "LORD said to Joshua." There is no question of the command's origin. The LORD has spoken many times to Joshua throughout the book (1:1; 3:7; 4:1, 15; 5:9; 6:2; 7:10; 8:1, 18; 10:8; 11:6), but here a different word is used (from *dbr* rather than *'mr*). It is a subtle difference but, interestingly, also the same word used when "the LORD said to Moses" in Numbers 35:1. This increases the referentiality to the commands given in that chapter. Joshua is to communicate the commands "as I instructed you through Moses." The "you" here is plural and refers to all Israel. Joshua serves (as did Moses) in a prophetic role, communicating God's words to the people. That these words were originally given "through Moses" and are now enacted through Joshua attests to his fulfillment of his predecessor's ministry. God is with Joshua as he was with Moses (1:5). Israel has covenanted obedience to the law of Moses; they are now to obey Joshua as they did Moses (1:17–18).

The command is that Israel "designate" cities of refuge. "Designate" is the Hebrew word most often translated in Joshua as "give" (from *ntn*) and is a key word in the book (see Explain the Story, Chapter 1). God has "given" Israel the land. Now they have the opportunity to give land as well, setting aside cities within their tribal allotments. Their response is one of obedience and demonstrates their commitment to justice for the manslayer. Coming as this chapter does after Israel has received the gift of land, their response is also one of gratitude for that good gift.

The cities are for the protection of the non-culpable killer. Joshua includes an abbreviated rendition of the earlier command as given in Numbers and Deuteronomy (see Listen to the Story above) and utilizes the language of those texts. The death is "accidental" (vv. 3, 9), "unintentional" (vv. 3, 5; in Hebrew, "without knowledge"), and "without malice" (v. 5). The killer is to "flee" (vv. 3, 4, 6, 9) for protection from the "avenger of blood" (vv. 3, 5, 9) and "stand trial" (vv. 4, 6, 9) before the "assembly" (vv. 6, 9). The innocent fugitive must not be surrendered to the avenger, and the penalty endures until the high priest's death.

In the Numbers and Deuteronomy iterations, the law has a dual purpose. First, it prevents the defilement of land through bloodshed (see Listen to the

Story above). This is not the focus in Joshua 20, although the reference to the death of the high priest suggests a concern for purifying the land from bloodguilt. This however is not stated, but must be gleaned from the earlier narration of the law. Second, the law in Numbers and Deuteronomy provides justice for the manslayer. This is the primary focus in Joshua 20, which speaks of protection for the killer and the conduct of a trial (vv. 4, 6, 9). A trial is only briefly referenced in Numbers (35:12, 24) and not at all in Deuteronomy. Joshua explicates how the trial is conducted: an initial statement before the city elders in the gate, admittance and preservation until a trial, a trial held before the assembly, and ensured protection until the death of the high priest.

After outlining the purpose and conduct of the law, the cities are selected. West of the Jordan, they are in the north (Naphtali), central highlands (Ephraim), and south (Judah), ensuring equitable access as prescribed in Deuteronomy 19:2. Notably, only three cities are appointed, not the possible six (Deut 19:8–9). The potential of six cities assumed a scenario in which God enlarged Israel's territory because they "carefully follow all the laws" (Deut 19:9). The limit of three cities is then a negative comment on Israel's obedience and ability to take the land, adding another note of failure in Israel's land possession.

East of the Jordan, the cities earlier appointed by Moses are named. These also are found in the north, central, and south Transjordan. The western cities are "set apart" (from *qdsh*), a word of consecration and holiness describing places (1 Kgs 9:3), people (Jer 1:5), or objects (Exod 28:38; Lev 22:2; Deut 15:19) set aside for holy purposes. By contrast, the eastern cities are only "designated" (v. 8; from *ntn*; it is also the word used for the designation of all the cities in 20:2). In such close proximity to the reference to the western cities which are "set apart," the different word appears to distinguish between the cities in the promised land and the concessionary Transjordanian land.

In a final note, the cities are part of a system of justice for Israelites and for "any foreigner residing among them" (v. 9; Num 35:15). The concern for non-Israelites is especially noteworthy in Joshua, especially in light of the *herem* command. It is a reminder that land possession does not include the total annihilation of all inhabitants. More, land possession envisions justice for all inhabitants, Israelite and foreigner.

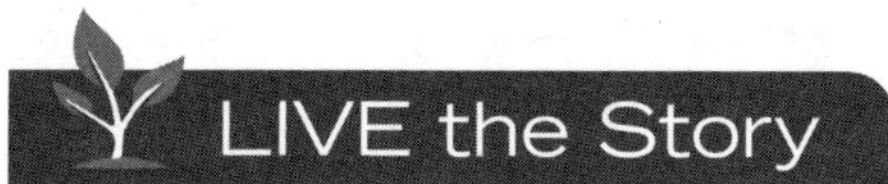


### Precious Life Redeemed

The cities of refuge and the due process they enshrine reveal that human life is precious to God. Both the life of the one unintentionally killed and the life of the manslayer are honored in this law. There is even provided, upon the death of the high priest, a redemption of sorts for the manslayer.

Despite the uncertainty of the mechanism by which the high priest's death in this passage effects redemption, figural interpretive traditions see in it a foreshadowing of Christ's own death by which sin is forgiven. Jerome's *Defense Against the Pelagians* argues that the passage's unintentional killer figures those who sin in ignorance. They are to wait in a city of refuge (although Jerome does not specifiy what this is, it may be a time of prayer or, for the unbaptized, the time of catechesis) until

> the death of the high priest, that is to say, until he is redeemed by the blood of the Savior, either in the house of baptism or by repentance, which supplies the efficacy of the grace of baptism through the ineffable mercy of the Savior who does not wish anybody to perish. Nor does he find his delight in the death of sinners, but rather that they be converted from their way and live.[3]

Jerome's comment reveals that he views the high priest's death as having a more expansive effect than releasing only those who sin in ignorance. By noting those who are called to repentance and conversion, Jerome includes all who sin, whether in ignorance or intentionally.

Jerome's expansive figural reading aptly captures the passage's commitment to the precious value of life and provides an insightful Christological reading. In Christ, our great high priest, all who sin can find refuge and release. Christ has entered the holy place and made atonement for all sin by his death. The certainty of this redemption is noted in Hebrews:

> We have this hope as an anchor for the soul, firm and secure. It enters the inner sanctuary behind the curtain, where our forerunner, Jesus, has entered on our behalf. He has become a high priest forever, in the order of Melchizedek. (Heb 6:19–20)

### The Response to God's Gifts: Obedience and Gratitude

These verses are added after a clear conclusion to the chapters of land distribution (19:51) and might be considered an awkward addendum. Their placement is not haphazard, however. Certainly, the designation of the cities demonstrates Israel's obedience to God's command. But, placed after God's action of gifting the land, it suggests the chapter is more than merely a demonstration of obedience. Coming after the gift of land—a land described

3. Jerome, *Defense Against the Pelagians* 1.33 cited in Franke, ed., *Joshua, Judges, Ruth, 1–2 Samuel*, 88–89.

as good, filled with cities, houses, vineyards, and all things needed for life (Deut 6:10–11)—the chapter's placement also suggests obedience flows from gratitude for the gift of land.

Gratitude in response to God's gifts is common throughout Scripture. Often, it is expressed in songs of worship. For instance, when the ark was brought into the temple after many years in the tabernacle, it was a time of great rejoicing: musicians and singers gave praise and thanksgiving to God in song, proclaiming the goodness of God's love which "endures forever" (2 Chr 5:11–13). The same refrain occurs in Psalm 100, in which a grateful Israel gives praise for God's sovereignty in creating and caring for Israel. Psalm 136 repeatedly responds to God's many gifts of creation, deliverance, protection, land, and provision with a refrain praising his enduring, steadfast love.

Gratitude also is expressed through material gifts given to God. In the desert, Israel gave freewill offerings to build the tabernacle in grateful response to God's deliverance and his presence in their midst (Exod 35:20–29). Their gratitude was so great, the leadership had to stop the gift-giving, which exceeded all expectation and need (Exod 36:2–7). Elsewhere, Naaman, a foreign enemy, was healed through God's prophet. In response, Naaman sought to lavish gifts upon the prophet (2 Kgs 5). Elisha's refusal of the gifts moved Naaman to a deeper and longer-lasting expression of gratitude by which he worshiped the God of Israel.

For the Christian, God's greatest gift is in the giving of his Son for the life of the world. The freedom of life in Christ precipitates the same response of gratitude, expressed in the ways observed in the Old Testament. The New Testament is filled with worship in song (Luke 1:46–55, 68–79; Acts 2:47; 13:2; Eph 5:19; Rev 5:9–14), material gifts of gratitude (1 Cor 16:1–2; 2 Cor 8:9–15; 9:6–7), and obedience to Christ as a demonstration of love (John 14:15).

These realities are each present in Paul's letter to the Philippians. Not only does this letter preserve a great song of praise to Christ (2:5–11), but Paul rejoices and calls the believers to rejoice because of God's great gift in Christ (1:18; 2:17–18; 3:1; 4:4). Paul also commends the believers for providing for Paul's material needs. These gifts he considers to be fragrant offerings made to God (4:18) and are the Philippians' response of gratitude to the gospel. Finally, Paul calls believers to obedience to Christ's example (2:1–5)—an example that is held before them in the lives of Timothy and Epaphroditus (2:19–30) and even Paul's own life (3:7–16).

The cities of refuge reveal gratitude for God's good gift of land. Designating the cities tacitly acknowledges there would be need for them—manslaughter would occur. The cities prevent vengeance and vigilante justice, affirming the value of human life and the necessity of due process. The cities, given in gratitude and obedience, were one means of safeguarding God's vision of rest in the land—of wholeness and peace for all peoples (Israelite and foreigner).

The Christian, too, lives in the rest of God. This rest is not found now in the geography of a land but in life lived in union with Christ (Rom 8:1–11). Freed from the tyranny of sin, the Christian receives the Spirit in token of the fullness of the eschatological life. All this is received without money and without cost. A life lived in response to this great gift is a life of gratitude. The Christian life—of the individual and expressed in the community of the church—demonstrates gratitude and attests to the rest in which they live. Such lives stand as witnesses to God's astounding generosity and gifts.

CHAPTER 19

# Joshua 21:1–45

## LISTEN to the Story

[1]Now the family heads of the Levites approached Eleazar the priest,
Joshua son of Nun, and the heads of the other tribal families of Israel [2]at
Shiloh in Canaan and said to them, "The LORD commanded through
Moses that you give us towns to live in, with pasturelands for our live-
stock." [3]So, as the LORD had commanded, the Israelites gave the Levites
the following towns and pasturelands out of their own inheritance:

[4]The first lot came out for the Kohathites, according to their clans.
The Levites who were descendants of Aaron the priest were allotted thirteen towns from the tribes of Judah, Simeon and Benjamin. [5]The rest of
Kohath's descendants were allotted ten towns from the clans of the tribes
of Ephraim, Dan and half of Manasseh.

[6]The descendants of Gershon were allotted thirteen towns from
the clans of the tribes of Issachar, Asher, Naphtali and the half-tribe of
Manasseh in Bashan.

[7]The descendants of Merari, according to their clans, received twelve
towns from the tribes of Reuben, Gad and Zebulun.

[8]So the Israelites allotted to the Levites these towns and their pasturelands, as the LORD had commanded through Moses.

[9]From the tribes of Judah and Simeon they allotted the following towns
by name [10](these towns were assigned to the descendants of Aaron who were
from the Kohathite clans of the Levites, because the first lot fell to them):

[11]They gave them Kiriath Arba (that is, Hebron), with its surrounding pastureland, in the hill country of Judah. (Arba was the forefather of
Anak.) [12]But the fields and villages around the city they had given to Caleb
son of Jephunneh as his possession.

[13]So to the descendants of Aaron the priest they gave Hebron (a city
of refuge for one accused of murder), Libnah, [14]Jattir, Eshtemoa, [15]Holon,
Debir, [16]Ain, Juttah and Beth Shemesh, together with their pasturelands—
nine towns from these two tribes.

[17]And from the tribe of Benjamin they gave them Gibeon, Geba,
[18]Anathoth and Almon, together with their pasturelands—four towns.

[19]The total number of towns for the priests, the descendants of Aaron, came to thirteen, together with their pasturelands.

[20]The rest of the Kohathite clans of the Levites were allotted towns from the tribe of Ephraim:

[21]In the hill country of Ephraim they were given Shechem (a city of
refuge for one accused of murder) and Gezer, [22]Kibzaim and Beth Horon,
together with their pasturelands—four towns.

[23]Also from the tribe of Dan they received Eltekeh, Gibbethon,
[24]Aijalon and Gath Rimmon, together with their pasturelands—four
towns.

[25]From half the tribe of Manasseh they received Taanach and Gath Rimmon, together with their pasturelands—two towns.

[26]All these ten towns and their pasturelands were given to the rest of the Kohathite clans.

[27]The Levite clans of the Gershonites were given:

from the half-tribe of Manasseh,

Golan in Bashan (a city of refuge for one accused of murder) and Be Eshterah, together with their pasturelands—two towns;

[28]from the tribe of Issachar,

Kishion, Daberath, [29]Jarmuth and En Gannim, together with their
pasturelands—four towns;

[30]from the tribe of Asher,

Mishal, Abdon, [31]Helkath and Rehob, together with their pasturelands—four towns;

[32]from the tribe of Naphtali,

Kedesh in Galilee (a city of refuge for one accused of murder), Hammoth Dor and Kartan, together with their pasturelands—three towns.

[33]The total number of towns of the Gershonite clans came to thirteen, together with their pasturelands.

[34]The Merarite clans (the rest of the Levites) were given:

from the tribe of Zebulun,

Jokneam, Kartah, [35]Dimnah and Nahalal, together with their pasturelands—four towns;

[36]from the tribe of Reuben,

Bezer, Jahaz, [37]Kedemoth and Mephaath, together with their pasturelands—four towns;

[38]from the tribe of Gad,
Ramoth in Gilead (a city of refuge for one accused of murder),
Mahanaim, [39]Heshbon and Jazer, together with their pasturelands—four
towns in all.

[40]The total number of towns allotted to the Merarite clans, who were
the rest of the Levites, came to twelve.

[41]The towns of the Levites in the territory held by the Israelites were
forty-eight in all, together with their pasturelands. [42]Each of these towns
had pasturelands surrounding it; this was true for all these towns.

[43]So the LORD gave Israel all the land he had sworn to give their ancestors, and they took possession of it and settled there. [44]The LORD gave
them rest on every side, just as he had sworn to their ancestors. Not one
of their enemies withstood them; the LORD gave all their enemies into
their hands. [45]Not one of all the LORD's good promises to Israel failed;
every one was fulfilled.

*Listening to the Text in the Story*: Genesis 49:4–7; Exodus 32:25–29; Numbers 3–4; 18:20–21; 26:62; 35:1–8; Deuteronomy 10:8–9; Lists of Ramesses III (Papyrus Harris I); Alalakh Land Grant *AT*456; Alalakh Transfer of Ownership *AT*56

## The Levitical Status

The Levites have a special status within Israel. They serve in various cultic roles and transport and care for the tabernacle (Num 1:48–53; 3–4). They also have a duty to teach the law (Deut 33:8–11).

In their cultic role, the Levites hold the honored place of Israel's first-born sons who belong to God and represent Israel before God (Num 3:12–13, 41, 45; 8:14–19; cf. Exod 13:2, 12–13; 22:29; 34:19–20; Lev 27:26; Num 18:15; Deut 15:19). The Levites were not, however, the first-born son of Jacob; Reuben was. Reuben lost the position, for he defiled his father's bed and so would "no longer excel" (Gen 49:4). Simeon and Levi, the second- and third-born sons of Jacob, were judged for their violence (Gen 34:25–31) and dispersed in Israel (Gen 49:5–7). Simeon's dispersal is effected in its absorption into Judah. Levi's dispersal is through the system of Levitical cities.

For both Simeon and Levi, the dispersal is a judgment for their actions. Yet Levi's dispersal, placing them throughout Israel to teach and represent Israel before God, is an honor rather than a judgment. The judgment is redeemed, and Levi receives the place of honor because of their role in the golden calf episode. When Israel worshiped the golden calf (Exod 32:8), the Levites remained true to God. They rallied to Moses and carried out God's judgment against apostasy. For this act, they are "set apart to the LORD" and blessed (Exod 32:25–29).

### Provisions for the Levites

The Levitical cities were commanded by God (Num 35:1–8). Moses appointed forty-eight cities, although they are not named until Joshua 21. Six of the cities are also cities of refuge. In Numbers 35, the cities of refuge are noted after the Levitical cities. In Joshua, the order is reversed: the Levitical cities follow the cities of refuge. The reordering suggests the importance of the Levites' teaching and cultic role within Israel's life of obedience and worship. Joshua has emphasized the centrality of obedience and worship to life in the land; it is fitting that land allocation ends with this important tribe.

Levitical cities are granted proportionally from each tribal group (Num 35:8). The cities include "pasturelands around the towns" (Num 35:2–5). Pastureland would support livestock and contribute to the Levites' material needs. This is a necessary provision, for the Levites are excluded from the land inheritance received by all Israel. Instead, the LORD and his service (which includes the tithes and offerings from Israel) are their inheritance (Num 18:20–21; 26:62; Deut 10:9). The Levitical exclusion from land inheritance is a repeated theme throughout Joshua 13–21 (13:14, 33; 14:3–4; 18:7).

### Cities for Temple Personnel

It was common throughout the ancient Near East that grants of land and/or cities contributed to the upkeep of temple personnel. The twelfth century BC grant of Ramesses III to the temple of Amun in Canaan included cities in Canaan and Egypt.[1] This was not the same system as Joshua 21, where the towns were gifted proportionally from all the tribes and motivated by gratitude to the deity. The Egyptian bequest was by the king's *fiat* and out of his personal benefaction toward a particular temple cult. Nevertheless, each system attended to the material needs of cultic functionaries.

The parceling of towns "with their pasturelands" is repeated throughout Joshua 21. Similar language is attested in the Middle Bronze *AT456* where a list of gifted cities begins with, "The city of Emar together with its pasture lands."[2] Similarly, in the land transfer *AT56*, cities are cited "with their districts."[3]

1. *ANET*, 260–62; See also Kitchen, *On the Reliability*, 182.
2. *COS* 2.137:369–70.
3. Hess, "A Typology," 160–70; see especially 162–63.

## EXPLAIN the Story

Joshua 20–21 is an epilogue to the allocation of tribal lands (chs. 13–19), providing detail of the cities of refuge (ch. 20) and Levitical cities (ch. 21). These cities were commanded by Moses while Israel was in Moab (Num 35:1) and are gifted out of the tribal allotments (Num 35:2, 8). These chapters present Israel's response to the good gift of land received in chapters 13–19. That the cities are located on both sides of the Jordan is an additional reminder that the Transjordanian and Cisjordanian tribes comprise all Israel.

The provision of the Levitical cities is concluded in 21:41–42. A further conclusion (vv. 43–45) follows and ends chapters 13–21. This further conclusion highlights the LORD's fulfillment of all the promises made to Israel in respect of the land. Additionally, by citing the "rest" Israel experiences, verses 43–45 anticipate the eastward return of the Transjordanian tribes who had committed to fight alongside their western brothers until "the LORD gives them rest" (1:15). Thus verses 43–45 provide a bridge to the book's epilogue (chs. 22–24) in which the first event is the Transjordanian return.

The allocation of the Levitical cities is a highly structured account:[4]

- Overview of the Levitical allocations (21:1–8)
    - The Levites request the allocation (21:1–2)
    - The Israelites give Levitical cities (21:3–8)
        - The lot for the Kohathites (21:4–5)
        - The lot for the Gershonites (21:6)
        - The lot for the Merarites (21:7)
        - Conclusion: the commandment is fulfilled (21:8)
- Detail of the Levitical allocations (21:9–42)
    - Allocation for the Aaronide Kohathites (21:9–19)
        - Concluding summary (21:19)
    - Allocation for the non-Aaronide Kohathites (21:20–26)
        - Concluding summary (21:26)
    - Allocation for the Gershonites (21:27–33)
        - Concluding summary (21:33)
    - Allocation for the Merarites (21:34–40)
        - Concluding summary (21:40)
    - Conclusion: Forty-eight towns allocated (21:41–42)
- Conclusion to chs. 13–21: All the LORD's promises fulfilled (21:43–45)

4. See Chapter 13 above to set this chapter into the larger context of the third section of Joshua.

Key words appear throughout the chapter, connecting it to ideas present throughout chapters 13–21 and the book of Joshua. First, the idea of "giving" (from *ntn*) the cities underlies the chapter. Israel is commanded to "give" cities to the Levites (v. 2), and the overview of the allocation to all branches of the Levites indicates it does so (v. 3, 9 ["allotted" in NIV], 11, 13, 21).[5] The importance of this word lies in the fact that the land is "given" Israel by God. Not only did the book begin with this reality (1:2), but the conclusion to chapters 13–21 emphasizes all that is given by God (21:43 [2x], 44). Thus, Israel gives out of the abundance of what it has received as gift.

A second key word is the allocation of land superintended by God through the "lot" (*goral*). The word appears eight times in Joshua 21, translated in NIV as both "lot" (vv. 4, 10) and "allotted" (vv. 4, 5, 6, 8, 20, 40). As noted (see Chapter 13 above), this word characterizes the allocation of all western lands. Although the Levitical cities are not part of the tribal allocations per se, they are part of God's design for the equitable distribution of the land. Here, it is the Levitical presence in Israel that is equitably distributed for Israel's benefit.

Finally, while the Levitical bequests are differentiated from the tribal inheritance, they are an intrinsic element of "possessing" (from *yrsh*; see Chapter 13 above) the land. This is apparent for after the bequests are given the word appears in the summarization of all that is possessed (v. 43).

## Overview of the Distribution (21:1–8)

The distribution of Levitical cities is spurred by the initiative of the Levites. They "approach" (from *ngsh*), as did the Judahites before them (14:6). Only these allotments are initiated by a tribe "approaching" Eleazar, Joshua, and the heads of the tribal families (14:1, 6; 21:1), the leaders tasked with overseeing the western allocations (Num 34:16–29; Josh 14:1; 17:4; 19:51). Although the Levites do not inherit a tribal portion, they are yet part of all Israel and thus receive land from the same leaders as distributed the tribal allocations. The Levitical allocation takes place at Shiloh (v. 2), as did the allocations in chapters 18–19. The location is a reminder that all that occurs is "in the presence of the LORD" and thus under his direction (19:51). Confirming the LORD's direction, the Levitical allocation is made (as were the other western allotments) by lot (vv. 4 [2x], 5, 6, 8).

The overview focuses on two things: the LORD's command (vv. 2, 3, 8) and Israelite obedience (vv. 3, 8). The Levites recall the LORD's command (v. 2), and the Israelites respond "as the LORD had commanded" (v. 3). The overview concludes by again noting the allotment occurred "as the LORD had

---

5. The word also appears in verse 8. The Hebrew reads, "the Israelites gave by lot." NIV smooths the translation to "the Israelites allotted."

commanded" (v. 8). The command is "through Moses" (vv. 2, 8) and fulfilled by Joshua as Moses' successor.

Israelite obedience is immediate, as verse 3 indicates. The Hebrew differs from the NIV translation for it notes the Israelite response first, making their obedience clear: "*Israel gave to the Levites from their inheritance* as the LORD had commanded" (emphasis added). Israelite obedience is not only immediate, but costly. The cities are bestowed out of Israel's "own inheritance" (*nahalah*; v. 3), that is, from the very land gifted to them by God's promise. Forty-eight towns are to be gifted as specified in Numbers 35:6, together with their "pasturelands" (*migrash*), an area surrounding the city on which livestock can be grazed (Num 35:4–5). The chapter emphasizes the necessary inclusion of each city's pasturage, using the term after each Levitical city named.[6]

Finally, the overview summarizes the allotments given the sons of Levi who (by birth order) are Gershon, Kohath, and Merari (Num 3:17). The allotments, however, do not follow this order; the NIV notes "the first lot came out for the Kohathites" (v. 4; cf. v. 10). The Kohathites are given pride of place because this clan includes the priestly line of Aaron. This line receives the first allocation (v. 4), and then the non-Aaronide Kohathites receive towns (v. 5). After this, the overview takes up the birth order again (Gershon, Merari; vv. 6–7). This same order is followed in the detailed account of the allocations (vv. 9–40).

All the Kohathite cities are located west of the Jordan. The Aaronide Kohathites receive thirteen towns from the southern tribes of Judah, Simeon, and Benjamin. This locates them close to Jerusalem where the temple will later be situated, allowing ready access for their priestly service. The non-Aaronide Kohathites are located north of their Aaronide kin, receiving ten towns from Ephraim, Dan's original allotment, and the western half-tribe of Manasseh. The Gershonite cities are located across the north of Israel, including Asher and Naphtali west of the Jordan and the eastern half-tribe of Manasseh in Bashan. The Merarites receive twelve towns, distributed across Zebulun, west of the Jordan, and Reuben and Gad east of the Jordan and south of Manasseh.

Forty-eight towns in total are allocated, and the overview concludes with reference to fulfillment of the LORD's command through Moses, given in Numbers 35:6–7.

---

6. The term occurs fifty-seven times in Josh 21, occurring (in the Hebrew) with each Levitical city named. NIV simplifies the translation, using it only after each group of cities. The term is found elsewhere in Joshua only in 14:4, another reference to Levitical cities. In the Old Testament, the term occurs a total of one hundred fourteen times with almost exclusive reference (one hundred nine times) to Levitical cities (Lev 25:34; Num 35:2–7 [5x]; Josh 14:4; 21 [57x]; 1 Chr 6 [42x]; 1 Chr 13:2; 2 Chr 11:14; 31:19) and five times for non-Levitical usage (1 Chr 5:16; Ezek 27:28; 45:2; 48:15, 17).

## Distribution Details (21:9–42)

The more detailed list of Levitical cities proceeds in sections according to the order of the overview: Aaronide Kohathites (vv. 9–19), non-Aaronide Kohathites (vv. 20–26), Gershonites (vv. 27–33), and Merarites (vv. 34–40). Each section begins by naming the branch of the Levites and the contributing tribe(s), followed by a list of the gifted cities.[7] Each individual tribal contribution list concludes with a tally of towns (vv. 16, 18, 22, 24, 25, 27, 29, 31, 32, 35, 37, 39). For each Levitical group, a concluding summary tallies the total number of cities received (vv. 19, 26, 33, 40). That summary provides four pieces of information:

- An introduction that includes the word *kol*, translated as "total" or "all" (vv. 19, 26, 33, 40). This reference to totality is taken up both in the conclusion to the Levitical allotments (v. 41, "forty-eight in all") and repeatedly in the conclusion to chapters 13–21, which emphasizes the Lord gave "all" the land (vv. 43–45; see the discussion below). This pervasive use of "all" within the Levitical allocations and the summative conclusion reveals the Levitical allocations are, indeed, rightly considered part of the Lord's gift of land;
- The branch of the Levites receiving the gift;
- The tally of cities from all contributing tribes; and
- The notice that the cities are contributed "together with their pasturelands."

The allocation of the forty-eight Levitical cities includes the six cities of refuge (although only five are specifically noted as such [vv. 13, 21, 27, 32, 38]; Bezer is not specified [v. 36; see 20:8]). The six cities are evenly distributed among the three branches of the Levitical family:

Hebron, a Levitical and refuge city, is in the Aaronide allotment. It alone, of all the cities in chapter 21, is described with more than its name (vv. 11–13). Hebron was already granted to Caleb as an "inheritance" (*nahalah*; 14:13) and a "portion" (*heleq*; 15:13). The same city is clearly in view here for it, too, has a dual name (Kiriath Arba/Hebron) and is associated with Arba. To account for the one city being gifted twice, an explanation is provided. That is, the actual city and its surrounding pasturelands are gifted to the Levites; to Caleb went his "possession" (*'ahuzzah*; v. 12), which was only the city's fields and villages.

7. Virtually all of the cities listed in the chapter have already appeared in the book. A full listing of these references can be found in Hess, *Joshua*, 311–12. Hess also provides some suggestions for those town names that are uncertain.

| The Kohathites | |
|---|---|
| Aaronide Kohathites | Hebron in Judah |
| Non-Aaronide Kohathites | Gezer in Ephraim |
| The Gershonites | Golan in half-Manasseh (eastern) |
| | Kedesh in Naphtali |
| The Merarites | Bezer in Reuben |
| | Ramoth in Gad |

The explanation does not wholly satisfy, for it seems to contradict what was so clearly stated when the city was gifted to Caleb by Joshua. In what way might only the surrounding fields and villages be considered "Hebron"? Do the different words used to describe Caleb's relationship to Hebron signal a nuance that is unrecoverable ("inheritance" [*nahalah*; 14:13], "portion" [*heleq*; 15:13], "possession" [*'ahuzzah*; v. 12 ])?[8] Is some sort of shared claim in view that sees Caleb and the Levites both holding Hebron but in different capacities? The challenge remains.

**Promises Fulfilled (21:43–45)**

As the lengthy third section of Joshua closes (chs. 13–21), the land has been distributed east and west of the Jordan. Attention has been given to equitable distribution among the tribes who together remain "all Israel." The importance of ongoing Israelite obedience has been made clear. Appointed cities have dispersed Levites throughout Israel and ensured shelter for manslayers. Now, the section's conclusion (vv. 43–45) evokes the words of Deuteronomy 1:8 and Joshua 1:2–6 and recalls the primary themes of the book of Joshua.

The conclusion focuses firmly on God's initiative, and action and can be diagrammed as follows:

The LORD gave Israel all the land he had sworn to give their ancestors
(and)
The LORD gave them rest on every side, just as he had sworn to their
ancestors
Not one of their enemies withstood them;
The LORD gave all their enemies into their hands

8. Hawk, *Joshua*, 223, pursues this avenue, suggesting a conceptual difference between the allotment of a city and its possession.

Not one of the LORD's good promises to Israel failed
(and)
Every one was fulfilled

Two acts of God begin the conclusion. Both are "sworn to the ancestors." First, the land is "given" (v. 43 [2x]) by the LORD according to his oath to the ancestors (vv. 43, 44; see Gen 12:1–3; 15:18–21; 22:17–18; 24:7; 26:3; 50:24). Second, the LORD gives Israel "rest" (Deut 12:10; 25:19). Both are acts promised to Joshua as the book began (1:2, 3, 6, 11, 13, 15) and now pronounced fulfilled. With the fulfillment of these promises, the epilogue is anticipated, for its events occur after entering this "rest" (22:4; 23:1).

The land, and rest in it, are due to God's presence and action on Israel's behalf. This action is stated negatively ("Not one of their enemies withstood them") and positively ("the LORD gave all their enemies into their hands," v. 44). One can recall God's powerful interventions at Jericho and during the pursuit of the southern kings, or Caleb's honest boast that with "the LORD helping me" (14:12) he would drive out the inhabitants. Both supernaturally and through his peoples' exploits, God "gave all their enemies into their hands" (v. 44).

Finally, the conclusion returns to the idea of God's oath to the ancestors that has already been twice noted (vv. 43–44). Now, these "good promises to Israel" are likewise recalled negatively ("Not one failed") and positively ("every one was fulfilled," v. 45). The sworn oath is described as "the good promises" (*hadabar hatob*), a phrase which here is used in a very positive context. The exact phrase will appear later as "good things" (23:15) with the same positive reference of fulfillment, but with an ominous juxtaposition to the potential "evil things" (*hadabar hara'*) that God may in the future bring upon Israel (see Explain the Story at Josh 23:15 [Chapter 21] ). For now, however, no ominous note undermines the conclusion of land distribution.

The conclusion focuses on the totality of God's actions on behalf of Israel, signified by the repetitive use of *kol* ("all," "every"):

- He gave Israel "all" (*kol*) the land;
- Rest is given "just as (in Hebrew, "according to all [*kol*]") he had sworn";
- "Not one of (Hebrew, "none of all [*kol*]") their enemies withstood them";
- The LORD gave "all (*kol*) their enemies" to Israel;
- "Not one of all (*kol*) the LORD's promises failed";
- "Every one (*kol*) was fulfilled."

The emphasis lies on the complete fulfillment of God's promise of the land: all the land is given, all enemies subdued, and rest experienced on every side.

Israel, therefore, "took possession" (from *yrsh*; see Chapter 13) and "settled" in the land (v. 43).

The affirmation of possession does not mean no further work remains to be done. The book has presented a picture of incomplete possession and even directly contradicts the statement that Israel possesses the land (13:1; 23:5). Several failures to take the land have been noted (15:63; 16:10; 17:12–13) as well as Josephite reluctance to do so (17:14–18). Dan has even abandoned its allotted inheritance, seeking an illicit "conquest" elsewhere (19:47).

The difficulty of these concluding verses is obvious: in what way can it affirm Israel's complete possession and rest, and the fulfillment of "all the LORD's good promises," in light of several statements indicating incompleteness? The tension between these two realities is real and an intended part of the book's message. To account for the tension, two possibilities present themselves. First, one can consider the tension between what God has done and what Israel has done. God has done what he promised: the LORD has been faithful and fully given the land. His presence has defeated every enemy and provided Israel rest. On the other hand, Israel has not been faithful and so undercut all God's promises. Israel's disobedience and unfaithfulness account for any non-fulfillment of these promises in the book.

Second, one can consider the tension as between the real and the ideal. The ideal is set out as full possession and complete rest. But the real reckons with Israel's failure and lack of possession. The real also reckons with the ongoing process toward the ideal. Israel has made military claim over portions of the land, but much remains to be taken and the ideal of habitation, full possession, and rest remains in the future. As the narrative continues, the tension between the real and the ideal likewise continues. Should Israel hope to experience in reality the ideal presented in this conclusion, its portion must be full obedience and faithfulness; nothing else will work.

Both these readings take note of the place of Israel's obedience and faithfulness vis-à-vis God's promises and thus provide a fitting conclusion to the third section of Joshua, in which the land is distributed in prospect of habitation. It is this reality that becomes the focus of the book's epilogue: only true devotion to God can ensure Israel's life in the land.

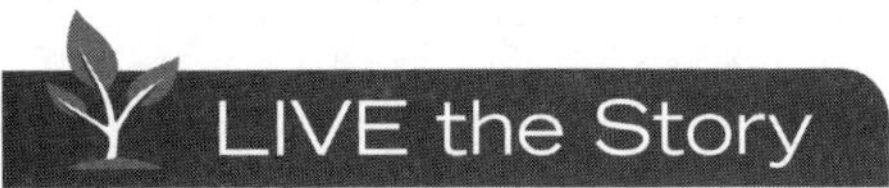


**Providing for Needs: Physical and Spiritual**

Compared to chapter 20, the designation of the Levitical cities is longer and much more detailed, suggesting the great importance of the Levites in Israel.

They are spread throughout the nation and, in their cultic and teaching roles, provide a witness to the covenant. Their influence on the lives of ordinary Israelites has great potential to influence Israelite covenant faithfulness.

Their chosen status within Israel is evident, for the LORD is their inheritance (13:33; 18:7). This special status includes more than just a unique relationship to the LORD. It also attends to their material needs of life (13:14)—it is difficult to provide spiritual leadership if you have to worry about how to feed a family! Together with the offerings the Levites receive, their cities and surrounding lands provide for their material livelihood. Nation and Levites work together for the common life: Israel contributes to the Levites' material needs; the Levites care for Israel's spiritual life.

A similar model is upheld in the New Testament. Jesus dispatches his disciples into the harvest field. They are to heal the sick and preach the kingdom of God, receiving the food and drink the people give them for "the worker deserves his wages" (Luke 10:1–9). Paul likewise affirms this principle of providing the material needs of those whose labor focuses on upholding the spiritual lives of God's people (1 Tim 5:17–18). In Corinth, Paul initially divides his time between manual labor and preaching; with the arrival of Silas and Timothy, their labor frees Paul to focus on preaching the gospel (Acts 18:1–5). Paul also finds his material needs met through the gifts of the Philippian church as he works to further the gospel (Phil 4:10–18).

It seems that this model for ministry is a biblical practice that undergirds the healthy common life of God's people. Today, however, those who enter pastoral ministry may not be assured that a congregation can adequately support a full-time minister. Students graduating seminary know this, and bivocational ministry is a consideration. Bivocational ministry may at times be a second-best option, but it can also be a preferred option arising from a congregation's missional vision.[9] In the same way that the Levites lived among the people, balancing work on their Levitical lands with their cultic responsibilities, a bivocational minister more intentionally shares his or her time between church and community. It can be incredibly difficult to balance the claims of pastoral ministry with the claims of secular employment, but current missional discussions argue that a bivocational model can be not just a second-best financial choice, but an intentionally chosen, missional choice. Paul did at times work to support his ministry (Acts 18:3–4); at other times

---

9. Bivocational pastoral ministry is noted as a new trend in church planting, and as having real benefits within a missional context, although its potential as a second-best option is not overlooked. See discussions at http://www.christianitytoday.com/pastors/2013/january-online-only/five-perks-to-being-bi-vocational.html and http://www.christianitytoday.com/edstetzer/2016/february/trend-2-for-future-of-church-planting-bivocational-ministry.html.

he chose not to receive payment that he could rightly claim as due him (1 Cor 9:9–15). In both cases, Paul's actions were missional—for the sake of the gospel in the world.

## The Now-and-the-Not Yet

The final verses of land distribution (vv. 43–45) end this large section in decided tension. Every one of God's promises is fulfilled, Israel has rest on every side, and has taken possession of the land. Yet chapters 13–21 have repeatedly shown that much land still remains to be taken. The land is *not* fully possessed. This tension has long troubled interpreters, yet it is a tension that the Christian church likewise knows. It is the tension of the now-and-the-not yet, the tension between what God has promised and fully provided, and what his people now experience.

In the cross of Christ, God won the victory. Jesus' words, "It is finished" and his sacrificial death mark the complete end of the power of sin and death. In the death of Christ, the new age of God's rule has broken in to the present age, and the outpoured Spirit stands as proof of the kingdom's inauguration.

At the same time, the Spirit is a downpayment of a fuller reality yet to come. The church prays "your kingdom come, your will be done, on earth as it is in heaven" (Matt 6:10). This is an acknowledgement that we await the establishment in our midst of the kingdom in all its fullness. The church knows too well the tension: sin and death are overcome; sin and death are still realities. Although we have the "firstfruits of the Spirit," with the whole of creation, we

> groan inwardly as we wait eagerly for our adoption to sonship, the redemption of our bodies. For in this hope we were saved. But hope that is seen is no hope at all. Who hopes for what they already have? But if we hope for what we do not yet have, we wait for it patiently. (Rom 8:23–25)

In her volume, *The Liturgical Year: The Spiraling Adventure of the Spiritual Life*,[10] Joan Chittister discusses the season of Advent (from Latin, meaning "coming"). In this four-week season immediately before Christmas, the church reflects on the first and second coming of Christ. It is a season filled with the tension of the now and not yet reality of God's economy. Long observed in liturgical settings, Advent is finding a new place in non-liturgical churches, often as a way to challenge the dominant consumerist message that precedes Christmas.[11]

10. Joan Chittister, *The Liturgical Year: The Spiraling Adventure of the Spiritual Life* (Nashville: Thomas Nelson, 2009).

11. See, for instance, the resources at www.adventconspiracy.org which, working largely through social media, has argued four tenets for a good advent: worship Jesus fully, spend less, give more, and love all.

Chittister writes that Advent calls our attention to three aspects of Christ's coming, each of which acknowledges the now and not yet in which the church lives. First, Advent prepares the church to remember and celebrate Christ's first coming in frail infancy. Second, Advent reflects on God coming to his church in Scripture, through the Eucharist, and in the Spirit-born community. It is the third aspect of Advent's waiting that especially speaks to the church living in the now and not yet tension:

> The final coming to which Advent points us is the Second Coming, the Parousia. It is this coming that whets the desire of the adult soul. At the end of time, Jesus has promised and the Christian believes that the Son will return in glory. Then the reign of God for which we strive with every breath will come in all its fullness. This is the coming for which we wait. This is the fullness for which we long. This is what we really mean when the choir sings into the dark, "Maranatha."[12]

Interestingly, Chittister's comment also reflects on the church's responsibility during this waiting time: the church is to "strive with every breath" for the coming kingdom. The church is to live *for* the kingdom: thinking, speaking, and acting in the ways of the kingdom's justice and peace. Not surprisingly, this was also to be Israel's attitude as they received all that God had promised, while still awaiting the full realization of that promise. In obedience and faith, they were to think, speak, and act according to the rest God had promised them. In this, the tension of their liminal time was similar to the church's own time of waiting. The kingdom is promised; the kingdom is yet to come. In the meantime, we await its coming, living in obedience to the King for whom we wait.

12. Chittister, *The Liturgical Year*, 65.

CHAPTER 20

# Joshua 22:1–34

## LISTEN to the Story

[1]Then Joshua summoned the Reubenites, the Gadites and the half-tribe of Manasseh [2]and said to them, "You have done all that Moses the servant of the LORD commanded, and you have obeyed me in everything I commanded. [3]For a long time now—to this very day—you have not deserted your fellow Israelites but have carried out the mission the LORD your God gave you. [4]Now that the LORD your God has given them rest as he promised, return to your homes in the land that Moses the servant of the LORD gave you on the other side of the Jordan. [5]But be very careful to keep the commandment and the law that Moses the servant of the LORD gave you: to love the LORD your God, to walk in obedience to him, to keep his commands, to hold fast to him and to serve him with all your heart and with all your soul."

[6]Then Joshua blessed them and sent them away, and they went to their homes. [7](To the half-tribe of Manasseh Moses had given land in Bashan, and to the other half of the tribe Joshua gave land on the west side of the Jordan along with their fellow Israelites.) When Joshua sent them home, he blessed them, [8]saying, "Return to your homes with your great wealth—with large herds of livestock, with silver, gold, bronze and iron, and a great quantity of clothing—and divide the plunder from your enemies with your fellow Israelites."

[9]So the Reubenites, the Gadites and the half-tribe of Manasseh left the Israelites at Shiloh in Canaan to return to Gilead, their own land, which they had acquired in accordance with the command of the LORD through Moses.

[10]When they came to Geliloth near the Jordan in the land of Canaan, the Reubenites, the Gadites and the half-tribe of Manasseh built an imposing altar there by the Jordan. [11]And when the Israelites heard that they had built the altar on the border of Canaan at Geliloth near the Jordan on the Israelite side, [12]the whole assembly of Israel gathered at Shiloh to go to war against them.

13So the Israelites sent Phinehas son of Eleazar, the priest, to the land of Gilead—to Reuben, Gad and the half-tribe of Manasseh. 14With him they sent ten of the chief men, one from each of the tribes of Israel, each the head of a family division among the Israelite clans.

15When they went to Gilead—to Reuben, Gad and the half-tribe of Manasseh—they said to them: 16"The whole assembly of the Lord says: 'How could you break faith with the God of Israel like this? How could you turn away from the Lord and build yourselves an altar in rebellion against him now? 17Was not the sin of Peor enough for us? Up to this very day we have not cleansed ourselves from that sin, even though a plague fell on the community of the Lord! 18And are you now turning away from the Lord?

"'If you rebel against the Lord today, tomorrow he will be angry with the whole community of Israel. 19If the land you possess is defiled, come over to the Lord's land, where the Lord's tabernacle stands, and share the land with us. But do not rebel against the Lord or against us by building an altar for yourselves, other than the altar of the Lord our God. 20When Achan son of Zerah was unfaithful in regard to the devoted things, did not wrath come on the whole community of Israel? He was not the only one who died for his sin.'"

21Then Reuben, Gad and the half-tribe of Manasseh replied to the heads of the clans of Israel: 22"The Mighty One, God, the Lord! The Mighty One, God, the Lord! He knows! And let Israel know! If this has been in rebellion or disobedience to the Lord, do not spare us this day. 23If we have built our own altar to turn away from the Lord and to offer burnt offerings and grain offerings, or to sacrifice fellowship offerings on it, may the Lord himself call us to account.

24"No! We did it for fear that some day your descendants might say to ours, 'What do you have to do with the Lord, the God of Israel? 25The Lord has made the Jordan a boundary between us and you—you Reubenites and Gadites! You have no share in the Lord.' So your descendants might cause ours to stop fearing the Lord.

26"That is why we said, 'Let us get ready and build an altar—but not for burnt offerings or sacrifices.' 27On the contrary, it is to be a witness between us and you and the generations that follow, that we will worship the Lord at his sanctuary with our burnt offerings, sacrifices and fellowship offerings. Then in the future your descendants will not be able to say to ours, 'You have no share in the Lord.'

[28]"And we said, 'If they ever say this to us, or to our descendants, we
will answer: Look at the replica of the LORD's altar, which our ancestors
built, not for burnt offerings and sacrifices, but as a witness between us
and you.'
[29]"Far be it from us to rebel against the LORD and turn away from him
today by building an altar for burnt offerings, grain offerings and sacrifices,
other than the altar of the LORD our God that stands before his tabernacle."
[30]When Phinehas the priest and the leaders of the community—
the heads of the clans of the Israelites—heard what Reuben, Gad and
Manasseh had to say, they were pleased. [31]And Phinehas son of Eleazar,
the priest, said to Reuben, Gad and Manasseh, "Today we know that the
LORD is with us, because you have not been unfaithful to the LORD in
this matter. Now you have rescued the Israelites from the LORD's hand."
[32]Then Phinehas son of Eleazar, the priest, and the leaders returned
to Canaan from their meeting with the Reubenites and Gadites in Gilead
and reported to the Israelites. [33]They were glad to hear the report and
praised God. And they talked no more about going to war against them
to devastate the country where the Reubenites and the Gadites lived.
[34]And the Reubenites and the Gadites gave the altar this name:
A Witness Between Us—that the LORD is God.

*Listening to the Text in the Story*: Numbers 13–14, 25, 32; Deuteronomy 12

## Revisiting the Wilderness

Joshua 22 consciously evokes several events of the wilderness generation. The first is the Transjordanian request for the eastern lands (Num 32) to which the eastern tribes now return. That request was earlier explored in this commentary (Listen to the Story, Chapter 1).

A second event that is evoked is Israel's refusal to enter the land; this event has already been discussed as background to Joshua 2 (see Listen to the Story, Chapter 2). The refusal to enter the land is characterized as "rebellion" (Num 14:9; from the Hebrew root *mrd*), and it is this same Hebrew root that in Joshua 22 repeatedly characterizes the altar-building (vv. 16, 18, 19 [2x], 22, 29). In Numbers and Joshua, it is only in these two places that this important word is utilized. By characterizing the altar-building as "rebellion," Joshua 22 implicitly likens it to the great sin of the wilderness. The altar-building holds the same threat to Israel's life as the earlier wilderness sin.

Yet a third event of the wilderness generation is evoked in Joshua 22. It is the "sin of Peor" (Josh 22:17), a reference to events in Numbers 25 where the Israelites sinned sexually with Moabite women and worshiped Baal of Peor. Israel's sin aroused God's anger, and he ordered the death of the sinful leaders. In addition, a plague appeared in the camp as judgment against Israel. The action of Phinehas, the son of Eleazar, turned God's anger away and the plague ended. It is this same Phinehas who takes the lead in Joshua 22.

The sin of Baal Peor and the building of the altar are both characterized as "unfaithful" or "breaking faith" (the same noun, *ma'al,* is used in Num 31:16; Josh 22:16, 20, 22, 31). In a further comparison, the sin of Achan is likewise *ma'al* (Josh 7:1). These past events and the devastating judgment they precipitated are indelibly imprinted upon Israel's memory. By likening the altar-building to the heinous sins at Baal Peor and Jericho, the delegation expresses their fear that the altar will likewise bring God's judgment upon his people (22:20, 31).

### One Place for Sacrifice

Both the delegation (v. 19) and the Transjordanian tribes (vv, 23, 26–29) are clear that should the altar be for the purpose of sacrifice, it would violate God's command. That command is expressed clearly in passages such as Deuteronomy 12. The specification that sacrifice be limited to the place "where God would put his name" underlies the tabernacle's erection at Shiloh. See further discussion of this background issue in Listen to the Story in Chapter 17.

## EXPLAIN the Story

Joshua 22 begins the concluding fourth section of the book. God's words to Joshua in chapter 1 set the agenda for each section of the book (see Explain the Story, Chapter 1). In the first section (1:1–5:12), Israel "crossed" the Jordan as God had commanded (1:2). In the second (5:13–12:24), Israel finds success in taking the land; none is able to withstand them (1:3–5). In the third section, the land is distributed as Israel's inheritance (13:1–21:45). Finally, section four takes up God's command that the Book of the Law govern Israel's life (1:7–9). In chapter 22 Joshua urges the Transjordanians to wholly "serve" (from *'bd*) God (v. 5); they affirm they will "worship" (in Hebrew, "perform the service" [both using the root *'bd*]) the LORD (v. 27).[1] In the conclusion's consternation over the Transjordanian altar, in Joshua's final address (ch. 23), and in the

1. The Hebrew root noted here has already been used in the book, particularly to describe Moses, the "servant" of the LORD. But only in this final section is the root used in the sense of "worship," occurring twenty-one times in three chapters (22:5, 27 [2x]; 23:7, 16; 24:2, 14 [3x], 15 [4x], 16, 18, 19, 20, 21, 22, 24, 31).

covenant renewed at Shechem (ch. 24), Israel's adherence to the law of Moses is explored through the paradigms of right worship and covenant obedience. Only by these can Israel remain in the land.

Joshua 22–24 closes the book with many partings. Not only do the Transjordanian tribes depart east to their territory, but Joshua prepares for his departure with an address reminiscent of Joshua 1 (ch. 23) and with a renewal of the covenant (ch. 24). In his final words, Joshua calls the Israelites to continue to worship and serve God after his departure. In the book's final verses, Joshua and Eleazar die (24:29–33). Whether Israel upholds Joshua's call to obedient service after Israel's key leaders die is left to the book of Judges.

Finally, Joshua 22–24 revisits the ongoing question of the identity of "Israel" and whether it includes the Transjordanian tribes. This concern was present as the book began (see above, Chapter 1), was visited throughout, and remains as the book concludes. Joshua clearly includes the Transjordanians with their "fellow Israelites" (22:3), and therefore his summons of "all Israel" includes them (23:2). They are pointedly part of the covenant renewal as Joshua summons "all the tribes" (24:1). But in chapter 22, the altar-building, the dispatch of the delegation, and the conversation that ensues reveal this unity continues highly disputed, and the eastern tribes are a suspect part of Israel. Ultimately, the chapters reveal that there is more to being "Israel" than living within the promised land or (as demonstrated by those such as Rahab, Achan, and the Gibeonites) being ethnically Israelite. The book's concluding section points to right worship and covenant obedience as the true hallmarks of God's people.

## Heading Home (22:1–9)

In a passage that reveals the tension surrounding the Transjordanian status within Israel, Joshua releases the two and a half tribes to their eastern territory. Their return home is precipitated by the "rest" Israel now experiences (21:44; 22:4). It is this rest that signals the fulfillment of the Transjordanian pledge to assist their fellow Israelites (1:14–15). The two and a half tribes will "return" (vv. 8, 9) to their land on "the other side" (from *'br*). As Israel once "crossed" (from *'br*) the Jordan, the Transjordanian tribes will now affect their own crossing—not to the promised land given by God (1:2; 22:4) but to concessionary land given by Moses (v. 4; see Chapter 1 above, on 1:1–9). The different status of this land might be signaled by the word used to describe it. It is an *'ahuzzah* ("land" in NIV; vv. 4, 9, 19). The term is not necessarily negative (for the western land is also called an *'ahuzzah* in v. 19), but never in this chapter is the eastern land called an "inheritance" (as it has been elsewhere; see 13:23, 28).

Despite the problematic Transjordanian land choice, Joshua commends them in several ways. They have responded fully to all that "Moses the servant of the LORD commanded" and obeyed "in everything I [Joshua] commanded" (v. 2). The commandment is central in Joshua's words to the Transjordanians, being referenced six times in five verses (either nominally or verbally).[2] The centrality of the commandment accounts for the frequent reference to Moses in these verses (five times in vv. 1–9), for the Transjordanians pledged obedience to Moses by whom God gave the "Book of the Law" (see Listen to the Story, Chapter 1). Moses is here the "servant of the LORD" (vv. 2, 4, 5) as he has been throughout Joshua (see Listen to the Story, Chapter 1). Joshua has throughout the book fulfilled Moses' ministry and will himself be named the "servant of the LORD" as the book closes (24:29).

Reference to the commands given by Moses and Joshua recalls Joshua's exchange with the eastern tribes in chapter 1 (vv. 13, 16). The Transjordanians pledged that "Just as we fully obeyed Moses, so we will obey you" (1:17). Joshua affirms that they have remained committed for a very long time, without deserting the Israelites. They "have done" what they pledged and "carried out" the "mission" (vv. 2–3). Each of these three words arises from the Hebrew root (*shmr*)[3] and speaks positively of their past faithfulness. Later, using the same root, Joshua will twice urge them to prospective faithfulness by "keeping" (from *shmr*) the commandments (v. 5).

Joshua's commendation considers the Transjordanians part of all Israel. The western tribes are their "fellow Israelites" (v. 3) and "your brothers" (v. 4; NIV reads only "them"). They are fully Israel because God repeatedly is referenced as "your God" (vv. 3, 4, 5). A defining mark of their inclusion is their obedience to the law of Moses—the law given for all Israel.

Two commissions follow the commendation. The first releases them to return home (v. 4). Although that home is outside the promised land, Joshua releases them to it in recognition of their obedience. The second commission starts this new venture in the same way the book began: with a call for obedience to the law (v. 5). While Joshua does not specify that such obedience equals success (as he himself was told; 1:7, 8), the implication is there nonetheless.

Joshua charges them to "be very careful to keep the commandment and the law that Moses the servant of the LORD gave you" (v. 5). This law given by

2. V. 2 "Moses . . . *commanded*" and "I *commanded*"; v. 3 "carried out the mission the LORD your God gave you" renders the Hebrew phrase "carried out the mission of the *commandment* of the LORD your God"; v. 5 "the *commandment* . . . that Moses . . . *commanded* you . . . to keep his *commands*." Emphasis added.

3. A wooden translation of the Hebrew shows how the verbal and nominal forms relate and reflect a similar idea: "they guarded/kept" what they pledged and "guarded/kept" the "thing to be guarded/kept."

Moses is, in context, the law of Deuteronomy (see Listen to the Story, Chapter 1). Despite their settlement outside of the promised land, they are held to the same law as given all Israel. It is not surprising, then, that this charge draws on the language of Deuteronomy, calling them to:

- Love the Lord your God (Deut 6:5; 11:13, 22; 19:9; 30:6, 16, 20);
- To walk in obedience to him (in Hebrew, "to walk in [all] his ways"; Deut 8:6; 10:12; 11:22; 19:9; 30:16);
- To keep his commands (Deut 4:40; 8:2, 11; 13:4[5], 18[19]; 26:18; 28:1, 15; 30:10, 16);
- To hold fast to him (Deut 10:20; 11:22; 13:4[5]; 30:20); and
- To serve him (Deut 6:13; 11:13).

The final element in this charge, "to serve him" (from *'bd*), introduces the key word for chapters 22–24. Service, or worship, is a wholehearted act. Echoing Deuteronomy 6:5, service requires "all your heart and all your soul."

The commission ended, Joshua releases them and they return home (v. 6). At this moment of departure, a brief explanation on the divided Manassite tribe raises the conflicted status of Israel again. Only one half of Manasseh makes the journey; the rest remain "with their fellow Israelites" west of the Jordan (v. 7). Yet, the great wealth of the eastern tribes forestalls any conclusion that their choice of land resulted in God withholding plunder from them. Their "great wealth" includes "large herds," diverse and precious metals, and "great quantities of clothing" (v. 8). Earlier, Israel was to "divide" the land among the tribes; now the eastern tribes are to "divide" the plunder with their "fellow Israelites." These "fellow Israelites" may be the western tribes identified in verse 7. If so, the reason for such sharing is uncertain. More likely, the "fellow Israelites" are those Transjordanians who remained east of the Jordan when the men of war went to battle (Num 32:27; see similarly 1 Sam 30:24). To call them "fellow Israelites" is an intentional inclusion of easterners within Israel.

Joshua's final act toward them reveals they are indeed worthy Israelites: he blesses them. The action is striking and twice noted (vv. 6, 7). Elsewhere, Joshua has blessed only Caleb. This places the Transjordanians (despite their choice of land) in the company of a very faithful man. Rather than denigrating the Transjordanians, Joshua's blessing honors them.

Though blessed, the tension surrounding the Transjordanians remains in the narrative conclusion (v. 9). On one side of the Jordan are the "Israelites," those who are in "Shiloh in Canaan." This is the place of the tabernacle. On the other side are "the Reubenites, the Gadites, and the half-tribe of Manasseh," those who are in Gilead. It is "their own land," given by God. But it came through Moses, not the divinely-supervised lot. As the chapter progresses,

"Canaan" (vv. 9, 10, 11, 32) and "Gilead" (vv. 9, 13, 15, 32) designate the western and eastern lands, respectively.

### Altar Wars (22:10–31)

The tension signaled in verse 9 becomes the main story in these verses. Joshua had summoned the eastern tribes by name (v. 1) but includes them alongside their "fellow Israelites" (v. 3) as part of all Israel. The ongoing narrative does not continue this inclusive spirit; the eastern tribes will be named only as "Reubenites, Gadites, and the half-tribe of Manasseh" (vv. 10, 11 ["they" in NIV], 13, 15, 21; also "Reubenites and Gadites" [vv. 25, 32, 33, 34] and "Reuben, Gad, and Manasseh" [vv. 30, 31]). By contrast, the western tribes will be named in terms that suggest they alone comprise Israel. Rarely, the labeling is ambiguous as to whether western or eastern tribes are in view. These labels will be noted as this commentary proceeds.

Enroute home, the two and a half tribes build an altar on the Jordan's western side. The altar's location is described ambiguously, and translations vary as to whether it is east or west of the Jordan. The NIV clearly places it on the western side, which is the more natural reading of the various descriptors. This seems consistent with the response of the western tribes: if they understand the eastern side to somehow be "less Israel," it is difficult to account for their visceral reaction. They are concerned with the purity of the LORD's land and unconcerned about the "defiled land" of the east (v. 19); in their eyes, the altar erected west of the Jordan threatens the purity of the promised land.

It is revealed later that the tension between eastern and western tribes is the impetus behind the altar (vv. 24–25). For now, however, no reason is given. The altar is "imposing" and clearly designed to be seen and noticed—but by whom is not stated. The structure is not a stone marker or memorial such as has appeared already in Joshua (4:8–9; 7:25–26; 8:29; 10:27). It is an altar—a *mizbeah*—a structure whose purpose is sacrifice. That this is the usual intended use of a *mizbeah* both tribes agree (vv. 19, 26).

The altar is built, and word reaches "the Israelites"—clearly, the western tribes (v. 11). The sense that they alone comprise Israel is strengthened as it is said the "whole assembly of Israel" gathers at Shiloh (v. 12).[4] Although

4. The ensuing commentary discussion engages the different ways the community is labelled in vv. 12, 16, 17, 18, and 20. For ease of comparison, the Hebrew transliteration, and NIV translation of each phrase is here provided:

v. 12, *kol-ʿadat bene yisrael* (the whole assembly of Israel);
v. 16, *kol ʿadat yhwh* (the whole assembly of the LORD);
v. 17, *baʿadat yhwh* (on the community of the LORD);
v. 18, *kol-ʿadat yisrael* (the whole community of Israel);
v. 20, *kol-ʿadat yisrael* (the whole community of Israel).

gathered at Shiloh, no mention is made of inquiry at the tabernacle "before the Lord." Instead, warfare is immediately determined "against them"—the eastern tribes (v. 12).

Before war is engaged, Israel exercises some restraint. They dispatch a delegation led by Phinehas the priest and including representatives from the ten tribes. From Shiloh in Canaan they head east, catching up with the eastern tribes in Gilead. In matters of cultic violation, Phinehas has shown himself "zealous" for the Lord's honor (Num 25:11), acting swiftly against the guilty (Num 25:7–8). Now, he acts in restraint and a series of questions are posed—although less in the spirit of discovery than accusation. The delegation assumes the worst: that the altar is for sacrifice and thus contravenes the law and Israel's covenant life.

The delegation is a messenger for "the whole assembly of the Lord" (v. 16). The phrase is similar to that of verse 12 and refers to the western tribes—another telling exclusionary identification. The delegation's message begins with four severe questions (vv. 16–18a). These questions are followed by an expression of fear (v. 18b), and a proposed solution (v. 19). Finally, the delegation rests its case with a powerful illustration of the consequences they fear (v. 20).

The four questions demand:

1. "How could you break faith with the God of Israel like this?" (v. 16). To "break faith" (here using the nominal and verbal form of *m'l*) indicates sin or disloyalty and (as here) is against God rather than humans. Other places where both noun and verb appear together speak of being "unfaithful to the Lord" (Lev 5:15; 6:2[5:21]), or of "unfaithfulness . . . toward me [the Lord]" (Lev 26:40), or of one who is "unfaithful to the Lord" (Num 5:6). Elsewhere, the verbal usage speaks of those who "broke faith with me [the Lord] . . . at the waters of Meribah" (Deut 32:51), or of those who enticed Israel "to be unfaithful to the Lord in the Peor incident" (Num 31:16).
2. "How could you turn away from the Lord and build yourselves an altar in rebellion against him now?" (v. 16). This question has two parts. The first is the accusation they "turn away" from the Lord and is asked again in question four. The second part of the question accuses them of "rebellion"—the consequence of "turning away"—demonstrated in altar-building. As noted in Listen to the Story above, the Hebrew root *mrd*, from which comes "rebel" and "rebellion," is utilized in Numbers and Joshua only in Numbers 14:9 and in Joshua 22 where it occurs six times (as a verb in vv. 16, 18, 19 [2x], 29; as a noun in v. 22).

The association reveals the western tribes count the altar-building to be as heinous as the disastrous wilderness rebellion; might they even fear that a similarly disastrous response from God is therefore in the offing? Their final words reveal this to be so (v. 31).

3. "Was not the sin of Peor enough for us?" (v. 17). There is pathos and frustration in these words that compare the magnitude of sinful altar-building to the sin of Peor. The events of Peor involved Israel with the Baal of Peor and sexual sin. The sin brought plague upon Israel and death to the sinners in their midst (Num 25:4–5). Despite the pathos and frustration of this question, the western tribes apparently plan to execute a similar judgment by going to war against their eastern brothers.

   The western tribes acknowledge the ongoing taint of that past event, despite the plague that fell on "the community of the LORD" (v. 17). The "community of the LORD" is the same phrase that appears in verse 16, where it is clearly the western tribes that are identified. By using the same phrase to now recall the past community, is the delegation's understanding of past events shifting? Baal Peor affected the LORD's community—Israel. In the delegation's eyes, is this now only the western tribes?
4. "Are you now turning away from the LORD?" (v. 18). This is the final question, posing the second question again, and once again equating turning away with rebellion (vv. 16, 18). "Turning away" is later denied more than once (vv. 23, 29).

Instead of pausing for a response, the delegation rushes on to voice its first fear: that rebellion will rouse God's anger against the "whole community of Israel" (v. 18). But what community do they have in mind? The western tribes only? The phrase is very similar to that of verse 12, and not wholly dissimilar to that of verses 16 and 17. In verses 12 and 16, the western tribes are in view but in verse 17 it is not as clear. Is the reference in verse 18, then, another indication that the western tribes are redefining the identity of the "whole community of Israel" to exclude the Transjordanians? The ambiguity creates tension regarding the definition of "Israel."

The delegation now turns from voicing fear to voicing its proposed solution. It urges the eastern tribes to relocate to the "LORD's land" where the "LORD's tabernacle stands" (v. 19). The Shiloh altar is the authorized altar of the "LORD *our* God" and is contrasted to the unauthorized altar built "for yourselves" (v. 19, emphasis added). The contrast pits the legitimate altar commanded for Israel against the illegitimate altar built "for yourselves." But is there also an assertion of a proprietary relationship of the western tribes to the LORD *our* God? In light of the exploration in this section of the various ways the western tribes define the community, it is possible that they are claiming themselves the true Israel, and thus God as *their* God.

Despite the ambiguity, what is clear from the delegation's words is that they consider the Jordan a fixed boundary. The Transjordanians are urged to worship on the right side of that boundary, in the undefiled land of promise.

Finally, to illustrate the severity of the threat posed by the altar-building, the delegation voices a concluding fear of potential consequences. It is tied to the memory of the sin of Achan. Through Achan's sin, Israel acted "unfaithfully" (Josh 7:1); this is the accusation against the eastern tribes (vv. 16, 22, 31). The fear is that as occurred then, so God's wrath will come now upon the "whole community of Israel" (v. 20). Once again, how should this community be identified? Certainly, in the Achan narrative, God's wrath came upon all the tribes, and thus one might so define the "whole community of Israel" in verse 20. But the phrase is identical to that of verse 18, and a similar ambiguity could be understood here. Is the delegation's fear on behalf of the western tribes alone? Despite the ambiguity around the community's identification, what is clear is the fear that, for the (perceived) sin of the altar, many will die.

The narrative's ambiguity regarding the identification of the "assembly" and "community" of Israel is intentional and a further reflection of the uncertainty regarding the Transjordanian status throughout Joshua (for instance, in chs. 1, 4, 13). Can the Transjordanians, east of the Jordan, be truly part of Israel? Does their unauthorized altar—by violating covenant law—attest to their outsider status? It is this very question that the eastern tribes address in their response.

"Reuben, Gad, and the half-tribe of Manasseh" respond vehemently and express their heightened distress by twice invoking God as "the Mighty One, God, the LORD" (v. 22). Invoking a mighty God, they assert he has power to know the truth; by invoking the LORD, they assert he is the covenant God with whom they stand in covenant relationship. The Transjordanians also call "Israel" to know the truth, ironically adopting the western tribes' own characterization of themselves as "Israel."

Positing the possibility that they are guilty as charged, they affirm that Israel should "not spare" them (v. 22). By this, they acknowledge the seriousness of the charges. More forcefully, they plead that the "LORD himself [will] call us to account" (v. 23). In this, they place their case before a judge who is higher and more powerful than the western tribes. Using the language of the charges leveled against them, they sketch the imputed offense as "rebellion" (*mrd*; v. 22; charged in vv. 16, 18, 19), "disobedience" (*mʿl*; v. 22; charged in

vv. 16 ["breaking faith"], 20, 31 ["unfaithful"]), and "turning away" (v. 23; charged in vv. 16, 18).

Their denial is a sharp "No!" followed by a twice-repeated argument. They state the purpose of the altar in both negative and positive terms and repeat their motivating fear three times. Their argument can be sketched as follows:

- First statement of argument (vv. 24–27)
  - Motivation: fear of future exclusion and loss of worship (vv. 24–25)
    - Answer: build an altar (v. 26)
      - Negative purpose: not for sacrifice (v. 26)
      - Positive purpose: as a witness (v. 27)
        - Witness to worship the Lord
        - Witness for sacrifices at sanctuary
  - Motivation: fear of future exclusion (v. 27b)
- Second statement of argument (v. 28)
  - Motivation: fear of future exclusion and loss of worship (v. 28)
    - Answer: proof of the altar (v. 28)
      - Negative purpose: not for sacrifice (v. 28)
      - Positive purpose: as a witness (v. 28)
- Summary statement: denial of all charges (v. 29)

Their motivation is clearly stated. They fear future western generations will deny Transjordanian participation in Israel and relationship with Israel's God (vv. 24, 27, 28). They anticipate the Jordan boundary will eventuate in this rejection and lead to the charge they have "no share" in the Lord (vv. 25, 27). The "share" denied them is the same word (from *hlq*) found throughout Joshua 13–21. It describes both Israel "dividing" the land and the "portion" that all should receive. Ironically, the fear is that those who received such a "share" will now deny the Transjordanian share—not in the land, but in the One who gives the land. This fear underlies the Transjordanian's greater anticipation: that the rejection will lead to them to stop "fearing the Lord" (v. 25). That is, they fear they will not fulfill Joshua's commission to them (v. 5).

The altar is erected as a witness against these future charges. It is emphatically stated that the altar is *not* for sacrifice (vv. 26, 28). This negation is even further emphasized, for they add that the altar's witness is that they will conduct all such sacrifice at the Lord's sanctuary (v. 27). Positively, the altar *is* a witness to Transjordanian commitment to "worship the Lord." Again, this takes up Joshua's charge to the Transjordanians (v. 5).

The conclusion of the argument revisits the charges made by the western tribes. The Transjordanians strongly aver the altar is neither rebellion nor turning away from the Lord. Rather, its witness is that they will offer sacrifices only at the LORD's altar—not any other altar but the one "before his tabernacle" (v. 29). Notably, they claim the LORD as "our God," firmly rejecting any exclusive claim to the LORD made by the western tribes (v. 19).

The Transjordanian's argument does not address why an altar was erected (rather than a memorial stone), nor does the narrative affirm the veracity of the Transjordanian claim. But the Transjordanian argument is enough for the delegation. They accept—or choose to accept—the proffered explanation. Yet their response is not entirely free of the ambiguities that aroused the Transjordanian fear of exclusion. Phinehas rejoices that the "LORD is with us"—with no clear indication as to who is included in that "us." He removes the charge that the Transjordanians have been unfaithful (v. 31) and voices palpable relief that "you have rescued the Israelites." But are the Israelites here the western tribes according to the earlier words of the delegation, or does Phinehas now broaden that group to include their eastern brothers? The tension is not fully resolved, and the stage remains set for the very exclusion the Transjordanians fear.

### Heading Home with a Witness (22:32–34)

Much "turning" and "returning" has taken place in this narrative. It began with Transjordanians released to "return" home (vv. 8, 9; using the Hebrew root *shwb*). When they built the altar, they were accused of and denied "turning" from the LORD (vv. 16, 18, 23, 29; using the same root). Now, the delegation "returns" home and "reports" (v. 32; literally, "returns a word"). The western tribes are pleased and "praise" God (v. 33), which is the same word as when Joshua "blessed" the Transjordanians (vv. 6, 7). War is averted, leaving the Reubenites and Gadites in the "country where [they] lived." It is a rapprochement, but one that does not wholly heal the rift between the two groups.

Throughout the narrative, the tension between eastern and western tribes has been overtly attested and covertly suggested. As this chapter concludes, that tension remains. The delegation returns to Canaan, leaving the Reubenites and Gadites in Gilead. The dividing line of the Jordan remains intact. The NIV takes up the sense of this tension well, noting that the delegation reports to the "Israelites" (v. 32; the Hebrew reads only "them"). War is averted and the westerners praise God. But the final line of the narrative returns to the altar. It is named by the easterners: "A Witness between Us—that the LORD is God" (v. 34). It is both a hopeful and an ominous ending.

It is hopeful in that the Transjordanians have voiced their commitment to God and affirm the altar as testimony to their word. Their part in the book began with them affirming their commitment to their word (1:16–17), and the book attests they fulfilled their word. One hopes the same commitment will arise out of the altar that witnesses they will worship the LORD rightly, and that the one Lord will be worshiped as God by both easterners and westerners. But the altar as witness is also ominous. Built out of fear of exclusion, it stands at the Jordan boundary. It remains to be seen whether the altar's witness will overcome that dividing line. Will the Jordan become a marker of who comprises Israel? Will Israel remain united as eastern and western tribes? The undercurrents of the chapter suggest the unity of "all Israel" will not hold.

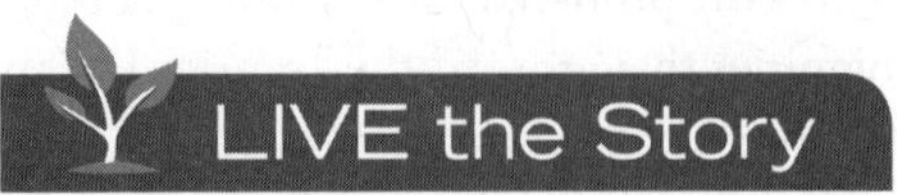


**Beyond the Jordan, but not Forgotten**

Joshua 22 reveals once again the ambiguity surrounding the Transjordanian tribes. Their status is openly challenged and not fully resolved. The immediate confrontation is amicably resolved, and the Transjordanians are present at the subsequent covenant renewal (24:1). But what of the Transjordanians *after* the book of Joshua? Does their choice of land outside the promised land cause them to fade from view? Is the ambiguity with which they are associated in Joshua continued, or even resolved on the negative side of the ledger? Do they continue in the worship of the one, true God? It is true that the rest of the Old Testament does not focus on the Transjordanians, but they are certainly present. A quick survey reveals their ongoing participation in Israel.

The book of Judges focuses west of the Jordan, but the Transjordanian tribes are not wholly overlooked. Deborah chides Reuben and Gilead for non-participation in battle (Judg 5:15–17), which suggests the west expected them to stand as military allies. Gilead falls under Ammonite oppression (10:6–8), and two judges arise from Gilead: the minor judge Jair (10:3) and the major judge Jephthah (11:1).

The Transjordan plays a role in the monarchic era as well. Its fighting men support David at Hebron (1 Chr 12:8, 37–38 [9, 38–39]) and, during Absalom's rebellion, David seeks refuge east of the Jordan (2 Sam 17:27; 19:3). David's control extends to the Transjordan, as evidenced by his census of its fighting men (2 Sam 24:5–6). Solomon also exercises control over the Transjordan, incorporating it into his new administrative system (1 Kgs. 4:13–14, 19).

In the ninth century BC, Israelite control extends east over the Jordan. Israel engages its northern enemy, Aram, at Ramoth Gilead, an eastern Levitical city (2 Kgs 9:15). In that city, Jehu is anointed king over Israel and returns west of the Jordan to overthrow the ruling dynasty of Ahab (2 Kings 9–10). Although successful in his coup, God punishes Jehu for his cultic sins. This is realized through the reduction of Israel's Transjordanian territory as Hazael "overpowered Israelites throughout their territory east of the Jordan in all the land of Gilead (the region of Gad, Reuben and Manasseh)" (10:32–33). Those territories are recovered (likely by Jeroboam II; 2 Kgs 14:25), only to be lost again in the eighth century BC to Assyria (1 Chr 5:26). It is in the eighth century BC that Israel experiences increased monarchic instability. In rapid succession, different families and factions hold power, and two of these kings come from the Transjordan: Shallum (2 Kgs 15:13) and Pekah (2 Kgs 15:25).

The Transjordan also figures in prophetic ministry. For instance, the anointing of Jehu as king over Israel fulfills God's word to the great prophet Elijah, who is from Gilead (2 Kgs 17:1). This prophet serves as God's instrument against apostate Israel, ministering west of the Jordan.

Finally, the prophet Ezekiel definitively addresses the tenuous status of the Transjordanian tribes. Sketching boundaries of an idealized Israel, the Jordan is the unequivocal eastern boundary (Ezek 47:15–20). Manasseh (with only one portion), Reuben, and Gad are located with all Israel west of the Jordan (48:4, 6, 27). Ezekiel's vision of a perfected, ideal Israel removes the ambiguity surrounding these tribes that is evident throughout Joshua. They are placed where God had always envisioned them, within the promised land.

The land of the Transjordan is never the primary focus of the Old Testament, which accords with its limited role in Joshua. But (as in Joshua) the Transjordan is not forgotten in the Old Testament. As part of all Israel, it plays a role in its spiritual, military, and monarchic leadership. Ultimately, it is Ezekiel's vision that repairs the ambiguity surrounding the Transjordan. His full inclusion of it into the promised land reflects God's own testimony which is recorded twice in the Psalter (60:7 [9]; 108:8 [9]): "Gilead is mine, and Manasseh is mine."

In moving to the New Testament, the categories of "Transjordanian" and "Cisjordanian" do not apply. Israel is one entity, a Roman province that spans the Jordan River. But, as the categories of "Transjordanian" and "Cisjordanian" do not apply, neither does the ambiguity apparent in Joshua. The Transjordanian land is honored, for Jesus' ministry is not limited to west of the Jordan. Significant events take place east, "beyond the Jordan," and this liminal space is often for Jesus a place of safety against those from west of the Jordan. So, Jesus is baptized "at Bethany on the other side of the Jordan, where John was baptizing" (John 1:28–34). He calls his first disciples in the same place (John 1:35–51; cf. 10:40–42). Significant ministry takes place at Bethsaida (Mark 8:22–26), on the eastern shores of Galilee (Mark 5:1–20; Luke 8:26–29), in the Decapolis (Mark 7:31–37), in Caesarea Philippi (Matt 16:13–20), and in the region of Judea on the other side of the Jordan (Matt 19:1–12)—all in the ancient Transjordanian lands. Mary and Martha send word to Jesus who is "across the Jordan," where he has sought safety from the

Jews (John 10:40–11:16). Even the great crowds that follow Jesus include many from the Transjordan (Matt 4:25; 19:1–2; Mark 3:8; 10:1).

Jesus' baptism "beyond the Jordan" and his public ministry there accords with God's word in the above psalms and the full inclusion of the Transjordanians as "all Israel" in Joshua. There is no ambiguity: Jesus does not avoid the eastern territory because it is outside the promised land or because of its history. Along with Jerusalem (the heart of the promised land), and Galilee, Tyre, and Sidon (the realm of the gentiles), the Transjordan receives Christ's message and is hallowed by his presence.

### If You Think You Are Standing Firm, Be Careful!

The return of the Transjordanians should be a time of celebration: the land is taken, and Joshua sends the eastern tribes home, blessing them for their faithfulness. All Israel can now enjoy the rest the land provides. The threat of the altar turns the event from celebration to cautionary tale.

Referencing the great wilderness sin of Israelite refusal to enter the land, pairing it with the sin of Baal Peor, and throwing in the sin of Achan for good measure, the description of the altar's dangerous potential is made clear. As the book draws to a close, this chapter is a reminder that falling away from the covenant can easily occur. The first message of the epilogue is this: Israel is not guaranteed its life in the land. Should the altar be for sacrifice in contravention of the law, it will be a sin as egregious as that of the wilderness, of Baal Peor, and of Achan. Israel can again stand under God's wrath and suffer severe discipline. The celebration this chapter *should* engage is overcast with warning: in the teeth of promises fulfilled, be careful that you do not sin again! It is a fitting warning to begin an epilogue that calls Israel to right worship.

In 1 Corinthians 8–10, the apostle Paul writes a fledging church living in the midst of an idolatrous culture. It is a situation not dissimilar to Israel's as it enters the land. Paul warns the church to flee idolatry and live so they are not tempted away from true worship. Again, the parallel to the moment recorded in Joshua 22 is striking.

To illustrate the danger of sin and its consequences, Paul draws on examples from Israel's history. The examples are apt, Paul says, because "these things happened to them as examples and were written down as warnings for us, on whom the culmination of the ages has come" (1 Cor 10:11). Paul anticipates the examples will keep the church "from setting our hearts on evil things as they did" (v. 6).

Two of the examples Paul chooses are those that appear in Joshua 22: the wilderness refusal to enter the land and Baal Peor. It seems that these two events are, both for ancient Israel and for Paul, paradigmatic examples of covenant unfaithfulness. Referencing the refusal to enter the land, Paul comments, "Nevertheless, God was not pleased with most of them; their bodies were scattered in the wilderness" (v. 5). This aligns with the judgment pronounced in Numbers 14:29, 32–33. Paul may also refer to this event when he later references the sinful grumbling and the violent punishment by the "destroying angel" (v. 10; see Num 14:2, 29, 37), although the events of Numbers 16 seem better suited to the sudden death Paul cites (Num 16:2, 41–49). Referencing Baal of Peor, Paul warns that "we should not commit sexual immorality, as some of them did—and in one day twenty-three thousand of them died" (v. 8; see Num 25:1, 9). Along with these sins, Paul also references the golden calf of Sinai (v. 7; see Exod 32:5–6) and Israel's testing of God, visited with punishment by snakes (v. 9; see Num 21:4–9).

Joshua 22 opens the epilogue of the book with a warning. Called to worship only the true and living God, Israel is surrounded by idolatry; it is a threat to Israel's covenant worship. Within such a context, Joshua 22, paired with the call to committed worship and covenant renewal in the book's epilogue, stands as a warning and prescription against sin. For an exilic audience pondering how covenant sinfulness led to exile, these chapters provide an answer. They also reveal the way back to covenant life: turning from idolatry, standing firm against its temptation, and renewing covenant commitments.

Paul's message to the church seems clear. He speaks to people of the new covenant, embarking on the life of Christ. He warns that when we think we stand secure, we must be careful that we are not tempted to sin. We, like ancient Israel, face "temptations . . . common to mankind" (1 Cor 10:13). Paul illustrates from Israel's history the grave effects of sin. The danger is real. Sin must be marked and resisted for the full experience of covenant life—whether that covenant life is that of Israel or of the church. The good news is that always, God is faithful and "will not let you be tempted beyond what you can bear. But when you are tempted, he will also provide a way out so that you can endure it" (1 Cor 10:13).

In a final resonance with Joshua 22, Paul's illustrations are closely followed by instruction on the Lord's Supper (1 Cor 11:23–34). As in the epilogue of Joshua, the warning against sin is followed by the call to covenant renewal (Josh 24). For both Israel and the church, faithful covenant life is a matter of turning from sin and temptation and being renewed in covenant commitment and life.

### Suspicion and Judgment

"How good and pleasant it is when God's people live together in unity!" Psalm 133 begins with an observation that could easily be applied to Joshua 22.

The friction between the eastern and western tribes is not about whether the altar is sinful if intended for sacrifice. Both sides agree on the sinfulness of such an altar (vv. 19, 23, 26–29). The friction of this chapter arises out of attitudes and beliefs the eastern and western tribes hold toward one another.

The Cisjordanians assume the worst of the Transjordanians, apparently basing their suspicion and judgment on the Transjordanians' choice of land outside the promised land. The Cisjordanians think of themselves as the real representatives of God's people—the insiders. They decide to go to war against the easterners and confront them with harsh accusations. Only the Transjordanians' spirited protestation forestalls battle. The Transjordanians likewise assume the worst of the Cisjordanians, reckoning they will in the future reject their eastern kin as part of Israel. The book of Joshua has given evidence that their fear is well-founded, but the Transjordanians assume the inevitability of such western action, so they build the altar.

Suspicion and judgment are shared on both sides of the Jordan and are not fully assuaged even when confrontation and explanation are made. The question of the Transjordanian status remains a real issue, even as the chapter closes. Yet the ongoing participation of Transjordanians in the life of Israel (see Beyond the Jordan above) suggests that while tension may have remained, Israel largely (and favorably) resolved the status of the eastern tribes.

One cannot help but hear, perhaps, echoes of the conduct of past and present church disagreements in this chapter's conflict. Even when agreement is held on essentials (as was the case in Josh 22 regarding the essential of where sacrifice appropriately could be made), different ways of thinking about and living out those essentials can lead to vicious suspicion and judgment. The status of the "other" and their place in the church is sometimes challenged and undermined.

One current example might be the status within the church of Christians who identify as same-sex attracted. Some do argue that Scripture does not preclude engaging in same-sex sexual relations. But there are same-sex attracted Christians who hold to the church's traditional reading of Scripture in regard to sexual relations. They uphold that God intends it to be heterosexual, monogamous, and covenanted. Submitting to the teaching of Scripture, these same-sex attracted believers argue that faithful discipleship calls them to celibacy.

The church struggles regarding the status of same-sex attracted Christians in its midst. This is the case even when there is shared agreement on the scriptural prohibition of same-sex sex. Some simply refuse to engage the conversation. Some argue that such attraction is sinful per se, denying that one can be Christian and also same-sex attracted. Some admit the teaching of Scripture but argue for same-sex sexual relationships on other grounds.

Some honor same-sex attracted Christians as fellow brothers and sisters, seeking to support them in their celibate life. While there is irenic and thoughtful engagement around these questions,[5] such is not always the case. One sees the worst examples of "Christian" conversation on this issue. Assumptions and judgments are forwarded about the other "side": their ability to think credibly, their evangelical credentials, even their salvation.

As in Joshua 22, the church also has its dividing lines, even around issues where agreement on essentials is shared. Across such dividing lines, "how good and how pleasant" it would be if we could debate and disagree in a Christian manner, living in the tension of disagreement while honoring those with whom we disagree, as members of one body.

To the church in Ephesus, torn over the question of the inclusion of gentiles in the church, Paul writes passionately about the one body of Christ. His words are a good guide for conduct when the church is in agreement on essentials but in disagreement on how to live in light of such essentials:

> [L]ive a life worthy of the calling you have received. Be completely humble and gentle; be patient, bearing with one another in love. Make every effort to keep the unity of the Spirit through the bond of peace. There is one body and one Spirit, just as you were called to one hope when you were called; one Lord, one faith, one baptism; one God and Father of all, who is over all and through all and in all. (Eph 4:1–6)

---

5. For thoughtful engagement from different perspectives on this question, see Preston Sprinkle, ed., *Two Views on Homosexuality, the Bible, and the Church*, Counterpoints (Grand Rapids: Zondervan, 2016). For an accessible treatment of the biblical texts with a view to the very human face of the question see Preston Sprinkle, *People to be Loved: Why Homosexuality is Not Just an Issue* (Grand Rapids: Zondervan, 2015). For a personal account of a New Testament scholar who is same-sex attracted and committed to celibacy see Wesley Hill, *Washed and Waiting: Reflections on Christian Faithfulness and Homosexuality* (Grand Rapids: Zondervan, 2010) and "Washed and Still Waiting: An Evangelical Approach to Homosexuality," *JETS* 59 (2016): 323–38. For a different personal story and commitment see Justin Lee, *Torn: Rescuing the Gospel from the Gays-vs.-Christians Debate* (New York: Jericho Books, 2012). For a brief response to Lee's account see Wesley Hill, "The Love We Dare Not Ignore," *CT* (http://www.christianitytoday.com/ct/2012/october/love-we-dare-not-ignore.html?start=1), 2012.

# CHAPTER 21

# Joshua 23:1–16

## LISTEN to the Story

[1]After a long time had passed and the LORD had given Israel rest from
all their enemies around them, Joshua, by then a very old man, [2]sum-
moned all Israel—their elders, leaders, judges and officials—and said to
them: "I am very old. [3]You yourselves have seen everything the LORD your
God has done to all these nations for your sake; it was the LORD your God
who fought for you. [4]Remember how I have allotted as an inheritance
for your tribes all the land of the nations that remain—the nations I
conquered—between the Jordan and the Mediterranean Sea in the west.
[5]The LORD your God himself will push them out for your sake. He will
drive them out before you, and you will take possession of their land, as
the LORD your God promised you.

[6]"Be very strong; be careful to obey all that is written in the Book of
the Law of Moses, without turning aside to the right or to the left. [7]Do
not associate with these nations that remain among you; do not invoke
the names of their gods or swear by them. You must not serve them or
bow down to them. [8]But you are to hold fast to the LORD your God, as
you have until now.

[9]"The LORD has driven out before you great and powerful nations;
to this day no one has been able to withstand you. [10]One of you routs a
thousand, because the LORD your God fights for you, just as he promised.
[11]So be very careful to love the LORD your God.

[12]"But if you turn away and ally yourselves with the survivors of these
nations that remain among you and if you intermarry with them and
associate with them, [13]then you may be sure that the LORD your God will
no longer drive out these nations before you. Instead, they will become
snares and traps for you, whips on your backs and thorns in your eyes, until
you perish from this good land, which the LORD your God has given you.

[14]"Now I am about to go the way of all the earth. You know with all
your heart and soul that not one of all the good promises the LORD your

God gave you has failed. Every promise has been fulfilled; not one has failed. [15]But just as all the good things the LORD your God has promised you have come to you, so he will bring on you all the evil things he has threatened, until the LORD your God has destroyed you from this good land he has given you. [16]If you violate the covenant of the LORD your God, which he commanded you, and go and serve other gods and bow down to them, the LORD's anger will burn against you, and you will quickly perish from the good land he has given you."

*Listening to the Text in the Story*: Genesis 48–49, 50:22–26; Deuteronomy; 1 Samuel 12:1–25; 1 Kings 2:1–9; 8:12–61; 17:7–23; Hittite Treaties between Mursilis and Duppi-Tessub of Amurru, Suppiluliumas and Kurtiwaza, and Tudḫaliya IV with Kurunta of Tarḫuntašša.

## Saying Goodbye

Joshua delivers his farewell speech as he prepares to "go the way of all the earth" (v. 14). In it, he reviews past history and instructs Israel for an anticipated future. Other biblical characters have delivered such speeches as they approached death. To varying degrees, these speeches also reflect on the past and prepare for the future.

In Genesis 48–49, Joseph's death-bed speech is lengthy. It includes future blessings pronounced over Joseph's sons Ephraim and Manasseh (48:8–20), as well as over Jacob's other sons (49:1–28). All of this is preceded by his reflection on God's past blessing and promise (48:3–4) and concluded by instructions for his own burial (49:29–32).

In comparison to Jacob's lengthy death-bed speech, Joseph's is very brief (50:22–26). No retrospective is provided beyond reference to the promise of land made to the patriarchs. He anticipates the promise's future fulfillment and, in hope, instructs his bones be "carried up from this place" (v. 25).

The farewell speech of Moses—the great covenant mediator—comprises the whole book of Deuteronomy. He provides a full retrospective of God's saving acts (chs. 1–3) before providing extensive instruction for successful life in the land (chs. 4–26). He ratifies a new covenant with Israel, with further instructions providing for the continuance of the covenant's precepts (chs. 27–30). Before he dies, Moses transfers leadership to Joshua (ch. 31), sings praise to God (ch. 32) and gives his own blessing on the tribes of Jacob's descendants (ch. 33). Throughout, Moses' final words urge adherence to the law contained in the book.

Reflecting the same Deuteronomic language and themes as Moses' farewell speech, David's charge to Solomon occurs "when the time drew near for David to die" (1 Kgs 2:1). No retrospective history is provided. Instead, David urges Solomon to Deuteronomic obedience and gives sly permission to dispose of David's (and Solomon's) enemies (1 Kgs 2:2–9).

Besides these deathbed speeches, other significant speeches occur in books shaped by the language and themes of Deuteronomy. They share the retrospective and prospective shape established in Moses' speech. Samuel is "old and grey" (1 Sam 12:2) when he delivers his swan song—although his death is not recorded until much later (1 Sam 25:1; 28:3). He reviews Israel's history from Moses to the present and anticipates different possible futures for Israel. As in Joshua 23, the future is open to either blessing or curse, depending on Israel's adherence to the law (12:14–15, 20–25). A similar pattern is found in Solomon's dedicatory speech of the temple. Israel's past is recalled with particular focus on the temple (1 Kgs 8:16–21), and Israel is called to a future of faithful prayer (8:22–53) and wholehearted obedience to the law (8:56–61).

A final text is a "speech" made not by a biblical character but by the narrator of 1–2 Kings (2 Kgs 17:7–23). In it, a sad retrospective of Israel's sins is recounted and the resultant exile of the northern kingdom. No explicit prospective is provided although it is implicit in the embedded warning to Judah (vv. 13, 19). Should Judah continue in disobedience to the law, they too will be exiled.

### Curse You; Bless You

Joshua 23 is Joshua's farewell speech; the covenant is not renewed until chapter 24. But Joshua's farewell includes potential curses that involve failure to take the land, harassment by the inhabitants, the Lord's anger and destruction of his people, and Israel perishing from the land (vv. 12–13, 15–16). These are heavy words that reveal God's future response to Israel's actions under the covenant. The language of cursing and blessing reflects the book's ancient context, where the blessings or curses of deities are invoked in treaty documents. Although the blessings and curses are not identical to those in Joshua, as in Joshua they are exercised by the deity.

The treaty between Tudḫaliya IV with Kurunta of Tarḫuntašša puts it very succinctly:

> If you, Kurunta, fail to comply with these treaty clauses . . . then may these oath-deïties destroy you together with your posterity. But if you, Kurunta, take to heart the words of this tablet . . . then may these same

> deities take good care of you, and may you grow old under the protection of My Majesty.[1]

With a little more description, Mursilis invokes the deities against Duppi-Tessub:

> The words of the treaty and the oath that are inscribed on this tablet—should Duppi-Tessub not honor these words of the treaty and the oath, may these gods of the oath destroy Duppi-Tessub together with his person, his wife, his son, his grandson, his house, his land and together with everything that he owns.
>
> But if Duppi-Tessub honors these words of the treaty and the oath that are inscribed on this tablet, may these gods of the oath protect him together with his person, his wife, his son, his grandson, his house (and) his country.[2]

### Reflecting on the Past, Anticipating the Future

The epilogue (chs. 22–24) continues in this chapter with Joshua's sermonic farewell. Joshua commissions Israel to future action as he himself was commissioned by God (Josh 1). The dual commission provides a framework for the book, revealing that both taking and dividing the land (Josh 1) and continued existence in the land (Joshua 23) require the same attitudes and responses to God.

As in chapter 13, Joshua is described as a "very old" man (13:1; 23:1–2). Yet as each chapter begins, Israel's relationship to the land is described in fundamentally different ways. While much land remains to be taken in 13:1, in 23:1 the Lord has given Israel rest from all its enemies around them. It might be that two different eras in Joshua's old age are envisioned, as chapter 23 remarks that "a long time had passed," but the conundrum can be better explained.

As the chapters proceed, they both agree that Israel has not fully "possessed" (23:5) or "taken over" (13:1) the land. The Lord is still to "drive out" the peoples (23:5, 9). Each of these words derives from the same Hebrew root (*yrsh*; see Chapter 13 above). Israel has had success in conquest and has placed a claim on the land but still needs to possess it through habitation, and expand its boundaries to all that God has promised. God has driven peoples out and

1. *COS* 2.18:105.
2. Treaty provisions 20–21 in *ANET* 205 (also in *COS* 2.17B:98).

will continue to do so. Both chapters agree on the incompleteness of Israel's "possession" or habitation of the land.

What, then, of the "rest" (from *nwh*) Israel has from all its enemies in 23:1? Rest was promised in 1:13, 15 and proclaimed in 21:44 and 22:4. The contradiction between this "rest" and Israel's failure to possess the land is apparent, not real. The "rest" here proclaimed focuses on the completeness of God's acts to fulfill his promise of land. It also reckons the "rest" as an anticipatory ideal to be experienced by Israel in its future (see the larger discussion above, Chapter 20 at 22:43–45).

In the rest provided by God, Joshua summons "all Israel," a group in which he has specifically included the Transjordanian tribes (see above, Chapter 20 at 22:1–9). All Israel is here present in its representative "elders, leaders, judges, and officials" (v. 2). Each of these has appeared in various capacities throughout Joshua, but it is only here and at the covenant ceremony (24:1) that all four appear together, reflecting the crucial nature of these gatherings.[3]

Joshua's words to Israel reveal the interconnectedness of past events, present action, and potential future. In verses 3–5 he first recalls past events before moving to future anticipation. In this, he focuses on God's action as follows:

In the past (v. 3):
- They have seen everything the LORD your God has done
- The LORD's action was to all these nations
- The LORD fought for you

In the future (v. 5):
- The LORD your God will push them out
- He will drive them out
- You will take possession as the LORD your God promised.

All this has been—and will be—accomplished by God on behalf of Israel. Between God's past and future action, Joshua notes his own past action (v. 4), which reviews the first two sections of the book. He conquered the nations (chs. 1–12) and allotted the inheritance of the promised land (chs. 13–21). No mention is made of the eastern lands, for these were divided by Moses while Israel was yet in the wilderness. Anticipating God's future action, Joshua notes the allotment was of the "nations that remain" (v. 4), a reference that

3. At the earlier covenant ceremony (8:30–35), three of the representative groups were present (elders, judges, and officials; 8:33). Named alone or with others of this group are: "elders" in 7:6, 33; 9:11; 20:4; 23:2; 24:1, 31; "leaders" (literally, "heads" as in NIV) in 8:10; 14:1; 19:51; 21:1; 22:14, 21, 30; "judges" in 8:33; 23:2; 24:1; "officials" (sometimes "officers" in NIV) in 1:10; 3:2; 8:33; 23:2; 24:1.

acknowledges the land is not fully taken (cf. vv. 7, 12). God's future action is required, and its surety rests in the LORD's promise (v. 5).

In response to God's past fulfillment of his promises and the anticipation of their further fulfillment, Joshua details Israel's present responsibility (vv. 6–13). It is a responsibility that is itself bound to both past and future, as noted below. Throughout, Joshua's language echoes that of Deuteronomy, the law of Moses (see discussion at Josh 22:5 in Chapter 20 above).

As Joshua prepares to die, he passes on to Israel what he himself received from God (1:7). Israel is to be "strong" and "be careful to obey" without "turning aside to the right or to the left" (v. 6). Israel's obedience, like Joshua's, is to the "Book of the Law of Moses" (1:8). This is the same book that Joshua read in its entirety at Ebal and Gerizim (8:30–35). To this same law, Israel is now commended.

That initial commendation proceeds to a series of prohibitions detailing particular aspects of Israel's obedience (v. 7). Israel is not to associate with the nations, a prohibition repeated in verse 12 where it includes the intimacy of marriage. The underlying concern is that of Deuteronomy 7:1–4: intermarriage presents an inherent danger that Israel will be drawn away from the worship of the LORD. For this reason, Deuteronomy commanded Israel to totally destroy the nations (Deut 7:1–4). Joshua's speech takes up the Deuteronomic concern but, strikingly, makes no mention of destroying the nations. Instead, the concern is the inherent danger intermarriage presents to the ongoing worship of the LORD.

This concern is further expressed in the second prohibition: that Israel offer no allegiance with the nations' gods. Israel is to invoke neither their names nor swear by them. "Invoking" these gods carries the idea of remembering (from *zkr*) their names in praise. This is strictly forbidden Israel (Exod 23:13), for such invocation should be of God alone (Pss 45:17; 71:16). Neither is Israel to affirm an oath using the names of these gods. Rather, they are to swear only in the LORD's name (Deut 6:13; 10:20) as already illustrated in Joshua (2:12; 9:18).

The final prohibition is emphatically expressed through the dual "you must not serve them or bow down to them" (v. 7). This is the prohibition (although in reverse order) of the second commandment (Exod 20:5; Deut 5:9) and Joshua repeats it in verse 16. This prohibition returns to the epilogue's key word "serve/worship" (*'bd*; 22:5, 27 [2x]; 23:7, 16; 24:2, 14 [3x], 15 [4x], 16, 18, 19, 20, 21, 22, 24, 31).

After saying what they must *not* do, Joshua returns to what they *must* do. Israel is to "hold fast" to their covenant God (v. 8). This was the charge earlier directed to the Transjordanians (22:5; cf. Deut 10:20; 11:22; 13:4[5];

30:20). Joshua concludes this charge by urging them to replicate past obedience, holding fast to the Lord "as you have until now" (v. 8). The affirmation of Israelite covenant faithfulness appears to contradict the charge in Joshua 24 that Israel "throw away" their gods (24:14–15, 23). The contradiction suggests that Joshua 23 uses a rhetorical strategy. In a similar way, Paul's letters ascribe positive action to the recipients before demanding change.

Joshua's charge to Israel charts a way into the future. Israel is to (1) obey the law of Moses (v. 6); and (2) hold fast to God (v. 8). These are the commands of Deuteronomy 11:22, which promises such obedience will be met by God's action. God will "drive out all these nations before you, and you will dispossess nations larger and stronger than you" (Deut 11:23). Reminding Israel that they have obeyed "until now" (v. 8) leads to the concomitant past action on God's part: he has "driven out . . . great and powerful nations" (v. 9). Israel's past obedience was met by God's power on their behalf. None have withstood Israel; it has routed its thousands (v. 10). The equation between past obedience and past success is clearly drawn.

Therefore, should Israel hope to see what is promised in verse 5—God *in the future* driving out the nations—the implication is likewise clear. They must obey God's law. Only then can they expect God will continue to drive out "great and powerful nations." Israel's obedience is not to be one of legalism, however. It is grounded in a covenant with a God who chose, rescued, and sustained a people so that the larger purposes of the promise to Abraham would be fulfilled. Joshua closes his charge, then, with the response to which Israel is ultimately called: "be very careful to love the Lord your God" (v. 11). This is the central command of Deuteronomy 6:5 and is the essence of the covenant relationship. As such, it is the foundation of Israel's life and the way into an anticipated future.

So crucial is this covenant relationship to the fulfillment of God's plans through Israel, Joshua repeats his charge. He does so by exploring its flip-side, detailing the anticipated outcomes of Israel's disobedience (vv. 12–13). In a book that is often mischaracterized as depicting total destruction of the inhabitants, Joshua's command reveals this is not the case. The inhabitants remain, and Israel is commanded not to ally or marry with them; of note, no command for total destruction is here issued. Joshua has already stressed Israel's religious commitments, and it is in this context that alliances with the inhabitants are prohibited. This is the same context as the prohibition against alliance and intermarriage in Deuteronomy 7:3, for "they will turn your children away from following me to serve other gods" (Deut 7:4). The intent is not xenophobia but religious purity. This is the point on which Joshua has already cautioned them (v. 7). Israel knows this danger from the experience of Baal Peor (Num 25:1–3), and (sadly) it will be amply illustrated in Solomon's downfall (1 Kgs 11:1–3).

The certain outcome of Israel's disregard is communicated through an emphatic grammatical construction here translated "you may be sure that" (v. 13). If the result of obedience is God's commitment to drive out the nations, the result of disobedience is that he will "no longer drive out these nations before you." With the nations still in the land, the threat remains that through alliance and intermarriage Israel will become apostate, worshiping other gods. This potential is stated through several graphic, dire images. First, the inhabitants will be "snares and traps" (v. 13). To be caught in a "snare" (*pah*) leads to death (Prov 7:23); the psalmist rejoices to escape from one (Ps. 91:3; 124:7). A "trap" (*moqesh*) traps birds but is also used metaphorically to describe the outcome of making treaties with the inhabitants (Exod 34:12) or worshiping their gods (Exod 23:33; Deut 7:16; Judg 2:3). Second, the inhabitants will be "whips on your backs and thorns in your eyes," a parallel phrase that is very similar to Numbers 33:55:

| | |
|---|---|
| Josh 23:13 | whips (*shotet*) on your backs (*tsiddim*) and thorns (*tseninim*) in your eyes |
| Num 33:55 | barbs (*sikkim*) in your eyes and thorns (*tseninim*) in your sides (*tsiddim*) |

This is the only occurrence of "whips" in the Old Testament, and "thorns" appear only in these two passages. Both passages speak of the inherent danger of not driving out the inhabitants, and both name the end result: they will "perish from this good land" (v. 13). Although gifted with "this good land" (vv. 13, 15; cf. v. 16 where the Hebrew is slightly different), Moses made this threatened result clear in his final words (Deut 4:25–31; 8:19–20; 28:20–22; 30:17–18). Joshua reiterates the threat: gifted land can be lost. Israel can perish off it. Of course, the ongoing history of Israel reveals they do not heed this caution and come to worship the gods of Canaan such as Baal, Asherah, and others. In the end, they do perish from the land through the exile to Assyria and Babylon (2 Kgs 17, 25).

Joshua concludes by telling Israel of his impending death (v. 14). Perhaps he hopes for the persuasive power of a successful leader's final words. He may even hope for a response such as the Transjordanians had earlier given: "Whatever you have commanded us we will do" (1:16). He revisits God's past work, reminding Israel that all that was promised has now been accomplished (v. 14). Israel knows this "with all your heart and soul," a clear allusion to the Deuteronomic command to love the LORD "with all heart and with all your soul and with all your strength" (Deut 6:5). By this, Joshua connects what they know to the very thing he had earlier commanded them: the natural outcome of knowing past events should be covenant love (v. 11).

What they know is stated three times, both negatively and positively (v. 14):

> Not one of all the good promises (*hadebarim hatobim*) . . . has failed
> Every promise has been fulfilled
> Not one has failed.

These assertions recall the conclusion of the third section of Joshua (21:45) where

> Not one of the LORD's good promises (*hadabar hatob*)[4] to Israel failed
> Every one was fulfilled.

Assuming their present knowledge leads to covenant love and thus obedience, they are assured of the LORD's continued action on their behalf. Just as this is so, the reverse is also true. In the same way God brought all the promised "good things" (v. 15; *hadabar hatob*), so he will surely bring all the promised "evil things" (*hadabar hara'*). Knowledge of the past should inform ongoing action. Which action they choose will determine what their future experience will be: more "good things" or threatened "evil things."

The determining factor is Israel's response to their covenant God. Covenant love is demonstrated by obedience; covenant violation lies in "serv[ing] other gods and bow[ing] down to them" (v. 16). The result is heighted by a grim word-play of two words that differ by only one letter: should they "serve" (*'abad*) these gods, God's anger will be roused, the covenant-curses activated, and they will "perish" (*'abad*) from the good land.

Although they are to perish "quickly" (v. 16), in actual fact sinful Israel remains in the land for several centuries. Repeatedly, God sends prophets to call them back to covenant. Israel, however, continues to reject God's word. In consequence, the northern kingdom is exiled to Assyria in 722 BC, and the southern kingdom is exiled to Babylon in 597 BC and 586 BC. Joshua's words seek to prevent the eventuality of exile, yet when that eventuality comes about, God's covenant love to a sinful people is such that his "good promise" does not fail. To an exiled people God speaks of a love that remains even through and beyond exile:

> "The days are coming," declares the LORD, "when I will fulfill the good promise (*hadabar hatob*) I made to the people of Israel and Judah." (Jer 33:14)

4. The difference (in the Hebrew text) in phrasing between the two passages is that 21:45 is singular while 22:14 pluralizes the phrase. In the next verse (22:15), "the good things" is the singular form of the phrase, *hadabar hatob*. The phrase in its singular form occurs only elsewhere in Jer 33:14.

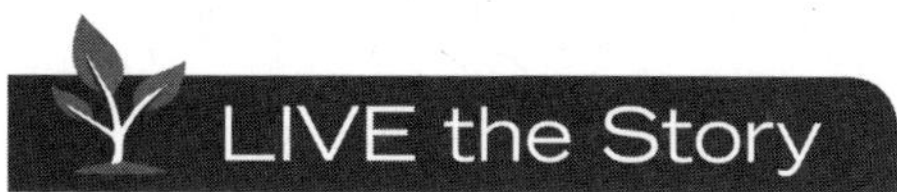


**The Farewell of Jesus, the True Joshua**

Joshua's farewell words are given in light of the rest into which Israel has entered, at a time when Joshua is old and about to die (Josh 23:1). It is curious, in light of these two contexts, that Origen's homilies make no connection between this chapter and Jesus' own words as he approaches death. This commentary has explored the figural analogy made between Joshua and Jesus in Origen's homilies (see Live the Story, Chapters 1, 3–4). The analogy relies on the fact that Joshua and Jesus are the same name in Greek and draws on the typological work of Hebrews 4, in which Jesus provides the rest Joshua was unable to provide.

Despite Origen's neglect of Joshua 23, it readily lends itself to a figural reading. Joshua calls Israel to love God and walk in obedience to his commands. This is a message Jesus himself gave (see Show Me Your Love below). How might a figural reading be applied to the analogy of a farewell message in the context of rest provided by God?

One could point to different "farewell" messages of Jesus: his words from the cross, his parting words at the ascension, his words to his disciples the night of his arrest (John 14–17). Each of these could be considered a farewell message and compared to that of Joshua. But another "farewell" message could be considered: the words spoken at Jesus' last supper with his disciples. This is the real farewell before his death. It is recorded in all three synoptic gospels (Matt 26:26–29; Mark 14:22–25; Luke 22:14–20), and the subject is treated in John's feeding of the multitude discourse (John 6:1–59).

In the synoptic tradition, the meal as Jesus' farewell message is, as in Joshua, a message that looks to the past (see Listen to the Story above). It is contextualized in the past events surrounding Israel's Passover festival. Luke's account intensifies the meal's connection to past events, noting the cup is a "cup of the new covenant in my blood" (Luke 22:20). This is a citation of Jeremiah's past oracle (Jer 31:33), given shortly before Israel's exile. Even the command that the bread be done "in remembrance of me" sets its ongoing observance in an orientation to the past event of Christ's life and death.

The meal as Jesus' last message reveals it is a message grounded in all that God has done before. It is a message that is meant to recall the church's attention to this past.

It is also a message that anticipates the future. The citation of Jeremiah's new covenant oracle looks back, but Jeremiah's oracle is itself anticipatory of future hope and covenant life. Jesus shares the meal in anticipation of that hope's culmination in the coming kingdom (Luke 22:16, 18). Paul, giving instruction for the ongoing observance of the meal, also anticipates the future kingdom. He commands the meal be done into the future and until the Lord returns saying, "whenever you eat this bread and drink this cup, you proclaim the Lord's death until he comes" (1 Cor 11:26). Paul even captures the meal's past-and-future orientation when he says, "I received from the Lord what I also passed on to you" (1 Cor 11:23).

The past-and-future orientation of this last message of Jesus is recognized as the church observes the ordinance of the meal. In hymns and readings, the event of Christ's death is recalled, and his return to share the meal in the future kingdom of God is anticipated. In a eucharistic setting, the liturgy around the Lord's Table often includes a congregational response that reflects this understanding. Asked to "proclaim the mystery of faith" the congregation responds, "Christ has died. Christ is risen. Christ will come again." For those who share the meal, it is always a moment at the hinge of time, between past and present. As the church shares the meal and "remembers Christ's death until he comes," it hears and sees again his last message, ever new and ever needed.

Considering the Lord's Table within the figural reading of Joshua-as-Jesus also finds resonance with Joshua's call to Israel to love God (vv. 8, 11) and follow in his way (v. 6). The Lord's Table is, for the church, the constant reminder of God's redeeming love, and of the new covenant into which God brought his people. The Christian life lived in light of cross and redemption is a call to live in the ethic of Christ. In gratitude for all it has received, the church is to live out Christ's life in winsome ways, drawing others to a mercy it has itself received.

Finally, Joshua's farewell message is given in the context of rest achieved in the land. It is a rest given by God in keeping with his purposes. But, as Hebrews 4 argues, it is a rest that did not last, because of Israel's disobedience. The promise of rest in the land finds it fulfillment in the rest made available by God's own work in Christ. At the Lord's Table, the church recalls, lives in, and anticipates the goodness of this rest. Christ has done the work and brings us into his own Sabbath rest.

### Show Me Your Love by Your Obedience

Joshua calls Israel to two commitments. First, they are to "hold fast to the Lord" (v. 8) by "loving the Lord your God" (v. 11). The heart of the covenant is love and relationship. Out of this arises the second commitment to which Israel is called, to "obey all that is written in the Book of the Law of Moses" (v. 6).

In Joshua 23, the call to love and the command to obey are inextricably intertwined, unable to exist in isolation. It is no accident that verse 11 brings Joshua's words back to the great truth of Deuteronomy that Israel should "love the LORD your God" (v. 11; Deut 6:5). Deuteronomy (and all of the Old and New Testaments) never coerces Israel's loving response. Rather, Deuteronomy calls Israel to love God in response to God's prior love that redeemed Israel out of bondage. It is in this matrix that obedience is placed. How does Israel show love and gratitude to this electing, redeeming God? By walking in ways that please him. By so doing, Israel knows the rest and joy of covenant life. Additionally, Israel's life of holiness communicates God's uniqueness to the foreigner in Israel's midst and to the nations around it. In this priestly role is the hope that those outside of Israel would come to know, and join themselves to, Israel's God.

The relationship of love and obedience remains for the New Testament people of God. As Jesus prepares for the cross—providing redemption out of the bondage of sin, just as the exodus redeemed Israel from Pharaoh—he shares his heart with his disciples, comforting them (John 14:1–13). Describing the relationship of love between the Father and the Son, Jesus speaks of his own obedience to the Father's will (14:9–14). He then gives a startling word to those he seeks to comfort: "If you love me, keep my commands" (v. 15). It is a word that binds together love and obedience and is reiterated a few verses later: "Whoever has my commands and keeps them is the one who loves me" (v. 21).

Jesus binds together love and obedience. Love leads to obedience, and obedience is the proof of love. As in the Old Testament, love and obedience arise in the matrix of redemption. In the context of love and obedience, Jesus further comforts his disciples by extending the relationship of love between Father and Son to the disciples. He says, "The one who loves me will be loved by my Father, and I too will love them and show myself to them" (v. 21). Additionally, the comfort of the "Spirit of truth" is promised, for he will be "with you and will be in you" (v. 17).

As in the Old Testament, love and obedience arise as response to God's redemption. Obedience is requisite to the life of faith, and it stands as *proof* of that faith. This is perhaps not very popular in the church today. Some of this unpopularity is due to currents of anti-authority at work. They make the church loathe to attribute to God standards to which he calls, and by which he judges, his people. Some is due to legalism that abuses and caricatures God's call to obedience. Some is due to our fascination with feel-good discipleship that looks for blessing and finds obedience passé or onerous. Christ's call to obedience doesn't "sell" well in such so-called discipleship. Whatever the cause, leaving obedience aside undercuts true discipleship and its freedom and joy.

Joshua's farewell words remind Israel and the church that obedience is not optional for covenant people. God has purchased his people out of bondage and invites a response of obedience. Obedience opens the door to enjoy the life of the covenant. It protects Israel in the land (and God's people today), from all the false gods that seek to lead God's people away from the fullness of covenant life.

Kathleen Norris, writing in *Amazing Grace: A Vocabulary of Faith*, reflects on the necessary relationship of obedience and love. Her words reconfigure unhelpful ideas of covenant obedience:

> When I'm made aware that I've broken one of the commandments—and that coming to awareness in itself has come to seem a grace—I've also been forced to pay attention to the trouble that follows, the loss of trust and the capacity to love that dogs broken relationships. I have begun to see the commandments in the light of an underlying covenant, as essential to the relationship that God is establishing with Israel, and with us.
>
> "Jealously" is a loaded word, and I used to cringe when I would hear the Ten Commandments begin with the injunction against idolatry: "You shall not bow down to [idols] or worship them for I the Lord am a jealous God" (Exod. 20:5). Human jealousy is a sign of fear. Often, it indicates immaturity, or a maladaption of the ability to love. God's jealousy is a different matter, more like mother-love, the protective zeal of a lioness or mother bear for her young. The word "jealousy" has its root in "zealous," denoting extreme enthusiasm and devotion, and God's jealousy retains the word's more positive aspects. It helps us to trust. Who, after all, would trust a God, a parent, spouse, or love, who said to us, "I really love you, but I don't care at all what you do or who you become?"[5]

5. Kathleen Norris, *Amazing Grace: A Vocabulary of Faith* (New York: The Berkley Publishing Group, 1998), 86.

CHAPTER 22

# Joshua 24:1-33

## LISTEN to the Story

[1]Then Joshua assembled all the tribes of Israel at Shechem. He summoned the elders, leaders, judges and officials of Israel, and they presented
themselves before God.
[2]Joshua said to all the people, "This is what the LORD, the God of Israel,
says: 'Long ago your ancestors, including Terah the father of Abraham and
Nahor, lived beyond the Euphrates River and worshiped other gods. [3]But
I took your father Abraham from the land beyond the Euphrates and led
him throughout Canaan and gave him many descendants. I gave him
Isaac, [4]and to Isaac I gave Jacob and Esau. I assigned the hill country of
Seir to Esau, but Jacob and his family went down to Egypt.
[5]"'Then I sent Moses and Aaron, and I afflicted the Egyptians by what
I did there, and I brought you out. [6]When I brought your people out of
Egypt, you came to the sea, and the Egyptians pursued them with chariots
and horsemen as far as the Red Sea. [7]But they cried to the LORD for help,
and he put darkness between you and the Egyptians; he brought the sea
over them and covered them. You saw with your own eyes what I did to
the Egyptians. Then you lived in the wilderness for a long time.
[8]"'I brought you to the land of the Amorites who lived east of the
Jordan. They fought against you, but I gave them into your hands.
I destroyed them from before you, and you took possession of their land.
[9]When Balak son of Zippor, the king of Moab, prepared to fight against
Israel, he sent for Balaam son of Beor to put a curse on you. [10]But I would
not listen to Balaam, so he blessed you again and again, and I delivered
you out of his hand.
[11]"'Then you crossed the Jordan and came to Jericho. The citizens of
Jericho fought against you, as did also the Amorites, Perizzites, Canaanites,
Hittites, Girgashites, Hivites and Jebusites, but I gave them into your
hands. [12]I sent the hornet ahead of you, which drove them out before
you—also the two Amorite kings. You did not do it with your own sword

and bow. [13]So I gave you a land on which you did not toil and cities you did not build; and you live in them and eat from vineyards and olive groves that you did not plant.'

[14]"Now fear the LORD and serve him with all faithfulness. Throw away the gods your ancestors worshiped beyond the Euphrates River and in Egypt, and serve the LORD. [15]But if serving the LORD seems undesirable to you, then choose for yourselves this day whom you will serve, whether the gods your ancestors served beyond the Euphrates, or the gods of the Amorites, in whose land you are living. But as for me and my household, we will serve the LORD."

[16]Then the people answered, "Far be it from us to forsake the LORD to serve other gods! [17]It was the LORD our God himself who brought us and our parents up out of Egypt, from that land of slavery, and performed those great signs before our eyes. He protected us on our entire journey and among all the nations through which we traveled. [18]And the LORD drove out before us all the nations, including the Amorites, who lived in the land. We too will serve the LORD, because he is our God."

[19]Joshua said to the people, "You are not able to serve the LORD. He is a holy God; he is a jealous God. He will not forgive your rebellion and your sins. [20]If you forsake the LORD and serve foreign gods, he will turn and bring disaster on you and make an end of you, after he has been good to you."

[21]But the people said to Joshua, "No! We will serve the LORD."

[22]Then Joshua said, "You are witnesses against yourselves that you have chosen to serve the LORD."

"Yes, we are witnesses," they replied.

[23]"Now then," said Joshua, "throw away the foreign gods that are among you and yield your hearts to the LORD, the God of Israel."

[24]And the people said to Joshua, "We will serve the LORD our God and obey him."

[25]On that day Joshua made a covenant for the people, and there at Shechem he reaffirmed for them decrees and laws. [26]And Joshua recorded these things in the Book of the Law of God. Then he took a large stone and set it up there under the oak near the holy place of the LORD.

[27]"See!" he said to all the people. "This stone will be a witness against us. It has heard all the words the LORD has said to us. It will be a witness against you if you are untrue to your God."

[28]Then Joshua dismissed the people, each to their own inheritance.

[29]After these things, Joshua son of Nun, the servant of the LORD, died

at the age of a hundred and ten. [30]And they buried him in the land of his inheritance, at Timnath Serah in the hill country of Ephraim, north of Mount Gaash.

[31]Israel served the LORD throughout the lifetime of Joshua and of the elders who outlived him and who had experienced everything the LORD had done for Israel.

[32]And Joseph's bones, which the Israelites had brought up from Egypt, were buried at Shechem in the tract of land that Jacob bought for a hundred pieces of silver from the sons of Hamor, the father of Shechem. This became the inheritance of Joseph's descendants.

[33]And Eleazar son of Aaron died and was buried at Gibeah, which had been allotted to his son Phinehas in the hill country of Ephraim.

*Listening to the Text in the Story*: Genesis 35:1–4; Deuteronomy 6:10–15; 26:3–10; Apology of Ḫattušili III; Treaty between Muršili and Duppi-Tešub

## Shechem and "Foreign Gods"

Joshua's charge that Israel put away its "foreign gods" recalls Jacob's return from Paddan Aram. Renamed "Israel" following his all-night wrestling match, Jacob/Israel declares he "saw God face to face" (Gen 32:30). Shortly after, while Jacob was at Shechem, God instructs him to return to Bethel. There, God had earlier made great promises to Jacob (Gen 28), which now are fulfilled. Jacob prepares to return to Bethel, acknowledging God "answered me in the day of my distress and . . . has been with me wherever I have gone" (Gen 35:3). Signifying his commitment to this faithful God, Jacob commands his household to put away their "foreign gods." The gods are buried under the oak at Shechem before Jacob sets out for Bethel (Gen 35:1–4).

In Joshua 24, Israel (now the nation) is again at Shechem. Using the same terminology, Joshua commands Israel to put away their "foreign gods." As with its forefather Jacob, Israel is to do so in response to God's past action on its behalf. Thus, Israel (the nation) entered the land as did Israel (the man): with a call to commitment signified by turning from "foreign gods."

## Reciting the Past as a Call to Present Worship

As in chapter 23, Joshua again recalls past events. Now the recital reaches further back to begin with Abraham. God is the primary actor throughout this historical review. Whereas the recitation in chapter 23 focused on past events to evoke present action toward an anticipated future, the recitation in chapter 24 has a different function. It is for the sole purpose of eliciting Israel's present renewal of its covenant relationship, evidenced in the sole worship of the LORD. They are called to choose "this day" (v. 14) and they make a covenant with the LORD on "that day" (v. 25). The future implications of their commitment are real and referenced in verse 20, but the focus is securely on the call to present covenant commitment and the worship that entails.

A similar review of history occurs in Deuteronomy 26:5–9. It begins with Jacob, the one who called Israel to put away foreign gods (see above, Shechem and "Foreign Gods"). Deuteronomy's recitation begins with Jacob's journey to, and sojourn in, Egypt. It is when the recitation recalls Israel's oppression in Egypt that God is introduced as a primary actor. Israel cries out to the LORD, and he delivers his people out of Egypt and gives the land. As in Joshua 24, the recital in Deuteronomy is connected to worship, for it is made by an individual who brings an offering to the LORD. The recital in Joshua 24 and Deuteronomy 26 serve as a reminder that worship is always the response to God's acts of choosing, redeeming, and providing for his people.

## The Danger of the Land

Joshua highlights the truth that the land is gifted by God. Israel receives it without toil and does not build its cities or plant its vineyards and olive groves (v. 13). Joshua's words are those of Moses, who said Israel would enter

> a land with large, flourishing cities you did not build, houses filled with all kinds of good things you did not provide, wells you did not dig, and vineyards and olive groves you did not plant. (Deut 6:10–11)

Moses describes the goodness of the land, but goes on immediately to speak of its inherent danger:

> then when you eat and are satisfied, be careful that you do not forget the LORD, who brought you out of Egypt, out of the land of slavery. (Deut 6:11–12)

To prevent this forgetfulness, Moses immediately urges Israel to

> Fear the LORD your God, serve him only and take your oaths in his name. Do not follow other gods, the gods of the peoples around you. (Deut 6:13–14)

Finally, Moses cites the reason Israel should serve only the LORD:

> for the LORD your God, who is among you, is a jealous God and his anger will burn against you, and he will destroy you from the face of the land. (Deut 6:15)

Joshua's dialogue with Israel uses Moses' words. He explicitly cites the land's goodness. He makes a covenant with Israel lest they live out the inherent danger of the land: forgetfulness. He calls them to fear and serve the LORD (v. 14–15) and cites the same motivation referenced by Moses (v. 19–20). By taking up Moses' words at this crucial juncture of Israel's life in the land, Joshua proves once again to be Moses' faithful successor. Crafting a covenant on the basis of these concerns makes him, like his predecessor, a covenant mediator between the people and God. This is Joshua's crowning achievement as Moses' successor. He is therefore rightly ascribed with Moses' title, the "servant of the LORD" (v. 29).

## As for Me and My House

Joshua commits himself and his household to God. The idea of an individual making a corporate devotion to a deity is attested in the Apology of Ḫattušili III.[1] A supporter of the Ishtar cult, Ḫattušili has a dream in which the goddess requests he and his house become her servants. Ḫattušili complies, "so the goddess' servant with my household I became."

Joshua calls all Israel to similar commitment to the LORD, confirming it by covenant renewal (v. 25). Within the chapter's dialogue are found elements common to ancient Near Eastern treaties, such as the fourteenth century BC Hittite treaty between Muršili and Duppi-Tešub.[2] These elements at times are altered in Joshua but still discernible:

| | |
|---|---|
| **Preamble** | The Hittite king initiates the treaty; in Joshua 24, God does not initiate the treaty. He had done so in the past; now the emphasis lies on Israel's freely-made recommitment in response to God's past actions |
| **Historical Prologue** | An account of past history that informs the present treaty; Josh 24:2b–13 |
| **Stipulations** | An outline of the expectations placed upon the vassal and overlord (including military and extradition clauses); Joshua 24 stipulates only that Israel is to "fear the LORD and serve him with all faithfulness," attested by the disposal of foreign gods (v. 14–15). The covenant "reaffirms decrees and laws" (v. 25), likely those contained in covenants made by Moses, particularly Deuteronomy. Departing from the treaty form, no stipulations are stated on the LORD's part |

1. *COS* 1.77:202.
2. *ANET*, 203–205; also found in *COS* 2.17B:96–98.

| | |
|---|---|
| **Provisions** | Includes provisions for the storage, display, and reading of the document; Josh 24:26–27 |
| **Blessings and Curses** | Invocation of the gods' power for compliance and non-compliance; Josh 24:20 |
| **Witnesses** | Hittite gods are invoked as witnesses; Joshua sets both the people (v. 22) and the stone (v. 27) as witnesses |

Incorporated into the larger narrative of Joshua, the chapter does not stand as a de facto treaty document. However, by utilizing treaty elements, the narrative account communicates the serious and binding nature of Israel's commitment. The form serves the chapter's sole emphasis: that Israel is called to devoted commitment to the LORD alone. This is presented as the natural response to God's past gracious acts.

## EXPLAIN the Story

The book's climactic chapter takes up the call for Israel to "serve" (*'bd*) the LORD, a concern explored throughout the epilogue (see Explain the Story, Chapter 20). Joshua 22 focuses on the service of the LORD through the threat of the Transjordanian altar. Joshua's farewell sermon (ch. 23) urges Israel to respond to God's past actions with present obedience to the law of Moses. They are to "hold fast" to the LORD and not serve other gods (vv. 7, 16), so as to enjoy in the future the LORD's good promises. In the final chapter, Joshua calls Israel to serve the LORD rather than foreign gods. This is the necessary commitment for continued life in the land (v. 20) and is the natural response to God's past actions on Israel's behalf (vv. 2–13).

In Joshua, the choice to serve the LORD alone is presented as the final, identifying act of Israel. Thus, the chapter speaks to the question raised throughout Joshua, namely, *Who can be an Israelite*? The question has been answered in two ways thus far. First, regardless of ethnicity, all who respond to God's power and grace can be included in Israel (such as Rahab and the Gibeonites). Second, those who respond in obedience to the law of Moses, whether they reside east or west of the Jordan, can be included in Israel. Thus, Transjordanian obedience shows them included in Israel despite their eastern habitation, while Achan's disobedience shows him excluded from Israel despite his western habitation. The call in this present chapter is for all Israel to commit to the LORD alone as the determining feature of its identity. Ratification of that commitment by covenant is Joshua's last act before his death.

## God Acted for Israel (24:1–13)

Joshua assembles "all the tribes of Israel" at Shechem. Israel had earlier gathered at Shiloh (18:1) and the narrative context suggests the intervening chapters have also taken place at Shiloh. No reason is given for the relocation to Shechem, but an earlier covenant ceremony was held in its vicinity, at Ebal and Gerizim (8:30–35).[3] The second ceremony is set shortly before Joshua's death rather than after Israel's early success in the land.

Holding covenant ceremonies at Shechem can be explained by that location's long cultic history in Israel. There, at the great tree of Moreh, Abraham first built an altar to God in response to the promises of land, descendants, and blessing (Gen 12:7). Joshua's historical recital begins with Abraham and traces the fulfillment of the promises. Shechem's association with the first statement of those promises makes it a fitting place to recite their fulfillment and to respond by covenant. Shechem is also the place at which Jacob and his household forsook their foreign gods, burying them under a tree, perhaps the same oak.[4] Joshua now calls upon Jacob's descendants to follow his example.

The people gather "before God," a further reference to the cultic associations of Shechem. The ark is not mentioned; it may remain at Shiloh. Given the importance of the ark's progression in the book (chs. 3–4, 18), had it now been transported to Shechem, some notice of its further progress might be expected. However, the ark is the symbol of God's presence and here the people gather "before God." Further, the ark was in the midst of the people at the earlier renewal ceremony (8:33). For both these reasons, it is appropriate to assume the ark's presence at Shechem. Perhaps it is not mentioned so that the focus remains on the words: God's actions in history calling forth Israel's present response.

As at the earlier ceremony at which all the people attended (8:32, 33, 35), the emphasis lies on the totality of Israel. "All the tribes of Israel" assemble, which includes the Transjordanians. Speaking for the tribes are their representative "elders, leaders, judges, and officials." Only here and in Joshua 23:2 do all these leaders appear together, signifying the chapters' importance to Israel.[5]

Joshua rehearses Israel's history beginning with Abraham and tracing significant steps toward the fulfillment of God's promises to the patriarch. Throughout the recitation, the focus is firmly on God as the primary actor. This is evident in the distribution of the finite verbs within the recitation:

---

3. The relationship of the covenant ceremonies in Josh 8:30–35 and Josh 24 is contested; see the discussion in Explain the Story, Chapter 8. This commentary understands the two chapters as separate ceremonies.

4. Shechem appears elsewhere in significant accounts in Israel's history. See for example Gen 34:2–26; 37:12, 14; Judg 8:31; 1 Kgs 12:1–25; Jer 41:5; Hos 6:9.

5. See Explain the Story, Chapter 21 at 23:2 for discussion of the named representatives and their appearance elsewhere in Joshua.

**God acts:**

In first-person verbs (twenty times in vv. 3–6, 7b–8, 10–13);
In third-person verbs (three times in v. 7);
Through his agent, Balaam (once in v. 10; the blessing is by God's power and direction; see Num 23:5, 16; 24:2, 13);
Through his agent, the hornet (once in v. 12);
**Total acts of God = 25**

**Israel acts:**

In the past generation (seven times in vv. 2–7);
In the present generation (four times in vv. 8–13). There are also three acts in v. 13 that Israel did *not* do [they did not drive out inhabitants, did not toil, did not build]. By implication, these are things God did for them);
**Total acts of Israel = 11** (plus three things they did not do; God did).

**The Inhabitants act:**

Six times in vv. 8–11.

**Egypt acts:**

Once in v. 6.

God is credited with twenty-three direct actions, two actions through an agent and three actions by implication (v. 13). He is clearly the main actor in the recitation, revealing the breadth of God's favor toward his chosen people.

Three key words reveal several themes in the history. Each is noted initially in respect of Abraham. He "lived" (from *yshb*) "beyond" (from *'br*) the Euphrates (vv. 2–3). There, although Abraham "worshiped" (from *'bd*) other gods, God chose him. Later, it is the Amorites who "lived" (*yshb*) "east" (*'br*) of the Jordan (v. 8). In contrast to these places "beyond" and "east," Israel "crossed" (*'br*) the Jordan. Significantly, *'br* ("beyond," "east," and "cross") is the key word used throughout Joshua for crossing the Jordan (see Chapter 3 above). Having crossed, Israel "lives" (*yshb*; v. 13) in the promised land. In verses 14–15 Joshua charges Israel with the logical response to a history that moved them from "living beyond" and "other gods" to the LORD and crossing the Jordan: it is the response of worship (from *'bd*) of the LORD alone. Joshua's charge will include each of these three key words, as noted below.

A fourth key word highlights God's gracious act of giving (from *ntn*). With one exception, what is given is land and descendants in fulfillment of the promise to Abraham. Esau is the only recipient named who is not in the direct line of the patriarchal promise:

Descendants:

God **gave** Isaac to Abraham (v. 3)
God **gave** Jacob and Esau to Isaac (v. 4)

Land:

God **assigned** Seir to Esau (Hebrew reads, "God **gave** to Esau the hill country of Seir to possess it"; v. 4)
God **gave** the land of the Amorites to Israel (v. 8)
God **gave** the (land of) the western nations to Israel (v. 11)
God **gave** the land in which Israel lives (v. 13)

The focus on giving the land revisits the emphasis noted in Joshua 1 (vv. 2, 3, 6, 11, 13, 15). The book begins with God's promise of giving the land. Its fulfillment is noted in 21:43–45, and Joshua's historical review indicates the gifting of land (and descendants) brings the ancient promises to completion.

Joshua begins the history with the standard prophetic messenger formula, "This is what the LORD says." With a nod to the covenant, he further identifies the LORD as the "God of Israel" (v. 2). By this device, the subsequently enumerated call of Abraham is heard in the context of the promise's outcome in the chosen nation of Israel. While both Abraham and Nahor are cited as Israel's "ancestors," God's selection is apparent, as it is the line of Abraham that is traced. God acts to take Abraham from a foreign land "beyond the Jordan" to Canaan, the "land I will show you" (Gen 12:1).

The promise of "many descendants" is sketched through reference to Isaac, Jacob, and Esau. Esau is assigned land, and the review quickly passes from him to the promised line and Jacob. Despite having the promise of land, Jacob "went down to Egypt," delaying fulfillment of that promise.

Moses, Aaron, and the escape out of Egypt are reviewed quickly; throughout, the "you" of the present generation is included, thus closely identifying them with their history (vv. 5–7). The account is a minimalist presentation. It focuses only on the main steps in God's initiative ("I afflicted," "what I did there," "I brought you out"), without reference to the many miracles within that initiative.

At the moment of the powerful Red Sea crossing, the recital changes from God's perspective ("I brought you out") to Israel's, revealing what they see in the event. "They" cry out and "he put darkness between you and the Egyptians; he brought the sea over them and covered them" (v. 7). Israel can only "[s]tand firm and . . . see the deliverance the LORD will bring you today" (Exod 14:13). Then, Joshua's words return to God's perspective of the event, while still reflecting what Israel experienced: "you saw with your own eyes what I [God] did to the Egyptians" (v. 7b).

The recitation holds two surprising omissions at this point. First, the account skips over Sinai and the law. This lacuna keeps the emphasis firmly on God's gracious acts toward Israel, rather than on what Israel might do under the law. More, it is a reminder that the promises this history traces were given to Abraham before the law was instituted. Second, the account glosses over the wilderness sins. The forty years of the wilderness generation are simply a "long time in the wilderness." That time is only a stopping point en route to the land of God's promise, and the wilderness sins are insufficient to eliminate God's promises. These lacunae are a reminder that Israel's history begins and is sustained by God's gracious acts. To this, Joshua will call Israel to only one response (vv. 14–15): a commitment to worship the God who acts in promise and grace.

From the wilderness, God brings Israel to the Transjordan, the "land of the Amorites." Like Abraham who "lived beyond," they "live east" (the Hebrew terms are the same)—that is, they do not "live across" the Jordan in the promised land. The term "Amorites" is used generically in this passage to describe eastern (v. 8) or western nations (vv. 15, 18), to specify one of the seven western nations (v. 11), or to describe Sihon and Og (v. 12).[6] In a history that relates the fulfillment of promises made to Abraham, reference to "Amorites" has particular meaning. God had promised Abraham that his descendants would return to Canaan after four generations, for "the sin of the Amorites has not yet reached its full measure" (Gen 15:16). The usage in Joshua 24 is another reference to the fulfillment of God's promise.

Success against the Amorites is achieved only by God's action. He "gave them into your hands" and "destroyed them." Israel's action is simply to "take possession" (v. 8; here, the familiar root *yrsh* occurs; see Chapter 13 above). Later, the settlement in the promised land itself will be more fully described (v. 13).

The engagements east of the Jordan are represented only by Balak's preparation for war (v. 9). The gist of that preparation is that Balak "sent" for the prophet Balaam, just as God had "sent" Moses and Aaron to redeem Israel (v. 5). For a second time in Joshua (see Chapter 14 at 13:22) Balaam appears. He is an odd inclusion in this history of significant historical junctures but serves as a powerful commentary on the fulfillment of God's promises to Abraham. Despite Balak's designs for Balaam to curse Israel, God controls the outcome. He "would not listen," and so Balaam repeatedly "blessed" Israel.

---

6. This replicates the pattern of usage throughout Joshua. "The Amorites" is a generic descriptor of the eastern (9:10) or western nations (5:1; 7:7; 10:5–12), one of the seven western nations (3:10; 9:1; 11:3; 12:8; 13:4), or Sihon and Og as "Amorite kings" (2:10; it is more often Sihon who is the "king of the Amorites"—12:2; 13:10, 21).

Thus, God "delivered you out of his hand." Effectively, the deliverance from "his hand" has reference to Balak. The closer reference, however, is Balaam, not Balak. Deliverance is from Balaam's hand: his repeated attempts to curse God's people as part of Balak's war preparations. Now the point of including Balaam becomes clear, for the comment proves the many blessings promised Abraham, which included nationhood and land (Gen 12:1–7). Out of the mouth of a foreign prophet, the final blessing recorded in the book (v. 10; cf. 8:33; 14:13; 17:14; 22:6–7, 33) prepares Israel to receive the blessing of land God promised to Abraham.

The Red Sea crossing began the wilderness journey, and the Jordan crossing marked its end. In Joshua 3–4 the account uses words and phrases descriptive of the Red Sea crossing, marking the two events as bookends to the wilderness years. Now, however, the two chapters that earlier depicted the great river crossing are condensed to a few words. Pointedly, Israel's only action is crossing the Jordan and coming to Jericho. The statement that "Jericho fought against you" contrasts with Joshua 6, in which no battle is engaged. This suggests the selective account given in chapter 6 and its focus on God's power that overcomes all opposition so that Israel need not engage in battle. Whatever battle took place at Jericho, the city is here included with others who resisted and fought Israel.

God is the one who acts against these nations. He "gave them" into Israel's hands and "sent the hornet" to drive out the nations as it had Sihon and Og. The "hornet" appears only here and in Exodus 23:28 and Deuteronomy 7:20. In each passage, the context is God's action against the inhabitants.

The limited occurrences of the "hornet" make its identity uncertain. Perhaps the best understanding is that it refers to terror, fear, or discouragement—all effectual agents for removing the inhabitants. At Jericho, the inhabitants were terrified by the report of the LORD's actions (2:9; cf. 5:1). Israel targeted cities in its campaigns (as the list in Josh 12 suggests), leaving much of the surrounding countryside untouched. Fear would drive the inhabitants into the countryside, away from the urban centers and battle zones. The effective terror is by God's design, and Joshua emphasizes the point: Israel "did not do it with [their] own sword and bow" (v. 12).

God's action against the inhabitants is so that he might "give" the land, fulfilling the promise to Abraham. The land, its cities, vineyards, and olive groves are all gifts of God, a fact emphasized by three negatives: Israel "did not toil" for the land, "did not build" the cities, and "did not plant" its crops. God alone fulfills the promise of the good land. Abraham had "lived beyond" (from *yshb* and *'br*) the Euphrates; through God, Israel "crossed" (*'br*) the Jordan and "lives" (*yshb*; v. 13) in the land.

**A Covenant at Shechem (24:14–28)**

Joshua now speaks in his own voice, moving from his prophetic first-person voice of God. He calls Israel to a consequent response (vv. 14–15) indicated by "Now" (*'attah*). Joshua formulates the response using the history's key words and themes (see the discussion at vv. 1–13 above).

Joshua calls Israel to the only appropriate response. He signals this by a series of imperative commands. They are to "fear" and "serve" the LORD "with all faithfulness"—that is, completely and with fidelity (v. 14). They are also commanded to "throw away" the gods worshiped "beyond the Euphrates and in Egypt." Apparently, there is lingering adherence to ancestral gods and those brought out of Egypt (Lev 17:7; Ezek 20:7; 23:3, 8; Amos 5:25–26). After the command to throw these gods away, they are again commanded to "serve" the LORD (v. 14). Each imperative seeks a response of total commitment to serve, or worship (*'bd*), the LORD alone. The centrality of this commitment is echoed in the ensuing dialogue. In it, the Hebrew root *'bd* is used fourteen times to speak of serving the LORD or not serving foreign gods.[7] The same root has already occurred once in the historical recital. The history began with Abraham worshiping (*'bd*) other gods beyond the river. God chose Abraham *while he was worshiping other gods*, gave him promises, and acted graciously to fulfill them. Israel, too, has received and experienced God's gracious fulfillment of these promises. Now Israel is called to respond as did Abraham, who worshiped God, building an altar to "call on the name of the LORD" (Gen 12:8).

Joshua commands the natural and logical response, but it cannot be coerced. He presents three options for Israel to "choose for yourselves this day." They can:

1. Serve the LORD; or if undesirable
2. Serve the gods of your ancestors beyond the Euphrates; or
3. Serve the gods of the Amorites, in whose land you are living.

The choices call Israel to a demarcation noted in the history and throughout the ensuing dialogue. It is this: the ancestors "beyond the River" (v. 2), the nations who lived "east of the Jordan" (v. 8), and the Amorites "in whose land you are living" are those who serve other gods. Israel, however, has been taken from the land "beyond the River" (v. 3) and has "crossed the Jordan" (v. 11). They are a chosen people in a gifted land that really belongs to God. Should they choose option two, they should reject the gift and live outside

7. Positively, to "serve" the LORD in 24:14 (2x), 15 (3x), 18, 19, 21, 22, 24; negatively the worship of other gods in 24:14, 15, 16, 20. One other occurrence in the dialogue refers to the land of "slavery" (v. 17). Two additional occurrences round out the chapter in v. 29 ("servant of the LORD") and v. 31 ("Israel served the LORD").

the land where such gods are served. Should they choose option three, they would reject their identity as God's people if they live as Amorites and serve their gods in the land. Only with option one can they be God's people, living in God's gifted land. To signal that they choose the first option, they must throw away the other gods and worship the LORD.

A choice for any god other than the LORD is antithetical to their history. Joshua understands this correlation and commits himself and his house to "serve the LORD" (v. 15). The peoples' response reveals a similar understanding. They recap Joshua's history, remembering the deliverance from "slavery" (from *'bd*), protection through all the nations they "passed through" (from *'br*), and entry into a land won for them by God. They draw the obvious corollary: God has chosen them, so they promise not to "forsake" God (v. 16). Earlier, God had made the same commitment to not forsake Israel (Deut 31:6). Israel joins Joshua in commitment: "We too will serve the LORD, because he is our God" (v. 18)

Rather than renew the covenant on the strength of this affirmation, Joshua denies their ability to serve the LORD. This negative word contradicts his earlier invitation to serve the LORD and appears to be testing their resolve, rhetorically demonstrating the seriousness of the commitment they are making (v. 19). He reminds them that serving other gods cannot be countenanced by a holy, unique God; he is the only God! Nor will divided loyalty be received by a jealous God; he is the only God! For this specific "rebellion and sin," God—whose very character is to "forgive rebellion and sin" (Exod 34:7; Num 14:18; cf. Lev 16:21)—will *not* do so (v. 19).

Joshua next states their inability as a future condition, one that Joshua apparently considers inevitable. Should Israel break their pledge to not forsake God (*'zb*; vv. 16, 20), and they serve "foreign gods," judgment will come upon them. His words should be heard in the context of Deuteronomy 31:16–18, where the phrase "foreign gods" (*'elohe nekar*) also appears.[8] There, the LORD says the people will in the future prostitute themselves to "foreign gods," "forsaking" (*'zb*) God. In judgment, God says he will "forsake" (*'zb*) them, hiding his face from them. Disasters will come upon them and they will be destroyed (Deut 31:16–18). God's own words lie behind Joshua's present word of judgment. Much later, Jeremiah will answer the people who wonder how the exile occurred, "As you have forsaken (*'zb*) me [God] and served foreign gods in your own land, so now you will serve foreigners in a land not your own" (Jer 5:19). The tragedy of Joshua's words, spoken at Shechem, is that long ago Jacob/Israel had committed to God, burying the "foreign gods" at

8. The phrase appears only here in Joshua, Gen 35:2, 4; Deut 31:16; and Jer 5:19.

Shechem (Gen 35:1–4). Israel will make the same commitment to God, but will not adhere to it.

Despite Joshua's negative words, the people commit a second time to "serve the LORD." Their commitment is more emphatically stated in Hebrew as "The LORD, we will serve" (v. 21). Their agreement to stand as witnesses against themselves further strengthens the intentionality of their commitment (v. 22).

Having twice given their response to serve the LORD, they have effectively agreed to two of the three imperatives of Joshua's challenge (vv. 14–15; "fear and serve God"). That challenge began with "Now" (*'attah*), and Joshua concludes the dialogue by returning to that "Now" (v. 23). He takes up the remaining imperative to "throw away" the "foreign gods" (*hanekar*). This is proof of their commitment to serve the LORD. Ominously, the narrative records no disposal of the foreign gods (as earlier Jacob/Israel had done at Shechem).

The commitment to serve "the LORD, the God of Israel" and to dispose of foreign gods can only arise from a yielded heart. "Yield your hearts" is thus Joshua's final charge to them (v. 23). As before, the people respond emphatically, "The LORD, we will serve." To this, they add their pledge to also "obey him," which reads in Hebrew, "We will listen to his voice."

Later in Israel's history, the prophet Jeremiah preaches to people experiencing the judgment Joshua predicted (v. 20). Jeremiah's words reveal how quickly Israel fell away from their commitment to "serve the LORD our God and obey him" (v. 24). Jeremiah says that even before Joshua's generation, the people "did not listen" to God's voice and did not "pay attention." Instead, they "followed the stubborn inclinations of their evil hearts" (Jer 7:24). Apparently, Joshua's final charge to yield their hearts was quickly abandoned (or never taken up). They failed to yield their hearts, and by not listening, failed to yield their ears, proving the truth of Joshua's warning.

Despite the anticipated failure, Joshua ratifies Israel's commitment with a covenant. This includes reaffirming "decrees and laws." Often, this phrase is applied to the law code in Deuteronomy (Deut 4:1, 5, 8, 14, 45; 5:1; 11:32; 12:1; 26:6). Elsewhere, it can refer to the law of Sinai (Lev 26:46). Given the focus on the Book of the Law of Moses in Joshua, it is likely that the Deuteronomic law is in view here. Joshua makes a record of "these things" in this same book (although here given a slightly different title of "Book of the Law of God"). The record of the people's commitment may simply be added as an appendix to the Book of the Law of Moses. With this act of writing, Joshua exercises once more the ministry of Moses, the writer of the law (Deut 31:9).

Finally, a stone is set up under the oak, near the "holy place of the LORD" (v. 26). The site has already been marked as a "holy place," for Israel has gathered there "before God" (v. 1). It is an ancient holy site, for there the LORD appeared to Abraham (Gen 12:7) and spoke to Jacob/Israel (Gen 35:1). At the very least, the stone serves as a memorial marker for future generations (see Judg 9:6), as have other memorial stones in Joshua (3:7; 7:26; 10:27). More powerfully, the stone functions as a witness, much as the pillar erected by Laban and Jacob witnessed a mutual covenant of non-aggression (Gen 31:45–49). The stone in Joshua is not simply a reminder *that* the covenant was made. It is a reminder *of what the covenant contains*. As if a living witness, it has heard the LORD's words and Israel's response. It stands to query all passersby: "Are you true or untrue to your commitment to serve the LORD?"

Initially, Joshua includes himself with the people. He says the stone will witness "against us," having heard all the words spoken "to us." Then, as if reaffirming the steadfastness of his own commitment and the improbability of the peoples' commitment, he repeats the words with a telling alteration: "It will be a witness *against you* if you are untrue to *your* God" (v. 27, emphasis added). In the future, Israel is untrue. Joshua began the covenant ceremony with the prophetic "this is what the LORD, the God of Israel, says." Now, he ends it with a prophetic forecasting of Israel's covenant failure.

The covenant ratified, Joshua releases the people, each to the inheritance given by God.

### Retiring the Past; Anticipating the Future (24:29–33)

The book's concluding words begin "after these things." In the immediate context, it is a reference to the covenant renewal Joshua has enacted with the people. But "these things" should be read also as a reference to all that has occurred in the book of Joshua: entry to the land and its possession and distribution. Even more broadly, in light of Joshua 24's historical recital, "these things" recall the promise made to Abraham. In that way, these final verses conclude not just the book of Joshua but all of the pentateuchal history.

This earlier history and the promise of land made to Abraham is referenced by the interment of Joseph (v. 32) who, like Joshua, died at one hundred and ten years of age (Gen 50:22). The interment of Joseph takes place at Shechem, in land Joseph's father Jacob bought from Hamor the Hivite, an inhabitant of Canaan (Gen 33:18–20; 34:2a). To commemorate the purchase, Jacob built an altar, acknowledging that "El Elohe Israel" (God is the God of Israel; Gen 33:20). It marked a claim on the land, and trust in God's promises to Abraham.

On his deathbed, Joseph spoke of God's promise, saying, "God will surely come to your aid and take you up out of this land to the land he promised on oath to Abraham, Isaac, and Jacob" (Gen 50:24). In certain hope of that promise, he commanded the Israelites, "you must carry my bones up from this place" (Gen 50:25). Shechem, then, is not only the place of covenant renewal under Joshua. It is also, as the place of Joseph's interment, witness to the fulfillment of the ancient promise of land in which Abraham, Jacob, and Joseph trusted.

God's promise of land, given to Abraham, trusted by the patriarchs and Joseph, and fulfilled under the leadership of Moses and Joshua (Josh 1:1–9) has now been fulfilled. The work of Joshua and Eleazar is finished and a significant chapter in Israel's history closes with their death. Joshua is buried in the inheritance granted him (19:49–50). Eleazar likewise is buried within his tribal allotment of Ephraim, in land given to Phinehas his son. Joshua is accorded honor as he is named once again by his full patronym and also identified by a new title, "servant of the LORD." In obedience to the law of Moses, he led Israel into the land and distributed it among them. Like Moses, he renewed Israel's commitment to the LORD through a covenant ceremony; like Moses, he recorded that covenant in a book. All these reveal he is the true successor of Moses, and so he receives the title reserved to Moses throughout the book (see Listen to the Story, Chapter 1).

Not only does the death of Joshua and Eleazar close a chapter of Israel's history, but the death notice for each (vv. 29–31, 33) includes an openness to the future. During the lifetime of Joshua and the elders, Israel "served the LORD." This is the final occurrence of the key word "serve" in the chapter. It is a hopeful attestation to Israel's commitment to the covenant they have just made. Because this statement is placed within the death notice of Joshua, it raises the obvious question: will Israel still "serve the LORD" after he is gone? Will the covenant hold?

In the notice of Eleazar's death, his son Phinehas is named. Phinehas led the delegation that confronted the Transjordanians for the altar they built (ch. 22). Commitment to worship at the LORD's altar was voiced, and the union between eastern and western tribes was preserved, although signs of strain remained. Will the tribes continue in their commitment to worship the LORD at the LORD's altar? Will the identity of Israel be preserved?

The answers to the questions raised as Joshua and Eleazar die are left to the future. Israel's history and its experience during land entry and possession do not speak well for an affirmative answer, but there is hope for Israel's future in the land. The ancient promise of blessing for all nations through Abraham's descendants is in process. God remains Israel's God by covenant. In these two certainties lies future hope.

### That "Our Hearts May Surely There Be Fixed"

Joshua closes with a recitation of history that shows that all God's promises are fulfilled. From its beginning in Abraham to the possession of the land, the history's focus remained firmly on God's initiative and gracious enactment of what he had promised. Abraham is chosen while serving other gods. Redemption out of Egypt is by God's power. Israel's wilderness sin is glossed over while by God's provision they "lived in the wilderness for a long time" (v. 7). Land is given by God, and Israel neither toils nor builds. Blessings trump intended curses, and the land's fruitfulness is proof of the rest provided by God.

In light of all Israel has received and in light of all that Israel is to be in the midst of the nations, Joshua calls them to the only faithful response—indeed, the only logical response! Serve the LORD! They are the people of God, redeemed by his grace. What other response could be contemplated in light of God's mercies?

The fulfillment of the promises to Abraham does not end with Israel in the land. It goes on to the greater fulfillment of the blessing to all nations through Abraham's "seed," Jesus Christ. He is the one in whom is found the true rest (of which the land was but a shadow and copy). And, as Joshua's historical recital shows the amazing grace of God toward an undeserving people, so too the greater fulfillment. Paul writes to the church in Rome, sketching out for the people of God the wonder of the church—the merciful inclusion of Jew and gentile as co-heirs in Christ. So great is the mystery of God's will and so undeserving the grace of it that Paul, having sketched out its history, breaks into wonder-filled doxology:

> Oh, the depth of the riches of the wisdom and knowledge of God!
> How unsearchable his judgments, and his paths beyond tracing out!
> Who has known the mind of the Lord? Or who has been his counselor?
> Who has ever given to God, that God should repay them?
> For from him and through him and for him are all things.
> To him be the glory forever! Amen. (Rom 11:33–36)

One might consider that in light of Paul's doxology the only faithful—the only logical—response is to serve the LORD. But for the church as for Israel, commitment to faithful worship of the one, true God is not simply a response of logic. In the end, the issue of "[choosing] . . . this day whom you will serve" (v. 15) is one of the heart. For this reason, Joshua urges the Israelites to "yield your hearts to the LORD, the God of Israel" (v. 23).

Bob Dylan had it right when he sang that "it may be the devil or it may be the Lord/But you're gonna have to serve somebody."[9] The choice is the same for God's people through all time: choose whom you will serve. The "foreign gods" with which the church grapples are not those of ancient Israel, but they entice our allegiance just the same: money, power, prestige, consumer culture. These are just some of the foreign gods demanding our loyalty today.

The poet Christina Rosetti wrote, "What can I give him, poor as I am? . . . give my heart."[10] She recognized what true worship rightly requires. Thankfully, even a yielded heart is not something that relies entirely on our own doing. There is the call to "choose," but the church has always coupled the ability to so choose with the gracious work of the one who enables the choosing. In the fifth century AD, the Roman bishop Gelasius collected prayers together in a book known as a sacramentary. One of his prayers asks of God a yielded heart, that true worship might be enabled. The language is old and perhaps a little strange to us, but it is good theology. Such a prayer might be one to pray daily, so that our hearts remain fixed on the LORD, the gracious redeemer:

> Almighty God, which dost make the minds of all faithful [people] to be of one will; grant unto thy people, that they may love the thing which thou commandest, and desire that which thou dost promise; that among the sundry and manifold changes of the world, *our hearts may surely there be fixed*, where true joys are to be found; through Christ our Lord.[11]

## Household Legacies

"As for me and my household, we will serve the LORD." (v. 15)

My paternal great-grandparents served overseas as missionaries with The British and Foreign Bible Society in the late nineteenth century before moving to Canada to shepherd a church. We still have my great-grandfather's Bible, marked in the margins with his comments. It is one legacy of his faith. My paternal grandparents and my own dad were Christians of quiet but influential faith. I remember one Sunday in my preteen years, as my dad and I sat together in church before the service began. I was grousing about church being boring. He listened and then said something that has shaped my life over the years: "Worship isn't about you being entertained. It's about you bringing something to offer to God." It was a gentle observation; an invitation to consider faith

9. https://www.azlyrics.com/lyrics/bobdylan/gottaservesomebody.html

10. Christina Rossetti, "In the Bleak Midwinter," https://www.poetryfoundation.org/poems-and-poets/poems/detail/53216.

11. Emphasis added. The prayer of Gelasius was adapted by Thomas Cranmer for the Book of Common Prayer. This translation is found in C. Frederick Barbee and Paul F.M. Zahl, *The Collects of Thomas Cranmer* (Grand Rapids: Eerdmans, 1999), 58.

in a new light. Later, in my teen years, my family experienced its own revival: I, my mom, my two sisters, and several cousins were "marvelously saved." I sometimes wonder what role the faithfulness of my forebears had in preparing the hearts of our family for that time of revival. I wonder how the present generation of my family's faith will influence family members who come after.

In any family, there is no guarantee that faith will transfer unhindered down a family line. Applying the proverbial "train a child in the way they should go, and when they are old they will not turn from it" (Prov 22:6)[12] as a guarantee in matters of faith is a misunderstanding of the proverbial form. Proverbs are *general* truths, not guarantees. The misunderstanding has caused much grief in families who have raised children in the faith, only to have those children reject the faith.

Joshua made a declaration that included his whole household. It was a declaration to worship the LORD alone, suggesting his was a household in which God came first. From the evidence of Joshua's words in this chapter, it was a household in which God's story was known and in which God's law was honored. Given the fallenness of humanity, it would not have been a sinless household. But in its commitments and in the living out of a lively faith, it would have provided a fertile ground for the faith of those who came after. As subsequent generations heard or read the account in Joshua, each of its members would hear the call to "choose for yourselves whom you will serve."

Faith is not hereditary, but a household of faith that chooses to serve the LORD provides an environment where faith might naturally be caught and someday owned by the next generation.

### How Wretched I Am!

Despite Joshua's insistence that Israel is not able to serve the LORD (v. 19), Israel presses its desire to renew the covenant, saying, "We will serve the LORD our God and obey him" (v. 24). It is not as if only now Israel is charged as being unable or unwilling to walk in its covenant relationship. When the covenant was first made at Sinai, the people repeatedly voiced their commitment to "do everything the LORD has said" (Exod 19:8; 24:3, 7), all while God tested them by his presence, so that "the fear of God will be with you to keep you from sinning" (Exod 20:20). Then, immediately after the covenant was forged, Israel forged the golden calf and turned from God.

Israel seems willing and desirous of covenant but utterly unable or unwilling to walk in it. Joshua's insistence on the peoples' inability to keep the

12. This familiar statement of the proverb relies on the NIV 1984 translation (here utilizing non-gendered language). The 2011 NIV translates the proverb, "Start children off on the way they should go, and even when they are old they will not turn from it."

covenant, and their equal insistence to renew the covenant, highlights the problem. The surprise is that God, knowing this, enters into covenant at all. The further surprise is that God continues in covenant with Israel, despite its sinfulness. The fact that God proceeds with Israel from Sinai, and that he continues with it through the years of the wilderness wanderings, reveals how committed God is to sinful people.

It is during the golden calf episode that God provides the essential statement of his character: compassionate and gracious, slow to anger, abounding in love and faithfulness, maintaining love to thousands, and forgiving wickedness, rebellion and sin (Exod 34:6–7). This is the kind of God that a sinful people needs: one who plays the long game, sticking with the covenant even when the covenant partner, Israel, does not. When Israel sins, God remains true to his covenant character of forgiveness, although his character also means that sin is not left unpunished (Exod 34:7).

God redeems sinful people. The Old Testament also clearly shows that within a sinful nation there were faithful people: Moses, David, Huldah, Jeremiah. The countless named and unnamed individuals who, as a faithful remnant, were grasped by, and responded to, God's saving presence. People who (like Joshua) chose to serve God. People who were not perfect but had faith in what they hoped for and assurance for what they did not see (Heb 11:1).

Paul addresses the problem of sinful people covenanted to a sinless God. In Romans, he speaks of the new covenant made through Christ. By it, people are set free from sin and death. Yet Paul realistically recounts the Christian's continuing struggle with sin, even under the new covenant. What he describes will be true until sin and death are done away with at the end of this age (1 Cor 15:20–28). His words might also describe the experience of Israelites who desire to be in covenant with God, but who sin:

> So I find this law at work: Although I want to do good, evil is right there with me. For in my inner being I delight in God's law; but I see another law at work in me, waging war against the law of my mind and making me a prisoner of the law of sin at work within me. What a wretched man I am! Who will rescue me from this body that is subject to death? (Rom 7:21–24)

Paul sketches the conundrum of the Christian experience: wanting to serve God, but seeming unable to do so. In the face of the cry, "Wretched man that I am . . . who will save me?" the apostle turns to the great newness of the new covenant and proclaims the gospel: "Thanks be to God, who delivers me through Jesus Christ our Lord!" (Rom 7:25). God plays the long game with sinful Israel and with a sinful church because of the work of his Son, Jesus Christ. Anticipated under the old covenant and fulfilled in the new, in Christ sin is forgiven and set aside.

Joshua was right. None is able on their own to serve a holy God. But God takes the initiative and covenants himself to sinful people. Now in Christ, all who say, "Who will rescue me from this body of death?" can be saved. This is good news, indeed. Thanks be to God.

### What Remains for the Future?

The book of Joshua concludes with the death of its leaders Joshua and Eleazar. These strong leaders have shaped Israel's life and have led it to possess the land. Is it possible for Israel to continue in covenant with God without them? The answer must be a definite "yes." Leaders are important, for they model and encourage faithfulness, but faithfulness is not dependent on them alone. Israel has committed in covenant to remain true to its redeeming God (ch. 24). Israel has the law of Moses to show the way of life (ch. 1) and repeated urgings to remain in the law. Most importantly, the nation has a God who has covenanted himself to Israel, abiding with his people. Whatever leaders might lead Israel in the future, the covenant, the law, and God remain. What more can be needed for Israel to go into the future, continuing in the rest it enjoys in the land?

The answer to this second question is a more sobering one. What is needed for Israel to enter that future, secure in covenant blessing, is its own continuing choice to serve the Lord. Will Israel yield its heart to its covenant God (Josh 24:23)? The ongoing history shows that it does not.

Through Israel's choice, the rest achieved in the land begins to disintegrate. Yet for each generation of Israel's history, the choice presents itself anew—as it continues to present itself today. God remains the God of the covenant. Choose whom you will serve. Yield your heart. Enter into the rest provided by God. For all that the book of Joshua contains, this is its enduring message.

# Scripture Index

## Genesis

**Exodus**

**Leviticus**

**Deuteronomy**

### Joshua

**Judges**

**Ruth**



**1 Samuel**

**2 Samuel**



**1 Kings**

**2 Kings**

**1 Chronicles**



**2 Chronicles**



**Job**



**Psalms**

**Proverbs**



**Isaiah**

**Jeremiah**



**Lamentations**



**Ezekiel**



**Daniel**



**Hosea**

**John**



**Acts**



**Romans**



**1 Corinthians**

**2 Corinthians**



**Galatians**



**Ephesians**



**Philippians**



**Colossians**



**1 Thessalonians**



**1 Timothy**



**2 Timothy**



**Hebrews**

**James**



**1 Peter**



**1 John**



**Jude**



**Revelation**

# Subject Index

# Author Index